The Grand Scribe's Records

VOLUME VII

The Memoirs of Pre-Han China

The Grand Scribe's Records

VOLUME VII

The Memoirs of

Pre-Han China

by Ssu-ma Ch'ien

William H. Nienhauser, Jr.
Editor

Tsai-fa Cheng, Zongli Lu,
William H. Nienhauser, Jr., and
Robert Reynolds
Translators

With the Assistance of Chiu-ming Chan

INDIANA UNIVERSITY PRESS

Bloomington & Indianapolis

The maps for this volume were prepared by Francis Stanton of
Eagle Eye Maps, Madison, Wisconsin.

The paper used in this publication meets the minimum requirements
of American National Standard for Information Science—Permanence
of paper for Printed Library Materials, ANSI Z39.48-1984.

Manufactured in the United States of America

Library of Congress Cataloging-in-Publication Data
(Revised for volume 7)

SSu-ma, Ch' ien,   ca. 145-ca. 86 B.C.
The grand scribe's records.

Includes bibliographical references and index.
Contents: v. 1, 7. The basic annals of pre-Han China.
1. China—History—To 221 B.C. 2. China—History—Ch' in dynasty,
221-207 B.C. 3. China—History-—Han dynasty, 202 B.C.-220 A.D.
I. Nienhauser, William H. II. Cheng, Tsai Fa. III. Title.
DS741.3.S6813 1994
931—dc20   94-18408
ISBN 0-253-34021-7 (v. 1)
ISBN 0-253-34027-6 (v. 7)

1 2 3 4 5 00 99 98 97 96 95 94

TABLE OF CONTENTS

This volume is dedicated to Wang Shu-min 王叔岷.

ACKNOWLEDGMENTS

Although we owe debts to many colleagues for their assistance, we would like to first acknowledge the generous financial support we received. The Council for Cultural Planning and Development 文建會 in Taiwan was our main benefactor through the first three years of this translation. The Graduate School Research Committee of the University of Wisconsin-Madison, the Center for Chinese Studies 漢學中心, National Central Library (Taipei), and the Pacific Cultural Foundation have also subvented major portions of our work. We are grateful to each of these organizations for their support.

The following colleagues deserve our special gratitude: Stephen Durrant read most of the early chapters of our manuscript and provided numerous useful suggestions. David Knechtges shared his broad knowledge of early Chinese texts in a detailed critique of the first five chapters. C. S. Goodrich read several chapters, offered us the wisdom of his years and experience, and was always ready with sound advice. Allyn Rickett made a number of improvements in our version of "Kuan Yi-wu and Yen Ying" 官晏列傳. Hsü Cho-yün 許倬雲 read several early drafts and lent us direction during our first year. Jens O. Petersen suggested a number of revisions to Chapters 61, 62 and 65. Robert G. Henricks helped us with useful suggestions on the first several chapters. Victor H. Mair read "Lao Tzu and Han Fei" 老子韓非列傳 and lent us the experience of his work on these figures. A. F. P. Hulsewé made several important corrections to our rendition of "Po Yi" 伯夷列傳. Juan Chih-sheng 阮芝生 provided us with a number of his own studies on the *Shih chi* 史記. Han Zhaoqi 韓兆琦 and Wu Shuping 吳樹平 have sent elusive texts and sound criticism from Beijing. Wang Ch'iu-kuei 王秋桂 gave us important advice as we began our work. Tu Cheng-sheng 杜正勝 allowed us to consult with him on a variety of problems.

A number of librarians in this country and abroad have helped us. During the first few months of our work, Raymond Nai-wen Tang 湯迺文 of the East Asian Collection at the University of California-Berkeley Library and Eugene Wu 吳文津 of the Harvard-Yenching Library aided us in locating and understanding the primary and secondary sources we needed. James Ching Su 蘇精 of the Rare Books Department and Rui-lan Ku 辜瑞蘭 of the Liaison Division, Center for Chinese Studies (both at National Central Library, Taipei) directed us in the use of their collections. Tai-loi Ma 馬泰來 of the University of Chicago and Wei-ying Wan 萬維英 of the University of Michigan have directed our searches for periodical articles. Tim Connor of the Harvard-Yenching Library has provided ready access to the Dynastic History Data Base. The director of Academia Sinica (Taiwan), Kuan Tung-kuei 管東貴 was always generous in allowing us to consult the same corpus.

Particular notice is in order for Chan Chiu-ming 陳照明 who did first drafts of nearly a dozen of the translations in this volume in the two years he worked with us. Jeff Bissell has assisted in typing parts of the text, solved various problems through long days in the library, and done a careful proofreading of much of this volume. Jiang Shuyong 蔣樹勇 contributed in a number of ways to this volume and compiled a draft of the Index. Lance Halvorsen did a draft translation of a chapter (105) to appear in a future volume, typed some chapters, and helped to facilitate production of camera-ready copy. Donna Jahnke directed our search for financial support and Terry Nealon administered the monies we received, both with their usual good humor and skill.

Another colleague, John Gallman, Director of Indiana University Press, has been an early and consistent supporter of our endeavor.   To John and his staff we are sincerely grateful.

Finally, we would like to thank Wang Shu-min 王叔岷, whose *Shih chi chiao-cheng* 史記斠證 (10v.; Taipei: Chung-yang Yen-chiu Yüan, Li-shih Yü-yen Yen-chiu So, 1982. *Chung-yang Yen-chiu Yüan, Li-shih Yü-yen Yen-chiu So chuan-k'an* 中央研究院，歷史 語言研究所專刊, No. 87) was one of our main sources, and who impressed us equally by his gentlemanly decorum and his knowledge of the text and context of the *Shih chi*.   To Professor Wang and his work this volume is dedicated.

INTRODUCTION

I. History of the Project

In Chinese thought seven (*ch'i* 七) is sometimes associated with eight (*pa* 八) suggesting commotion or confusion. It may be disconcerting for the reader, therefore, to learn that this seventh volume (of a proposed nine) represents the beginning of our efforts to translate the *Shih chi* 史記 (The Grand Scribe's Records) by Ssu-ma Ch'ien 司馬遷 (145-*ca.* 86 B.C.). Although all of the translators had been interested in the text prior to 1989 (see the Introduction to Volume 1), we began to work together under a three-year grant (1989-1992) from the Council for Cultural Planning and Development (文建會) in Taiwan. Our initial goal was to translate the 30 chapters not included in the early major *Shih chi* translation projects by Burton Watson and Édouard Chavannes (1865-1918).[1] As our own work progressed, encouragement from other scholars emboldened us to expand our goals. We have now completed translations of 44 chapters--28 in this volume, 7 in Volume 1 (to be published concurrently), and 9 more for future volumes.

II. Contents of This Volume

The "Introduction" to Volume 1 discusses the text, its history and the author of the *Shih chi.* However, some general summary of this great narrative is required here. The *Shih chi* is a history of the "known world" from the Chinese perspective through the end of the first century B.C. Kenneth Rexroth claimed the *Shih chi* "was at least as important as Gibbon's [history]" and "played a far greater role in the formation of the historical consciousness of a far larger number of people."[2] The work is arranged in five historical forms or subgenres: the first 12 chapters are the *pen-chi* 本紀 (basic annals), the next 10 the *piao* 表 (tables), followed by the 8 *shu* 書 (treatises), 30 *shih-chia* 世家 (hereditary houses) and finally the 70 *lieh-chuan* 列傳 (memoirs). This volume presents the first 28 of the *lieh-chuan* which take us from the early Chou 周 dynasty (1122-256 B.C.), in Chapter 61, Po Yi 伯夷, through the end of the Ch'in 秦 dynasty (traditionally 256-212 B.C.), in Chapter 88, Meng T'ien 蒙恬.

The nature of the term *lieh-chuan,* which we have rendered "memoirs," has elicited many explanations by modern scholars. The major modern arguments have been put forward by Burton Watson in "Memoirs" (in *Ssu-ma Ch'ien, Grand Historian of China* [New York: Columbia University Press, 1958], pp. 120-131), by Pierre Ryckmans in "A New Interpretation of the Term *Lieh-chuan* as Used in the *Shih-chi*" (*PFEH,* 5 [1972], 135-147), and

---

[1] Chavannes translated Chapters 1-47 in his *Les mèmoires historiques de Se-ma Ts'ien* (5v.; Paris: E. J. Brill, 1895-1905); three more chapters (48-50) were published posthumously in a sixth volume (Paris: Adrien Maisonneuve, 1969) along with two additional chapters by Max Kaltenmark (51-52); Watson translated Chapters 7-12, 16-20, 28-30, 48-59, 84, 89-104, 106-125, 127 and 130 in his *Records of the Grand Historian of China,* 2v., *V. I: Early Years of the Han Dynasty, 209-141 B.C., V. 2: The Age of Emperor Wu, 140 to Circa 100 B.C.* (New York: Columbia University Press, 1961) and an additional five chapters (61, 66, 82, 85 and 86) in his *Records of the Grand Historian, Chapters from the Shih chi of Ssu-ma Ch'ien* (New York: Columbia University Press, 1969). Last year Watson published a third volume, *Records of the Grand Historian: Qin Dynasty* (Hong Kong and New York: *Renditions* and Columbia University Press, 1993), with versions of chatpers 5, 6, 15 (partial), 68, 71-73, 79, 85-88, and 126 (partial).

[2] See Rexroth's *More Classics Revisited,* Bradford Morrow, ed. (Rpt. New York: New Directions, 1989), p. 23.

Mizusawa Toshitada's 水澤利忠 "Retsuden kaisetsu" 列傳解說 (in *Shiki* 史記, Mizusawa *et al.*, trans. [Tokyo: Meiji Shoten, 1990], v. 8, pp. 1-29) among others.[3] Burton Watson, although noting that *lieh* meant "to arrange, to set forth" ("Memoirs," p. 121) and *chuan* something like "tale" (following James R. Hightower), settled on the translation "memoir" because "the chapters on the history of foreign peoples and lands" could not be called biographies. In fact, Watson often uses "biography" to translate *lieh-chuan* in his *Records of the Grand Historian of China* and the term may remain viable, since, as Arnaldo Momigliano points out, there are parallels to its broader use in the West:

> *Bios* was not a word reserved for the life of an individual man. In Hellenistic and Roman times there existed works, such as *Bios 'Ellados* (life of Greece), vita populi romani (life of the Roman people) . . . . Furthermore, we know that biography developed in the Hellenistic age in conjunction with philological commentaries.[4]

Our dissatisfaction with other translations stems more from the basic understanding of the term *lieh-chuan*. Many of the early Chinese attempts to define it (see Yang, *Li-tai*, pp. 157-176) approach the term as if it were a generic concept. Although *lieh-chuan* certainly *became* a genre, in Ssu-ma Ch'ien's mind is seems to have been more a functional, structural term. The Grand Scribe himself describes his writing of the *lieh-chuan* as follows:

> We [i.e., Ssu-ma T'an and Ssu-ma Ch'ien] collected the old lost traditions from around the world and, searched from beginning to end for the reasons a king's deeds were accomplished in order to see how a house prospered and how it declined, and we investigated the ways things were done. We surveyed the Three Dynasties, took notes on Ch'in and Han, accounting for the history back to Hsüan-yüan, The Huang-ti, and down to the present, and wrote the twelve Basic Annals. Although history had been so outlined, because things recorded in the same or different ages were dated differently or dated unclearly, we made the ten Chronological Tables. Because the norms and music have altered, measurements and the calendar have been changed, and the art of war, the tactics of planning, mountains and rivers, spirits and gods, and the things concerning heaven and man have been improved and made to work, we wrote the eight Treatises. As the twenty-eight constellations revolve about the North Star, or the thirty spokes from the same hub turn round it all the way, so the assistant and supporting vassals are instated to serve the lord with their faithfulness and effectiveness, therefore we wrote the thirty Hereditary Houses. There were those who, upholding righteousness and being unrestricted in spirit, refused to miss their opportunities and achieved merit and fame in the world, thus we wrote the seventy memoirs.[5]

The clear association between these five sections--and especially between the *pen-chi* and the *lieh-chuan*--was apparent to scholars from very early times. Liu Hsieh 劉勰 (*c.* 465-*c.* 520)

---

[3] Takigawa Kametarō's headnote to "Po Yi lieh-chuan" (61:1285D-1286C) and Yang Yen-ch'i 楊燕起 *et al.*, *Li-tai ming-chia p'ing Shih chi* 歷代名家評史記 (Peking: Shih-fan Ta-hsüeh, 1986), esp. pp. 157-195 are excellent sources for traditional comments on *lieh-chuan*. Further useful discussions can be found in Denis C. Twitchett, "Chinese Biographical Writing," in *Historians of China and Japan*, W. G. Beasley and E. G. Pulleyblank, eds. (London: Oxford University Press, 1961), pp. 95-6 and A. F. P. Hulsewé, "Notes on the Historiography of the Han Period," *Ibid.*, pp. 31-43, esp. pp. 35ff.

[4] Arnaldo Momigliano, *The Development of Greek Biography* (Cambridge: Harvard University Press, 1971), p. 13.

[5] *Shih chi*, 130:3319.

offers what seems to be the earliest extant statement on *lieh-chuan* in his *Wen-hsin tiao-lung* 文心雕龍 (The Literary Mind and the Carving of Dragons):

> When we observe how Mr. Tso tied together events, [we see] they were appended to [the text of] the classic [i.e., the *Spring and Autumn Annals*] and spaced out and placed in a style made concise, so that it was difficult to see clans clearly, until each of the *chuan* of Ssu-ma Ch'ien's *The Grand Scribe's Records* [the narrative] was first divided by individuals, so that [their lives] could easily be observed in detail.[6]

"Mr. Tso" is Tso Ch'iu-ming 左丘明, the reputed author of the historical work *Tso chuan* 左傳 which was conventionally seen as a "commentary" to the laconic *Ch'un ch'iu* 春秋 (Spring and Autumn Annals). Each of the entries in the *Tso chuan* was affixed to a corresponding passage in the *Annals*, thus "they were spaced out according to the [text of the] classic." Similar ideas are expressed by Liu Chih-chi 劉知幾 (661-721) in his *Shih t'ung* 史通 (Mastery of History):

> The *chuan* were written for the *Spring and Autumn Annals* to explain the classic; in *The Grand Scribe's Records* and the *History of the Han Dynasty, chuan* were written to explicate their annals.[7]

*   *   *   *   *

> If there is some great event which is worthy of documenting, it appears in [its proper] year and month [in the basic annals]. When one writes on the details of an event, it is committed to the memoirs.[8]

Our understanding of *chuan* 傳 is similar to that of Liu Chih-chiu: *chuan* is a "continuation" or "supplementation." *Chuan* also has the connotation of commentary (an extension of the idea of "supplementation" or "continuation") in titles such as *Tso chuan* 左傳 and *Mao chuan* 毛傳.[9] As Liu Chih-chi argued, "when one writes on the details of an event, it is committed to the *lieh-chuan*." The *lieh-chuan* supplement or complement the narrative line presented in the *pen-chi*. *Lieh* 列, in our understanding, is a plural marker as in the expression *lieh-kuo* 列國 "the [various] states." Thus none of the previously suggested translations--biography, memoir, vitagraph, tradition[10]--is a completely apt rendering of *lieh-chuan*.

We realize that "the [various] supplements [to the basic annals]" is not a practical rendering of *lieh-chuan* and therefore turn back to Ssu-ma Ch'ien for further clarification of his intent. In the "Po Yi lieh-chuan," the first of the *lieh-chuan* and considered by some a preface to the *lieh-chuan* section, he writes:

---

[6] Wang Li-ch'i 王利器, ed., *Wen-hsin tiao-lung chiao-cheng* 校證 (Shanghai: Shang-hai Ku-chi, 1980), Ch. 4, "Shih-chuan" 史傳, p. 107.

[7] "Lieh-chuan" 列傳, *Shih-t'ung t'ung-shih* 史通通釋 (*SPPY*, 2:13b).

[8] *Shih t'ung t'ung-shih* (2:7a-8b, *SPPY*).

[9] On the "Mao Commentary" to the *Shih ching* see Legge, 4, Chapter 1, Section 2, pp. 7-13.

[10] "Vitagraph" is Stuart H. Sargent's rendering (see his "Understanding History and the Narration of Events," in *The Translation of Things Past, Chinese History and Historiography,* George Kao, ed. (Hong Kong: Chinese University Press, 1982), p. 29, n. 10; "tradition" is the translation preferred by Stephen W. Durrant in his as yet unpublished manuscript on Ssu-ma Ch'ien.

I have climbed Mount Chi 箕山, on whose summit supposedly lies the tomb of Hsü Yu 許由. Confucius narrated the deeds of virtuous sages and worthy men of old; for those such as Wu T'ai-po 吳太伯 and Po Yi 伯夷, he did so in detail. From what I have heard, [Hsü] Yu and [Wu] Kuang 務光 were men of the highest principles, yet in Confucius' writings and speech they are scarcely seen. Why is this?[11]

* * * * *

Though Po Yi and Shu Ch'i 叔齊 were worthy men, their names became even more brilliant when they obtained the Master's help.

Though Yen Yüan 顏淵 was devoted to study, his actions became even more renowned when he attached himself to the stallion's tail.

When the gentlemen of cliffs and caves choose and reject [official positions], it is with such careful timing; when their names are buried and unspoken, it is sorrowful, isn't it?

When men from village gates and lanes wish to polish their actions and establish their names, unless they attach themselves to a man of the highest rank, how can these [actions and names] reach later ages?[12]

The solution to the problems of why Hsü Yu and Wu Kuang were "scarcely seen in Confucius' writing and speech" or how the names of the gentlemen of the cliffs and caves or men from villages who acted well and achieved rank "can reach later ages" is, of course, *The Grand Scribe's Records*. To evade this responsibility, he tells us, would be the greatest offense.[13] The desire to prolong history's *memory* of "men of the highest integrity" by recording the "details of events" in their lives suggests to us that the word *memoir* is the best available translation.

The 28 chapters in this volume span approximately a millennium from Po Yi's death in the 11th century B.C. to the end of the Ch'in in the late 3rd century B.C. Stories of more than a hundred men are included. We have set off sections of the major accounts with subtitles in each chapter, thus under "Kuan Yi-wu and Yen Ying" there are separate sections for "Kuan Yi-wu" and "Yen Ying," and in "Su Ch'in" (Chapter 69) there are sections for both "Su Ch'in" and his brother, "Su Tai." A "Translators' Note," which often addresses the relationship of the text to adjoining and other chapters, is appended to each *lieh-chuan*.

III. Method of Translation

Most of these translations were first prepared by a single individual. Each of the translators did at least several drafts, but the majority for this volume were done by Chan Chiu-ming and Robert Reynolds over a period from late 1989 through early 1992. Beginning in the spring of 1992, Lu Zongli, William H. Nienhauser, Jr. and Reynolds met several times a week to revise these drafts. Tsai-fa Cheng, who was concurrently doing the drafts of the "basic annals," then read and commented on many of the drafts.

In our translation, we used the Chung-hua edition (1959, 10v.) of the *Shih chi*. This text is based on the Chin-ling shu-chü 金陵書局 edition compiled by Chang Wen-hu 張文虎 (1808-1855) and revised primarily according to Chang's *Chiao-k'an Shih chi "Chi-chieh,"*

[11] *Shih chih*, 61:2122.
[12] *Shih chi*, 61:2127.
[13] See his comments in the autobiographical final chapter, *Shih chi*, 130:3299.

"So-yin," "Cheng-yi," cha-chi 校刊史記集解索隱正義札記 (2v.; Peking: Chung-hua, 1977). But two important texts, the Northern Sung Ching-yu (1034-37 A.D.) [Kuo-tzu] Chien 景祐[國子]監 edition (the so-called "Chien-pen" 監本) of the *Shih chi* and the Po-na 百衲 edition, were not employed by Chang. Thus we have consulted these two editions as well as the important suggestions in the commentaries by Wang Nien-sun 王念孫 (1744-1817) and Liang Yü-sheng 梁玉繩 (1745-1819)[14] in our work. In addition, we have relied on the following texts: Takigawa Kametarō 瀧川龜太郎 (1865-1946), *Shiki kaichūkōshō fu kōho* 史記會注考證附校補 (Rpt. of Tokyo, 1934 ed. with supplementary collation notes by Mizusawa Toshitada 水澤利忠 [Shanghai: Shang-hai Ku-chi, 1986]), Wang Shu-min 王叔岷, *Shih chi chiao-cheng* 史記斠證 (10v.; Taipei: Chung-yang Yen-chiu Yüan, Li-shih Yü-yen Yen-chiu So, 1982), Wang Li-ch'i 王利器, ed.,[15] *Shih chi chu-i* 史記注譯 (4v.; Sian: San Ch'in, 1988), Ōgawa Tamaki 小川環樹, trans., *Shiki retsuden* 史記列傳 (Rpt. Tokyo: Chikuma Shobō, 1986 [1969]), Mizusawa Toshitada, *Shiki* 史記, V. 8, *Retsuden (ichi)* 列傳 (一), (Tokyo: Meiji Shoten, 1990), and the Western-language translations by Burton Watson, trans. *Records of the Grand Historian of China, from the Shih chi of Ssu-ma Ch'ien* (2v. New York: Columbia University Press, 1961), *Records of the Grand Historian, Chapters from the Shih chi of Ssu-ma Ch'ien* (New York: Columbia University Press, 1969), Yang Hsien-yi and Gladys Yang, *Records of the Historian* (Rpt. Hong Kong: The Commercial Press, 1985), and the various partial translations listed in Timoteus Pokora's "Bibliographie des traductions du *Che ki*" (in Édouard Chavannes, trans. *Les Mémoires historiques de Se-ma Ts'ien* [V. 6; Paris: Adrien Maisonneuve, 1969], pp. 113-46). Burton Watson's new translations just published by The Chinese University Press (Hong Kong) and Columbia University Press arrived just as we were completing our work, but we have compared our translations to those of his in his *Qin Dynasty* volume (v. 3). We have not seen R. V. Viatkin's sixth volume of his *Istoricheskie Zapiski ("Si tszi")* (Moscow: Nauka, 1972-), which we understand is "in press." A further discussion of important sources for rendering official titles, locating places, etc., can be found in "On Using This Book" below.

Drafts of a number of chapters were also sent to various colleagues with expertise in the *Shih chi* (see Acknowledgments). Each of the chapters was revised several times by our team. Upon the completion of a "second draft"--which often took into consideration the suggestions of our colleagues outside Madison--the translations were distributed to all four of the translators for further comments.

Thus this volume is truly a collaborative effort. In editing, efforts to standardize the language and annotation have been stressed; using an extensive glossary prepared by Robert Reynolds and revised by Tsai-fa Cheng, we have aimed at translating the same expression in a consistent manner (thus *peng* 崩 is "pass away," *tsu* 卒 "expire," *and ssu* 死 "die"). In a larger sense, we have aimed at a translation that would be as readable as possible while attempting to render all words and nuances of the original text. It would diminish the Grand Scribe and the style of the *Shih chi* to claim that we have been even slightly successful in this endeavor. On the contrary, in studying and translating the *Shih chi* we have come to hold the pioneers who single-handedly worked on the text in greater awe and dedicate this volume to

---

[14] Wang Nien-sun, "*Shih chi* tsa-chih 史記雜志," in v. 1 of Wang's *Tu-shu tsa-chih* 讀書雜志 (Rpt. Taipei: Shih-chieh, 1963), Liang Yü-sheng, *Shih chi chih-i* 史記志疑 (3v.; Peking: Chung-hua, 1981).

[15] This volume was done with no participation from the "editor" by a group of graduates from Beijing University and scholars from Hunan Province (the key figures seem to have been from Hunan, but graduated from Beijing University in the early 1960s).

one of their rank: Wang Shu-min 王叔岷. The final revisions, and the responsibility for any remaining errors, were left to the Editor.

William H. Nienhauser, Jr.
Madison, 31 March 1994

ON USING THIS BOOK

Sinological Convention has dictated a number of decisions in preparing this book. For example, we have used the term "hegemon," even though we do not feel it an apt rendering for the original *pa* 霸. There is an entry on *pa* which addresses the problem--midst an assembly of other problematic terms--in our **Glossary,** now in draft form, which we plan to publish in the final volume.

Most **Texts** are cited by chapter and page in a particular edition--*Shih chi* 62:2185 indicates *chüan* 卷 62, page 2135 of the Chung-hua edition (see **List of Abbreviations**)--but references to the *Lun yü* 論語 (Analects of Confucius) and *Meng Tzu* 孟子 (Mencius) are according to chapter and verse (學而時習之 is thus *Lun yü* 1/1) and to *Lao Tzu* 老子 (Lao Tzu) by section. When comments in a modern critical edition are relevant, however, we cite it. All dynastic history references are to the modern punctuated editions from Chung-hua Shu-chü 中華書局. For most other citations we have referred to the ***Ssu-pu pei-yao*** 四部備要 or ***Ssu-pu ts'ung-kan*** 四部叢刊 **Editions** to allow the reader to more easily locate the passage.

In one important aspect we have deviated from accepted practice--**Names.** In the pre-Ch'in period there were four basic types of name--*hsing* 姓, *shih* 氏, *ming* 名 and *tzu* 字--one more than in later eras. The *ming,* given at birth, and the *tzu,* given at maturity in a male and marriage in a female, posed no new problems. The hsing has also remained the name given to those related by blood throughout Chinese history. But the *shih* is unique to pre-Ch'in times. Originally it was used to designate separate clans within the same *hsing.* The *shih* were usually created by using the official position (Ssu-ma 司馬), location (Chao 趙), noble title (Kung-tzu 公子), or profession (Shih 史) of the clan leader. In earliest times *shih* were only held by nobles, but during the Warring States era they were more widely held until *shih* and *hsing* became virtually indistinguishable (thus causing confusion for later scholars, including Ssu-ma Ch'ien). Given this extra name, and because we were not satisfied that any translation norms were universally followed for these terms, we have adopted a new scheme based primarily on Roman practice: "The Romans generally bore three names, the *praenomen,* corresponding to our Christian name; the *nomen,* the name of the *gens* or clan; the *cognomen,* the name of the family . . . . a fourth name was sometimes added, the *agnomen*" (cf. Sir Paul Harvey, "Names of Persons," in Harvey's *The Oxford Companion to Classical Literature* [Rpt. Oxford: Oxford University Press, 1980], pp. 284-5). Well aware that there is not a perfect correspondence between these four name-types and those of pre-Ch'in China, we have adopted these terms: thus *hsing* is *cognomen, shih* is *nomen, ming* is *praenomen,* and *tzu* is *agnomen.*

For **Personal Names** in the early chapters we have hyphenated those two-syllable names we cannot analyze (e.g., Ch'a-fu 差弗), but separated those with titles or honorifics (e.g. Kung Liu 公劉). We have followed Ssu-ma Ch'ien's penchant for using several types of names to refer to the same character in a single chapter, but tried to alert the reader to this practice in our notes.

Locations of **Place Names** are based on T'an Ch'i-hsiang 譚其驤, ed. *Chung-kuo li-shih ti-t'u chi* 中國歷史地圖集, *Vol. I: Yüan-shih she-hui--Hsia, Shang, Hsi Chou, Ch'un-ch'iu, Chan-kuo shih-ch'i* 原始社會一夏，商，西周，春秋，戰國時期, *Vol. II: Ch'in, Hsi Han, Tung Han shih-ch'i* 秦，西漢，東漢時期 (Shanghai: Ti-t'u Ch'u-pan-she, 1982). T'an's identifications are not without problems, but they have been adopted by a number of large projects in China (such as the *Chung-kuo ta pai-k'o ch'üan-shu* 中國大百科全書) and provide the only practical means to attempt to identify the great number of place names in the *Shih chi*. On occasion we have added information from Ch'ien Mu's 錢穆 *Shih chi ti-ming k'ao* 史記地名考 (Rpt. Taipei: San-min Shu-chü, 1984), or Wang Hui's 王恢 *Shih chi pen-chi ti-li t'u-k'ao* 史記本紀地理圖考 (Taipei: Kuo-li Pien-i Kuan, 1990). Chinese characters for the major states of pre-Ch'in China (Chao 趙, Cheng 鄭, Ch'i 齊, Chin 晉, Ch'in 秦, Ch'u 楚, Han 韓, Lu 魯, Shu 蜀, Sung 宋, Wu 吳, Yen 燕, Yüeh 越, etc.) are generally not given. Wei 魏 is distinguised from Wey 衛 by romanization. We have found it difficult to decide when to translate a place name. Our basic principle has been to translate names which seem to still have meaning in the *Records* and to leave untranslated those which were understood by Ssu-ma Ch'ien primarily as toponyms. Where we were unsure, we gave a translation at the first occurence only. Words like *yi* 邑, *ch'eng* 城 or *chün* 郡 (in two-syllable compounds) are treated as suffixes and transliterated rather than translated. For example, place names like An-yi 安邑, Tung-ch'eng 東城, and Nan-chün 南郡, in which *yi, ch'eng* and *chün* are similar to the "-ton" in Washington or "-ville" in Nashville, are transliterated as An-yi, Tung-ch'eng, and Nan-chün, rather than translated as An Town, East City or Southern Commandery. For modern cities and provinces we have used the postal-system romanization (Peking, Szechwan, etc.). Ssu-ma Ch'ien is fond of using two names (primarily Wei 魏 and Liang 梁 or Ching 荊 and Ch'u 楚) to refer to the same state, a practice that can be confusing to the reader.

Another difficulty is, of course, that the location of many of these places is tentative at best. Although we have not been able to resolve such problems, we have given attention to the logic of locations within a given passage. In other words, if an army fought first at Point A and then took Point B, we have attempted to follow modern identifications which would accord with these events. Where the narrative lends support to a group of locations, we have provided rudimentary **Maps.**

Official Titles have posed a particular problem. Charles O. Hucker's *A Dictionary of Official Titles in Imperial China* (Stanford: Stanford University Press, 1985) is often useful, but many of the titles we encountered do not occur in his guide or represent positions different from that in later eras. Thus we have made reference to *Chung-kuo ku-tai chih-kuan ta tz'u tien* 中國古代職官大辭典 , Chang Cheng-lang 張政烺, ed. (Chengchow: Ho-nan Jen-min Ch'u-pan-she, 1990), to Hsü Lien-ta 許連達, ed., *Chung-kuo li-tai kuan-chih tz'u-tien* 中國歷代官制詞典 (Hofei: An-huei Chiao-yü Ch'u-pan-she, 1991), to the traditional commentators, and to works such as Miao Wen-yüan 繆文遠, ed., *Ch'i-kuo k'ao ting-pu* 七國考訂補 (2v.; Shanghai: Shang-hai Ku-chi, 1987). Official titles are cross listed (by translated title and romanized title) in the **Index.**

Weights and Measures are generally given in romanization only. More information is often provided in the notes and especially in the "Weights and Measures" section below (pp. xxi-xxiv).

Dates given according to the sexagenary cycle have been romanized: *chia-tzu jih* 甲子日 becomes "the *chia-tzu* 甲子 day." Reign periods preceded by an asterisk indicate that the dates given are those of the *Shih chi* but have been revised by modern scholars (see "A Note on Chronology" below).

We have used a slightly modified version of Wade-Giles' **Romanization:** *i* is written throughout as *yi* to avoid the confusion between the English first-person pronoun and Chinese proper names. For Chinese passages over four characters in length, romanization is usually not provided. Reconstructed pronunciation follows that of Li Fang-kuei 李方桂.

Our **Base Edition** has been that edited by Ku Chieh-kang 顧頡剛(1893-1980) *et al.* and entitled *Shih chi* 史記. It was based on the Chin-ling Shu-chü 金陵書局 edition and published in ten volumes by Chung-hua Shu-chü in 1959. References to this edition are given by chapter and page (69:2250) in the notes and by page numbers in brackets in the translation itself [2250]. We have also consulted the Po-na 百衲 and Chien-pen 監本 editions regularly (see also Introduction).

In citing the standard three **Commentaries**--"Chi-chieh" 集解, "Cheng-yi" 正義 and "So-yin" 索隱--page numbers are given only if the reference is to a chapter other than that being translated. In other words, in the translation of 61:2124 no page number is provided for a citation from the "Cheng-yi" if that citation occurs on 61:2124 or 61:2125, since the reader should easily be able to locate it. If a "Cheng-yi" comment is provided from another section or chapter of the *Shih chi*, we use the following format: 4:120.4, indicating *Chüan* 4, p. 120, n. 4. A brief introduction to these commentaries can be found in the front-matter to Volume 1.

Our **Annotation** has attempted to identify major textual problems, place names, book titles, rituals, unusual customs, individuals and groups of people. We provide, however, only one base note for those items which occur repeatedly in the text (such as Jung and Ti--n. 10 to Chapter 4) and the reader is expected to use the index for help in locating the base note.

Abbreviated titles and words can be found in the **List of Abbreviations** in the front-matter.

Chinese Characters are given at their first occurence and repeated only in personal names in that person's "biography." In other words, the characters 張儀 are given at their first occurrence (69:2250) and again in Chang Yi's memoir (Chapter 70).

The translation of each chapter is followed by a **Translators' Note** and a short **Bibliography**. The former may provide a summary of analyses from traditional commentators, point out problems in the text, or discuss its relations to other chapters. The latter includes the major studies and translations. Outdated translations, such as that by E. Hübotter (1912), are not listed.

A **General Bibliography** is appended.

A NOTE ON CHRONOLOGY

Although Ssu-ma Ch'ien's "Memoirs" begin with Po Yi and Shu Ch'i, two recluses who predate the establishment of the Chou dynasty, his focus for the first 28 chapters is firmly on the Eastern Chou. After Chapter 67, we have left the Spring and Autumn period behind, and are well into the Warring States period, ending with the Ch'in dynasty in the last two chapters of our translation.

The history of the Warring States period is complex, and although we have many sources for this era, there remain many questions we are unable to answer. The *Shih chi* is undoubtedly the most important textual source for the Warring States period. Nonetheless, it incorporates numerous errors which later scholars have corrected, based primarily on archaeological discoveries. The reason for the large number of errors in Ssu-ma Ch'ien's accounts of this era undoubtedly lies in the fragmentary nature of the records to which he had access. The records of most of the feudal states in this period were probably destroyed at the end of the Ch'in dynasty. Lacking complete records, Ssu-ma Ch'ien relied on the materials that had survived, most prominently the records of Ch'in, and in a remarkable feat of scholarship, reconstructed the entire Warring States chronology.

Since it is at least partially a reconstruction, and not based solely on first hand documents, there are numerous points on which Ssu-ma Ch'ien's chronology was in error. Doubtless there are many errors which we are still unable to correct. The fact that we are able to correct any errors is due largely to the discovery in 281 A.D. of what was apparently an almost intact official history of the state of Wei, which came to be known as *Chu-shu chi-nien* 竹書紀年 (Bamboo Annals). A version of this history survives today, but great controversy surrounds its authenticity. What remains uncontroversial is the authenticity of extracts of this document preserved in two of the three major commentaries on the *Shih chi*. The authors of these two commentaries, "So-yin" and "Cheng-yi," compared at least some sections of the Wei history with the *Shih chi* records, and recorded at least some of the major discrepancies. The Sung dynasty compilers of the monumental annals of China, the *Tzu-chih t'ung-chien* 資治通鑑 (Comprehensive Mirror for Aid in Governing), also apparently consulted either the *Chu-shu chi-nien* or the *Shih chi* commentaries, for their reconstruction of the period, while based primarily on *Shih chi*, also incorporates some changes which most scholars believe are based on the *Chu-shu chi-nien*.

Over the centuries, scholars working on the chronology of this era have continued to propose revisions, and in recent decades three major works, summarizing both pre-modern research and the results of modern discoveries and study have been published on Warring States chronology: *Hsien Ch'in chu-tzu hsi-nien* 先秦諸子繫年 by Ch'ien Mu 錢穆, *Liu-kuo chi-nien* 六國紀年 by Ch'en Meng-chia 陳夢家, and *Chan-kuo shih* 戰國史 by Yang K'uan 楊寬.[1] We have chosen the Yang K'uan as the basis for the dates we provide in our annotations, not because it is unquestionably correct in all cases, but because Yang provides the most comprehensive revision of Ssu-ma's dates in a relatively convenient form.

The most troubled chronologies for the Warring States period are those of the states of Ch'i, Yen, Wei, and Han. There are two particularly important mistakes that Ssu-ma Ch'ien makes here. First, he was in error on the dates of King Hui 惠 and King Hsiang 襄 of Wei. According to Ssu-ma Ch'ien, King Hui's dates are 370-335 B.C. and King Hsiang's dates are 334-319 B.C. In addition, Ssu-ma Ch'ien also lists a King Ai 哀, whose dates he gives as

[1] On Ch'ien Mu and Yang K'uan, see our "List of Abbreviations." *Liu-kuo chi-nien* was published by Shanghai Jen-min in 1957. Yang's dating is in his Appendix III (pp. 553-84).

318-296 B.C.   Based largely on the *Chu-shu chi-nien*, Yang K'uan gives completely new dates. For King Hui, he gives 369-319 B.C. For King Hsiang, he gives 318- 296 B.C. As for King Ai, Yang K'uan simply eliminates him altogether.[2] It appears that Ssu-ma Ch'ien "invented" King Ai to fill the gap created by the incorrect dates for King Hui and King Hsiang. This is an interesting point which we will return to below. King Hui is an important figure in several of the Memoirs, and this problem has clearly affected the way Ssu-ma Ch'ien has put together a number of his narratives. Even more crucial, however, are the errors Ssu-ma Ch'ien made for the state of Ch'i's kings. The most important errors here are the dates for King Wei 威, King Hsüan 宣, and King Min 湣. Ssu-ma Ch'ien's dates are as follows: King Wei, 378-343 B.C.; King Hsüan, 342-324 B.C.; King Min, 323-284 B.C.[3] Yang K'uan's dates, on the other hand are: King Wei, 356-320 B.C.; King Hsüan, 319-301 B.C.; King Min, 300-284 B.C. These discrepancies are apparently due to the omission of an earlier ruler, Marquis Shan 剡. The omission forced Ssu-ma Ch'ien to push the other rulers back two decades and stretch out their reigns to cover the gap. In any case, this error has interesting consequences for a number of chapters, in particular, Chapter 75, the Memoir of the Lord of Meng-ch'ang, who lived in Ch'i in the middle of this period.

The chronologies with the fewest problems, on the other hand, appear to be those of Ch'in and Ch'u. That is not to say that there are not many individual problems in the histories of these states, but the main lines of sovereignty at least are not disputed. As an appendix to this volume, we provide a list of dates for all rulers of these states, according to Yang K'uan's work, together with Ssu-ma's dates in cases where the two are at odds. We have also given reign dates in the text to help keep the reader oriented without making constant reference to this table, but in the reign dates given in the text, we give the dates according to Ssu-ma Ch'ien and use an asterisk to indicate those dates for which Yang offers corrections.

Our rationale for this practice is based on conclusions we have reached on Ssu-ma Ch'ien's composition of the Memoirs, and his means for indicating dates there. We believe that Ssu-ma first constructed his chronology of the Warring States period, and then composed the Memoirs using this chronology. Rather than choosing the reign dates of one particular kingdom as a standard for indicating chronology, he frequently inserts the name of the ruler of the state where a particular event he wishes to narrate took place. Sometimes he will mention instead a specific event as occurring at the same time as the main event of his narrative. We believe that in general Ssu-ma's source material, particularly for the more complex narratives, did not originally contain either of these clues to dating. This belief is based on general practices in narratives incorporated in the *Chan-kuo ts'e* 戰國策, which, if they did not serve as Ssu-ma Ch'ien's direct sources, are unquestionably similar to the materials which he used; in addition to the evidence of sources such as *Chan-kuo ts'e*, the structure of the Memoirs themselves, where such dating material generally occurs between stories rather than as an integral part of a narrative, also suggests that the majority of such references came from Ssu-ma Ch'ien. The clearest evidence of the fact that at least some of these dating references came from Ssu-ma himself lies in the mention of King Ai of Wei in Chapters 69 and 70. This king is apparently unique to the *Shih chi*. As we have seen, he filled a very particular hole in the

---

[2] See Yang (rev. ed., 1986), pp. 720-727 for his sources and arguments. Many of these corrections were not, of course, Yang's discoveries. D.C. Lau, in the appendix to his *Mencius* (New York: Penguin Books, 1970), pp. 205-209 gives a very useful summary of how and when these dates were gradually corrected.

[3] NB: Because of its relative consistency within the *Shih chi*, we follow Ssu-ma Ch'ien's dating in our translation, but alert the reader to dates which have been corrected by modern scholars by placing an asterisk before them: e.g., King Min 湣 of Ch'i (r. *323-284 B.C.).

Shih chi chronology. King Ai's appearance in these chapters then is strong evidence that these references, at least, came from Ssu-ma Ch'ien himself.

This being the case, we must be wary of simply incorporating the corrected reign dates into the Memoirs without due consideration. The consequences of this may be seen from the *Shih chi*'s description of the travels of Su Ch'in 蘇秦 in his attempt to bind the states of China in alliance against Ch'in. This chapter is often cited as an example of the massive historical contradictions found in Ssu-ma Ch'ien's narratives, but consider the sequence of kings found here, according to Ssu-ma's own chronology. The kings Su Ch'in visits are: King Hsien 顯 of Chou (368-321 B.C.), King Hui 惠 of Ch'in (336-311 B.C.), Marquis Wen 文 of Yen (361-332 B.C.), Marquis Su 肅 of Chao (349-326 B.C.), King Hsüan 宣 of Han (332-312 B.C.), King Hsiang 襄 of Wei (334-319 B.C.), King Hsüan 宣 of Ch'i (342-324 B.C.), and King Wei 威 of Ch'u (339-329 B.C.) This gives us a rather precise date for Su Ch'in's travels, centering around 332 B.C.; this is necessary to accommodate both Marquis Wen of Yen and King Hsüan of Han. There are no contradictions apparent, and if we make the reasonable assumption that Ssu-ma Ch'ien took his own chronology seriously, then from his point of view, he has written a narrative marred by no major anachronisms. If we use the corrected dates of King Hsüan of Ch'i (319-301 B.C.) and King Hsiang of Wei (318-296 B.C.), however, this produces a marked anachronism: these men were not on the throne until at least a decade after all the other rulers mentioned, and they are mentioned in the biography as being addressed prior to King Wei of Ch'u, who died ten years before they were enthroned.

It may very well be that the account of Su Ch'in's travels which Ssu-ma Ch'ien gives is incorrect (though as we will discuss below, we doubt that Su Ch'in himself was a fictional character), but it is important to note that Ssu-ma is at least being internally consistent here, and this is what we suggest by providing the dates Ssu-ma Ch'ien postulates for these kings. Since Yang K'uan's corrections to the *Shih chi* chronology do have merit, however, we feel we would be remiss in failing to point out that there is a problem here, hence our use of the asterisk with all these dates, with footnotes discussing the problem in more detail when appropriate.

Another interesting instance where correct dates would create anachronisms occurs in Chapter 75, when T'ien Wen 田文 tells his father T'ien Ying 田嬰: "Your Lordship has wielded power and served as prime minister of Ch'i for the reigns of three kings now." Using the sequence of Ch'i kings which Ssu-ma Ch'ien followed, these kings must have been Wei, Hsüan, and Min. Yet when the correct dates are supplied, it turns out to have been impossible for T'ien Ying to have served under any three kings. What is particularly interesting here is that this reference comes in the middle of speech, suggesting either that others committed a mistake similar to his, or that Ssu-ma Ch'ien has changed or composed this speech himself, a charge which is otherwise generally quite hard to prove.

We do not mean to overstate the internal cohesion of the *Shih chi*; there are many contradictions between the different sections. Some of these must be laid to Ssu-ma Ch'ien. Others are certainly due to textual corruption. But some are also products of a failure to look closely at the way Ssu-ma Ch'ien recorded events.

An interesting problem which apparently has been little noted lies in the method of counting Ssu-ma Ch'ien used. The western tradition has always been to begin with "zero" and count up. In the Chinese tradition, however, it appears that dates could also be calculated by beginning with "one" and continuing up. The western style we will thus call "exclusive" (the number you begin with is excluded), while the Chinese style is "inclusive." Thus a child is born aged one "sui," and a king's reign begins with the "yüan" year; there is good evidence from the oracle bone inscriptions that days were also sometimes counted in this way, so that the span between the tenth day and the twentieth day of the sixty day cycle, for instance, was not ten days, but eleven days.

It would not do, of course, to claim that this is the method being used every time there is a one year difference in dates between different *Shih chi* chapters. But it is almost certain that something like this is going on when almost every date given by counting years in a particular chapter is off by one year! This in fact turns out to be the case in several chapters: in particular Chapters 66, 68, and perhaps 72. Chapter 68 is a straightforward example, if we compare the years given there and the years as given in Ssu-ma Ch'ien's table in Chapter 15. For instance, on 68:2232 Shang Yang 商鞅 is said to attack the state of Wei at An-yi 安邑; in Chapter 15, this is put in the year 352 B.C. Chapter 68 then says that "three years later," Shang Yang built new palaces and towers at the city of Hsien-yang, following which the state of Ch'in moved its capital there. Yet Chapter 15 dates this to 350 B.C. (two years later), not 349 B.C. According to Chapter 68, "four years later" he cut off the nose of the king's son for violating the law. Chapter 15, however, dates this to 347 B.C. (three years after 350 B.C.), not 346 B.C. Chapter 68 then records that "five years later" the Chou Son of Heaven gave the Ch'in king meat from the sacrifices to the Chou ancestors. Chapter 15 dates this to 343 B.C., four years after 347, not five years. Thus the records in Chapter 68 are completely consistent with Chapter 15; they are always one year off.

Another problem which we can deal with here has to do with Ssu-ma Ch'ien's failure to mention a time lapse between two events. Thus for the last date mentioned above, in Chapter 68, the next three sentences run as follows:

> After five years had passed [343 B.C.], the people of Ch'in were wealthy and powerful. The Son of Heaven presented sacrificial meat to Duke Hsiao, and the feudal lords all offered their congratulations.
> The next year, Ch'i defeated Wei's troops at Ma-ling ,

According to Chapter 15, Ch'i defeated Wei at Ma-ling 馬陵 in 341 B.C. If the Son of Heaven presented the sacrificial meat in one year, and Ch'i defeated Wei the "next year" this apparently contradicts our date of 343 B.C. which we arrived at by using the "inclusive" counting method. A closer look at Chapter 15 reveals a curious sequence, however: according to 15:743, in the row for Chou, we find that Chou "conferred hegemony on Ch'in" in 343 B.C. This is another reference to "presenting sacrificial meat." Then in the Ch'in row for 342 B.C., we read that "The feudal lords all offered their congratulations. [Ch'in] convened the feudal lords at Tse." If we accept this date and return to Chapter 68, we will see that "the next year" here must refer not to the conferring of the sacrificial meat, but to the congratulations of the feudal lords, and one year after 342 is indeed 341. Ssu-ma Ch'ien simply neglected to tell us that a year elapsed between the presentation of the meat and the feudal lords' congratulations. It certainly is *odd* that the feudal lords would congratulate Ch'in a year after it received the sacrificial meat, but regardless of whether this was actually the case or not, Ssu-ma Ch'ien seems to have been at pains to offer a consistent set of dates for Chapters 15 and 68. This sort of "run on" dating is frequent throughout the *Shih chi*.

A final point worth mentioning here relates to the problem of the Ch'in calendar. According to *Shih chi,* 6:237, when the King of Ch'in declared himself the First Emperor, he changed the calendar so that the beginning of the year (*sui-shou* 歲首) fell in the tenth month. What this meant was that the year of the king's reign was calculated from the beginning of the tenth lunar month, rather than from the beginning of the first lunar month. This practice is evident in Ssu-ma Ch'ien's records after this date, but there are also apparently records of such a calendar prior to 221 B.C. As the Translator's Note to Chapter 73 attempts to show, the Memoir for Pai Ch'i 白起 can only be interpreted if we assume such a calendar, yet the events depicted there occurred in the reign of King Chao 昭 of Ch'in (r. 306-251 B.C.) It is also very odd that although the dates of Chapter 73 are clear, the Ch'in Basic Annals in Chapter 5 ignores this and lumps all these events into one year, as if the compiler of Chapter 5 was unaware of the narrative in Chapter 73. Perhaps here we have evidence of the separate roles of Ssu-ma Ch'ien and his father, Ssu-ma T'an, in the composition of the *Shih chi*. This is quite speculative, of course. At any rate, the incongruity between the calendar of Ch'in and the calendars of the other states seems to have left its mark in several curious gaps of thirteen months between various events.

Thus despite the inconsistencies, apparent and real, in Ssu-ma Ch'ien's dates, it seems that he usually had evidence to support his narratives. This is in contrast to the views of many Western historians and sinologists who have examined the *Shih chi* since Édouard Chavannes first began his path-breaking translation, and who seem to have adopted the working assumption that unless there is independent evidence to support the veracity of the events Ssu-ma narrates, particularly for the Warring States period, Ssu-ma Ch'ien either composed fiction himself or made uncritical use of fiction. We question this assumption on general grounds. It is far from clear that the idea of fiction was even present during the time of Ssu-ma Ch'ien, much less in earlier times. In particular, the assumption that writers created many Warring States personalities from whole cloth is a quite remarkable idea. Thus James I. Crump, Jr., in a preface to his translation of a speech from *Chan-kuo ts'e*, labels the famous persuader Fan Sui 范雎 a fictional creation, a claim that has been disproved when recently excavated historical records dating to the pre-Ch'in era record the date of death of both Fan Sui and his patron Wang Chi 王稽. Even as eminent an authority as Ch'ien Mu leapt to the conclusion that the Ch'i general Sun Pin 孫臏 was created by Ssu-ma Ch'ien due to his errors in interpreting ancient documents, a theory that became untenable when a copy of Sun Pin's works dating back to before the composition of the *Shih chi* came to light. Sun Pin still might not be a historical figure, but the blame for his creation cannot be laid on Ssu-ma Ch'ien.

In general, therefore, even when we have not found positive evidence to support the *Shih chi*, our assumption has been that Ssu-ma Ch'ien himself believed in the historicity of the figures in the Memoirs, with a cautious acknowledgement that in most cases he had reason to believe this.

Robert Reynolds

WEIGHTS AND MEASURES

Throughout the text we have given words indicating weights and measures in their romanized form followed (at the first occurrence) by the Chinese character (e.g., *jen* 仞). This is in part because there are no standards for each era or each region dealt with in the "basic annals." Yet most of the values given in the following charts were fairly stable from the Warring States era into the early Han in most states.

Generally speaking, the basic unit of length, the *ch'ih* 尺, was the most stable. It varied from 23.1 cm in Warring States to about 23.2 cm in the Western Han. In terms of volume, one *sheng* 升 was roughly equal to 200 cc throughout the period. The greatest variance can be seen in weights, but even there we can assume that one *chin* 斤 remained equal to approximately 250 g through the era.

However, in order to avoid confusion between *chin* 金 (which when preceded by a number indicated so many *yi* 鎰 of bronze or copper [1 *yi* = 20 *liang* 兩]) and *chin* 斤 (the standard measure for gold or *huang-chin* 黃金 which consisted of 16 *liang*), we refer to the former as *chin* and the latter as "catties."

The following list is arranged by category (Length, Capacity, etc.) and under each category by the importance of the term. Variances are listed with the most ancient value first. A selected list of sources (along with a key to the abbreviated sources cited in the list) is appended.

Length

Unit Name	Western Equivalent (Era)	Source (see appended Bibliography)
ch'ih 尺	22-23 cm (Ch'u) 23.1 cm (Wey Yang's standard in Ch'in) 23-23.7 cm (Western Han)	Ch'en Meng-chia Ch'eng Meng-chia *K'ao-ku hsüeh*
ts'un 寸	1/10th *ch'ih*	
pu 步	8 *ch'ih* = 184.8 cm (Chou) 6 *ch'ih* = 138.6 cm (Ch'in-Han) 138 cm	*Tz'u-hai* *Tz'u-hai* "Han Weights and Measures"
jen 仞	8 *ch'ih* (Chou dynasty) 7 *ch'ih* (Western Han)	*Ku-tai wen-hua* *Ku-tai wen-hua*
hsün 尋	8 *ch'ih*	*Ku-tai wen-hua*
chang 丈	10 *ch'ih*	
ch'ang 常	16 *ch'ih*	*Ku-tai wen-hua*

Length (continued)

Unit Name	Western Equivalent (Era)	Source (see appended Bibliography)
ch'un 純	4 *tuan* 端 (of cloth; 1 *tuan* = 2 *chang*)	"Chi-chieh" (*Shih chi*, 69:2250)
yin 引	10 *chang*	
li 里	415 m	"Han Weights and Measures"
	416 m = 300 *pu* or 180 *chang*)	*Ku-tai wen-hua*
she 舍	30 *li*	

Area

mu 畝	100 *pu*^{2} (342.25 m.^{2,}, Chou)	*Ku-tai wen-hua*
	160 *pu*^{2} (Ch'in, Chin, Fan, Chung-hang)	*Ku-tai wen-hua*
	200 *pu*^{2} (Han, Wei)	*Ku-tai wen-hua*
	240 *pu*^{2} (Chao)	*Ku-tai wen-hua*
	240 *pu*^{2} (Warring States, Ch'in, Han;	*Ku-tai wen-hua*
	457.056 m.^{2})	"Han Weights and Measures"
	0.1139 English acre	
li 里	often stands for x-*li on a side* (i.e.,	
	x by x *li*)	

Capacity

sheng 升	201.25 cc (Wey Yang's standard)	*K'ao-ku hsüeh*
	202.15 cc (Wey Yang's standard)	*Ku-tai wen-hua*
	199.69 cc (Wey Yang's standard)	Ch'en Meng-chia
	205.8 cc (state of Ch'i)	*K'ao-ku hsüeh*
	from 194-216 cc (later in Ch'in)	
yüeh 龠	1/2 *ho* = about 10 cc	
ho 合	1/10 *sheng* = about 20 cc	
	19.968 cc.	"Han Weights and Measures"
t'ung 桶	6 *sheng* (Warring States era)	*Shih chi tz'u-tien*
tou 斗	10 *sheng* = about 2000 cc	
	1900 cc (Ch'in dynasty)	Ch'en Meng-chia
hu 斛	10 *tou* = about 20,000 cc	
	19,968 cc.	"Han Weights and Measures"

Unit Name	Western Equivalent (Era)	Source (see appended Bibliography)
yü 庾	16 *tou* (Spring and Autumn era)	*Tso chuan,* Chao 26
fu 釜	20,460-20,580 cc	*K'ao-ku hsüeh*, Ch'en Meng-chia

Weight

chin 斤	256.26 g (Warring States, Ch'in)	Ch'en Meng-chia
	251.53 g (Ch'u)	Ch'en Meng-chia
	234.6-273.8 g (Ch'in)	*K'ao-ku hsüeh*
	244-268 g (Western Han)	Ch'en Meng-chia
	245 g (Western Han)	"Han Weights and Measures"
liang 兩	1/16 *chin*--about 15.625 g	
	15.36 g	"Han Weights and Measures"
chu 銖	1/24 *liang*--about 0.651 g	
	0.64 g	"Han Weights and Measures"
tzu 錙	6 *chu*	
	1/4 *liang* = about 3.906 g	
yi 溢	20 *liang*	See introduction to "Weights and Measures" above
chün 鈞	30 *chin* = about 7,500 g	
	7,350 g	"Han Weights and Measures"
tan 石	120 *chin* = about 30 kg	
	29.5 kg	"Han Weights and Measures"
chin 金	= *yi* (of copper or bronze, in pre-Ch'in times)	See introduction to "Weights and Measures" above
	1 *chin* = 1 $ts'un^3$ of gold = 238-251 g (Ch'in-Han)	

Key to Abbreviated Sources

Ch'en Meng-chia

Ch'en Meng-chia 陳夢家. "Chan-kuo tu-liang-heng shih-lüeh shuo" 戰國度量衡史略說, *K'ao-ku*, 6.6(1964), 312-14.

"Han Weights and Measures"

"Han Weights and Measures," in *The Cambridge History of China, Volume 1, The Ch'in and*

	Han Empires. Denis Twitchett and Michael Loewe, eds. Cambridge: Cambridge University Press, 1986, p. xxxviii.
K'ao-ku hsüeh	*Chung-kuo ta pai-k'o ch'üan shu, K'ao-ku hsüeh* 中國大百科全書，考古學．Peking and Shanghai: Chung-kuo ta pai-k'o ch'üan shu Chu-pan-she, 1986.
Ku-tai wen-hua	*Ku-tai wen-hua ch'ang-chih* 古代文化常識．Yang Tien-k'uei 楊殿奎 *et al., eds.* Tsinan: Shan-tung Chiao-yü Ch'u-pan-she, 1984, pp. 271-92.
Shih chi tz'u-tien	*Shih chi tz'u-tien* 史記辭典. Ts'ang Hsiu-liang 倉修良, ed. Tsinan: Shan-tung Chiao-yü Ch'u-pan-she, 1984
Tz'u-hai	*Tz'u-hai* 辭海．3v. Shanghai: Shang-hai Tz'u-shu Ch'u-pan-she, 1979.

Selected Bibliography

Ho Ch'ang-ch'ün 賀昌群．"Sheng tou pien" 升斗辨, *Li-shih yen-chiu*, 1958.6, 79-86.

Hulsewé, A. F. P. "Ch'in-Han Weights and Measures," in Hulsewé, *Remnants of Ch'in Law.* Leiden: E. J. Brill, 1985, p. 19.

_____. "Weights and Measures in Ch'in Law," in *State and Law in East Asian: Festschrift Karl Bünger*. Dieter Eikemeier and Herbert Franke, eds. Wiesbaden: Harrassowitz, 1981, pp. 25-39.

Kuo-chia Chi-liang Tsung-chü 國家計量總局. *Chung-kuo ku-tai du-liang-heng t'u-chi* 中國古代度量衡圖集. Peking: Wen-wu 文物, 1981.

Loewe, Michael. "The Measurement of Grain during the Han Period," *TP*, 49(1961), 64-95.

Tseng Wu-hsiu 曾武秀．"Chung-kuo li-tai chih-tu kai-shu" 中國歷代尺度概述, *Li-shih yen-chiu,* March 1964, esp. pp. 164-166 and 182.

Wang Chung-ch'üan 王忠全．"Ch'in-Han shih-tai chung, hu, tan hsin-k'ao" 秦漢時代鐘，斛，石新考, *Chung-kuo-shih yen-chiu,* 1988.1, 11-23.

Wu Ch'eng-lo 吳承洛．*Chung-kuo tu-liang-heng shih* 中國度量衡史. Shanghai: Shangwu, 1937.

Yang K'uan 楊寬．*Chung-kuo li-tai ch'ih-tu k'ao* 中國歷代尺度考. Shanghai: Shang-wu, 1955.

Lu Zongli

LIST OF ABBREVIATIONS

I. Books

Ancient China — *Ancient China: Studies in Early Civilization*. David T. Roy and Tsuen-hsuin Tsien, eds. Hong Kong: The Chinese University Press, 1978.

Bodde, "Ch'in" — Derk Bodde. "The State and Empire of Ch'in," in Denis Twitchett and Michael Loewe, eds., in *The Cambridge History of China. Volume 1, The Ch'in and Han Empires*. Cambridge: Cambridge University Press, 1986, pp. 20-102.

Bodde, *Festivals* — Derk Bodde. *Festivals in Classical China*. Princeton: Princeton University Press, 1975.

Bodde, *Statesman* — Derk Bodde. *Statesman, Patriot and General in Ancient China*. New Haven: American Oriental Society, 1940.

Bodde, *Unifier* — Derk Bodde. *China's First Unifier, A Study of the Ch'in Dynasty as Seen in the Life of Li Ssu*. Leiden: E. J. Brill, 1938.

Chang Cheng-lang — Chang Cheng-lang 張政烺. *Chung-kuo ku-tai chih-kuan ta tz'u-tien* 中國古代職官大辭典. Chengchow: Ho-nan Jen-min 河南人民, 1990.

Chang Ta-k'o, *Lun-tsan* — Chang Ta-k'o 張大可. *Shih chi lun-tsan chi shih* 史記論贊輯釋. Sian: Shan-hsi Jen-min 陝西人民 Ch'u-pan-she, 1986.

Chang Wen-hu — Chang Wen-hu 張文虎 (1808-1855). *Chiao-k'an Shih chi "Chi-chieh," "So-yin," "Cheng-yi," cha-chi* 校刊史記集解索隱正義札記. 2v. Rpt. Peking: Chung-hua 中華, 1977.

Chavannes — Édouard Chavannes, trans. *Les Mémoires historiques de Se-ma Ts'ien*. 5v. Paris, 1895-1905; rpt. Leiden: E. J. Brill, 1967. V. 6 Paris: Adrien Maisonneuve, 1969.

Ch'en Chih — Ch'en Chih 陳植. *Shih chi hsin cheng* 史記新證. Tientsin: T'ien-chin Jen-min 天津人民 Ch'u-pan-she, 1979.

"Cheng-yi" — Ssu-ma Chen 司馬貞 (*fl.* 745). "*Shih chi* cheng-yi" 史記正義, as found in the *Shih chi*.

Ch'eng Shu-te   -   Ch'eng Shu-te 程樹德 (1877-1944). *Lun-yü chi-shih* 論
                                          語集釋. 4v. Peking: Chung-hua, 1990.

Cheng T'ien-t'ing   -   Cheng T'ien-t'ing 鄭天挺 *et al., eds. Chung-kuo li-shih
                                          ta tz'u-tien: Ch'in Han shih* 中國歷史大辭點: 秦漢史.
                                          Shanghai: Shang-hai Tz'u-shu 上海辭書 Ch'u-pan-she,
                                          1990.

Chiang Liang-fu   -   Chiang Liang-fu 姜亮夫. *Li-tai jen-wu nien-li pei-chuan
                                          tsung-piao* 歷代人物年里碑傳綜表. Rpt.; Hong Kong:
                                          Chung-hua, 1976.

"Chi-chieh"   -   P'ei Yin 裴駰 (*fl*. 438). "*Shih chi* chi-chieh" 史記集解,
                                          as found in the *Shih chi*.

Ch'ien Mu, *Chu-tzu*   -   Ch'ien Mu 錢穆 . *Hsien Ch'in chu-tzu hsi-nien* 先秦諸
                                          子繫年. 2v. Rpt. Peking: Chung-hua Shu-chü, 1985.

Ch'ien Mu, *Ti-ming k'ao*   -   Ch'ien Mu. *Shih chi ti-ming k'ao* 史記地名考. Rpt.
                                          Taipei: San-min 三民 Shu-chü, 1984.

Chu Tsu-keng   -   Chu Tsu-keng 諸祖耿. *Chan-kuo ts'e chi-chu hui-k'ao* 戰
                                          國策集注彙考. 3v. Nanking: Chiang-su Ku-chi 江蘇
                                          古籍, 1985.

Crump   -   James I. Crump, Jr., trans. *Chan-kuo Ts'e*. 2nd rev. ed.;
                                          San Francisco: Chinese Materials Center, Inc., 1979.

Dolby   -   William Dolby and John Scott, trans. *Sima Qian, War-
                                          Lords, Translated with Twelve Other Stories from His
                                          Historical Records*. Edinburgh: Southside, 1974.

Fang Hsüan-ch'en   -   Fang Hsüan-ch'en 方炫琛. "*Tso-chuan* jen-wu ming-hao
                                          yen-chiu" 左傳人物名號研究. Ph.D. dissertation, Cheng-
                                          chih University (Taiwan), 1983.

Haenisch, *Gestalten*   -   Erich Haenisch. "Gestalten aus der Zeit der chinesischen
                                          Hegemoniekämpfe: Übersetzungen aus Sze-ma Ts'ien's
                                          Historischen Denkwürdigkeiten," *Abhandlungen für die
                                          Kunde des Morgenlandes*, XXXIV.2. Wiesbaden: Har-
                                          rassowitz, 1962.

Haenisch, *Der Herr*   -   Erich Haenisch. *Der Herr von Sin-ling, Reden aus dem
                                          Chan-kuo ts'e und Biographien aus dem Shi-ki*. Stuttgart:
                                          Reclam, 1965.

Han Chao-ch'i	-	Han Chao-ch'i 韓兆琦. *Shih chi hsüan-chu hui-p'ing* 史記選注匯評. Chungchow: Chung-chou Ku-chi 中州古籍 Ch'u-pan-she, 1990.
Ho Chien-chang	-	Ho Chien-chang 何建章. *Chan-kuo Ts'e chu-shih* 戰國策注釋. 2v. Peking: Chung-hua, 1990.
Hucker	-	Charles O. Hucker. *A Dictionary of Official Titles in Imperial China.* Stanford: Stanford University Press, 1985.
Kierman	-	Frank A. Kierman, Jr. *Ssu-ma Ch'ien's Historiographical Attitude as Reflected in Four Late Warring States Biographies.* Wiesbaden: Harrassowitz, 1962.
Knoblock	-	John Knoblock. *Xunzi, A Translation and Study of the Complete Works.* 2v. Stanford: Stanford University Press, 1988 and 1992.
Ku-shih pien	-	Ku Chieh-kang 顧頡剛 (1893-1980) *et al.*, ed. *Ku-shih pien* 古史辨. 7v. Peking: K'ai-ming Shu-tien 開明書店, 1926-38.
Lau, *Analects*	-	D. C. Lau, trans. *Confucius, The Analects.* Harmondsworth, England: Penguin, 1979.
Legge	-	James Legge, trans. *The Chinese Classics.* 5v. Rpt. of 2nd rev. ed. Taipei: Southern Materials Center, 1985.
Liang Yü-sheng	-	Liang Yü-sheng 梁玉繩. *Shih chi chih-i* 史記志疑. 3v. Peking: Chung-hua, 1981.
Liu Pao-nan, *Cheng-yi*	-	Liu Pao-nan 劉寶楠 (1791-1855). *Lun-yü cheng-yi* 論語正義. *SPPY*.
Mizusawa	-	Mizusawa Toshitada 水澤利忠. *Shiki* 史記. V. 8. *Retsuden (ichi)* 列傳 (一). Tokyo: Meiji 明治 Shoten, 1990.
Miao Wen-yüan	-	Miao Wen-yüan 繆文遠, ed. Tung Yüeh 董說 (1620-1686). *Ch'i-kuo k'ao ting-pu* 七國考訂補. 2v. Shanghai: Shang-hai Ku-chi 上海古籍, 1987.
Needham	-	Joseph Needham. *Science and Civilization in China.* V. 1- . Cambridge: Cambridge University Press, 1956- .
Nyitray	-	Vivian-Lee Nyitray. "Mirrors of Virtue: Four 'Shih chi' Biographies." Unpublished Ph. D. dissertation, Stanford

University, 1990.

Ōgawa   -   Ōgawa Tamaki 小川環樹, Imataka Makoto 今鷹真, and Fukushima Yoshihio 福島吉彦, trans. *Shiki retsuden* 史記列傳. Rpt. Tokyo: Chikuma Shobō, 1986 (1969).

Panasjuk   -   V. Panasjuk. *Syma Czjan', Izbrannoe*. Moscow, 1956.

"Pien-nien chi"   -   "Pien-nien chi" 編年紀 in *Shui-hu-ti Ch'in mu chu chien* 睡虎地秦墓竹簡. Shui-hu-ti Ch'in mu chu chien cheng-li hsiao-tsu 整理小組, ed. Peking: Wen-wu 文物 Ch'u-pan-she, 1978.

Pokora, "Traductions"   -   Timoteus Pokora. "Bibliographie des traductions du *Che ki*," in Édouard Chavannes, trans. *Les Mémoires historiques de Se-ma Ts'ien*. V. 6. Paris: Adrien Maisonneuve, 1969, pp. 113-46.

Shen Chung   -   Shen Chung 沈重 *et al.*, ed. *Chung-kuo li-shih ti-ming tz'u-tien* 中國歷史地名辭典. Nanchang: Chiang-hsi Chiao-yü 江西教育 Ch'u-pan she, 1988.

Shih chi   -   *Shih chi* 史記. Ku Chieh-kang 顧頡剛 (1893-1980) *et al.*, eds. 10v. Peking: Chung-hua Shu-chü, 1963.

Shih Chih-mien   -   Shih Chih-mien 施之勉. *Shih chi hui-chu kao-cheng ting-pu* 史記會注考證訂補. Taipei: Hua-kang 華岡, 1976.

SKCS   -   *Ssu-k'u ch'üan-shu* 四庫全書. Rpt., Taipei: Shang-wu.

"So-yin"   -   Chang Shou-chieh 張守節 (*fl.* 725-735). *"Shih chi* so-yin" 史記索隱, as found in the *Shih chi*.

SPPY   -   *Ssu-pu pei-yao* 四部備要.

SPTK   -   *Ssu-pu ts'ung-k'an* 四部叢刊.

Su Chen-shen   -   Su Chen-shen 蘇振申. *Shih-chi "Chung-ni ti-tzu lieh-chuan" shu-cheng* 史記仲尼弟子列傳疏證 (Taipei: Chung-kuo Wen-hua Hsüeh-yüan 中國文化學院 Ch'u-pan-pu, 1965.

Takigawa   -   Takigawa Kametarō 瀧川龜太郎. *Shiki kaichūkōshō fu kōho* 史記會注考證附校補. Rpt. of Tokyo, 1934 ed. with supplementary collation notes by Mizusawa Toshitada 水澤利忠. Shanghai: Shang-hai Ku-chi, 1986.

T'an Ch'i-hsiang   -   T'an Ch'i-hsiang 譚其驤, ed. *Chung-kuo li-shih ti-t'u chi* 中國歷史地圖集. *V. I: Yüan-shih she-hui--Hsia, Shang, Hsi Chou, Ch'un-ch'iu, Chan-kuo shih-ch'i* 原始社會一夏，商，西周，春秋，戰國時期. *V. II: Ch'in, Hsi Han, Tung Han shih-ch'i* 秦，西漢，東漢時期. Shanghai: Ti-t'u 地圖 Ch'u-pan-she, 1982.

T'ang Yen   -   T'ang Yen 唐晏 (1857-1920). *Liang Han San-kuo hsüeh-an* 兩漢三國學案. Wu Tung-min 吳東民, ed. Peking: Chung-hua Shu-chü, 1986.

Tsung-heng-chia shu   -   *Chan-kuo tsung-heng-chia shu* 戰國縱橫家書. Peking: Wen-wu, 1976.

Vandermeersch   -   Léon Vandermeersch. *La formation du Légisme, recherche sur la constitution d'une philosophie politique caractéristique de la Chine ancienne.* Paris: Ecole Francaise d'Extreme-Orient, 1965.

Waley, *Analects*   -   Arthur Waley, trans. *The Analects of Confucius.* London: George Allen and Unwin, 1938.

Wang Hui   -   Wang Hui 王恢. *Shih chi pen-chi ti-li t'u-k'ao* 史記本紀地理圖考. Taipei: Kuo-li Pien-i Kuan 國立編譯館, 1990.

Wang Li-ch'i   -   Wang Li-ch'i 王利器, ed. *Shih chi chu-i* 史記注譯. 4v. Sian: San Ch'in, 1988.

Wang Li-ch'i, *Jen-piao*   -   Wang Li-ch'i 王利器 and Wang Chen-min 王貞珉. *Han shu ku-chin jen-piao shu-cheng* 漢書古今人表書證. Tsinan: Ch'i Lu 齊魯 Shu-she, 1988.

Wang Nien-sun   -   Wang Nien-sun 王念孫 (1744-1817). "*Shih chi* tsa-chih 史記雜志," in V. 1 of Wang's *Tu-shu tsa-chih* 讀書雜志. Rpt. Taipei: Shih-chieh, 1963.

Wang Shu-min   -   Wang Shu-min 王叔岷. *Shih chi chiao-cheng* 史記斠證. 10v. Taipei: Chung-yang Yen-chiu Yüan, Li-shih Yü-yen Yen-chiu So, 1982. *Chung-yang Yen-chiu Yüan, Li-shih Yü-yen Yen-chiu So chuan-k'an* 中央研究院，歷史語言研究所專刊, No. 87.

Watson   -   Burton Watson, trans. *Records of the Grand Historian of China, from the Shih chi of Ssu-ma Ch'ien.* 2v. New York: Columbia University Press, 1961.

Watson, *Chapters*   -   Burton Watson, trans. *Records of the Grand Historian,
                                    Chapters from the Shih chi of Ssu-ma Ch'ien*. New York:
                                    Columbia University Press, 1969.

Watson, *Qin*   -   Burton Watson, trans. *Records of the Grand Historian:
                                    Qin Dynasty*. V. 3. Rev. ed. Hong Kong and New
                                    York: The Research Centre for Translation, The Chinese
                                    University of Hong Kong and Columbia University Press,
                                    1993.

Watson, *Ssu-ma Ch'ien*   -   Burton Watson. *Ssu-ma Ch'ien, Grand Historian of
                                    China*. New York: Columbia University Press, 1958.

Yang, *Li-tai*   -   Yang Yen-ch'i 楊燕起, Ch'en K'o-ch'ing 陳可青, Lai
                                    Chang-yang 賴長揚, eds. *Li-tai ming-chia p'ing Shih chi*
                                    歷代名家評史記. Peking: Pei-ching Shih-fan Ta-hsüeh
                                    北京師範大學, 1986.

Yang, *Lun-yü*   -   Yang Po-chün 楊伯峻. *Lun-yü yi-chu* 論語譯注. Peking:
                                    Chung-hua, 1980.

Yang, *Tso-chuan*   -   Yang Po-chün. *Ch'un-ch'iu Tso-chuan chu* 春秋左傳 注.
                                    4v. Peking: Chung-hua, 1982.

Yang, *Tz'u-tien*   -   Yang Po-chün and Hsü T'i 徐提. *Ch'un-ch'iu Tso-chuan
                                    tz'u-tien* 春秋左傳辭典. Peking: Chung-hua, 1985.

Yang Chia-lo   -   Yang Chia-lo 楊家駱, ed. *Shih chi chin-shih* 史記今釋.
                                    Taipei: Cheng-chung 正中 Shu-chü, 1971.

Yang K'uan   -   Yang K'uan 楊寬. *Chan-kuo shih* 戰國史. 8th printing.
                                    Shanghai: Shang-hai Jen-min 上海人民, 1991.

Yangs   -   Yang Hsien-yi and Gladys Yang. *Records of the Histo-
                                    rian*. Rpt. Hong Kong: The Commercial Press, 1985.

II. Journals

AM   -   *Asia Major*

BIHP   -   *Bulletin of the Institute of History and Philology*
                                            (Academia Sinica, Taiwan)

BMFEA   -   *Bulletin of the Museum of Far Eastern Antiquities*

BSOAS   -   *Bulletin of the School of Oriental and African Studies*

CAJ	-	*Central Asiatic Journal*
CLEAR	-	*Chinese Literature: Essays, Articles, Reviews*
EC	-	*Early China*
HJAS	-	*Harvard Journal of Asiatic Studies*
JA	-	*Journal asiatique*
JAH	-	*Journal of Asian History*
JAOS	-	*Journal of the American Oriental Society*
JAS	-	*Journal of Asian Studies*
JOS	-	*Journal of Oriental Studies*
JCP	-	*Journal of Chinese Philosophy*
MS	-	*Monumenta Serica*
NAA	-	*Narody Azii i Afriki*
OE	-	*Oriens Extremus*
PFEH	-	*Papers on Far Eastern History*
Ritsumei bungaku	-	*Ritsumei bungaku* 立命文學
Shingaku kenkyū	-	*Shingaku kenkyū* 支那研究
TP	-	*T'oung Pao*
Yü-wen hsüeh-hsi	-	*Yü-wen hsüeh-hsi* 語文學習
ZDMG	-	*Zeitschrift der Deutschen Morgenländischen Gesellschaft*

III. Other

ArC	-	Archaic Chinese
ed.	-	editor
mss.	-	manuscript
n.	-	note

no.	-	number
rev. ed.	-	revised edition
rpt.	-	reprint
trans.	-	translator
transl.	-	translation
v.	-	volume

The Grand Scribe's Records

VOLUME VII

*The Memoirs of
Pre-Han China*

Po Yi, Memoir 1[1]

[61:2121[2]] Scholars possessing the broadest of [historical] records and [other] written workss still use the *Six Arts* to determine which of them are failthful records.[3] Among the *Six Arts,*] though the *Odes* and *Documents* are incomplete, the writings of Yeu 虞 and Hsia 夏 can be known.[4]

When Yao 堯 wished to leave the throne, he yielded it to Shun 舜 of Yeu 虞. From Shun to [Shun's successor] Yü 禹, all the Chiefs and Shepherds recommended them [as fit to rule];[5] only then were they tried on the throne. They held office for decades, until their merit was established; only then were they given the reins of government.[6] By this it was shown that the world is a vital vessel,[7] the kingship a great tradition, and the transfer of the world a matter as difficult as this.

Yet speculators[8] also say that Yao yielded the world to Hsü Yu 許由, but Hsü Yu would not accept it. Humiliated at Yao's offer, he fled into hiding.[9] When it came to the time

[1] The title and content of this chapter vary in different editions. By decree of the T'ang Emperor Hsüan-tsung in A.D. 735, the first part of *Shih chi* Chapter 63, relating to Lao Tzu and Chuang Tzu, was placed at the beginning of this chapter. The resulting text was, in one edition, retitled "Lao Tzu Po Yi lieh-chuan" 老子伯夷列傳. The remaining part of Chapter 63 was then renamed "Shen Pu-Hai Han Fei lieh-chuan" 申不害韓非列傳. This rearrangement was no doubt due to the T'ang imperial family's claim to be descendants of Lao Tzu, and perhaps to some readers' objections to the pairing of the founder of Taoism with the most infamous of the Legalist philosophers (see n. 1 to our translation of *Shih chi* Chapter 63). Some later editions which keep the original sequence of biographies still combine the old and new titles of *Shih chi* Chapter 63 as "Lao Chuang Shen Han lieh-chuan" 老莊申韓列傳.

[2] As explained in the front-matter, these numbers refer to the chapter and page of the Chung-hua Shu-chü edition of the *Shih chi* (1959). Only the first reference in each chapter notes the chapter number.

[3] "Six Arts" was another name for the Confucian "Six Classics": *Shih [ching]* 詩[經] (The [Book of] Odes, an anthology of early Chinese poetry), *Shu [ching]* 書[經] (The [Book of] Documents, a collection of essays and speeches attributed to early Chinese rulers, also referred to as the *Shang shu* 尚書 [Ancient Documents]), *Yi [ching]* 易[經] (The [Book of] Changes, a divination manual of the Chou court, also known as *Chou Yi* 周易 [The Changes of Chou]), *Li* 禮 (The Rites, a general term for a number of early works on rites), *Yüeh* 樂 (The Music, a general term for early works on music, none of which have survived), and *Ch'un-ch'iu* 春秋 (The Spring and Autumn Annals, a chronology of the state of Lu 魯).

[4] The place name Yü 虞 is written Yeu to distinguish it from the personal name Yü 禹. Yeu and Hsia 夏 here may specifically refer to the reigns of Emperors Shun 舜 and Yü 禹. Yeu was reputedly either the former state or home village of Shun (see *Shih chi*, 1:31 and our note on that passage). Hsia was the dynasty founded by Shun's successor, Yü.

We translate *wen* 文 as "writings," but recognize it can be taken in the broader sense of both written works and moral teachings (*wen-chiao* 文教). "Cheng-yi" suggests *wen* refers to the chapters of the *Book of Documents* related to Yao, Shun, and Yü, but this is too narrow an interpretation.

[5] According to the accounts of Yao and Shun given in the *Book of Documents*, the *Ssu-yüeh* 四岳 (Chiefs of the-Four Sacred Mountains) and the *Chou-mu* 州牧 (Shepherds of the Divisions) were among the highest positions in their courts (see also n. 91to our translation of *Shih chi* 1 in Volume I).

[6] See *Shih chi* chapters 1 and 2 for Ssu-ma Ch'ien's version of Yao and Shun's yielding the throne.

[7] References to the world as a "vessel" occur in the pre-Ch'in philosophical works *Lao Tzu* 老子, sec. 29, where it is called a *shen-ch'i* 神器 "holy vessel," and in the "Jang wang" 讓王 chapter of *Chuang Tzu* 莊子 (9:10a, *SPPY*), where it is a *ta-ch'i* 大器 "great vessel." The "Wang pa" 王霸 chapter of *Hsün Tzu* 荀子 (7:3b-4a, *SPPY*) says "The state is the world's great vessel, its heavy burden. One must be careful in choosing a place for it and only then placing it."

[8] "Speculators" is our translation for *shuo-che* 說者 which we understand as those thinkers who "meditated on or pondered a subject" (the basic meaning of "to speculate"). This term includes the *chu-tzu* 諸子, those of the *shuo-che* who left written records.

of Yü's 禹 dynasty] Hsia, there were [men such as] Pien Sui 卞隨 and Wu Kuang 務光.[10] For what reason are these men [Hsü Yu, Pien Sui and Wu Kuang] spoken of?

His Honor the Grand Scribe[11] says: "I have climbed Mount Chi 箕山,[12] on whose summit supposedly lies the tomb of Hsü Yu. Confucius narrated the deeds of virtuous sages and worthy men of old; for those such as Wu T'ai-po 吳太伯 and Po Yi 伯夷, he did so in detail.[13] From what I have heard, [Hsü] Yu and [Wu] Kuang were men of the highest principles, yet in Confucius' writings and speech they are scarcely seen. Why is this?

[2122] "Confucius said, 'Po Yi and Shu Ch'i 叔齊 did not dwell on old offenses and thus they harbored little resentment.'[14] 'They sought virtue and obtained it. After all what did they have to resent?'[15] I was profoundly moved by Po Yi's resolve, but when I saw a neglected poem of his, it was rather different from this.[16] Their biographies read as follows":[17]

[2123] Po Yi and Shu Ch'i were two of the sons of the Lord of Ku-chu 孤竹.[18] Their father wanted Shu Ch'i to be enthroned; when he died, Shu Ch'i yielded [the throne] to Po Yi. Po Yi said, "It was father's command [that Shu Ch'i take the throne]," and fled. Shu Ch'i was unwilling to take the throne and he, too, fled. The men of their state enthroned the king's middle son.[19]

---

[9] See *Chuang Tzu* (1:5b-6a, *SPPY*).

[10] These figures are more obscure than Hsü Yu. The longest pre-Ch'in stories are in the "Jang-wang" chapter of *Chuang Tzu* (9:10a-17b, *SPPY*), where the founder of the Shang dynasty, T'ang, approaches them for help in overthrowing the Hsia dynasty. They refuse, and when T'ang succeeds in deposing the Hsia and offers the world to them, they drown themselves.

[11] Much has been written about the term *T'ai-shih kung* 太史公. The basic problem is that *kung* is an honorific referring to someone senior in age (or according that person such status). Whether Ssu-ma Ch'ien uses it to refer to his father, Ssu-ma T'an 司馬談 (d. 110 B.C.) or it has been applied to Ssu-ma Ch'ien himself by later editors, the term is not identical to *T'ai-shih,* the Grand Scribe. We have translated it throughout as "His Honor the Grand Scribe."

Ssu-ma Ch'ien also introduces comments with the phrase "His Honor the Grand Scribe says" in the middle of *Shih chi* Chapters 49 and 124 where he makes more general observations before the main texts.

[12] Mount Chi is located in the southeastern part of Teng-feng 登封 county in present-day Honan (Ch'ien Mu, *Ti-ming k'ao,* pp. 149-50).

[13] Wu T'ai Po was the eldest son of Tan-fu 亶父 (also known as T'ai Wang 太王), the grandfather of King Wen. He supposedly fled south from Chou into the state of Wu 吳 in order to ensure that his younger brother became the Chou king (see *Shih chi,* 31:1445). The *Lun yü* 論語 (Analects of Confucius, 8/1) says, "As for T'ai Po, he can be said to have had supreme virtue. He yielded the world three times and the common people were unable to acclaim him for it." For the *Lun yü* references to Po Yi and Shu Ch'i, see n. 17 below.

[14] *Lun yü,* 5/23. Another interpretation (apparently first proposed by Hsing Ping 邢昺 (932-1010) and cited in *Lun yü cheng-yi* 論語正義, [6:19a, *SPPY*]) would say that "others bore them little resentment." Ssu-ma Ch'ien seems to follow the interpretation given in the translation.

[15] *Lun yü,* 7/15.

[16] The phrase *yi-shih* 軼詩 (with *yi* 軼 equivalent to *yi* 逸) is often applied to ancient poems which were not included in, or dropped out of, the *Book of Odes* (see n. 2 above); this is the interpretation most commentators have adopted. Based upon the context of the word in *Shih chi* Chapters 61 and 62 we have adopted the translation "neglected."

[17] The main body of the *lieh-chuan* 列傳 follows.

Other versions of the Po Yi-Shu Ch'i story occur in *Lun yü* (5/23, 7/15, 16/12 and 18/8), *Meng Tzu* (2A/2, 3B/10, 4A/13, 5B/1, 6B/6, 7A/22 and 7B/15), *Han Fei Tzu* (4:17b, *SPPY*) and *Chuang Tzu* (9:16b-17a and 10:17b-25a, *SPPY*).

[18] In the southern part of modern Lu-lung 盧龍 county in extreme northeast Hopei (T'an Ch'i-hsiang, 1:16).

[19] Po 伯 and Shu 叔 are generational titles (Yi the Elder and Ch'i the Younger). Since translating the names in this way would render them difficult to recognize for many readers, we continue to romanize them, but omit the hyphen (Po Yi instead of Po-yi).

After this, Po Yi and Shu Ch'i heard that Ch'ang 昌, the Earl of the West,[20] cared well for the old. "Why not turn to him?"

When they arrived, the Earl of the West had died and [his son] King Wu 武 was leading an expedition east against Chow 紂,[21] carrying the wooden spirit tablet [of the Earl of the West], whom he called King Wen 文.[22] Po Yi and Shu Ch'i pulled on his horse's reins and admonished him.

"Your father is dead and you have not buried him.[23] Instead you resort to buckler and bill. Can this be called filial? For a vassal to kill his lord, can this be called humane?"

The attendants wanted to cut them down. T'ai-kung 太公[24] said, "These are men of principle." He had [his attendants] help them up and sent away.

When King Wu had quelled the disorders of Yin, the world took [King Wu's dynasty] Chou 周 as its leader; but Po Yi and Shu Ch'i were ashamed to. Their principles would not allow them to eat the grain of Chou,[25] so they hid on Mount Shou-yang 首陽,[26] where they plucked ferns to eat. When their hunger had brought them to the verge of death, they made a song.[27] Its words are:

> We climb that West Mountain,
> pluck its ferns
> He replaces tyranny with tyranny,
> without knowing his error.
> The Shen Nung 神農 (The Divine Farmer),[28]
> Yeu, and Hsia have perished,

[20] The Earl of the West was the title of King Wen of the Chou dynasty prior to Chou's destruction of the Shang dynasty (see *Shih chi*, 3:106).

[21] The last ruler of the Shang dynasty (see *Shih chi*, 4:105-109). We spell his name Chow to avoid confusion with the name of the Chou 周 dynasty which replaced him.

[22] See *Shih chi*, 4:120: "In his ninth year, King Wu sacrificed at Pi. He reviewed his troops to the east up to the Ford of Meng. He made a wooden spirit tablet for the King Wen and carried it in his chariot in the middle of the army. King Wu called himself the Heir Fa, and said that he was serving King Wen in launching the expedition, that he did not dare to act on his own accord."

[23] One of the objections to this story is that in *Shih chi*, 4:120 King Wen died nine years before this expedition. That King Wen had not yet buried him after such a long time was therefore rejected as preposterous. Burials in traditional China, however, were often delayed for years while a suitable gravesite was sought.

[24] T'ai-kung, also known as Lü Shang 呂尙, was one of King Wu's advisors. *Shih chi*, 32:1477 describes his background, role at the Chou court, and enfeoffment with the state of Ch'i 齊. He supposedly received the title T'ai-kung wang 太公望 (Our Grandfather's Hope) when King Wen first met him and exclaimed "Our grandfather, the late ruler, once said 'There will be a sage coming to Chou, and Chou will be revitalized through him.' Are you truly that man? Our grandfather has hoped for you for a long time now." 吾太公望子久矣. See also n. 49 to our translation of *Shih chi* Chapter 4 above.

[25] Another objection to this story has been that "even the ferns belonged to the Chou state" so that Po Yi was inconsistent in refusing to eat grain grown there. As a number of scholars have noted, however, the term "grain" here is to be understood as "official salary," which in pre-modern China was usually calculated in terms of grain. See also Liu Chia-yü 劉家鈺, "Po Yi Shu Ch'i 'pu-shih Chou su' pien" 伯夷叔齊不食周粟辨, *Jen-wen tsa-chih*, 1984.1, 107.

[26] As "Cheng-yi" notes, there are at least five locations given for this mountain in various sources. Tan Ch'i-hsiang (1:19) locates it about 5 miles south of the modern city of Yung-chi 永濟 in Shansi. Ch'ien Mu (*Ti-ming k'ao*, p. 77) believes that yang in Shou-yang probably refers to the south side of Mount Shou and that there is no way to definitely determine its location.

[27] The "neglected poem" referred to above.

[28] See *Shih chi*, 1:3 and our translation of Chapter 1 above.

We understand Shen Nung here as referring to the head of a clan and translate it therefore, on the analogy of the way Scottish clan heads are addressed (i.e., The Bruce), as "The Shen Nung"; when it refers to a clan, we render it "the Shen Nung" (see also n. 3 to our translation of *Shih chi* Chapter 1 above).

where shall we go, where to turn?
Alas, it's all over,
our lot nears its end!

Then they died of starvation on Mount Shou-yang.

"Judging from this, did they harbor resentment, or not?

[2124] "Some say, 'Heaven's way favors none, but always sides with good men.'[29] Can men such as Po Yi and Shu Ch'i be called good then, or bad? They accumulated such virtue, kept their actions this pure, and died of starvation.

"Of his seventy disciples, Confucius recommended only Yen Yüan 顏淵 as 'fond of learning.'[30] But 'Hui 回 [Yen Yüan] was often poor,' and did not get his fill of even rice dregs and husks, finally dying young.[31] How then does Heaven [*2125*] repay good men?

"The Bandit Chih 盜跖 killed innocent men daily, made delicacies from men's flesh,[32] was cruel and ruthless, willful and arrogant, gathered a band of thousands of men and wreaked havoc across the world, yet finally died of old age.[33] From what virtue did this follow?

"These are just the most notorious and best known examples. As for more recent times, men who do not follow what is proper in their actions, and do nothing but violate taboos are still carefree and happy for all their lives and wealthy for generations without end; men who choose carefully how they tread, wait for the right time to offer their words,[34] in walking do not take shortcuts,[35] and except for what is right and fair do not vent pent-up emotions, still encounter disaster and catastrophe in numbers beyond counting. I am deeply perplexed by all this. Perhaps this is what is meant by 'the Way of Heaven.' Is it? Or isn't it?[36]

[2126] "The Master said, 'Those whose ways are not the same do not take counsel with each other.'[37] This is just to say that each follows his own intentions. Thus he said, 'If wealth and rank could be sought, though it were as a knight holding a whip,[38] I too would do it. If they could not be sought, I would follow what I love.'[39]

[29] *Lao Tzu,* section 79. Wang Shu-min (61:2000) cites several other pre-Ch'in and early Han works which express similar sentiments.

[30] In *Lun yü,* 6/3 and 11/7.

[31] See *Lun yü,* 11/7 and 11/18; on Yen Yüan see also *Shih chi* Chapter 67.

[32] The phrase *kan jen chih jou* 肝人之肉 is difficult to interpret. The "Tao-chih" 盜跖 chapter of *Chuang Tzu* (9:18a, *SPPY*) says "[he] minced men's livers and ate them." 膾人肝而餔之. Takigawa (61:12) would thus read *kan* 肝 in the *Shih chi* as an error for *k'uai* 膾. Our translation is an attempt to take *kan* in a putative sense: "he treated men's flesh as [a delicacy or snack similar to] liver."

[33] The Bandit Chih is a stock figure in philosophical literature of the Warring States period. The longest essay on him is found in chapter 29 of the *Chuang Tzu* (9:17b-25a, *SPPY*) We have found no other early references to the Bandit Chih dying of old age. The "P'ien-mu" 駢拇 chapter of *Chuang Tzu* (4:4b, *SPPY*) says that "the Bandit Chih died for the sake of profit on the Eastern Hill," contradicting Ssu-ma Ch'ien's claim.

[34] Perhaps derived from *Lun yü,* 14/13: "The master waited for the right time and only then spoke."

[35] *Lun yü,* 6/14.

[36] The interpretation of the word *tang* 儻 is problematic. One common meaning of *tang* is "if." This would require us to read *so-wei t'ien Tao* 所謂天道 as one clause, and *shih yeh fei yeh* 是邪非邪 as a second clause: "If this is the so-called Way of Heaven, is it right, or wrong?" This is the most common interpretation. Another meaning for *tang,* however, is "perhaps." Thus "Cheng-yi" says "*tang* is a particle indicating uncertainty." 儻, 未定之詞. Such a usage is also found in *Shih chi,* 47:1914: "Although Pi is small, perhaps it is close enough!" 今費雖小, 儻庶幾乎 (see also Wang Yin-chih 王引之, *Ching-chuan shih-tz'u* 經傳釋詞 [Peking, Chung-hua Shu-chü, 1956], p. 138). Our translation follows this interpretation. Wang Shu-min (61:2006) notes that a T'ang mss. of this chapter reads 儻所謂天道邪, 非是邪, but regards this as an error for 儻所謂天道, 非邪,是邪.

[37] *Lun yü,* 15/40.

"'When the year is cold, only then does one know that the pine and cypress are the last to lose their leaves.'[40] When a whole age is muddy, the pure knight stands out. Could it be because he esteems the pine and cypress and scorns the mire of his era?[41]

[2127] "'A gentleman loathes leaving the world with his name unspoken.'"[42] Master Chia [Yi] 賈[宜] said,

The greedy man sacrifices himself for wealth,
the ardent knight for a name.
He who blusters dies for power,
and the common masses cling to life.[43]

"The same brilliances illuminate each other, the same kinds seek each other. 'The clouds follow the dragon, the wind follows the tiger. But when a sage arises, the universe can be seen.'[44]

"Though Po Yi and Shu Ch'i were worthy men, their names became even more brilliant when they obtained the Master's help.

"Though Yen Yüan was devoted to study, his actions became even more renowned when he attached himself to the stallion's tail.[45]

"When the gentlemen of cliffs and caves[46] choose and reject [official positions],[47] it is with such careful timing; when their names are buried and unspoken, it is sorrowful, isn't it?

[38] Liu Pao-nan 劉寶楠 (1791-1855), in his *Lun yü cheng-yi* 論語正義 (8:6a-b, *SPPY*), gives two possible explanations for the phrase *chih pien chih shih* 執鞭之士 "the knight holding the whip": 1) a guard at a market place; 2) an attendant charged with "clearing the road" *pi tao* 躍道 for a noble's carriage. Another possibility is a military officer charged with maintaining discipline when soldiers drill. At any rate, in archaic Chinese *pien* 鞭 "whipping cane" and *ts'e* 策 "horsewhip or riding crop" are usually distinct. By Ssu-ma Ch'ien's time, however, the two were becoming interchangeable (see *Shih chi*, 109:2871, where *pien* is used to describe whipping a horse). Ssu-ma Ch'ien himself seems to refer this passage to a chariot driver (see *Shih chi*, 62:2137).

[39] *Lun yü*, 7/12. The original reads *fu erh k'o ch'iu* 富而可求, here it reads *fu kuei erh k'o ch'iu* 富貴如可求. This famous passage presents some difficulties. It seems preferable to take *fu* here as Ssu-ma Ch'ien understood it, implying not just wealth. Despite James Legge's strictures in his translation of *The Analects of Confucius* (Legge, 1:198), it is also preferable to understand *k'o* 可 as "morally acceptable" or even "morally good," as Arthur Waley (*The Analects of Confucius*, [London: George Allen and Unwin, 1938], p. 125) and D.C. Lau (*Analects*, p. 87) do.

[40] *Lun yü*, 9/28.

[41] This is a particularly difficult sentence to interpret: 豈以其重若彼，其輕若此哉. Our translation takes *yi* 以 as describing the manner in which the "pure knight" becomes famous. If this is correct, then *ch'i* 其 also must refer to the "pure knight." *Ch'i* in turn is the subject of *chung* 重 and *ch'ing* 輕 which we interpret as putative verbs which are nominalized here: "that which is treated as weighty" and "that which is treated as light." The antecedents of *pi* 彼 "such" and *tz'u* 此 "so" are difficult to determine; see Wang Li-ch'i (61:1607) for a summary of the traditional views. It is not clear, however, that the traditional commentators took *yi* or *ch'i* in the way we have here. Wang Shu-min (61:2008-9) follows an interpretation similar to the one proposed here.

[42] *Lun yü*, 15/20.

[43] This is from Chia Yi's 賈誼 (200-168 B.C.) "Fu-niao fu" 鵩鳥賦 (Rhapsody on an Owl, see *Shih chi*, 84:2500).

[44] This is a reference to the "Wen Yen" 文言 section of the *Book of Changes*: "The Master said, 'The same sounds echo each other; the same essences seek each other. Water flows to the wetlands, fire takes to the dry places. Clouds follow the dragon, winds follow the tiger. But when the sage arises, the universe is seen.'" (*Chou Yi cheng-yi* 周易正義, 1:9a, *SPPY*); see also *The I Ching*, Richard Wilhelm, trans., English transl. by Cary F. Baynes [Princeton: Princeton University Press, 1968], p. 382). Thus the sage illuminates not just one or two things, but the entire universe.

[45] Based on the maxim "a fly which attaches itself to the stallion's tail travels one-thousand *li*"; the stallion's tail here is Confucius (see also Wang Li-ch'i, 61:1607n. and *Shih chi*, 95:2673.

[46] A common term for hermits who have retired from the world.

"When men from village gates and lanes wish to polish their actions and establish their names, unless they attach themselves to a man of the highest rank,[48] how can these [actions and names] reach later ages?"

---

[47] *Ch'ü-she* 趣舍 can be taken in two ways: either "advancing and halting" (this is perhaps a military metaphor: "when to charge and when to make camp?") or "taking and discarding" (in which case these are loan characters for *ch'ü* 取 and *she* 捨).

There is a textual variant here in the T'ang manuscript version, which reads 趣舍時有若此類而名堙滅而不稱悲夫. As Wang Shu-min (61:2011) points out, this must have been similar to the version "Cheng-yi" used, since the commentary there reads 言隱處之士時有附驥尾而名曉達. In addition, there are also two punctuations for the current text: the Chung-hua edition breaks after *jo tz'u* 若此, forcing *lei* 類 to be taken in the sense of "good." This is contrary to the general usage of *lei* in *Shih chi.* Takigawa (61:17) breaks after *yu shih* 有時, taking *lei* in its more common sense of "type, kind." This seems to have been the traditional punctuation.

[48] Literally, "a man of the green clouds" *(ch'ing-yün chih shih* 青雲之士). There are a number of interpretations of this phrase. "Cheng-yi" paraphrases it as "a man of great rank" *(kuei-ta chih shih* 貴大之士). This is the best documented meaning of the term, particularly during the Han period, and the basis of our translation. See also n. 62 to our translation of *Shih chi* Chapter 1 above.

TRANSLATORS' NOTE

The "Memoir of Po Yi" is one of the most important works extant for understanding the thought of Ssu-ma Ch'ien, but the subtle indirection he employs here have also made it one of the most difficult chapters to understand in the entire *Shih chi*. Central to this chapter, in our reading, are the concepts of "Heaven's way" *t'ien-tao* 天道 and "Heaven's fate" *t'ien-ming* 天命, or "divine justice" and "blind fate" as Ch'ien Chung-shu 錢鍾書 translates them (Ch'ien Chung-shu, *Kuan-chui pien* 管錐編 [Hong Kong: Chung-hua Shu-chü, 1980], vol. 1, p. 306). Ssu-ma Ch'ien was deeply moved by the failure of good men to come to good ends. As a moralist, this posed difficult questions for him, yet he could not bring himself to wholly reject the idea of "divine justice." As a historian, it also raised dilemmas; morality was central to his vision of history, yet throughout his book, he cannot help but note how often the subjects of his history were mediocrities, whose historical importance was due to "blind fate." Ssu-ma Ch'ien certainly intended his work to make up, at least in part, for the random chance of "blind fate," yet we suggest that this chapter also reflects his acknowledgement that this was not to be done at the price of distorting history.

Because of the wide-ranging nature of Ssu-ma Ch'ien's comments here, many scholars view this chapter as almost a general preface to the memoir section of the *Shih chi*. This is justified, not only by the amount of space Ssu-ma Ch'ien devotes to his musings, as opposed to the exceedingly brief account of his putative subjects, but also by the way in which the language of this biography echoes throughout the entire memoir section of the *Shih chi*. Ssu-ma Ch'ien's quote in this chapter from Confucius, "If wealth and rank could be sought, though it were as a knight holding a whip, I too would do it," is certainly echoed in the next chapter (62), "The Biography of Kuan Chung and Yen Ying," where the final sentence reads, "If Master Yen were still alive, though I were only holding the whip for him, I would be pleased with it." Another quotation from Confucius in this chapter, "Those whose ways are not the same do not take counsel with each other," is repeated in an ironic form in "The Biography of Lao Tzu and Han Fei" (63). The remark "I was profoundly moved by Po Yi's resolve" is repeated again in the "Biography of Ch'ü Yüan and Chia Yi" (84): "When I read "Li-sao," "T'ien-wen" "Chao-hun" and "Ai-ying" I was profoundly moved by his resolve." The comment on how Yen Yüan "attached himself to the stallion's tail" is amplified in the concluding remarks to "The Biography of Fan, T'eng, Li, and Kuan" (95) to include not just Confucius, but great historical figures such as Liu Pang 劉邦, founder of the Han dynasty: "When [these men] were wielding their cleavers, butchering dogs, and selling silk, could they have known that by attaching themselves to the stallion's tail they would be able to leave their names in the courts of Han, and pass on their merit to their descendants?" Such subtle echoes and repetitions, scattered throughout his work, are typical of Ssu-ma Ch'ien's writing and present one of the greatest difficulties in its translation.

There are many complaints about the ahistoric nature of the *Shih chi* version of the Po Yi-Shu Ch'i story, which Liang Yü-sheng (27:1182-4) has summarized under ten points, several of which we have mentioned in the text. These complaints seem to be largely irrelevant to Ssu-ma Ch'ien's purpose in repeating the story. An interesting discussion of various versions of the Po Yi and Shu Ch'i story may be found in Aat Vervoorn's recent work on the Chinese eremitic tradition (see "Bibliography: Studies" below).

BIBLIOGRAPHY

I. Translations

Mizusawa Toshitada 水澤利忠. *Shiki* 史記. V. 8. *Retsuden (ichi)* 列傳 (一). Tokyo: Meiji Shoten, 1990, pp. 31-41.

Ōgawa Tamaki 小川環樹, trans. *Shiki retsuden* 史記列傳. Rpt. Tokyo: Chikuma Shobō, 1986 (1969). pp. 5-7.

Watson, Burton. *Records of the Historian, Chapters from the Shih chi of Ssu-ma Ch'ien*. Rpt. New York: Columbia University Press, 1969, pp. 11-15.

II. Studies

Allan, Sarah. *The Heir and the Sage*. San Francisco: Chinese Materials Center, 1981.

Berkowitz, Alan. "Patterns of Reclusion in Early and Medieval China: A Study of the Formulations of the Practice of Reclusion in Early China and Its Portrayal." Unpublished Ph.D. dissertation, University of Washington, 1989.

Chen Chu 陳柱. "*Shih chi* 'Po Yi lieh-chuan' chiang-chi" 史記伯夷列傳講記, *Hsüeh-shu shih-chieh* 學術世界, 2.2 (November 1936), 112-3.

Graham, A. C. "The Tillers' Version of the Legend of Po Yi 伯夷 and Shu Ch'i 叔齊," in A. C. Graham, *Studies in Chinese Philosophy and Philosophical Literature*. Singapore: The Institute of East Asian Philosophies, 1986, pp. 86-90.

Juan Chih-sheng 阮芝生. "'Po Yi lieh-chuan' hsi-lun" 伯夷列傳析論. *Ta-lu tsa-chih* 大陸雜誌, 62 (1981), 3, 37-42.

_____. "'Po Yi lieh-chuan' fa-wei" 伯夷列傳發微. *Wen-shih-che hsüeh-pao* 文史哲學報, 34 (1985), 1-20.

Vervoorn, Aat. "Boyi and Shuqi: Worthy Men of Old?" *Papers in Far Eastern History*, 28 (September 1983), 1-22.

_____. *Men of the Cliffs and Caves: The Development of the Chinese Tradition to the End of the Han Dynasty*. Hong Kong: The Chinese University Press, 1990.

Kuan [Yi-wu] and Yen [Ying], Memoir 2

Kuan Yi-wu

[62:2131] Kuan Chung 管仲 (*ca.* 720-645 B.C.) Yi-wu 夷吾[1] was a native of the Ying 潁 River region.[2] When he was young, he went abroad[3] with Pao Shu-ya 鮑叔牙,[4] so Pao Shu-ya knew that he was worthy. Kuan Chung was impoverished and often took advantage of Pao Shu-ya, but Pao Shu-ya always treated him well, never mentioning any of these [matters].[5] Shortly thereafter, Pao Shu-ya served the Noble Scion[6] Hsiao-po 小白,[7] while Kuan Chung served the Noble Scion Chiu 糾.[8] When Hsiao-po was established as Duke

[1] Kuan was the *nomen* (the Kuans had the royal *cognomen,* Chi 姬), Yi-wu was the *praenomen,* Chung was the *agnomen,* and Ching 敬 was Kuan's posthumous name (see also Wang Shu-min, 62:2013, and Fang Hsüan-chen, entry 1920, pp. 557-8).

[2] We read Ying as the name of the river and *shang* 上 indicating "along" or "on the shores of" (see Wang Li-ch'i, 62:1611). Although the Chung-hua *Shih chi* editors, Wang Shu-min (62:2013) and other modern scholars treat Ying-shang as a place name (perhaps misreading "So-yin," which says Kuan was born near what is in T'ang times [and today still is] Ying-shang County 潁上縣, located near the confluence of the Ying and the Huai 淮 rivers in western Anhwei), in the late eighth century B.C. when Kuan Chung was born, there was no place named "Ying-shang" (see Ch'ien Mu, *T'i-ming k'ao*, p. 439, and T'an Ch'i-hsiang, 1:29-30).
  In the seventh century B.C. this region was occupied by several small states, but the Ying generally divided Sung 宋 from Ch'u 楚 (see T'an Ch'i-hsiang, 1:21, 29-30). Kuo Sung-t'ao 郭嵩燾 (1818-1891) claims this was the territory of the state of Cheng 鄭, but he doubts that Kuan Chung's lineage can really be traced to Ying-shang (see his *Shih chi cha-chi* 史記札記 [Taipei: Shih-chieh, 1963], 5:234-5).

[3] *Yu* 遊 usually means "to go abroad to study," "to learn," but given the story below, it is "to engage in trade" here.

[4] In this text and elsewhere Pao is often referred to as Pao Shu 鮑叔, but Shu-ya 叔牙 is apparently his *praenomen,* since on *Shih chi,* 32:1486 Pao refers to himself as "Shu-ya." "Cheng-yi" cites a commentary by Wei Chao 韋昭 (208-273) which supports this reading. Fang Hsüan-chen, entry 2214, pp. 626-7, believes that "Shu" designates his generational rank ("middle brother") and "Ya" was his *praenomen.*

[5] "So-yin" cites a passage from the *Lü-shih ch'un-ch'iu:* "Kuan Chung and Pao Shu-ya engaged in trade together at Nan-yang. When they divided the profits, Kuan Chung often took advantage of Pao Shu-ya and got a bigger share. Pao Shu, knowing that he had a mother [to support] and that he was poor, did not consider him greedy." 管仲與鮑叔同賈南陽, 及分財利, 而管仲嘗欺鮑叔, 多自取, 鮑叔知其有母而貧, 不以為貪也. However, this passage cannot be found in modern editions of the *Lü-shih ch'un-ch'iu,* see Chiang Wei-ch'iao 蔣維喬 *et al., Lü-shih ch'un-ch'iu hui-chiao* 會校 (Shanghai: Chung-hua, 1937), p. 664.

[6] *Kung-tzu* 公子 (Noble Scion) was a formal title given to all legitimate male offspring of any feudal lord except the designated successor who was called Greatest Scion or "Heir" (*T'ai-tzu* 太子, Yang, *Tz'u-tien,* p. 99).

[7] Both Hsiao-po and Chiu were sons of Duke Hsi 僖 of Ch'i (r. 730-698 B.C.) by a concubine. Chiu was older than Hsiao-po (see Yang, *Tso chuan,* Chuang 8, p. 176, commentary). It is generally accepted that they were brothers, but in *Kuan-tzu* 管子 ("Ta-k'uang" 大匡, 7:1b, *SPPY*) Kuan Chung said: "The people of this country detest Jiu's [Chiu's] mother and extend this [detestation] to Jiu himself, whereas they pity Xiaopo [Hsiao-po] for being motherless" [W. Allyn Rickett, trans., *Guanzi* (Princeton: Princeton University Press, 1985), p. 285]. Their half-brother, Chu-erh 諸兒, was probably older (cf. the order in which the brothers are listed in the "Ta K'uang" chapter of *Kuan-tzu* [7:1a]). He was the son of the Duke's legitimate wife, succeeded his father, Duke Hsi, in 698 B.C. and ruled as Duke Hsiang 襄 until he was murdered in 686 B.C. His murderer, a cousin named Wu-chih 無知, usurped power in Ch'i until he was killed in 685 B.C. (Yang, *Tso chuan,* Chuang 9, p. 177). Wu-chih's death precipitated the struggle between Chiu and Hsiao-po.

[8] There are several passages which describe these events in more detail. The *Tso chuan* (Yang, *Tso chuan,* Chuang 8, p. 176) notes that when Duke Hsiang first took office he was "without constancy" (*wu ch'ang* 無常). This has been interpreted either as referring to his administration (Tu Yü 杜預) or to his personal morals (as in Ssu-ma Ch'ien's account of how he murdered Duke Huan of Lu among others and slept with Huan's wife and a number of other women in the "Hereditary House of Ch'i T'ai-kung" (*Shih chi,* 32:1485). Indeed, his entire reign was constant only in the improprieties and illegalities he perpetrated.

Huan 桓 (r. 685-643 B.C.), Noble Scion Chiu died[9] and Kuan Chung was imprisoned.[10] Thereupon, Pao Shu-ya recommended Kuan Chung [to the Duke].[11]   Once employed, Kuan Chung was entrusted with the administration of Ch'i and Duke Huan thereby became Hegemon, assembling the feudal lords together[12] and completely rectifying the world.[13]   These were all the plans of Kuan Chung.

Kuan Chung once remarked, "Earlier when I was in adversity, I engaged in trade with Pao Shu-ya and, in dividing the profits, I gave myself more, but Pao Shu-ya never considered me [*2132*] greedy, because he knew I was impoverished.[14]   I planned affairs for Pao Shu-ya and they became worse, but Pao Shu-ya did not consider me ignorant, because he knew that for all affairs there are opportune and inopportune times.   Several times I gained office and several times I was dismissed by my lords, but Pao Shu-ya did not consider me unacceptable, because he knew that my time had not come.   I was in battle several times and I ran several times,[15] but Pao Shu-ya did not consider me cowardly, because he knew that I had an aged mother.   When the Noble Scion Chiu was defeated, Shao Hu 召忽 died for him while I suffered the humiliation of being imprisoned,[16] but Pao Shu-ya did not consider me shameless,

The *Tso chuan* proceeds to relate that Pao Shu-ya foresaw a rebellion and fled to the tiny principality of Chü 莒 (near modern Chü County in southeastern Shantung) with Hsiao-po, while Kuan Chung fled with Chiu to Lu 魯. Their destinations proved of consequence. Hsiao-po in Chü was nearer to the Ch'i capital and subsequently he was the first to reach Lin-tzu 臨淄 after Wu-chih's death. Chiu sought the support of the larger state of Lu and was able to lead their troops against Hsiao-po. Yet the decision to flee to Lu was perhaps a poor one, since under Duke Hsiang, relations between Lu and Ch'i were very bad and the people of Ch'i were certain to reject anyone attempting to gain power supported by Lu.

[9] After Hsiao-po defeated the army of Lu which was supporting Chiu, he forced them to put Chiu to death.

[10] According to the *Tso chuan* (Yang, *Tso chuan*, Chuang 10, p. 180), Pao Shu-ya led the Ch'i army into Lu and asked the Duke of Lu to execute Chiu and to turn over Kuan Chung to Pao Shu-ya. The Duke agreed and Kuan Chung was held prisoner until Pao Shu-ya had returned to T'ang-fu 堂阜, on the Ch'i-Lu border, where he was released.

[11] "Cheng-yi" cites the "Hereditary House of Ch'i T'ai-kung" (*Shih chi*, 32:1486): Pao Shu-ya said [to Duke Huan]: "If my lord wishes to rule Ch'i, Kao Hsi [a fellow official] and I will be sufficient. But if you would serve as Hegemon to the king, you must have Kuan Yi-wu. In whatever country Kuan Yi-wu resides, that country will be weighty, so we should not lose him. At this Duke Huan went along with him."

[12] Reading *chiu* 糾 (*kjegw*) "assembled" for *chiu* 九 (*kjegw*); *chiu-ho chu-hou* 糾合諸侯 is a common phrase (see Wang Shu-min, 62:2014).

[13] *Yi-k'uang t'ien-hsia* 一匡天下 can also be found in the *Lun yü*, 14/17) in a well known passage: "The Master said, 'When Kuan Chung served as chief minister to Duke Huan, [the latter] became Grand Duke over the feudal lords and completely rectified the world. Down to the present day people have received benefits from him. If there had been no Kuan Chung, we might be wearing our hair unbound and buttoning our coats from the left [both as the barbarians do]." The parallelism between *chiu* 九, literally "nine," and *yi* 一, literally "one," though common in early texts (see Wang Shu-min, 62:2014), operates here only at the surface level.

[14] In a comment on another similar passage in the *Shuo-yüan* 說苑 ("Fu-en p'ien" 復恩篇 2 [Peking: Chunghua, 1987], 6:132), Hsiang Tsung-lu 向宗魯 (1895-1941) notes several other parallel versions for this entire speech in various pre-Ch'in works and concludes that this narrative is allegorical.

[15] In Hsü Kan's 徐幹 (170-217) *Chung-lun* 中論 (B:29b, *SPPY*) we are told that "In ancient times Kuan Yi-wu fought three battles and every time was put to rout, so that the people all said he was without courage." Wang Shu-min wryly observes that perhaps Pao Shu-ya was the only person who did not consider Kuan Chung cowardly (62:2015). On losing three battles see also the account of Ts'ao Mo in *Shih chi*, 86:2515-6.

[16] Shao Hu was a friend of Kuan Chung and Pao Shu-ya. He had gone with Kuan Chung to Lu in support of Noble Scion Chiu. His own decision to die is described in *Kuan Tzu* ("Ta-k'uang," 7:5a-b, *SPPY*). There he provides in essence one of the pretexts which have been used to explain Kuan Chung's unconventional acceptance of a position under the lord who defeated his own liege: "I have not died because I have been waiting for things to be settled. Now that they have been settled, [the new duke] will make you chief minister of the left in Ch'i. He would certainly make me chief minister of the right, but for him to employ me after killing my prince would be a double shame for me. You become a live minister, but I shall be a dead one. I shall die knowing that I might

because he knew that I would not be embarrassed by these trivial observances [of social codes], but would consider it shameful if my accomplishments and fame were not made known to the entire world.[17] It was my parents who gave birth to me, but it is Master Pao who understands me."

After he had recommended Kuan Chung, Pao Shu-ya himself worked under Kuan. His descendants for generations received official emoluments in Ch'i, those who were given fiefs held them for more than ten generations,[18] and often they became famous high officials. Throughout the world people thought less of Kuan Chung's worthiness, but much of Pao Shu-ya's ability to appreciate men.[19]

Once Kuan Chung was put in charge of the administration and became Prime Minister[20] of Ch'i, he took the tiny territory of Ch'i on the seacoast[21] and exchanged commodities so as to accumulate wealth, enriching the country and strengthening its armies, sharing with the common people their likes and dislikes. Therefore he proclaimed[22]: "When the granaries are full, the people will understand [the value of] social codes and moderation. When their food and clothing are adequate, they will understand [the distinction between] honor and disgrace.[23] If the sovereign practices the restrictions [set by the social codes],[24] the six relationships will be secure.[25] If the four ties are not extended, the nation will perish.[26] The orders handed

have had [charge of] the government of a 10,000-chariot [kingdom]; in this way, Noble Scion Chiu may be said to have had a minister who died for him. But you will live [to raise to power] a Hegemon; in this way, Noble Scion Chiu may be said to have had a minister who lived for him. . . . And so as they were crossing the border into Ch'i, he cut his own throat and died . . . ." [trans. revised slightly from Rickett, *Guanzi*, pp. 291-2].

[17] In the "Ta-k'uang" chapter of *Kuan Tzu* (7:4a, *SPPY*) this is explained more explicitly in the words of Pao Shu, "That Yi-wu [Kuan Chung] did not die for Noble Scion Chiu was because he wanted to make Ch'i's altars of soil and grain secure"[slightly revised from Rickett, *Guanzi*, p. 290].

Ssu-ma Ch'ien also records Lu Chung Lien's 魯仲連 sympathetic attitude toward Kuan in a letter Lu wrote to a general of Yen: "Kuan Tzu did not take it as shameful to be tied up in prison; he was only ashamed that the empire was not in order. He did not consider not dying for Noble Scion Chiu as shameful; he was only ashamed that his prestige had not spread among the feudal lords" (*Shih chi*, 83:2467-8).

[18] Takigawa (62:4), following Hung Liang-chi 洪亮吉 (1746-1809), points out that "So-yin" erroneously lists ten generations of the lineage of the Kuans here, when the text suggests that Pao Shu-ya's descendants are meant; Takigawa identifies two of these descendants, Pao Mu 鮑牧 and Pao Yen 鮑晏, both officials of Ch'i.

[19] Duke Huan himself was grateful to Pao Shu for recommending Kuan Chung and with each of Kuan's great accomplishments the Duke would reward Pao first (see "Tsan-neng" 贊能, *Lü-shih ch'un-ch'iu* [24:3b, *SPPY*]).

[20] Sydney Rosen has argued that in the *Tso chuan*, the earliest depiction of Kuan Chung's career, it is likely that *hsiang* 相 meant only "to hold office as a general advisor, with perhaps special advisory functions in the field of interstate relations" (see her "The Historical Kuan Chung," *JAS*, 35.3 [May 1976], p. 431).

[21] This language echoes that on *Shih chi*, 6:282: "But Ch'in, with its tiny territory and force of one-thousand chariots, had been able to command the other eight lands and bring the lords of equal rank to its court for more than one-hundred years" (see the translation by Chavannes, 2:6:231). In ancient times China was supposedly divided into nine *chou* 州 or "lands": Yung 雍 (Ch'in territory), Chi 冀, Yen 兗, Ch'ing 青, Hsü 徐, Yang 揚, Ching 荆, Yü 預, and Liang 梁 (see Wang Li-ch'i, 1:42).

[22] "So-yin" comments here: "This is that which Yi-wu had written into a book that is called *Kuan Tzu*. As his book contains these words, [Ssu-ma Ch'ien] briefly cites their essential points." Rickett (*Guanzi*, "The Origin of the Present Text," pp. 14-24) has carefully outlined the development of the current text. This first chapter Rickett believes to be "certainly one of the earlier chapters" (p. 51), and dates it "from the early or middle part of the fourth century B.C." (p. 52).

[23] Rickett (*Guanzi*, p. 52, n. 2) observes that "Jung ju" 榮辱 (Honor and Disgrace) is a chapter title in the *Hsün Tzu* and discusses comments by Hsün Tzu and Meng Tzu on "honor and shame."

[24] This passage also occurs at the onset of the first section ("Mu-min" 牧民 [Shepherding the People]) of the *Kuan Tzu* (1:1a, *SPPY*). Fang Hsüan-ling's 房玄齡 (578-648) commentary glosses *fu* 服 as *hsing* 行, "to carry out, to practice," and *tu* 度 as *li-tu* 禮度, "restrictions of the social norms." Although there are a number of explications of this passage in the various *Shih chi* commentaries, our translation follows Fang's reading which addresses the text in its fuller context. The translation is revised accordingly from Rickett, *Guanzi*, p. 52.

down are like the source of a river [which follows a natural course] so that they will be in accord with the hearts of the people."[27] Therefore, what he advocated was modest and easy to put into effect.[28] Whatever the masses desired, he would accordingly give them. Whatever they rejected, he would accordingly abolish.

[2133] As for his political strategies, he excelled in creating blessings from disasters and in turning failure into success. He gave great importance to the weight [of coins] and was careful about the standards of scales.[29] When Duke Huan was in fact angry with Shao Chi 少姬 and raided south into Ts'ai 蔡,[30] Kuan Chung took advantage of the situation to launch a punitive expedition against Ch'u, which he accused of failing to present "bound reeds" as tribute to the Chou House.[31] When Duke Huan was in fact leading a campaign north against

[25] We follow Wang Pi's 王弼 (226-249) opinion quoted in "Cheng-yi": "[The six relationships are those with] father, mother, elder brother, young brother, wife, and children" (See Rickett, *Guanzi*, p. 52, n. 3).

[26] This is a quotation from the first chapter of the *Kuan Tzu*, "Mu-min" (trans. modified slightly from Rickett, *Guanzi*, p. 52-3). The *ssu-wei* 四維 or "four ties" refer "to the four guy lines or ropes used to support a target or lines attached to the four corners of a fish net to pull it in" (Rickett, p. 52, n. 4). They are subsequently explained in "Mu-min" as *li* 禮 (social codes), *yi* 義 (righteousness), *lien* 廉 (purity) and *ch'ih* 恥 (sense of shame). Rickett thus renders the term "the four cardinal virtues."

[27] This last section is slightly revised from *Kuan-tzu*, 1:2b (*SPPY*); the translation is again based on Rickett, *Guanzi*, p. 55.

[28] "Cheng-yi" presents another reading: "Which is to say 'His administrative orders were humble and few, and the common people were easily able to put them into effect.'"

[29] "So-yin" (*Shih chi*, 62:2133) comments: "'Light and heavy' refers to coins. In the present *Kuan Tzu* there is a 'Light and Heavy Section.'" "Cheng-yi," however, reads this passage metaphorically: "Light and heavy refer to shame and dishonor; the weight and beam [of the scale] refers to gains and losses. When there were [matters involving] shame and dishonor, he took them as very important; when there were [matters involving] gains and losses, he was very cautious [in dealing] with them."

This section is one of eight into which an unknown person (possibly Liu Hsiang) divided the *Kuan Tzu*; "Light and Heavy" makes up the final section of the work (ch. 24, *SPPY*) and is concerned mainly with economics (see Rickett, *Guanzi*, p. 5). It appears "to be quite late" and is "often associated with the scholars representing the tradition of the famous Salt and Iron debates in 81 B.C." (Rickett, "*Kuan-tzu* and the Newly Discovered Texts on Bamboo and Silk," in *Chinese Ideas about Nature and Society*, Charles LeBlanc and Susan Blader, eds. (Hong Kong: Hong Kong University Press, 1987), p. 243, n. 18. In personal correspondence Rickett concurs that our reading for *ch'ing-chung* might be correct here, but cautions that "in the *Guanzi* [the term] is much more complex. There it refers to the manipulation of goods to control prices and production. It also appears to involve a rudimentary quantitative theory of money."

[30] Shao Chi, literally the "Chi, the Younger," is referred to elsewhere as Ts'ai-chi 蔡姬, "Chi from Ts'ai" (Chi was the *cognomen* of the Ts'ai rulers). "So-yin" comments: "It is our opinion that this refers to his being angry with the 'rocking-boat consort,' who when she was sent back [to Ts'ai] was not divorced. The people of Ts'ai had her remarried."

The basic story is told in the *Tso chuan* (656 B.C.; Yang, *Tso chuan*, Hsi 3, p. 286): "The Marquis of Ch'i [Duke Huan] was boating with the Consort from Ts'ai in [his] park when she rocked the duke. The duke was frightened, changed color, and forbade her [from this], but she wouldn't stop. The duke became angry and sent her back [to Ts'ai] without divorcing her. The people of Ts'ai remarried her."

Ts'ai is located near modern Hsin Ts'ai 新蔡 on the Ju River 汝水 in southeast Honan about 360 miles southwest of the Ch'i capital at Lin-tzu on the northeastern border of Ch'u (see T'an Ch'i-hsiang 1:20-21 and 29-30). Therefore, to attack Ch'u the allies would have to pass through (or very near to) Ts'ai.

In several later accounts, including those in *Shih chi* 32:1489 and 35:1566, this event is amplified and related to the concerted attack on Ts'ai by the feudal lords reported in the account of the following year (656 B.C.) in the *Tso chuan*.

Yang Po-chün (*Tso chuan*, Hsi 4, p. 289) recounts several versions of this story including that which says Duke Huan summoned the feudal lords on the pretense of wanting to punish Ch'u, but then swung his armies about and attacked Ts'ai. But he concludes that these are merely accounts by later "persuaders" (*shui-k'o* 說客) and that the *Tso chuan*, which does not link the two incidents, should be considered the most reliable account.

[31] *Fa* 伐 were "punitive expeditions" ostensibly undertaken on behalf of the Chou king. The reason for this ex-

the Jung [tribe] of the Mountains,[32] Kuan Chung took advantage of the situation to order the lord of Yen to cultivate the [model] government of Duke of Shao 召.[33] When Duke Huan intended to break his agreement with Ts'ao Mo 曹沫 after the convention of K'o 柯, Kuan Chung took advantage of the situation and made him faithful to his word,[34] and through this the feudal lords all submitted to Ch'i.[35] Therefore, it is said that "Knowing that 'to give is to receive' is the most precious thing in governing."[36]

[2134] Kuan Chung's wealth was comparable to that of a ducal house. He held [the privilege of] "three returns"[37] and of using the cup-stand,[38] but the people of Ch'i did not

pedition was ostensibly that Ch'u had stopped submitting *pao-mao* 包茅 or 苞茅, reeds which were bound and used to filter wine for sacrifice.

[32] Shan-Jung 山戎 (Mountain Jung) were a non-Chinese tribe, sometimes equated with the Pei 北 or "Northern" Jung, who lived in the mountainous regions of what is today Hopei province (see also n. 10 to our translation of *Shih chi* Chapter 4 above).

[33] According to *Shih chi*, 32:1488, "In the twenty-third year [of Duke Huan, i.e., 663 B.C.] the Jung [tribe] of the Mountains made a punitive expedition against Yen, and Yen reported the danger to Ch'i. Duke Huan of Ch'i went to Yen's rescue, leading a punitive expedition against the Jung of the Mountains and reaching Ku-chu before returning. Duke Chuang of Yen then saw off Duke Huan until they entered the Ch'i border. Duke Huan said, 'Unless it is the Son of Heaven, the feudal lords in seeing one another off do not leave their borders. I cannot act without propriety towards Yen.' Thereupon, he demarcated the land the Lord of Yen had reached with a ditch and gave it to Yen, ordering the lord of Yen to reinstate the government of Duke of Shao and to pay tribute to Chou as in the days of [Kings] Ch'eng 成 (c. 1067-1031 B.C.) and K'ang 康 (c. 1030-1005 B.C.). When the feudal lords heard of this, they all followed Ch'i."

[34] These events took place in the fifth year of Duke Huan's rule (681 B.C.). None of the sources, which provide two basically different accounts, is without errors of some sort (see Yang, *Tso chuan*, Chuang 13, pp. 193-4, esp. the commentary on p. 194). Nevertheless, the accounts agree that Duke Chuang 莊 of Lu (r. 693-662 B.C.) met with Duke Huan at K'o (southwest of Tung-k'o hsien 東柯縣 in modern northwest Shantung, Wang Li-ch'i, 62:1080) "to swear a covenant" as a means to settle hostilities between Lu and Ch'i. Lu presented Ch'i with the city of Sui 遂 (20 miles southeast of T'ai-an 泰安 at the foot of Mount T'ai, 10 miles north of the Wen River 汶河 and some 40 miles north of Ch'ü-fu 曲阜, the Lu capital [*ibid.*]). Some texts (*Shih chi*, 32:1487 and 86: 2515) then describe how Ts'ao Mo leapt onto the earthen altar and held a dagger to Duke Huan to compel him to return the city to Lu. After the duke consented and Ts'ao Mo released him, he wanted to renege on his agreement and kill Ts'ao Mo, but Kuan Chung pointed out the larger gain of support from the feudal lords which could be had by the duke's keeping his word. Liang Yü-sheng (27:1184-5) is skeptical that any of these three events (i.e., the raid on Ts'ai, the campaign against the Mountain Jung, and the incident with Ts'ao Mo) actually took place.

[35] The seventh year of Duke Huan's reign (679 B.C.) is generally accepted as the year he became Hegemon (see "Hereditary House of Ch'i T'ai-kung," *Shih chi*, 32:1487). Sydney Rosen ("Changing Conceptions of the Hegemon in Pre-Ch'in China," in *Ancient China*, pp. 99-114) has summarized the final steps in Ch'i's ascendancy as follows: "In 684 Duke Huan extinguished the small state of T'an, the ruler of which had offended him. In 683 he married a Chou princess. In 681 there was a meeting of the states to consider disorder in Sung. Commentators assert that it was called by Ch'i, although that is not clear in the text of the *Tso chuan*. The little state of Sui did not send a representative and that summer Ch'i extinguished Sui. In the winter of the same year Lu concluded a peace pact with Ch'i. The Ch'i ruler requested troops from the king and thus, with royal armies, led the feudal lords under the king's banner, in a disciplinary action, against Sung. The state of Sung submitted. And in 679, at a meeting of the feudal lords, Ch'i 'for the first time was *pa*' [citing the "Hereditary House of Ch'i T'ai-kung" here]."

[36] This saying is also found in the "Mu-min" chapter of *Kuan Tzu* (1:2b, *SPPY*; trans. by Rickett, *Guanzi*, p. 54). A similar saying is also found in *Lao Tzu* (Section 36): "If you wish to snatch something from it [the Way], you must give something to it" 將欲奪之, 必固與之. The current text of *Lao Tzu* reads *to* 奪 "to snatch" for *ch'ü* 取 "to take." Chu Ch'ien-chih 朱謙之 (*Lao Tzu chiao-shih* 老子校釋 [Hong Kong: T'ai-p'ing Shu-chü, 1962], p. 144) reviews the various arguments and prefers *to*. Here *ch'ü* may be used because of the rhyme with *yü* 與 "to give." Regardless of the exact wording, our text refers to Kuan Chung's strategy of giving back to Lu what it wanted so as to gain for Ch'i the confidence of other feudal states, including eventually Lu itself.

[37] *San-kuei* 三歸 "three returns" has been variously interpreted. "Cheng-yi" says: "The 'three returns' are women of three cognomens. A woman refers to getting married as a 'return' [to her home]." Panasjuk (p. 55)

consider him extravagant. After Kuan Chung died, the country of Ch'i followed his policies and Ch'i was often stronger than the other feudal states. Over one-hundred years later, Master Yen was there.[39]

Yen Ying

Yen P'ing 晏平, Chung Ying 仲嬰,[40] was a native of Yi-wei 夷維 in Lai 萊.[41] He served Duke Ling 靈 (r. 581-554 B.C.), Duke Chuang 莊 (r. 553-548 B.C.) and Duke Ching 景 (r. 547-490 B.C.) [of Ch'i] and because of his moderation[42] and vigor was esteemed in Ch'i. Even after he became Prime Minister of Ch'i, he did not have two servings of meat[43]

follows this reading. But Kuo Sung-t'ao refutes the "Cheng-yi" claim in his *Shih chi cha-chi* (5A:235-6), pointing out that this explanation is based on a commentary (by Ho Yen 何晏 [d. 249]) to the *Lun yü* (3/22). Kuo goes on "According to the social code, when the feudal lords first took a wife, a country of the same cognomen used her nieces as servants [for the bride]. [But] in one marriage [to take] wives of three surnames, was unheard of according to the social code . . . ." Kuo's conclusion is that *san-kuei* referred to a *return* of *three* parts of ten from profits in the market place and he cites passages from the "Ch'ing-chung" section of the *Kuan-tzu* (24:2b, *SPPY*) and several other supporting texts. Wang Li-ch'i (62:1612) assembles most of the other theories concerning "three returns," which include (1) the name of a tower, (2) the name of a city, and (3) three homes (to return to) and adopts "three homes." Wang Shu-min (62:2018) endorses Kuo Sung-t'ao's conclusions, as do we.

[38] Takigawa (62:6) notes that *fan-tien* 反坫 were "cup-stands" placed between two pillars where the lords placed empty cups after drinking to seal a pledge or vow. Cheng Hsüan 鄭玄 (127-200) argues in his commentary to the *Li chi* 禮記 (8:3a, *SPPY*) that the stands were used after a toast to a visiting lord. This *Li chi* passage is in the context of various privileges which had been usurped from the king by the feudal lords. Perhaps in response to this, Confucius criticized Kuan Chung for having both a cup-stand and the three returns (see *Lun yü*, 3/22).

[39] As Wang Li-ch'i (62:1612) observes, Kuan Chung died in B.C. 645 while Yen Ying was first appointed to a position in Duke Ling's court in 556 B.C., only eighty-nine years after Kuan's death. However, since Yen Tzu served in the Ch'i court for a long period (he died in 500 B.C.--*Shih chi*, 32:1505), Ssu-ma Ch'ien might have intended here that "over one-hundred years later Yen Tzu was there [in charge of the Ch'i government]."

[40] P'ing was his posthumous name, Chung his *agnomen,* and Ying his *praenomen* (see "So-yin"). Fang Hsüan-chen (entry 1352, p. 425) comes to similar conclusions, except for Chung, which she calls his "generational rank" (*hang-tz'u* 行次).

[41] "Chi-chieh," following Liu Hsiang 劉向 (57-6 B.C.), identifies Lai with what was known as Tung Lai 東萊, i.e., most of the tip of the Shantung Peninsula north and east of modern Tsingtao. T'an Ch'i-hsiang (1:27) and Yang Po-chün (*Tso chuan*, Hsüan 7, p. 690) observe that Lai was the region southeast of modern Ch'ang-yi 昌邑 in northern Shantung. Yi-wei is near modern Kao-mi 高密, about 40 miles northwest of Tsingtao (see also Ch'ien Mu, *T'i-ming k'ao*, p. 663). Lai was annexed by Ch'i in 567 B.C. (see Yang, *Tso chuan*, Hsiang 6, p. 946).

[42] Concerning Yen Ying's moderation there is a relevant passage in the *Li chi* (12:19a-b, *SPPY*) which Wang Shu-min (62:2019) cites: "Confucius said, 'Kuan Chung engraved his sacrificial grain vessels and colored his hat strings red [usurping royal privilege--see the commentary to a similar passage, *Ibid.*, 7:16b]. He set out trees [to screen his gate] and used cup-stands. He had hills fashioned on his pillars and had duckweed painted on his roof beams. He was a virtuous official, but it was not easy to be his superior [since he usurped so many privileges of his superior].'

'Yen P'ing-chung in sacrificing to his ancestors used the shoulder of a suckling pig which did not cover the platter. He was a virtuous official, but it was difficult to be his subordinate'" [see also the translation by James Legge, *Li chi, Book of Rites* (Rpt. New Hyde Park, New York: University Books, 1967), v. 2, p. 165].

In the *Lun yü* (5/18) the man who "had hills fashioned on his pillars and had duckweed painted on his roof beams" was Tsang Wen-chung 臧文仲 (d. 617 B.C.), a minister of Lu.

Takigawa (62:7) cites a further relevant passage from the *Li chi* (3:6b-7a, *SPPY*): "Yen Tzu had a single fox coat for thirty years."

[43] Both Wang Li-ch'i (62:1613) and Georges Margouliès ("Biographies de Kouan [Tchong] et de Yen [Ying]," *Le Kou-wen chinois* [Paris: Guethner, 1926], p. 81) read 重 as *ch'ung*, an adjective meaning "double." See also the "So-yin shu-tsan" 述贊 (*Shih chi, 62:2137*).

and his concubines did not wear silk. When he was at court, if the duke said something which praised him, he would speak warily, if the duke said something which did not praise him, he would act warily.[44] If the Way prevailed in the country, he would follow orders. If it did not, he would weigh the orders [before deciding whether to obey].[45] For these reasons, he was renowned among the feudal lords during the three reigns [he served in Ch'i].

[2135] Father Yüeh Shih[46] 越石父 was a worthy man who was [tied up] in black ropes[47] [as a prisoner].[48] When Master Yen set out and met him along the road, he unharnassed the horse to the left [from his team of four], ransomed him [with it], and took him home in his carriage. There without properly taking leave, Master Yen went into his chambers. After a long while, Father Yüeh Shih asked to bid farewell to him. Master Yen was surprised. Straightening his hat and clothes, he apologized, "Although I might not be a benevolent man, I have freed you from your distress. Why do you seek to bid me farewell so soon?" Father Shih replied, "This is not the case. I have heard that a gentleman is wronged by one who does not appreciate him, but trusts one who does. Now when I was in the black ropes, those people did not appreciate me. Since you, sir, sensed [my worth] and ransomed me, you are someone who appreciates me. For even one who appreciates me to act improperly [towards me] is certainly worse than being in the black ropes." Thereupon, Master Yen invited him to enter his home as his honored guest.

Once when Master Yen was Prime Minister of Ch'i and went out, the wife of his driver peeked out through a crack in the door at her husband. Her husband, as the Prime Minister's driver, was holding a large umbrella and whipping the team of four horses; striking a haughty pose, he was extremely pleased with himself. After some time he returned home and his wife requested that he let her leave him. When her husband demanded a reason, she answered, "Master Yen, though barely five-feet tall,[49] personally acts as Prime Minister of Ch'i and his fame is known among the feudal lords. Just now I watched him leave, deep in thought, as if there was always something which humbled him. As for you, you are six-feet tall and yet you serve others as a driver and seem content with yourself--this is why I want to leave you." After this, her husband became more self-effacing. When Master Yen wondered [at his change] and asked him about it, the driver told him the facts of the matter. Master Yen subsequently recommended him to be a Grand Master.

---

[44] See also Rainer Holzer, *Yen Tzu und das Yen Tzu ch'un-ch'iu* (Frankfurt: Peter Lang, 1983), pp. 8-9. Takigawa (62:7) cites the *Lun yü* (14/3) for comparison: "When the Way prevails in a state, words should be bold. When the Way does not prevail, actions should be bold, [but] words should be unassuming."

[45] Takigawa (62:7) cites a gloss by Li Li 李笠 to the effect that *heng* 衡 was interchangeable with *heng* 橫, "to refuse." Margouliès follows this reading (p. 81). But Takigawa prefers to understand *heng* 衡 here according to "Cheng-yi" as *ch'eng* 秤 "to weigh, consider."

[46] *Fu* 父 is an honorific designation for an old man here. Yüeh Shih is unknown except in the series of parallel passages dealing with this incident (see note 49) and a (probably spurious) speech recorded in the *Shuo yüan* (17:13b-14a, *SPPY*).

[47] "Black ropes" were used to bind prisoners (see "Cheng-yi" and *Lun yü* [5/1]).

[48] "Cheng-yi" cites a parallel passage from the *Yen Tzu ch'un-ch'iu*. But this passage (as "Cheng-yi" admits) differs in detail from the *Shih chi*. It seems more likely that Ssu-ma Ch'ien took his material from the *Lü-shih ch'un-ch'iu* (16:4b-5a, *SPPY*) passage which more closely approximates this text (or from another common source).

[49] A "foot" (*ch'ih* 尺) was about 7.839 inches (or 19.91 cm) during the Chou (see Wu Ch'eng-lo, chart p. 64). This would make Master Yen less than four-feet in height and the driver about five feet three inches tall. However, there were several standards of linear measurement at that time (Wu Ch'eng-lo, p. 59) so it is impossible to fix the exact heights intended. The translation is therefore not literal (reading "five" for "six" and "six" for "eight"), but conveys the meaning of the original closely.

[2136] His Honor the Grand Scribe says: "I have read Mr. Kuan's 'Mu min" 牧民 (Shepherding the People), 'Shan kao' 山高 (The Mountains are High),[50] 'Ch'eng ma' 乘馬 (Chariots and Horses),[51] 'Ch'ing chung' 輕重 (Light and Heavy),[52] and 'Chiu fu' 九府 (Nine Bureaus)[53] and the *Spring and Autumn of Yen Tzu.*[54] With such detail have they [Kuan and Yen] spoken of things.[55] Since I have seen their writings, I wanted to observe the way they put things into practice[56] and have for this reason composed[57] memoirs of them.[58] As for their writings, many people today have copies, and because of this I have not included them, but instead have included some neglected stories.[59]

"Kuan Chung was what the world refers to as a worthy official, but Confucius belittled him.[60] Could it be because he considered that the Way of the Chou House was in decline and Duke Huan was worthy, yet Kuan Chung did not exhort him to become king, but rather to proclaim himself Hegemon? The saying goes: '[A gentleman] guides [his ruler] in accordance with [his ruler's] merits and rectifies [him] in order to redeem him from his excesses.[61] For

---

[50] *Shan-kao* are the first words in the second chapter of the present *Kuan Tzu* text, known today as "Hsing-shih" 形勢 (On Conditions and Circumstances, see Rickett, *Guanzi,* p. 6, n. 13).

[51] As Rickett (*Guanzi,* p. 114) points out, the term *ch'eng ma* appears in the titles of chapters I.5, XXI.68, 69 and 70 (the last mentioned is no longer extant). A widely accepted reading understands *ch'eng* and *ma* as accounting terms and the chapter-title as "on government finances." Rickett proposes to read 乘 as *sheng* and believes the term refers to an early system of military taxes (*sheng-ma chih fa* 乘馬之法).

[52] Rickett (*Guanzi,* p. 6, n. 15) observes that some scholars feel the "Ch'ing chung" section (which contains the last nineteen chapters of the present text) was written during the Han dynasty and that Ssu-ma Ch'ien may be referring to other chapters here (see also note 31 above). Yet it is also possible that Ssu-ma Ch'ien's statement here lends support to scholars such as Hsü Ch'ing-yü 徐慶譽 who believe the "Ch'ing chung" predates *Han Fei Tzu.*

[53] This chapter has been lost (see "Cheng-yi"). "So-yin" argues that the "Chiu-fu" were treasuries. On *Shih chi,* 129:3255, Kuan Chung is said to have "set up the [system of] light and heavy and the nine bureaus" 設輕重九府. "Cheng-yi" argues that "light and heavy" here refers to money and that the bureaus were financial agencies (see also Rickett, *Guanzi,* p. 6, n. 16). On the general textual history of the *Kuan-tzu* see Rickett, *Guanzi,* pp. 3-25.

[54] Wu Tse-yü 吳則虞 (*Yen Tzu ch'un-ch'iu chi-shih* 晏子春秋集釋 [2v.; Peking: Chung-hua, 1982], pp. 18-21) believes the text was compiled in the mid-third century B.C. by a scholar from Ch'i, possibly Ch'un-yü Yüeh 淳于越.

[55] Here the *chih* 之, literally "those things," presumably refers to the subjects discussed in the *Kuan-tzu* and *Yen Tzu ch'un-ch'iu* which both Ssu-ma Ch'ien and his readers know so well they need not be mentioned.

[56] Possibly paraphrasing Confucius' comments on assessing men (*Lun yü,* 5/10): "Tsai Yü was taking a nap. The Master said, 'Rotten wood cannot be carved, a wall of dung-filled earth cannot be troweled. As for Yü, what use is there to reprimand him?'
[Another time] the Master said, 'At first [my attitude] towards people was to listen to their words and then trust them to put them into action. Now [my attitude] towards people is to listen to their words and then observe their actions. On Tsai's account I have changed this."

[57] *Tz'u* 次 does not mean "to arrange" as some have argued (Wang Li-ch'i, 62:1613, for example), but, similar to *hsü* 序 or *lun* 論, "to put words into order," i.e., "to compose," as in the translation by Chang Ta-k'o 張大可 (*Lun-tsan,* p. 251: *pien-hsieh* 編寫).

[58] *Chuan* 傳 is read here similar to its use in the title *Tso chuan.* Ssu-ma Ch'ien seems to suggest that his *chuan* will focus on the actions of Kuan Chung and Yen Ying, thereby complementing their words as recorded in the *Kuan Tzu* and *Yen Tzu ch'un-ch'iu.* See also the discussion of *chuan* in the Introduction to this volume.

[59] See n. 15 to our translation of *Shih chi* Chapter 61 above.

[60] As Takigawa (62:10) observes this probably refers to Confucius' comment, "Small indeed was Kuan Chung's capacity!" (*Lun yü,* 3/22). Margouliès (p. 82, n. 33) believes that Confucius may have been jealous of the grandeur that Kuan Chung gave to Ch'i, a rival of Confucius' home state of Lu.

[61] "Cheng-yi" understands *ch'i* 其 as referring to the people and the state, thus "[A gentleman] guides [his ruler] in accordance with the merits of the people [or "the state"] and rectifies [him] in order to redeem their excesses . . . ." Panasjuk (p. 55) follows this interpretation in his rendition.

this reason the one above and the one below are able to develop a close relationship.'[62] Does-n't this refer to Kuan Chung?

"When Master Yen fell down upon the corpse of Duke Chuang, he would not leave un-til he completed his ritual duties [according to the social code] for his lord.[63] Could we say that he was 'one who regards seeing what was right but not doing it as cowardice'?[64] When it came to remonstrating, he did not care [*2137*] about saving his lord's face, and he was one whom we might refer to as 'exhausting his every thought in how to be loyal as he comes to court, and in how to remedy his [ruler's] faults as he withdraws.'[65] If Master Yen were still alive, though I were only holding the whip for him, I would be pleased with it."[66]

[62] This is from the *Hsiao ching* (8:2a-b, *SPPY*): "The Master said, 'A gentleman in serving his ruler, exhausts his every thought in how to be loyal as he comes to court, and in how to remedy his [ruler's] faults as he with-draws. [He] guides [his ruler] in accordance with [his ruler's] merits, ...'"

[63] This story is told in the *Tso chuan* (Yang, *Tso chuan*, Hsiang 25, pp. 1095-9) and took place in 548 B.C. Ts'ui Shu 崔述 killed Duke Chuang in his home because the Duke had carried on an affair with Ts'ui's wife. When Master Yen, who had been waiting outside, went in and found the Duke slain, he lay down on his body and wept and then performed the ritual three leaps before leaving. One of Ts'ui Shu's men urged that Master Yen be killed, but Ts'ui spared him in order to bring the people of Ch'i to his side (see also *Shih chi*, 32:1500-1, which follows the *Tso chuan* account).

On what appears to be a motif of falling upon the body of one's lord, see C. S. Goodrich, "Ssu-ma Ch'ien's Biography of Wu Ch'i," *MS*, 35(1981-3), pp. 202 and 225, n. 42.

[64] Alluding to the *Lun yü* (2/24): "To sacrifice to a spirit not related to oneself is flattery. To see what is right but not do it is cowardice."

[65] From the *Hsiao ching* 孝經 (8:2a-b, *SPPY*), see n. 64 above.

[66] Here Ssu-ma Ch'ien seems to concur with Master Yen's driver who was content simply to "hold the whip for him." See also the Translators' Note to Chapter 61.

TRANSLATORS' NOTE

The association between Kuan Yi-wu and Yen Ying is evident in a number of pre-Ch'in texts. But Ssu-ma Ch'ien, by selecting several incidents with which to depict the two men, has thereby revealed some striking parallels between them. Both were, of course, ministers to the dukes of Ch'i who brought their lords and their nation glory. In this respect, Kuan's achievements exceeded Yen's. Yet Ssu-ma Ch'ien, in speculating about Confucius's motive in belittling Kuan, observes that Duke Huan was a worthy man whom Kuan Yi-wu could have helped to rise even higher than he did.

Although not the first of the memoirs, this chapter is important in that it introduces two important techniques found often in subsequent accounts: (1) rhetorical repetition and (2) paired or parallel biographies. Here the former (*chih jen* 知人) provides both structure and theme for each of the biographies (on this sort of repetition in the *Shih chi* see also Tanaka Kenji 田中謙二, "*Shiki* ni okeru hyōgen no hampuku" 史記における表現の反覆, *Tōhō Gakuhō,* 27(1957), 1-30). This concept of perceiving a man's worth is certainly also related to Ssu-ma Ch'ien's concern in "Po Yi" (Memoir 61) that worthy men have been neglected in the past. Kuan Chung's career thus comes as a result of Pao Shu-ya's appreciation of his talents--after he had been bound and imprisoned. Kuan Yi-wu himself is not shown to be able to appreciate others and his lack of judgment in this respect is perhaps suggested by his under-evaluation of Duke Huan. Yen Ying, though known as a witty, clever minister elsewhere, is distinguished here for being able to fully appreciate Father Yüeh Shih, who was also bound and imprisoned. Ironically, it is the wife of Yen's driver who seems to be most perspicacious in this narrative.

BIBLIOGRAPHY

I. Translations

Margouliès, Georges.   "Biographies de Kouan [Tchong] et de Yen [Ying]," *Le Kou-wen chinois.* Paris: Guethner, 1926, pp. 77-83.

Mizusawa Toshitada 水澤利忠. *Shiki* 史記. V. 8. *Retsuden (ichi)* 列傳 (一). Tokyo: Meiji Shoten, 1990, pp. 42-53

Morgan, Evan, trans. "The Lives of Kuan Chung and Yen Tzu," in *A Guide to Wenli Styles and Chinese Ideals.* London: Probsthain and Co., 1931, pp. 117-127.

Ōgawa Tamaki 小川環樹, trans. *Shiki retsuden* 史記列傳. Rpt. Tokyo: Chikuma Shobō, 1986 (1969). pp. 8-10.

Panasjuk, V. *Syma Czjan', Izbrannoe.* Moscow, 1956, pp. 51-5.

II. Studies

Forke, Alfred.   "Yen Ying, Staatsman und Philosoph, und das Yen-tse Tch'un-ts'iu," *AM, Hirth Anniversary Volume* (London: Probsthain and Co., 1924), pp. 101-44.

Henry, Eric. "The Motif of Recognition in Early China," *HJAS,* 47(1987), 5-30.
    The first third of this study examines recognition in this memoir.

Holzer, Rainer. *Yen-tzu und das Yen-tzu ch'un-ch'iu.* Frankfurt: Lang, 1983.
    In "Yen-tzus Biographie," pp. 2-7, Holzer translates the opening paragraphs of the *Shih chi* biography as well as the remarks of the Grand Scribe.

Liang Ch'i-ch'ao 梁起超. *Kuan Tzu chuan* 傳. Rpt. Taipei: Chung-hua, 1963.

Rickett, W. Allyn, trans. *Guanzi: Political, Economic, and Philosophical Essays from Early China*. V. 1. Princeton: Princeton University Press, 1985.

_____. "*Guanzi xuekan,*" in *Early China*, 14(1989), 201-11.

Rosen, Sydney H. "In Search of the Historical Kuan Chung." Unpublished Ph. D. dissertation, University of Chicago, 1973.

_____. "In Search of the Historical Kuan Chung,"*JAS*, 25(1976), 431-40.

Walker, R. L. "Some Notes on the *Yen-tzu Ch'un-ch'iu,*" *JAOS*, 73(1953), 156-63).

Lao Tzu and Han Fei, Memoir 3

Lao Tzu

[63:2139] Lao Tzu 老子 was a native of the hamlet of Ch'ü-jen 曲仁 in the village of Li 厲鄉 in Hu County 苦縣 of [the state of] Ch'u.[1] His *praenomen* was Erh 耳, his *agnomen* Tan 聃, and his *cognomen* Li 李.[2] He was a scribe in the Chou office of archives.[3]

[2140] Confucius went to Chou,[4] intending to ask Lao Tzu about the rites. Lao Tzu said, "Those of whom you speak have all already rotted away, both the men and their bones. Only their words are here. Moreover, when a gentleman obtains his season, he will harness his horses. When he does not obtain it, he will move on like tumbleweed rolling in the wind.[5] I have heard that

An able merchant has the deepest storerooms, but they look empty;[6]
A gentleman has the fullest virtue, but he appears foolish.[7]

[1] Other early sources have "Ch'ü" instead of "Ch'ü-jen hamlet." The name *li* 厲 is also sometimes written *lai* 賴 (see Wang Shu-min, 63:2028). Liang Yü-sheng (27:1185) notes that an Eastern Han inscription claims Lao Tzu was from Hsiang 相 county (just west of modern Huai-pei 淮北 city in Anhwei on the Honan border [T'an Ch'i-hsiang, 1:39]); Hsiang was in approximately the same area as Hu, which was east of modern Lu-yi 鹿邑 county in Honan (T'an Ch'i-hsiang, 1:29). The statement that Hu prefecture was part of the state of Ch'u is anachronistic and has occasioned lengthy debate. To summarize the argument, the city of Hu 苦邑 was a part of the state of Ch'en 陳 until Ch'en was destroyed by Ch'u in 479 B.C. If Lao Tzu lived in Hu when it belonged to Ch'u, he could not have met with Confucius, who according to tradition died in 479 B.C.

[2] The *cognomen* Li 李 is not attested in works earlier than the last half of the Warring States period. The lack of early attested examples of the *cognomen* Li is disturbing for those who regard Lao Tzu as an authentic figure living at the same time as Confucius. Various suggestions have been made to explain Ssu-ma Ch'ien's statement. Kao Heng 高亨 thinks *li* (Archaic Chinese [hereafter ArC] *leg*) and *lao* (ArC *legw*) were phonetically close enough to be confused ("*Lao Tzu cheng ku* ch'ien-chi" 老子正詁前記, in *Ku-shih pien*, 4:351-353); as the reconstructions *leg* and *legw* (following Li Fang-kuei 李方桂) show, this is unlikely. T'ang Lan 唐蘭 suggests the character *li* is a textual error, but is unable to produce convincing evidence that there was ever a text which wrote *lao* for *li* ("Lao Tan te hsing-ming ho shih-tai k'ao" 老聃的姓名和時代考 in *Ku-shih pien*, 6:332-35). A number of scholars follow T'ang in his belief that Lao was actually the *cognomen* of Lao Tzu, since the honorary suffix *tzu* usually follows the *cognomen* for most pre-Ch'in philosophers. The use of *lao* as a *cognomen* or *nomen*, however, is poorly documented. Fang Hsüan-chen (entries 796-7, p. 293) cites two cases from the *Tso chuan* where it is claimed to be a *nomen* or part of a *cognomen*. More interesting is the instance on *Shih chi*, 122:3131 of the phrase *Lao shih* 老氏 (Mr. Lao [?]) which clearly refers to Lao Tzu.

[3] *Chuang Tzu* (5:16a, *SPPY*) describes Lao Tzu as a *Cheng-ts'ang shih* 徵藏史, "scribe of acquisition and collection." The *Lieh-hsien chuan* 列仙傳 (A:4A, *Pai-pu ts'ung-shu chi-ch'eng*) says he was a *chu-hsia shih* 柱下史, a "scribe under the pillar" (see Wang Shu-min, 63:2030). "So-yin" speculates that "under the pillar" refers to the location of the archives.

[4] Whether Confucius actually went to Chou is highly conjectural as Ssu-ma Ch'ien himself suggested in *Shih chi*, 47:1909)

[5] *P'eng* 蓬 in archaic Chinese refers sometimes to artemisia and sometimes to bitter fleabane (*erigeron acris*). Here it refers to the latter. According to Lu T'ien's 陸佃 (1042-1102) *P'i-ya* 埤雅 (15:4a, *SKCS*), "the *p'eng*'s stem is much longer than its root; it is readily uprooted by the wind and spins in the air." We take *lei* 累 as "to roll" here, following the interpretation in "Cheng-yi."

[6] We take *ts'ang* 藏 as a noun meaning "vault, cellar."

[7] There are a number of versions of this saying. The earliest extant version seems to be in *Ta Tai Li* 大戴禮 "Tseng Tzu chih-yen, shang" 曾子制言上, which reads 良賈深藏如虛, 君子有盛教如無 (5:2b, *SPTK*; Takigawa, 63:5, misquotes or uses a different edition). The original rhymes quite well in ArC (虛 *xjag* and 無 *mjag*), while the *Shih chi* version does not (虛 *xjag* and 愚 *ngjug*). The rhyming of ArC *ug* and *ag* is the rule in the Han period (see Lo Chang-p'ei 羅常培 and Chou Tsu-mo 周祖謨, *Han Wei Chin Nan-pei ch'ao yün-pu yen-pien*

Cast off your arrogant airs and many desires, sir, your contrived posturing and your over-weening ambition.[8] All of these are of no benefit to your person. What I have to tell you is this, and nothing more."

Confucius departed. He told his disciples, "Birds I know can fly, fish I know can swim, and beasts I know can run. For that which runs, one can make snares. For that which swims, one can cast lines. For that which flies, one can make arrows with strings attached. As for the dragon, I can never know how it mounts the wind and clouds and ascends into the sky. Today I have seen Lao Tzu; is he perhaps like the dragon?"[9]

[2141] Lao Tzu cultivated the Way and its virtue.[10] His teachings emphasized hiding oneself and avoiding fame. After living in Chou for a long time, he saw Chou's decline, and left. When he reached the pass, the Prefect of the Pass Yin Hsi 尹喜[11] said, "Since you are going to retire from the world, I beg you to endeavor to write a book for us." Lao Tzu thus wrote a book in two sections which spoke of the meaning of the Way and its virtue in five thousand and some characters[12] and then departed. No one knows where he finally ended.[13]

Some say [Lao Tzu] was Lao Lai Tzu 老萊子, also a man of Ch'u. He composed a book in fifteen sections which spoke of the ideas of Taoism and was a contemporary of Confucius.

[2142] Supposedly, Lao Tzu lived to be a 160 years old, some say over 200; his great longevity came through cultivating the way.[14]

yen-chiu 漢魏晉南北朝韻部演變研究 [Peking: K'o-hsüeh Ch'u-pan-she, 1958], pp. 9-15), and this fact suggests the *Shih chi* version of this expression may be as late as the Han period.

[8] *Chuang Tzu* (9:3a, *SPPY*) quotes a similar remark addressed to Confucius by Lao Lai-tzu: "Ch'iu, cast off your self pride and your disguised wisdom; this is what makes a gentleman."

[9] A completely different version of the conversation between Lao Tzu and Confucius occurs in *Shih chi*, 47:1909: "Confucius took his leave and Lao Tzu saw him off. 'I have heard that wealthy and noble men give parting gifts of money, and the most virtuous men give parting gifts of words. I have not been able to achieve wealth or nobility, so I shall presume on the title of "most virtuous" and give you a parting gift of words. Percep-tive, observant and close to death, this is a man fond of criticizing others. Knowledgeable, perspicacious, and en-dangering his life, this is a man who reveals others' blemishes. As a son, do not think of oneself, as another man's vassal, do not think of oneself.'"

In *Chuang Tzu* (5:25a, *SPPY*) Confucius also compares Lao Tzu to a dragon.

[10] *Te* 德 "virtue" is the quality of each person and thing acquired from *Tao* 道 "the Way."

[11] The phrase *kuan ling yin hsi yüeh* 關令尹喜曰 presents a number of problems (see Liu Pen-tung's 劉本棟 unpublished master's thesis, "*Shih chi* 'Lao Chuang Shen Han lieh chuan' shu-cheng" 史記老莊申韓列傳疏證 [Taipei: T'ai-wan Sheng-li Shih-fan Ta-hsüeh Kuo-wen Yen-chiu-so, 1966], pp. 37-42). There is a strong tradi-tion, dating back at least to Liu Hsiang in the Western Han period, that the gatekeeper's name was Hsi, which we have chosen to follow in our translation. A number of scholars take *kuan-ling* as Hsi's title, i.e.," prefect of the pass." This title is attested in other texts. The word *yin* is either rejected as an error or made into his *cognomen*. Others prefer to take *ling-yin* as his title. This is odd, since *ling-yin* was the state of Ch'u's equivalent to prime minister which we render "premier." The "pass" here is identified as either the San-kuan 散關 (in the western part of modern Shensi province a few miles south of Pao-chi 寶雞 City, [T'an Ch'i-hsiang, 2:58]) or Han-ku-kuan 函谷關 (a few miles northeast of modern Ling-pao 靈寶 in Honan near the southern bank of the Yellow River, [T'an Ch'i-hsiang, 1:35]).

[12] This refers to the famous text *Lao Tzu* (also known as the *Tao te ching* 道德經), which is traditionally di-vided into two parts. In the modern version, the first begins with the word *tao* and the second with the word *te*. In the Han-dynasty version recovered at Ma-wang tui, however, the order is reversed.

[13] Contrary to Ssu-ma Ch'ien's statement, *Chuang Tzu* (2:3a-b, *SPPY*) describes the funeral of Lao Tzu.

[14] Lao Lai-tzu appears in *Chuang Tzu* (9:3a, *SPPY*). He is also mentioned in "Chung-ni Ti-tzu" ("Confucius's Disciples," *Shih chi*, 67:2186): "Those who Confucius served as a student: in Chou there was Lao Tzu, in Wey, Chü Po-yü, in Ch'i, Yen P'ing-chung [Yen Ying], in Ch'u, Lao Lai-tzu, in Cheng, Tzu-ch'an, in Lu, Meng

The scribes record that 129 years after Confucius died Tan 儋, the Grand Scribe of Chou, had an audience with Duke Hsien 獻 of Ch'in (r. 384-362 B.C.) and said, "In the beginning Ch'in and Chou were united. After 500 years of union, they separated. Seventy years after they have separated, a Hegemon will emerge there [Ch'in]."[15] Some say that Tan was Lao Tzu. Others say he was not. Our generation does not know the truth of the matter.

Lao Tzu was a gentleman who retired from the world.[16] The *praenomen* of Lao Tzu's son was Tsung 宗. Tsung was a general of Wei. He was enfeoffed at Tuan-kan 段干.[17] Tsung's son was Chu 注. Chu's son was Kung 宮. Kung's great-great-grandson was Chia 假. Chia served as an official to Emperor Hsiao-wen 孝文 of Han (r. 180-157 B.C.) [*2143*] and Chia's son Chieh 解 was the Grand Mentor[18] to [Liu] Ang 卬, King of Chiao-hsi 膠西 (r. 164-154 B.C.),[19] at which time he took up residence in Ch'i.

Those nowadays who study Lao Tzu denigrate Confucianism, and Confucianism also denigrates *Lao Tzu*. Can this be what is meant by "Those whose ways are not the same do not take counsel with each other?"[20] Li Erh "did nothing, and [the people] transformed themselves, kept still, and [the people] rectified themselves."[21]

Chuang Tzu

Chuang Tzu 莊子 was a native of Meng 蒙.[22] His *praenomen* was Chou 周. Chou once served as a functionary at Ch'i-yüan 漆園 in Meng.[23] He was a contemporary of King Hui 惠 of Liang (r. *370-335 B.C.) and King Hsüan 宣 of Ch'i (r. *342-324 B.C.). There was nothing on which his teachings did not touch, but in their essentials they went back to the words of Lao Tzu. Thus his works, over 100,000 characters, all consisted of allegories. He wrote "Yü-fu" 漁父 (The Old Fisherman), "Tao Chih" 盜跖 (The Bandit Chih), and "Ch'ü-ch'ieh" 胠篋 (Ransacking Baggage), [*2144*] in which he mocked the likes of Confucius and made clear the policies of Lao Tzu.[24] Keng Sang Tzu" 亢桑子 (Master Keng Sang) from the

Kung-ch'o." While the paragraph above is not clear, it is obvious from this passage that Ssu-ma did not identify Lao Tzu and Lao Lai-tzu as the same person. He was apparently mentioned here because he too was regarded as a teacher of Confucius and perhaps also because of his title of *lao*. In the last sentence of this paragraph, we read *yang* 養 as *chang* 長, following Wang Shu-min, 63:2034.

[15] There is a parallel passage (with important distinctions) on *Shih chi*, 4:159. The reference there is either to Duke Hsien of Ch'in or perhaps even the First Emperor of Ch'in (see our n. 246 to *Shih chi* Chapter 4 above).

[16] The scribe Tan's visit to Ch'in is described in almost identical terms in *Shih chi*, 4:159, 5:201, 28:1364).

[17] About 30 miles north of the Yellow River near modern Hsia 夏 County in Shansi (Ch'ien Mu, *Ti-ming k'ao*, p. 404).

[18] *T'ai Fu* 太傅.

[19] Liu Ang was a grandson of the founder of the Han dynasty, Liu Pang (see *Shih chi*, 52:2011).

[20] This is a quote from *Lun yü*, 15/40.

[21] Several scholars believe this sentence is an interpolation from Ssu-ma Ch'ien's postface to the *Shih chi* (130:3313), which uses identical language (borrowed perhaps from *Lao Tzu*, Section 59) to describe Lao Tzu, but there is no textual evidence to support this (see Wang Shu-min, 63:2035-6).

[22] A few miles north of modern Shang-ch'iu 商丘 City in Honan (T'an Ch'i-hsiang, 1:25).

[23] According to "Cheng-yi" Chi-yüan was located 17 *li* north of Yüan-chü 冤句 county in Ts'ao 曹 Prefecture (near modern Tung-ming 東明 in Shantung, about 50 miles northeast of Kaifeng, [T'an Ch'i-hsiang, 5:45]).

[24] The first two of these chapters, "The Fisherman" and "The Bandit Chih," are probably the chapters Ssu-ma Ch'ien is referring to when he speaks of "mocking the likes of Confucius." They include two famous dialogues in which Confucius is soundly trounced in debate. "Ransacking Baggage," on the other hand, is probably what Ssu-ma Ch'ien refers to when he speaks of "illustrating the policies of Lao Tzu." In this chapter, which as A. C. Graham (*Chuang-tzu: The Inner Chapters* [London: George Allen & Unwin, 1981], p. 209) notes has parallels

Wilderness of Wei-lei 畏累 and others were all fictions without any truth.[25] Yet he was skilled in composing works and turning phrases, in veiled reference and analogy, and with these he flayed the Confucians and Mohists. Even the most profound scholars of the age could not defend themselves. His words billowed and swirled without restraint, to please himself, and so from kings and dukes down, the great men could not utilize him.

[2145] King Wei 威 of Ch'u (r. 339-329 B.C.) heard that Chuang Chou was a worthy man. He sent a messenger with lavish gifts to induce him to come and promised him the position of prime minister. Chuang Chou smiled and told Ch'u's messenger, "A thousand *chin*[26] is great profit, and a ministership an exalted position, but can it be that you have not seen the sacrificial cow used in the suburban sacrifices? After feeding it for several years, it is dressed in figured brocade and sent into the Great Temple. When things have reached this point, though it might wish to become an untended pig, how could it attain this? Go quickly, sir, do not pollute me. I would rather romp at my own pleasure in a slimy ditch than be held in captivity by the ruler of a state. I won't take office for as long as I live, for that is what pleases my fancy most."[27]

Shen Pu-hai

[2146] Shen Pu-hai 申不害 (d. *ca.* 337 B.C.)[28] was a native of Ching 京.[29] He was a lowborn vassal of the old state of Cheng 鄭. He practiced the arts of politics and thus sought

with *Lao Tzu*, the writer vigorously condemns "lusters after knowledge" for causing confusion in the world, with the consequence that instead of remaining settled, as they used to, people will abandon their homes in the hope of obtaining better living conditions. The solution, according to the writer, is in removing the distractions of ideas and sophistries from the people's minds. Graham claims that "The Old Fisherman" and "The Bandit Chih," were "Yangist," but thinks "Ransacking Baggage" was "primitivist" (see his "How Much of the *Chuang Tzu* Did Chuang Tzu Write?" in Graham's *Studies in Chinese Philosophy and Philosophical Literature* [Singapore: The Institute of East Asian Philosophies, 1986], pp. 307-313).

[25] This is probably a reference to Chapter 23 of *Chuang Tzu*, titled "Keng-Sang Ch'u" 庚桑楚 rather than 亢桑. Keng Sang was "a servant of Lao Tan" 老聃之役, who "obtained part of the *tao* of Lao Tzu and resided to the north, in the mountains of Wei-lei" 偏得老子之道，以北居畏累之山 (*Chuang Tzu*, 23:8a, *SPPY*). Thus it would seem that Wei-lei is a place name. "So-yin," however, claims that "Wei-lei hsü" is the name of a section in *Chuang Tzu*, and that Wei Lei was a disciple of Lao Tan. The Chung-hua edition punctuates in accord with this reading. There is, however, no chapter "Wei Lei" in any extant edition of *Chuang Tzu*, and "So-yin" goes on to cite the commentator Ssu-ma Piao 司馬彪 (240-306) that "Wei-lei is modern Tung-lai 東萊," i.e., eastern Shantung province. Thus at least one early commentator does not share the opinion expressed in "So-yin." "Cheng-yi" claims that this passage means Ssu-ma Ch'ien believed that the "Miscellaneous Chapters" in *Chuang Tzu* following "Keng-sang Ch'u" "are all empty theorizing without any true facts." The point in Ssu-ma Ch'ien's assertion here, however, is probably a more specific statement of disbelief in the anecdotes in *Chuang Tzu* relating to Lao Tzu.

[26] The phrase *ch'ien chin* 千金 (or *pai chin* 百金) occurs frequently throughout the *Shih chi*. According to Chao Ch'i's 趙岐 (d. 201 A.D.) commentary on the *Mencius* (quoted in Chiao Hsün's 焦循 (1763-1820) *Meng Tzu cheng-yi* 孟子正義 [8:7a, *SPPY*], in the pre-Ch'in period the word *chin* 金 preceded by a number indicated so many *yi* 鎰 of bronze or copper; an *yi* consisted of twenty *liang* 兩. Gold, on the other hand, is usually referred to in the *Shih chi* as *huang-chin* 黃金, and is measured in units of *chin* 斤, which consisted of sixteen *liang*. In order to avoid confusion between *chin* 金 and *chin* 斤, we refer to the former as *chin* and the latter as "catties" (see also "Weights and Measurements" in the front-matter).

[27] There is a short version of this story in *Chuang Tzu* (10:12a-b, *SPPY*): "Someone sent gifts to engage Chuang Tzu. Chuang Tzu responded to the messenger, "Have you seen the sacrificial cow, sir? It is dressed in fine brocades and fed with grass and grain. When it is led into the Great Temple, though it might wish to be an untended calf, how could it attain to it?"

[28] There are several problems associated with the dates of Shen Pu-hai. According to *Shih chi*, 15:723, Shen

office from Marquis Chao 昭 of Han (r. *358-333 B.C.). Marquis Chao employed him as prime minister. Within the state, he labored on regulating and instructing the people. Abroad, he treated with the feudal lords for fifteen years. During the life of Shen Tzu, the state was well run, its troops strong, and none trespassed against Han.

The teachings of Shen Tzu were based on those of Huang-Lao 黃老,[30] and emphasized "dispositions and designations."[31] He composed a book in two sections, which was called *Shen Tzu*.

Han Fei

Han Fei 韓非 (d. 233 B.C.) was one of the Noble Scions of Han. He enjoyed the study of "dispositions and designations" and "legitimation and the arts of politics," but his essentials go back to [the teachings of] Huang-Lao. Fei was a stutterer and could not recite his own advice, but he was skilled at composing written works. He and Li Ssu 李斯 (d. 208 B.C.)[32] both followed His Excellency Hsün 荀 (d. *ca.* 238 B.C.) as their teacher. [Li] Ssu himself felt he was not the equal of [Han] Fei.

[2147] [Han] Fei saw the gradual waning of Han and admonished the King of Han in letters several times, but the King of Han could not use his advice. Thus Han Fei came to loathe that in regulating the state [the king] did not labor to improve and clarify its laws and institutions, nor did he exercise his power to direct his subjects, and that in enriching the state and strengthening its forces, though he meant to seek out men and employ the worthy, instead he raised up frivolous, dissolute parasites and placed them above those with merit and substance. He felt that "Confucians use decorum to disorder the laws, and knight-errants violate the prohibitions with their violence."[33] "When times are slack they coddle men with high reputations and when times are dire they use knights with armor and helmets. Those who are now cultivated are not those whom the ruler uses and those whom the ruler uses are not those

Pu-hai became Prime Minister of Han in the eighth year of the reign of Marquis Chao of Han, and died in the twenty-second year of his reign (*Shih chi*, 15:747). This is repeated in *Shih chi*, 45:1869 ("Hereditary House of Han"). The problem is that the date of Marquis Chao's accession is not certain. According to Ssu-ma Ch'ien, the Marquis Chao became ruler of Han in 358 B.C. (*Shih chi*, 15:721), so that Shen became prime minister in 351 B.C. and died in 337 B.C. Ch'ien Mu suggests that the correct date for Marquis Chao's accession was 362 B.C. (*Chu-tzu*, pp. 200-2). Ch'en Meng-chia 陳夢家 in his *Liu-kuo chi-nien* 六國紀年 (Shanghai: Hsüeh-hsi Sheng-huo Ch'u-pan-she, 1955, pp. 70-1) argues it was 361 B.C. In handling the problem of dates, we have taken the chronology given in Yang K'uan's 楊寬 *Chan-kuo shih* 戰國史 (rev. ed., [Taipei: Ku-feng Ch'u-pan-she, 1986], pp. 672-719) as our standard, and have not attempted to form our own judgments (see "Note on Chronology" in the front-matter).

Despite his suggestion that Marquis Chao's dates be revised, Ch'ien Mu accepts the date 337 B.C. for Shen's death. This would contradict the *Shih chi* text above, which says that Shen was prime minister for fifteen years.

[29] About 15 miles southwest of modern Chengchow in Honan (T'an Ch'i-hsiang, 1:36).

[30] The phrase "Huang-Lao" refers to a school of thought prevalent in Western Han times which attempted to synthesize Taoist and Legalist concepts. Apparently The Huang-ti (see our translation of *Shih chi* Chapter 1 in the first volume of this translation) was enlisted by the writers of this school as an early exemplar of their ideas, hence the term Huang-Lao. A great deal more is now known about this school, following the recovery at Ma-wang Tui of several mss. by Huang-Lao writers (see Tu Wei-ming, "The 'Thought of Huang-Lao': A Reflection on the *Lao Tzu* and *Huang Ti* Texts in the Silk Manuscripts of Ma-wang Tui," *JAS,* 39 (1979), 95-110 and Jan Yün-hua "Tao, Principle, and Law: The Three Key Concepts in the Yellow Emperor Taoism," *JCP,* 7 (1980), 205-228).

[31] For a detailed discussion of the term *hsing-ming* 刑名, see H. G. Creel, "The Meaning of *Hsing-ming*" in *Studia Sinica Bernhard Karlgren Dedicata,* edited by Egerod Soren (Copenhagen: E. Munksgaard, 1959).

[32] See his biography in *Shih chi* Chapter 87 and Ch'ien Mu's "Li Ssu, Han Fei k'ao" 考 (*Chu-tzu,* pp. 477-9).

[33] This is a quote from *Han Fei Tzu* (19:4b, *SPPY*).

whom he cultivates."[34] He mourned for the upright who were not tolerated by wicked and perverse vassals and observed the successes and failures of the past; thus he wrote "Ku-fen" 孤憤 (Pent-up Emotions of a Solitary Man), "Wu-tu" 五蠹 (Five Parasites), "Nei-wai ch'u" 內外儲 (The Inner and Outer Congeries), "Shuo-lin" 說林 (The Forest of Advice), and "Shuo-nan" 說難 (The Difficulty of Advice), totaling over 100,000 characters.[35]

[2148] But although Han Fei knew the difficulty of advice and described it quite thoroughly in his work, "The Difficulty of Advice," he died in Ch'in in the end, and was unable to avoid this [difficulty] himself. "The Difficulty of Advice" says,[36]

What is difficult in advising is not a difficulty with gaining the knowledge providing the means to advise, nor is it a difficulty with the arguments illustrating my intent,[37] nor is it a difficulty in daring to exhaust my abilities without reserve.[38] What is difficult in advising is knowing the mind which I seek to advise, and matching my advice to it.

[2149] If the one being advised is motivated [by the desire] for a great reputation, and you advise him concerning great profit, you will appear to be unprincipled, and to treat him as a base man.[39] You are then sure to be driven off. If the one being advised is motivated [by the desire] for great profit and you advise him concerning a great reputation, you will appear unperceptive and out of touch with reality. You are then certain not to be accepted. If the one being advised actually seeks great wealth while publicly seeking a great reputation and you advise him concerning a great reputation, then he will openly accept you while in fact ignoring you. If you advise him concerning extravagant wealth, then he will secretly follow your words while publicly abandoning you. These are matters one cannot but know.

Tasks are accomplished through secrecy, and counsel fails when it is revealed. Although [the adviser] might not reveal it himself, if [the adviser's] counsel touches on that which [the nobleman] seeks to conceal, he is in danger.[40] [*2150*] If the nobleman has occasions on which he errs, and the adviser openly offers good suggestions which highlight these errors, the adviser is in danger. If [the adviser] has not yet attained [the nobleman's] good graces, and speaks with all his wisdom, then if his advice is used and [the nobleman] is successful, his merit will be lost; if his advice

[34] This is a reworking of *Han Fei Tzu* (19:5a-b, *SPPY*): "When the state is at peace, [the ruler] cultivates scholars and knight-errants. When troubles arrive, he employs men of arms. What is of benefit to him he does not use and what is of use to him he does not treat as beneficial."

[35] "Pent-up Emotions of a Solitary Man" reflected Han Fei's inability to be employed. "Five Parasites" referred to those men employed in his stead. "The Inner and Outer Congeries" and "The Forest of Advice" were collections of anecdotes. "The Difficulty of Advising" refers again to Han Fei's problems in impressing the King of Han.

[36] Han Fei's essay "The Difficulty of Advising" also appears in the modern version of *Han Fei Tzu* (4:5b-10b, *SPPY*), but there are substantial differences between the *Shih chi* and *Han Fei Tzu* versions. The *Shih chi* version is shorter and appears to have at least one lacuna, as noted below. Because of the numerous differences between these two versions, only the most important variations are pointed out in the notes which follow. Other English translations of this essay include W. K. Liao, *The Complete Works of Han Fei Tzu* (London: Arthur Probsthain, 1959), pp. 106-112; Burton Watson, *Han Fei Tzu: Basic Writings* (New York: Columbia University Press, 1964), pp. 73-79; and Arthur Waley, *Three Ways of Thought in Ancient China* (London: Allen & Unwin, 1939), pp. 242-7. Both Liao and Watson translate the *Han Fei Tzu* version, while Waley claims to have used both versions in his translation.

[37] Omitting the word *nan* 難 in the *Shih chi* text.

[38] Reading *heng-shih* 橫失 as *heng-yi* 橫佚.

[39] Reading *yü* 遇 as *ou* 偶.

[40] In this paragraph, the *Han Fei Tzu* text lists seven ways in which the persuader can endanger himself (4:6b-7a, *SPPY*). The *Shih chi* text omits the third of these and changes the order somewhat. The wording is also frequently different.

is not used and [the nobleman] fails, he will be doubted, and again he is in danger. If the nobleman obtains a plan and wishes to take credit for it himself, if the adviser knows of this, he is in danger. If [the nobleman] openly proposes something when his intentions are on something else, if the adviser knows of this, he is in danger.[41] If [the adviser] would force something on him which he is certain not to do, or if [the adviser] would stop him from something he cannot help but do, [the adviser] is in danger.

Thus it is said, "If you speak to him of great men, he will think you are criticizing him. If you speak to him of humble men, he will think you are selling positions." If you speak of what he loves, he will think you are manipulating him. If you speak of what he hates, he will think you are taunting him. If you shorten your advice, then he will think you ignorant and demote you. If you are verbose in your writings, then he will think they are too numerous and take too long to read. If you follow his wishes in presenting your opinions, he will say you are timid and remiss. If you weigh matters broadly, he will say you are uncouth and arrogant. These are the difficulties of advising, you cannot but know them.

[2151] What is essential in advising is to know how to embroider on that which the one being advised is proud of and to obscure that which he is ashamed of.[42]

If the advised feels his own plan is wise, then do not tax him with its shortcomings.[43] [*2152*] If he has confidence in his decision then do not anger him by discussing its faults.[44] If he exalts in his own strength then do not attack him with difficulties. Commend other events which involve similar plans, cite as exemplars other men who had similar actions. If the adviser embroiders with these, he can escape harm.[45] If there are others who have made the same errors, then openly defend them as without error.

Your crucial ideas should not offend, your elegant speech should not affront. Only then can you extend your intellect and discrimination for him. This is the difficulty of attaining to unhesitating trust and exhausting one's wisdom.

After many days have passed, after you have gained the nobleman's good graces, you may plan deeply without being doubted, and argue without offending. Only then can you openly evaluate cost and benefit, and attain merit through this; only then can you directly point out right and wrong and excuse yourself through this. When the adviser and the nobleman rely on each other for these things, that is the successful culmination of advising.

[2153] Yi Yin 伊尹[46] was a cook and Pai-li Hsi 百里奚[47] was a slave, but it was through [their occupations] that they approached their masters.[48] Thus these two men

---

[41] Reading the character *yeh* in the phrase 迺自以為也故 as either an error or loan for *t'a* 他.

[42] The word *ching* 敬 can occasionally mean "to take pride in." That this is the meaning intended here is shown by the *Han Fei Tzu* text (4:7b, *SPPY*), which reads *chin* 矜 "to be proud of" for *ching*, and *ch'ih* 恥 for the *Shih chi*'s *ch'ou* 醜. Following this sentence, the *Shih chi* version omits a section in the *Han Fei Tzu* text describing how to ingratiate oneself with "the nobleman."

[43] This paragraph follows the next "Commend other events . . ." in the *Han Fei Tzu* version (4:7b, *SPPY*). Its sentences are also not exactly in the order found here.

[44] The *Shih chi* text reads *ti* 敵. The *Han Fei Tzu* text reads *che* 謫 (4:8b, *SPPY*). T'ao Hung-ch'ing 陶鴻慶 (quoted in Ch'en Ch'i-yu 陳奇猷, *Han Fei Tzu chi-shih* 韓非子集釋, [Taipei: Han-ching Wen-hua Shih-yeh Yu-hsien Kung-ssu, 1983], p. 232, n. 35) notes that the Han-era dictionary *Fang-yen* 方言 explains *che* 謫 as *kuo* 過 "error" and suggests that the *Shih chi* variant is a phonetic loan. We follow his suggestion.

[45] Our translation simply follows the *Shih chi* text as it stands. The *Han Fei Tzu* version (4:9a, *SPPY*) reads "If there were others who shared his faults, be sure to vigorously defend them as harmless. If there were others who shared his failures, be sure to clearly defend them as blameless." 有與同汙者，則必以大飾其無傷也. 有與同敗者，則必以明飾其無失也. It seems possible that the phrase 有與同汙者 has simply dropped out of the *Shih chi* text.

[46] Yi Yin used his culinary skills to persuade King T'ang, founder of the Shang, to follow the Way of the King (see *Shih chi*, 3:93ff.).

were both sages, and yet they were unable to avoid servitude and occupations as base as these. This is not something capable men would be ashamed of.[49]

[2154] There was a wealthy man in Sung, whose wall collapsed because of the rain. His son said, "If you do not rebuild it, there will be bandits." An elder of his neighborhood also said this. That evening, [the wealthy man] did indeed lose much of his property. His family thought the man's son wise, but harbored doubts about their neighborhood elder.

Long ago, Duke Wu 武 of Cheng (r. 769-743 B.C.) wanted to attack [the state of] Hu 胡,[50] so he gave his daughter [to the Hu ruler] in marriage. Then he asked his assembled vassals, "We wish to put our weapons to use. Who could we attack?" Kuan Ch'i-ssu 關其思 said, "We could attack Hu." The duke then executed Kuan Ch'i-ssu. "Hu is our brother state, what do you mean by saying we should attack them?" When the Hu ruler heard this, he thought that Cheng was friendly towards him and did not prepare against him. The men of Cheng attacked the Hu unexpectedly and captured [their city].

These two advisers were both adequate in their wisdom, but in the graver case one was punished, while in the lighter case, one was doubted. Wisdom is not difficult then, but using it is difficult indeed.

Long ago, Mi Tzu Hsia 彌子瑕[51] was the beloved of the ruler of Wey. The law of Wey was that whoever harnessed the ruler's carriage without authorization could be punished by removal of the foot. Mi Tzu's mother became sick after a while, however, and when someone heard of this, he traveled overnight to tell Mi. Mi Tzu forged an order, harnessed the king's carriage, and went out. The king thought him an honorable man when he heard of this and said, "How filial! For the sake of his mother, he risks the penalty of removal of a foot!" Mi once traveled with the ruler to an orchard. Mi Tzu ate a peach and thought it sweet, so he offered it to the ruler without finishing it. The ruler said, "How he loves me! He forgets his own appetite and remembers mine!" When Mi Tzu had lost his looks and the king's affection had slackened, he finally offended the king. The king said, "After all, this is the one who forged an order to harness my carriage and gave me a half-eaten peach."

Thus Mi Tzu's behavior did not change, yet he was valued as worthy at first, then condemned at last as a criminal. This is the great change which love and hate undergo. Thus when one is loved by the ruler, then when one's wisdom is appropriate, one is even more trusted, and when one is disliked by the ruler then when the offense is appropriate one is even more distrusted. Therefore, men who would advise cannot but look first at the loves and hates of the ruler and only then advise him.

[2155] The dragon is the sort of creature which can be tamed and even ridden. But underneath his chin he has scales that curl outward, each a yard in diameter, and if you tug him by one, he will kill you. The rulers of men also have curling scales; to advise them without tugging on one is close to success."

---

[47] See *Shih chi,* 5:186ff.

[48] This paragraph is longer in the *Han Fei Tzu* version (4:9a, *SPPY*) and occurs before the preceding paragraph in *Shih chi.*

[49] The *Han Fei Tzu* text (4:9a, *SPPY*) reads, "If one were to be made a cook or a slave and through this could be listened to and shake the world, this would not be something an able man would feel ashamed of." 今以吾(言)為宰虜而可以聽用而振世，此非能仕之所恥也. We are unable to make sense of the *Shih chi*'s reading here of *she* 設 for *ch'ih* 恥 (perhaps "this is not something which an able man plans for" ?), and therefore adopt *ch'ih* from *Han Fei Tzu.*

[50] Located near modern Kuei-yang City 歸陽市 in northwestern Anhwei (T'an Ch'i-hsiang, 1:45 and Ch'ien Mu, *Ti-ming k'ao,* 382-3). This is not a reference to the non-Chinese tribes north of China.

[51] Mi Tzu Hsia is mentioned once in the *Chan-kuo ts'e* (10.5b, *SPTK*).

Someone brought Han Fei's works to Ch'in. When the King of Ch'in had seen the works "Pent-up Emotions of a Solitary Man" and "Five Parasites," he said, "Alas, If We could only see this man and make his acquaintance, We would not regret it even if it meant death." Li Ssu said, "These are the writings of Han Fei." The King of Ch'in thus vigorously attacked Han. The King of Han at first had not employed Fei, but when things grew dire, he at last sent Fei as an emissary to Ch'in. The King of Ch'in was pleased with him, but did not trust him enough to employ him. Li Ssu and Yao Chia 姚賈[52] attacked and slandered him, saying "Han Fei is one of the Noble Scions of Han. Your Majesty wishes to subdue the feudal lords now, but Han Fei will always work for Han, not Ch'in. This is the nature of human emotions. Yet now Your Majesty does not employ him, but allows him to linger here for a long time and then return [to Han]. This is simply leaving yourself open for trouble. It would be better to punish him for breaking a law." The king thought they were right and sent down officials to deal with Fei. Li Ssu sent someone to give Fei poison, allowing [Han Fei] to kill himself. Han Fei wished to present his case, but could not arrange an audience. The King of Ch'in later regretted his decision and sent someone to pardon him, but Fei had already died.[53]

Shen Tzu and Han Tzu both composed books which have been passed down to later generations, and many scholars possess these. I, however, am saddened that Han Tzu could write "The Difficulty of Advice," but could not extricate himself from his own plight.

[2156] His Honor the Grand Scribe says: "The Way that Lao Tzu valued was devoid of all form and reacted to change with inaction,[54] thus when he wrote his work, his rhetoric and terminology were abstruse and difficult to understand. Chuang Tzu abandoned morality and let loose his opinions, but his essence, too, lies mainly in spontaneity. Shen Tzu treated the lowly as befit the lowly, applying this [principle] to relating [official] titles to the reality [of their duties].[55] Han Tzu snapped his plumb line, cut through to the truth of things, and made clear true from false, but carried cruelty and harshness to extremes, and was lacking in kindness. All of these sprang from the idea of 'the Way and its virtue,' but Lao Tzu was the most profound of them all."

---

[52] Yao Chia appears three times in *Chan-kuo Ts'e* (3.80a; 6.70a and 7.28a, *SPTK*), twice as a minister of Ch'in and once working for the state of Chao. The first of these stories relates how Han Fei slandered Yao after he successfully completed a mission for the King of Ch'in. When the King of Ch'in summoned Yao Chia to answer Han Fei's allegations, he defended himself so successfully that the king "employed" Yao and "punished" [*chu* 誅] Han Fei. If *chu* is read as "execute" then this story contradicts the *Shih chi* account of Han Fei's death.

[53] *Shih chi*, 6:232 states that Han Fei's mission to Ch'in and death both took place in 233 B.C. *Shih chi*, 15:754 repeats this, but *Shih chi*, 45:1878 gives the date of his mission and execution as 234 B.C.

[54] Action (*wei* 為) in *Lao Tzu* means to act according to one's own ideas. Inaction (*wu wei* 無為) is to act only according to the forces of nature.

[55] We read *pei pei* 卑卑 as *pars pro toto* for *pei pei kuei kuei* 卑卑貴貴, "he treated the lowly as was befit the lowly and the noble as was befit the noble" (referring to social practice) and extended this principle to his concept of government. Although the term *ming shih* 名實 is found in the works of a number of pre-Ch'in philosophers (*Meng Tzu, Mo Tzu, Chuang Tzu, Lieh Tzu* and *Hsün Tzu* among them), Shen Pu-hai seems to have understood it as an extension of the Confucian *cheng ming* 正名 "rectification of names" applied to Legalist administrative practice. The Legalists were especially interested in clarifying language so that the duties of a position (its *shih* 實) would conform exactly to the title (*ming* 名) of that position (see the "Ting fa" 定法 chapter of *Han Fei Tzu*, 17:5b-7a, *SPPY*).

TRANSLATORS' NOTE

There is an immense literature on the historicity and identity of Lao Tzu. A selection of earlier Chinese articles on this problem can be found in v. 4 of *Ku-shih pien,* Lo Ken-tse 羅根澤, ed., pp. 403-61 and v. 6, pp. 387-684. An even wider range of articles on all aspects of Lao Tzu is excerpted in Liu Pen-tung's 劉本棟 unpublished master's thesis, "*Shih chi* 'Lao, Chuang, Shen, Han lieh-chuan' shu-cheng" 史記老莊申韓列傳疏證 (Taipei: T'ai-wan Sheng-li Shih-fan Ta-hsüeh Kuo-wen Yen-chiu-so, 1966). Articles in English include H. H. Dubs, "The Date and Circumstances of the Philosopher Lao-dz," *JAOS,* 61 (1941), 215-221, and D.C. Lau, *Lao Tzu Tao Te Ching,* "Appendix 1: The Problem of Authorship" (Middlesex: Penguin Books, 1963); probably the most influential article in English, however, has been A. C. Graham, "The Origins of the Legend of Lao Tan," *Studies in Chinese Philosophy and Philosophical Literature* (Singapore: National University of Singapore, Institute of East Asian Philosophy, 1986), pp. 111-124.

Opinion on Lao Tzu is divided into essentially two groups: those who believe he was a historical figure who was the author of the text *Lao Tzu* and those who regard him as a legendary figure, originating as an exemplar in either Taoist or Confucian anecdotes.

Among those who think there was a historical Lao Tzu, there is further disagreement as to which of the tentative identifications made by Ssu-ma Ch'ien in this biography is correct. Many Chinese scholars and most Western scholars now believe that Lao Tzu was a legendary figure. D. C. Lau suggests that Lao Tzu was created by the Taoists as a spokesman for attacking Confucius. A.C. Graham suggests that Lao Tzu, or Lao Tan, was originally a character from Confucian hagiography, whom the Taoists borrowed to attack the Confucians.

We suggest that in the name Lao Tzu, *lao* was a prefix denoting venerable age. Examples can be found of *lao* appearing before names, as in the Lao P'eng 老彭 of *Lun yü* (7/1), Lao Yang Tzu 老陽子 of *Tso chuan* (Chao 12; Yang Po-chün 1335), and Lao Lung Chi 老龍吉 in *Chuang Tzu* (7.27b, *SPPY*; also referred to as "Lao Lung" 老龍 in the same passage). A later example from *Shih chi,* 8:347 where an old woman is referred to as *lao-yü* 老嫗 is even more suggestive: *yü* itself means an old lady; *lao* was added very possibly by analogy or by the productivity of this prefixation. See also Fu Ssu-nien's 傅斯年 views, cited in Wang Shu-min (63:2028-9).

Thus this chapter combines traditions of three, distinct "Lao Tzu." Ssu-ma Ch'ien is careful to qualify his account of Lao Lai Tzu with *yün* 云, "some say," and to introduce the third Lao Tzu (whose son had the *praenomen* Tsung) with *kai* 蓋, "supposedly." Any attempt to read this biography as a description of a single Lao Tzu is, therefore, certain to lead to contradictions.

A good introduction to the information available on Chuang Tzu--and the consistency between the "historical" sources and the man found in the "inner chapters" of *Chuang Tzu*--can be found in the first few pages (3-4) of A. C. Graham's "Introduction" to his *Chuang-tzu, The Seven Inner Chapters and Others Writings from the Book Chuang-tzu* (London: George Allen & Unwin, 1981). Liu Pen-tung's study (see Bibliography) is also useful.

The major work on Shen Pu-hai in English is H. G. Creel, *Shen Pu-hai* (Chicago: University of Chicago Press, 1974); see also Leon Vandermeersch's commentary and translation of this chapter: "Biographies de Shen Buhai et de Shen Dao," *La formation du Légisme* (Paris: École Française d'Extrême-Orient, 1965), pp. 45-60.

On Han Fei see Leon Vandermeersch's commentary and translation of this chapter: "Biographie de Han Fei zi," in his *La formation du Légisme,* pp. 57-69; see also Ch'ien Mu's comments (*Chu-tzu,* pp. 477-79), which Vandermeersch discusses in detail.

A number of commentators have found Ssu-ma Ch'ien's pairing of the founders of Taoism and the most infamous of the Legalist philosophers unusual, or even offensive, and this may have influenced the changes this chapter has undergone in various editions (see n. 1 to our translation of *Shih chi* Chapter 61). In fact, Ssu-ma Ch'ien's choice in this respect was not unique. Yang Hsiung 揚雄 (53 B.C.-A.D. 18) in his *Fa-yen* 法言 (4:5b, *SPPY*), for instance, pairs Han Fei and Chuang Tzu. This pairing reflects the fact that in the Western Han period, and in Ssu-ma Ch'ien's time in particular, Taoism and Legalism were closely related.

A final note on chronology. On. p. 23 above (translation of *Shih chi,* 63:2143) we read: "He [Chuang Tzu] was a contemporary of King Hui 惠 of Liang (r. *370-335 B.C.) and King Hsüan 宣 of Ch'i (r. *342-324 B.C.)." The asterisks here indicate that the dating is Ssu-ma Ch'ien's, but has been revised by later scholars (the revised dates for these two kings are 369-319 B.C. and 319-301 B.C., respectively). Since we have found a degree consistency to Ssu-ma Ch'ien's chronology which would often be destroyed by revising his dates, we maintain them in our translation, but warn the reader with the asterisk whenever reign periods have been corrected by modern scholars (see also the "Note on Chronology" and "On Using This Book" in the front-matter).

BIBLIOGRAPHY

I. Translations

There are a number of translations of this chapter by noted sinologists such as H. A. Giles, Arthur Waley, and Richard Wilhelm listed in Pokora, "Traductions," pp. 130-131. We have included here recent translations (those since Pokora's list was published in 1969) and those we judge to be of the most use.

Chan, Wing-tsit. *The Way of Lao Tzu.* Indianapolis: Bobbs-Merrill, 1963, pp. 36-37.

Lau, D. C. *Lao tzu, Tao te ching.* Baltimore: Penguin, 1963, pp. 8-10 (Lao Tzu).

Mizusawa Toshitada 水澤利忠. *Shiki* 史記. V. 8. *Retsuden (ichi)* 列傳 (一). Tokyo: Meiji Shoten, 1990, pp. 54-77.

Ōgawa Tamaki 小川環樹, trans. *Shiki retsuden* 史記列傳. Rpt. Tokyo: Chikuma Shobō, 1986 (1969). pp. 11-16.

Vandermeersch, Leon. *La formation du légisme, recherches sur la constitution d'une philosophie politique caractéristique de la Chine ancienne.* Paris: Publications de l'École française d'Extrême-Orient, 1965 (Shen Pu-hai and Han Fei).

II. Studies

Bodde, Derk. "Further Remarks on the Identification of Lao Tzu," *JAOS,* 64 (1944), 24-27.

———. "The New Identification of Lao Tzu," *JAOS,* 62 (1942), 8-13.

Chan, Wing-tsit. *Op cit.,* pp. 37-59. Reviews the scholarship on this biography.

Dubs, Homer H. "The Date and Circumstances of the Philosopher Lao-dz," *JAOS,* 61 (1941), 215-221.

———. "The Identification of the Lao-dz," *JAOS* 62 (1942), 300-304.

Graham, A. C. "The Origins of the Legend of Lao Tan," in *Studies in Chinese Philosophy and Philosophical Literature*. Singapore: Institute of East Asian Philosophies, 1986, pp. 110-24.

Ishida Hiroshi 石田博士. "*Shiki* no kijutsu to Kan Pi" 史記の記述と韓非, *Kambun Gakkaihō* 漢文學惠報, 28(1983).
        Not seen.

Kao Heng 高亨. "*Lao Tzu cheng ku* ch'ien-chi" 老子正詁前記, in *Ku-shih pien*, v. 4, pp. 351-3.

_____. "*Shih chi* 'Lao Tzu chuan' chien-chien'" 史記老子傳箋證, in *Ku-shih pien*, v. 6, pp. 441-73.

Kusuyama Haruki 楠山春樹. *Rōshi densetsu no kenkyū* 老子傳説の研究. Tokyo: Sōbunsha 創文社, 1979.

Lau, D. C. "The Problem of Authorship," *Op cit.*, pp. 147-162.

Liu Pen-tung's 劉本棟. "*Shih chi* 'Chuang Tzu lieh-chuan' shu-cheng'" 史記莊子列傳疏證, *Yu-shih hsüeh-chih* 幼獅學誌, 5.2(1966), 42 pp. (no continuous pagination).

_____. "*Shih chi* 'Lao, Chuang, Shen, Han lieh-chuan' shu-cheng" 史記老莊申韓列傳疏證. Taipei: T'ai-wan Sheng-li Shih-fan Ta-hsüeh Kuo-wen Yen-chiu-so, 1966.

Lo Ken-tse 羅根測. "Lao Tzu chi *Lao Tzu* shu te wen-t'i" 老子及老子書的問題, in *Ku-shih pien*, v. 4, pp. 449-461.

Marshal Jang-chü, Memoir 4

[64:2157] Marshal Jang-chü 穰苴 was a descendant of T'ien Wan 田完.¹ In the reign of Duke Ching 景 of Ch'i (r. *547-490 B.C.), [the state of] Chin attacked O 阿 and Chüan 鄄, and [the state of] Yen invaded Ho-shang 河上.² The forces of Ch'i were defeated. Duke Ching was dismayed. Yen Ying 晏嬰 (d. 500 B.C.) then presented T'ien Jang-chü [to the duke].

"Although Jang-chü is a son of a concubine of the T'ien clan, he is a man whose refined manner can win the loyalty of his hosts and whose martial spirit can awe his adversaries. I would hope my lord might try him."

Duke Ching summoned Jang-chü and spoke with him of military strategy; he was delighted with him, made him commander of the army³ and had him lead troops to resist the forces of Yen and Chin.

Jang-chü said, "Your servant has always been a low and humble man. My Lord having lifted me from among the village gates and ranks and set me above his grand masters, the officers and men have not yet been won over and the families of the hundred cognomens do not trust me; my status is lowly and my authority slight. I hope I might obtain one of my lord's favored vassals, respected by [men of] the capital, as Supervisor of the Army.⁴ Only this will do." Duke Ching granted his request and appointed Chuang Chia 莊賈 to go.

When Jang-chü took his leave, he made an appointment with Chuang Chia. "Let us meet at the gate of the army's camp midday tomorrow." Jang-chü sped before Chia to his camp. He set up a sundial gnomon, poured water in a clepsydra, and waited for Chia.

Chia had always been arrogant because of his rank. He thought that since the troops being commanded were his state's and he himself was supervisor, there was no great need for urgency.⁵ When his friends, relatives, and attendants saw him off, he remained to drink. At midday Chia had not arrived. Jang-chü knocked down his gnomon, released the water from his clepsydra, and entered his camp. He marshaled the army, drilled the troops, and

---

¹ From this sentence and the accounts that follow, we know that T'ien was Jang-chü's *nomen*. It is however uncertain whether Ssu-ma was his *cognomen* as it was Ssu-ma Ch'ien's. According to this biography, he was once a *Ta ssu-ma* 大司馬, which Hucker translates as Minister of War (Hucker, #5713) and we render "Grand Marshal." Therefore, the title of this piece may be rendered as "The Memoir of Marshal [T'ien] Jang-chü."

² O was located at modern O-ch'eng 阿城, Shantung (T'an Ch'i-hsiang, 1:39-40). Chüan was about 10 miles north of modern Chüan-ch'eng 鄄城, Shantung (T'an Ch'i-hsiang, 1:39-40; Ch'ien Mu, *Ti-ming-k'ao*, p. 256). "So-yin" notes that both were Ch'i cities. "Cheng-yi" notes that Ho-shang was located south of the Yellow River and covered the area between Ts'ang-chou 滄州 in modern Hopei and Te-chou 德州 in Shantung (see also Wang Li-ch'i, 64:1629). Liang Yü-sheng (27:1192) observes that in *Chan-kuo ts'e*, Jang-chü was said to be killed by Duke Min 湣 (r. *323-284 B.C.) (see *Chan-kuo ts'e*, 4:50b, *SPTK*). He also points out that O, Chüan and Ho-shang did not belong to Ch'i during the time of Duke Ching, and that these invasions by Chin and Yen are not recorded in *Tso chuan*. He concludes that the historicity of these wars is dubious. But, since the "Biographies of Sun-tzu and Wu Ch'i" in *Shih chi* (see *Shih chi*, 64:2166), "Tsa-shang" 雜上 in *Yen-tzu ch'un-ch'iu* (5.6b-7a, *SPPY*) and "Cheng-chien" 正諫 in *Shuo-yüan* (9:9b, *SPPY*) all associate Jang-chü with Duke Ching or other persons of the Warring States period, Liang concedes that one cannot say for sure that Jang-chü did not flourish during Duke Ching's time.

³ "So-yin" notes that *chiang-chün* 將軍 originally meant "to command troops" and that only in the middle Warring States period was it used as an official title. Ku Yen-wu 顧炎武 (1613-1682--quoted in Takigawa, 64:2-3) argues that it was used as a title in the late Ch'un-ch'iu period.

⁴ *Chien-chün* 監軍.

⁵ Takigawa (64:3) reads 將已之軍, 而己為監不甚急. "The general having gone to his army, there was no great urgency for him, as supervisor."

announced the standing orders. The standing orders having been set, it was dusk when Chuang Chia arrived.

Jang-chü asked, "Why did you miss the appointed time?"

Chia apologized: "This unworthy one's grand masters, friends and relatives saw me off, so I stayed."

Jang-chü said, "The day a commander receives his appointment, he forgets his household. When he faces the army and sets the standing orders, he forgets his family. When he takes up the drum stick and sounds a tattoo, he forgets himself.[6] Enemy states have invaded deep into our land and there is turmoil within the country. The officers and men suffer on the borders, our lord takes no comfort from lying on his sleeping mat and no pleasure from his food's flavor. The fate of the families of the hundred cognomens lies in your hands. What do you mean they were seeing you off?"

[2158] Jang-chü summoned the Judge Advocate,[7] and asked, "What is the military code for those who arrive after the appointed time?"[8]

"The sentence is beheading," he replied.

Chuang Chia was frightened and dispatched a man to report to Duke Ching as quickly as possible, asking for help. After the man left, [Jang-chü] quickly beheaded Chuang Chia before [the messenger] could return, as a warning to the three divisions[9] of the army. The soldiers of the three divisions all trembled with shock.

After some time, Duke Ching sent a messenger carrying his tally to pardon Chia. The messenger sped into the army's camp. Jang-chü said, "When a commander is in his camp, there will be orders from his sovereign he will not accept."[10]

He then asked the Judge Advocate, "What is the military code for speeding into the army's camp?"

"The sentence is beheading," the judge said.

The messenger was terrified.

Jang-chü said, "He is our lord's messenger; we cannot kill him." He cut off the driver's head, the chariot's left support,[11] and the head of the left horse as a warning to the army. He dispatched the messenger back to report on his mission, then set off.

He personally saw to the officers' and men's campsites and shelters, wells and stoves, food and drink, and medical care and treatment. He took all of the provisions for the commanding general and feasted his troops, taking a share for himself equal to that of his officers and men. He was closest to those who were thin and sick. After three days, he drilled the troops. All of those who were ill pleaded to join and eagerly jumped forward to go and fight for him.

When the forces of Chin heard this, they withdrew. When the forces of Yen heard this, they crossed the river[12] and dispersed. He pursued and attacked them, recovered the territory that had been lost, and restored the old borders, then led his troops back.

---

[6] A similar saying is found in "Wu-i" 武議 of *Wei Liao Tzu* 尉繚子 (see *Wei Liao Tzu* 2:5b; *SKCS* 726:79).

[7] *Chün-cheng* 軍正.

[8] A famous parallel is the suicide of the Han general Li Kuang 李廣 (d. 119 B.C.) caused by his failure to arrive at a rendezvous on time (see *Shih chi*, 109:2874-6).

[9] On *san-chün* 三軍 see Sawyer, p. 381, n. 18.

[10] Similar sayings are found in the "Chiu-pien" 九變 chapter of *Sun Tzu* (8:7b, *SPPY*), and *Shih chi*, 65:2161 and 57:2074.

[11] According to "So-yin," this was a kind of brace holding up the mud-flaps on the chariot.

[12] "Cheng-yi" says this was the Yellow River. Takigawa (64:6) points out that the *Ch'ün-shu chih-yao* 群書治要 (12:3b, *SPTK*) quotation of this line reads "the Yi River 易水" (in modern Yi-hsien 易縣, Hopei [T'an Ch'i-hsiang, 1:38]).

Before they reached the capital [of Ch'i], he disbanded the troops, released them from their standing orders, and swore a covenant, then entered the capital. Duke Ching and his great officers welcomed them in the suburbs, feasted their forces, and fulfilled the rites. Only then did [Duke Ching] return [to his residence] and retire to his bedchamber. When he granted Jang-chü an audience, he made him marshal. The T'ien clan's honor increased daily in Ch'i.

[2159] After a short while, the Grand Masters Pao 鮑, Kao 高 and Kuo 國 became jealous of him and slandered him before Duke Ching. Duke Ching dismissed Jang-chü. Jang-chü became ill and died. T'ien Ch'i 田乞, T'ien Pao 田豹 and their followers thus bore a grudge against Kao, Kuo and the others. Afterwards, when T'ien Ch'ang 田常 killed Duke Chien 簡 (481 B.C.), he exterminated the entire clans of Masters Kao and Kuo. In the course of time, Ch'ang's great-grandson Ho 和 enthroned himself (386 B.C.) and [Ho's grandson] Yin 因 became King Wei 威 of Ch'i (r. *378-343 B.C.).[13] In commanding his troops and marshaling his might, [King Wei] imitated the methods of Jang-chü on a grand scale, and the feudal lords paid homage to Ch'i.

[2160] King Wei of Ch'i ordered his ministers to compile and edit the old *Ssu-ma Ping-fa* 司馬兵法 (The Marshal's Arts of War) and to append Jang-chü's [works] to them. The book was thus entitled *Ssu-ma Jang-chü Ping-fa* 司馬穰苴兵法 (Marshal Jang-chü's Arts of War).[14]

His Honor the Grand Scribe says: "I have read *The Marshal's Arts of War*. Broadly encompassing, deeply profound, even the expeditions and campaigns of the Three Dynasties could not have exhausted its rituals or followed its refinements. All that is somewhat exaggerated. As for Jang-chü, he merely marshaled the forces of a small country. How could he find time for the bows and salutes of *The Marshal's Arts of War*?[15] Since our generation preserves much of *The Marshal's Arts of War*, I have not included it here, but instead have written a memoir of Jang-chü."

---

[13] The original reads 至常曾孫和，因自立為齊威王 "In the course of time, [T'ien] Ch'ang's great-grandson [T'ien] Ho thus established himself and became King Wei of Ch'i." Liang Yü-sheng (27:1192) believes the text is corrupt and would change it to 至常曾孫和自立．因為齊威王 *chih Ch'ang tseng sun Ho tzu li; Yin wei Ch'i Wei-wang*. This is the reading we adopt.

On T'ien Ch'ang killing Duke Chien see *Shih chi*, 46:1883-4.

[14] In the *SPTK* and *SPPY* editions of Jang-chü's *Ssu-ma fa* 司馬法, there are only five short chapters in three *chüan*. In the *Ssu-k'u ch'üan-shu* edition, there are four chapters in one *chüan*. The discussion and history of this text are beyond the scope of our study (see also *Han shu* "I-wen chih" 藝文志 (10:1709), *Sui shu* "Ching-chi chih" 經籍志 (3:1012), Ling T'ing-k'an's 凌廷堪 (1757-1809) *Chiao-li T'ang wen-chi* 校禮堂文集 (24:14b in *An-hui ts'ung-shu* 安徽叢書 [Taipei: Yi-wen, 1968]), Yü Chia-hsi 余嘉錫 (1883-1955), *Ssu-k'u t'i-yao pien-cheng* 四庫提要辨證 [Rpt. Hong Kong: Chung-hua, 1974], p. 589), and Takigawa (64:7-8).

[15] These sentences are unclear. We have adopted Mizusawa's interpretation (see Mizusawa, p. 86). The interpretation in "So-yin" differs: "*The Marshal's Arts of War*, in its elaboration of the maneuver of troops, manifests the rites which comprise the principles of the three dynasties and yet the Ch'i was just a small country and the time was the Warring States period. Therefore, it says here that "it is quite an exaggeration" (*Shih chi*, 64:2160).

TRANSLATORS' NOTE

Among the early *lieh-chuan* chapters, it is clear that both *Shih chi* Chapter 61 and Chapter 63 are expository, the first arguing some of Ssu-ma Ch'ien's basic principles of historiography and the second presenting what could be read (in the long citation of the "Difficulty of Advising") as a preface to the several biographies of advisers which follow (see Chapters 68-70). Chapter 62 is built upon several short narratives.

This, therefore, is the first of the *lieh-chuan* in which there is a developed plot and extensive use of dialogue. The text is based essentially on a single event or chain of events--here the execution of Chuang Chia and Ch'i's victory over the forces of Chin and Yen. Although the piece, in part no doubt for this reason, has not been a popular selection in anthologies, it demonstrates Ssu-ma Ch'ien's skill in rhetoric. First he uses Yen Ying to introduce Marshal Jang-chü as a man of "whose refined manner [文] can win the loyalty of his hosts and whose martial spirit [武] can awe his adversaries," then he provides actual examples of how the Marshal used this manner (in the Marshal's conversations with the Duke and his treatment of his men) and this spirit (as his men all eagerly wanted to fight for him) in tandem to defeat Yen and Chin.

This chapter also sets the tone for the harsh actions of other military men such as Sun Wu and Wu Ch'i (see Chapter 65). Marshal Jang-chü is sometimes linked with another man who made his mark primarily through a single act in *Shih chi,* T'ien Tan 田單 (see *Chan-kuo ts'e,* 3.61a, *SPTK* and T'ien Tan's biography in Chapter 82 below).

Ch'ien Mu (see Bibliography--Studies below) believes that although T'ien Jang-chü was an actual historical figure, Ssu-ma Ch'ien has erred in placing him in the reign of Duke Ching and attributed events from T'ien Chi's 田忌 life to him.

BIBLIOGRAPHY

I. Translations

Mizusawa Toshitada 水澤利忠. *Shiki* 史記. V. 8. *Retsuden (ichi)* 列傳 (一). Tokyo: Meiji Shoten, 1990, pp. 78-86.

Ōgawa Tamaki 小川環樹, trans. *Shiki retsuden* 史記列傳. Rpt. Tokyo: Chikuma Shobō, 1986 (1969). pp. 17-18.

Sawyer, Ralph D. *The Seven Military Classics of Ancient China.* Boulder: Westview Press, 1993, pp. 112-114.

II. Studies

Ch'ien Mu 錢穆 . *Hsien Ch'in chu-tzu hsi-nien* 先秦諸子繫年. 2v. Rpt. Peking: Chung-hua Shu-chü, 1985, v. 1, pp. 263-4.

Sun Tzu and Wu Ch'i, Memoir 5

Sun Wu

[65:2161] Sun Tzu Wu 孫子武[1] was a native of Ch'i. He was granted an audience by Ho-lu 闔廬, King of Wu (r. 514-496 B.C.) because of his arts of war.

Ho-lu said, "I have read all of your thirteen chapters.[2] Could you give a small demonstration of their use in drilling troops?"

"I could," he replied.

Ho-lu said, "Could you demonstrate them with women?"[3]

"I could," he said.

At this, Ho-lu granted him permission [to proceed][4] and had the palace beauties come out, obtaining 180 women. Sun Tzu divided them into two companies,[5] made the king's two favorite ladies the company commanders, and had them all hold up halberds. He issued his orders. "Do you know where your front, left, right, and rear is?"

The women said, "We do."

Sun Tzu said, "When you go forward, face to the front. When you go left, face your left hand. When you go right, face your right hand; When you go back, face behind you."

The women said, "Yes, sir."

---

[1] Sun was his *cognomen* and Wu probably his *praenomen*. It was common during the pre-Ch'in era to use the honorific suffix *tzu* 子 after the *nomen* or *cognomen*; if the *praenomen* was also mentioned, it usually followed *tzu*, as it does here.

Beginning with Yeh Shih 葉適 (1150-1223) scholars have doubted the historicity of Sun Wu (see Yeh Shih, *Hsi-hsüeh chi yen* 習學記言, 46:1a-2a, *SKCS*). Some have even suggested that Sun Wu and Sun Pin were the same person. For a summary of traditional views with a selected bibliography, see Tsun Hsin 遵信, "*Sun Tzu ping-fa* te tso-che chi ch'i shih-tai" 孫子兵法的作者及其時代 in Yin-ch'üeh-shan Han-mu chu-chien cheng-li hsiao-tzu 銀雀山漢墓竹簡整理小組, ed., *Yin-ch'üeh Shan Han-mu chu-chien Sun Tzu ping-fa* (Peking: Wen-wu, 1976; hereafter, *Chu-chien Sun Tzu)*, pp. 127-40; see also Yü Chia-hsi, *Ssu-ku t'i-yao pien-cheng*, pp. 584-8). With the discovery of a very early version of the *Sun Tzu ping-fa* and a previously unknown work, *Sun Pin ping-fa* 孫臏兵法, at a Han tomb of the second century B.C., most scholars now accept both Sun Wu and Sun Pin as historical figures.

[2] "Thirteen chapters" refers to the *Sun Tzu ping-fa* 孫子兵法 (Sun Tzu's Art of War). In the "Yi-wen chih" 藝文志 chapter of Pan Ku's *Han shu* 漢書, *Sun Tzu ping-fa* is said to have 82 chapters (see *Han shu,* 30:1756). The *Sun Tzu ping-fa* discovered recently in a tomb (see n. 1 above) also contains thirteen chapters which, despite some textual differences, correspond closely to the modern edition (see Wu Chiu-ling 吳九龍, "Chien-pen yü ch'uan-pen *Sun Tzu ping-fa* pi-chiao yen-chiu" 簡本與傳本孫子兵法比交研究, *Sun Tzu hsin-t'an: Chung-wai hsüeh-che lun Sun Tzu* 孫子新探: 中外學者論孫子 [Peking: Chieh-fang Chün, 1990], pp. 176-188). Thus, despite the reference in the "Yi-wen chih," we now know that Ssu-ma Ch'ien was correct when he referred to the existence of a work by Sun Wu in thirteen chapters in the second century B.C.

[3] A longer version of this story can be found in the recently discovered *Yin-ch'üeh Shan Han-mu chu-chien Sun Tzu ping-fa* 銀雀山漢墓竹簡孫子兵法 (Peking: Wen-wu, 1976), pp. 106-8 in which Sun Tzu offers to demonstrate the arts of war with the noble, the ignoble, or with women. There is a translation of this section in Roger Ames, trans., *Sun-tzu, The Art of Warfare* (New York: Ballantine Books, 1993), pp. 193-6.

[4] Mizusawa (p. 89) thinks that Sun Tzu is the subject of the first clause in this sentence and Ho-lu the subject of the second: "[Sun Tzu] having granted [the King's request], [the king] called out . . . ." We follow the traditional reading.

[5] There are various suggestions of how many soldiers were in a *tui* 隊, ranging from 50 to 200 (see Yang, *Tso chuan,* p. 975). This account seems to suggest about 100, since there were 2 *tui* with 180 women.

The standing orders having been proclaimed, he set out axes. then repeated the signals four or five times.[6] After this, he gave the drum beat for a right turn. The women burst out laughing.

Sun Tzu said, "When the standing orders are not clear, and the signals not familiar, it is the commander's fault."

Once more, he repeated the signals four or five times, then gave the drum beat for a left turn. Once more the women burst out laughing.

Sun Tzu said, "When the standing orders are not clear, and the signals not familiar, it is the commander's fault. When they are clear yet are not followed, it is the officers' fault."

He prepared to behead the left and right company commanders.

The King of Wu had been observing from his terrace. When he saw that they were preparing to behead his favorite ladies he was aghast and hastily dispatched a messenger to pass on his orders. "We already know you can command troops, general. Without these two ladies, Our food will be tasteless. We prefer you do not behead them."

Sun Tzu said, "Your servant has already received his appointment as commander. 'When a commander is in his camp, there will be orders from his sovereign he will not accept.'"[7]

He then beheaded the two company commanders as a warning, made the next in line the company commanders, and once more beat the drum. When the women went left, right, forward, back, knelt, and stood, [their movements were as if] marked out by a carpenter's square, compass, and plumb line. [*2162*] None dared make a sound. After this, Sun Tzu sent a messenger to report to the king: "The troops having been trained, Your Majesty might try coming down to observe them; however Your Majesty would like to employ them, even marching them through fire and water, could all be done."

The King of Wu said, "Enough, general. Retire to your hostel, We do not wish to come down and observe."

Sun Tzu said, "The king only loves the words, he cannot make use of the reality."

After this, Ho-lu knew that Sun Tzu could command troops and in the end appointed him commander. [Later when Wu] defeated mighty Ch'u to its west and entered its capital Ying 郢,[8] awed Ch'i and Chin to its north[9] and spread its fame among the feudal lords,[10] it was due in part to Sun Tzu.[11]

---

[6] We tentatively suggest that *shen-ling* 申令 meant "military orders transmitted by drums and gongs" as opposed to *hao-ling* 號令, which were verbal orders. A similar instance of *shen-ling* appears in *Sun Pin ping-fa* (see Hsü P'ei-ken 徐培根, *Sun Pin ping-fa chu-shih* 孫臏兵法注釋 [Taipei: Li-ming Wen-hua, 1976], p. 115: *shen-ling yi chin ku* 申令以金鼓).

[7] This is a quote from the "Chiu-pien" 九變 chapter of *Sun Tzu* (*Sun Tzu*, 8:7a, *SPPY*). The Yin-chüeh Shan manuscript of *Sun Tzu* lists four conditions under which a commander could legitimately reject the king's orders (see *Chu-chien Sun Tzu*, pp. 98-100).

[8] This took place in 506 B.C. For Wu's capture of Ying, see *Shih chi*, 66:2171-84. On Ying in general, see n. 70 to our translation of Chapter 69 below.

[9] This probably refers to Wu's meeting with the Duke of Lu in 488 B.C., its attack on Lu in 487, and its victory over Ch'i at Ai-ling. The date of this latter battle is in question. See the Translators' Note to *Shih chi* Chapter 66 for a discussion of some of the problems involved.

[10] This probably refers to a meeting of several of the feudal lords convened in 482 B.C. at Huang-ch'ih 黃池 by Ho-lu's son Fu-ch'ai 夫差 (see *Shih chi*, 31:1473 and 66:2181).

[11] The coda beginning "After this, Ho-lu . . . " summarizes events narrated in more detail in *Shih chi* Chapter 66.

This account is also recorded in *Wu Yüeh ch'un-ch'iu*, 吳越春秋 (*Wu Yüeh ch'un-ch'iu*, 4:12b-13a, *SPPY*) and in a chapter in the *Chu-chien Sun Tzu* which the collators title "Chien Wu-wang" 見吳王. In a note, the collators observe that the style of this chapter is different from the other thirteen chapters and conclude it may have

Sun Pin

More than a hundred years after Sun Wu died there was Sun Pin 孫臏.[12] Pin was born between O 阿 and Chüan 鄄.[13] He was a descendant of Sun Wu.[14] Sun Pin once studied the arts of war together with P'ang Chüan 龐涓. After P'ang Chüan took up service in Wei, he obtained a command under King Hui 惠 (r. *370-335 B.C.), but thought his own ability inferior to Sun Pin's and secretly had [a man] summon Sun Pin. When Pin arrived, P'ang Chüan grew fearful that [Sun] was more worthy than himself. Jealous of him, he had both his feet cut off and his face tattooed as punishment by law, hoping [Sun] would retire and refuse to appear.

An envoy from Ch'i went to Liang.[15] Sun Pin, since he was a convict who had suffered the punishment of mutilation, met with the Ch'i envoy in secret and advised him. The Ch'i envoy thought him remarkable and secretly carried [Pin] to Ch'i with him in his carriage. Ch'i's general T'ien Chi 田忌 thought much of [Sun Pin] and made him his guest. Chi raced horses and gambled heavily with the Noble Scions of Ch'i several times. Sun Tzu[16] noticed that the horses' speed was not much different and that the horses fell into into high, middle and low grades. After this, [*2163*] Sun Tzu told T'ien Chi, "Just bet heavily, My Lord, and I can make you the winner."

T'ien Chi confidently agreed and bet a thousand *chin* with King [Wei 威, r. *378-343 B.C.] and the Noble Scions [of Ch'i] on a race. Just before the wager Sun Tzu said, "Now match their high-grade horses with your low-grade horses, take your high-grade horses to match their middle-grade horses and take your middle-grade horses to match their low-grade horses."

been a later addition (see *Chu-chien Sun Tzu*, pp. 106-11).

[12] *Pin* usually means "kneecap," but can also refer to leg mutilations inflicted on criminals. Judging from textual usage, these ranged from cutting off the toes to amputating the entire lower leg. (In one scholastic tradition, *pin* is supposed to refer to "removal of the kneecap.") Here *pin* simply refers to the mutilation inflicted on Sun; it is not his *praenomen*.

[13] O was located at O-ch'eng 阿城, about 15 miles northeast of modern Yang-ku 陽穀 county in Shantung (Ch'ien Mu, *Ti-ming k'ao*, p. 258; T'an Ch'i-hsiang, 1:39-40). Chüan was about 10 miles north of modern Chüan-ch'eng 鄄城 in Shantung (T'an Ch'i-hsiang, 1:39-40).

[14] According to the "Tsai-hsiang shih-hsi piao" 宰相世系表 of the *Hsin T'ang-shu* 新唐書 (73B:2945) and Teng Ming-shih's 鄧名世 (*fl.* 1160) *Ku-chin hsing-shih pien-cheng* 古今姓氏辨證 (7:11b, *SKCS* 922, p. 90), Sun Pin's father was Sun Ming 孫明, and Sun Ming was one of the three sons of Sun Wu. Since the battle of Kuei-ling (see below), in which Sun Pin was military counselor, took place in 353 B.C., 153 years after the battle of Ying, it is seems unlikely that Sun Pin could be Sun Wu's grandson. For a discussion of other anachronisms in these two sources see Hsü P'ei-ken, *op. cit.*, pp. 7-8.

[15] Wei was often referred to as Liang after King Hui moved his capital from An-yi 安邑 (about 5 miles northwest of modern Hsia-hsien 夏縣, Shansi [T'an Ch'i-hsiang, 1:35-36]) to Ta Liang 大梁 (about 5 miles northwest of modern K'ai-feng 開封, Honan, T'an Ch'i-hsiang, 1:35-36). According to *Shih chi*, 14:1847, the move took place in 340 B.C. The "Basic Annals of the First Emperor of Ch'in" (*Shih chi*, 6:203) gives the date 352 B.C. If *Shih chi* 14:1847 were correct, the reference to Wei as Liang here is an anachronism. However, the *Chu-shu chi-nien* 竹書紀年 records that King Hui moved to Ta Liang in 364 B.C. (some versions have 361 B.C., see Fang Shih-ming 方詩銘 and Wang Hsiu-ling 王修齡, *Ku-pen Chu-shu chi-nien chi-cheng* 古本竹書紀年輯證 [Shanghai: Shang-hai Ku-chi, 1981], pp. 110-1). Wang Shu-min (65:2072-3) thinks that *Chu-shu chi-nien* is wrong, but in the *Sun Pin ping-fa* excavated at Yin-ch'üeh Shan, there is a chapter entitled "Ch'in P'ang Chüan" 擒龐涓 in which Sun Pin advises T'ien Chi to "hasten to the west suburb of Liang" 西馳梁郊. In the same text, King Hui is called ruler of Liang 梁王 (see *Sun Pin ping-fa*, p. 32). It thus seems possible (despite *Shih chi*, 6:203) that by 353 B.C., when the battle of Kuei-ling 桂陵 occurred, Wei had moved its capital to Liang. See also n. 270 to our translation of *Shih chi* Chapter 4 above.

[16] Note that from here on "Sun Tzu" refers to Sun Pin, not Sun Wu.

After they raced the three grades [of horses], T'ien Chi lost once but won twice and eventually gained the king's thousand *chin*. After this, Chi presented Sun Tzu to King Wei. King Wei questioned him on the arts of war and made him his counselor.[17]

Some time later, Wei attacked Chao. Chao was hard pressed and sought help from Ch'i. King Wei of Ch'i wanted to make Sun Pin commander but Sun Pin declined: "A mutilated criminal will never do." [King Wei] then made T'ien Chi commander and Sun Tzu his counselor.

[Sun] occupied a wagon[18] where he sat and drew up plans and strategies. T'ien Chi wanted to lead the troops to Chao. Sun Tzu said, "To untangle a snarled mess, one does not raise his fists and to stop a fight one does not grab or bind.[19] Seize him at his throat[20] and charge him where he is defenseless; his formations attacked, his power constrained, he will retire of his own accord. Liang and Chao are attacking each other now; their swift soldiers and picked troops are sure to be exhausted outside [on the battlefield], their aged and infirm exhausted inside [the cities]. It would be better for My Lord to lead the troops in a rush to Ta Liang; block its roads and highways, and strike it when still undefended. Liang is sure to release Chao and save itself. We would thus in one swoop raise the siege of Chao and exhaust Wei [i.e., Liang]."

T'ien Chi followed his advice and Wei did indeed leave Han-tan 邯鄲[21] and fought with Ch'i at Kuei-ling 桂陵.[22] [Ch'i] crushed the Liang army.

[2164] Thirteen years later, Wei and Chao attacked Han. Han informed Ch'i of its straits. Ch'i had T'ien Chi take command and go [to Han's rescue]. He rushed straight to Ta Liang. Wei's commander P'ang Chüan heard this, left Han and returned [to Wei], but Ch'i's army had already passed him and [advanced] west [into Wei].

Sun Tzu told T'ien Chi, "These troops of Three Chin 三晉[23] have always been both fierce and courageous, and have little regard for Ch'i, [since] Ch'i has a name for cowardice.

---

[17] The text reads *shih* 師. Wang Li-ch'i suggests that *shih* here means "teacher," while the *shih* appearing in the next paragraph means "military counselor" *chün-shih* 軍師 (65:1636-7). Ogawa seems to share his view, rendering the first *shih* as 師 and the second as 軍師 in their translations (see Ogawa, p. 47).

[18] See n. 48 to our translation of *Shih chi* Chapter 72 below.

[19] There are two interpretations of the word *chi* 撠. The first, proposed by "So-yin," is that it means "to stab with a halberd" (the Chung-hua "So-yin" text is probably corrupt; see Wang Shu-min, 65:2071). This interpretation is adopted by Tatsuma Shosuke 立間祥介 (see his *Son Shi* 孫子 [Tokyo: Shueisha 集英社, 1984], p. 24). As Wang Nien-sun has noted, however, this probably means "to hold down or hold back," while the word po 搏 here means "to tie up" (see his *Tu-shu tsa-chi*, 3:4b-5a).

[20] Takigawa (65:8) and Wang Li-ch'i (65:1636-7) both interpret *p'i* 批 as "to avoid" and *k'ang* 亢 as "fullness (in strength)." "So-yin" reads *k'ang* as 抗 "to resist." As a number of other scholars have noted, however, *k'ang* probably is a phonetic loan for *k'eng* 吭 "throat" (see Wang Shu-min, 65:2071-2).

[21] The capital of Chao (modern Han-tan 邯鄲 in Hopei, T'an Ch'i-hsiang, 1:38).

[22] According to T'an Ch'i-hsiang (1:35-6), Kuei-ling was at about 10 miles northwest of modern Ch'ang-yüan 長垣, Honan. Ch'ien Mu, however, believes that it was located northeast of modern Ho-tse 荷澤, Shantung (*Ti-ming k'ao*, p. 431). On *Shih chi*, 15:722 the battle is said to have taken place in 353 B.C. There is also an account in the "Ch'in P'ang Chüan" 擒龐涓 chapter of *Sun Pin ping-fa* (pp. 31-3). There, P'ang Chüan is said to have been captured in this battle at Kuei-ling (rather than killing himself after his defeat at the battle of Ma-ling in 341 B.C. as recorded later in this biography). Hsü P'ei-ken thinks that this chapter was authored by Sun Pin himself. He points out that in *Chan-kuo ts'e* (7:9b, *SPTK*) the Wei commander at the battle of Ma-ling was the Heir, Shen 申, not P'ang Chüan, as recorded here. He therefore concludes that Ssu-ma Ch'ien, who apparently had not seen *Sun Pin ping-fa*, has made a mistake here (see *Sun Pin ping-fa chü-shih*, pp. 31-2). See also Lao Kan 勞榦, "Chan-kuo shih-tai te chan-cheng" 戰國時代的戰爭, *BIHP*, 36(1966), 801-28.

[23] *San Chin* generally refers to the three states of Han 韓, Chao 趙 and Wei 魏 which were created by the old Chin aristocracy after the fall and partition of that state in the early years of the Warring States Era (453-256

A skilled fighter acts according to the situation and directs the course of events by offering [the enemy] advantages. According to the arts of war, 'when one races after advantage for a hundred *li*, the commander falls; when one races after advantage for fifty *li*, only half the army arrives.'[24] When Ch'i's army enters Wei territory, have them make cooking fires for a hundred thousand; the next day make fires for fifty thousand, and the day after make fires for thirty thousand."

On the third day of P'ang Chüan's march, [P'ang] rejoiced. "I knew Ch'i's troops were cowards; three days after entering our territory, over half their officers and men have fled." He abandoned his infantry and covered two days' distance in one day with lightly armed picked soldiers, pursuing Ch'i's troops. Sun Tzu judged that they would reach Ma-ling 馬陵[25] at dusk. The road through Ma-ling was narrow and there were numerous barriers on both sides where troops could be hidden. [Sun] stripped the bark off a great tree and carved on it, "P'ang Chüan died at the foot of this tree." After this he ordered the best archers in Ch'i's army to hide along both sides of the road with ten-thousand crossbows and arranged a signal. "When you see a brand at dusk, fire in concert."

As he expected, P'ang Chüan reached the foot of the stripped tree at night, saw the inscription, and struck a fire to illuminate it. Before he had finished reading Sun's inscription, the Ch'i army's ten-thousand crossbows[26] all fired at once and Wei's army was thrown into chaos and confusion. P'ang Chüan, realizing that he had been outwitted and his troops defeated, cut his throat: "Now this whelp's name is made!"

The Ch'i army, following up on their victory, crushed P'ang's army, captured Wei's Heir, Shen 申, and returned. Sun Pin's name was renowned throughout the world because of this; his [*2165*] *Ping fa* 兵法 (Arts of War)[27] is transmitted by the present generation.

Wu Ch'i

Wu Ch'i 吳起 was a native of Wey. He loved to command troops. He once studied under Tseng Tzu 曾子,[28] [then] served the Lord of Lu. When the men of Ch'i attacked Lu (408 B.C.),[29] Lu intended to make Wu Ch'i its general, but Wu Ch'i had married a woman of Ch'i[30] and Lu distrusted him. Wu Ch'i wanted to win fame and killed his wife, showing by

B.C.); see also n. 241 to our translation of *Shih chi* Chapter 4 above. Here, however, Three Chin refers metonymically to the state of Wei.

[24] A similar saying is found in the "Chün cheng" 軍爭 chapter of *Sun Tzu* (7:5b-8a, *SPPY*).

[25] On this battle which took place in 341 B.C. about 30 miles southeast of modern Ta-ming 大名, Hopei (T'an Ch'i-hsiang, 1:39-40 and Ch'ien Mu, *Ti-ming k'ao*, pp. 256-7) see also Lao Kan 勞幹, "Chan-kuo shih-tai te chan-cheng" 戰國時代的戰爭, *BIHP*, 36(1966), 801-28.

[26] Sawyer (p. 387, n. 52) argues that the battle of Ma-ling saw the first recorded use of crossbows in Chinese history.

[27] For a translation and a summary of the history of this text see Sawyer, pp. 145-186 and 420-453.

[28] Wang Li-ch'i (65:1638) notes that this was Tseng Shen 曾參, a favorite student of Confucius (see his biography in *Shih chi* Chapter 67). However, Ch'ien Mu believes that the Tseng Tzu who studied with Confucius was born in 505 B.C. and died in 436 B.C. while Wu Ch'i was born in 440 B.C. and that this is therefore a different Tseng Tzu (see Ch'ien Mu, *Chu-tzu, p. 156)*.

[29] Ch'i Kuang 齊光 observes that this refers to Ch'i's attack of Lu in 408 B.C. In the battle Lu lost Ch'eng 郕 (see Ch'i Kuang, *Wu Ch'i ping-fa chin-i* 吳起兵法今譯 [Hong Kong: Chung-hua, 1982], p.1).

[30] In *Han Fei Tzu*, Wu Ch'i had already had a wife when he was in Wu. He later divorced her because she failed to sew for him a *tsu* 組 (waist band?) with the exact measurements he demanded. At the request of the wife's younger brother, the King of Wei intervened and tried to make Wu Ch'i take his wife back. Wu Ch'i did not want to comply and left Wei for Ch'u (see *Han Fei Tzu*, 13:11a, *SPPY*).

this that he was not a partisan of Ch'i. Lu finally made him general, and he commanded the attack against Ch'i, crushing its troops.

A man in Lu denounced Wu Ch'i. "Ch'i is by nature a suspicious and ruthless man. When he was young, his family saved up thousands of *chin*. He traveled abroad seeking office without success, and beggared his family. His neighbors laughed at him and Wu Ch'i killed more than thirty of those who had ridiculed them, then departed east through the gate of Wey's outer city wall. When he bade farewell to his mother, he bit his arm and swore an oath. 'If I, Ch'i, do not win high office, I will never again enter Wey.'[31] After this, he served Tseng Tzu [as a disciple]. After a short time had passed his mother died, but Ch'i never went home. Tseng Tzu was contemptuous of such behavior, and broke off with Ch'i. Ch'i then went to [the capital of] Lu, studied the arts of war, and sought service with the Lord of Lu.[32] When the Lord of Lu distrusted him, he sought the position of general by killing his wife. Now Lu is a small country, but having gained fame as a victor in battle, the feudal lords will plot against Lu. Moreover, Lu and Wey are brother states,[33] but by employing [Wu] Ch'i My Lord abandons Wey." The Lord of Lu distrusted Wu Ch'i and declined [to employ] him.[34]

[2166] After this, Wu Ch'i heard that Marquis Wen 文 of Wei (r. 424-387 B.C.) was worthy and decided to seek service with him.[35]

Marquis Wen asked Li K'o 李克,[36] "What kind of man is Wu Ch'i?"

Li K'o said, "Ch'i is greedy and lecherous, but in commanding troops, even Marshal Jang-chü 穰苴[37] cannot surpass him."

After this, Marquis Wen of Wei made him general and he attacked Ch'in, taking five walled cities.

As general, Wu Ch'i wore the same clothes and ate the same food as officers and men of the lowest rank. When sleeping he did not spread out a mat, and when marching he did not ride a horse or carriage. He carried his own provisions and shared his officers' and men's labors and hardships. One of his foot soldiers suffered from an abscess; [Wu] Ch'i sucked it clean for him. When the soldier's mother heard this she wailed.

A man said, "Your son is a foot soldier, and the general himself sucked his abscess clean. What are you wailing for?"

The mother replied, "It is not as you think. Last year Master Wu sucked his father's abscess clean and his father fought without turning until he died before the enemy. Now Master Wu has sucked my son's abscess clean, too, but I do not know where [my son] will die. This is why I wailed."[38]

---

[31] *Han Fei Tzu* gives a completely different reason for Wu Ch'i leaving Wei, see n. 31 above.

[32] Liang Yü-sheng believes that the character *Lu* 魯 in this sentence and the one that follows are interpolations (27:1195). Wang Shu-min (65:2176) speculates that it is a an error for *wu* 吾, "my."

[33] As Wang Li-ch'i (65:1638) points out, the royal family of Lu was descendant of the Duke of Chou's 周公 son, while that of Wei descended from the Duke's younger brother. Therefore, the two states could be called *hsiung-ti* 兄弟 states.

[34] As Chauncey S. Goodrich, "The Biography of Wu Ch'i," *MS,* 35(1981-83), p. 204, points out, the statement that "the Lord of Lu distrusted Wu Ch'i and declined to employ him" contradicts the previous statement that he fought against Ch'i for Lu. It might be possible to interpret *hsieh* 謝 as "dismiss" (Jens O. Petersen, personal communication), but we have found no other examples of this usage in *Shih chi.*

[35] The first meeting between Marquis Wen and Wu Ch'i is recorded in *Wu Tzu* (see *Wu Tzu* A:1a-2a, *SPPY*).

[36] Also known as Li K'uei 悝, he served the Marquis Wen of Wei as Prime Minister (see Wang Li-ch'i, *Jen-piao*, pp. 217-8 and 324) and was noted for his contributions to that state's agriculture (*Shih chi,* 30:1442); see also Timoteus Pokora, "The Canon of Laws by Li K'uei: A Double Falsification?" *AO,* 27(1959), 96-121.

[37] See his biography in *Shih chi* Chapter 64.

[38] A similar account is found in *Han Fei Tzu* (11:7b, *SPPY*).

Because of Wu Ch'i's skill in commanding troops, his integrity and impartiality, and his ability to win his men's total loyalty, Marquis Wen appointed him Governor of Hsi Ho 西河 (West Ho),[39] to resist Ch'in and Han. After the Marquis Wen of Wei died, Ch'i served his son, the Marquis Wu 武 (r. 386-371 B.C.).

The Marquis Wu floated down the Hsi Ho.[40] In midstream, he turned around and told Wu Ch'i, "How beautiful, these mountain and river strongholds! These are the treasures of the state of Wei!"

Ch'i replied, "[Its treasures] lie in virtue, not in redoubts. In ancient times The San-miao 三苗[41] had Lake Tung-t'ing 洞庭[42] to his left and Lake P'eng-li 彭蠡[43] to his right.[44] He did not cultivate virtue or righteousness, and Yü 禹 B.C.[45] destroyed him. The dwelling of Chieh 桀 of Hsia[46] had the Yellow River and the Chi 濟[47] River to its left, Mount T'ai-hua 泰華[48] to its right; Mount Yi-ch'üeh 伊闕[49] was to its south and the Yang-ch'ang 羊腸[50] Path was to its north. [Chieh] practiced government without humanity, and T'ang 湯[51] banished him. The capital of Chow 紂 of Yin [*2167*] had Mount Meng-men 孟門[52] to its left, the T'ai-hang 太行 Mountains[53] to its right. Mount Ch'ang 常[54] was to its north and the Great Ho [River] 大河 passed through its south. He practiced government without virtue, and King Wu 武[55] killed him. Judging from this, [the state's treasures] lie in virtue, not in redoubts. If My Lord does not cultivate virtue, [even] the people in this boat will go over to your enemies."

"Well put," said Marquis Wu said, and enfeoffed Wu Ch'i.[56]

[39] A commandery bordering the Yellow River to the west in eastern Shensi running as far north as the Liang 梁 Mountains (T'an Ch'i-hsiang, 1:35).

[40] The section of the Yellow River that flows south dividing modern Shensi and Shansi provinces (T'an Ch'i-hsiang, 1:35).

[41] The leader of an ancient tribe in South China during the time of the legendary emperor Shun (see also T'an Ch'i-hsiang, 1:9-10 and n. 111 to our translation of *Shih chi* Chapter 1 above).

[42] Modern Lake Tung-t'ing in northern Hunan province (T'an Ch'i-hsiang, 1:35-6).

[43] Modern Lake P'o-yang 鄱陽 in northern Kiangsi province (T'an Ch'i-hsiang, 1:45-6).

[44] There is a parallel text for this speech in *Chan-kuo ts'e* (7:3b-4b, *SPTK).* As a number of commentators have observed, the speech appears to be modeled on a passage in the *Tso chuan.* An interesting point to note is that the "left" and "right" of the *Shih chi* version are reversed in the *Chan-kuo ts'e* text. (The place names are also slightly different, as Goodrich, *op. cit.,* p. 221, n. 21, notes.) The *Chan-kuo ts'e* text is close to Warring States period usage, in which left referred to east and right referred to west.

[45] Legendary founder of the Hsia dynasty (traditionally, 2205-1767 B.C.); see also our translation of *Shih chi* Chapter 2 above.

[46] Last ruler of the Hsia Dynasty; see also our translation of *Shih chi* Chapter 2 above.

[47] Near the course of the modern Chi River in northern Honan (T'an Ch'i-hsiang, 1:35-6).

[48] Modern Hua-shan 華山 in eastern Shensi (T'an Ch'i-hsiang, 1:35-6).

[49] About 10 miles south-southeast of modern Loyang, Honan (T'an Ch'i-hsiang, 1:35-6).

[50] A path in the T'ai-hang 太行 Mountains about 40 miles west of modern An-yang 安陽, Honan (T'an Ch'i-hsiang, 1:35-6).

[51] Founder of the Yin or Shang dynasty; see our translation of *Shih chi* Chapter 3 above.

[52] About 25 miles west of modern Hui-hsien 輝縣, Shansi (T'an Ch'i-hsiang, 1:35-6).

[53] Forming the border between the modern provinces of Shansi and Hopei/Honan for over 100 miles (T'an Ch'i-hsiang, 1:37).

[54] Better known as Heng-shan 恆山 about 30 miles north-northwest of modern Ch'ü-yang 曲陽, Hopei (T'an Ch'i-hsiang, 1:37-7).

[55] Founder of the Chou dynasty (1122-256 B.C.); see also our translation of *Shih chi* Chapter 4 above.

[56] The Chung-hua editors punctuate these lines as follows: 武侯曰　"善!" [即封] 吳起為西河守. They follow Liang Yü-sheng (27:1196) in this emendation [the bracketed text indicates what the Chung-hua editors believe to be interpolations or other textual errors]. Our translation follows the emended punctuation suggested by Wang Shu-min (65:2079) which breaks the line after Wu Ch'i.

As Governor of Hsi Ho, [Wu Ch'i] had a great reputation. When Wei established the position of Prime Minister, he appointed T'ien Wen 田文. Wu Ch'i was displeased, and spoke to T'ien Wen.

"I ask your permission to discuss merit with you, sir. May I?"

"You may," said T'ien Wen.

Ch'i said, "In commanding the entire army, making the soldiers and troops rejoice in dying, and enemies fearful of plotting [against Wei], how do you compare with me, sir?"

"I am not your equal, sir," said Wen.

Ch'i said, "In governing the hundred officials, cherishing the multitudes, and filling the treasuries and arsenals, how do you compare with me, sir?"

"I am not your equal, sir," said Wen.

Ch'i said, "In governing Hsi Ho, so that Ch'in's troops do not dare face east and Han and Chao follow as clients, how do you compare with me, sir?"

"I am not your equal, sir," said Wen.

Ch'i said, "In all these three, sir, you come out below me. Why then is your position above me?"

Wen said, "When the ruler is young and the country unsettled, when the great vassals have not yet given their loyalty, or the families of the hundred cognomens their trust, at a time such as this, should the country be entrusted to you, or should it be entrusted to me?"

Ch'i was silent for a long while.

"It should be entrusted to you, sir."

Wen said, "That is why I hold a position above you."

Wu Ch'i then realized he was not T'ien Wen's equal.

After T'ien Wen died, Kung-shu 公叔 became Prime Minister. Although he had married a princess of Wei, he envied Wu Ch'i. Kung-shu's driver said, "Ch'i would be easy to get rid of."

"What would you do?" Kung-shu said.

His driver said, "Wu Ch'i is by nature pompous and self-satisfied.[57] My Lord can thus first tell the Marquis Wu, 'This Wu Ch'i is a worthy man, but the Marquis's state [*2168*] is small and shares a border with mighty Ch'in. Your servant secretly fears that [Wu] Ch'i might not intend to stay.' The Marquis Wu will ask, 'What would you do?' My Lord can then tell the Marquis Wu, 'Try offering him a princess; if Ch'i intends to stay he is sure to accept her. If he does not intend to stay, he is sure to decline. By this we can divine [his intention].' Then you summon Wu Ch'i and take him to your home; if you make [your wife] the princess angry enough to humiliate you, then Wu Ch'i, seeing that [one] princess treats you so meanly, is sure to decline [the other]."

After this, Wu Ch'i, seeing that the princess treated the Prime Minister of Wei so meanly, did indeed decline Marquis Wu of Wei's offer. Marquis Wu became suspicious and no longer trusted him. Wu Ch'i, fearing punishment, promptly left Wei and went to Ch'u.

King Tao 悼 of Ch'u (r. 401-381 B.C.) had long heard that [Wu] Ch'i was worthy. When [Wu Ch'i] arrived, he became Prime Minister of Ch'u. He fostered and nurtured knights for battle by clarifying the laws and scrutinizing the ordinances, removing unnecessary official posts, and disenfranchising the more distant [members] of the ducal clan. He emphasized strengthening the army and crushing the traveling rhetoricians who talked of alliances and counter alliances.[58] After this, he pacified the Pai-yüeh 百越[59] in the south, annexed

---

[57] We follow Wang Nien-sun (3:5a) in excising *ming* 名 here. *Lien* 廉, usually "incorrupt" or "possessing integrity," it is a non sequitur here and we tentatively translate it as "pompous" (see *Shih chi*, 104:2775 and 122:3138 for similar usages).

Ch'en 陳 and Ts'ai 蔡[60] and drove off the Three Chin in the north, and attacked Ch'in in the west. The feudal lords were dismayed at the might of Ch'u.

The former nobles and ducal relatives of Ch'u all wanted to kill Wu Ch'i. When King Tao died, members of the ducal house and the great vassals revolted and attacked Wu Ch'i. Wu Ch'i ran to the body of the king and lay on it. The mob attacking Ch'i thus shot and stabbed Wu Ch'i, and at the same time hit King Tao. After King Tao was buried and his Heir[61] enthroned, [the Heir] then ordered the premier[62] to execute all those who, in shooting Wu Ch'i, had also hit the king's body. More than seventy families of those who were implicated in the shooting of Ch'i were wiped out.

His Honor the Grand Scribe says, "When the common folk of our generation speak of divisions and brigades, they all mention Sun Tzu's thirteen chapters[63] and Wu Ch'i's *Ping fa* 兵法 (Arts of War).[64] Many of our generation possess [their writings], so I have not included any of them, but have instead included their actions and accomplishments. A saying goes, 'Those who can do it can't necessarily talk of it, those who can talk of it can't necessarily do it.' Sun Tzu was brilliant in his calculations against P'ang Chüan, but could not save himself earlier from [*2169*] the disaster of mutilation. Wu Ch'i advised Marquis Wu that tactical disposition and power were not equal to virtue, yet when he put [his advice] into practice in Ch'u, he destroyed himself through his harsh tyranny and lack of mercy. Tragic indeed, wasn't it?"

---

[58] On *ho-tsung* 合縱 and *lien-heng* 連橫 refer to the Translators' Note in Chapter 69 (Su Ch'in).

[59] Also written as *Pai Yüeh* 百粵. Literally the "Hundred Yüeh," this was a collective term for the various tribes of a people known as the Yüeh, who lived south of the Yangtze River.

[60] Just southwest of modern Shang-ts'ai 上蔡 in Honan (T'an Ch'i-hsiang, 1:29)

[61] He became King Su 肅 (r. 380-370 B.C.).

[62] *Ling-yin* 令尹, a title used only in the state of Ch'u.

[63] The identity of "Sun Tzu" here is not very clear. Elsewhere in this paragraph, Ssu-ma Ch'ien is commenting on Sun Pin and Wu Ch'i, thus "Sun Tzu" here should be understood as Sun Pin. However, the *Thirteen Chapters*, as it appears in the first paragraph of this biography, is usually a reference to the *Arts of War* by Sun Wu.

[64] Known as *Wu Tzu* 吳子 it was included in the Sung-dynasty *Wu-ching ch'i-shu* 五經七書 (and subsequently in *SPPY* and *SPTK;* see also *Han shu*, 30:1757 where a *Wu Ch'i* is listed in 48 *p'ien* 篇 and Sawyer, pp. 191-225 and 453-60).

TRANSLATORS' NOTE

In treating three more military geniuses, this chapter has resonances with that of Marshal Jang-chü above (see *Shih chi* Chapter 64). As with the preceding chapter, each of the protagonists here demonstrates his talent and is characterized through a clever stratagem: Sun Wu in his ruthless treatment of Ho-lu's courtesans, Sun Pin's brilliant ambush at Ma-ling, and Wu Ch'i's tactical death which eventually brought down all his enemies. A pattern for treating military men through one (or but a few) maneuvers has been established in these two chapters which is later emulated in Ssu-ma Ch'ien's treatment of "T'ien Tan" (Chapter 82).

This chapter and Chapter 64 above mark the transition from the Spring and Autumn era to that of the Warring States. As persuasion was perhaps the civil means to success during this period, strategy was that which might win a military man favor.

The structure of the chapter deserves note. Viewed overall it resembles the *lei-chuan* 類傳 (classified biographies, such as the "Tz'u-k'o" 刺客 [Assassin-Retainers]) which appear later in the *lieh-chuan* section with the classification here being military strategists. Internally, there is also a basis for the order of the biographies. Sun Tzu Wu is the earliest of the three men and is logically presented first (most of the classified biographies are arranged chronologically). Sun Pin, however, whose life was the latest of the three men discussed in this chapter, was perhaps placed second because he was related to Sun Tzu Wu. Or perhaps he was inserted second to initiate the subplot which binds Sun Pin and Wu Ch'i as men (in the Grand Scribe's own words) who "can talk of it but not necessarily do it."

As Roger Ames has observed (see Bibliography below), almost the entire section on Sun Tzu in this memoir is probably based on the version discovered at Yin-ch'üeh Shan or an account similar to it. Ssu-ma Ch'ien has essentially abridged and polished the story.

BIBLIOGRAPHY

I. Translations

Ames, Roger, trans. *Sun-tzu, The Art of Warfare, the First English Translation Incorporating the Recently Discovered Yin-ch'üeh-shan Texts*. New York: Ballantine Books, 1993 [Sun Tzu].

Dolby, William and John Scott, trans. *Sima Qian, War-Lords, Translated with Twelve Other Stories from His Historical Records*. Edinburgh: Southside, 1974, pp. 55-66 [Sun Tzu, Sun Pin, and Wu Ch'i].

Goodrich, Chauncey S. "The Biography of Wu Ch'i," *MS*, 35 (1981-83), 197-233 [Wu Ch'i].

Griffith, S. B., trans. *Sun Tzu: The Art of War*. Cambridge: Cambridge University Press, 1963, pp. 57-62 [Sun Tzu].

Mizusawa Toshitada 水澤利忠. *Shiki* 史記. V. 8. *Retsuden (ichi)* 列傳 (一). Tokyo: Meiji Shoten, 1990, pp. 87-113.

Ōgawa Tamaki 小川環樹, trans. *Shiki retsuden* 史記列傳. Rpt. Tokyo: Chikuma Shobō, 1986 (1969). pp. 19-24.

Sawyer, Ralph D. *The Seven Military Classics of Ancient China*. Boulder: Westview Press, 1993, pp. 193-6 [Wu Ch'i].

II. Studies

Ames, Roger. "Sun Wu as a Historical Person," and "An Interview with the King of Wu,"
    op. cit., pp. 32-35 and 190-6, respectively.

Chan Li-po 詹立波. "Lüeh t'an Yin-ch'üeh-shan Han-mu chu-chien *Sun Tzu ping-fa*" 略談銀
    雀山漢墓竹簡孫子兵法, in *Yin-ch'üeh-shan Han-mu chu-chien Sun Tzu ping-fa.*
    Peking: Wen-wu, 1976, pp. 10-18.

Ch'ien Mu 錢穆. *Hsien Ch'in chu-tzu hsi-nien* 先秦諸子繫年. 2v. Rpt. Peking: Chung-hua
    Shu-chü, 1985, pp. 164-5 and 190-1.

Konrad, N. T. *Wu-tzu: Trattat o voennom iskusstve, perevod y kommentarij.* Moscow:
    Izdatel'stvo Vostochnoi Literatury, 1958.
        Gives a brief biography of Wu Ch'i in the Introduction to this translation of *Wu
    Tzu.*

Li Ling 李零. "Kuan-yü Yin-ch'üeh-shan chien-pen *Sun Tzu* te shang-ch'üeh" 關於銀雀山漢
    墓竹簡孫子的商榷, *Wen shih,* 7 (1979), 23-34.

Petersen, Jens O. "On the Expressions Commonly Held to Refer to Sun Wu, the Putative
    Author of the Sunzi Bingfa," *Acta Orientalia,* 53(1992), 106-21.

_____. "What's in a Name? On the Sources Concerning Sun Wu," *AM, Third Series,*
    5.1(1992), 1-31.

Wu Chiu-lung 吳九龍. "Chien-pen yü ch'uan-pen *Sun-tzu ping-fa* pi-chiao yen-chiu" 簡本與
    傳本孫子兵法比交研究, *Sun Tzu hsin-t'an: Chung-wai hsüeh-che lun Sun Tzu* 孫子新
    探: 中外學者論孫子. Peking: Chieh-fang Chün, 1990, pp. 176-188.

Wu Tzu Hsü, Memoir 6

Wu Tzu Hsü

[66:2171] Wu Tzu Hsü 伍子胥[1] was a native of Ch'u. His *praenomen* was Yün 員. Yün's father was Wu She 伍奢; his elder brother was Wu Shang 伍尚. His ancestor was Wu Chü 伍舉, famous for serving King Chuang 莊 of Ch'u (r. 613-591 B.C.) with straightforward admonition;[2] because of this, [Wu] Chü's descendants were renowned in Ch'u.

King P'ing 平 of Ch'u (r. 528-516 B.C.) had an Heir whose *praenomen* was Chien 建. [King P'ing] made Wu She [the Heir's] Grand Mentor and Fei Wu-chi 費無忌 [his] Lesser Mentor.[3]

Wu-chi was disloyal to the Heir Chien. King P'ing sent Wu-chi to bring back a bride from Ch'in for the Heir. The Ch'in woman was striking. Wu-chi sped back and reported to King P'ing: "The Ch'in woman is beautiful beyond compare. Your Majesty should marry her yourself and get another wife for the Heir."

King P'ing married the Ch'in woman himself and loved and favored her above all others. [She] gave birth to a son, Chen 軫. [The king] found another wife for the Heir.[4]

Having ingratiated himself with King P'ing through the Ch'in woman, Wu-chi left the Heir to serve King P'ing. He feared that once King P'ing had died and the Heir was enthroned, [the Heir] would kill him. He therefore took every occasion to slander the Heir Chien. Chien's mother was a woman from [the state of] Ts'ai. She was not favored by King P'ing. King P'ing gradually became more and more estranged from Chien and sent him to guard Ch'eng-fu 城父[5] and maintain the border troops.

[2172] In a short while, Wu-chi was again speaking of the Heir's faults to the king day and night. "Because of the matter of the Ch'in woman, the Heir has to feel rancor. I would hope Your Majesty might make some preparations for your own sake. Since the Heir has taken up residence in Ch'eng-fu, he has taken command of the troops and is in contact with the feudal lords abroad. Soon he will enter [the capital] to raise a revolt."

King P'ing then summoned the Grand Mentor, Wu She, and interrogated him. Wu She knew that Wu-chi had been slandering the Heir to King P'ing and said, "Your Majesty, why

---

[1] We take Hsü as Wu's *agnomen* and Tzu as an honorific suffix (see n. 1 of our translation of Chapter 65). In a number of places in this biography, and in other works as well, he is also referred to as Wu Hsü. Throughout *Kuo-yü*, he is referred to as Shen Hsü 申胥. According to Wei Chao's *Kuo-yü chieh* (19:1a, *SPPY*), Shen was his fief in Wu. See also Fang Hsüan-ch'en, pp. 269-70.

[2] According to Tu Yü 杜預 (see Yang, *Tso chuan*, Chao 19, p. 1401), Wu Chü was Tzu Hsü's grandfather. It is very unlikely, however, that Chü would have lived long enough both to serve King Chuang and to have a son who served King P'ing. This is highlighted by Ssu-ma Ch'ien's record of Wu Chü admonishing King Chuang in 611 B.C., 85 years prior to the events narrated here (*Shih chi*, 40:1700). In the *Tso chuan*, Tzu Hsü's great-grandfather, Wu Ts'an 伍參, is several times referred to as a minister of King Chuang, in contrast to Wu Chü, who primarily served King Kang 康 (r. 559-545 B.C.) and King Ling 靈 (r. 544-529 B.C.). It is thus likely that Ssu-ma Ch'ien has confounded Wu Ts'an and Wu Chü, but he may have noticed the chronological difficulty here, since he says that Wu Chü was Wu Tzu Hsü's "ancestor" rather than "grandfather."

[3] *T'ai Fu* 太傅 and *Shao Fu* 少傅; *Tso chuan* (Yang, *Tso chuan*, Chao 19, p. 1401) says *Shih* 師 (Tutor) and *Shao Shih* 少師 (Lesser Tutor).

[4] The *Tso chuan* (Yang, *Tso chuan*, Chao 19, p. 1401) says that Fei Wu-chi "was not favored by the Heir." *Shih chi* (14:654 and 40:1712) places Fei Wu-chi's mission in 527 B.C., the year after King P'ing's ascension to the throne. It is worth noting that according to *Shih chi*, 40:1712, the Heir was fourteen years old at the time.

[5] About 5 miles northwest of modern P'ing-ting Shan 平頂山 City in central Honan (T'an Ch'i-hsiang, 1:29-30).

have you allowed yourself to become estranged from your own flesh and blood by a slanderous, malicious, menial slave?"

Wu-chi said, "If Your Majesty does not now restrain him, his scheme will succeed, and Your Majesty will soon be taken." Enraged, King P'ing imprisoned Wu She and sent the Marshal of Ch'eng-fu, Fen Yang 奮揚, to go kill the Heir. Before he reached [Ch'eng-fu], Fen Yang sent a man in advance to tell the Heir: "Fly quickly, Heir, or you will be executed!" Heir Chien, fled to Sung.[6]

Wu-chi said to King P'ing, "Wu She has two sons, both of them worthy. If they are not executed, they will be Ch'u's sorrow. You can summon them by using their father as a hostage. If not, they will be Ch'u's trouble."

The king sent a messenger to tell Wu She, "If you can bring your sons here, you live. If not, you die."

Wu She replied, "Shang is by nature humane. If called, he is sure to come. Yün is by nature relentless and ruthless, able to bear opprobrium, capable of accomplishing great things. If he sees that on coming they will both be taken, he is sure not to come."

The king would not listen. He sent a man to summon the two sons. "Come, and I will spare your father. Fail to come, and I will kill [Wu] She today."

Wu Shang decided to go. Yün said, "Ch'u summons us two brothers, not because he intends to spare our father; he fears that one might escape and give rise to trouble afterwards. Thus with the father as a hostage, he deceitfully summons the two sons. When the two sons arrive, father and sons will die together. How can this save father from death? If we go, it will only make it impossible for us to avenge this wrong. It would be better to flee to another state and borrow its strength to wipe out father's disgrace. To perish together is of no avail."

Wu Shang said, "I know that going could never save father's life. But I would regret it if I did not go when father summoned me to save his life and, unable later to wipe out his disgrace, I wound up a laughingstock before the entire world."

"You may fly!" he told Yün. "You can avenge father's murder. I shall go back to die."

Shang having surrendered himself, the emissary placed Wu Hsü under arrest. Wu Hsü bent his bow, nocked an arrow and aimed at the emissary. The emissary did not dare advance, and Wu Hsü fled. Hearing that Heir Chien, was in Sung, he went there to serve him.[7]

When [Wu] She heard of Tzu Hsü's escape, he sighed. "Ch'u's king and his vassals will soon feel the sword."

When Wu Shang reached [the capital of] Ch'u, Ch'u killed both [*2173*] She and Shang.[8]

When Wu Hsü reached [the state of] Sung, Sung was in the midst of the rebellion of the Hua 華 clan.[9] He fled to [the state of] Cheng with Heir Chien. The people of Cheng thought very highly of them. Heir Chien, then went to [the state of] Chin.

Duke Ch'ing 頃 of Chin (r. 525-512 B.C.) said, "Since the Heir is highly regarded in Cheng, Cheng will trust him. If the Heir could respond for us inside, and we attacked it

---

[6] A kingdom at modern Shang-ch'iu 商丘 in Honan (T'an Ch'i-hsiang, 1:29-30).

[7] *Tso chuan* (Yang, Chao 20, pp. 1407-8) relates the same story with some variations.

[8] According to *Shih chi,* 14:656 and 40:1712, the Heir's transfer to Ch'eng-fu, the execution of Wu She and Wu Shang, and the flight of Tzu Hsü and the Heir Chien all occurred in 522 B.C. *Shih chi* Chapter 14, however, says that the Chien went first to Sung, then to Cheng, and that Wu Tzu Hsü went directly to Wu. This contradicts the events described below in this biography.

[9] This refers to the rebellion of Hua Hai 華亥, Hua Ting 華定, and Hsiang Ning 向寧 in 522 B.C. For details, see Yang, *Tso chuan,* Chao 20, pp. 1409-10 and *Shih chi,* 38:1630.

outside, the destruction of Cheng would be certain. Once Cheng is destroyed, we will enfeoff you, Heir." The Heir then returned to Cheng. Before a chance for the plot came, it chanced that the Heir wanted to kill one of his attendants over a personal matter. The attendant knew of the plot, and informed Cheng. Duke Ting 定 of Cheng (r. 529-514 B.C.) and [his prime minister] Tzu Ch'an 子產 executed the Heir Chien.[10]

Chien had a son whose *praenomen* was Sheng 勝. Wu Hsü feared [for Sheng's life]. He fled to Wu with Sheng. When he reached Chao Pass 昭關,[11] the [officer of] Chao Pass prepared to seize him. Wu Hsü and Sheng fled together with only the clothes on their backs.[12] They were almost captured. His pursuers behind him, Wu Hsü reached the Chiang River. On the bank of the Chiang was an old fisherman in a boat. He realized Wu Hsü's plight, and took him across the river.

After Wu Hsü had crossed, he took off his sword and said, "This sword is worth a hundred *chin*. I give it to you, father."

"It is the law of Ch'u," the fisherman replied, "that whoever captures Wu Hsü will be granted fifty thousand *tan* of grain and the title of Jade-Baton Holder,[13] not just a sword worth a hundred *chin*." He refused to accept it.[14]

Before Wu Hsü reached Wu, he fell ill. He stopped on the way and begged for food.[15]

When he arrived in Wu, Liao 僚, King of Wu (r. 526-515 B.C.) was at war and the Noble Scion Kuang 光[16] was general. Wu Hsü therefore sought an audience with the King of Wu through Noble Scion Kuang.

[2174] Some time later, King P'ing of Ch'u became angry over clashes between the Ch'u border-town Chung-li 鍾離[17] and the Wu border-town, Pei-liang-shih 卑梁氏,[18] both of

[10] *Shih chi*, 42:1774 says that Chien was executed in 520 B.C. after plotting with Chin to attack Cheng. Following this, his son Sheng fled to Wu. This confirms the biography's account of Chien's death, but again contradicts the biography's claim that Wu Tzu Hsü followed Chien into exile and saved Chien's son, Sheng.

The *Shih chi* chronology for this period and the accounts in the related "Shih-chia" 世家 chapters are all consistent in saying that Wu Tzu Hsü went to Wu in 522 B.C., that Chien went to Sung and then to Cheng, that Cheng executed Chien for plotting with Chin (in either 520 or 519 B.C.), and that following this Chien's son fled to Wu. It may be that Ssu-ma Ch'ien is attempting to make Wu Tzu Hsü into a "loyal minister" after the fashion of the followers of Duke Wen of Chin during his exile, at the expense of both historical fact and internal consistency as well.

[11] Located on the Ch'u side of the Wu-Ch'u border on a hill called Hsiao-hsien 小峴 today (about 5 miles north of Han-shan 含山 County in southeastern Anhwei (Wang Li-ch'i, 66:1646).

[12] It seems that when Wu Tzu Hsü retired to the fields after Noble Scion Kuang refused to attack Ch'u, Sheng was with him. Towards the end of the chapter, Sheng seems to have stayed in Wu until Fu-ch'ai became king. Therefore, it is likely that they had escaped together. Accordingly, we read *yü* 與 as "together," and take *tu-shen* 獨身 as similar to our expression "with only the clothes on their back," meaning that they were not accompanied by attendants or carrying any valuables.

[13] *Chih-kuei* 執珪, a title of nobility in the state of Ch'u.

[14] In *Wu Yüeh ch'un-ch'iu*, (3:4a, *SPPY*), the fisherman is said to have drowned himself later so as to keep Wu Tzu Hsü's whereabouts a secret. For a detailed analysis of the Wu Tzu Hsü story--both in *Wu Yüeh ch'un-ch'iu* and other texts--see David Johnson, "The Wu Tzu Hsü *Pien-wen* and Its Sources: Part I," *HJAS*, 40.1(June 1980), 128-43.

[15] In *Wu Yüeh ch'un-ch'iu* (3:4a, *SPPY*) Wu was fed by a young woman beating silk by a river who later also drowned herself to assure him of her loyalty.

[16] He was Liao's cousin.

[17] This was located about 10 miles northeast of modern Feng-yang 鳳陽 County in Anhwei (T'an Ch'i-hsiang, 1:29-30; see also Ch'ien Mu, *Ti-ming k'ao*, pp.573-4).

[18] About 10 miles northwest of modern T'ien-ch'ang 天長 County in eastern Anhwei (T'an Ch'i-hsiang, 1:29-30).

which raised silkworms; [the clashes occurred] after a fight between two women over mulberry trees,[19] and resulted in the two states raising soldiers and attacking each other. Wu sent the Noble Scion Kuang to attack Ch'u. He returned after taking Chung-li and Chü-ch'ao 居巢.[20]

Wu Tzu Hsü spoke to Liao, King of Wu: "Ch'u's [army] could be defeated. I beg you to send Noble Scion Kuang once more."[21]

Noble Scion Kuang told the King of Wu, "This Wu Hsü's father and elder brother were killed by Ch'u; in urging Your Majesty to attack Ch'u, he only wishes to avenge his own grudge. If we attacked Ch'u, [its army] could not yet be defeated."

Wu Hsü realized that Noble Scion Kuang had ambitions inside the state, that he hoped to kill the king and take the throne himself, and that he could not yet be persuaded on matters abroad. He presented Chuan Chu 專諸[22] to the Noble Scion Kuang and retired to take up the plow in the countryside with the Heir Chien's son, Sheng.

Five years [later],[23] King P'ing of Ch'u died. The Ch'in woman whom King P'ing had earlier taken away from Heir Chien had given birth to a son, Chen 軫. When King P'ing died, Chen was eventually enthroned as his successor. He was known as King Chao 昭 (r. 515-489 B.C.).

Liao, King of Wu, taking advantage of Ch'u's mourning, sent two Noble Scions[24] to lead a surprise attack on Ch'u. Ch'u mobilized its troops and cut off the Wu troops' retreat. They were thus unable to return. With Wu's capital emptied [of its troops], Noble Scion Kuang had Chuan Chu attack and stab Liao, King of Wu,[25] then took the throne himself. He was known as Ho-lu 闔廬,[26] King of Wu (r. 514-496 B.C.).

Ho-lu having taken the throne and realized his ambition, he summoned Wu Yün, made him Officer of Foreign Affairs[27] and consulted with him on affairs of state.

Ch'u executed its great vassals Hsi Yüan 郤宛 and Po Chou-li 伯州犁.[28] Po Chou-li's grandson Po Hsi 伯嚭[29] fled to Wu. Wu made Po Hsi a grand master, too.

[2175] The two Noble Scions whom the King, Liao, had earlier sent to lead the troops in the attack against Ch'u were unable to return because their retreat was cut off. After they

---

[19] According to *Shih chi,* 31:1462, there was first a fight between two women which led to clashes between their families, their towns and, eventually, their states.

[20] Wang Li-ch'i (66:1647) holds that Chü-ch'ao was located in modern Ch'ao county in Anhwei and is now submerged in the Ch'ao Lake. T'an Ch'i-hsiang (1:29-30) locates it about 30 miles southeast of modern Shou 壽 County in central Anhwei (see also Ch'ien Mu, *Ti-ming k'ao,* p. 174).

[21] There is a parallel account of this story on *Shih chi,* 31:1462.

[22] See his biography in *Shih chi* Chapter 86.

[23] See the Translators' Note at the end of the chapter.

[24] *Shih chi* Chapters 40 and 86 say they were King Liao's brothers, Kai-yü 蓋餘 and Chu-yung 屬庸. *Tso chuan*, however, has Yen-yü 掩餘 instead of Kai-yü (Yang, *Tso chuan,* Chao 27, p. 1485).

[25] This took place in 515 B.C. For a record of the assassination, see *Shih chi,* 31:1463 and 86:2516.

[26] Elsewhere (*Shih Chi,* 14:1463 and *Wu Yüeh ch'un-ch'iu,* 4:1a-13a, *SPPY*) Ho-lu is written as Ho-lü 闔閭. Wang Shu-min (66:2067) observes that *lu* and *lü* were interchangeable.

[27] *Hsing-jen* 行人.

[28] Observing that Hsi Yüan was killed in 514 B.C. while Po Chou-li died in 540 B.C., Liang Yü-sheng believes that the first "Po Chou-li" in these two sentences is an interpolation (Liang Yü-sheng, 27:1198). According to *Shih chi,* 40:1714-5, Hsi Yüan's clan name was Po and Po Hsi was his son. Liang Yü-sheng disputes this and suggests that they belonged to the same faction rather than the same clan.

[29] The reading "Hsi" is based on "So-yin." In *Wu Yüeh ch'un-ch'iu* (ch. 4 and 5, *SPPY*), Po's name is given as Po Hsi 白喜.

heard that Ho-lu had murdered the King, Liao, and enthroned himself, they surrendered with their troops to Ch'u. Ch'u enfeoffed them at Shu 舒.[30]

In the third year of Ho-lu's reign (512 B.C.), [Ho-lu] mobilized his troops and attacked Ch'u together with Wu Hsü and Po Hsi. He took Shu and captured the two renegade commanders of Wu. After this, he wanted to advance to Ying 郢.[31]

His commander, Sun Wu 孫武,[32] said, "With the people exhausted, it is not yet possible. Wait for a while." [Ho-lu] then returned.

In [Ho-lu's] fourth year (511 B.C.), Wu launched an expedition against Ch'u and took Liu 六[33] and Ch'ien 灊.[34]

In his fifth year (510 B.C.), [Wu] launched an expedition against Yüeh and defeated it.

In his sixth year (509 B.C.), King Chao of Ch'u sent the Noble Scion Nang Wa 囊瓦[35] to lead troops in an expedition against Wu. Wu sent Wu Yün to meet the attack. He crushed Ch'u's army in Yü-chang 豫章[36] and took Ch'u's [city] Chü-ch'ao.

In his ninth year (506 B.C.), Ho-lu, King of Wu said to Wu Tzu Hsü and Sun Wu, "Earlier, you gentlemen said that we could not yet enter Ying. What do you say now?"

The two gentlemen replied, "Ch'u's general Nang Wa is greedy; both T'ang 唐[37] and Ts'ai resent him. If Your Majesty insists on launching a great campaign against Ch'u, you must first gain T'ang and Ts'ai [as allies]. Only this will do."

Ho-lu heeded them. He mobilized all his forces and launched a campaign against Ch'u with T'ang and Ts'ai. [*2176*] [Wu] and Ch'u drew up in formation and faced each other across the Han River 漢水, .

The King of Wu's younger brother, Fu-kai 夫概, led in his troops. He asked for permission to follow [the king]. The king refused. [Fu-kai] attacked Ch'u's general Tzu Ch'ang 子常 with the five thousand men under his command. Tzu Ch'ang was routed and fled to Cheng. After this Wu advanced, following up on its victory. After five battles, they reached Ying. On the *chi-mao* 己卯 day,[38] King Chao of Ch'u left [Ying] and fled his state. On the *keng-ch'en* 庚辰 day of the cycle, the King of Wu entered Ying.

King Chao left [Ying] and fled into the marshes of Yün-meng 雲夢.[39] Bandits attacked the king and the king fled to [the state of] Yün 鄖.[40] Huai 懷, the younger brother of the Duke

[30] Southwest of modern Lu-chiang 廬江 County in Anhwei (T'an Ch'i-hsiang, 1:29-30).

[31] The capital of Ch'u. T'an Ch'i-hsiang locates it about 10 miles northeast of modern Sha-shih 沙市 in Hupei (T'an Ch'i-hsiang, 1:29-30). See also n. 70 to our translation of Chapter 69 below.

[32] See his biography in *Shih chi* Chapter 65.

[33] About 5 miles northeast of modern Liu-an 六安 County, Anhwei (T'an Ch'i-hsiang, 1:29-30).

[34] About 25 miles southwest of modern Huo-shan 霍山 County in southwestern Anhwei (T'an Ch'i-hsiang, 1:29-30). In his annotation, Wang Li-ch'i (66:1647) notes that Ch'ien is northeast of Huo-shan (see also Ch'ien Mu, *Ti-ming K'ao*, p. 572-3).

[35] Both "So-yin" and Liang Yü-sheng (27:1198-9) observe that Nang Wa should not be titled *Kung-tzu* 公子, "Noble Scion."

[36] Ch'ien Mu (*Ti-ming k'ao*, pp. 567) cites Ku Tung-kao 顧棟高 (1679-1759), a Spring and Autumn era specialist, to the effect that Yü-chang was a large area straddling the Yangtze and extending north almost to the Huai River. Chü-ch'ao was located at the easternmost part of this region (see also T'an Ch'i-hsiang, 1:29-30, Wang Li-ch'i, 66:1647 and our n. 20 above).

[37] T'ang was a small neighbor state of Ch'u located around modern T'ang County in Hopei (T'an Ch'i-hsiang, 1:29-30).

[38] A sixty-unit cycle known as *t'ien-kan ti-chih* 天干地支 was used for indicating both days and years in ancient China. This day was the sixteenth in the cycle. The *keng-ch'en* day (mentioned in the following line) was the seventeenth.

[39] Located between the Yangtze and Han 漢 rivers west of modern Wuhan in southern Hupei (T'an Ch'i-hsiang,

of Yün, said, "King P'ing killed our father.[41] Wouldn't it be fitting if we killed his son?" The Duke of Yün feared that his younger brother would kill the king and fled with the king to [the state of] Sui 隨.[42]

The troops of Wu besieged Sui and told the men of Sui, "Ch'u exterminated all of the descendants of Chou by the Han River."[43]

The people of Sui decided to kill the king. Prince Tzu Ch'i 子綦[44] hid the king and went in his place, posing as the king. The people of Sui divined on whether to give the king to Wu. [The result] was inauspicious. They then refused Wu and would not surrender the king.

Earlier, Wu Yün and Shen Pao-hsü 申包胥 had been friends. When Yün fled, he told Pao-hsü, "I must overthrow Ch'u." Pao-hsü said, "I must preserve it." When the troops of Wu entered Ying, Wu Tzu Hsü sought King Chao. Not finding him, he dug up King P'ing of Ch'u's tumulus, removed his corpse, and whipped it three-hundred times before he stopped.[45]

Shen Pao-hsü had fled into the mountains. He sent a man to tell Tzu Hsü, "You go too far in your vengeance! I have heard that men, when numerous, can prevail over Heaven, but Heaven's order can also crush men. You were once King P'ing's vassal, sir, and you faced north and served him in person. Now you even expose a dead man. Is this not an utter lack of Heaven's Principles?"

Wu Tzu Hsü said, "Apologize to Shen Pao-hsü for me [*2177*] and tell him, 'My day is late and my road a distant one. I had to take shortcuts and move against the current.'"

After this, Shen Pao-hsü hastened to Ch'in and informed it of [Ch'u's] plight. He begged for help from Ch'in. Ch'in refused. Shen Pao-hsü stood in the court of Ch'in and wailed day and night. The sound of his wailing did not stop for seven days and seven nights.

Duke Ai 哀 of Ch'in (r. 536-501 B.C.) took pity on him. "Although Ch'u is devoid of principle, he has an official such as this. How can we refuse to preserve him?" He then dispatched five-hundred chariots to rescue Ch'u and attack Wu. In the sixth month,[46] they defeated Wu's troops at Chi 稷.[47]

1:45).

[40] A small state occupied by Ch'u and located at modern An-lu 安陸 County in Hupei about 60 miles northwest of Wuhan (T'an Ch'i-hsiang, 1:29).

[41] Their father's name was Tou Ch'eng-jan 鬥成然. According to *Tso chuan*, he was killed by the King of Ch'u in 527 B.C. (Yang, *Tso chuan*, Chao 12, p. 1336).

[42] Modern Sui-chou 隨州 City in Hupei (T'an Ch'i-hsiang, 1:29-30). *Tso chuan* records the Duke of Yün's remarks on why one should not take revenge on one's ruler (Yang, *Tso chuan*, Ting 4, p. 1546), but since Ssu-ma Ch'ien has structured his narrative around that motive, he omits them here. Ssu-ma Ch'ien also ignores evidence (see *Ku-liang chuan* 穀梁傳 [19:4b, *SPPY*] and *Kung-yang chuan* 公羊傳 [8b:9a, *SPPY*]) that Wu Tzu Hsü turned down Ho-lu's offer to help him gain revenge, choosing to wait until Wu was asked by Ts'ai for help against Ch'u.

[43] Takigawa (66:11) observes that both Wu and Sui shared the same surname as the house of Chou. Thus this message apparently suggests that Ch'u was a common enemy to all states of the Chou surname.

[44] *Shih chi*, 40:1715 refers to Tzu-ch'i as "the king's attendant" (*wang ts'ung-ch'en* 王從臣). In *Tso chuan* and *Kuo-yü*, "Tzu-ch'i" is written as 子期. According to Tu Yu 杜佑 (735-812 A.D.), he was an elder brother of King Chao and his *praenomen* was Chieh 結 (Yang, *Tso chuan*, Ting 4, p. 1547). Tu's theory that he was King Chao's elder brother is generally accepted, thus we read "Wang tzu ch'i" 王子綦 as an error for "Wang-tzu Tzu-ch'i" 王子子綦 (Prince Tzu-ch'i) and follow the Chung-hua editors in taking Tzu-ch'i 子綦 as a personal name.

[45] Liang Yü-sheng (27:1199) points out that neither *Tso chuan* nor *Kung-yang chuan* mention the excavation of King P'ing's grave. He further observes that in *Ku-liang chuan* and *Shih chi*, 14:665, 40:1715 and 100:2729, Wu Tzu Hsü only whipped King P'ing's tomb, not his corpse. Liang, therefore, suspects that Ssu-ma Ch'ien errs here. Wang Shu-min, however, argues that the discrepancies in the Shih chi simply indicate that Ssu-ma Ch'ien had two different versions of the story and that he chose to follow faithfully the original sources without resolving their differences (Wang Shu-min, 66:2089).

The King of Wu remained in Ch'u for a long time, seeking King Chao. Ho-lu's younger brother, Fu-kai, fled back [to Wu] and enthroned himself as king. When Ho-lu heard of this, he let Ch'u be and returned to Wu, where he attacked his younger brother Fu-kai. Fu-kai was routed and fled to Ch'u. Seeing there was civil strife in Wu, King Chao of Ch'u re-entered Ying and enfeoffed Fu-kai at T'ang-hsi 棠谿.[48] He was known as "The T'ang-hsi." Ch'u fought with Wu again and defeated it. The King of Wu returned to Wu.

In the second year after this (504 B.C.),[49] Ho-lu sent the Heir, Fu-ch'ai 夫差, to command troops in an expedition against Ch'u. He took P'o 番.[50] Ch'u feared that Wu would come again in great force. He left Ying and moved his capital to Jo 鄀.[51] At this time, Wu, through the counsel of Wu Tzu Hsü and Sun Wu, crushed mighty Ch'u in the west, awed Ch'i and Chin in the north and subdued the Yüeh people in the south.

[2178] Four years after this (500 B.C.), Confucius became the Prime Minister of Lu.[52]

In the fifth year after this (496 B.C.), Wu attacked Yüeh. Kou-chien 句踐, the King of Yüeh (r. 497-465 B.C.), met the attack. He defeated Wu at Ku-su 姑蘇[53] and wounded Ho-lu's toe. The army retreated. Sick from his wound, Ho-lu was about to die. He said to his Heir, Fu-ch'ai, "Will you forget that Kou-chien killed your father?"

Fu-ch'ai replied, "I dare not forget." That evening, Ho-lu died.

After Fu-ch'ai was enthroned as king (r. 495-477 B.C.), he made Po Hsi grand steward,[54] and drilled [his troops] in battle and archery. Two years later (494 B.C.), he attacked Yüeh and defeated him at Fu-chiao 夫湫.[55] Kou-chien, the King of Yüeh, took refuge with his remaining five-thousand troops on top of [Mount] K'uai-chi 會稽[56] and sent Grand Master Chung 種[57] to seek peace by presenting lavish gifts to Wu's Grand Steward, Hsi; he begged to

---

[46] According to *Shih chi,* 14:665, this was in 505 B. C.

[47] About 5 miles east of modern T'ung-po 桐柏 County in southern Honan (T'an Ch'i-hsiang, 1:29-30).

[48] About 20 miles southwest of modern Hsi-p'ing 西平 County in Honan (T'an Ch'i-hsiang, 1:29-30).

[49] Beginning here many of the dates in this chapter differ from other accounts of the same events by one year. In this case, since Ch'in rescued Ch'u in 505 B.C., two years thereafter would seem to be 503 B.C. But the date of 504 B.C. for this attack is fairly secure (see *Shih chi,* 14:666). See the Translators' Note at the end of this memoir.

[50] Modern pronunciation would be "Fan," but traditional scholars argue it should be pronounced "P'o." According to Wang Li-ch'i (66:1649), it was located at modern P'o-yang 波陽 County in Kiangsi. Ch'ien Mu, however, says it was northwest of modern Feng-t'ai 鳳臺 County, also in Kiangsi (see *Ti-ming k'ao*, p. 578). T'an Ch'i-hsiang has no record of it.

[51] About 20 miles southeast of modern Yi-ch'eng 宜城 in central Hupei (T'an Ch'i-hsiang, 1:29-30).

[52] The date of 500 B.C. is controversial, and many scholars now doubt that Confucius ever held such a high position.

[53] About 15 miles west of modern Soochow in Kiangsu (T'an Ch'i-hsiang, 1:29-30). According to *Tso chuan*, the battle took place at Tsui-li 檇李 (Yang, *Tso chuan,* Ting 14, p. 1593), which was about 20 miles south of modern Chia-hsing 嘉興 County in Kiangsu (T'an Ch'i-hsiang, 1:29-30) or perhaps (Wang Li-ch'i, 66:1649 and Yang, *Tz'u-tien,* p. 937) southwest of Chia-hsing County.

[54] *T'ai-tsai* 太宰.

[55] Name of a mountain now surrounded by T'ai-hu 太湖 (Lake T'ai), it is about 25 miles southeast of modern Soochow in Kiangsu (T'an Ch'i-hsiang, 1:29-30).

Two separate parallel accounts of the following story about the relations between Wu and Yüeh are found in *Kuo-yü* (19:2b, 3a-4b, and 20:1b-2a, *SPPY*).

[56] A mountain about 10 miles southeast of modern Shao-hsing 紹興 in central Chekiang (T'an Ch'i-hsiang, 1:29-30).

[57] This was Wen Chung 文種; on his mission to seek peace with Fu-ch'ai see also *Shih chi,* 41:1740-41 and Wang Li-ch'i, *Jen-piao,* p. 312-13.

offer up his state as slaves to [Wu]. The King of Wu decided to grant his request. Wu Tzu Hsü admonished the king.

"The King of Yüeh is the sort of man who can endure hardship and bitterness. If Your Majesty does not destroy [his state] now, you are sure to regret it later."

The King of Wu did not listen. He adopted Grand Steward Hsi's plan and made peace with Yüeh.

Five years after this (490 B.C.), the King of Wu heard that Duke Ching 景 of Ch'i (r. 547-490 B.C.) had died and that his great vassals were struggling for favor, while the new lord was weak.[58] He mobilized his forces and launched an expedition north against Ch'i. Wu Tzu Hsü admonished the king.

"At his meals, Kou-chien does not have more than one dish with spices. He mourns for the dead and asks after the sick. He will soon have a use [for his people]. If this man does not die, he is sure to be Wu's sorrow. Wu suffers from Yüeh like a man suffering from a disease of the bowels and heart. [*2179*] Yet Your Majesty does not place Yüeh first, but occupies yourself with Ch'i. Is this not a great error?"

The King of Wu did not listen to him. He attacked Ch'i, crushed its forces at Ai-ling 艾陵 (489 B.C.),[59] and returned after awing the rulers of Tsou 鄒 and Lu.[60] He became more and more disenchanted with Tzu Hsü's counsel.

Four years after this (485 B.C.), the King of Wu decided to launch an expedition north against Ch'i. Kou-chien, the King of Yüeh, adopted Tzu-kung's 子貢 counsel,[61] and led his host to Wu's aid, while presenting precious treasures to Grand Steward Hsi.

Grand Steward Hsi having received several bribes from Yüeh, his affection for and trust in it was complete. Day and night, he spoke on its behalf to the King of Wu. The King of Wu confidently adopted Hsi's plans. Wu Tzu Hsü admonished the king.

"Yüeh is a sickness of the bowels and heart, yet now you believe this hollow rhetoric and deceitful pretense and covet Ch'i. If you crushed Ch'i, it would be a rocky field; you could never put it to use. As 'The Announcement of Pan K'eng' says, '[If] there are people who confound, transgress or disregard [our orders], we will cut off their noses and utterly exterminate them so that they will not have any children leave behind. We will not allow them

---

[58] For the details of the power struggle in the Ch'i court, see *Shih chi* Chapters 32 and 46.

[59] Ai-ling was situated about 20 miles northeast of modern Lai-wu 萊蕪 County in Shantung (see Ch'ien Mu, *Ti-ming k'ao*, pp. 265-6).

The date of the battle of Ai-ling is not uniform, even in the *Shih chi*. *Shih chi*, 31:1471 and 41:1743 recount it during the 7th year of Fu-ch'ai, 489 B.C. But in *Shih chi* Chapter 41--"Yüeh-wang Kou-chien shih-chia" 越王句踐世家 (The Hereditary House of the King of Yüeh, Kou-chien)--Wu Tzu Hsü dies subsequent to the battle of Ai-ling, causing Chavannes (4:426, n. 1) to speculate that, since Wu Tzu Hsü died in 485 B.C., the battle should have taken place in that year. *Shih chi*, 36:1583 dates Ai-ling during the 16th year of Duke Min 湣 of Ch'en, 486 B.C. *Ch'un-ch'iu* and *Tso chuan*, however, clearly ascribe the battle to the 11th year of Duke Ai, 484 B.C. (Yang, *Tso chuan*, Ai 11, pp. 1657 and 1663), one year after Wu Tzu Hsü's death.

Wang Shu-min's comment on the date of the encounter (36:1409) is not useful, since he assumes only that the *Shih chi* should adhere to the chronology in the *Tso chuan* without recognizing that Ssu-ma Ch'ien had a distinct, but normally consistent, system of dates. See also "Chronology" in the front-matter above.

[60] "Awing the rulers of Tsou and Lu" probably refers to an incident in 488 B.C. in which the Duke of Lu met with Fu-ch'ai and Fu-ch'ai demanded a feast with one-hundred *T'ai-lao* sacrifices (*Shih chi*, 14:675).

[61] Tzu-kung was a disciple of Confucius. For a brief account of his life and how he assisted Yüeh to become Hegemon, see *Shih chi* Chapter 67. Although a number of traditional scholars doubt the reliability of this story (for a summary, see Takigawa, 66:26-7), Wang Shu-min (66:2094), in view of the attention that Ssu-ma Ch'ien gives to this story in Chapter 67, believes that Ssu-ma Ch'ien probably had come across the story and chose to preserve it out of his fondness of unusual tales.

to transplant any seeds [of their kind] to this city."[62]   This was how Shang 商 rose to power. I would hope that Your Majesty might let Ch'i be and place Yüeh first. If you do not, it will be too late for regrets later."

The King of Wu did not listen and sent Tzu Hsü as an ambassador to Ch'i. On the eve of his journey [back to Wu], Tzu Hsü told his son, "I admonished the king many times, but the king would not use [my counsel]. I will soon see the fall of Wu. For you to fall with it would be of no benefit." He then entrusted his son to Pao Mu 鮑牧[63] of Ch'i and returned to report to Wu.

Now that there was bad blood between Wu's Grand Steward Hsi and Tzu Hsü, [Hsi] slandered [Tzu Hsü]:

"Tzu Hsü is by nature relentless and cruel, lacking in mercy, mistrustful and malicious. His rancor, I fear, will mean deep trouble. In days past when Your Majesty was about to at-tack Ch'i, Tzu Hsü thought that it could not be done, yet Your Majesty in the end attacked and achieved great success. Tzu Hsü was ashamed that his plans and counsel were not adopted, and harbored resentment. Now Your Majesty attacks Ch'i again, and Tzu Hsü, firm in his own opinions, is unyielding in his admonitions. He attacks and denigrates the campaign and would take pleasure only in the defeat of Wu, for this would vindicate his plans and counsel. Now Your Majesty sets out in person, leading an attack against Ch'i with the military might of the entire state, but Tzu Hsü, his admonitions unheeded, declines [to go] and, feigning illness, refuses to set out. Your Majesty must prepare. It would not be difficult for trouble to arise. Moreover, I have had a man secretly observing him, and during his mission to Ch'i, he en-trusted his son to the Pao Clan of Ch'i. This fellow is [your] vassal, yet dissatisfied at home, he relies abroad on the feudal lords; he thinks of himself as your father's councilor, [*2180*] but now that he is unheeded, he is constantly seething with rancor. I would hope my lord might take measures against him as soon as possible."

The King of Wu said, "Even without your words, sir, I, too, have suspected him." He then sent an envoy to bestow on Wu Tzu Hsü a chu-lou 屬鏤 sword.

"You are to die with this."[64]

Wu Tzu Hsü looked up at the heavens and sighed.

"Alas! This slanderous slave Hsi subverts the state, yet the king executes me! I made your father Hegemon. From the time before you were made [Heir] and the Noble Scions struggled for appointment, I argued for you before the late king, offering to die, and even then you almost were not made Heir. When you were made Heir, you wanted to share the

[62] This is an abridged quotation from *The Book of Documents*. The entire section reads: "If there are people who are evil and unprincipled, who confound, transgress or disregard [our orders] and who, taking advantage of this brief season, act treacherously, we will cut off their noses or utterly eliminate them so that they will not have any children leave behind. We will not allow them to transplant any seeds [of their kind] to this city" ("Pan-keng, B" 盤庚下 [*Shang shu*, 5:6a, *SPPY*]; see also Legge, 3:241). At first reading this quotation of someone con-founding and transgressing orders seems somewhat out of place here. Even if read as an insinuation to Po Hsi, it is a little forced and is not very consistent with Wu Tzu Hsü's other remarks. However, we suspect that Wu Tzu Hsü meant to take the character *yüeh* 越 ("transgress") here as a pun for the name of Wu's enemy, which is actu-ally the same Chinese character. If this is the case, the extended meaning of the first part of the quotation would become: "There is rebellious Yüeh, which is not respectful [to Wu]. We should cut off their noses or utterly eliminate them . . . ."

[63] Pao Mu had already been dead for four years by this time (see Wang Li-ch'i, *Jen-piao*, p. 753). Scholars generally believe that this is a mistake for Pao Shih 鮑氏, or "the Pao Clan" as at the end of *Shih chi*, 66:2179--two paragraphs down in our translation).

[64] In *Kuo-yü* (19:4b-5a, *SPPY*) Wu Tzu Hsü draws his own swords and commits suicide without prompting from Fu-cha'i; his death occurs immediately after Wu's victory at Ai-ling, not several years later as in this text.

kingdom of Wu with me. I turned away and did not even dare consider it. Yet now you heed the words of a sycophantic slave and kill your elder!"

He then told his houseman,[65] "Be sure to plant some catalpa trees at my grave so that there will be material for my coffin. Pluck out my eyes and hang them above the east gate of Wu so that I can watch the Yüeh invaders enter [the city] to destroy Wu."[66] Then he cut his throat and died.

When the King of Wu heard this he was enraged, took Wu Tzu Hsü's corpse, put it in a wineskin[67] and let the Chiang carry it away.[68] The people of Wu pitied him, and erected a shrine for him on the bank of the Chiang; after this they called the place Mount Hsü 胥.[69]

[2181] The King of Wu having executed Wu Tzu Hsü, then attacked Ch'i (485 B.C.). The Pao Clan of Ch'i had killed their lord, Duke Tao 悼 (r. 488-485 B.C.),[70] and installed Yang-sheng 陽生.[71] The King of Wu wanted to punish Ch'i's rebels, but left after failing to gain victory.

In the second year after this (483 B.C.), the King of Wu summoned the rulers of Lu and Wei to a meeting at T'o-kao 橐皋.[72]

The next year he then went north and held a great meeting with the feudal lords at Huang-ch'ih 黃池[73] (482 B.C.), which he then used to issue orders to the House of Chou.

---

[65] *She-jen* 舍人.

   In *Kuo-yü* (19:5a, *SPPY*) Wu Tzu Hsü speaks directly to Fu-ch'ai.

[66] In *Lü-shih ch'un-ch'iu* (23:5b-6a, *SPPY*), it was Fu-ch'ai who scooped out Wu Tzu Hsü's eyes.

[67] Most annotators says that *ch'ih yi* 鴟夷 (owl and pelican) is a "wineskin" without further explanation. Yang Hsiung's "Chiu chen" 酒箴 (Admonition on Wine) may provide a clue: "The 'owl and pelican' [i.e., "wineskin"] is round about, / Its belly like a big pot." 鴟夷滑稽, 腹如大壺 (see *Yang Hsiung chi* 揚雄集 in *Han-Wei Liu-ch'ao san-pai-chia chi* 漢魏六朝三百家集, 8:18b-19a, *SKCS*, 1412:200). The skin apparently was shaped pear-shaped, resembling the anatomy of these birds.

   Timoteus Pokora has devoted the "Appendix" (pp. 165-72) in his "The Etymology of *Ku-chi* (or *Hua-chi*) 滑稽," *ZDMG*, 122(1972), 149-72 to a study of *ch'ih yi*. Although his ruminations move far and wide through ancient Chinese literature, his conclusion that the term connotes "adaptability" is of interest, since Wu Tzu Hsü in his search for revenge was able to adapt himself to a variety of situations and tribulations. Similarly, his observation that these are both birds "waiting for opportunity" may be seen as ironic in view of Wu Tzu Hsü's patience in seeking revenge against the King of Ch'u and his desire to overlook a second revenge by having his eyes view the ultimate defeat of Wu by Yüeh.

[68] David Johnson speculates that Wu Tzu Hsü's fate is a distant echo of the Liao people's practice of stuffing a sacrificial victim into a sack and casting this image of Hun-tun, the creating principle of the universe, into a river so as to insure the fertility of their fields (see Johnson, "Epic and History in Early China: the Matter of Wu Tzu Hsü," *JAS*, 40.2[February 1981], 263 [255-71]).

[69] According to Ch'ien Mu (*Ti-ming k'ao*, p. 586), it was located southwest of modern Wu 吳 County in eastern Kiangsu (T'an Ch'i-hsiang, 1:29-30). Traditional scholars generally think that Hsü-shan had already existed before the death of Wu Tzu Hsü and was not named after him (see Wang Shu-min, 66:2097).

[70] Liang Yü-sheng (27:1202) points out that according to *Tso chuan* Duke Tao was not killed by the Pao Clan. However, since Ssu-ma Ch'ien consistently labels the murderers of Duke Tao as "the Pao Clan" in *Shih chi* Chapters 14, 31, 32, 37 and 46 as well as in this biography, Wang Shu-min argues that Ssu-ma Ch'ien must have his own source which was different from *Tso chuan* (66:2097-8).

[71] This obviously is a mistake because Yang-sheng was the name of Duke Tao himself. According to *Shih chi*, 14:677 and 32:1508, Yang-sheng's son, Jen 壬 (i.e., Duke Chien 簡 of Ch'i [r. 484-481 B.C.]), was the one established. Wang Shu-min (66:2098) believes that "Yang-sheng" should read "Jen" here. There is also the possibility that the two characters "erh li" 而立 are an interpolation and the line should read "the Pao Clan of Ch'i had killed their ruler Duke Tao, Yang-sheng."

[72] Modern T'o-kao city, about 15 miles northwest of Ch'ao county in eastern Anhwei (T'an Ch'i-hsiang, 1:29-30).

[73] About 15 miles north of modern Kaifeng in Honan (T'an Ch'i-hsiang, 1:25).

Kou-chien, King of Yüeh, launched a surprise attack, killed Wu's Heir, and crushed the Wu forces. Upon hearing this, the King of Wu returned home and sent an emissary with lavish gifts to make peace with Yüeh. Nine years later, Kou-chien, the King of Yüeh, destroyed Wu and killed its king, Fu-ch'ai. He also executed Grand Steward [Po] Hsi because he was disloyal to his lord, accepted lavish gifts from abroad and conspired with Kou-chien.

The Magistrate of Pai, Sheng

Sheng 勝, the son of Chien 建, the former Heir of Ch'u, with whom Wu Tzu Hsü had earlier fled, lived in Wu. In the reign of Fu-ch'ai, King of Wu, King Hui 惠 of Ch'u (r. 488-432 B.C.) decided to summon Sheng back to [*2182*] Ch'u.[74] The Magistrate[75] of She 葉 admonished [King Hui]: "Sheng admires boldness and secretly seeks men willing to die [for him]. He probably has some personal interests in mind." King Hui did not heed him. He summoned Sheng and sent him to live in Ch'u's border-town Yen 鄢.[76] His title was the Magistrate of Pai 白.[77] In the third year after the Magistrate of Pai had returned to Ch'u (485 B.C.), Wu executed Wu Tzu Hsü.[78]

The Magistrate of Pai, Sheng, having returned to Ch'u, and harboring resentment against Cheng for killing his father, secretly nurtured men willing to die [for him], and sought to repay Cheng.

In the fifth year after his return to Ch'u (483 B.C.), he asked permission to attack Cheng.[79] The Premier of Ch'u, Tzu Hsi 子西, gave his assent. Before the troops set out, Chin attacked Cheng. Cheng begged for aid from Ch'u. Ch'u sent Tzu Hsi to aid it. He swore a covenant with Cheng and returned. The Magistrate of Pai, Sheng, was angry: "It is not Cheng that is my enemy, it is Tzu Hsi." Sheng personally sharpened his sword. A man asked him, "What are you going to do with it?"

Sheng said, "I'm going to kill Tzu Hsi with it."

Tzu Hsi heard this and laughed. "Sheng is [my] egg.[80] What can he do?"

[74] According to *Shih chi,* 14:675-6, this occurred in 487 B.C., but it was Tzu Hsi, King Hui's uncle, who invited Sheng to return (Wang Shu-min, 66:2098).

[75] *Kung* 公, which in the general scheme of pre-Ch'in titles meant "duke," referred to the Grand Master who governed a city in the state of Ch'u (see "Chi-chieh," *Shih chi,* 40:1719, Tung Yüeh, pp. 77-78, and n. 17 to our translation of *Shih chi* Chapter 6). For a somewhat different view of the term see Abe Michiko 阿部道子 "Shunjū kōki no So no kō ni tsuite 春秋後期の楚の「公」について, *Tōyōshi kenkyū* 東洋史研究, 45(1986).

[76] About 5 miles northwest of modern Yen-ling, Honan (T'an Ch'i-hsiang, 1:29-30; see also Ch'ien Mu, *Timing K'ao,* p. 339).

[77] According to Wang Li-ch'i (66:1651), Pai was the name of his fief and was located southwest of modern Hsi 息 County in Honan.

[78] Lord Pai returned to Ch'u in 487 B.C. while Wu Tzu Hsü was killed in 485 B.C. (see *Shih chi,* 14:677 and Wang Li-ch'i, 66:1651).

[79] Again, some scholars, based on *Tso chuan,* think that "five" should read "eight" (i.e., 480 B.C.) here (for a summary of their ideas, see Wang Shu-min, 66:2099). However, as Wang Shu-min observes, the date in this biography is consistent with the one given on *Shih chi,* 14:678.

[80] It is unclear what is meant by the term *luan* 卵 (egg) here. A parallel text in *Tso chuan* (Yang, *Tso chuan,* Ai 16, p. 1701) reads: "Sheng sharpened his sword himself. Tzu-ch'i's son P'ing saw him and said, 'Why are you sharpening it yourself, Prince?' 'I gained renown for my directness; if I did not tell you, that would be no directness at all. I am going to kill your father with it.' P'ing told Tzu-hsi of this. Tzu-hsi said, 'Sheng is like an egg I have hatched and raised. If I die, who should be premier or marshal in the state of Ch'u if not Sheng?' Sheng heard this and said, 'The premier is mad. If he dies a natural death, it will not be because of me!'"

Although there is some uncertainty in the interpretation of this passage, it seems that Tzu-hsi is claiming a pa-

Four years after this (479 B.C.), the Magistrate of Pai, Sheng and Shih Ch'i 石乞 launched a surprise attack, killing Ch'u's Premier, Tzu Hsi, and Marshal Tzu Ch'i 子綦 at court. Shih Ch'i said, "It would be best to kill the king." They carried the king off to Kao-fu 高府.[81] Shih Ch'i's attendant,[82] Ch'ü Ku 屈固, put King Hui of Ch'u on his back and fled to the residence of [the Queen Dowager], Lady Chao 昭夫人.[83] When the Magistrate of She heard that the Magistrate of Pai had rebelled, he led the men of his state to attack the Magistrate of Pai. The Magistrate of Pai's men were defeated and he fled into the mountains where he killed himself. They captured Shih Ch'i and asked him the location of the Magistrate of Pai's corpse.

"If you do not speak, you shall boil!"

Shih Ch'i said, "If the affair had succeeded, I'd be a minister. Since it has not, boiling is all I can expect." In the end he refused to tell them the location of the corpse. They then boiled Shih Ch'i, sought out King Hui, [*2183*] and reinstated him.

His Honor the Grand Scribe says: "How terrible is hatred and resentment in a man! If a king cannot give cause for it among his vassals and subordinates, how much more is this so for men of the same rank! If Wu Tzu Hsü had accompanied [his father] She in death, how would he differ from an ant or mole-cricket? Casting aside a lesser duty, he wiped clean a great disgrace, and his name has endured through later generations. Moving indeed, isn't it? When Tzu Hsü was trapped on the bank of the Chiang, and begged for food by the roadside, did he for a single moment forget Ying? Endurance ending in merit and fame; if not a man filled with ardor, who could attain this?

"If the Magistrate of Pai had not installed himself as lord,[84] his merit and counsel, too, would be beyond recounting."

---

ternal interest in Sheng's career, and is thus unable to believe ill of him.

[81] Apparently (see "Chi-chieh," *Shih chi,* 40:1719) an alternate royal residence in Ch'u.

[82] *Shih chi,* 40:1718, says Ch'ü-ku was King Hui's follower.

[83] She was King Chao's concubine and King Hui's mother.

[84] This biography does not mention that the Magistrate of Pai made himself king, but *Shih chi,* 40:1718 says he ruled for more than a month after his *coup d'etat.*

TRANSLATORS' NOTE

David Johnson's studies of Wu Tzu Hsü (see Bibliography below) have shown that much that is known about Wu other than that presented in this chapter. Ssu-ma Ch'ien maintains, however, at least a skeleton of most of the major events of Wu's story (he mentions "begging for food" in his comments at the end of the chapter almost in passing--the incident where a woman gives him something to eat was not recounted in the text--since he seems to assume that his readers were familiar with the overall story). Instead of a "life" we have here an essay on resentment (*yüan* 苑) and revenge and the disasters it fosters. Wu Tzu Hsü, of course, seeks revenge on King P'ing of Ch'u for the murder of his father and brother. But this basic story is embedded in the larger struggle between Wu and Yüeh, a struggle that is also built upon a desire for revenge (the father of Fu-ch'ai, King of Wu, having been killed by Kou-chien, the King of Yüeh). Finally, there is the story of Sheng and his revenge to serve as a more immediate and apparent foil to that of Wu Tzu Hsü. All three revenge seekers meet tragic ends.

Although scholars laud Ssu-ma Ch'ien for his juxtaposition of these stories, the chronological structure of the chapter has elicited criticism. A number of studies propose various corrections and explanations. We note two reasons for the controversy over dating and suggest that a simpler method than textual emendation can account for most of the problems.

First, it is clear that Ssu-ma Ch'ien had a generally consistent chronology for the events of this period, and that this chronology is reflected in the "Shih-chia" 世家 (Hereditary Houses) and "Nien-piao" 年表 (Chronological Tables) of the *Shih chi*. Unfortunately, this chronology often contradicts the other major source for this period, the *Tso chuan*. This is a primary cause of disagreement among scholars. Many, most notably Liang Yü-sheng, have attempted to resolve the inconsistencies between the *Shih chi* and the *Tso chuan* by assuming that textual corruption and interpolation has made the *Shih chi* less reliable. But in Liang's treatment of each error individually, he fails to see the forest for the trees. There is an internal consistency to the *Shih chi* chronology. Ssu-ma Ch'ien may be wrong in his dating for the Ch'un-ch'iu period, but the consistency generally displayed in the *Shih chi* dispels the idea of massive corruption or interpolation. Second, the method of dating in the this chapter is unusual, misleading many scholars. We tentatively suggest that this chapter uses the ancient counting method in which calculation does not begin with zero, but with one. This sort of inclusive counting may also occur in *Shih chi* Chapters 68 and 72. The reader is referred to the footnotes of our translation and to the section on "Chronology" in the front-matter for further details.

BIBLIOGRAPHY

I. Translations

Jäger, Fritz. "Die Biographie des Wu Tzu-hsü, 66. Kapitel des *Shih-chi*)," *OE,* 7 (1960), 12-16.

Mizusawa Toshitada 水澤利忠. *Shiki* 史記. V. 8. *Retsuden (ichi)* 列傳 (一). Tokyo: Meiji Shoten, 1990, pp. 114-44.

Ōgawa Tamaki 小川環樹, trans. *Shiki retsuden* 史記列傳. Rpt. Tokyo: Chikuma Shobō, 1986 (1969). pp. 24-30.

Rudolph, Richard Casper. "The *Shih chi* Biography of Wu Tzu-hsü," *OE,* 9 (1962), 106-120.
_____. "Wu Tzu-hsü, His Life and Posthumous Cult: A Critical Study of *Shih chi* 66."
    Unpublished Ph. D. dissertation, University of California, 1942. Contains a
    translation and an analysis of the text.
Watson, Burton. *Records of the Historian. Chapters from the Shih chi of Ssu-ma Ch'ien.*
    New York: Columbia University Press, 1969, pp. 16-29.

II. Studies

Johnson, David. "Epic and History in Early China: The Matter of Wu Tzu-hsü," *JAS,* 40.2
    (February 1981), 255-271.
_____. "The Wu Tzu-hsü *Pien-wen* and Its Sources: Parts I and II," *HJAS,* 40.1 (June 1980),
    and 40.2 (December 1980), 93-156 and 465-505, respectively.

Confucius's Disciples, Memoir 7[1]

[67:2185] Confucius said, "Of those who received my teachings, there are seventy-seven who are conversant with them."[2] They were all scholars of unusual talent.[3]

Among those who studied virtuous actions were Yen [Tzu-]yüan 顏子淵, Min Tzu-ch'ien 閔子騫, Jan Po-niu 冉伯牛 and [Jan] Chung-kung 冉仲弓. Among those who studied government affairs were Jan [Tzu-]yu 冉子有 and Chi [Tzu-]lu 季子路. Among those who studied speech and conversation were Tsai [Tzu-]wo 宰子我 and [Tuan-mu] Tzu-kung 端木子貢. Among those who studied literature and learning were [Yen] Tzu-yu 言子游 and [Pu] Tzu-hsia 卜子夏.[4] (11/3)

Chuan-sun Shih 顓孫師 was pretentious. Tseng Shen 曾參 was slow. Kao Ch'ai 高柴 was stubborn. Chung Yu 仲由 [=Chi Tzu-lu] was rude. (11/18)

Yen Hui 顏回 [=Yen Tzu-yüan] was often poor. Tuan-mu Tz'u 端木賜 [=Tuan-mu Tzu-kung] did not accept his lot. He was interested in trades and often speculated correctly. (11/19)

[2186] Among those whom Confucius respected and served were Lao Tzu 老子 in Chou,[5] Ch'ü Po-yü 蘧伯玉 in Wei,[6] Yen P'ing-chung 晏平仲 in Ch'i,[7] Lao Lai Tzu 老萊子 in Ch'u,[8] Tzu Ch'an 子產 in Cheng[9] and Meng Kung-ch'o 孟公綽 in Lu.[10]

[1] This chapter contains many quotat... ...alects. There are numerous commentaries and studies on the *Analects,* but the ...1-1855), as found in his *Lun yü cheng-yi* 論語正義, have been a major influe... ...n our normal notation for the *Analects* (Chapter/verse--see "On Using This ... ...ace to the *Lun yü cheng-yi* commentary (SPPY) is also provided (abbreviated a...

The most extensive modern work ... ...hen-shen's 蘇振申 *Shih chi "Chung-ni ti-tzu lieh-chuan" shu-cheng* 史記仲尼彐... ...Wen-hua Hsüeh-yüan Ch'u-pan-pu, 1965; hereafter "Su Chen-shen").

[2] The source of this quotation is nc... ...vere seventy or seventy-two disciples.

[3] The quotation below from *Lun yi... ...s chapter, with the first ten disciples introduced in the same order as in the qu... ...ections dealing with each disciple. Rather than provide notes for each of the di... ...s (based, unless otherwise noted, on the traditional dates for Confucius, and the ... ...regarding how many years younger the disciples were than Confucius), *agnome... ...r the disciples can be found under each later entry. In this chapter, as in the *Analects*, the disciples are sometimes referred to by full name, sometimes by *agnomen*, and sometimes by *praenomen*. Here, for instance, Yen Yüan is referred to by his *cognomen* and *praenomen*. Directly below, however, he is referred to by his *cognomen* and *agnomen*, Hui 回. The honorific suffix *tzu* 子 is also sometimes used with the *cognomen* of a major disciple.

[4] In the *Analects,* the order of these four categories is virtuous actions, speech and conversation, government affairs, and literature and learning. Liu Pao-nan, *Cheng-yi* (14:3a-b, *SPPY*) believes that the *Shih chi* order is the correct one .

[5] See his biography in *Shih chi* Chapter 63.

[6] Po-yü was his *agnomen*. His *cognomen* was Yüan 瑗 (see Ch'ien Mu, *Chu-tzu*, pp. 28-29). According to *Ta Tai Li-chi* 大戴禮記 (6:9a, *SPTK*), he was a man who was "lenient outside and forthright inside. He found pleasure in reclusion" 外寬而內直, 自娛於隱括之中. In the *Analects*, Confucius praises him, saying "When the Way prevails in the country, he takes office. When the Way does not prevail, he will roll it up and keep [the Way] in his breast" 邦有道則仕, 邦無道則可卷而懷之 (15/7).

[7] This is Yen Ying 晏嬰, the famous Prime Minister of Ch'i. See his biography in *Shih chi* Chapter 62.

[8] See the brief reference to him in *Shih chi* Chapter 63.

[9] Tzu Ch'an was the Prime Minister of Cheng. A brief notice of Tzu-ch'an is given in *Shih chi* Chapter 119. The *Analects* records that Confucius praises Tzu Ch'an as a gentleman who "conducted himself in a respectful manner, served his superior with respect, nurtured the people with generosity and employed them with righteous-

He often spoke of Tsang Wen-chung 臧文仲,[11] Hui 惠 of Liu-hsia 柳下,[12] Po-hua of T'ung-ti 銅鞮伯華,[13] and Chieh-shan Tzu-jan 介山子然.[14] Confucius lived after them; they were not his contemporaries.

1.

[2187] Yen Hui 顏回 (521-481 B.C.) was a native of Lu. His *agnomen* was Tzu-yüan 子淵. He was thirty years younger than Confucius.[15]

Yen [Tzu-]yüan[16] asked about humaneness.[17] Confucius said, "Restrain yourself and revert to the norms, and the world will consider you humane." (12/1)

Confucius said, "Worthy indeed is Hui! A bamboo bowl of food and a gourd cup of drink in a shabby alley: other men could not bear such sorrow, but Hui does not vary in his joys." (6/11)

"Hui seems foolish. When I observe his private conduct after he has taken his leave, it is sufficient to illustrate [my teachings]. Hui is no fool." (2/9)

"'When employed, practice your Way. When set aside, treasure your Way.' Only you and I can do this." (7/11)

ness" 其行己也恭，其事上也敬，其養民也惠，其使民也義 (5/16; Liu Pao-nan, *Cheng-yi,* 6:13a-b, *SPPY*).

[10] He is mentioned once in the *Tso chuan,* when, during Ch'i's invasion of Lu in 548 B.C., he correctly predicted that Ch'i would withdraw (Yang, *Tso chuan,* Hsiang 25, p. 1095). Confucius did not seem to have a very high opinion of him. In the *Analects,* Confucius says that "Meng Kung-ch'o would make an excellent steward to noble families like Chao or Wei, but he could not be a grand master [even] for [small states such as] T'eng or Hsüeh" (14/12; Liu Pao-nan, *Cheng-yi,* 17:7a-8a, *SPPY*).

[11] A minister of Lu in the seventh century B.C. In the *Analects,* Confucius expresses doubts on his intelligence (5/18; Liu Pao-nan, *Cheng-yi,* 6:13b-15b, *SPPY*). In *Tso chuan* (Yang, *Tso chuan,* Wen 2, pp. 525-6), Confucius is even quoted as saying Tsang was neither humane (*pu-jen* 不仁) nor intelligent (*pu-chih* 不知). It thus seems odd that Confucius should be respectful of him. Wang Shu-min (67:2105) suggests Tsang Wu-chung 臧武仲 is intended here, rather than Tsang Wen-chung, and cites various sources to show Confucius's high opinion of Tsang Wu-chung.

[12] His *cognomen* was Chan 展, his *praenomen* Huo 獲, and his *agnomen* Ch'in 禽. He was a minister of Lu. Liu-hsia was his fief and Hui was his posthumous title (see Wang Li-ch'i, 67:1659, Mizusawa, p. 147, and Lau, *Analects,* p. 242). Confucius showed admiration for his wisdom and integrity in various places in the *Analects* (e.g., *Analects* 15/14, 18/2, and 18/8).

[13] According to "So-yin" and "Chi-chieh," he was a minister of Chin. He was called Yang She-ch'ih 羊舌赤. Po-hua was probably his *agnomen.* T'ung-ti was his fief. In a lost paragraph of the *Ta-Tai li-chi* quoted in "Chi-chieh," Confucius says that "when the Way prevails in the country, his word can prosper [the country], when the Way does not prevail in the country, his silence can embrace [the country]" 國家有道，其言足以興；國家無道，其默足以容.

[14] In Takigawa's punctuation, there is a comma after Chieh-shan Tzu and the *jan* heads the following phrase. Takigawa believes that this Chieh-shan Tzu was the Chin minister Chieh Chih-t'ui 介之推. Chieh-shan was his fief (see Takigawa, 67:4). For Chieh Chih-t'ui, see also Fang Hsüan-ch'en, pp. 140-141.

[15] According to tradition Confucius was born in 551 B.C. Dates in this chapter are based on several sources, including Ch'ien Mu's *Chu-tzu,* pp. 615-20 and Chiang Liang-fu.

[16] The *tzu* 子 in the *agnomens* of many of these disciples is a problem. Ssu-ma Ch'ien first tells us Yen Hui's *agnomen* was "Tzu-yüan," and then immediately refers to him as "Yen Yüan." It is possible, therefore, that the *tzu* here is the honorific often used preceding *agnomens* during the Spring and Autumn Era (see our n. 1 in Chapter 65). However, since Ssu-ma Ch'ien specifically labels *tzu* part of the *agnomen,* we have added the missing *tzu* in brackets throughout this chapter.

[17] For Confucius the concept of *jen* 仁 was broader than that of Mencius (where "benevolence" may be a good translation) and included compassion, reason, prudence, and righteousness--all the qualities needed for the ideal human being.

[2188] Yen Hui was only twenty-nine when his hair turned white. He died young. Confucius wailed bitterly,[18] saying, "Ever since I have had Hui, my disciples have grown closer to me."

Duke Ai 哀 of Lu (r. 494-476 B.C.) asked, "Who among your disciples loves to learn?" Confucius replied, "There was a Yen Hui who loved to learn. When he was angry over one matter, he did not transfer his anger to another matter. Nor did he repeat his mistakes. Unfortunately his life was short, and he died. Now there are none." (6/3)

2.

Min Hsün's 閔損 (b. 536 B.C.) *agnomen* was Tzu-ch'ien 子騫. He was fifteen years younger than Confucius.

[2189] Confucius said, "What a filial son Min Tzu-ch'ien is! No one would dispute what his parents and brothers have to say of him."[19] (11/5)

[Min Hsün] would not serve as a knight to a grand master and refused to take the wages of a corrupt lord.

[When the Grand Master Chi offered him the stewardship of Pi 費], he said, "If anyone should come summon me again, I shall certainly go live on the banks of the Wen 汶 river."[20] (6/9)

3.

Jan Keng's 冉耕 (b. 544 B.C.) *agnomen* was Po-niu 伯牛.[21] Confucius considered him a man of virtuous conduct.

When Po-niu was seriously ill, Confucius went to ask after him. He held his hand through the window and said, "It is fate, isn't it! Such a man, yet with such a disease! It is fate, isn't it!"[22] (6/10)

---

[18] *The Analects* (11/7-10) also records that Confucius wept bitterly at Yen Hui's death (see Liu Pao-nan, *Cheng-yi*, 14:6b, *SPPY*).

[19] Liu Pao-nan (*Cheng-yi*, 14:4a-b, *SPPY*) asserts that people did not dispute the good words that his parents and brothers had to say of him because he was not blindly obedient and would not let his parents do things that would give them bad names. He also cites a story from *Shuo-yüan* (this story is lost in the extant version of *Shuo-yüan* but quoted in *Yi-wen lei-chü* 藝文類聚 [Peking: Chung-hua, 1965 ed.] 24:369) to support his claim. The gist of the story is that his stepmother gave him thin clothes to wear in the winter while her own sons had warm and thick clothes. When his father learned this, he wanted to expel the stepmother, but Min Tzu-ch'ien begged his father to let the stepmother stay so that the other sons would not suffer. Eventually, the stepmother was moved by his filiality and reformed.

[20] Liu Pao-nan, *Cheng-yi* (7:7b-8a, *SPPY*) points out that there were two Wen rivers and it is not clear to which one Min Tzu-ch'ien is referring. One theory is that by living on the banks of Wen, Min Tzu-ch'ien means he would leave Lu and go to Ch'i if pressed to serve the Chi family.

[21] On Jan Po-niu see also Donald Leslie, "Note on the *Analects*," *TP*, 49(1961), p. 26f.

[22] There are different theories on the direction Jan Keng was lying. Liu Pao-nan, *Cheng-yi* (7:8a-9b, *SPPY*) believes that he was lying on the east side of the house. Different theories are also proposed to explain why Confucius did not enter the house but held Jan Keng's hand through the window instead. Mao Ch'i-ling 毛奇齡 (1623-1713) says that Jan Keng had a disease called *lai* 癩, which Legge believes is "leprosy" (see Mao Ch'i-ling as quoted in Liu Pao-nan, *Cheng-yi* (7:9a, *SPPY* and Legge, 1:188, n. 8). He therefore would not see people. Chu Hsi says that sick people were usually placed on the north side of the house and when the ruler visited him, he would be moved to the south so that the ruler could face south. When Confucius visited, Jan Keng's friends wanted to receive him in this manner, but Confucius avoided this and would not enter the house (see *Lun yü chi-chü* 論語集注, 3:11a, *SPPY*).

4.

Jan Yung's 冉雍 (b. 522 B.C.) *agnomen* was Chung-kung 仲弓.

[2190] Chung-kung asked about [humane] government. Confucius said, "Go out of your gate as if receiving an important guest. Employ the common people as if officiating at a great sacrifice. You will not incur complaints when you are serving the state, nor will you incur complaints when you are serving a noble family."[23] (12/2)

Confucius considered Chung-kung a man of virtuous conduct and said, "[Jan] Yung could be given the seat facing south." (6/1)

Chung-kung's father was of humble origin. Confucius said, "If the calf of a plough ox has a sorrel coat and well-formed horns, would the [spirits of the] mountains and rivers refuse to accept it even though people may not want to use it [as sacrifice]?"[24] (6/6)

5.

Jan Ch'iu's 冉求 (b. 522 B.C.) *agnomen* was Tzu-yu 子有. He was twenty-nine years younger than Confucius. He was the steward[25] of the Chi 季 family.

Chi K'ang-tzu 季康子 asked Confucius, "Is Jan Ch'iu a humane man?" [Confucius] said, "Ch'iu can be charged with the duties of managing the military levies of a city of a thousand households and those of a family of a hundred chariots. As to whether he is humane, I cannot say."

[Chi K'ang-tzu] asked again, "Is Tzu-lu humane?" Confucius replied, "He is like Ch'iu."[26] (5/8)

[2191] Jan Ch'iu asked, "When one hears of something he should do, should he act immediately?" Confucius said, "Act immediately!"

Tzu-lu asked, "When one hears of something he should do, should he act immediately?"

Confucius said, "You have your father and elder brother [to consult], how can you act upon what you hear immediately?"

---

[23] See Liu Pao-nan, *Cheng-yi,* 15:2a-b, *SPPY.* In the *Lun yü,* Chung-kung asked about humaneness rather than government. Since the other sections before and after this in the *Lun yü* concern *jen,* Liu Pao-nan argues that the *Shih chi* version is wrong. The two versions are compatible, however, if we read *cheng* here as *jen-cheng* 仁政 (humane government).

[24] Liu Pao-nan, *Cheng-yi,* 7:5a-7a, *SPPY.* Some scholars interpret the word *li* 犁 as "brindled" and take it in a metaphorical sense as "of a mixed moral character." For these scholars, Confucius is saying that although Chung-kung's father was a man of bad character, people should not overlook the virtue of Chung-kung himself. Liu Pao-nan rejects this reading. He takes *li-niu* 犁牛 as "a plough ox," which he interprets as a metaphor for Chung-kung's humble origins, rather than a reference to his father's character. Thus Confucius is saying that though Chung-kung came from a humble family, his virtue should not be overlooked. Sorrel calves with well-formed horns were best suited for use in sacrifices.

[25] *Tsai* 宰.

[26] This is a mixture of two sentences in the following paragraph of the *Analects*: Meng Wu Po asked, "Is Tzu-lu humane?" Confucius said, "I do not know." Meng repeated the question. Confucius said, "Yu [i.e. Tzu-lu] can be charged with the duties of managing the military levies of a country of a thousand chariots. But I do not know whether he is humane." Meng asked, "How about Ch'iu?" Confucius said, "Ch'iu can be appointed the steward of a city of a thousand households and a family of a hundred chariots. I do not know whether he is humane." 孟武伯問："子路仁乎？" 子曰："不知也。" 又問．子曰："由也，千乘之國，可使治其賦．不知其仁也。" "求也何如？" 子曰："求也，千室之邑，百乘之家，可使為之宰也．不知其仁也" (Liu Pao-nan, *Cheng-yi,* 6:5b-7b, *SPPY*).

Tzu-hua 子華 was puzzled and asked, "May I ask why you gave different answers to the same question?"

Confucius said, "Ch'iu holds himself back, so I urged him forward. Yu tends to exceed what a man is supposed to do, so I held him back." (11/22)

6.

Chung Yu's 仲由 *agnomen* (542-480 B.C.) was Tzu-lu 子路. He was a native of Pien 卞.[27] He was nine years younger than Confucius.

Tzu-lu was blunt. He delighted in prowess and strength and was forthright in disposition. Wearing a rooster-hat and carrying a sword ornamented with pig-skin, he bullied and humiliated Confucius. Confucius established the rites and gradually influenced Tzu-lu. Later, Tzu-lu dressed as a scholar, presented his pledge,[28] and asked to become a student through one of the Master's disciples.

Tzu-lu asked about government. Confucius said, "Act ahead of the people. Urge them to work hard." He asked for more [advice]. [Confucius] said, "Do this untiringly." (13/1)

[2192] Tzu-lu asked, "Does a gentleman exalt prowess?"

Confucius said, "Righteousness comes above all else. If a gentleman delights in prowess and lacks righteousness, disorder results. If a small man delights in prowess, and lacks righteousness,

If Tzu-l[u] [ ] should do] but had not been able to do it, his one fear was to hea[r]

Confuc[ius] [ ] a legal suit on the basis of the words of one side, isn't that Yu?"

"Yu's c[ ] [ ]ine. He is no material I can use."[30] (5/7)

[27] On the Ssu 泗[ ] [ ]) from Lu's capital (modern Ch'u-fu 曲阜 in Shantung--T'an Ch'i-hsiang, 1:39[ ]

[28] The presentat[ion] [ ]h as a bird, marked the submission of vassal to lord in pre-Ch'in China. Thi[ ] [ ]ituals used by disciples in acknowledging a particular teacher as their master.

[29] Liu Pao-nan, [ ] that Pao Hsien 包咸 (6 B.C.-65 A.D.) and Han Yü 韓愈 (768-824) interpre[ ] [ ], reputation). If this were correct, the sentence could be rendered as "If Tzu-l[ ] [ ]g] which he could not live up to, he would only fear having a reputation."

[30] To understand this sentence, one must examine the original *Analects* passage: Confucius said, "If the Way does not prevail and I were to get upon a raft and float about on the sea, Yu will probably be the person to accompany me." Tzu-lu was overjoyed when he heard this. Confucius said, "Yu esteems feats of physical strength higher than I do. He is no material I can use [for my raft]." 子曰：「道不行，乘桴浮于海，從我者，其由與？」子路聞之，喜．子曰：「由也，好勇過我，無所取材．」 (Liu Pao-nan, *Cheng-yi*, 6:5a-b, *SPPY*). The meaning of the phrase *wu so ch'ü ts'ai* is ambiguous. An ancient scholar, quoted by Cheng Hsüan 鄭玄 (127-200), understood *ts'ai* as *tsai* 哉 (see Liu Pao-nan, *Cheng-yi*, 6:5a, *SPPY*). In this reading, the sentence quoted here in *Shih chi* can be rendered as "Yu esteems feats of physical strength higher than I do. Don't I have anyone else to take with me?" Another meaning of the word is suggested by Cheng Hsüan, who glosses the phrase as *wu so ch'ü yü fu ts'ai* 無所取于桴材. He apparently takes *ts'ai* as *mu-ts'ai* 木材 (wooden material for the raft). Legge understands Cheng Hsüan's phrase as "my meaning is not found in the raft" (Legge, 1:175, n. 5). However, Liu Pao-nan glosses the same phrase of Cheng Hsüan as *wu so ch'ü ts'ao wei fu* 無所取材為桴 (cannot be taken as the material for the raft). Our translation is based on Liu Pao-nan's understanding of Cheng Hsüan: "Yu esteems feats of physical strength more than I do. He is no material I can use [for my raft]." According to Liu Pao-nan, Confucius was chiding Tzu-lu because his joy in the Master's remark revealed that he failed to understand that Confucius himself did not really want to withdraw from the world (*Cheng-yi*, 6:5a, *SPPY*). A third interpretation, as suggested by Chu Hsi, is to read *ts'ai* as *ts'ai* 裁 (to measure, to judge, see *Lun yü chi-chu*, 3:2b, *SPPY)*. In this

"One like Yu will not be able to die a natural death." (11/13)

"To wear a tattered robe padded with old silk floss and stand with one wearing fox and badger furs without feeling ashamed, isn't that Yu?" (9/27)

"Yu has already ascended to the hall; he has not yet entered the chamber."[31] (11/15)

Chi K'ang-tzu asked, "Is Chung Yu humane?" Confucius said, "He can be sent to manage the military taxes of a thousand-chariot state. I do not know whether he is humane."[32] (5/8)

Tzu-lu loved to accompany [Confucius] on his travels. He met Chang Chü 長沮, Chieh Ni 桀溺 and the old man carrying a staff over his shoulder.[33]

[2193] When Tzu-lu had become the steward of the Chi family, Chi Sun 季孫 asked, "Can Tzu-lu be called a great vassal?" Confucius said, "He can be called a vassal for ceremonial purposes."[34] (11/24)

When Tzu-lu became a Grand Master of P'u 蒲,[35] he took leave of Confucius. Confucius said, "P'u has many strong knights and moreover will be difficult to rule. But let me tell you this: 'Be respectful in your modesty; this is how you can hold onto the courageous. Be lenient in your justness; this is how you can draw the multitudes. Be serene in your modesty and justness; this is how you can repay your superior.'"

Earlier, Duke Ling 靈 of Wey (r. 534-493 B.C.) had a favorite consort called Nan Tzu 南子. K'uei-k'uei 蕢聵, Duke Ling's Heir, offended Nan Tzu; fearing he would be executed, [K'uei-k'uei] fled to another state. When Duke Ling expired, his wife wanted to enthrone Noble Scion Ying 郢. Ying was unwilling: "There is Che 輒, son of the exiled Heir." After this, Wey enthroned Che as its lord. He was known as Duke Ch'u 出 (r. 492-481 B.C). Twelve years after Duke Ch'u was enthroned, his father K'uei-k'uei lived abroad and was unable to enter [Wey].

Tzu-lu became the town steward of Wey's Grand Master K'ung K'uei 孔悝. K'uei-k'uei and K'ung K'uei rebelled. [K'uei-k'uei] plotted to enter the house of K'ung K'uei and then, together with his followers, to attack Duke Ch'u without warning. Duke Ch'u fled to Lu and K'uei-k'uei entered [the ducal residence] and was enthroned. He was known as Duke

---

reading, one may translate the last sentence as "He is lacking in judgment" as D. C. Lau (*Analects,* p. 77) does.

[31] Liu Pao-nan, *Cheng-yi,* 14:9a-b, *SPPY)* points out that this is a metaphor for the progress one makes in cultivating the Way (*yü hsüeh tao yu ch'ien shen* 喻學道有淺深).

[32] See n. 17 above.

[33] This refers to two incidents found in the *Analects.* In the first, Confucius sent Tzu-lu to ask Chang Chü and Chieh Ni the way to a ford. Upon learning that it was Confucius who was making the inquiry, Chang Chü said that he did not have to ask where the ford was. When Tzu-lu asked Chieh Ni the same question, he advised Tzu-lu to follow a man who "runs away from the world altogether" (meaning a recluse like himself) rather than a gentleman who "keeps running away from men" (referring in this context to Confucius). Confucius later commented that "one cannot associate with birds and beasts." He further said that as long as the Way might be found in the world, he would not change places with a recluse like Chieh Ni. In the second incident, Tzu-lu fell behind Confucius and met with the old man carrying the basket. The latter said Tzu-lu did not seem to be unable to toil with his limbs nor to tell one kind grain from another and wondered who his teacher could be. When Tzu-lu reported this to Confucius, he observed that he must be a recluse. Tzu-lu then commented that a gentleman should take office in order to do his duty regardless of whether the Way could be put into practice. Both incidents show early Confucian belief that one's foremost concern should be the human society and not personal reclusion; see Liu Pao-nan, *Cheng-yi,* 21:5b-7b, *SPPY.*

[34] Liu Pao-nan, *Cheng-yi,* 14:13b-14b, *SPPY.* Confucius defines *ta-ch'en* 大臣 as a minister who serves his lord according to the Way and will resign if this cannot be done.

[35] A city-state 35 miles northeast of modern Kaifeng in Honan (T'an Ch'i-hsiang, 1:23).

Chuang 莊 (r. 480-476 B.C.). When K'ung K'uei rebelled, Tzu-lu was abroad. When he heard of it, he raced back. He met Tzu-kao 子羔 going out of Wey's city gate.

[Tzu-kao] told Tzu-lu, "Duke Ch'u has left and the gate has already been closed. You may go back, sir. Do not share your lord's misfortune in vain."

Tzu-lu said, "One who eats his lord's food will not avoid involvement in his calamity." Eventually Tzu-kao left. A messenger entered the city and the city gate was opened. Tzu-lu followed him in. He went to see K'uei-k'uei. K'uei-k'uei ascended the terrace with K'ung K'uei.

Tzu-lu said, "Why does My Lord employ K'ung K'uei? I ask for permission to kill him." K'uei-k'uei did not listen. Thereupon, Tzu-lu attempted to burn the terrace. K'uei-k'uei was frightened. He thus sent down Shih Ch'i 石乞 and Hu Yen 壺黶 to attack Tzu-lu. They attacked him and cut apart his cap-strings. Tzu-lu said, "When a gentleman dies, he does not let his cap fall off." He then tied his cap-strings and died.

[2194] When Confucius heard of the rebellion in Wey, he said, "Alas, Yu will die." Shortly after he did indeed die.[36]

Thus Confucius said, "Ever since I have had Yu, I have not heard malicious words." It was at this point that Tzu-kung went on his mission to Ch'i for Lu.

7.

Tsai Yü's 宰予 (520-481 B.C.) *agnomen* was Tzu-wo 子我. His speech was quick and his language perspicuous. Having received instruction, he asked, "Isn't a mourning period of three years too long? If a gentleman does not practice the rites for three years, the rites will certainly be in ruins. If he does not practice the music for three years, the music will certain collapse. The old grain has fallen, the new grain has risen, and fire is renewed after the different woods have been burned;[37] after one year, it may be ended."

Confucius said, "Would you feel at ease?"

"I would," he said.

Confucius said, "If you would feel at ease, then do it. When a gentleman is in mourning, he eats delicacies and they are not sweet; he listens to music and is not happy. Thus he does not do these things."

After Tsai [Tzu-]wo had gone out, the master said, "Yü is not humane! Three years after a child is born, only then can it be released from its parents' bosoms. Three years of mourning is a universal duty throughout the world."[38] (17/21)

[2195] Tsai Yü fell asleep in the daytime. The master said, "Rotten wood cannot be carved and a wall of dirty mud cannot be trowelled." (5/10)

---

[36] For another version of this rebellion, see *Tso chuan* (Yang, *Tso chuan,* Ai 15, pp. 1695-6). From *Tso chuan* we know that K'ung K'uei's mother was K'uei-k'uei's (written 蒯聵 in *Tso chuan*) elder sister. K'ung was dragged out of his privy and was forced to join the rebellion. Tzu-lu rushed to the scene in order to rescue him. In *Tso chuan*, he managed to get into the city when a messenger came out (not when he entered, as *Shih chi* records). He tried to convince K'uei-k'uei that K'ung K'uei was not useful to his course and that even if he killed K'ung, there would be someone to fill his position (Tzu-lu did not ask to kill K'ung K'uei himself as he did in the *Shih chi* account). Apparently, he was trying to persuade K'uei-k'uei to release K'ung K'uei. His threat to burn the terrace served the same purpose.

[37] Different kinds of wood are drilled to get fire in different seasons (see Bodde, *Festivals,* pp. 294ff).

[38] As Liu Pao-nan's annotations (*Cheng-yi,* 20:14b-17a, *SPPY*) have shown, "three years" here only covers a period of twenty-five to twenty-seven months. Also, contrary to Confucius' claim, the examples Liu Pao-nan cites show that the three-year mourning period was not universally practiced.

Tsai [Tzu-]wo asked about the virtues of the Five Sage Emperors. The master said, "I am not the right person [to ask]."

Tsai [Tzu-]wo became a Grand Master of Lin-tzu 臨淄 and participated in the rebellion of T'ien Ch'ang 田常.[39] As a consequence, his clan was exterminated, and Confucius was ashamed of him.

8.

Tuan-mu Tz'u 端沐賜 (b. 520 B.C.) was a native of Wey. His *agnomen* was Tzu-kung 子貢.[40] He was thirty-one years younger than Confucius.

Tzu-kung's speech was quick and his language skilled. Confucius often rejected his arguments.

Confucius asked, "Who do you think is better, you or Hui?"

Tzu-kung replied, "How dare I compare myself to Hui? When Hui hears one thing, he will know ten. When I hear one thing, I will know two." (5/9)

[2196] Tzu-kung having received instruction, he asked, "What kind of person am I?"

Confucius said, "You are a vessel."

"What kind of vessel?"

"A jade sacrificial vessel."[41] (5/4)

Ch'en Tzu-ch'in 陳子禽 asked Tzu-kung, "Who did Chung-ni 仲尼 (Confucius) learn from?"

Tzu-kung said, "The way of Wen and Wu has not fallen to the ground. It is still found among men. The more worthy understand its greater points and the less worthy understand its minor ones. All possess the Way of Wen and Wu. Who does the master *not* learn from? Yet what constant teacher does he have?"[42] (19/22)

[Ch'en] also asked, "Whenever Confucius arrives in a state, he is sure to hear of its government. Does he seek this [knowledge], or is it given to him?" Tzu-kung said, "Our Master obtains it through his gentleness, goodness, modesty, restraint and yielding. Our Master's seeking is perhaps different from other men's seeking." (1/10)

Tzu-kung asked, "'Wealthy but lacking arrogance, poor yet lacking servility', how would this do?" Confucius said, "It would do. 'Poor but rejoicing in the Way, wealthy but delighting in the rites' would be better." (1/15)

[2197] T'ien Ch'ang intended to instigate a rebellion in Ch'i, but he was afraid of the Kao 高, Kuo 國, Pao 鮑 and Yen 晏 families. He thus transferred the troops [of these families] and prepared to use them in an attack on Lu.[43] When Confucius heard this, he told his

---

[39] T'ien Ch'ang's rebellion took place in 481 B.C. (*Shih chi*, 14:679, 46:1883-5; see also Yang, *Tso chuan*, Ai 14, pp. 1683ff). There is no other record of Tsai Tzu-wo participating in this rebellion.

[40] The *mu* in the name Tuan-mu Tz'u is often written as 木. Liang Yü-sheng (28:1213) suggests that the word *kung* (which means "to tribute") in his *agnomen* should be *kan* 贛, which means "to give" and matches his *praenomen ssu*, which means "to grant, to give."

[41] Liu Pao-nan, *Cheng-yi*, 6:3a-b, *SPPY*. "Vessel" is *ch'i* 器 in the original. Confucius also said that "A gentleman is not a vessel" (*chün tzu pu ch'i yeh* 君子不器也, see Liu Pao-nan, *Cheng-yi*, 2:10a, *SPPY*). Vessel is a metaphor for a person with one specialized skill, to be contrasted to a gentleman whose knowledge is more catholic. However, though Tzu-kung was a "vessel," he was an important one.

[42] Liu Pao-nan, *Cheng-yi*, 22:7a-b, *SPPY*. In the *Analects*, it was Kung-sun Ch'ao 公孫朝 who asked this first question, the next was put by Ch'en Tzu-ch'in.

[43] In this struggle, Ch'i attacked Lu in 487 B.C. (see *Shih chi*, 14:677). Liang Yü-sheng (28:1214) points out that when Ch'i attacked Lu, T'ien Ch'ang was not yet in power.

disciples, "Lu is the site of [our ancestors'] tombs and graves, the state of our parents. With the state in such danger, why don't you gentlemen go out?"

Tzu-lu asked permission to set forth. Confucius stopped him. Tzu-chang and Tzu-shih 子石 asked to set out.[44] Confucius would not permit it. Tzu-kung asked permission to set out. Confucius granted his request.[45]

Tzu-kung set out. When he reached Ch'i,[46] he advised T'ien Ch'ang: "My Lord's attack on Lu is an error. Lu is a country that is difficult to attack. Its city walls are low and thus thin. Its moat is shallow and thus narrow.[47] Its ruler is stupid and without compassion. Its great vassals are pretentious and useless. Its knights and commoners loathe matters of the sword and armor. You cannot fight them. My Lord would be better off attacking Wu. The city walls of Wu are thick and thus high. Its moat is deep and thus wide. Its armor is new and thus hard. Its troops are well fed and thus well trained. It is filled with heavy weapons and picked troops, and has sent an enlightened grand master to guard [its capital]. This is easy to attack."

T'ien Ch'ang flushed angrily. "Your difficult, sir, is other men's easy, and your easy, sir, other men's difficult. Why do you instruct me thus?"

Tzu-kung said, "Your servant has heard that 'Those whose worry lies within attack the mighty; those whose worry lies without attack the weak.' My Lord's worry lies within. I have heard that My Lord sought enfeoffment three times, and three times failed because there were those among the great vassals who were opposed. If you now enlarge Ch'i by crushing Lu, My Lord, if you make your ruler arrogant by triumphing in battle, and exalt his vassals by defeating a state, yet can claim no share of the merit, you will grow more estranged from your ruler day by day. In this way, My Lord makes his ruler above arrogant, and his vassals below unrestrained. If you seek to accomplish your grand scheme by these means, it will be difficult indeed! If your sovereign is arrogant, he will be unrestrained. If his vassals are arrogant, they will be contentious. Thus above there will be bad blood between My Lord and his ruler, and below there will be contention between My Lord and the great vassals. This being the case, My Lord's status in Ch'i will be hazardous indeed.

"Thus I said it would be better to attack Wu. If you attack Wu and do not gain victory, the people will die abroad and the great vassals will be defenseless at home. Thus above My Lord will have no mighty vassals as equals and below will have no people as critics. Isolate the ruler, take control of Ch'i; there is only you, My Lord."

T'ien Ch'ang said, "Well said. However, our troops are already committed against Lu. If they leave for Wu, the great vassals will suspect me. What might be done?"

Tzu-kung said, "Hold your troops, My Lord, and do not attack. Allow me to go on a mission to the King of Wu. I will have him [*2198*] rescue Lu and attack Ch'i. My Lord may then meet him with troops." T'ien Ch'ang granted his request and sent Tzu-kung south to see the King of Wu [Ho-lu 闔廬, r. 514-496 B.C.].

[Tzu-kung] advised [the King of Wu]. "Your servant has heard that 'A man fit to be king will not cut off a succession; a man fit to be hegemon has no mighty foes.' [But] a

[44] Towards the end of this biography, Tzu-shih is given as the *cognomen* of Kung-sun Lung (b. 498 B.C.). If this is the case, when Ch'i attacked Lu in 487 B.C. he would have been still a boy not likely to have been entrusted with this mission.

[45] There are a number of anachronistic elements in the following account of Tzu-kung's diplomatic activities (for a summary see Liang Yü-sheng, 28:1213-5). Scholars generally tend to doubt its authenticity (see Su Chen-shen, pp. 101-107).

[46] He arrived in Ch'i in 480 B.C. after Ch'i and Lu made peace (Liang Yü-sheng, 28:1214).

[47] We read this phrase as *ch'i ch'ih hsia yi ch'ien* 其池狹以淺, as Wang Nien-sun suggests (4:6a-b).

weight of a thousand *chün* will move when [something as light as] one *chu* or *liang* is added. Now if Ch'i, with its ten-thousand chariots, occupies Lu, with its thousand chariots, and then contends for power with Wu, I privately feel this is dangerous for Your Majesty. Moreover, in rescuing Lu, you can spread your fame and in attacking Ch'i, you can gain great profit. By this means, you can placate the feudal states on the banks of the Ssu 泗, punish savage Ch'i and force mighty Chin into submission. Nothing could be more profitable than this. In name, you preserve fallen Lu, but in fact you constrain mighty Ch'i. A wise man would not hesitate."

The King of Wu said, "Well put. However, I once fought with Yüeh and trapped him on top of K'uai-chi. The King of Yüeh mortifies his body and nurtures his troops. He has a mind to repay us. Wait until we have attacked Yüeh, sir, and then we will heed you."

Tzu-kung said, "Yüeh is no stronger than Lu and Wu no more powerful than Ch'i. If Your Majesty puts Ch'i to one side and attacks Yüeh, Ch'i will soon have pacified Lu. Moreover, Your Majesty now seeks fame by restoring fallen states and continuing severed successions. To attack tiny Yüeh and fear mighty Ch'i, this is not courage. A man with courage will not avoid difficulties, a man with compassion will not insist on the letter of an agreement, a man with wisdom will not miss the right moment, and a man fit to be king will not end a line. This is how they establish their principles.

"If you now allow Yüeh to survive, you show the feudal lords your compassion. If you save Lu, attack Ch'i and awe Chin, the feudal lords will follow each other to pay homage to Wu, and your goal of hegemony is achieved. If Your Majesty must needs fear Yüeh, your servant asks permission to seek an audience east with the King of Yüeh to have him send out his troops as your allies. This will effectively empty Yüeh [of its troops], while ostensibly making them allies of the feudal lords in the expedition." The King of Wu was delighted and sent Tzu-kung to Yüeh.

The King of Yüeh [Kou-chien 句踐, r. 497-473 B.C.] cleared the roads [for Tzu-kung] and greeted him in the suburbs. He personally drove Tzu-kung to the guesthouse and asked, "Ours is a barbarian state. Why have you, Grand Master, humbled yourself and come in person?"

Tzu-kung said, "Today I advised the King of Wu to save Lu and attack Ch'i. He wanted to, but feared Yüeh. So he said, 'Wait until We have attacked Yüeh; only then can it be done.' This being the case, the defeat of Yüeh is certain. If one has no intention of repaying another, yet arouses his suspicion, this is clumsy. If one has the intention of repaying another, yet lets him know it, this is fatal. If the matter is not yet ripe, yet is learned of beforehand, this is perilous. These three [*2199*] are the greatest hazards of rebellion."

Kou-chien struck his forehead against the ground twice. "I once failed to assess my strength, did battle with Wu, and was trapped at K'uai-chi. It pains me to the marrow; day and night my lips are parched and my tongue dry. I want only to die together with the King of Wu. This is my wish." He asked Tzu-kung [for advice].

Tzu-kung said, "The King of Wu is by nature savage and ruthless; his assembled vassals cannot stand him. His country is worn out by many battles; his officers and men cannot bear it. The families of the hundred cognomens resent their sovereign, the great vassals rebel at home. Tzu Hsü was killed for his admonitions[48] and Grand Steward Hsi exercises power. He secures his personal affairs by going along with his lord's errors. This is a rule fit to cripple the state. If Your Majesty could humor his desire by sending troops to aid him, please his heart with rich treasures, and exalt his status with humble speech, the attack on Ch'i is certain.

---

[48] See his biography in *Shih chi* Chapter 66.

If he does not gain victory in battle, that is Your Majesty's great fortune. If he does gain victory in battle, he is sure to confront Chin with his troops. Your servant asks permission to obtain an audience in the north with Chin, and to have him attack Wu in concert [with you]. The weakening of Wu is certain. His picked troops used up in Ch'i, his armored troops trapped in Chin, if Your Majesty seizes him in his weariness, the destruction of Wu is certain."

The King of Yüeh was delighted and consented. He gave Tzu-kung a parting gift of one-hundred yi of gold, a sword, and two fine spears. Tzu-kung declined them and set out.

He reported to the King of Wu: "I respectfully told the King of Yüeh Your Majesty's words. The King of Yüeh was terrified and said, 'I am an unhappy man! I lost my father in youth and at home failed to assess my own strength, incurring the punishment of Wu. My troops defeated, my person humiliated, I was trapped atop K'uai-chi and my state was laid waste. Through the Great King's grace, I am allowed to hold the sacrificial dish and platter and continue the sacrifices to spirits and ancestors. I dare not forget, even after death. What plots would I dare harbor!'"

Five days later, Yüeh's emissary, Grand Master Chung 種[49] struck his head against the ground and spoke to the King of Wu. "The slave Chung, emissary of humble Kou-chien, your servant from the Eastern Sea 東海, ventures to inquire as a lowly functionary among the court attendants. I have privately heard, Great King, that you are about to mobilize in great righteousness to punish the mighty and save the weak, to press cruel Ch'i and succor a member of the House of Chou. I ask permission to mobilize all three-thousand troops within my borders. I humbly ask permission to myself don stout armor, grasp a sharp weapon, and to be first to suffer arrow and stone. I present, through this lowly slave of Yüeh, Chung, the stored weapons of my ancestors: twenty suits of armors, ch'ü-lu 屈盧 halberds and [*2200*] pu-kuang 步光 swords[50] as gifts to the officers of your army."

The King of Wu was delighted and told Tzu-kung, "The King of Yüeh wants to accompany Us himself on the attack against Ch'i. Will this do?"

Tzu-kung said, "It will not. To empty another state [of its goods], to summon off its hosts, and then to lead away their lord, this is unrighteous. Accept their gifts, My Lord, consent to their troops, but decline their lord." The King of Wu consented and refused the King of Yüeh. After this, the King of Wu mobilized the troops of nine commanderies to attack Ch'i.

Tzu-kung then left for Chin. He told the Lord of Chin, "Your servant has heard that 'Without plans set beforehand, there will be nothing with which to meet surprise. Without weapons prepared beforehand, there will be nothing with which to overcome an enemy.' Ch'i and Wu are about to do battle. If [Wu] does not triumph in battle, Yüeh's invasion of [Wu] is certain. If [Wu] does battle with Ch'i and triumphs, it is sure to confront Chin with its troops."

The Lord of Chin was terrified. "What's to be done?"

Tzu-kung said, "Prepare for them by repairing your weapons and resting your troops." The Lord of Chin consented.

Tzu-kung left for Lu. As expected, the King of Wu fought with Ch'i at Ai-ling, crushed the forces of Ch'i, and captured the troops of seven [Ch'i] generals, but did not return [to Wu].[51] As expected, he confronted Chin with his troops, and met on equal terms with the men of Chin on the banks of Huang-ch'ih 黃池.[52]

---

[49] See also n. 57 to our translation of Shih chi Chapter 66 above.

[50] We omit the word fu 鈇 (see Wang Shu-min, 67:2119).

[51] On the battle at Ai-ling see our translation of Shih chi Chapter 66. Liang Yü-sheng (28:1214) observes that

Wu and Chin contended for power. The men of Chin attacked and crushed the troops of Wu. When the King of Yüeh heard this, he crossed the Chiang, launched a surprise attack against Wu, and camped seven *li* away from the walls [of Wu's capital]. When the King of Wu heard this, he left Chin, returned [to Wu], and fought with Yüeh at Wu-hu 五湖.[53] After Wu had fought three times without victory, the city gates fell. Yüeh then besieged the king's palace, killed Fu-ch'ai and executed his prime minister. Three years after defeating Wu (470 B.C.), Yüeh faced east and became Hegemon.

[2201] Thus in one trip, Tzu-kung preserved Lu, troubled Ch'i, defeated Wu, strengthened Chin and made Yüeh Hegemon. With one mission, Tzu-kung made them break their own forces, and within ten years,[54] each of the five states was undone.

Tzu-kung was fond of buying and selling and adjusted to market changes in controlling the flow of his goods and capital. He liked to praise others' virtues but could not cover up others faults. He was once Prime Minister of Lu and Wei and his family property amounted to thousands of *chin*. He died in the end in Ch'i.

9.

Yen Yen 言偃 (506-443 B.C.) was a native of Wu. His *agnomen* was Tzu-yu 子游. He was forty-five years younger than Confucius.

After Tzu-yu received [Confucius'] teachings, he became the steward of Wu-ch'eng 武城.[55] Confucius passed by the town and heard the sound of a stringed instrument and singing. Confucius smiled good-humoredly and said, "Why use an ox-cleaver to kill a chicken?"

Tzu-yu said, "I once heard this from the Master, 'If a gentleman learns from the Way, he will be kind to people. If a small person learns from the Way, he will be easy to command.'" Confucius [*2202*] said, "Students, what Yen says is right. My remark just now was made only in jest." (17/4)

Confucius considered Tzu-yu well-versed in literature and learning.

10.

Pu Shang's 卜商 (507-425 B.C.) *agnomen* was Tzu-hsia 子夏. He was forty-four years younger than Confucius.

Tzu-hsia asked, "What is the meaning of the lines,
'Oh the lovely smile dimpling,
The beautiful eyes flashing,
White silks can be made into colored [prints].'"[56]

according to the *Tso chuan*, Wu captured only five generals.

[52] See n. 73 to our translation of Chapter 66.

[53] Modern T'ai-hu 太湖 in Kiangsu (T'an Ch'i-hsiang, 1:45).

[54] From Ch'i's attack on Lu in 487 B.C. to Yüeh's occupation of Wu in 473 B.C., fifteen years had passed, not ten (see Liang Yü-sheng, 28:1214).

[55] Although it seems this place must have been in Lu and although many scholars (T'an Ch'i-hsiang, 1:39, places it about 25 miles west-southwest of modern Fei 費 County in Shantung) have postulated its location there, the evidence to support this claim is not strong (see the long note to *Lun yü*, 6/12 in Ch'eng Shu-te 程樹德, *Lun yü chi-shih* 論語集釋 [4v.; Peking: Chung-hua, 1990], 1: 329-333, which discusses at least four possible sites).

[56] The translation is ours; the first two lines in this quote are from *Shih ching* (*Mao* #57, Legge, 4:95). The third line was apparently originally part of the *Shih ching* (see the *Shuo-wen* 說文 entry for *hsüan* 絢), but is not part of extant versions.

Confucius said, "The coloring comes after the white cloth."

Tzu-hsia asked, "Then does the practice of rites come afterwards?"

Confucius said, "With [Pu] Shang one can begin to discuss *The Odes*."[57] (3/8)

[2203] Tzu-kung asked, "Who is more worthy, [Chuan-sun] Shih or [Pu] Shang?"

Confucius said, "Shih has gone beyond [the mean] while Shang has not reached it."

"Then is Shih better?"

Confucius said, "To go beyond it is the same as not reaching it." (11/16)

Confucius said to Tzu-hsia, "You should be a gentleman ritualist, not a petty ritualist."[58] (6/13)

After Confucius died, Tzu-hsia resided at Hsi Ho 西河[59] and lived by teaching. He became the teacher of Marquis Wen 文 of Wei (r. 445-396 B.C.).[60] When his son died, he cried so much that he lost his eyesight.[61]

11.

Chuan-sun Shih 顓孫師 (503-447 B.C.) was a native of Ch'en 陳.[62] His *agnomen* was Tzu-chang 子張. He was forty-eight years younger than Confucius.

[2204] Tzu-chang asked how to attain office. Confucius said, "Hear much, leave out what is doubtful, and speak cautiously about the rest. Then you will incur few complaints. Watch much, leave out those examples that cause danger and practice the rest. Then you will have few regrets. Incur few complaints with your words, incur few regrets with your practices, herein lies the way of attaining office."[63] (2/18)

On another occasion, he accompanied [Confucius] on the road between Ch'en and Ts'ai. When they encountered difficulties, he asked how one should conduct oneself.[64] Confucius said, "If one's words are sincere and trustworthy and his deeds earnest and reverent, then even if he is among the barbarians of the South or North, he can go forward. If one's words are neither sincere nor trustworthy and his deeds are neither earnest nor reverent, even though he is in his home country, can he go forward? When standing, envision these

[57] Liu Pao-nan, *Cheng-yi*, 3:7a-8a, *SPPY*.

[58] Liu Pao-nan, *Cheng-yi*, 7:10b, *SPPY*. The word *ju* 儒 eventually became a synonym for the Confucians. But in Confucius' time and earlier it designated those who conformed to established procedures and institutional norms and were often consulted on these procedures and norms.

[59] "So-yin" and "Cheng-yi" both want to place Hsi Ho near its usual Warring States Era location. "Cheng-yi" prefers a site near the portion of the Yellow River which swings north around the Ordos, "So-yin" the commandery just west of this region. Following "Cheng-yi," Tzu-hsia lived in a "stone house" 石室 and taught there near Fen-chou 汾州 (modern Fen-yang 汾陽 in Shansi (T'an Ch'i-hsiang, 5:46-7), upriver from the state of Wei's old capital at An-yi 安邑 (T'an Ch'i-hsiang, 1:34). Nevertheless, there seems to be an earlier tradition which would place Tzu-hsia's later residence much nearer to Lu, south and west of modern Nei-huang 內黃 in Honan (see the *Erh-ya* 爾雅 citation given in "Cheng-yi"). Ch'ien Mu has a lengthy disquisition (*Chu-tzu*, pp. 125-9) in support of the Honan location.

[60] Scholars have pointed to the discrepancy of the dates of Confucius' death (481 B.C.), Pu Shang's life (507-420 B.C. [according to Ch'ien Mu, *Chu-tzu*, p. 661; Chiang Liang-fu, p. 3, gives 507-400 B.C.) and the dates of Marquis Wen's reign (445-396 B.C.). However, Ch'ien Mu (*Chu-tzu*, pp. 124-5) shows convincingly that this discrepancy has been overstated and it is quite possible Pu Shang taught the Marquis.

[61] The "T'an-kung" 檀弓 chapter of *Li chi* (2:9b, *SPPY*) records a similar anecdote.

[62] Near the modern city of Huai-yang 淮陽 in Honan (T'an Ch'i-hsiang, 1:45).

[63] In the *Analects*, *wen* 問 "asked about" reads *hsüeh* 學 "[wanted to] learn about" (Liu Pao-nan, *Cheng-yi*, 2:13a-b, *SPPY*).

We have translated *kan-lu* 干祿 as "to seek a salary" following Cheng Hsüan and Liu Pao-nan.

[64] This took place about 489 B.C. (see Lau, *Analects*, p. 174).

principles as if they are rising upright in front of you. In your carriage, envision them as if they are resting across the handbar. Then you can go forward." Tzu-chang wrote this down on his sash.[65] (15/6)

Tzu-chang asked, "What must a scholar be like before he can be said to be accomplished?"

Confucius asked, "What do you mean by 'accomplished?'"

Tzu-chang replied, "When serving the state, he will be renowned; when serving a noble family, he will also be renowned."

Confucius said, "That is 'renowned,' not 'accomplished.' An 'accomplished' man is one whose nature is unbending and who loves righteousness. He examines others' words, observes others' expressions, and, after thinking them over, defers to others. Thus he is sure of accomplishments when serving both a state and a noble family. As for a 'renowned' man, he appears humane, then diverges from it in his actions, yet has no hesitation in claiming it. Thus he is sure of 'renown' when serving both a state and a noble family."[66] (12/20)

12.

[2205] Tseng Shen 曾參 (505-436 B.C.) was a native of South Wu-ch'eng 南武城.[67] His *agnomen* was Tzu-yü 子輿. He was forty-six years younger than Confucius.

Confucius thought that he had a thorough understanding of filial piety and thus gave him instruction. [Tseng Shen] compiled the *Hsiao ching* 孝經 (Classic of Filial Piety). He died in Lu.

13.

T'an-t'ai Mieh-ming 澹臺滅明 (b. 512 B.C.) was a native of Wu-ch'eng. His *agnomen* was Tzu-yü 子羽. He was thirty-nine years younger than Confucius.

[2206] His appearance was quite ugly. He wanted to serve Confucius [as a disciple] and Confucius thought that he was limited in talent. After he had received [Confucius'] teaching, he retreated and cultivated his conduct. He did not take shortcuts and would not go to see ministers or grand masters unless he was on official business.[68]

He traveled south to the Chiang and had three-hundred followers. He perfected [his manner] of receiving, giving, retreating and advancing, and his name spread among the feudal lords. When Confucius heard this, he said, "I judged people by their speech and was mistaken in the case of Tsai Yü; I judged people by their appearance and was mistaken in the case of Tzu-yü."

14.

Fu Pu-ch'i's 宓不齊 (b. 521 B.C.) *agnomen* was Tzu-chien 子賤. He was thirty years

[65] Liu Pao-nan, *Cheng-yi,* 18:4a-5a, *SPPY.* Waley understands *heng* 衡 (handbar) as *o* 軛 (yoke). However, as Liu Pao-nan has pointed out, *o* is not correct; Liu observes that *ts'an* 參 means *chih* 直 (rising upright); since *heng* can mean "horizontal" and since it is used in juxtaposition with *ts'an* here, we believe it also means "horizontal" here.

[66] Liu Pao-nan, *Cheng-yi* (15:13a-14a, *SPPY*).

[67] This was another term for Wu-ch'eng--see n. 54 above.

[68] While Tzu-yu was steward of Wu-ch'eng, Confucius visited him and asked him whether he had discovered any good men there. This was his reply (*Lun yü,* 6/12; Liu Pao-nan, *Cheng-yi,* 7:10b-11b, *SPPY*).

younger than Confucius.

[2207] Confucius said, "What a gentleman Tzu-chien is! If there were no gentlemen in Lu, then where could he have acquired such [qualities]?" (5/3)

Tzu-chien was the steward of Shan-fu 單父.[69] On his return [to Lu], he told Confucius this, "In this place there are five people who are better than me and teach me how to govern." Confucius said, "What a pity! The place that you govern is too small. If you could have a larger area to govern, that would be perfect."

15.

Yüan Hsien's 原憲 (b. 525 B.C.[70]) *agnomen* was Tzu-ssu 子思.

Tzu-ssu asked about the shameful. Confucius said, "If the Way prevails in the state, accept government emolument. If the Way does not prevail in the state, to accept government emolument is shameful."[71] (14/1)

Tzu-ssu said, "Can checking one's inclinations to vanquish others, to brag about himself, to bear grudges and to covet be called humane?"

Confucius said, "It may be called 'difficult.' But I don't know if it is humane." (14/1)

[2208] After Confucius died, Yüan Hsien hid among the grasses and marshes. Tzu-kung became the Prime Minister of Wey. Leading an array of horses, he pushed his way through weeds and brambles. He entered the shabby lane and visited Yüan Hsien. Yüan Hsien tidied his tattered gown and cap and received Tzu-kung. Tzu-kung found it shameful and asked, "Are you infirm?" Yüan Hsien said, "I have heard that one who does not have property is said to be poor, one who studies the Way but cannot practice it is said to be infirm. As for me, I am poor, but I am not infirm."

Tzu-kung was ashamed and left in displeasure. For the rest of his life, he was ashamed of the impropriety of his words.[72]

16.

Kung-yeh Chang 公冶長 was a native of Ch'i. His *agnomen* was Tzu-chang 子長.[73]

Confucius said, "[Kung-yeh] Chang is a man to whom one can marry his daughter. Even if he should be tied up in prison, it would not be because of any fault of his own." Accordingly, he married his daughter to him. (5/1)

17.

Nan-kung K'uo's 南宮括[74] *agnomen* was Tzu-jung 子容.

[69] About 50 miles southwest of the modern city of Chi-ning 濟寧 at Shan 單 County in Shantung (T'an Ch'i-hsiang, 1:39); Shan-fu at that time was in the state of Sung.

[70] Ch'ien Mu, *Chu-tzu*, pp. 172-6.

[71] Liu Pao-nan, *Cheng-yi*, 17:1a, *SPPY*.

[72] A similar account of Tzu-kung's visit to Yüan Hsien is found in the "Jang-wang" 讓王 chapter of *Chuang-tzu* (9:13b, *SPPY*).

[73] According to "So-yin" his *praenomen* was Ch'ang 萇; other sources give Shih 師 (see Wang Li-ch'i, *Jen-piao*, p. 199). Although there seems to be no further information on Confucius marrying his daughter to Kung-yeh Chang, there are numerous accounts of the latter's ability to understand the language of birds (see Ch'eng Shu-te, pp. 285-6).

[74] *K'uo* is written 适 in the *Analects*.

[2209] He asked Confucius, "[Isn't it true that] though Yi 羿 excelled in archery and Ao 奡 could move a boat along on land,[75] neither of them were able to die a natural death, while Yü 禹 and Chi 稷 personally took part in farming and [finally] possessed the world?"

Confucius did not reply. After [Tzu-]jung left, Confucius said, "What a gentleman this man is! How highly virtuous this man is! (14/5)

"If the Way prevails in the state, he will not be cast aside; if the Way does not prevail, he can be spared punishment." (5/2)

[Tzu-jung] recited over and over again the verse about the white-jade scepter.[76] [Confucius] married his elder brother's daughter to him.[77] (11/6)

18.

Kung-hsi Ai's 公晳哀 *agnomen* was Chi-tz'u 季次.[78]

Confucius said, "The world's scholars have lost their standard of conduct. Many of them are household managers or serve in cities. Only Chi-tz'u has never served."[79]

19.

[2210] Tseng Tien's 曾蒧 *agnomen* was Hsi 晳.[80]

He was waiting on Confucius when Confucius said, "Tell me what you like to do."

Tseng Tien said, "When the spring clothes have been made, I would like, together with five or six youths and six or seven boys, to bathe in the Yi 沂 River[81] and enjoy the breeze at the Rain-dance Altar and chant poems along the way back."

Confucius heaved a long sigh and said, "I agree with you."[82] (11/26)

20.

Yen Wu-yu's 顏無繇 (b. 545 B.C.) *agnomen* was Lu 路.[83] He was Yen Hui's father.

[75] For an attempt to trace these allusions, see Ch'eng Shu-te, *op. cit.,* 3:953-6.

[76] Liu Pao-nan, *Cheng-yi,* 14:4b, *SPPY.* "The verse about the white jade scepter" refers to *Shih ching* (*Mao* #256; Legge, 4:513). Stanza five reads: "Demand your officials and people, / To attend your princely measures, / Thus to prepare for unforseeable dangers. / Be careful with what you say, / Be reverential in your composure. / In nothing should you be want of gentleness and finesse. / A flaw in a white jade sceptre, / May be ground away; / A flaw in your speech, / May not be done away." 質爾人民，謹爾侯度，用戒不虞，慎爾出話，敬爾威儀，無不柔嘉，白圭之玷，尚可磨也，斯言之玷，不可為也．

[77] In *Lun yü,* 5/2, this sentence immediately followed Confucius's comment that Nan-kung Kuo could escape punishment even if the Way did not prevail (see Liu Pao-nan, *Cheng-yi,* 6:2a-b, *SPPY*). The association between the recitation of the Ode and the marriage appears only in *Lun yü,* 11/6.

[78] See also *Shih chi,* 124:3181.

[79] This statement may seem strange, since Confucius and a number of his disciples sought to serve. But, as Ch'ien Mu, *Chu-tzu,* p. 81 suggests, there were two groups of Confucian disciples--those who studied with him before he left Lu, and those who studied with him after his return. The first group was oriented toward government service, the second towards scholarship. This attribution of these words to Confucius is certainly from one of the later disciples.

[80] His *praenomen* is also written Tien 點; he was Tseng Shen's father (Wang Li-ch'i, *Jen-piao,* pp. 199-200).

[81] Running north to south in modern south-central Shantung (T'an Ch'i-hsiang, 1:39).

[82] Liu Pao-nan, *Cheng-yi,* 14:15a-23b, *SPPY.* This is the final portion of an exchange between Confucius, Tseng Tien, Tzu-lu, Jan Ch'iu and Kung-hsi Ch'ih. The comments of other disciples, and Confucius' reactions to them, have been omitted.

Yü 雩 was a rain ceremony usually performed in spring.

Father and son each served Confucius at different times.

When Yen Hui died (481 B.C.), Yen Lu, who was impoverished, asked for Confucius' carriage to pay for [Yen Hui's] funeral. Confucius said, "Be they gifted or not, we each praise our own son. When [my son] Li 鯉 (532-483 B.C.) died,[84] he had a coffin but no enclosure. I would not [sell my carriage and] go on foot in order to provide for his coffin enclosure because I was in line with the grand masters and it would have been improper for me to go on foot."[85] (11/8)

21.

[2211] Shang Ch'ü 商瞿 (b. 522 B.C.) was a native of Lu.[86] His *agnomen* was Tzu-mu 子木. He was twenty-nine years younger than Confucius.

Confucius transmitted the *Book of Changes* to Shang Ch'ü, Shang Ch'ü transmitted it to a native of Ch'u, Han Pi 馯臂, whose *agnomen* was Tzu-hung 子弘.[87] Tzu-hung transmitted it to a native of Chiang-tung 江東,[88] Chiao Tz'u 矯疵, whose *agnomen* was Tzu-yung 子庸. Chiao Tz'u transmitted it to a native of Yen, Chou Shu 周豎, whose *agnomen* was Tzu-chia 子家. Chou Shu transmitted it to a native of Ch'un-yü 淳于,[89] Kuang Yü 光羽, whose *agnomen* was Tzu-ch'eng 子乘. Kuang Yü transmitted it to a native of Ch'i, T'ien Ho 田何, whose *agnomen* was Tzu-chuang 子莊. T'ien Ho transmitted it to a native of Tung-wu 東武,[90] Wang T'ung 王同, whose *agnomen* was Tzu-chung 子中. Wang T'ung transmitted it to a native of Tzu-ch'uan 菑川,[91] Yang Ho 楊何. During the Yüan-shuo 元朔 period (128-123 B.C.), Yang Ho was made a Regular Grand Master of the Han 漢 [dynasty] because of his expertise in the *Book of Changes*.[92]

22.

[2212] Kao Ch'ai's 高柴 *agnomen* was Tzu-kao 子羔.[93] He was thirty years younger than Confucius.

Tzu-kao was less than five *ch'ih* tall. He received instruction from Confucius. Confucius considered him slow.

---

[83] Sometimes referred to as Yen Yu 由 (Wang Li-ch'i, *Jen-piao*, p. 206).

[84] For a study of the dates of K'ung Li and Yen Hui, see Ch'ien Mu, *Chu-tzu*, pp. 51-53.

[85] Liu Pao-nan, *Cheng-yi*, 14:5a-6a, *SPPY*.

[86] See also Wang Li-ch'i, *Jen-piao*, pp. 206-7.

[87] On this transmission see also Ch'ien Mu, "K'ung-men ch'uan Ching k'ao" 孔門傳經考, *Chu-tzu*, pp. 83-88.

[88] A region (later commandery) stretching south of T'ai-hu across the modern provinces of Anhwei and Kiangsu (T'an Ch'i-hsiang, 1:45).

[89] A few miles northeast of the modern city of An-ch'iu 安丘 in central Shantung (T'an Ch'i-hsiang, 1:40); it was a part of Ch'i.

[90] Also known as Wu-ch'eng 武城, it is near the modern city of that name on the Hopei-Shantung border (T'an Ch'i-hsiang, 1:38; see also n. 55 above).

[91] Ch'ien Mu (*Ti-ming k'ao*, p. 284) places it in Hsüeh 薛 County in what was then Ch'i (modern Shantung).

[92] According to *Han shu* (58:3597), he was appointed to the post during the Yüan-kuang 元光 period (134-129 B.C.).

[93] He is supposed to have been a native of Wey, but some accounts claim he was from Ch'i (see "So-yin" and "Cheng-yi"). See also Wang Li-ch'i, *Jen-piao*, p. 205 and Fang Hsüan-chen, pp. 445-6. He was also known as Chi Kao 季羔 and appears twice in the *Tso chuan* (Yang, *Tso chuan*, Ai 15, pp. 1696 and 1711) in the accounts of events in 480 and 478 B.C.

Tzu-lu appointed Tzu-kao steward of Pi [Hou] 費 [郈].[94] Confucius said, "You are ruining another man's son."

Tzu-lu said, "There are the common people and the altars to the spirits of the land and
grain. Why must one study books before he can be considered to have learned?"

Confucius said, "This sort of talk has made me detest glib talkers." (11/25)

23.

[2213] Ch'i-tiao K'ai's 漆雕開 (b. 540 B.C.) *agnomen* was Tzu-k'ai 子開.

Confucius wanted Ch'i-tiao K'ai to take office. He replied, "I do not have enough confidence in this yet." Confucius was pleased. (5/6)

24.

Kung-po Liao's 公伯繚 *agnomen* was Tzu-chou 子周.[95]

[2214] Tzu-chou slandered Tzu-lu to Chi Sun 季孫.[96] Tzu-fu Ching-po 子服景伯[97] reported this to Confucius and said, "My master has certainly been swayed, but I still have the
influence to have his corpse exposed in a public place."

Confucius said, "If the Way prevails, it is destiny; if the Way comes to ruin, it is destiny. What can Kung-po Liao do to destiny?" (14/36)

25.

Ssu-ma Keng's 司馬耕 *agnomen* was Tzu-niu 子牛.[98]

[Tzu-]niu was talkative and impetuous. He asked Confucius about humaneness. Confucius said, "A humane man speaks with difficulty."

[Tzu-niu] said, "One can be said to be a humane man just because he speaks with difficulty?" Confucius said, "It is difficult to be a humane man so how can one not find it difficult
to speak humanely?" (12/3)

[Tzu-niu] asked about the gentleman. Confucius said, "The gentleman neither worries
nor fears."

[Tzu-niu] said, "One can be said to be a gentleman just because he neither worries nor
fears?" Confucius said, "If, in examining oneself, one does not have any [*2215*] regrets,
why should he worry or fear?" (12/4)

26.

Fan Hsü's 樊須 (b. 505 B.C.) *agnomen* was Tzu Ch'ih 子遲.[99] He was thirty-six years
younger[100] than Confucius.

---

[94] In the *Analects*, Tzu-kao was assigned to Pi, not Pi-hou. Following Liu Pao-nan, *Cheng-yi* (14:14b-15a,
SPPY), we read Hou as an interpolation. Pi is a few miles north of modern Pi County in southern Shantung (T'an
Ch'i-hsiang, 1:39).

[95] See Wang Li-ch'i, *Jen-piao*, p. 302.

[96] Chi Sun was the head of one of the three most powerful clans in Lu.

[97] A member of the powerful Meng 孟 family (see Ch'eng Shu-te, *op. cit.*, 4:1022).

[98] The sentence "Niu was talkative and impetuous" is not found in the *Analects* (Liu Pao-nan, *Cheng-yi*,
15:2b-3a, *SPPY*), but a similar description is found in *K'ung-tzu chia-yü* (9:3a, *SPPY*); see also Wang Li-ch'i,
Jen-piao, p. 204. See also Donald Leslie's "Note on the *Analects*," *TP*, 49(1961), p. 26f.

Fan [Tzu-]ch'ih asked for instructions on how to plant crops. Confucius said, "[On this subject], I am not as good as an old farmer." He asked for instructions on how to plant vegetables. Confucius said, "I am not as good as an old gardener." Fan [Tzu-]ch'ih left.

Confucius said, "What a small man Fan Hsü is! If the one above loves the rites, people will not be disrespectful. If the one above loves righteousness, people will not dare to be disobedient. If the one above loves fidelity, then people will not dare to be untruthful. If one is like such [a gentleman], people from the four quarters will carry their children on their backs and come to him. What need has he to learn to plant crops?"[101] (13/4)

Fan [Tzu-]ch'ih asked about humaneness. Confucius said, "Love the people." He asked about wisdom. Confucius said, "Know the people." (12/22)

27.

Yu Jo 有若 (508-457 B.C.)[102] was forty-three years younger than Confucius.[103] Yu Jo said, "When you practice the rites, prize harmony most. Of the ways of the former kings, this is best. Following this in all matters, great and small, [*2216*] is not always the way to proceed. To harmonize because you know how to, without the measures of the rites, one cannot go this way, either.[104] (1/12)

"Stay close to what is righteous when making promises, and you may make good on your word. Stay close to propriety in deferring to others, and you may keep disgrace and humiliation at a distance. Maintain without fail a proper relationship when others seek your good offices, and ⸳ ⸳⸳⸳der "[105] (1/13)

After Con⸳   ⸳sed him. Yu Jo looked like Confucius. Together, the discip⸳   ⸳l served him as they served Confucius when he
was alive.

One day,   ⸳tion, saying, "Once when the Master was about
to go out, he tol⸳   ⸳raincoats. Later, it rained as he expected. We
[want to] ask, 'H⸳   ⸳it will rain?'"

"The Ma⸳   f Odes says, "When the moon is in the Hyades, /
There will be a ⸳   ⸳e moon in the Hyades the night before?' On another day the m⸳   ⸳did not rain after all.

"Shang ⸳   d [still] did not have a son. His mother found
[another] wife f⸳   ⸳o Ch'i, but his mother asked that he be excused.

"Confuc⸳   i will have five sons after forty.' Later, it turned
out to be so. We would like to ask ⸳⸳⸳ Master knew it?"

Yu Jo was silent and could not offer an answer. The disciples stood up and said, "Let Master Yu vacate the seat, it is not for you."[107]

[99] See also Wang Li-ch'i, *Jen-piao*, pp. 203-4. Fan is also mentioned in the *Tso chuan* account of events in 484 B.C. (Yang, *Tso chuan*, Ai 11, p. 1659).

[100] *K'ung-tzu chia-yü* (9:2a, *SPPY*) says "*forty-six* years younger."

[101] Liu Pao-nan, *Cheng-yi*, 16:5a-6a, *SPPY*. According to Ma Jung 馬融 (79-166 A.D.), the "planting of the five grains is called *chia* while the planting of vegetables is called *p'u*" 樹五穀曰稼, 樹菜蔬曰圃 (16:5a).

[102] See also Wang Li-ch'i, *Jen-piao*, p. 202.

[103] *K'ung-tzu chia-yü* (9:2a, *SPPY*) says "*thirty-six* years younger."

[104] Liu Pao-nan, *Cheng-yi*, 1:14b-15a, *SPPY*.

[105] Liu Pao-nan, *Cheng-yi*, 1:15a-16a, *SPPY*.

[106] *Mao* #232; Legge, 4:422.

[107] Both stories occur in the *K'ung-tzu chia-yü* (9:3a, *SPPY*). The first, about the umbrellas, is set in Confucius' time. In it one of the Master's disciples, Wu-ma [Tzu-]ch'i 巫馬子期 (see n. 110 below), asks Confucius how he

28.

[2217] Kung-hsi Ch'ih's 公西赤 (b. 509) *agnomen* was Tzu-hua 子華.[108]   He was forty-two years younger than Confucius.

Tzu-hua had been sent to Ch'i. Jan Yu asked for grain on behalf of his mother. Confucius said, "Give her one *fu* 釜." Jan asked for more. Confucius said, "Give her one *yü* 庾." Jan Yu gave her five *ping* of grain.[109]

Confucius said, "Ch'ih, when going to Ch'i, rode in carriages pulled by fat horses and wore light furs. I have heard that 'A gentleman helps one who is in dire need but does not add to the wealth of the rich.'" (6/4)

29.

[2218] Wu-ma Shih's 巫馬施 (b. 521 B.C.) *agnomen* was Tzu-ch'i 子旗.[110]   He was thirty years younger than Confucius.

Ch'en Ssu-pai 陳司敗[111] asked Confucius, "Does Duke Chao 昭 of Lu (r. 541-510 B.C.) know the rites?" Confucius said, "He knows the rites."

[After Confucius had left, Ch'en Ssu-pai] bowed to Wu-ma Shih and said, "I have heard that 'A gentleman is not partial.' Will a gentleman be partial after all? The Lord of Lu took a daughter of Wu for his wife and called her Meng Tzu 孟子. Meng Tzu's *cognomen* was Chi 姬. To avoid calling her by her *cognomen* which was the same as his, he called her Meng Tzu. If the Lord of Lu knows the rites, who does not?"

Wu-ma [Tzu-]ch'i repeated this to Confucius. Confucius said, "I am a fortunate man. If I should make a mistake, other people will surely notice it." (7/31)

An official was not allowed to talk about the wrongdoing of his lord. [Confucius'] avoidance of this conformed to the rites.

30.

Liang Chan's 梁鱣 (b. 522 B.C.) *agnomen* was Tzu-yü 子魚.[112]   He was twenty-nine years younger than Confucius.[113]

---

knew it was going to rain. The second story is also framed differently. In it another disciple, Liang Chan 梁鱣, wanted to send his wife away because she had not given him a son. Shang Ch'ü then dissuades him from doing so by relating how Confucius admonished him to wait. After two years Liang Chan's wife did give birth.

More significantly, it can be seen from the obvious Yin-yang influence that these stories are more recent date than the *Analects* and strive to exhalt qualities not sought by the orthodox followers of Confucius.

[108] See also Wang Li-ch'i, *Jen-piao,* pp. 201-2.

[109] One *fu* equals about 12 liters; one *yü* about 31 liters; five *ping* amounts to 1,550 liters (see Mizusawa, p. 190).

[110] See also Wang Li-ch'i, *Jen-piao,* p. 204 and n. 107 above.

[111] Some scholars believe that *Ssu-pai* is an official title and that Ch'en refers to the state of that name (Liu Pao-nan, *Cheng-yi,* 8:14b-15b, *SPPY*).

Marriage between people sharing the same *cognomen* was not allowed.

[112] See n. 107 above.

[113] *K'ung-tzu chia-yü* (9:3a, *SPPY*) says "*thirty*-nine years younger."

31.

Yen Hsing's 顏幸 (b. 505 B.C.) *agnomen* was Tzu-liu 子柳. He was forty-six years younger than Confucius.

32.

[2219] Jan Ju's 冉孺 (b. 501 B.C) *agnomen* was Tzu-lu 子魯. He was fifty years younger than Confucius.

33.

Ts'ao Hsü 曹恤 (b. 501 B.C.) *agnomen* was Tzu-hsün 子循. He was fifty years younger than Confucius.

34.

Po Ch'ien's 伯虔 (b. 501 B.C.) *agnomen* was Tzu-hsi 子析. He was fifty years younger than Confucius.

35.

Kung-sun Lung's 公孫龍 (b. 498 B.C.) *agnomen* was Tzu-shih 子石.[114] He was fifty-three years younger than Confucius.

[2220] Thirty-five disciples, up to Tzu Shih, have their dates and names, the instruction they received, and the deeds they performed recorded in historical documents. The remaining forty-two disciples, whose dates are not known and whose deeds are not recorded in historical documents, are listed as follows:

Jan Chi's 冉季 *agnomen* was Tzu-ch'an 子產.
Kung-tzu Kou-tzu's 公祖句茲 *agnomen* was Tzu-chih 子之.
Ch'in Tzu's 秦祖 *agnomen* was Tzu-nan 子南.
Ch'i-tiao Ch'ih's 漆雕哆 *agnomen* was Tzu-lien 子斂.
[2221] Yen Kao's 顏高 *agnomen* was Tzu-chiao 子驕.
Ch'i-tiao Hsi-fu 漆雕徒父.
Jang-ssu Ch'ih's 壤駟赤 *agnomen* was Tzu-hsi 子徒.
Shang Tse 商澤.
Shih-tso Shu's 石作蜀 *agnomen* was Tzu-ming 子明.
Jen Pu-ch'i's 任不齊 *agnomen* was Hsüan 選.
Kung-liang Ju's 公良孺 *agnomen* was Tzu-cheng 子正.
[2222] Hou Ch'u's 后處 agnomen was Tzu-li 子里.
Ch'in Jan's 秦冉 *agnomen* was K'ai 開.
Kung-hsia Shou's 公夏首 *agnomen* was Ch'eng 乘.
Hsi-jung Chen's 奚容箴 *agnomen* was Tzu-hsi 子皙.

[114] *K'ung-tzu chia-yü* (9:3b, *SPPY*) says he was from Wey. See also Wang Li-ch'i, *Jen-piao*, p. 303-4.

Kung-chien Ting's 公肩定 *agnomen* was Tzu-chung 子中.

Yen Tzu's 顏祖 *agnomen* was Hsiang 襄.

[2223] Ch'iao Shan's 鄡單 *agnomen* was Tzu-chia 子家.

Kou Ching-chiang 句井疆.

Han-fu Hei's 罕父黑 *agnomen* was Tzu-so 子索.

Ch'in Shang's 秦商 *agnomen* was Tzu-p'i 子丕.

Shen Tang's 申黨 *agnomen* was Chou 周.

Yen Chih-p'u's 顏之僕 *agnomen* was Shu 叔.

Jung Ch'i's 榮旂 *agnomen* was Tzu-ch'i 子祈.

[2224] Hsien Ch'eng's 縣成 *agnomen* was Tzu-ch'i 子祺.

Tso-jen Ying's 左人郢 *agnomen* was Hsing 行.

Yen Chi's 燕伋 *agnomen* was Ssu 思.

Cheng Kuo's 鄭國 *agnomen* was Tzu-hsi 子徒.

Ch'in Fei's 秦非 *agnomen* was Tzu-chih 子之.

Shih Chih-ch'ang's 施之常 *agnomen* was Tzu-heng 子恆.

Yen K'uai's 顏噲 *agnomen* was Tzu-sheng 子聲.

Pu-shu Ch'eng's 步叔乘 *agnomen* was Tzu-ch'e 子車.

[2225] Yüan K'ang-chi 原亢籍.

Yüeh K'ai's 樂欬 *agnomen* was Tzu-sheng 子聲.

Lien Hsieh's 廉絜 *agnomen* was Yung 庸.

Shu Chung-hui's 叔仲會 *agnomen* was Tzu-ch'i 子期.

Yen Ho's 顏何 *agnomen* was Jan 冉.

Ti Hei's 狄黑 *agnomen* was Hsi 皙.

Pang Hsün's 邦巽 *agnomen* was Tzu-lien 子斂.

[2226] K'ung Chung 孔忠.

Kung-hsi Yü-ju's 公西輿如 *agnomen* was Tzu-shang 子上.

Kung-hsi Chen's 公西蒧 *agnomen* was Tzu-shang 子上.

His Honor the Grand Scribe says: "Scholars often speak of the seventy disciples. Those who praise them have probably exaggerated the facts, while those who criticize them have probably stretched the truth. When I weigh one against the other, I find that they chose their words without having seen their subjects. The *Ti-tzu chi* 弟子籍 (Register of Disciples) came from the ancient writings of Confucius's household; it is close to the truth. I took the names of the disciples, then gathered all the records concerning them from among the questions posed by the disciples in the *Analects* and arranged the information in one chapter. I have left out the dubious."

TRANSLATORS' NOTE

The position this chapter occupies in the *Shih chi* is interesting. One reason it appears here, rather than before or after Chapter 63, on Taoist-Legalist philosophers, is the connection between Tzu-kung and the wars involving Wu, Yüeh and Ch'u. This is also the connecting thread of the previous two chapters; Chapter 65, for instance, begins with Sun Tzu, one of the generals commanding Wu's attack on Ch'u, and Chapter 66 is devoted primarily to Wu Tzu Hsü, one of the chief participants in these wars. Although the long story in this chapter on Tzu-kung's mission to Ch'i, Wu, Yüeh, and Chin is historically dubious, as we have pointed out in the footnotes to the translation, its inclusion seems to be one of the best reasons for explaining the sequence of chapters Ssu-ma Ch'ien has chosen here. In addition, the inclusion of this story may also shed light on why this chapter is followed by three more devoted to the great persuaders Kung-sun Yang, Su Ch'in and Chang Yi. Ssu-ma Ch'ien seems to be implying something very interesting about the origins of this class of traveling rhetoricians, successors, in his view, to a tradition that originated with Confucius's disciples.

There are a number of specialized studies of this chapter in Chinese. We list only selected and significant works in the bibliography below. There are, however, no English translations or studies (except for a translation of Ssu-ma Ch'ien's comments at the end of the chapter, in Burton Watson's *Ssu-ma Ch'ien, the Grand Historian of China* [New York: Columbia University Press, 1958], p. 190). The "Prolegomena" to James Legge's translation of the *Analects* contains a study of 86 people traditionally believed to be Confucius' disciples (see Legge, 1:112-27). D. C. Lau's translation of the *Analects* also has an appendix on "The Disciples as They Appear in the *Analects*" (Lau, *Analects*, pp. 197-219).

BIBLIOGRAPHY

I. Translations

Mizusawa Toshitada 水澤利忠. *Shiki* 史記. V. 8. *Retsuden (ichi)* 列傳 (一). Tokyo: Meiji Shoten, 1990, pp. 145-195.

Ōgawa Tamaki 小川環樹, trans. *Shiki retsuden* 史記列傳. Rpt. Tokyo: Chikuma Shobō, 1986 (1969), 31-42.

Plath, H. *Confucius und seiner Schüler, Leben und Lehre,* v. III, "Die Schüler des Confucius" (Munich, 1873), pp. 1-98. Not seen.

Watson, Burton. *Ssu-ma Ch'ien: Grand Historian of China.* New York: Columbia University Press, 1958, p. 190 [The Grand Scribe's Comments only].

II. Studies

Ch'ien Mu 錢穆. "K'ung-tzu Ti-tzu t'ung-k'ao" 孔子弟子通考, *Hsien Ch'in chu-tzu hsi-nien* 先秦諸子繫年. 2v. Rpt. Peking: Chung-hua Shu-chü, 1985, v. 1, pp. 60-83.

Su Chen-shen 蘇振申. "*Shih chi* 'Chung-ni Ti-tzu lieh-chuan' shu-cheng" 史記仲尼弟子列傳 疏證. M.A. Thesis, China Culture College (Taiwan), 1964.

Takahashi Hitoshi 高橋均. "'Chūji Teishi retsuden' ni tsuite" 仲尼弟子について, *Tōkyō Kyōiku Daigaku Bungakubu kiyō--Kokubungaku kambungaku ronsō* 東京教育大學文學部紀 --要國文學漢文學論集, 77(1970), 79-116.

The Lord of Shang, Memoir 8

[68:2227] The Lord of Shang 商[1] was a scion[2] of the ducal family of Wey 衛[3] by a concubine. His *praenomen* was Yang 鞅 and his *cognomen* Kung-sun 公孫; his ancestors originally had the *cognomen* Chi 姬. Since youth, Yang had loved the study of "dispositions and designations."[4] He served the Prime Minister of Wei 魏, Kung-shu Tso 公叔座, as Counselor of the Palace.[5] Kung-shu Tso knew his worth, but had not recommended him when Tso happened to fall ill. King Hui 惠 of Wei (r. *370-335 B.C.) went in person to inquire after his illness.

"If your illness, Kung-shu, takes a turn for the worse, what should be done for our altars of soil and grain?"[6]

Kung-shu said, "My Household Headmaster, Kung-sun Yang, though young in years, has remarkable talent; I would hope Your Majesty might present him with [affairs of] state and heed [his advice]."

The King was silent. When the King was about to leave, Tso dismissed his attendants and spoke: "If Your Majesty will not heed [me] and employ Yang, you must kill him; do not allow him to pass the border."

The King gave his word and left. Kung-shu Tso summoned Yang and apologized. "Today His Majesty asked who could serve as Prime Minister and I mentioned you, but His Majesty, from his expression, was going to refuse me. I then put lord before vassal and thus told His Majesty that if he did not employ you, Yang, he should kill you. His Majesty gave me his word. You can fly quickly, or you will soon be taken."

Yang said, "If this king could not take My Lord's advice to appoint me, how could he take My Lord's advice to kill me?" In the end, he did not leave.

After King Hui left, he told his attendants, "Kung-shu's illness is grave indeed. How sad! He wanted Us to heed Kung-sun Yang in [affairs of] state. Isn't that perverse?"[7]

[2228] After Kung-shu Tso died, Kung-sun Yang heard that Duke Hsiao 孝 of Ch'in (r. 361-338 B.C.) had issued an order to seek worthy people throughout his state, and that he intended to renew the enterprises of Duke Mu 繆 (r. 659-621 B.C.), and to recover Ch'in's captured lands in the east.[8] [Yang] promptly entered Ch'in in the west and sought an audience with Duke Hsiao through the offices of the duke's trusted vassal Ching Chien 景監.[9]

[1] Ch'ien Mu (*Chu-tzu*, pp. 53 and 617) gives his dates as *c.* 390-338 B.C.. Yang K'uan 楊寬 (*Shang Yang pien fa* 商鞅變法 [Shanghai: Shanghai Jen-min Ch'u-pan-she, 1955], pp. 21-2, n. 1) also believes that Kung-sun Yang was born around 390 B.C. (see also Li Yu-ning, ed. *Shang Yang's Reforms and State Control in China* [New York: M.E. Sharpe, 1977], p. 3 [this is an English translation of the 1973 edition of Yang K'uan's book with a long introduction by the editor and some useful appendices] and Kao Heng 高亨, *Shang-chün shu chu-shih* 商君書注釋 [Peking: Chung-hua, 1974], pp. 195-230).

[2] The phrase *chu-shu nieh-kung-tzu* 諸庶孽公子 is very odd. Wang Nien-sun (4:8b-9a) demonstrates that *nieh-tzu* 孽子 and *kung-tzu* 公子 are virtually synonymous and thus suggests that *kung-tzu* is an interpolation.

[3] Wey was a small kingdom located near modern Ch'i-hsien 淇縣 in northeast Honan (T'an Ch'i-hsiang, 1:17-8). King Wu of Chou first enfeoffed his younger brother K'ang-shu 康叔 there. It became a protectorate of Wei in the fourth century B.C. (see *Shih chi*, 37:1589-1605).

[4] *Hsing-ming* 刑名 was a branch of the Legalist school of philosophy; see n. 31 to our translation of *Shih chi* Chapter 63.

[5] *Chung shu-tzu* 中庶子.

[6] *She* 社 was the temple of the spirit of land and *chi* 稷 was the temple of the spirit of grains; the term *she-chi* was often used to refer *pars pro toto* to the state.

[7] A simpler version of this story is found in *Chan-kuo ts'e* (7:6a, *SPTK*) and *Lü-shih ch'un-ch'iu* (11:10a, *SPPY*).

Duke Hsiao having granted Wey Yang [i.e., the Lord of Shang] an audience, [Wey Yang] discoursed on matters at great length. Duke Hsiao frequently nodded off, and paid him no heed. [The audience] ended and Duke Hsiao was angry with Ching Chien. "Your retainer is just a fool, sir. What makes him worth employing?"

Ching Chien rebuked Wey Yang. Wey Yang said, "I advised the Duke on the way of an emperor, but his mind was closed and he did not understand." After five days, [Ching Chien] again sought to present Yang.

Yang was granted another audience with Duke Hsiao. He tried even harder, but still did not strike [Duke Hsiao's] fancy. The audience ended and Duke Hsiao once more rebuked Ching Chien.

Ching Chien in turn rebuked Yang. Yang said, "I advised the Duke on the way of a king, but he has not yet accepted it. Please seek to present me again."

Yang was granted another audience with Duke Hsiao. Duke Hsiao considered him good but still did not employ him. [The audience] ended and [Yang] left. Duke Hsiao said to Ching Chien, "Your retainer is good; I can talk with him now."

Yang said, "I advised the Duke on the way of a hegemon, and he wished to make use of it. If you could just present me again, I know [his interest] now."

Wey Yang was granted another audience with Duke Hsiao. The Duke talked with him, unconsciously moving forward till his knees were off his mat. They talked for several days without tiring.

Ching Chien said, "How did you strike My Lord's fancy? My Lord is happy indeed!"

Yang said, "I advised His Lordship on the ways of emperors and kings comparable to those of the Three Dynasties [Hsia, Yin and Chou]. His Lordship said, 'These take too long. I cannot wait. Moreover, worthy rulers all spread their fame across the world within their own lifetime. How could I bear to stew for decades or a hundred years waiting to become an Emperor or King?' I therefore advised His Lordship on the ways of strengthening the state and that is all it is that has pleased him so much. But it will be hard [for him] to compare in virtue with Yin and Chou."

[2229] Duke Hsiao having employed Wey Yang, Wey Yang wanted to change the laws, but [Duke Hsiao] feared that the world would censure him.

Wey Yang said,[10] "Indecision in one's actions will win no fame, indecision in one's enterprises will win no merit. Moreover, those whose actions are above the level of others are naturally abused by their age; those whose considerations are unique in their wisdom are sure to be despised by the common folk. The simple are blind to a task's successful conclusion, while the wise see it before it has begun. One cannot consider how to begin with the common people, one can only enjoy results with them. One who talks of the highest virtue will not be in accord with the vulgar, one who achieves great merit will not plan with the multitude.[11]

---

[8] For Duke Hsiao's order, see *Shih chi,* 5:202. Duke Mu had once gained control of the part of Ho-hsi 河西 region (west of the Yellow River in eastern Shensi (T'an Ch'i-hsiang, 1: 35-6) belonging to Chin, which Chin recovered after Duke Mu's death (*Shih chi,* 5:189).

[9] Many scholars interpret *chien* 監 in the sense of *t'ai-chien* 太監 or "eunuch." This is perhaps because in Ssu-ma Ch'ien's famous "Pao Jen An shu" 報任安書 (Letter Replying to Jen An; *Han shu,* 62:2727), he lists a number of incidents in which eunuchs were involved, among which is Wey Yang's success in gaining audience with King Hui through Ching Chien. However, J.J.L. Duyvendak, following "So-yin," thinks that Ching Chien was a member of a branch of the ruling house of Ch'u, apparently taking *chien* as his *praenomen* or *agnomen* (see Duyvendak, *The Book of Lord Shang* [London: Probsthain and Co., 1928], p. 11, n. 1).

[10] This debate took place in 359 B.C. (see *Shih chi,* 5:203). There is a parallel text of this debate in *Shang-chün shu* 商君書 (1:1a, *SPPY*).

[11] In *Shang-chün shu,* this saying (beginning "With the people . . .") is ascribed to Kuo Yen 郭偃, who served

Thus, if it might strengthen a state, the sage will not follow its precedents; if it might benefit the people, he will not observe their social norms."

"Well put!" said Duke Hsiao.

Kan Lung 甘龍 said, "Not so. A sage will teach without altering the people; a wise man will rule without changing the laws. Adapt to the people in teaching them, and success comes without labor. Follow the laws in ruling, and the functionaries will be well versed while the common people will take comfort."

Wey Yang said, "What Lung has just said are the words of the vulgar. The common folk take comfort from precedent and custom, while the scholars are obsessed with what they have learned. One may fill offices and guard the laws with both of these, but they are not the ones with whom to discuss matters beyond the law. The [founders of the] Three Dynasties differed in their rites but became kings; the Five Hegemons[12] differed in their laws but won hegemony. The wise make laws and the simple are bound by them; the worthy change the social norms and the inferior are restrained by them."

Tu Chih 杜摯 said, "If the profit is not a hundredfold, one does not change the law; if the merit is not tenfold, one does does not change the [sacrificial] vessels. There is no error in following precedents; there is no evil in observing social norms."

Wey Yang said, "In ruling an age there is no one way, and in benefiting the state one does not ... 'ang 湯 [of Yin] and Wu 武 [of Chou] did not observe precede... Hsia 夏 and Yin 殷 did not alter social norms yet perished.[13] ... e condemned, and observing social practice is not worth praising.

"... He made Wey Yang Left Chief of Staff[14] and eventually decided o...

[22... nces, [he ordered that] the common people be put in groups of ... each member of the group guiding and watching the others and ...s' crimes. Whoever failed to report a criminal would be cut in h... ...rted a criminal would be granted the same reward as for beheadi... ...d a criminal would be given the same punishment as for surrende...

Com... ...males in their families who did not divide their household would have their military tax doubled. Whoever won military merit would be awarded higher rank according to his accomplishments, whoever engaged in a private feud would receive punishment according to its gravity.[15] Families, young and old, who labored at the fundamental professions, tilling and weaving, and produced much grain and silk, would be exempted from the corvée. Whoever engaged in secondary profit-making and whoever was poor because of laziness would be taken as government slaves.[16] Members of the royal family who did not win

Duke Wen 文 of Chin (r. 636-628 B.C.).

[12] Generally referring to Duke Huan 桓 of Ch'i (r. 685-643 B.C.), Duke Wen 文 of Chin (r. 636-628 B.C.), Duke Mu 穆 of Ch'in (r. 659-621 B.C.), King Chuang 莊 of Ch'u (r. 613-591 B.C.), and Duke Hsiang 襄 of Sung (r. 650-637 B.C.--see Wang Li-ch'i, 68:1690n.). On the variations in this grouping see Sydney Rosen, "Changing Conceptions of the Hegemon in Pre-Ch'in China," in *Ancient China*, pp. 99-114 and n. 375 to our translation of *Shih chi* Chapter 6 above.

[13] In *Shang-chün shu*, Wey Yang also draws examples from the Five Sage Emperors as well as King Wen and King Wu of the Chou dynasty here.

On kings T'ang and Wu, see our translations of *Shih chi* Chapters 3 and 4 above.

[14] *Tso Shu-chang* 左庶長.

[15] We follow Wang Shu-min (68:2173) in excising *shang* 上 "higher" here.

[16] The translations of Duyvendak (p. 15) and Wang Li-ch'i (68:1691) are almost the same as ours.

military merit would be punished by not entering them in the royal family's clan-register.[17] Positions, titles, and ranks were clarified according to social status; land and houses, male and female slaves and clothing were held according to family status. Those who won merit gained honor and prominence; those who did not win merit, even the wealthy, were denied any place to display [their wealth].

[2231] The ordinances having been drafted, they were still not issued. [Yang] feared that the people would not trust him.[18] He erected a three-*chang* pole at the south gate of the capital's market and advertised for men able to move [the pole] and set it up at the north gate. He offered ten *chin*. The commoners wondered at it, and no one dared move it.

Once more [Yang] said, "Fifty *chin* to the one who can move it."

A man moved it, and [Yang] immediately gave him fifty *chin* to show that he was not deceiving them. Finally, he issued the ordinances.[19]

When the ordinances had been in effect among the commoners for a year, the commoners of Ch'in who came to the capital to speak of the disadvantages of this first [set of] ordinances numbered in the thousands.

At this point, the Heir[20] violated the law. Wey Yang said, "That the laws have not taken effect is because the sovereign violates them." He decided to handle the Heir according to the law. The Heir was the lord's successor; he could not be mutilated. Instead, he mutilated [the Heir's] tutor, Noble Scion Ch'ien 虔, and tattooed his preceptor, Noble Scion Chia 賈. The next day, the men of Ch'in all hastened [to obey] the ordinances. After [the ordinances] had been in effect for ten years,[21] the commoners of Ch'in were delighted; no one picked up articles lost on the road,[22] there were no bandits or thieves in the mountains, households were well provided for and the people were well off. The commoners were brave in the duke's battles but cowardly in private feuds and the townships and cities were in good order. Some of the Ch'in commoners who had spoken of the disadvantages of the ordinances in the beginning now came to speak of the advantages of the ordinances. Wey Yang said, "These are all disturbers of the peace." He transported them all to border-towns. After this, none of the people dared to discuss the ordinances.

[2232] After this, [Duke Hsiao] made Yang a Grand Excellent Achiever.[23] He commanded troops in a siege of Wei's An-yi 安邑[24] and caused it to surrender (352 B.C).

Vandermeersch (p. 29) suggests that Kung-sun Yang's measure was applied only to merchants who were excessive in profit-making (l'abuse des benefices) and points out that neither the *Shang-chün shu* nor *Han Fei Tzu* (which also contains some records on Kung-sun Yang) lend support to Duyvendak's interpretation. His own translation differs little from that of Duyvendak.

[17] Vandermeersch observes that such a measure practically brought an end to hereditary privileges (see Vandermeersch, p. 29, n. 3).

[18] Chung-hua edition reads *yi* 巳 here. Most early editions read *ssu* 巳 which was often confused with both *yi* and *chi* 己 (the latter is our reading).

[19] There is a similar anecdote concerning Wu Ch'i 吳起 in *Lü-shih ch'un-ch'iu* (26:10a, *SPPY*). Kimura Eiichi 木村英一 speculates that Ssu-ma Ch'ien's account is copied from *Lü-shih ch'un-ch'iu*, substituting Shang Yang for Wu Ch'i (see Kimura, *Hōka shisō no kenkyū* 法家思想の研究 [Tokyo: Kōbundō, 1944], p. 48). This similarity of the two stories, Vandermeersch points out, seems to support the hypothesis that Wu Ch'i might have been an important influence on Kung-sun Yang (see Vandermeersch, pp. 24-5, and 30 and Ch'ien Mu, *Chu-tzu*, p. 227).

[20] Later King Hui-wen 惠文 of Ch'in (see our translation of *Shih chi*, 68:2236 below).

[21] Both Takigawa (68:10) and Wang Shu-min (68:2175) believe that "ten" (*shih* 十) is an error for "seven" (*ch'i* 七).

[22] As Duyvendak points out, the same phrase has also been used to describe the result of Confucius' administration of Lu (see Duyvendak, *The Book of Lord Shang*, p. 16, n., and *Shih chi*, 47:1917).

[23] *Ta Liang-tsao* 大良造.

After three years (350 B.C.),[25] he constructed "promulgation towers"[26] and palaces at Hsien-yang 咸陽 and Ch'in moved its capital there from Yung 雍.[27] Ordinances prohibited fathers and sons or elder and younger brothers from living under one roof. Small townships and cities were grouped into counties and prefects and assistants were appointed. There were thirty-one counties in all. [Wey Yang] marked out fields, removed the raised paths and boundary balks in the fields,[28] and the taxes[29] were levied equally. He also standardized the *tou* and *t'ung* measures, the balance measures, and the *chang* and *ch'ih* measures.[30]

[These measures] had been in effect for four years (347 B.C.) when Noble Scion Ch'ien again violated the regulations and his nose was cut off.

After five years had passed, the people of Ch'in were wealthy and powerful. The Son of Heaven presented sacrificial meat[31] to Duke Hsiao (343 B.C.). The feudal lords all offered their congratulations (342 B.C).

The next year (341 B.C.), Ch'i defeated Wei's troops at Ma-ling 馬陵, captured his Heir Shen 申, and killed his general P'ang Chüan 龐涓.[32]

The next year (340 B.C.), Wey Yang advised Duke Hsiao: "Ch'in and Wei can be compared to a man with a disease of the stomach and heart; if it is not Wei that annexes Ch'in,

[24] An-yi (about 5 miles northwest of modern Hsia-hsien 夏縣, Shantung, T'an Ch'i-hsiang, 1:36-7) was the capital of Wei until King Hui moved it to Ta Liang. Liang Yü-sheng (29:1240), Takigawa (68:11) and Wang Shu-min (68:2175-6) all agree that An-yi is a mistake for Ku-ling 固陵 (northwest of modern Huai-yang 淮陽, Honan [Ch'ien Ming, *Ti-ming k'ao*, p. 535]). But this seems unlikely since Ssu-ma Ch'ien makes clear elsewhere his belief that An-yi fell in 352 B.C. (*Shih chi*, 15:722) and Ku-ling in 351 B.C. (*Shih chi*, 15:723). Nevertheless, Ssu-ma Ch'ien does have Wey Yang speaking just five paragraphs below in 340 B.C. about Wei's "capital . . . at An-yi." We suggest, however, that this speech should have been placed in 352 B.C., after the battle at Kuei-ling (353 B.C.) instead of after the battle at Ma-ling (341 B.C.). See also n. 13 to our translation of *Shih chi* Chapter 65 above.

[25] The dating of this event (and later ones in this chapter) is taken from *Shih chi* Chapter 15. As the reader will notice, the number of years that elapsed between these events does not correspond with the dates in Chapter 15--they are regularly off by one year. This occurs in Chapter 66 as well. See the Translators' Note to Chapter 66 for a further discussion.

[26] "So-yin" observes that *chi-ch'üeh* 冀闕, also called *wei-ch'üeh* 魏闕, were high structures from which court orders were announced (see also n. 233 to our translation of *Shih chi* Chapter 5 above).

[27] Hsien-yang was about 15 miles northwest of modern Sian, Shensi (T'an Ch'i-hsiang, 1:43-4; see also Ch'ien Mu, *Ti-ming k'ao*, pp. 605-6). Yung was located just south of modern Feng-hsiang 鳳翔, Shensi (see T'an Ch'i-hsiang, 1:43-4).

[28] The usual interpretation of *ch'ien* 阡 and *mo* 陌 is that *ch'ien* are paths running from north to south while *mo* run from east to west. Vandermeersch (p. 33), however, suggests that *mo* are plots of land of one-hundred *mu* 畝 and *ch'ien* those of one-thousand *mu*. Ochi Shigeake's 越智重明, using bamboo slips excavated from a tomb of the Warring States period, argues similarly that *ch'ien* and *mo* were plots of land opened in outlying districts to be used as rewards (see Ochi Shigeake, *Sengoku Shin Kan shi kenkyū* 戰國秦漢史研究 [Tokyo: Chūgoku Shoten, 1988], pp. 431-46). See also n. 241 to our translation of *Shih chi* Chapter 5 above.

[29] Miyazaki Ichisada 宮崎市定 has argued that the revenues of *fu* were for military expenses while taxes from *shui* were for the use of the Court and the civil service (see his "Chung-kuo ku-tai fu shui chih-tu lun" 中國古代賦稅論 in Tu Cheng-sheng 杜鄭勝, ed., *Chung-kuo shang-ku shih lun-wen hsüan-chi* 中國上古 史論文選集, v. 2, (Taipei: Hua-shih Ch'u-pan-she, 1979), pp. 749-95; *fu-shui* could also be understood as a general term for taxes.

[30] Measures of volume, weight and length respectively (see also "Weights and Measures" in the front-matter).

[31] Liang Yü-sheng (29:1240) and Wang Shu-min (68:2177) propose that *chih tso* 致胙 (granted some sacrificial meat) should read *chih Po* 致伯 (granted the title of *Po*, or Earl). Duyvendak observes that "The sending of the sacrificial meat, which came from the sacrifices to King Wen and King Wu, was the solemn confirmation of this dignity [of bearing the title *po*]" (*The Book of Lord Shang*, p. 19, note 3). However, *Shih chi* records elsewhere the granting of sacrificial meat to someone long before the title of *Po* was conferred upon them (see *Shih chi*, 4:160 and 5:203).

[32] See *Shih chi* Chapter 65 for a more detailed account of these events.

it will be Ch'in that annexes Wei. Why is this so? Wei lies to the west of the dangerous ranges, its capital is at An-yi, it borders Ch'in along the Ho [River], but it monopolizes the profits from the East of the Mount. When Wei has the advantage, it will invade Ch'in in the west, and when exhausted, it will guard its land in the east. Now our state has prospered by relying on My Lord's virtue and sagacity, but Wei was crushed by Ch'i last year and the feudal lords have abandoned him. [Ch'in] can take advantage of this opportunity to attack Wei. When Wei is unable to withstand Ch'in, it is sure to move east. When it moves east, Ch'in will seize the fastnesses of the Ho and the mountains; facing east, it will control the feudal lords. This is a task for an emperor and king."

Duke Hsiao agreed and sent Wey Yang to command the attack against Wei. Wei sent Noble Scion Ang 卬 to command its counterattack [against Yang]. The two armies having confronted each other, Wey Yang dispatched a letter to the Wei commander, Noble Scion Ang.

"The Scion and I were on friendly terms before; now we are the commanders of our two states. I cannot bear to attack you; if I could meet face to face with you, Noble Scion, make a covenant, have a pleasant drink and [*2233*] withdraw our troops, we might thus bring peace to Ch'in and Wei."

Wei's Noble Scion Ang agreed. The meeting and covenant were concluded and they drank, but Wey Yang had concealed armored knights, and ambushed Wei's Noble Scion Ang, taking him prisoner. He then attacked his army, crushed it, and returned to Ch'in. King Hui of Wei's troops having been defeated several times by Ch'i and Ch'in, his state exhausted and [his territory] reduced from day to day, he was afraid. He sent a messenger to Ch'in, ceded the territory of Ho-hsi,[33] and made peace by presenting it to Ch'in. Wei thus abandoned An-yi and moved its capital to Ta Liang.[34] King Hui of Liang[35] said, "We regret that We did not take Kung-shu Tso's advice."

Wey Yang having returned after defeating Wei, Ch'in enfeoffed him with fifteen towns at Wu 於 and Shang 商;[36] his title was Lord of Shang.

The Lord of Shang was Prime Minister of Ch'in for ten years and many members of the royal family and nobility by marriage harbored rancor against him. Chao Liang 趙良 was granted an audience with the Lord of Shang.

The Lord of Shang said, "My meeting with you has come about through Meng Lan-kao 孟蘭皋. I ask permission to become your confidant; is this possible?"

Chao Liang said, "Your servant dares not hope for this. As Confucius said, 'Put forward men of worth and the man fit to revere will advance; gather men without worth and the man fit to be king will retreat.' Your servant is without worth; thus he does not dare to accept this command. Your servant has heard that, 'To occupy a position which is not rightfully his, this is coveting position; to win a name which is not rightfully his, this is coveting fame.' If your servant were to heed your lordship, he would fear to covet position and to covet fame. Thus, he dares not heed your lordship's command."

The Lord of Shang said, "Are you displeased with my government of Ch'in, sir?"

---

[33] Liang Yü-sheng points out that King Hui of Wei did not cede Ho-hsi until some time later (29:1240). Wang Shu-min (68:2178), however, argues that Wei ceded part of the region at this time and the rest later.

[34] For a discussion of the date Wei moved its capital to Ta Liang, see n. 24 above and n. 13 to our translation of *Shih chi* Chapter 65.

[35] I.e., King Hui of Wei. He was called the King of Liang after he moved the capital to Ta Liang.

[36] Both Wu and Shang were located about 25 miles southeast of modern Shang-hsien 商縣, Shensi (see T'an Ch'i-hsiang, 1:43-4).

Chao Liang said, "To turn listening inward is what is meant by keen-eared; to gaze within is what is meant by sharp-eyed; to control oneself is what is meant by able-bodied." As Shun of Yeu said, 'One who lowers himself is elevated.' It would be better for your lordship to [*2234*] follow the way of Shun of Yeu; do not inquire from your slave."

The Lord of Shang said, "In the beginning the people of Ch'in practiced the customs of Jung 戎 and Ti 翟.[37] There was no distinction between father and son; they shared the same room. Now I have changed their customs and made distinctions between their men and women; I have built order promulgation towers on a grand scale, constructed like those of Lu and Wey. In observing my government of Ch'in, sir, how does it compare in worth with that of the Five-Rams Grand Master?"[38]

Chao Liang said, "The skins of a thousand sheep are not as good as a single fox's white fur; the 'yes, yes' of a thousand men is not as good as a single knight's 'no, no.'[39] King Wu 武 [of Chou] prospered through 'no, no,' while Chow 紂 of Yin perished through 'mm, mm.'[40] If Your Lordship does not find fault with King Wu, I ask permission to speak directly all day without punishment; may I do so?"

The Lord of Shang said, "As the saying has it, 'superficial words are flowery, sincere words fruitful; bitter words are medicine, sweet words sickness. If you are indeed willing to speak directly all day long, sir, it will be my medicine. I am prepared to serve you [as your disciple] sir; why then do you decline it?"

Chao Liang said, "The Five-Rams Grand Master was a country rustic from Ching 荆.[41] When he heard that Duke Mu of Ch'in was worthy, he yearned to gaze upon him. He set out but had no traveling expenses, sold himself to a traveler from Ch'in, dressed in coarse cloth, and fed oxen. After a year, Duke Mu learned of this, lifted him from beneath the mouths of oxen and placed him above the families of the hundred cognomens. No one in Ch'in dared to bear him ill will. After serving as Ch'in's Prime Minister for six or seven years, he attacked Cheng in the east (627 B.C.),[42] established a lord for the state of Chin three times,[43] and once saved [Chin] from disaster at the hands of Ching.[44] He promulgated his instructions within the state, and the men of Pa 巴[45] offered tribute; his virtue reached to the feudal lords, and the eight Jung came to submit. When Yu Yü 由余[46] heard of it, he knocked at the pass to seek

[37] Ti, also written 狄, and Jung were terms referring to "barbarian" tribes living in the north and west of the Chinese states (see also n. 10 to our translation of *Shih chi* Chapter 4 above).

[38] *Wu-ku Tai-fu* 五羖大夫 refers to Pai-li Hsi 百里奚. Chao Liang's account given below differ substantially from the story as recounted on *Shih chi*, 5:186. See also Melvin P. Thatcher, "The Case of the Five Skeepskins Grandee," *JAOS*, 108(1988), 27-49.

[39] This saying seems to be proverbial (cf. *Shih chi*, 43:1792, and *Han-shih wai-chuan* 韓詩外傳, 7:6b, *SPTK*, for example). On white fox-fur see n. 28 to our translation of *Shih chi* Chapter 75 below.

[40] In *Han-shih wai-chuan (op. cit.)*, this sentence is ascribed to Chao Chien-tzu. However, *Shuo-yüan* 說苑 puts it into the mouth of Confucius (9:13b, *SPPY*).

[41] The older place-name Ching is sometimes used to refer to the state of Ch'u, particularly in Ch'in-dynasty documents. It is claimed that this is because of the name-taboo of the First Emperor of Ch'in's grandfather.

[42] This battle ended in Ch'in's defeat. Pai-li Hsi actually advised against this war (see *Shih chi*, 5:190-1).

[43] The three Chin rulers that Ch'in helped put on the throne were Duke Hui 惠 (r. 650-638 B.C.), Duke Huai 懷 (r. 637 B.C.), and Duke Wen 文 (r. 636-628 B.C., see *Shih chi*, 5:187-9).

[44] The reference is to the Battle of Ch'eng-p'u 城濮 (632 B.C.) in which Ch'in helped Chin to resist Ch'u's attempt to occupy Sung 宋 (see *Shih chi*, 14:596 and 39:1664-5).

[45] The eastern part of modern Szechuan province (see T'an Ch'i-hsiang, 1:43-4).

[46] Yu Yü was a descendant of a Chin citizen who had fled to the Jung. When the chieftain of the Jung heard of Duke Mu's good government, he sent Yu Yü to Ch'in to observe. Impressed by Yu Yü, Duke Mu succeeded in making the Jung chieftain suspicious of Yu Yü, who eventually joined the administration of Ch'in. As a result, Ch'in finally defeated the Jung (see *Shih chi*, 5:192-3).

audience. As Prime Minister of Ch'in, the Five-Rams Grand Master did not sit in his carriage when tired,[47] did not put up his canopy when hot; when driving about the capital, he had no entourage of carriages, and no guards armed with buckler and bill. His merit and fame are stored in the archives and his virtue and actions will reach to future generations. When the Five-Rams Grand Master died, the men and women of the state of Ch'in shed tears, the children stopped singing songs, and the grain-pounders ceased pounding rhythm for each other with their pestles. Such was the virtue of the Five-Rams Grand Master. Now when Your Lordship gained an audience with the King of Ch'in, it was through his favorite Ching Chien, who you took as patron[48]; this is not how fame is won. After you became Prime Minister of Ch'in, you did not concern yourself with the families of the hundred cognomens, but constructed promulgation towers on a grand scale; this is not how merit is earned. You inflicted mutilation and tattooing on the Heir's mentor and preceptor, and crippled and wounded the commoners with savage punishments; this is accumulating resentment and storing up calamities. Moral instructions' influence on commoners is more profound than decrees, and the commoners imitation of their superiors is swifter than ordinances. Now in addition, you establish [yourself] by improper means, My Lord, and change orders as soon as they come out; this is not how instruction is given. Furthermore, you face south and call yourself the lonely one,[49] My Lord, daily binding the Noble Scions of Ch'in. The *Odes* says,

> Look at the rat--it has limbs;
> Yet this man does not have propriety.
> Yet this man does not have propriety,
> Why does he not die quickly?[50]

Judging from the ode, this is not how a long life is secured. The Noble Scion Ch'ien has barred his door and refused to go out for eight years now. [*2235*] Since then, My Lord, has killed Chu Huan 枳懽 and tattooed Noble Scion Chia. The *Odes* says,

> One who wins over the people prospers,
> One who loses the people falls.[51]

These several actions are not how the people are won over. When you go out, My Lord, you are accompanied by more than ten chariots; each chariot accompanying you carries armored soldiers; those who are strongest and toughest[52] are your outriders, those bearing spears and wielding pole-hammers flank your chariot and sally forth. If you lack just one of these, My Lord, you cannot go out. The *Documents* says,

> One who relies on virtue prospers,
> One who relies on force perishes.[53]

---

[47] *An-ch'e* 安車, "rest carriages," had seats and canopies. They were normally reserved for elderly riders.

[48] See n. 9 above.

[49] Facing south means to become a ruler. The original for "become a lonely one" is *ch'eng kua jen* 稱寡人 (literally, "calling oneself 'I, the lonely one'"), *kua-jen* (the lonely one) the form by which a ruler referred to himself.

[50] See *Book of Odes*, Mao, #52, Legge, 4:84.

[51] These lines are not found in the extant text of the *Book of Odes*.

[52] Literally, "[men with] ribs joined together."

[53] Wang Li-ch'i (68:1694) believes that these lines are from a lost chapter of the *Shang-shu* (Book of Documents).

My Lord is as insecure as the morning dew; do you still hope to extend your years and prolong your life? Then why not return your fifteen towns, tend gardens in the suburbs, and advise the King of Ch'in to exalt the men of cliffs and caves, nourish the aged, preserve the orphaned, respect his elders, rank the meritorious, and honor the virtuous; thus you may gain some peace. If My Lord covets the wealth of Shang and Wu, plays along with the state of Ch'in's policies, and stores up the resentment of the families of the hundred cognomens, once the King of Ch'in deserts his guests and stands no more in court, it will not be on just one or two charges that the state of Ch'in arrests you, My Lord. One can await your fall standing on one foot."[54]

The Lord of Shang did not heed his advice.

[2236] Five months later (338 B.C.), Duke Hsiao of Ch'in expired and his Heir was enthroned.[55] The Noble Scion Ch'ien's followers accused the Lord of Shang of intending to rebel, and [the duke] dispatched functionaries to arrest the Lord of Shang. The Lord of Shang fled to the foot of the Pass. He sought to lodge in the traveler's lodge. The owner of the traveler's lodge did not know he was the Lord of Shang: "According to the laws of the Lord of Shang, one who puts up a person without identification will be prosecuted for it."

The Lord of Shang heaved a sigh and said, "Alas, [*2237*] that the disadvantages of making laws should come to this!"

He left for Wei. The men of Wei resented his treachery against the Noble Scion Ang and his defeat of the forces of Wei; they refused to accept him. The Lord of Shang prepared to go to another state. The men of Wei said, "The Lord of Shang is a criminal of Ch'in. Ch'in is mighty; to fail to return their criminal when he enters Wei will not do." They then had him enter Ch'in.

Having reentered Ch'in, the Lord of Shang fled to his manor of Shang, and together with his followers and subordinates, dispatched the manor's troops to attack Cheng 鄭 [County][56] in the north. Ch'in dispatched troops to attack the Lord of Shang and killed him at Cheng's Min-ch'ih 澠池 (338 B.C.).[57] King Hui 惠 of Ch'in (r. 337-310 B.C.) had him torn apart by chariots as a warning, and said, "Let no one rebel as did Yang of Shang." He then exterminated the Lord of Shang's household.

His Honor the Grand Scribe says: "The Lord of Shang was born by nature a harsh and relentless man. Mark well that in seeking favor from Duke Hsiao with "the arts of emperors and kings," he was merely making use of insincere speech! His true nature was otherwise. Moreover, it was through the offices of a favored slave [that he obtained his interviews]. Once employed, he mutilated Noble Scion Ch'ien, deceived Wei's commander Ang, and failed to follow Chao Liang's advice. This alone is enough to reveal the Lord of Shang's lack of mercy. I once read the Lord of Shang's writings, 'K'ai se' 開塞 (Breaking Open the Blocked Way)[58] and 'Keng-chan' 耕戰 (Agriculture and War),[59] and they were similar to the man's actions. The ill fame he eventually won in Ch'in was well founded, wasn't it?"

[54] In other words, before one has to put the other foot down to steady oneself, he will have fallen.

[55] He was to become King Hui-wen 惠文 of Ch'in (r. 337-310 B.C.).

[56] Located about 15 miles east of modern Hui-nan 渭南, Shensi (see T'an Ch'i-hsiang, 1:43-4).

[57] Located about 10 miles west of modern Min-ch'ih in Honan (T'an Ch'i-hsiang, 1:35-6). According to *Shih chi*, 15:726, Kung-sun Yang was killed at T'ung-ti 肜地 (about 15 miles southeast of modern Hui-nan), which was much closer to Cheng. Wang Li-ch'i therefore suspects that Min-ch'ih is a mistake for T'ung-ti (68:1694).

[58] Chapter 7 of the *Shang-chün shu*, traditionally believed to be written by Kung-sun Yang (for a study of the authorship of the book, see Kao Heng, *op. cit.*, pp. 6-11, and Duyvendak, *The Book of Lord Shang*, pp. 131-59).

[59] "The extant text of *Shang-chün shu* does not have a chapter by this title; it is generally believed that Chapter Three, "Nung chan" 農戰, is what Ssu-ma Ch'ien is referring to here.

TRANSLATORS' NOTE

This chapter is one of the most important sources we have for Kung-sun Yang, a central figure not just in the legal and political development of the state of Ch'in, but also in the legal and political development of all pre-Ch'in China. Ssu-ma Ch'ien seems to acknowledge that Yang's influence was not limited to Ch'in by placing him outside the sequence of chapters narrating the great statesmen and generals of pre-imperial Ch'in (*Shih chi,* Chapters 71-73). Instead, Kung-sun Yang precedes the great orators Su Ch'in and Chang Yi, famous for their oratory, for their inter-state activities, and for their completely amoral politics. It seems likely that there were other than strictly chronological reasons for this order. Perhaps Ssu-ma Ch'ien saw certain similarities between the careers of these men, none of whom attained success in their native states, but won power and fame in their travels abroad. Certainly he finds these men similarly repulsive in their policies and actions. In earlier sections we have seen politicians, philosophers, and generals grouped together. Here then, perhaps, we have Ssu-ma Ch'ien's grouping of villains. Kung-sun Yang, however, was unique in the repulsion he aroused in Ssu-ma Ch'ien; he receives one of the harshest judgments passed in *The Grand Scribe's Records.* Ssu-ma Ch'ien, we suggest, is even at pains to rebut some of the source material he uses in this chapter, which presents Kung-sun in a not completely unfavorable light. According to the account above, Kung-sun at least tries, in his first series of interviews with Duke Hsiao, to proposed more enlightened forms of government, but driven by his ambition, panders to the Duke's worst side when these do not meet with acceptance. To Ssu-ma, however, this is mere sophistry; a judgment in which later scholars have generally concurred.

BIBLIOGRAPHY

I. Translations

Duyvendak, J. J. L. *The Book of Lord Shang.* London: Probsthain and Co., 1928, pp. 8-31.
Mizusawa Toshitada 水澤利忠. *Shiki* 史記. V. 8. *Retsuden (ichi)* 列傳 (一). Tokyo: Meiji Shoten, 1990, pp. 196-223.
Ōgawa Tamaki 小川環樹, trans. *Shiki retsuden* 史記列傳. Rpt. Tokyo: Chikuma Shobō, 1986 (1969), pp. 42-48.
Vandermeersch, Léon. *La formation du Légisme, recherche sur la constitution d'une philosophie politique caractéristique de la Chine ancienne.* Paris: Ecole Francaise d'Extreme-Orient, 1965, pp. 23-39.
Watson, Burton. *Records of the Grand Historian: Qin Dynasty.* V. 3. Hong Kong and New York: The Research Centre for Translation, The Chinese University of Hong Kong and Columbia University Press, 1993, pp. 89-99.

II. Studies

Chu Yüan 朱瑗. "*Shih chi* 'Shang-chün lieh-chuan' shu-cheng" 史記商君列傳疏證, *Kuo-li Pien-i-kuan kuan-k'an* 國立編譯館館刊, 1 (1971.10), 39-58.
Sun Tz'u-chou 孫次舟. "*Shih chi* 'Shang-chün lieh-chuan' shih-liao chüeh-yüan" 史記商君列傳史料抉原, *Shih-hsüeh chi-k'an* 史學季刊, 1.2 (March 1941).

Su Ch'in, Memoir 9

[69:2241] Su Ch'in was a native of East Chou's Lo-yang 雒陽.[1] He served teachers to the east in Ch'i and practiced under the Venerable Kuei-ku 鬼谷.[2] After traveling for several years, he returned home in dire straits.[3] His older and younger brothers, sister-in-law and sisters, and [their] wives and concubines all privately laughed at him: "The custom of the men of Chou has been first of all to manage their property, to strive at crafts and commerce, and to pursue [a profit of] twenty percent. Now that you've abandoned your roots and work at your mouth and tongue, you're in straits. Isn't that fitting!"

Su Ch'in heard them and was ashamed. Feeling sorry for himself, he closeted himself in his room and would not come out. He pulled out all his books and looked at each one: "As a knight I have already bowed down my head and received [my Master's] writings. But if they can't be used to win high position and honor, even though they are numerous what use are they?"

After this, he obtained [*2242*] the Chou book *Yin fu* 陰符 (Secret Tallies). He huddled over it, reciting. After a year had gone by, he went out with it to plumb [men's intentions] and plan [his responses]. "With this I can advise the great lords of our times!"

He sought to advise King Hsien 顯 of Chou (r. 368-321 B.C.). King Hsien's courtiers had for a long time been familiar with Su Ch'in. They thought little of him, and did not trust him.

He then went west to Ch'in. Duke Hsiao 孝 of Ch'in (r. 361-338 B.C.) had expired. He advised [Duke Hsiao's son] King Hui 惠 (r. 337-311 B.C.): "Ch'in is a state of four barriers. It is cloaked by mountains and girded by the Wei 渭. To the east it has the passes and the Ho. To the west it has Han-chung 漢中.[4] To the South it has Pa 巴 and Shu 蜀.[5] To the

---

[1] King K'ao 考 of the Chou dynasty (r. 440-426 B.C.) divided the territory of the Chou royal house with his younger brother Chieh 揭, granting Chieh the title of Duke Huan 桓 of Chou. King K'ao kept the eastern portion of the royal territory, while Duke Huan received the area to the west, known as Ho-nan 河南. This area became known as West Chou. In 367 B.C., Duke Hui 惠 of West Chou enfeoffed his younger son with the land around Kung 鞏 (just southwest of modern Kung-hsien 鞏縣 in Honan [T'an Ch'i-hsiang, 1:36]) and granted his son the title of Duke Hui of East Chou. This area included the ancient site of Lo-yang. Modern Lo-yang city, however, is located about 10 miles west of ancient Lo-yang. For further discussion of East and West Chou, see our translation of *Shih chi* Chapter 5 above and Henri Maspero's *China in Antiquity*, Frank A. Kierman, Jr., trans. (Amherst: University of Massachusetts Press, 1978), pp. 242-3.

[2] According to "Chi-chieh" and "So-yin," Kuei-ku was a valley near Yang-ch'eng 陽城 (about 5 miles southeast of modern Teng-feng 登封 city in Honan [T'an Ch'i-hsiang, 1:36]) and the "Venerable Kuei-ku" was named after the place he lived. A number of other sources also refer to this person (see Wang Shu-min, 69:2191). However, modern scholars such as Chiang Po-ch'ien 蔣伯潛 and Ch'ien Mu have expressed doubts on the historicity of such a person (see Chiang Po-ch'ien, *Chu-tzu t'ung-k'ao* 諸子通考 [Taipei: Chung-cheng Shu-chü, 1961], p. 249; Ch'ien Mu, *Chu-tzu*, pp. 309-10) and Chiang has pointed out that there were no less than five places named Kuei-ku (pp. 245-50).

[3] A quite different version of Su Ch'in's attempt to persuade Ch'in appears in the *Chan-kuo ts'e* (3:2a-6a, SPTK). In the *Chan-kuo ts'e* version, Su Ch'in attempts to persuade King Hui 惠 of Ch'in (r. 337-311, B.C.) "ten times," and it is after his failure in Ch'in that he returns home to his family's obloquy, finding a mysterious text which inspires him to set out again and persuade the King of Chao. The *Chan-kuo ts'e* version does not include any of Su Ch'in's speeches in Chao or the other states thereafter (a number of these speeches do appear in *Chan-kuo ts'e*, as separate narratives), but skips directly to his return home and his family's apology for their previous behavior.

[4] Han-chung was the name of a commandery located to the south of Ch'in-ling 秦嶺 in modern Shensi (T'an Ch'i-hsiang, 1:43).

north it has Tai 代 and Ma 馬.⁶ This is Heaven's treasury. With the masses of Ch'in's knights and commoners, and their training in the arts of war, you can swallow the world, proclaim yourself Emperor, and rule."

The King of Ch'in said, "When feather and down have not yet grown, one cannot fly high. When culture and principle are not yet illustrious, one cannot annex." Having just executed Shang Yang, he loathed rhetoricians and did not make use of him.⁷

[2243] He then went east to Chao. Marquis Su 肅 of Chao (r. 349-326 B.C.) had made his brother Ch'eng 成 Prime Minister, titling him Lord of Feng-yang 奉陽.⁸ The Lord of Feng-yang didn't care for Su Ch'in.

He left and traveled to Yen. After more than a year, he obtained an audience. He advised Marquis Wen 文 of Yen (r. 361-333 B.C.)⁹: "To the east Yen has Ch'ao-hsien 朝鮮 and Liao-tung 遼東.¹⁰ To the north it has Lin Hu 林胡 and Lou-fan 樓煩.¹¹ To the west it has Yün-chung 雲中 and Chiu-yüan 九原.¹² To the south it has the Hu-t'o 滹沱 and Yi 易 Rivers. Its territory is more than two-thousand *li* [on a side], its armored soldiers number hundreds of thousands, its chariots six hundred, its horsemen six thousand, and its grain will last for several years. To the south it has the plentitude of Chieh-shih 碣石 and Yen-men 鴈門.¹³ To the north it has the benefit of dates and chestnuts. Even if its peasants do not labor in the fields they will have plenty of these. This is what is called Heaven's treasury.

[2244] "For peace without troubles, without defeat of its army or death of its generals, none can surpass Yen. Do you know why this is so, Great King? The reason that Yen has not encountered invaders or suffered from armored soldiers is because Chao acts as its screen to the south. Ch'in and Chao have fought five times. Ch'in triumphed twice and Chao three times. Ch'in and Chao have exhausted each other, and Your Majesty has controlled the aftermath with an unharmed Yen. This is why Yen has not encountered invaders. Moreover, for Ch'in to attack Yen, it must go over Yün-chung and Chiu-yüan, passing through Tai and Shang-ku 上谷, traveling thousands of *li*.¹⁴ Even though it might gain Yen's capital, Ch'in

---

⁵ Pa was located in the eastern part of modern Szechwan province. Shu was located in the central and western area of modern Szechwan.

⁶ This is not a description of Ch'in's borders at the beginning of King Hui-wen's reign, but at a much later period. We follow "So-yin" and most other scholars in taking "Ma" as the name of a city here, probably Ma-yi 馬邑, located in Shuo-hsien 朔縣 in modern Shansi (Ch'ien Mu, *Ti-ming k'ao*, p. 863).

⁷ Shang Yang was killed in 338 B.C. See his biography in *Shih chi* Chapter 68.

⁸ Ch'ien Mu (*Ti-ming k'ao*, p. 511) speculates that Feng-yang was near modern Wen-hsien 溫縣 in Honan province. Scholars generally identify the Lord of Feng-yang as Li Tui 李兌. Modern scholars such as Ch'ien Mu, however, believe that Li Tui was in fact a vassal of Marquis Su's successor, King Wu-ling 武靈(r. 325-299 B.C., see Ch'ien Mu, *Chu-tzu*, pp. 290-1).

⁹ There is a parallel text for the following speech in the *Chan-kuo ts'e* (9:2a-b, *SPTK*). *Shih chi*, 15:727 places Su Ch'in's trip to Yen in 334 B.C.

¹⁰ Ch'ao-hsien corresponds to modern Chi-lin and Hei-lung-chiang provinces, together with the Korean peninsula. Liao-tung corresponds to modern Liao-ning province.

¹¹ The Lin Hu and Lou Fan were the names of non-Chinese tribes who actually lived west of Yen, between Chao and Ch'in (T'an Ch'i-hsiang, 1:37).

¹² Chiu-yüan was located approximately 5 miles west of modern Pao-t'ou 包頭 city, in the Inner Mongolian Autonomous Region. Yün-chung was about 20 miles northeast of modern T'o-k'o-t'o 托克托 (T'an Ch'i-hsiang, 1:37).

¹³ Chieh-shih is a mountain approximately 30 miles east of the modern city of T'ang-shan 唐山 in Liao-ning (T'an Ch'i-hsiang, 1:41). Yen-men is another mountain, approximately 40 miles northeast of modern Ta-t'ung 大同 city in Shansi (T'an Ch'i-hsiang, 1:38).

¹⁴ Tai and Shang-ku were both commanderies of Yen, located northwest of modern Peking (T'an Ch'i-hsiang, 1:41).

must realize that it cannot hold it. It is clear then that Ch'in cannot harm Yen. But if Chao attacked Yen, from issuing orders and presenting commands, it would take less than ten days before an army of hundreds of thousands would be encamped in Tung-yüan 東垣.[15] After crossing the Hu-t'o and fording the Yi River, it would be less than four or five days before they faced the capital. Thus I say if Ch'in attacked Yen, it would fight a thousand *li* away [from Ch'in]. If Chao attacked Yen, it would fight within a hundred *li* [of Chao]. No plan could be more mistaken than to ignore a disaster a hundred *li* away and exalt a state a thousand *li* away. For this reason I hope, Great King, that you might join in alliance with Chao. When the world is as one, the state of Yen is sure to have no fears."

Marquis Wen said, "Your advice is acceptable, sir, but my state is small. To the west we are near mighty Chao, to the south we are close to Ch'i. Ch'i and Chao are mighty states. If you are set on forming an alliance to secure the safety of Yen, we ask permission to follow with our state."

[2245] He provided Su Ch'in with carriages, horses, gold, and silk to take to Chao. The Lord of Feng-yang, however, had already died, and instead he advised Marquis Su of Chao[16]: "For a long time indeed the world's high officials and lowly vassals, down to knights dressed in plain cloth, have all admired Your Worthiness's just actions and longed to receive your instructions and lay their advice before you for a long time indeed! The Lord of Feng-yang, however, was envious and My Lord would not entrust affairs to them. It was because of this that the guests and traveling knights did not dare to unburden themselves before you. Now that the Lord of Feng-yang has abandoned his hostels and houses, My Lord may once again grow close with his knights and commoners. Thus your servant dares to present his foolish thoughts.

"In laying plans for My Lord, I would say that nothing could surpass securing the people. Moreover, there is no need to trouble the people. The basis of securing the people lies in choosing one's alliances. If alliances are chosen well, the people will be secure. If alliances are not chosen well, then the people will know no security all their lives. Let me speak of your troubles abroad. When Ch'i and Ch'in are both your enemies, the people will know no peace. If you rely on Ch'in and attack Ch'i, the people will know no peace. If you rely on Ch'i and attack Ch'in, the people will know no peace.

"Thus, when one plots against another ruler, or attacks another state, one must always worry over letting slip a phrase which might sever relations. I beg My Lord to take care not to let slip such words. Distinguish between black and white; in this way, one may differentiate between the *yin* and the *yang*.[17] If My Lord can truly heed me, Yen is sure to present you with lands filled with felts and furs, dogs and horses, Ch'i is sure to present seas filled with fish and salt, Ch'u is sure to present gardens filled with tangerines and grapefruit, Han, Wei, and Chung-shan can all be made to present bath-towns,[18] and your consort's family and your own male relatives can all be given fiefs of marquises. To obtain land and embrace profit, the Five Hegemons sought this by destroying armies and seizing generals. To enfeoff their consorts' relatives as marquises, T'ang and Wu struggled for this by exiling and murdering [their

---

[15] Located in modern Cheng-ting 正定 County in Hopei (T'an Ch'i-hsiang, 1:38).

[16] A parallel to the following speech appears in *Chan-kuo ts'e* (6:9b-13a, *SPTK*).

[17] The punctuation and meaning of this passage is obscure. Most commentators agree with the suggestion of the *Chan-kuo ts'e* commentator Pao Piao 鮑彪 (*fl.* 1140; see Ho Chien-chang, p. 659) that *yin* and *yang* here refer to the "advantages and disadvantages" of alliance (see Wang Shu-min, 69:2196, for further discussion).

[18] *T'ang-mu yi* 湯沐邑 were fiefs within the royal domain given to various lords at which they were to cleanse themselves before attending court (see Hsü Lien-ta, p. 451).

sovereigns]. Now My Lord may raise up his arms, clasp his hands together, and have them both. This is what your servant desires for you.

[2246] "If you, Great King, ally with Ch'in, then Ch'in is sure to weaken Han and Wei. If you ally with Ch'i, then Ch'i is sure to weaken Ch'u and Wei. If Wei is weakened, it will cede Ho-wai 河外.[19] If Han is weakened, then it will present Yi-yang 宜陽.[20] When Yi-yang is presented, Shang-chün 上郡 [Commandery][21] will be cut off, and when Ho-wai is ceded, the roads [to Shang-chün] will be severed, and if Ch'u is weakened, it cannot assist. These three strategies must be given the most careful consideration.

"If Ch'in goes down the Chih 軹 Road, then Nan-yang 南陽 is in danger.[22] If it then threatens Han and surrounds Chou, then the clans of Chao must personally take up weapons.[23] If it then seizes Wey and takes Chüan 卷,[24] then Ch'i is sure to enter Ch'in and pay homage. When Ch'in has gained its desires East of the Mount,[25] it is sure to mobilize its troops and approach Chao. When the armored soldiers of Ch'in cross the Ho, ford the Chang 漳, and seize P'u-wu 番吾,[26] then soldiers are sure to clash under the walls of Han-tan 邯鄲. This is what your servant fears for My Lord.

[2247] In our time, not one of the kingdoms that have been established[27] East of the Mount is as mighty as Chao. Chao's territory extends over two-thousand *li* [on a side]. Its armored troops number in the hundreds of thousands, its chariots in the thousands, its horsemen in the tens of thousands, and its grain can last for several years. To the west, it has Mount Ch'ang 常,[28] to the south it has the Ho and the Chang, to the east the Ch'ing River

[19] Ho-wai ("outside the Ho River") refers to the northwest region of modern Honan province south of the Yellow River, as opposed to Ho-nei 河內, "inside the Ho River," which is the area north of the Yellow River (T'an Ch'i-hsiang, 1:35-36).

[20] Located in modern Yi-yang 宜陽 County in Honan, about 10 miles west of modern Yi-yang City (T'an Ch'i-hsiang, 1:35).

[21] Shang Commandery was located in the northern part of modern Shensi province.

[22] The Chih Road was a narrow mountain passage, near modern Chi-yüan 濟源 City in Honan, leading into Nan-yang, one of the most heavily populated areas of the state of Han, just north of the Yellow River in the southeast corner of modern Shansi province (T'an Ch'i-hsiang, 1:35-6).

[23] As the Ch'ing scholar Yü Ch'ang 于鬯 notes (cited in Ho Chien-chang, p. 659, n. 32), it makes little sense in these circumstances to say that Chao is menaced by an attack on the Nan-yang area of Han or East and West Chou. The most direct threat in such a case would be to the state of Wei.

[24] Other editions of the *Shih chi* have Chi Chüan 淇卷 instead of Chüan 卷. The Chung-hua edition follows Wang Nien-sun's (4:10b-11a) suggestion in excising the word Chi (see also Wang Shu-min, 69:2197). The *Chan-kuo ts'e* version of this passage has Chi. Chüan was about 10 miles west of modern Yüan-yang 原陽 City in Honan (T'an Ch'i-hsiang, 1:36).

[25] This refers to the area east of Mount Hsiao 郩 which was located about 15 miles east-southeast of modern San-men-hsia 三門峽 in western Honan (T'an Ch'i-hsiang, 1:35). Mount Hsiao and the Han-ku 函谷 Pass (often referred to as "the Pass"), about 20 miles southwest of San-men-hsia (*ibid.*), were the major natural barriers of the time, lands to the east being referred to as "Beyond the Pass" or "East of the Mount."

[26] The Chang, according to T'an Ch'i-hsiang (1:38), flowed south from what is now modern Shansi, turned east along the modern Hopei-Honan border just south of P'u-wu and the Chao Wall, and then flowed northeast to join the Ho, essentially providing a ring around Han-tan.

This place name was later fixed as P'u-wu 蒲吾, but there are textual variants which suggest that P'o-wu and P'an-wu are also possible (see "Cheng-yi," *Shih chi*, 43:1832). There were two places known as P'u-wu: one was to the southeast of P'ing-shan 平山 County in modern Hopei, one some 20 miles south of modern Han-tan County in Hopei (T'an Ch'i-hsiang, 1:38, locates it slightly further north). Takigawa (69:11) prefers the former identification. Yü Ch'ang (quoted in Ho Chien-chang, p. 333) prefers the latter, and we follow Yü.

[27] The phrase *chien-kuo* 建國 is puzzling. Ho Chien-chang (p. 660, n. 37) believes it is an error for *chan-kuo* 戰國.

[28] Located on the border between Hopei and Shansi provinces, 60 miles northwest of modern Pao-ting 保定

清河,[29] and to the north the state of Yen. Yen is a weak state, not worth fearing. There is no one Ch'in loathes more in the world than Chao, yet it does not dare to mobilize its troops to attack Chao. Why? It fears Han and Wei will make plans against its rear. Thus Han and Wei are Chao's southern screen. When Ch'in attacks Han and Wei, there are no barriers formed by famous mountains or great rivers, so that it gradually nibbles away at them, until it reaches the capitals of their states, and only then stops. Han and Wei, unable to resist Ch'in, are sure to enter Ch'in as vassals. When Ch'in is rid of the plotting[30] of Han and Wei, disaster is sure to strike Chao. This is what your servant fears for My Lord.

"Your servant has heard that Yao hadn't the allotment of three men, Shun hadn't an inch of land, and with these holdings they gained the world.[31] Yü hadn't even a village of a hundred, and with this he became ruler of the feudal lords.[32] T'ang and Wu's knights numbered no more than three thousand, their carriages no more than three hundred, and their foot soldiers no more than thirty thousand, and they became Sons of Heaven.[33] These [men] truly found the right Way. Thus an enlightened ruler measures the strength of his enemies abroad, and marks the worthiness of his knights at home. Without waiting for the clash of the two armies, victory and defeat, survival and destruction are already visible to his mind. How could he be confounded by the words of the masses and decide matters blindly?

[2248] "Your servant has consulted the maps of the world, and the territory of the feudal lords is five times greater than that of Ch'in. I estimate also that the foot soldiers of the feudal lords are ten times greater than Ch'in's. If the Six States were to unite, join their forces, face west and attack Ch'in, Ch'in's defeat would be certain. If you face west now and serve it, you will be made a vassal by Ch'in. To defeat or be defeated, to make a vassal or be made a vassal, these are as different as night and day!

"The advocates of counter-alliance all wish to cede the territory of the feudal lords to Ch'in. If Ch'in succeeds,[34] they will raise high terraces and pavilions, make beautiful houses and buildings, and listen to the music of pipes and zither. In the front of their estates will be lofty towers and high carriages,[35] in the rear, tall and comely beauties; and when their states suffer the disaster of Ch'in, they will not share in the sorrow. This is why Ch'in's persuaders strive day and night to terrify and threaten the feudal lords with the power of Ch'in, to seek territorial concessions from them. Thus I hope that you will consider this carefully, Great King.

(T'an Ch'i-hsiang, 1:38).

[29] According to Ch'ien Mu (*Ti-ming k'ao*, p. 272), Ch'ing-ho refers to the Chi River 淇水. According to Ho Chien-chang (p. 660, n. 42), however, it refers to what was formerly known as the Chi River 濟水 (T'an Ch'i-hsiang, 1:39). The latter seems preferable. As the text indicates, it was on the border between Chao and Ch'i.

[30] The meaning of *kuei* 規 here is unclear. Mizusawa, p. 239, suggests "plotting," perhaps because of parallel with *yi ch'i hou* 議其後 above. This is supported by another passage in the *Chan-kuo ts'e*, where the commentator Pao Piao glosses the word *kuei* in a similar usage as *mou* 謀, "plot" (see Ho Chien-chang, p. 455, n. 32); we have tentatively adopted this suggestion. The parallel *Chan-kuo ts'e* text for the current passage, however, reads *ko* 隔, "block, barrier."

[31] Yao and Shun were the first, perhaps mythical, pre-dynastic emperors of China; see our translation of *Shih chi* Chapter 1.

[32] Yü was the founder of the Hsia dynasty; see our translation of *Shih chi* Chapter 2.

[33] King T'ang was the founder of the Shang dynasty, King Wu of the Chou dynasty; see our translations of *Shih chi* Chapters 3 and 4.

[34] The *Chan-kuo ts'e* text is clearer: "The advocates of 'counter-alliance' all wish to cede the territory of the feudal lords to make peace with Ch'in. When they have made peace with Ch'in, ..."

[35] There are a number of interpretations of the phrase *hsüan-yüan* 軒轅 (see Wang Shu-min, 69:2200 and Ho Chien-chang, p. 662, n. 70).

[2249] "Your servant has heard that an enlightened ruler will sever all doubts and re-move all slander, close off the paths of idle rumor, block up the gates of partisan squabbling; thus your vassals will be free to place before you plans for exalting the ruler, broadening his territory and strengthening his army.

"Thus in planning for you, Great King, it would be best to unify Han, Wei, Ch'i, Ch'u, Yen, and Chao into one alliance, and fight back against Ch'in.

"Assemble the generals and ministers of the world on the bank of the Huan 洹,[36] ex-change pledges, disembowel a white horse, and swear an oath.[37] Let the oath say 'If Ch'in at-tacks Ch'u, Ch'i and Wei will each send out their best troops to aid it, Han will cut Ch'in's supply routes, Chao will ford the Ho and Chang, and Yen will hold the north of Mount Ch'ang.

"If Ch'in attacks Han and Wei, Ch'u will cut off its rear, Ch'i will send out its best troops to assist them, Chao will ford the Ho and Chang, and Yen will hold Yün-chung.

"If Ch'in attacks Ch'i, then Ch'u will cut off its rear, Han will hold Ch'eng-kao 城皋,[38] Wei will block its road, Chao will ford the Ho and Chang, and cross Po 博 Pass,[39] and Yen will send out its best troops to aid [Ch'i].

"If Ch'in attacks Yen, then Chao will hold Mount Ch'ang, Ch'u will occupy the Wu 武 Pass,[40] Ch'i will cross the Sea of Po-hai 勃海, and Han and Wei will send out their best troops to aid [Yen].

"If Ch'in attacks Chao, then Han will occupy Yi-yang, Ch'u will occupy the Wu Pass, Wei will occupy Ho-wai, Ch'i will ford the Ch'ing River, and Yen will send out its best troops to aid [Chao].

"If one of the feudal lords fails to follow the pact, the forces of the five states will jointly attack it.'

"If the Six States ally together and isolate Ch'in, the armored soldiers of Ch'in will not dare to come out of the Han-ku 函谷 [Pass] to harm the lands East of the Mount.[41] When this is done, the task of a Hegemon King is complete."

[2250] The King of Chao said, "We are youthful, and have not held the throne for long, so that we have never heard great plans for securing the altars of grain and soil. Now you, our honored guest, desire to preserve the world and secure the feudal lords. We respect-fully follow you with our state."

---

[36] A tributary of the Yellow River which passed just north of modern An-yang 安陽 City in Honan (T'an Ch'i-hsiang, 1:36).

[37] As part of the covenant, various animals were killed and their blood either drunk or smeared on the lips (*sha-hsieh* 歃血). The type of animal used in the covenant depended on the rank of those participating in the cere-mony. Thus, according to the ritual work *Chou Li* 周禮 (cited in "So-yin," *Shih chi*, 76:2367), the Chou king used cattle and horses, the feudal lords used dogs and boars, and their subordinates used chickens. The color of the animal to be killed was also important, with different colors appropriate for different sacrifices. Another fa-mous instance of a white horse used to conclude a covenant occurs in *Shih chi*, 9:400. Presumably in both these cases the rank of the participants was exalted enough that the use of a horse was justified. In *Shih chi*, 76:2367, we find all three types of animals used for a covenant that involved the King of Ch'u, a high ranking member of the nobility of Chao, and a number of his subordinates.

[38] Located in modern Ying-yang 滎陽 County in Honan (T'an Ch'i-hsiang, 1:36).

[39] Also known as Po-ling 博陵. Located northwest of modern Po-p'ing 博平 County in Shantung (T'an Ch'i-hsiang, 1:39).

[40] Located in modern Shang-nan 商南 County in Shansi (T'an Ch'i-hsiang, 1:44). This was one of the major routes from Ch'u into the state of Ch'in.

[41] Han-ku refers to a long, mountainous region located about 5 miles south of modern Ling-pao 靈寶 County in Honan (T'an Ch'i-hsiang, 1:35).

Su Ch'in then went to make alliance with the feudal lords, taking a hundred ornamented carriages, a thousand *yi* of gold, a hundred pairs of white jade-disks, and a thousand *ch'un* of embroidered brocade.

At this time, the Chou Son of Heaven presented the sacrificial meat for kings Wen and Wu to King Hui of Ch'in.[42] King Hui had the *Hsi-shou*[43] attack Wei; he captured Wei's general Lung Chia 龍賈, took Wei's Tiao-yin 雕陰,[44] and threatened to move east again. Su Ch'in feared Ch'in's troops reaching Chao, and infuriated Chang Yi 張儀, sending him into Ch'in.

He then advised King Hsüan 宣 of Han (r. *332-312 B.C.):[45] "To the north, Han has the fastnesses of Kung 鞏[46] and Ch'eng-kao. To the west it has the fortresses of Yi-yang and Shang-pi 商陂.[47] To the east it has Yüan 宛, Jang 穰, and the Wei 洧 River.[48] To the south it has Mount Hsing 陘.[49] Its territory is more than nine-hundred *li* [on a side], its armored soldiers number in the hundreds of thousands, and the world's strongest bows and most powerful crossbows all come from Han.

"The 'Shih-li' 時力 and 'Chü-lai-che' 巨來者, the 'Hsi Tzu' 谿子 and the 'Shao-fu' 少府 can all shoot more than six-hundred paces.[50] When the soldiers of Han push with their feet to cock their crossbows and fire, they do not stop once in a hundred shots. For those farther, arrowshafts pierce deep into their chests. For those closer, arrowheads are buried in their hearts.

[2251] "The halberds and swords of the Han foot soldiers all come from Mount Ming 冥, T'ang-hsi 棠谿, Mo-yang 墨陽, Ho-fu 合賻, Teng-shih 鄧師, Yüan-feng 宛馮, Lung-yüan 龍淵, and T'ai-o 太阿.[51] All are capable of sundering horses and cattle on land, of splitting geese and swans on water. When the enemy is met, they cut through sturdy chest armor and iron cuirasses. From leather finger guards to shield straps, there is nothing they lack.

"With the courage of a Han soldier, dressed in sturdy armor, cocking a powerful crossbow, carrying a sharp sword, one man holding back a hundred is not worthy of mention. With your wisdom, Great King, and the vigor of Han, to then face west and serve Ch'in, to make obeisance and submit, to disgrace your altars of grain and soil and to become the laughingstock of the entire world, nothing could be worse than this. Thus I hope you will carefully consider this.

[2253] "If you serve Ch'in, Great King, Ch'in is sure to seek Yi-yang and Ch'eng-kao. If you present them this time, next year it will seek more concessions of territory. If you give

[42] According to *Shih chi*, 15:7272, this occurred in 334 B.C.

[43] *Hsi-shou* 犀首 was originally a military title in the state of Wei, but it usually refers to Kung-sun Yen, who presumably held this title at one time. For a further notice of his activities, see our translation of *Shih chi* Chapter 70.

[44] Tiao-yin was located about 10 miles south of modern Kan-ch'üan 甘泉 City in Shensi (T'an Ch'i-hsiang, 1:35). According to *Shih chi* 15:728, this occurred in 333 B.C.

[45] A parallel text to this speech appears in the *Chan-kuo ts'e* (8:6b-8a, *SPTK*).

[46] Kung was a city located a few miles southwest of modern Kung County in Honan (T'an Ch'i-hsiang, 1:36).

[47] Shang-pi is a mountain, also known as 商山, located south of modern Shang 商 County in Shansi (T'an Ch'i-hsiang, 1:44).

[48] Yüan was a major city located south of modern Nan-yang 南陽 City in Honan (T'an Ch'i-hsiang, 1:29). Jang was a city located in modern Teng 鄧 County in Honan (T'an Ch'i-hsiang, 1:45). The Wei is a river now known as Shuang-chi Ho 雙洎河, located in Honan (T'an Ch'i-hsiang, 1:36).

[49] Located 20 miles southwest of modern Hsin Cheng 新鄭 County in Honan (T'an Ch'i-hsiang, 1:45).

[50] We follow Wang Shu-min (69:2203-4) in taking all four of these as the names of types of bows or crossbows.

[51] Some of these are obviously place names, and some may be the names of blacksmiths. There is no general agreement on which is which, or where these locations might have been.

it more, you will run out of land to give. If you do not, you cast aside your past merit [in granting land] and suffer future sorrows. Your land is limited, Great King, but Ch'in's demands are without end. To meet endless demands with limited land, this is what is called bartering for trouble and buying disaster. Your territory will be stripped from you without a struggle. Your servant has heard a country saying that goes, "Better to be a chicken's beak than a cow's rear." If you face west, make obeisance, and serve Ch'in, what difference is there between Han and a cow's rear? To possess wisdom such as yours, Great King, and to wield might such as Han's, yet to bear the name of cow's rear, this is something for which your servant would feel shame on your behalf."

The King of Han swelled in anger, his face flushed, he pushed up his sleeves, opened his eyes wide, grasped the handle of his sword, turned his head to the sky and sighed, "Although We may be unworthy, We shall never be able to serve Ch'in. You, My Lordship and Master, have informed me of the instructions of the King of Chao, and We respectfully offer up our altars of grain and soil and follow you."

Su Ch'in then advised King Hsiang 襄 of Wei (r. *334-319 B.C.):[52] "Your territory, Great King, to the south covers Hung-kou 鴻溝, Ch'en 陳, Ju-nan 汝南, Hsü 許, Yen 鄢, K'un-yang 昆陽, Shao-ling 召陵, Wu-yang 舞陽, Hsin-tu 新都, and [*2254*] Hsin-ch'i 新郪.[53] To the east you have the Huai 淮 and the Ying 潁 [rivers], Chu-tsao 煮棗 and Wu-hsü 無胥.[54] To the west you have the border of the Long Wall, to the north you have Ho-wai, Chüan, Yen 衍, and Suan-tsao 酸棗.[55] Your territory stretches a thousand *li* [on a side]. Although your lands are called small, the field houses and cottages are so numerous there is no place for grazing or herding. The people are so numerous and the carriages and horses so many, moving day and night without end, rumbling and rattling, that it seems as if a whole army were on the march. In your servant's private view, your state is the equal of Ch'u, Great King, yet the advocates of counter-alliance, without regard for the dire consequences, threaten Your Majesty into joining with the mighty tiger-and-wolf Ch'in to invade the states of the world, leaving you at last faced with the menace of Ch'in.

"To utilize the force of mighty Ch'in to threaten one's own ruler in his own kingdom, there is no crime greater than this. Wei is the mightiest state in the world, Your Majesty the worthiest king in the world. Yet now you intend to face west and serve Ch'in, calling yourself the 'eastern feudatory,' build summer palaces for the 'emperor,' adopt Ch'in hats and belts, and offer it sacrifices in the spring and autumn. Your servant privately feels shame for you, Great King.

---

[52] A parallel to the following speech appears in *Chan-kuo ts'e* (7:12a-14a, *SPTK*).

[53] All but the last of these places are located in modern Honan. The Hung-kou was an ancient canal. Ch'en was an ancient state, in the area of modern Huai-yang 淮陽 County in Honan. Ju-nan was located near modern Shang-ts'ai 上蔡 County in Honan. Hsü was an ancient state close to modern Ch'ang 昌 City in Honan. Yen was another ancient state located near modern Yen-ch'eng 鄢城 County in Honan. K'un-yang was a city located in modern Yeh 葉 (formerly read "She") County in Honan. Shao-ling was a city located east of modern Yen-ch'eng County in Honan. Wu-yang was a city in what is today Wu-yang County in Honan. There was a place called Hsin-tu, but it was located in the Nan-yang area of the state of Han, leading some scholars to suggest this is an error (see Wang Li-ch'i, 69:1705). Hsin-ch'i was a city northeast of modern Chieh-shou 界首 County in Anhwei (T'an Ch'i-hsiang, 1:29-30 and 45).

[54] Chu-tsao was a city located southwest of modern Ho-ts'e 菏澤 County in Shantung (T'an Ch'i-hsiang, 1:36). The location of Wu-hsü is not known.

[55] The "Long Wall" referred to here is probably the wall built between Wei and Ch'in (T'an Ch'i-hsiang, 1:35). Yen was a place name, located north of modern Chengchow 鄭州 in Honan. Suan-tsao was a city located southwest of modern Yen-chin 延津 County in Honan (T'an Ch'i-hsiang, 1:36).

[2255] "Your servant has heard that Kou-chien, King of Yüeh, fought with 3,000 worn-out soldiers and captured Fu-ch'ai at Kan-sui 干遂.[56] King Wu, with 3,000 soldiers and 300 leather-armored carriages overcame Chow at Mu-yeh 牧野.[57] It was not that their troops were many; they were truly able to exert their authority. Now I have privately heard that your troops, Great King, number 200,000 warriors, 200,000 blue turbans, 200,000 shock troops, 100,000 porters, 600 chariots, and 5000 horsemen.[58] This surpasses by far Kou-chien, King of Yüeh, and King Wu. Yet now you listen to the speeches of your vassals and wish to serve Ch'in. To serve Ch'in, you must cede territory to demonstrate honesty; thus without using force, the state will be depleted. Every one of your assembled vassals who speaks of serving Ch'in is a traitor and no loyal vassal. These 'vassals' would cede their ruler's territory to make connections abroad, seize a moment's merit without regard for the consequences, ruin the ducal family to build their private estates, and rely on the foreign influence of mighty Ch'in to threaten their ruler in his own state, in order to help it seek territorial concessions. I would hope you might carefully observe this, Great King.

[2256] "The *Documents of Chou* says, 'If you do not cut it when it is small, what can you do when it has spread? If you do not chop the twigs and branches, you must use a long-handled ax.'[59] If consideration is not taken beforehand, great disasters will come after, and what can be done then? If you can heed your servant, Great King, with the Six States as allies, with unity of mind, unity of strength, and unity of will, no disaster can come from mighty Ch'in. Thus our humble manor's King of Chao has sent his servant to present this foolish plan and offer the oaths of alliance. It depends on your writ to command this, Great King."

The King of Wei said, "We are unworthy, and have until now been unable to hear your illustrious instructions. Now that My Lord has proclaimed the writ of the King of Chao to Us, We respectfully follow with Our state."

Su Ch'in then went east and advised King Hsüan 宣 of Ch'i (r. *342-324 B.C.):[60] "To the south Ch'i has Mount T'ai 泰, to the east Lang-ya 琅邪,[61] to the west the Ch'ing River, to the north the Sea of Po-hai. This is what is called a state of four barriers. [*2257*] Ch'i's territory is over 2000 *li* [on a side]. Its armored troops number in the hundreds of thousands and its grain is heaped up in mountains and hills. With the quality of its army and its five-

---

[56] This is usually identified as a mountain near the city of Soochow in modern Chekiang province (Ch'ien Mu *Ti-ming k'ao*, p. 587).

[57] See our translation of Chapter 3.

[58] "So-yin" says *ts'ang-t'ou* 蒼頭 (our "blue turbans") refers to soldiers wearing dark turbans, but it offers no suggestion as to what role they played. "So-yin" further suggests that *ssu-t'u* 廝徒 "porters" were originally something like "grooms" who were later made foot soldiers. "Cheng-yi," however, merely says that they were responsible for "cooking, caring for the horses, and doing miscellaneous tasks." Yü Ch'ang (quoted in Ho Chien-chang, p. 5, n. 24) identifies them with the *jen-t'u* 人徒, who were generally slave and corvee laborers. Nakai Riken 中井履軒 (1732-1819--cited in Takigawa, 69:24) sees parallels between the Wei army with pre-modern Japanese military organization: thus he believes the *wu-shih* 武士 were equivalent to *samurai*, the *ts'ang-t'ou* were equivalent to the *ashigaru* 輕足 "foot soldiers," and the *ssu-t'u* were equivalent to *nimbu* 人夫 "carriers, coolies." Most writers take *fen-chi* 奮擊 as translated in the text: "shock troops, vanguard." Ho Chien-chang (p. 77, n. 8) notes that it can also be written *fen-chi* 奮戟. L. S. Perelomov, "O haraktere dvizhushchih sil vojny 209-202 gg. do. n. e. v Kitae," *NAA*, 1962.1, 79-90, believes that *ts'ang-t'ou* had a status not far from that of a slave.

[59] There is an almost identical passage which occurs in the *Yi Chou shu* 逸周書 (4:1b, *SPPY*). Our translation offers the most common interpretation, but there are several difficulties here. The *Yi Chou shu* is a collection of essays, which, in its current form, probably dates back to at least the Han period.

[60] A parallel text to the following speech appears in *Chan-kuo ts'e* (4:8b-10a, *SPTK*).

[61] Lang-ya was located south of modern Chiao-nan 膠南 County in Shantung (T'an Ch'i-hsiang, 1:45). This is on the coast of the Sea of Po-hai.

household conscript system,[62] it advances like darts and arrows, fights like thunder rumbling, and retires like rain dispersing. Even if challenged in battle, not once has [the enemy] gone over Mount T'ai, crossed the Ch'ing River, or forded the Sea of Po-hai.[63] There are 70,000 households in Lin-tzu 臨菑,[64] and your servant's private estimate is that there are no less than 3 adult males in each household--3 times 7[0,000] is 210,000, so that without depending on the mobilization of distant counties, Lin-tzu's foot soldiers are already sure to number that many. Lin-tzu is rich and well supplied. Not one of her people does not play the flute, strum the zither, strike the harp, beat the drum, fight cocks, race dogs, play *liu-po* 六博,[65] or kick a ball. On the roads of Lin-tzu, carts rub hubcaps and men rub shoulders; their blouses form a canvas wall. When they raise their sleeves it forms a tent. When they shake off their sweat it turns to rain. Families are rich, men are well off, their will high, their spirits soaring. With your wisdom, Great King, and the might of Ch'i, none in the world can match you. Yet now you face west and serve Ch'in. Your servant is privately ashamed for you, Great King.

[2258] "As to the reason Han and Wei fear and honor Ch'in, it is because their borders adjoin with Ch'in. When the troops issue forth and meet, in less than ten days, battle and victory, survival and destruction are decided. If Han and Wei fight and triumph over Ch'in, their troops will be reduced by half, and they will be unable to hold their borders. If they fight and do not triumph over Ch'in, their states' destruction will soon follow. This is why Han and Wei treat battle with Ch'in as a grave matter and vassalage to Ch'in as a light matter. But for Ch'in to attack Ch'i is a different matter. With its back to the territory of Han and Wei, it must pass over the Yang-chin 陽晉 road of Wey and climb over the slopes of K'ang-fu 亢父,[66] its carts unable to go two abreast, its horsemen unable to ride in pairs. With a hundred men holding the heights, a thousand would not dare to pass. If Ch'in entered too deeply it would have to keep glancing behind like a wolf, for fear that Han and Wei might plot against its rear. Fearful but putting on a fearsome front, arrogant but not daring to advance, it is clear that Ch'in is unable to harm Ch'i. [*2259*] Failing to perceive that Ch'in is unable to do anything to Ch'i, wishing to face west and serve it, this is the error of your assembled vassals' stratagems. You have not yet the name of vassal to Ch'in and still have the reality of a mighty state. Your servant thus wishes you to note this, Great King, and plan accordingly."

The King of Ch'i said, "We are dull-witted and hug the sea in a far off corner, in our state at the eastern border at the end of all roads, so that until now we have never heard a

[62] There are various explanations for the "five households" system referred to here. "So-yin" suggests that it refers to the soldiers of five states. Takigawa (69:26) believes that it refers to the "five household" system instituted by the early Ch'i minister Kuan Chung (this system is described in the *Kuo-yü*, 6:5b, *SPPY*). Finally, Yang K'uan (p. 113) argues that this refers to the *wu-tu* 五都 "five city" system used by Ch'i during the Warring States period.

[63] There are two interpretations here. "Cheng-yi" and Takigawa (69:27) both take this to mean that in all its wars, Ch'i has never been forced to levy troops from these areas. Wang Li-ch'i (69:1720) and Ho Chien-chang (p. 391, n. 11) take it in the sense given in the translation. Both interpretations present difficulties.

[64] Ch'i's capital a few miles east of the modern city of the same name in northern Shantung (T'an Ch'i-hsiang, 1:41).

[65] *Liu-po* was a kind of chess game played on a board resembling a sundial and containing many astrological symbols. See also Needham, 4.1:327, Yang Lien-sheng, "A Note on the So-called TLV Mirrors and the Game *Liu-po*," *HJAS*, 10(1947), 202-206, Yang's sequel, "An Additional Note on the Ancient Game *Liu-po*," *HJAS*, 15(1952), 124-39, and Fu Chü-yu 傅舉有, "Lun Ch'in-Han shih-ch'i te po-chü po-hsi chien-chi po-chü wen-ching 論秦漢時期的博具博戲兼及博局紋鏡, *K'ao-ku hsüeh-pao*, 1986.1, 21-42, which includes information derived from recent archaeological discoveries in China.

[66] Yang-chin was located west of modern Yün-ch'eng 鄆城 County in Shantung; K'ang-fu was located south of modern Chi-ning 濟寧 City in Shantung (T'an Ch'i-hsiang, 1:39).

whisper of your instructions. Now that the honored gentleman has instructed us with the writ of the King of Chao, We respectfully follow with our state."

Su Ch'in then went southwest and advised King Wei 威 of Ch'u (r. 339-329 B.C.):[67] "Ch'u is the mightiest state in the world. Your Majesty is the most sagacious king in the world. To the west you have Ch'ien-chung 黔中 and Wu Commandery 巫, to the east you have Hsia-chou 夏州 and Hai-yang 海陽, to the south you have Tung-t'ing 洞庭 and Ts'ang-wu 蒼梧, to the north you have Hsing-sai 陘塞 and Hsün-yang 郇陽.[68] Your territory is more than five-thousand *li* [on a side], your armored soldiers number one-hundred thousand, your carriages one thousand, your horsemen ten thousand, and your grain can last for ten years. These are the resources of a Hegemon King. With the might of Ch'u and Your Majesty's wisdom, no one in the world can resist you. If now you wish to face west and serve Ch'in, not one of the feudal princes but will face west and submit at the foot of the Illustrious Terrace.[69]

[2260] "There is none that Ch'in loathes more than Ch'u. When Ch'u is strong then Ch'in is weak. When Ch'in is strong then Ch'u is weak. The two cannot exist together. Thus in laying plans for you, Great King, the best move would be to form alliances and isolate Ch'in. If you fail to ally, Great King, Ch'in is sure to form two armies. One will emerge from the Wu Pass and one will descend into Ch'ien-chung. Then even Yen 鄢 and Ying 郢 will tremble.[70]

"Your servant has heard it said, 'Cultivate it before it grows wild, act before it comes into existence.' If disaster arrives and only then are you troubled, it is far too late to do anything. I thus hope that you will carefully consider this beforehand, Great King. If you can heed your servant, Great King, I ask your permission to have the states East of the Mount submit offerings for the four seasons in compliance with the Great King's illustrious writ, to have

[67] A parallel to the following speech appears in *Chan-kuo ts'e* (5:6b-8a, *SPTK*).

[68] Ch'ien-chung was a commandery covering parts of modern Szechwan, Kweichow, Hunan, and Hupei. Wu Commandery was on the eastern edge of modern Szechwan province. Hsia-chou was a very extensive area. Since the text refers to this as the eastern border of Ch'u, it apparently refers to the eastern end of Hsia-chou, located north of modern Han-yang 漢陽 County in Hupei. Hai-yang was located in modern T'ai 泰 County in Kiangsu. Tung-t'ing is a lake located in modern Hunan province, near the city of Yüeh-yang 岳陽. Ts'ang-wu was a Ch'u district located in the modern Ts'ang-wu County in Kwangsi Autonomous Region. Hsing-sai refers to a mountain located east of modern Lo-ho 漯河 City in Honan. Hsün-yang was located in modern Hsün-yang County in Shansi.

[69] The Chang-t'ai 章臺 was a pleasure palace, rather than a formal residence, hence to pay homage there, in front of the King of Ch'in's entertainers and concubines, was particularly humiliating. This was where King Huai of Ch'u was brought when he was forced to pay homage, and where Lin Hsiang-ju was sent for an audience (see our translation of Chapter 81).

[70] There is some confusion here due to the fact that wherever Ch'u built a new capital city, the place name was changed to Ying. (Perhaps *ying* was simply a Ch'u dialect word for capital.) Ch'u moved its capital a number of times, once to a place originally called Yen, so that most scholars now agree that *Yen-ying* was the name of this one particular city. There is a parallel to this in that Ch'u later moved its capital to a place called Ch'en 陳 which is also sometimes referred to as *Ch'en-ying*. We believe there are also cases, however, where *Yen-ying* refers to two different places, with "Yen" referring to the city located near modern Yi-ch'eng 宜城 in Hupei and "Ying" referring to the old capital city of Ch'u located near modern Chiang-ling 江陵 in Hupei (T'an Ch'i-hsiang, 1:45). In particular, this is the case for references throughout the *Shih chi* to the Ch'in general Pai Ch'i's attack on Ch'u, during which he captured *Yen-ying*. According to *Shih chi* 5:212-3, 15:742, and 73:2331, he captured Yen in 279 B.C., and Ying in 278 B.C. In these accounts, Yen and Ying were clearly two different places. (Ch'ien Mu, *Ti-ming k'ao*, p. 338, attempts to resolve these references so that "Yen Ying" still refers to Yen alone, unsuccessfully, in our opinion.) It is not as clear, however, that the current text refers to two places. "Cheng-yi" believes this to be so and would refer the "troops emerging from Wu Pass" to an attack on Yen and the "troops coming down through Ch'ien-chung" to an attack on Ying. We tentatively accept this interpretation here, and thus throughout the *Shih chi* translate *Yen-ying* as "Yen and Ying."

them entrust their altars of grain and soil, to offer up their ancestral temples, to train their knights and sharpen their weapons and to place them all at you disposal.

[2261] "If you can truly make use of your servant's foolish plans, Great King, Han, Wei, Ch'i, Yen, Chao, and Wey's finest sounds and most beautiful women will fill your back palaces, and the camels and stallions of Yen and Tai will fill your outer stables. Thus if alliance is joined then Ch'u will rule, and if counter-alliance succeeds then Ch'in will be emperor. To abandon now the task of a Hegemon King and take the name of servant to another, this is not what your servant would choose for you, Great King.

"Ch'in is a state of tigers and wolves, and has the ambition to swallow the world. Ch'in is the mortal enemy of the rest of the world. The advocates of counter-alliance all wish to serve Ch'in with concessions of territory from the feudal lords. This is what is called nourishing an enemy and serving a foe. To act as vassal to another, ceding his ruler's territory to ingratiate himself with the mighty tigers and wolves of Ch'in, leading into the invasion of the world, until finally the disaster of Ch'in strikes, yet ignoring this danger, or to make use of mighty Ch'in's majesty to threaten his ruler at home and to seek territorial concessions, the greatest faithlessness and disloyalty could not exceed this. Thus if alliances are made, the feudal lords will cede territory to serve Ch'u, and if counter-alliance is made, then Ch'u will cede territory to serve Ch'in. These two policies are far different. Of these two, which would you choose, Great King? Therefore, our humble manor's King of Chao has sent his servant to present his foolish plan, and present the oaths of alliance. May you issue the orders as you will, Great King!"

The King of Ch'u said, "Our state to the west adjoins the borders of Ch'in and Ch'in has a mind to take Pa and Shu and annex Han-chung. Ch'in is a state of wolves and tigers, and cannot be trusted. But Han and Wei are now faced with disaster from Ch'in, and we cannot consult closely with them. If we consulted closely with them, We fear that traitors would enter Ch'in with [our plans], and with consultations yet unrealized, our state would already be in danger. Our own estimate is that with Ch'u resisting Ch'in, victory is by no means certain. Consulting at home with our assembled vassals is not enough to rely on. We take no comfort from lying on our sleeping mat, no pleasure from our food's flavor. Our heart flutters like a dangling banner, with no place to tie it down. Now that My Lord and Master wishes to unify the world, gather the feudal lords, and preserve endangered states, We scrupulously offer up our altars of grain and soil and follow you."

After this, the Six States made alliance and joined their strength. Su Ch'in was master of the oaths of alliance and served as Prime Minister to all Six States. He went north to report to the King of Chao and passed on his journey through Lo-yang. The carriages and horsemen, heavy and light carts sent by each of the feudal lords to accompany him were so numerous that he was mistaken for a king. When King Hsien of Chou heard of it, he was [*2262*] terrified, cleared the roads, and sent men to feast him in the suburbs.

Su Ch'in's older and younger brothers and their wives averted their eyes and did not dare look up at him, but with their heads lowered, bowed down and served him food.

Su Ch'in laughed and said to his older brother's wife, "Why were you so arrogant before and so respectful now?"

His sister-in-law crawled over on her hands and knees, pressed her face to the ground, and apologized. "We see that your position is high and your gold abundant, Chi Tzu 季子."[71]

---

[71] Although several sources, apparently based on this passage, identify Su Ch'in's *agnomen* as Chi Tzu, this seems very unlikely since Chi has no semantic relationship with Su Ch'in's *praenomen* Ch'in, as was usually the case. Instead, we suggest that *chi* here has the common meaning of "youngest brother." This does leave open the difficult question of what Su Ch'in's relationship with Su Li and Su Tai was. *Shih chi* identifies them both as Su

Su Ch'in sighed deeply. "I am still the same man, but now that I am wealthy and noble, my own relatives fear me, while when I was poor and lowly they despised me. How much more so, then, for the masses of men? If I had had two *ch'ing* of farmland next to the inner city wall of Lo-yang, how could I ever have hung the ministerial seals of Six States from my belt!" He gave out a thousand in gold as a gift to his clan and friends.

Previously, when Su Ch'in had gone to Yen, he had borrowed a hundred coins from a man for his expenses. When he became wealthy and noble, he repaid him with a hundred in gold. He repaid all who had ever done him favors. Only one of his followers was not rewarded, so he went before Su Ch'in and mentioned this himself.

Su Ch'in replied, "I haven't forgotten you, sir. When you and I reached Yen together, several times you wanted to leave me by the bank of the Yi River. At the time I was in straits, so I hated you deeply. That is why I have left you till last. Now you too shall have your payment."

Su Ch'in, having joined the Six States in alliance, returned to Chao. Marquis Su of Chao enfeoffed him as the Lord of Wu-an 武安,[72] and sent the articles of alliance to Ch'in. The soldiers of Ch'in did not dare to peer out of the Han-ku Pass for fifteen years.[73]

[2263] Afterwards, Ch'in sent the *Hsi-shou* to deceive Ch'i and Wei into attacking Chao together with Ch'in, hoping to destroy the alliance. When Ch'i and Wei attacked Chao, the King of Chao berated Su Ch'in. Su Ch'in was afraid and asked to go on a mission to Yen, assuring the king that he would repay Ch'i. Su Ch'in left Chao and the alliances all collapsed.[74]

King Hui of Ch'in sent his daughter as wife to the Heir of Yen.[75] Marquis Wen died that year. The Heir succeeded him and became King Yi 易 of Yen (r. 332-321 B.C.). When King Yi was first enthroned, King Hsüan of Ch'i took advantage of Yen's funeral to attack Yen and took ten cities.[76]

King Yi said to Su Ch'in, "In days past when you reached Yen, the late king gave you money for an audience in Chao, from which you proceeded to effect the alliance of the Six States. Ch'i first attacked Chao and has now reached Yen. Because of you, sir, we are the laughingstock of the world. Can you win back for Yen our seized lands, sir?"

Su Ch'in was mortified. "Allow me to take them for Your Majesty."

Su Ch'in met with the King of Ch'i. He touched his forehead to the ground twice. Looking down, he congratulated the king. Looking up, he offered condolences.

The King of Ch'i said, "How is it that your congratulations and condolences follow so quickly on one another?"

Ch'in's younger brothers, but the Wei scholar Chiao Chou 譙周 (quoted in "So-yin," *Shih chi,* 69:2241) states they were Su Ch'in's older brothers, a view which has become more popular with the discovery of the silk manuscripts at Ma-wang-tui. Crump (p. 15), believing that Su Ch'in was a fictional character, reasserts Maspero's contention that the popularity of this literary creation inspired the addition of brothers for him, but it is impossible to show which of the texts mentioning the Su brothers is earliest, making this a difficult statement to justify.

[72] There were at least three Lords of Wu-an during the Warring States period: Su Ch'in, the Ch'in general Pai Ch'i (see our translation of Chapter 73), and the Chao general Li Mu (see our translation of Chapter 81). T'an Ch'i-hsiang (1:38) shows only one Wu-an, located in the state of Chao, near modern Wu-an City in Honan. This would be a possible fief location for both Su Ch'in and Li Mu, who were associated with the state of Chao, but not for Pai Ch'i. For a further discussion of the problems involved, see Ch'ien Mu, *Ti-ming k'ao,* p. 490.

[73] It is impossible to find 15 years during this period without military expeditions or attacks by Ch'in against the Six States.

[74] This apparently refers to the attack on Chao in 332 B.C., recorded in *Shih chi,* 15:728.

[75] The following story also appears in *Chan-kuo ts'e* (9:3b-4a, *SPTK*).

[76] This attack is not otherwise recorded in *Shih chi.*

Su Ch'in said, "Your servant has heard that the reason a hungry man goes hungry rather than eat [the poison herb] monkshood[77] is because it will fill his belly for the moment, but in the end is as disastrous as starving to death. Although Yen is small and weak, [its king] is the younger son-in-law of Ch'in. You coveted its ten walled cities, Great King, and are now forever an enemy of mighty Ch'in. If feeble Yen is in the vanguard, mighty Ch'in will follow behind it; thus might one attract the world's finest troops. This is the same as eating monkshood."

The King of Ch'i paled in dismay. "If that is the case, what's to be done?"

Su Ch'in said, "Your servant has heard that those skilled of old at controlling affairs turned bad luck into good fortune and established merit through defeat. If you can heed your servant's plan, Great King, then you will immediately return Yen's ten walled cities. When Yen obtains ten walled cities without any cause, it is sure to be pleased. When the King of Ch'in learns that you returned Yen's ten cities for his sake, he is also sure to be pleased. This is what is called casting aside enmity and gaining a relationship of stone. With Yen and Ch'in both serving Ch'i, when you issue orders to the world, Great King, none will dare to disobey. Thus Your Majesty can ally yourself to Ch'in through empty words and take the world with ten cities. This is the task of a hegemon king."

"Well put," said the king, [*2264*] and afterward returned Yen's ten cities.

Someone slandered Su Ch'in.[78] "Your courtier is selling out the state; he is a treasonous, treacherous vassal. He is going to rebel."

Su Ch'in was afraid he had offended the king and returned [to Yen], but the King of Yen did not put him in office again. Su Ch'in appeared before the King of Yen.

"Your servant is a rustic from East Chou, without an inch of merit, yet Your Majesty presented him before his ancestral temple and treated him with reverence in his court. Now your servant has repelled the troops of Ch'i and gained ten walled cities for Your Majesty. For this you should give even more trust. That I come and Your Majesty does not put me in office must be because someone has slandered me before Your Majesty as untrustworthy. My untrustworthiness is Your Majesty's good fortune. Your servant has heard 'those who are loyal and trustworthy are so for their own sakes. Those who advance and take profit do so for the sake of others.' Moreover, in speaking before the King of Ch'i I did not even deceive him. Your servant abandoned his aged mother in East Chou; naturally by doing so I put away action for my own sake and engaged in advancing and taking profit. If today there were men as filial as Tseng Shen, as incorruptible as Po Yi, as faithful as Venerable Wei 尾, if you could obtain three such men to serve you, Great King, how would that be?"[79]

"It would be enough," said the king.

"If a man were as filial as Tseng Shen, whose sense of duty did not permit him to leave his parents for one night, then how could Your Majesty make him walk a thousand *li* to serve the imperiled king of feeble Yen?

"If a man were as incorruptible as Po Yi, whose integrity did not permit him to succeed the Lord of Ku-chu, who was unwilling to become a vassal of King Wu, who did not accept the fief of a marquis, and who starved to death at the foot of Mount Shou-yang; if his

---

[77] *Wu-cho* 烏啄, also called *wu-t'ou* 烏頭 (*aconitum carmichaeli*); the drug from this plant is aconite.

[78] The following anecdote also appears in the *Chan-kuo ts'e* (9:4b-6a, *SPTK*). A portion of it also appears in the Ma-wang-tui silk manuscripts (see *Chan-kuo tsung-heng chia shu*, pp. 16-22).

[79] For Tseng Shen, see n. 23 to our translation of *Shih chi* Chapter 65, n. 23. For Po Yi, see our translation of Chapter 61. Venerable Wei arranged to meet a girl under a bridge; when she failed to appear and the water began to rise, he did not leave, but wrapped his arms around a pylon and drowned (*Chuang Tzu*, 29:9:21a, *SPPY*).

incorruptibility were such, how could Your Majesty make him walk a thousand *li* to engage in advancing and taking profit in Ch'i?

[2265] "If a man were as faithful as Venerable Wei, who agreed to meet with a woman beneath a bridge and, when the woman did not come and the water reached him, would not leave, but instead clung to the bridge pylon and died; if his faithfulness were such, how could Your Majesty make him walk a thousand *li* to repel the mighty army of Ch'i? This is what your servant meant by offending the sovereign through loyalty and faithfulness."

The King of Yen said, "You are simply disloyal and unfaithful. How could one offend through loyalty and unfaithfulness?"

Su Ch'in said, "Not so. Your servant heard of a man who as an official had to travel far. His wife took a lover. When her husband was going to return, the lover was worried. The wife said, 'Don't worry, I have already prepared poison wine to deal with him.' After three days, her husband arrived as expected. The wife had a slave present him with the poison wine. The slave wanted to speak of the poison in the wine, but feared her mistress would be driven away. She wanted to be silent, but feared she would kill her master. Thus she pretended to slip and dropped the wine. Her master was furious and beat her fifty strokes with a light cane. Thus with one stumble and some overturned wine, the slave saved her master above and her mistress below, yet she was not spared the cane. In what way then can loyalty and faithfulness never offend? Your servant's error was unfortunately of this sort."

The King of Yen said, "Resume your old office, Master."

King Yi's mother was the wife of Marquis Wen. She took Su Ch'in as her lover. When the King of Yen learned of this, he treated him even better. Su Ch'in feared punishment and advised the King of Yen.

"Living in Yen, your servant is unable to exalt Yen. If I were in Ch'i, then Yen would be sure to be exalted."

"Do whatever you feel best, Master," said the King of Yen. Su Ch'in then pretended to have offended Yen and fled to Ch'i. King Hsüan of Ch'i made him a Foreign Excellency.

When King Hsüan of Ch'i died, King Min 湣 (r. *323-284 B.C.) took the throne. [Su Ch'in] persuaded King Min to make the funeral an elaborate one in order to exalt his filial piety and to enlarge his palace and expand his parks in order to show he had gained his ambitions, hoping to exhaust Ch'i for the sake of Yen.

When King Yi 易 of Yen (r. 332-321 B.C.) died, K'uai 噲 of Yen (r. 320-312 B.C.) succeeded as king. Afterwards, many of Ch'i's grand masters struggled for favor with Su Ch'in. A man was sent to stab Su Ch'in, but he fled before Su Ch'in died. The King of Ch'i sent out men to catch the assassin, but did not get him. As Su Ch'in was dying, he told the King of Ch'i, "After I die, have me torn asunder by carts in the marketplace as a warning and say that 'Su Ch'in was stirring rebellion in Ch'i for Yen.' If you do this, then you are sure to catch my assassin."

[2266] They did as he said, and the killer of Su Ch'in did indeed emerge on his own. The King of Ch'i then executed the killer. Yen heard this and said, "Savage indeed was Ch'i's vengeance for Master Su!"[80]

After Su Ch'in died, his machinations were all uncovered. After Ch'i learned of them, it was furious with Yen. Yen was terrified. Su Ch'in's younger brother was Tai. Tai's

---

[80] The date of Su Ch'in's death is a controversial question. *Shih chi* (70:2289) seems to put it at 311 B.C., but that is impossible as far as this chapter is concerned, because that would mean that Su Ch'in outlived the King of Yen, K'uai, and in the following section, Su Ch'in's brother, Su Tai, addresses a speech to K'uai in the hopes of filling Su Ch'in's post. For a number of other theories on the date of Su Ch'in's death, see Ho Chien-chang, p. 11, n. 3, and the references at the end of this chapter.

younger brother was Su Li 蘇厲. They saw their older brother's success and both began their studies.

Su Tai

When Su Ch'in died, [Su] Tai [蘇]代 asked for an audience with the King of Yen, hoping to fill [Su Ch'in's] old post:[81] "Your servant is a rustic from East Chou. I have privately heard that your principles are most exalted, Great King. I am a dull-witted rustic and have laid aside my hoe and plow to seek you. When I reached Han-tan what I saw was not at all equal to what I had heard in East Chou, and I regretted my ambitions. When I reached the court of Yen, I saw Your Majesty's assembled vassals and lower officers. Your majesty is the world's most enlightened king."

The King of Yen said, "What is this enlightened king that you speak of like?"

He replied, "Your servant has heard that an enlightened king strives to hear of his faults and does not wish to hear of his virtues. Your servant asks permission to lay out Your Majesty's faults. Ch'i and Chao are the foes of Yen. Ch'u and Wei are the supporters of Yen. Your majesty now serves your foes in an attack against your supporters. This is not the way to gain advantage for Yen. If this was Your Majesty's own scheme, it was an error of planning, but that there were none from whom you could hear this, these were no loyal vassals."

The King of Yen said, "Ch'i is indeed our mortal enemy and the one whom we desire to attack, but we fear that in our state's exhaustion, our strength is not sufficient. If you can lead an expedition against Ch'i with Yen, we shall take up our state and entrust it to you, sir."

[Su Tai] replied, "There are seven warring states in the world today, and Yen is the weakest of them. If it fought alone, it would be unable. [But] if there were one it could ally itself to, that one would be exalted. If it allied itself to Ch'u in the south, Ch'u would be exalted. [*2267*] If it allied itself to Ch'in in the west, Ch'in would be exalted. If it allied itself to Han and Wei in the middle, Han and Wei would be exalted. If the state to which you ally yourself is exalted, you are sure to be exalted too, Your Majesty. Ch'i's ruler is worthy, but manages affairs himself.[82] He attacked Ch'u in the south for five years and his supplies were exhausted. He penned up Ch'in for three years and his troops were exhausted. He fought with the men of Yen to the north and lost three armies to capture two generals.[83] Yet now to

---

[81] There is a speech paralleling that which follows in *Chan-kuo ts'e* (9:6b-8a, *SPTK*).

[82] The phrase *ch'ang chu* 長主 is unclear. We tentatively follow Takigawa (44:30).

[83] These dates present a number of difficulties. For the "five years attacking Ch'u," Yü Ch'ang (quoted in Ho Chien-chang, p. 46, n.5) refers this to the period from 305 to 301 B.C. There is a record of a major attack by Ch'i, Ch'in, Han, and Wei on Ch'u in 301 B.C. (*Shih chi*, 15:736). It is not clear why he would have the five years start with 305 B.C., however. The commentators of *Chan-kuo tsung-heng chia shu* (p. 28, n. 2) point out that according to *Shih chi*, 40:1727, in 305 B.C. Ch'u reneged on a treaty with Ch'i, and, as a consequence, in 303 B.C. Ch'i, Wei, and Han attacked Ch'u. If we date the beginning of armed conflict in 303 B.C., however, five years would be either 299 or 298 B.C., depending on how we count, and again there are no records of fighting between Ch'i and Ch'u for the period 300-298 B.C. This date therefore cannot be regarded as satisfactorily resolved.

For the "three years" of penning up Ch'in, Ho Chien-chang (p. 229, n. 14) accepts Yang K'uan's reconstruction of these events (Yang K'uan, pp. 702-3), and puts this from 298-296 B.C., when Ch'i, Han, and Wei fought their way into the Han-ku Pass. Yang puts Ch'i's attack on Yen in 296 B.C. There is no other record of such an attack, however, and this suggestion is speculative. (For other suggestions, see Ho Chien-chang, p. 1102, n. 40.)

The difficulty with this speech is that these dates would place it during the reign of King Chao of Yen

face south with his remaining troops and capture great Sung, [a state with] five-thousand chariots, and then to clasp the twelve feudal lords, this is what [Ch'i's] lord desires to accomplish. With his people exhausted, how can he do it? Moreover, your servant has heard that 'after numerous battles, the people are exhausted, after invading in force, the troops are worn out.'"

The King of Yen said, "I have heard that Ch'i has the Clear Chi and the Muddy Ho which can stand as strongholds and the Long Wall and Great Barricade which can serve as fortresses. Is this so?"

[Su Tai] replied, "If Heaven's season is not with you, even with the Clear Chi and Muddy Ho, what strongholds will stand? If the people's strength is exhausted, even with the Long Wall and Great Barricade, what fortresses will serve?

"Moreover, in other days, Ch'i levied no troops west of the Chi; these were what it held in reserve against Chao. It levied no troops north of the Ho; these were what it it held in reserve against Yen. Now it has used up the levies both west of the Chi and north of the Ho, while within its borders it is exhausted. An arrogant lord is sure to love profit and the vassals of a doomed state are sure to be greedy for goods. If Your Majesty is not ashamed at making your maternal nephews and full brothers hostages and serving [Ch'i's] courtiers with treasure and jewels, jade and silk, they will owe Yen their gratitude and will think nothing of destroying Sung; then Ch'i can be destroyed."

The King of Yen said, "At last I have received Heaven's mandate through you, sir."

Yen then sent a hostage prince to Ch'i.[84] Su Li asked for a meeting with the King of Ch'i through the hostage prince. The King of Ch'i was angry with Su Ch'in and wanted to imprison Su Li. The Yen hostage prince apologized for him and [Su Li] then laid down his pledge as a vassal of Ch'i.

[2268] Yen's Prime Minister, Tzu-chih 子之, was related to Su Tai by marriage, but wanted to seize power in Yen. He sent Su Tai to accompany the hostage prince in Ch'i. Ch'i sent Tai to report to Yen, and K'uai, King of Yen, asked him, "Will the King of Ch'i become Hegemon?"

"He is incapable."

"Why?"

"He does not trust his vassals."

After this the King of Yen entrusted all power to Tzu-chih, later yielding the throne to him, and great strife broke out in Yen. Ch'i led an expedition against Yen, killing the king, K'uai, and Tzu-chih (314 B.C.). King Chao succeeded to the throne in Yen (311 B.C.), and after this Su Tai and Su Li did not dare to enter Yen. Finally they turned to Ch'i, and Ch'i treated them well.

Su Tai passed through Wei.[85] Wei seized [Su] Tai for Yen. Ch'i sent an envoy to tell the King of Wei, "Ch'i has asked to enfeoff the Lord of Ching-yang 涇陽[86] with the territory of Sung, but Ch'in is sure to refuse it. [*2269*] It is not that Ch'in does not think it would be to its advantage to have Ch'i's homage or obtain the territory of Sung, but it does not trust

(311-279 B.C.), rather than in the reign of K'uai (320-312 B.C.), yet in the paragraph after this, Su Tai is plotting with K'uai's Prime Minister Tzu-chih to persuade K'uai to give up the throne, an event which occurred in 316 B.C. (*Shih chi,* 15:732).

[84] A passage very similar to the following narrative occurs in *Chan-kuo ts'e* (9:13b, *SPTK*). On the use of hostages during this period, see Yang Lien-sheng, "Hostages in Chinese History," in *Studies in Chinese Institutional History* (Cambridge, Mass.: Harvard University Press, 1963), pp. 43-57.

[85] A passage similar to the following narrative appears in the *Chan-kuo ts'e* (9:14a, *SPTK*).

[86] The Lord of Ching-yang was the younger brother of King Chao of Ch'in. See *Shih chi,* 72:2323 and our translation of *Shih chi* Chapter 72.

the King of Ch'i and Su Tzu. But now that Ch'i and Wei's conflict has become so severe, Ch'i will not deceive Ch'in. If Ch'in trusts Ch'i, Ch'i and Ch'in will join together, and the Lord of Ching-yang will have the territories of Sung. This is not to the advantage of Wei. Thus Your Majesty would be better off sending Su Tzu eastward. Ch'in is sure to suspect Ch'i and distrust Su Tzu. If Ch'i and Ch'in do not get along, the world will not suffer any changes, and the conditions for an attack on Ch'i will be laid." They sent Tai out of the state. Su Tai went to Sung, and Sung treated him well.

Ch'i launched an attack against Sung. Sung was hard pressed and Su Tai sent a letter to King Chao of Yen which read:[87]

> To rank among the states with ten-thousand chariots and yet leave a pledge in Ch'i, this lowers your reputation and reduces your authority. To offer ten-thousand carriages to assist Ch'i's expedition against Sung, this will wear out your people and deplete your stores. To break Sung, ravage Ch'u's Huai-pei, and fatten great Ch'i, this will strengthen your enemy and wound your state. These three are all great defeats for your state, yet Your Majesty is still prepared to carry out all three, thinking you will thus earn Ch'i's trust. Yet Ch'i will trust Your Majesty even less and mistrust Yen even more. This is the error of Your Majesty's plan. Sung added to Huai-pei would be mightier than a state with ten-thousand carriages. When Ch'i annexes it, this will increase the number of Ch'i's by one. The Pei-Yi have seven-hundred *li* [on a side];[88] added to Lu and Wey, this would be mightier than a state with ten-thousand chariots. When Ch'i takes it, this will increase the number of Ch'i's by two. Faced with the strength of one Ch'i, Yen must look behind like a wolf and cannot resist it. For Yen to be confronted now with three Ch'i's, this disaster is sure to be even greater.
>
> [2270] Even so, a clever man in charge can make bad luck into good fortune and turn defeat into merit. The purple silk of Ch'i is made from worn raw silk, but its price is ten times greater. Kou-chien, King of Yüeh, was trapped on top of K'uai-chi, and later ravaged mighty Wu and became Hegemon of the world.[89] These were both cases of making bad luck into good fortune and turning defeats into merit.
>
> If Your Majesty wants to make bad luck into good fortune and turn defeat into merit, it would be best to support the Hegemon Ch'i and honor him, send a messenger to make a covenant [with Ch'i] in the court of the Chou, burn Ch'in's credentials,[90] and say [to Ch'i], "The best of all plans would be to defeat Ch'in. The next best would be to isolate it forever." The King of Ch'in would be sure to fear awaiting defeat in isolation. Ch'in has attacked the feudal lords for five generations. Now the inferior of Ch'i, if the King of Ch'in could attain his ambition of weakening Ch'i, he would not hesitate to award a state for [helping in] such an achievement. This being so, Your Majesty, why not send an eloquent knight to speak with King of Ch'in using this argument:
>
> "If Yen and Chao were to defeat Sung and fatten Ch'i, honoring Ch'i and becoming his inferiors, Yen and Chao see no benefit in this. That Yen and Chao are

---

[87] The following letter also appears in the *Chan-kuo ts'e* (9:19a-20b, *SPTK*), and the Ma-wang-tui silk manuscripts (*Chan-kuo tsung-heng chia shu*, pp. 85-90). The latter attributes it to Su Ch'in, rather than Su Tai, and presents it as a speech, rather than a letter.

[88] Wang Nien-sun (4:14b-15a) suggests that *pei* 北 is an error for *chiu* 九, and the *Chan-kuo tsung-heng chia shu* version of this passage does indeed read *chiu*.

  Yi was the name for a number of non-Chinese tribes in the eastern part of China.

[89] For Yüeh's defeat of Wu, see our translation of *Shih chi* Chapter 66.

[90] Diplomatic credentials took the form of tallies which were to be matched when the envoy of one state sought audience with the ruler of an allied state. Urging Yen to burn the tallies its emissary would need to see the King of Ch'in is equivalent to urging Yen to break off diplomatic relations with Ch'in.

prepared to do this even though it is not to their advantage is because they do not trust the King of Ch'in. This being so, why not send a trustworthy messenger to win over Yen and Chao; send the Lord of Ching-yang 涇陽 and the Lord of Kao-ling 高陵 into Yen and Chao;[91] if Ch'in changes, they can hold them as hostages, and then Yen and Chao will trust Ch'in. Ch'in will become the Western Emperor, Yen the Northern Emperor, and Chao the Middle Emperor, establishing three emperors to rule the world. If Han and Wei do not obey, then Ch'in will lead an attack on them. If Ch'i does not obey then Yen and Chao will lead an attack on him. Who in the world would dare not to obey? When the world has submitted and obeys [us], we can spur Han and Wei to attack Ch'i, demanding that Ch'i 'must return the territory of Sung and Ch'u's Huai-pei.' To return the territory of Sung and Ch'u's Huai-pei would benefit Yen and Chao. To be established as two of the three emperors would fulfill Yen and Chao's desire. In practical terms they would gain benefit; in terms of honor, they would gain their desires. Yen and Chao would cast Ch'i aside like throwing off straw sandals. If you do not win over Yen and Chao, Ch'i is sure to succeed as Hegemon. If the feudal lords support Ch'i and Your Majesty does not follow, your state will be attacked. [*2271*] If the feudal lords support Ch'i and Your Majesty does follow, your reputation will be lowered. If you win over Yen and Chao, your state will be safe and your name honored. If you do not win over Yen and Chao, your state will be threatened and your reputation lowered. To cast aside honor and safety, grasping danger and lowliness, a clever man would not do this.'

When the King of Ch'in hears such a speech, he is sure to be as if stabbed in the heart. Why then does Your Majesty not have an eloquent knight speak thus to Ch'in? Ch'in is sure to be won over and Ch'i is sure to suffer attack. To win over Ch'in will result in a strong tie. To attack Ch'i will yield pure profit. To exalt strong ties and to labor at pure profit, these are the affairs of a sage king.

King Chao of Yen thought his letter excellent. "Our late king once did the Su clan a favor. After the rebellion of Tzu-chih, the Su clan left Yen. If Yen is to gain revenge against Ch'i, only the Su clan can do this." He summoned Su Tai and treated him well once more, planning an expedition against Ch'i with him. In the end they broke Ch'i and King Min fled from his capital.

After some time, Ch'in summoned the King of Yen.[92] The King of Yen wanted to go, but Su Tai restrained the King of Yen. "Ch'u obtained Chih 枳 and lost its capital.[93] Ch'i obtained Sung and lost its capital.[94] Ch'i and Ch'u were not able to treat with Ch'in once they had Chih and Sung. Why was this? Whoever has achievements is the mortal foe of Ch'in. Ch'in would win the world not through the practice of righteousness, but through tyranny. Ch'in's tyrannical actions were openly announced to the world.

[2272] "He announced to Ch'u, 'The armored troops of our lands in Shu will travel by boat down the Wen 汶,[95] they will ride the summer floods down the Chiang and in five days

[91] For the Lord of Ching-yang, see n. 85 above. The Lord of Kao-ling was another brother of King Hui of Ch'in (see n. 3 above), named Hsien 顯. Kao-ling was located southwest of modern Kao-ling County in Shensi (T'an Ch'i-hsiang, 1:36).

[92] A parallel to the following speech appears in the *Chan-kuo ts'e* (9:29b-31a, *SPTK*).

[93] Chih was located in modern P'ei-ling 涪陵 County in Szechwan (T'an Ch'i-hsiang, 1:44). "Chi-chieh" suggests that Ch'u losing its capital refers to Pai Ch'i's attack on Ch'u in 279 B.C., and this suggestion is accepted by most commentators. No one, however, has explained the reference to "gaining Chih."

[94] As noted above, Ch'i destroyed the state of Sung in 286 B.C. "Lost its capital" apparently refers to the attack led by the state of Yen against Ch'i in 284 B.C. during which King Min of Ch'i was driven from his capital.

[95] This is taken by some commentators (e.g., Wang Li-ch'i, 69:1713) to refer to the Min River 岷江, a tributary of the Yangtze that begins south of Min mountain range of Szechwan, but as Ch'ien Mu, *Ti-ming k'ao*, p. 65-66

will reach Ying. The armored troops of Han-chung will set out by boat on the Pa, they will ride the summer floods down the Han and in four days reach Wu-tu 五都.[96] We will mass armored troops at Yüan 宛, we will take Sui 隨 in the east,[97] and the clever man will have no time to take counsel, the brave man will have no time to take anger; We will [attack you] like eagle hunters. If you intend to wait for the world to attack Han-ku Pass, isn't that far too distant, Your Majesty?' It is for this reason that the King of Ch'u has served Ch'in for seventeen years.

"Ch'in openly announced to Han, 'If we assemble [our troops] at Shao-ch'ü 少曲,[98] in one day we can sever [the road through] T'ai-hang 太行.[99] If we assemble [our troops] at Yi-yang 宜陽, and butt against P'ing-yang 平陽, in two days [troops] will be levied in every [Han county].[100] If we pass through the two Chou and butt against [Han's capital] Cheng 鄭,[101] in five days the capital will fall.' The royal clan of Han believed this and thus served Ch'in.

[2273] "Ch'in openly announced to Wei, 'If we capture An-yi 安邑, we will block Nü-chi 女戟, Han's T'ai-yüan 太原, and Chüan 卷.[102] If we come down the Chih Road [through] Nan-yang 南陽, Feng 封, and Chi 冀, we will encircle the two Chous.[103] We will ride the summer floods in light boats, with strong crossbows in front and sharp halberds in back, and when we breach the Ying 榮 Ford, Wei will no longer have [its capital] Ta Liang.[104] We will

points out, a passage from the Min to the Yangtze would take far longer than five days.

[96] There are a number of explanations of Wu-tu. "Chi-chieh," noting that the text refers to Tung-t'ing Lake, simply refers this to the area around Tung-t'ing. "So-yin" suggests that it refers to the area "between Yüan 宛 and Teng 鄧." Ho Chien-chang (p. 95, n. 48) seems to concur with this, suggesting it refers to Yen 鄢, Teng 鄧, Wu Commandery 巫, Hsi-ling 西陵, and Ying 郢. We have been unable to find any other source which offers such specific identifications, however.

[97] Yüan was located near modern Nan-yang 南陽 City in Honan (T'an Ch'i-hsiang, 1:29). The location of Sui approximates modern Sui-chou 隨州 City in Hupei (T'an Ch'i-hsiang, 1:45). Takigawa would read *Hsia Sui* as a place name. No other commentators have accepted this reading, although Crump (p. 540) seems to, translating "east of Yüan and Hsia-sui."

[98] Ho Chien-chang (p. 1132, n. 23) suggests that the area to which Shao-ch'ü refers was northeast of Chi-yüan 濟原, on the Shao River in modern Honan province.

[99] T'ai-hang is a mountain range north of the Yellow River, between Honan and Shansi provinces. The T'ai-hang mountains separated the northern part of Han (Shang-tang) from the southern part (T'an Ch'i-hsiang, 1:38).

[100] We follow Takigawa (69:56) in reading *yao* 繇 as *yao* 徭 "to levy a corvée." Wang Shu-min (69:2224) accepts this reading, but would further interpret it as meaning "to obey, to follow." This seems unnecessary.

P'ing-yang was located just southwest of modern Lin-fen 臨汾 City in Shansi. Yi-yang, as noted above, was west of modern Yi-yang City in Honan. These cities were about 100 miles apart, roughly on the southern and northern ends of Han's western border (T'an Ch'i-hsiang, 1:35-6).

[101] The two Chou refer to East Chou and West Chou (see n. 1 of this chapter). The capital of Han, Cheng, was located in modern Hsin Cheng 新鄭 County in Honan (T'an Ch'i-hsiang, 1:36).

[102] The text here seems flawed. Several interpretations have been proposed (see in particular Takigawa, 69:56, Wang Li-ch'i, 69:1714, and Ho Chien-chang, p. 1132). We have not attempted to resolve any of these problems in the translation.

[103] The geography here is confusing in that many of the places named here are said elsewhere to belong to Han, rather than Wei. We follow "So-yin" in reading Feng as a place name referring to Feng-ling 封陵, about 15 miles southwest of Yung-chi 永濟 City in Shensi (T'an Ch'i-hsiang, 1:35). Chi was located at modern Chi-shan 稷山 County in Shansi (T'an Ch'i-hsiang, 1:29). These seem to be the only possible identifications if we limit ourselves to within the generally known boundaries of Wei, but it is very difficult to understand what relation taking or threatening these two places would have with encircling the two Chous.

[104] The Ying is identified by "So-yin" as the Ying-tse 榮澤, an ancient wetland north of modern Chengchow 鄭州 City in Honan. "So-yin" and "Cheng-yi" both suggest that the word *chüeh* 決 here means "breach" and that the intent of breaching the "mouth" of this area was to inundate Ta Liang. It is not clear how this would work, since according to T'an Ch'i-hsiang (1:38), Ta Liang was about 50 miles away from Ying-tse. T'an Ch'i-

breach the Pai-ma 白馬 Ford and Wei will no longer have Wai-huang 外黃 or Chi-yang 濟陽.[105] We will breach the Hsiu-hsü 宿胥 Ford and Wei will no longer have Hsü 虛 or Tun-ch'iu 頓丘.[106] Attacking by land, we will strike Ho-nei. Attacking by water we will destroy Ta Liang.' The royal clan of Wei believed this and thus served Ch'in.

[2274] "Ch'in wanted to attack An-yi, but feared that Ch'i would come to its aid; he thus offered Sung to Ch'i, saying 'The King of Sung is bereft of [moral] principle. He made a wooden figure in Our image and shot its face. Our lands are cut off [from Sung], our soldiers distant [from it], and We cannot attack it. If you, Your Majesty, could defeat and take Sung, it would be as if We had taken it [ourselves].' Then when he had taken An-yi and blocked Nü-chi, he denounced Ch'i for the crime of destroying Sung.

"Ch'in wanted to attack Han, but feared that the world would come to its aid, thus he offered Ch'i to the world, saying, 'The King of Ch'i made treaties with us four times, deceived us four times, and led the troops of the world against us three times. If there is a Ch'i there can be no Ch'in. If there is a Ch'in, there can be no Ch'i. We must attack it. We must destroy it.' Then when he had taken Yi-yang 宜陽 and Shao-ch'ü, and won Lin 藺 and Li-shih 離石, he denounced the world for the crime of destroying Ch'i.[107]

[2275] "Ch'in wanted to attack Wei [but] was concerned over Ch'u, thus he presented [Han's territory of] Nan-yang to Ch'u, saying, 'We were already about to break relations with Han. Ravage Chün-ling 均陵, block Meng-ai 鄳隘;[108] if this is of benefit to Ch'u, it will be as if We had won [these benefits] for ourselves.' Wei abandoned its ally [Ch'u] and joined with Ch'in, and [Ch'in] then denounced Ch'u for the crime of blocking Meng-ai.

"His troops were trapped at Lin-chung 林中.[109] Concerned over Yen and Chao, he gave Chiao-tung 膠東 to Yen and Chi-hsi 濟西 to Chao.[110] Having reached terms with Wei, he sent the Noble Scion Yen 延 [to Wei], and through the offices of the *Hsi-shou* joined forces [with Wei] and attacked Chao.[111]

hsiang lists Ying-k'ou separately, apparently as a fording, or crossing point on the Yellow River just north of the Ying-tse area. The idea of diverting a river to destroy an enemy city is an old one, however. This was supposedly how the Ch'in general Pai Ch'i took the Ch'u capital of Yen (see our translation of Chapter 73, n. 13).

[105] According to T'an Ch'i-hsiang (1:36), Pai-ma K'ou was a Ford across the Yellow River located northeast of modern Hua-hsien 滑縣 in Honan (at the time, the bed of the Yellow River was north of its present location). Chi-yang was located northeast of modern Lan-k'ao 蘭考 in Honan. Wai-huang was located southeast of Lan-k'ao. Again, it is not clear how "breaching" the Yellow River at this point could inundate these cities, since Pai-ma K'ou was over 50 miles away.

[106] According to T'an Ch'i-hsiang (1:36), the Hsü-hsiu Ford was southwest of modern Hua-hsien, about 10 miles further up the Yellow River from the Pai-ma Ford. Hsü was a city about fifteen miles east of modern Yen-chin 延津 in Honan. Tun-ch'iu was located just west of modern Ch'ing-feng 清豐 also in Honan. The geography here is also puzzling, since Tun-ch'iu was over 50 miles northeast of Hsü.

[107] Li-shih was located near the city of the same name in modern Shansi province. Lin was about 10 miles west of Li-shih. Most editions of *Shih chi* read "Lin and Shih." The Chung-hua edition has changed Shih to Li-shih, probably following Liang Yü-sheng's suggestion (29:1249), which in turn is based on the text of Pao Piao's edition of the *Chan-kuo ts'e*. As Takigawa (69:58) points out, Lin and Shih were in Chao, not Ch'i.

[108] Chün-ling was an area located north of modern Chün-hsien 均縣 in Hupei and south of modern Lu-shih 盧氏 County in Honan. Meng-ai, also known as P'ing-ching Pass 平靖, was a major pass on the northern border of Ch'u, located south of modern Hsin-yang 信陽 County in Honan (T'an Ch'i-hsiang, 1:35-6).

[109] Lin-chung (also known as Lin) was the name of a Han city located about 5 miles west of modern Yu-shih 尉氏 in Honan (T'an Ch'i-hsiang, 1:36).

[110] Chiao-tung refers to the area east of the Chiao River in modern Shantung province. Chi-hsi refers to the area west of the now gone Chi River and east of where the Yellow River formerly flowed, along Ch'i's border with Chao (T'an Ch'i-hsiang, 1:38-9).

[111] The Noble Scion Yen is otherwise unknown.

"His troops were injured at Chiao-shih 譙石, he encountered defeat at Yang-ma 陽馬. Concerned over Wei, he presented She 葉 and Ts'ai 蔡 to Wei.[112] Having come to terms with Chao, he then threatened Wei, but Wei would not cede land to him. When [Ch'in] was trapped, [the king] sent the Queen Dowager's younger brother, the Marquis of Jang, to make peace. When [Ch'in] triumphed, [the king] deceived both his uncle and mother.

[2276] "He berated Yen saying, 'Because of Chiao-tung.' He berated Chao saying, 'Because of Chi-hsi.' He berated Wei saying, 'Because of She and Ts'ai.' He berated Ch'u saying, 'Because of blocking Meng-ai.' He berated Ch'i saying, 'Because of Sung.' His words are perfectly circular, he uses his troops like cutting grass.[113] His mother cannot control him, his uncle cannot restrain him.

"In the battle with Lung Chia 龍賈, in the battle at An-men 岸門, in the battle at Feng-ling 封陵, in the battle at Kao-shang 高商, and in the battle with Chao Chuang 趙莊, the people of the Three Chin killed by Ch'in numbered in the hundreds of thousands.[114] Those living there are all the orphans of those killed by Ch'in. Beyond the Hsi Ho 西河, and in the lands of Shang-lo 上雒 and San-ch'uan 三川,[115] the disasters engulfing the states of Chin have covered half of the Three Chin. This is how great the disasters caused by Ch'in have been. Yet Yen and Chao go to Ch'in and all strive to serve Ch'in and persuade its ruler. This is what your servant fears most of all."

King Chao of Yen did not go [to Ch'in]. Su Tai was again exalted in Yen. Yen sent him to form alliances with the feudal lords, as in the time of Su Ch'in. Some joined and some did not, but from this time, the world followed Su Ch'in's policy of alliance. Tai and Li both died of old age and were renowned among the feudal lords.[116]

---

[112] The Chan-kuo ts'e writes Chiao-shih as Li-shih 離石 and Yang-ma as Ma-ling 馬陵. As Wang Shu-min (69:2225) notes, there are at least two editions of the Shih chi which have Li-shih instead of Chiao-shih. As noted above, Li-shih was located in Chao. No commentators have succeeding in locating Yang-ma. According to the Ch'ing scholar, Ch'eng En-tse 程恩澤 (quoted in Ho Chien-chang, p. 1135, n. 70), the Chan-kuo ts'e reading of Ma-ling refers to a location near modern Shansi province's T'ai-ku 太谷. It is unclear what battles are referred to here. She was located in the northern part of Ch'u, near modern She-hsien 葉縣 in Honan. Ts'ai was also in the northern part of Ch'u, in the area of modern Shang-ts'ai 上蔡 County also in Honan (T'an Ch'i-hsiang, 1:37-8).

[113] This passage is very unclear, and there are a number of interpretations--see Takigawa, 69:60; Wang Shu-min, 69:2226; Ho Chien-chang, p. 1136, n. 77; Mizusawa, pp. 301-2. We follow the latter.

[114] Lung Chia was a general of Wei. According to Shih chi, 44:1848, Ch'in defeated Lung Chia in 330 B.C. An-men was a Han city located about 5 miles north of modern Hsü-ch'ang 許昌 City in Honan (T'an Ch'i-hsiang, 1:36). Shih chi, 45:1871 says Ch'in defeated Han at this location in 314 B.C.

Feng-ling belonged to Wei, as noted above (n. 102). According to Shih chi, 15:735, Ch'in took Feng-ling in 303 B.C.

There are no other references to Kao-shang in the Shih chi or Chan-kuo ts'e. Chao Chuang was a Chao general. According to "Chi-chieh," this refers to a battle between the forces of Ch'in and the forces of Chao, led by Chao Chuang, in 338 B.C. The text of "Chi-chieh" gives the date of the "eleventh year of Marquis Su of Chao, but as Wang Shu-min (69:2226) points out, this must be an error for the "twenty-second year" or 328 B.C. Shih chi, 45:1803 does record a battle between Ch'in forces and a general Chao Tz'u 疵 in 328 B.C. Since the name is wrong, it seems likely "Chi-chieh" is mistaken, and the reference here is to the Chao general Chao Chuang who was captured or killed by Ch'in in 313 B.C. (Shih chi, 15:733).

[115] The Hsi Ho refers to the section of the Yellow River which runs roughly north and south, along the border between modern Shansi and Shensi provinces. "Outside" this area would apparently mean west of this part of the Yellow River, an area which at the time belonged to Wei.

Shang-lo was the name of a Han city located southeast of modern Lo-nan 雒南 County in Shensi.

San-ch'uan was the name of the area south of the Yellow River in modern Honan province, which included the Yi 伊 River and the Lo 洛 River, hence the name San-ch'uan "three rivers." Together, the region from Shang-lo to the San-ch'uan area composed the southwestern corner of the state of Han.

[116] This paragraph also appears in a text parallel to this speech in the Chan-kuo ts'e (see n. 91 above).

[2277] His Honor the Grand Scribe says: "Su Ch'in and his two brothers all traveled among the feudal lords in search of fame. Their teachings were best suited for grasping the unexpected change, yet Su Ch'in died at the hands of an enemy agent. The world laughed at him and refused to study his teachings. But what our generation tells of Su Ch'in is often inconsistent, and similar matters from different times are all assigned to Su Ch'in. Su Ch'in rose up from the streets of a small hamlet to unite the Six States in alliance. His cleverness exceeded that of other men, thus I arranged his actions according to order, so that he would not merely suffer an ill reputation [because of these]."

TRANSLATORS' NOTE

In Su Ch'in, Ssu-ma Ch'ien introduces us to the type of figure often referred to as a "traveling persuader," "rhetorician," or "speculator." These men were political advisors who traveled from state to state seeking high office by advocacy of various policies. By the time of King Hui 惠 of Ch'in (337-311 B.C.), the state of Ch'in had assumed a dominant position in the Chinese political sphere, and the rhetoricians' policies soon came to reflect this fact. These policies were often subsumed under the general term *tsung-heng* 從橫. This phrase first appears in *Shih chi* Chapter 65 (p. 2168), and is generally translated as "vertical and horizontal alliances." The reason usually given for this translation is that the *tsung* alliances were between states in the north and south and were directed against the state of Ch'in, while the *heng* alliances were from east to west, and were orchestrated by the state of Ch'in to protect its interests and weaken its foes. We have chosen to depart from this translation, however, and replace it with "alliances and counter-alliances." We have two reasons for doing so.

First, we believe that *tsung* originally meant "ally" or "alliance." To show this, it is necessary to consider the Archaic Chinese pronunciation of the written form 從. This form had at least five different readings in Archaic Chinese, of which four are relevant here: **dzung, *dzungh, *tsung,* and **tsungh.* We believe that the form **dzungh* meant alliance. Etymologically, this meaning derived from **dzungh* "follower," itself a nominalized form of the verb **dzung,* "to follow." The word **tsung* "vertical," on the other hand, derived from **tsung* "warp" (as opposed to "woof"), and was generally a noun or adjective, which in turn has a verbal form, **tsungh,* "to send across, to let loose." Early phonetic glosses supplied by various commentators, provide support for the claim that the character 從 in phrases we are concerned with (合從, 從親, 約從) was read **dzungh,* rather than **tsung.* This in turn would support the etymology we suggest here.

Second, there are a number of places where **dzung* does not refer to north-south alliances, but instead includes the state of Ch'in. Moreover, the use of **dzung* to mean alliance may date as far back as the Spring and Autumn period, when the north-south and east-west axes it supposedly describes did not exist.

As to the use of *heng* to describe a political alliance, this clearly arose much later, and was much more limited than tsung. Here we do not dispute that the meaning of "horizontal" may have been intended, but it seems likely that it was chosen for its punning qualities rather than its geographic connotations. Since **dzungh* and **tsung* are phonetically similar and are often written with the same graph, it is not at all surprising that proponents of policies designed to counteract **dzung* "alliances" among the eastern states, alliances often directed against Ch'in, should call themselves advocates of *heng* "counter-alliances."

The historicity of Su Ch'in has been questioned by many scholars. Henri Maspero, in his article "Le Roman de Sou Ts'in" (see Bibliography), claims that the records concerning the life of Su Ch'in are often anachronistic, and concludes that both the alliances and part of Ssu-ma Ch'ien's account of Su Ch'n were more fictional than historical. Ch'ien Mu (*Chu-tzu,* pp. 285-94) has made similar observations and given further examples. James I. Crump, Jr. (*Intrigues--Studies of the Chan-kuo ts'e* [Ann Arbor: The University of Michigan Press, 1964], p. 29) extends this argument even further: "Henri Maspero . . . showed that this alliance against Ch'in must have dissolved one year earlier than it was founded! If the Vertical Alliance is fictional, so also is its counterpart, the Horizontal alliance which Ch'in was supposed to have arranged to nullify the league of the Chinese states. So also is Chang Yi, the clever minion of this powerful state and organizer of the counter-alliance, and so also is Su Ch'in, the brilliant rags-to-riches leader of the Chinese states who held the barbarian at bay for fifteen years, according to the *Intrigues* and the *Shih-chi*." Such a claim is more radical that Maspero's. Although Maspero claims that Ssu-ma Ch'ien's account of Su Ch'in is largely fictional, he never said Su Ch'in himself was not a historical person. Similarly, Ch'ien Mu says only that speeches were attributed to Su Ch'in and Chang Yi respectively because they were known to be advocates of such alliances, but he has not argued that Su Ch'in and Chang Yi were fictional.

BIBLIOGRAPHY

I. Translations

Maspero, Henri. "Le Roman de Sou Ts'in," *Études Asiatiques Publieé à l'occasion de vingt-cinquieme anniversaire de l'École française d'Extrême Orient*. Paris: G. Van Oest, 1925, v. 2, pp. 128-33 (127-41).

Mizusawa Toshitada 水澤利忠. *Shiki* 史記. V. 8. *Retsuden (ichi)* 列傳 (一). Tokyo: Meiji Shoten, 1990, pp. 24-304.

Ōgawa Tamaki 小川環樹, trans. *Shiki retsuden* 史記列傳. Rpt. Tokyo: Chikuma Shobō, 1986 (1969). pp. 48-63.

II. Studies

Fan Hsiang-yung 范祥雍. "Su Ch'in ho-tsung Liu-kuo nien-tai k'ao hsin" 蘇秦合縱六國年代考信 in *Chung-hua wen-shih lun-ts'ung* 中華文史論叢, 1985.4, 1-25.

T'ang Lan 唐蘭. "Su Ch'in shih-chi chien-piao" 蘇秦事跡簡表 in *Chan-kuo tsung heng chia shu* 戰國從橫家書, Beijing, 1976, pp. 145-153 [also in Ho Chien-chang, pp. 1345-51].

Yang Tsung-yüan 楊宗元. "Kuei-ku Tzu shu-k'ao chi 'Su Ch'in, Chang Yi lieh-chuan' shu-cheng" 鬼谷子書考及蘇秦張儀列傳疏證. M.A. thesis, Chinese Cultural College, 1962.

Chang Yi, Memoir 10

Chang Yi

[70:2279] Chang Yi 張儀 was a native of Wei. Earlier he and Su Ch'in 蘇秦[1] once served the Venerable Kuei-ku 鬼谷[2] [as disciples] and learned his arts [of politics]. Su Ch'in thought he had not attained to Chang Yi's [skill].

After Chang Yi finished his studies, he traveled around advising before the feudal lords. He once drank in the company of the Prime Minister of Ch'u. A short while later, the Prime Minister of Ch'u missed a jade disc. His retainers suspected Chang Yi and said, "Chang Yi is poor and unscrupulous. It must be this fellow who stole His Lordship the Prime Minister's jade disc." They seized Chang Yi and beat him several hundred times with a thin cane. Chang Yi did not confess and they released him.

His wife said, "Hmph! If you had not read all those books or traveled around talking, how would you ever suffer this sort of indignity?"

Chang Yi said to his wife, "See if my tongue is still there."

His wife laughed. "It is."

Chang Yi said, "Then all's well."

[2280] Su Ch'in had advised the King of Chao and obtained his agreement to form an alliance, but he feared that Ch'in would attack the feudal lords, defeat the alliance and afterwards [the feudal lords] would renege [on their treaties]. Concerned that there was no one who could be sent to serve in Ch'in, he sent someone to subtly persuade Chang Yi.

"Earlier, sir, you and Su Ch'in were on good terms. Now Ch'in holds a key post. Why not seek to realize your aspirations by going to visit him?"

Chang Yi then went to Chao. He sent in his name card, seeking an audience with Su Ch'in. Su Ch'in forbade his retainers to arrange an audience for him and also made it impossible for him to leave for several days. A short while later, he granted him an audience, seated him at the foot of the hall, granted him the rations of a servant or handmaid, and then rebuked him.

"With your talent and ability, sir, you have still brought yourself to this pass. It isn't that I could not make you a wealthy and noble man with just a word, but you are not worth taking in." He rejected him and sent him off. In coming, Chang Yi had thought of himself as an old friend seeking benefit. Instead, he had suffered humiliation. Angered, he decided that none of the feudal lords were worth serving and that only [the state of] Ch'in could trouble Chao. He then entered Ch'in.

A short while later, Su Ch'in said to his houseman, "Chang Yi is one of the worthiest men in the world; I am probably not his equal. I was fortunate enough to be employed first, but it is only Chang Yi who might be able to wield power in Ch'in. He is poor, however, and hasn't the means to advance himself. I was afraid that he would be content with petty profit and not seek advancement. Thus I roused his spirit by summoning, then humiliating him. Provide for him secretly on my behalf, sir."

[Su Ch'in] then advised the King of Chao who dispensed gold, silks, carriages, and horses, and sent his man to follow Chang Yi in secret. The man took up lodgings with him, gradually grew close with him, and provided him with carriages, horses and money.

---

[1] See his biography in *Shih chi* Chapter 69.

[2] See n. 2 to our translation of *Shih chi* Chapter 69 for a brief note on "Venerable Kuei-ku" and the place name Kuei-ku.

Whatever [Chang Yi] wanted he obtained for him, without further informing [Chao]. Chang Yi was then able to gain an audience with King Hui 惠 of Ch'in (r. 337-311 B.C.). King Hui made him Foreign Excellency and took counsel on expeditions against the feudal lords with him.

Su Ch'in's houseman took his leave.

Chang Yi said, "It was through you that I gained prominence. I was just about to repay your kindness, why are you leaving?"

The houseman said, "It was not I, your servant, who appreciated you, My Lord; it was Master Su. Master Su worried that Ch'in would attack Chao, ruining the alliance, and thought that no one other than you could wield power in Ch'in. Thus he incited you to anger and sent me to secretly provide you with money. All these were the plans of Master Su. Now that you are employed, my lord, I ask to return and report."

Chang Yi said, "Alas, this tactic was among the things I learned, but I did not realize [it had been used against me]. I cannot attain to Master Su; that is [*2281*] clear indeed! Moreover, I am but recently employed; how could I plot against Chao? Please tell Master Su for me, in the lifetime of Master Su, what would Chang Yi dare to say? As long as there is a Master Su, what can a Chang Yi do?"

After Chang Yi became Prime Minister of Ch'in,[3] he wrote a letter to the Prime Minister of Ch'u. "In earlier times when I drank in your company, I did not steal your jade disc, but you had me caned. Guard your state well, I will soon steal your cities!"[4]

Chü 苴 and Shu 蜀 attacked each other[5] and each came to inform Ch'in of its plight. King Hui of Ch'in wanted to send troops to attack Shu, but thought that because the road there was precipitous and narrow, [Shu] would be hard to reach, and that Han moreover might invade Ch'in. King Hui of Ch'in wanted to attack Han first and then attack Shu, but feared that the advantage would not be with him; he wanted to attack Shu first but he was afraid that Han would launch a surprise attack on an exhausted Ch'in. He hesitated and could not decide.

Ssu-ma Ts'o 司馬錯[6] and Chang Yi disputed before King Hui.[7] Ssu-ma Ts'o wanted to attack Shu. Chang Yi said, "It would be better to attack Han." The king said, "Allow me to hear your arguments."

[3] According to *Shih chi,* 69:2250, Su Ch'in humiliated Chang Yi then secretly helped him to go to Ch'in after King Hui of Ch'in received the *Wen-Wu tso* 文武胙 (sacrificial meat offered to King Wen and King Wu of the Chou) from the Chou court and also after Ch'in attacked Wei and took Tiao-yin 雕陰. According to *Shih chi* 15:727-8, we know that these two events took place in 334 B.C. and 333 B.C. respectively. Other sources (see n. 18 below), however, claim that Chang Yi did not become Ch'in's minister until 328 B.C. Probably reading this sentence here in the same breath with the previous one, which relates Chang Yi's conversation with Su Ch'in's aide immediately after he had successfully secured employment in Ch'in in 333 B.C., Liang Yü-sheng suggests that there is a mistake (29:1249). Wang Shu-min (70:2231) shares Liang Yü-sheng's observation and points out that *Ch'un-ch'iu hou-yü* 春秋後語 has *yung yü Ch'in* 用於秦 "was employed in Ch'in" instead of *hsiang yü Ch'in* 相於秦 "became Ch'in's Prime Minister." In an attempt to explain away the apparent mistake here, Nakai Riken (cited in Takigawa, 70:5) says that though Chang Yi became minister after Ch'in attacked Shu, Ssu-ma Ch'ien chooses to mention in advance his promotion to the Ch'in ministership and his letter to the minister of Ch'u so as to give a complete picture of the story of his conflict with the Ch'u minister before moving on to other events. Unfortunately, although his suggestion about Ssu-ma Ch'ien's intention is interesting, his statement that Chang Yi became minister *after* Ch'in's attack of Shu is wrong: Chang Yi became minister in 328 B.C., which is twelve years *before* Ch'in attacked Shu.

[4] Chang Yi is addressing the Ch'u Prime Minister with the familiar forms of the second person pronoun (*jo* 若, *erh* 而, and *ju* 汝), a deliberate insult.

[5] Chü was located northeast of modern Chien-ko 劍閣 in Szechwan; Shu was in central and western Szechwan (T'an Ch'i-hsiang, 1:43-4). According to "Cheng-yi," the King of Shu enfeoffed his younger brother at Hanchung and gave him the title Lord of Chü. The Lord of Chü later associated himself with the King of Pa, who was an adversary of his brother. The King of Shu thereupon launched an attack on the Lord of Chü.

[2282] Yi said, "Treat Wei as kin and treat Ch'u well. Dispatch troops to San-ch'uan 三川, seal the mouth of Shih-ku 什谷 and block the way to T'un-liu 屯留.[8] Have Wei cut off Nan-yang 南陽, have Ch'u confront Nan-cheng 南鄭, and have Ch'in attack Hsin-ch'eng 新城 and Yi-yang 宜陽.[9] This is how one may confront the two Chou's in their suburbs,[10] punish the crimes of the Chou king, and invade the territory of Ch'u and Wei. When Chou realizes it cannot be rescued, its nine cauldrons and precious vessels are sure to arrive. Seize the nine cauldrons, hold the maps and registers, and control the Son of Heaven; when you issue orders to the world, the world must heed you. This is a task fit for a king.

"Now Shu is a state of the distant west, the ilk of the Jung 戎 and Ti 翟.[11] If we wear out our swords and exhaust our hosts there, it will not be enough to achieve fame; if we gain its territory, it will not be enough to count profitable. Your servant has heard 'contend for fame at court, contend for profit at market.' San-ch'uan and the royal house of Chou are the world's court and market, yet Your Majesty does not contend there, but instead contends with the Jung and Ti; this is far indeed from a task fit for a king."[12]

[2283] Ssu-ma Ts'o said, "Not so. Your servant has heard that 'one who intends to enrich his state strives to broaden his territory; one who intends to strengthen his forces strives to enrich his people; one who intends to be king strives to extend his grace.' When these three resources are all available, kingship ensues. Now Your Majesty's territory is small and your masses poor. Thus your servant would hope to work first on what can be easily done.

"Shu is a state of the distant west, but it is the leader of the Jung and Ti, and suffers the strife of Chieh and Chow. To attack it with [the forces of] Ch'in, one might compare it to sending jackals and wolves to chase a flock of sheep. Acquiring its land would be enough to broaden our state; obtaining its property would be enough to enrich our masses. Ready our weapons, and without harming our hosts, it will soon have submitted. Seize a country, yet the world will not think it tyranny; exhaust the profits of the land of the western barbarians,[13] yet the world will not think it avarice. Thus in one stroke we gain both fame and profit, and

---

[6] See n. 268 to our translation of *Shih chi* Chapter 5 above.

[7] A parallel to the following debate appears in *Chan-kuo ts'e* (3:13a-14a, *SPTK*).

[8] San-ch'uan was the name of that part of the state of Han which was south of the Yellow River; it included the Yi 伊 River and the Lo 洛 River, hence the name San-ch'uan "three rivers." Shih-ku was about 10 miles northeast of modern Kung-hsien 鞏縣 in Honan. T'un-liu was a few miles south of modern T'un-liu in Shansi (T'an Ch'i-hsiang, 1:35-6).

[9] Nan-yang was one of the most heavily populated areas of the state of Han, just north of the Yellow River in the southeast corner of modern Shansi province. It was connected by narrow mountain roads to an area further north called Shang-tang. Here Chang Yi seems to suggest severing the mountain road and cutting off the Shang-tang area. Nan-cheng (often referred to as Cheng) was the capital of Han, located at modern Hsin-cheng 新鄭 County in Honan. Hsin-ch'eng was about a few miles southwest of modern Yi-ch'uan 伊川 County in Honan (T'an Ch'i-hsiang, 1:35-6). Yi-yang was located about 10 miles west of modern Yi-yang, also in Honan. These were both major cities in the San-ch'uan area (see n. 8 above).

[10] The two Chou's refer to East Chou and West Chou (see n. 1 to our translation of *Shih chi* Chapter 69).

[11] See n. 10 to our translation of *Shih chi* Chapter 4 above.

[12] Wang Nien-sun (4:17a-b) argues that the word *yeh* 業 is an interpolation and proposes to read *wang* 王 as a verb. Wang Shu-min (70:2233) shares this view. In such a reading, the sentence may be rendered as "you are far from becoming king [of the world]."

[13] In common usage, *hai* 海 means "sea." This is how Crump (p. 67) understands the term when he renders the term *hsi-hai* 西海 as "western sea." However, there is no sea in the west of China. "Cheng-yi" glosses the word as *hui* 晦 "dim, obscured" and asserts that it refers to dimwitted barbarians and that *li-chin hsi hai* 利盡西海 accordingly means "monopolize the profits of the western barbarians." Pao Piao mentions an edition of *Chan-kuo ts'e* which reads *ssu-hai* 四海 instead of *hsi-hai* (see 3:14a, *SPTK*) and in the "Shih-ti" 釋地 section of *Erh-ya* 爾雅 (6:6b, *SPPY*), we find the following explanation of *ssu-hai*: "[The lands of] the nine Yi tribes, the eight Ti tribes, the seven Jung tribes and the six Man tribes are called *ssu-hai*" 九夷八狄七戎六蠻謂之四海.

moreover have a name for suppressing tyranny and ending strife. If we now attack Han and take the Son of Heaven hostage, it would blight our name, yet would not necessarily be profitable, and, moreover, we will have a name for being unrighteous; to then attack that which the world does not want attacked would be dangerous indeed! Allow your servant to lay out the reasons. Chou is the ceremonial head of the world's clans and the ally of Ch'i and Han. If Chou realizes it must lose the nine cauldrons and Han realizes it must forfeit San-ch'uan, they will combine their strength and plan together. They will turn for support to Ch'i and Chao, seek relief from Ch'u and Wei, give the nine cauldrons to Ch'u, cede the land to Wei, and Your Majesty will be unable to stop them. This is what your servant means by danger. It is not as secure as attacking Shu."

[2284] King Hui said, "Well put. Allow Us to heed you, sir." In the end he raised troops, attacked Shu and in the tenth month took it.[14] He then pacified Shu, demoted the King of Shu, changing his title to marquis, and sent Ch'en Chuang 陳莊 as Prime Minister of Shu.[15] Shu having become Ch'in's appanage, Ch'in became more and more powerful and wealthy, and scorned the feudal lords.

In his tenth year (328 B.C.), King Hui of Ch'in sent the Noble Scion Hua 華 and Chang Yi to besiege P'u-yang 蒲陽.[16] They subdued it. Afterwards Yi told Ch'in to return it to Wei and to send Noble Scion Yu 繇 to Wei as a hostage.[17] Yi then advised the King of Wei.

"The King of Ch'in has treated Wei lavishly indeed. Wei must not lack courtesy." After this Wei presented Shang 上 Commandery and Shao-liang 少梁[18] to express its gratitude to King Hui of Ch'in. King Hui then made Chang Yi Prime Minister [of Ch'in] and renamed Shao-liang Hsia-yang 夏陽.[19]

When Chang Yi had been Prime Minister of Ch'in for four years King Hui established himself as a king (325 B.C.).[20] One year later (324 B.C.), serving as Ch'in's commander, he took Shan 陝 and fortified Shang-chün [Commandery].

In the second year after this (323 B.C.), [Ch'in] sent him to meet the Prime Ministers of Ch'i and Ch'u at Nieh-sang 嚙桑.[21] He then turned his carriage east and was removed as

---

[14] According to *Shih chi*, 5:207 and 15:732, Ch'in destroyed Shu in 316 B.C. This is subsequent to the events in the text below, so that this debate seems to have been placed out of chronological order.

[15] Ch'en Chuang was probably the same person as Chief of Staff Chuang 壯. See n. 6 to our translation of *Shih chi* Chapter 72 for details.

[16] P'u-yang was located in modern Shih-hsien 濕縣 in Shansi (Tan Ch'i-hsiang, 1:35). The Noble Scion Hua is otherwise unknown.

[17] The Noble Scion Yu was probably the same person as Noble Scion Yu-t'ung 繇通 (see Ma Fei-pai 馬非百, *Ch'in chi-shih* 秦集史 [Peking: Chung-hua, 1982], vol. 1, p. 118, and *Shih chi*, 5:207 and 15:733).

[18] Shang-chün Commandery was an area extending from the southeastern part of the modern Inner Mongolian Autonomous Region to the northwestern part of Shensi province (T'an Ch'i-hsiang, 1:37-8). Shao-liang was about 5 miles south of modern Han-ch'eng 韓城 in Shensi (T'an Ch'i-hsiang, 1:35-6).

According to *Shih chi*, 15:722, Shao-liang was ceded to Ch'in in 354 B.C. No mention of it being returned appears in the *Shih chi*, nor is it mentioned under the entries for 328 B.C. in *Shih chi* Chapters 5 and 44. Liang Yü-sheng (29:1250) and Wang Shu-min (70:2235) therefore argue that Shao-liang is an interpolation here. This ignores the fact that *Shih chi*, 15:729 does state that Wei gave Shao-liang to Ch'in in 330 B.C. Although this is not identical with the date given in this chapter, it does support the possibility that Wei gave Shao-liang to Ch'in more than once.

[19] *Shih chi*, 5:206 and 15:729 record 328 B.C. as the date Ch'in made Chang Yi Prime Minister. According to *Shih chi*, 5:206, Shao-liang was renamed Hsia-yang in 327 B.C.

[20] Although Ssu-ma Ch'ien calls the Ch'in rulers kings throughout the *lieh-chuan* section, their title was actually "duke" prior to this year. For a note on the discrepancy of the "four years" see n. 20 below.

[21] Nieh-sang was about 5 miles southwest of modern P'ei-hsien 沛縣 in Kiangsu (Tan Ch'i-hsiang, 1:39). Liang

[Ch'in's] prime minister, serving Wei as prime minister on behalf of Ch'in. He intended to first make Wei serve Ch'in so that the feudal lords would follow its example. [*2285*] The King of Wei was unwilling to heed Yi. The King of Ch'in angrily attacked and took Wei's Ch'ü-wo 曲沃 and P'ing-chou 平周,²² secretly treating Chang Yi more and more lavishly. Chang Yi was ashamed he had no means to repay his favor. He remained in Wei for four years until King Hsiang 襄 of Wei (r. *334-319 B.C.) died and King Ai 哀 (r. *318-296 B.C.) was enthroned.²³ Chang Yi once more advised King Ai, but King Ai did not heed him. After this Chang Yi secretly had Ch'in attack Wei. Wei fought with Ch'in and was defeated.²⁴

The next year (317 B.C.), Ch'i too came and defeated Wei at Kuan 觀 Ford.²⁵ Ch'in prepared to attack Wei again. It first defeated Han's army under Shen Ch'a 申差,²⁶ cutting off eighty-thousand heads. The feudal lords trembled in fear, and Chang Yi once more advised the King of Wei.²⁷

"Wei's territory covers no more than a thousand *li* [on a side] and its troops are no more than three-hundred thousand. Its land is level on all four sides, the feudal lords converge on it from all four directions like spokes on a hub, and there are no famous mountains or great rivers as barriers. From Cheng to Liang it is only a little more than two-hundred *li*. Chariots speeding and men racing, it requires no effort to reach here. Liang shares borders with Ch'u in the south, with Han in the west, with Chao in the north, and with Ch'i in the east. Its troops garrison the four quarters; those guarding watchtowers and forts are no fewer than a hundred thousand. Liang's topography is that of a natural battleground. If Liang allies with Ch'u in the south but not with Ch'i, Ch'i will attack it in the east; if it allies with Ch'i in the east but not with Chao, Chao will attack it in the north; if it does not join with Han, Han will attack it in the west; if it does not unite with Ch'u, Ch'u will attack it in the south. This is what is called the road to partition and division.

"Moreover, when the feudal lords made alliances, they intended by this means to secure their altars of grain and soil, exalt themselves as rulers, strengthen their troops and manifest their names. Now the allies have unified the world, bound themselves as brothers, and

Yü-sheng (10:1250-1) points out that the meeting at Nieh-sang took place in 323 B.C., one year after Chang Yi occupied Shan and proposes that "two years after this" should read "one year after this." As noted in the "Chrono-logy" in the front-matter, however, there are cases where *Shih chi* uses a counting system beginning with one rather than zero. This counting system is used quite consistently in some chapters (see the notes to our translation of *Shih chi* Chapter 66), but it is not clear that this is true of this chapter. For instance, the "four years" above apparently refers to the period 328-325 B.C., suggesting that this system is being used, but the "four years" below, apparently referring to 322-318 B.C., does not accord with such a system.

²² Ch'ü-wo was located about 10 miles northeast of modern Wen-hsi 聞喜 in Shansi (T'an Ch'i-hsiang, 1:35). P'ing-chou was located about 10 miles northwest of Chieh-hsiu 介休 in Shansi (T'an Ch'i-hsiang, 1:35).

According to *Shih chi*, 5:207 and 15:732, Chang Yi resigned his post as Prime Minister in Ch'in and took up his new post in Wei in 322 B.C. Ch'in's attack on Ch'ü-wo and P'ing-chou came in the same year.

²³ As we noted in the "Chronology," Ssu-ma Ch'ien made a number of errors in the chronology of the states of Wei and Ch'i, among others. In the corrected chronology we have adopted, that of Yang K'uan's *Chan-kuo shih*, there was in fact no King Ai in Wei. Rather, King Hui ruled from 369 to 319 B.C. and was succeeded by King Hsiang, who ruled from 318 to 296 B.C. This error seems to have been Ssu-ma Ch'ien's own mistake (at least we have no earlier textual sources for such a view), which in turn suggests that this summary of the chronology of the period was written by Ssu-ma Ch'ien himself, rather than taken from some other source.

²⁴ This attack on Wei is mentioned nowhere else in the *Shih chi*. Rather, 318 B.C. was supposedly the year in which the great five states joined together and attacked Ch'in.

²⁵ In *Shih chi*, 15:732, this place is called Kuan-tse 觀澤, but according to *Shih chi*, 45:1870 (and also *Tzu-chih t'ung-chien* 資治通鑑, 3:83, *SPPY*), Shen Ch'a was captured at Cho-tse 濁澤 (located, according to Ch'ien Mu, *Ti-ming k'ao*, p. 405, west of modern Hsieh-hsien 解縣 in Shansi).

²⁶ Otherwise unknown.

²⁷ A parallel to the following speech appears in *Chan-kuo ts'e* (7:23b-25a, *SPTK*).

made a covenant on the bank of the Huan River 洹水 by sacrificing a white horse.[28] This is how they strengthened themselves. Even among kin as close as brothers with the same father and mother, however, there still are some who fight over property. Yet they intend to rely on the leftover schemes of the deceitful, dishonest, treacherous, and treasonous Su Ch'in; that these could never succeed is clear indeed!

If you do not serve Ch'in, Great King, Ch'in will send down its troops to attack Ho-wai 河外 and seize Chüan 卷, Yen 衍, Yen 燕 and Suan-tsao 酸棗.[29] Threatening Wey, it will take Yang-chin 陽晉,[30] and Chao cannot [*2286*] go south. If Chao cannot go south, Liang cannot go north. If Liang cannot go north, then the road to the allies will be severed. If the road to the allies is severed, even if you wished to avoid peril to your state, you would be unable to do so, Great King. Ch'in will force Han to attack Liang. With Han cowed by Ch'in, Ch'in and Han will act as one, and you can wait standing up for the fall of Liang. This is what your servant fears for you, Great King.

"In planning for you, Great King, it would be best to serve Ch'in. If you serve Ch'in, Ch'u and Han are sure not to dare to move [against Liang]. With no distress from Ch'u and Han, you can lie down with your head on a high pillow, Great King, and your state will be free of sorrow.

"Moreover, of the states that Ch'in wants to weaken, there is none it wishes to weaken more than Ch'u, and there is no state which can weaken Ch'u more than Liang. Though Ch'u has a name for wealth and size, in reality it is hollow and empty. Though its troops are numerous, they readily run and can be easily defeated. They are unable to fight stoutly. If all the troops of Liang face south and attack it, victory over Ch'u is certain. Carving up Ch'u and fattening Liang, crippling Ch'u and pleasing Ch'in, shifting misfortune onto another, and securing your state, these are excellent things. If you do not heed your servant, Great King, Ch'in will send down its armored knights and attack to the east. Even if you wanted then to serve Ch'in, it would no longer be possible.

"Moreover, the men building alliances often exert themselves in eloquence, but are seldom to be trusted. By advising a feudal lord, they succeed in enfeoffment as marquises. This is why, day and night, traveling talkers all over the world, without exception, clutch their wrists, pop their eyes and gnash their teeth talking about the advantages of alliance and advising rulers. If a ruler admires their eloquence and is drawn by their advice, how can he not be confused?

[2287] Your servant has heard that

A pile of feathers will sink a boat,
A collection of light things will break an axle.
A multitude of mouths can melt metal,
A heap of slander can dissolve bone.

---

[28] The Huan-shui was the ancient name of the An-yang River 安陽河, which runs north of modern Honan province's An-yang city.

For further notes on the events leading up to this covenant and the rituals involved, see n. 36 to our translation of *Shih chi* Chapter 69.

[29] Ho-wai 河外 usually refers to an area belonging to the state of Wei south of the Yellow River. Chüan 卷 was about 25 miles west of modern Honan province's Yüan-yang 原陽 county. Yen 衍 was about 5 miles north of modern Chengchow 鄭州 in Honan (see Ch'ien Mu, *Ti-ming k'ao*, pp. 719-20). Yen 燕 was about 20 miles northwest of modern Yen-chin 延津 county in Honan. According to T'an Ch'i-hsiang (1:35-6), Suan-tsao 酸棗 was about 5 miles southwest of Yen-chin county, but Ch'ien Mu (*Ti-ming k'ao*, pp. 420-1) puts Suan-tsao north of Yen-chin county.

[30] Located about 5 miles west of modern Yün-ch'eng 鄆城 in Shantung (T'an Ch'i-hsiang, 1:39-40).

Thus I would hope that you might carefully decide on your plans, Great King, and that you might also grant me permission to retire from office and depart from Wei."

After this, King Ai reneged on his alliances and sought peace with Ch'in through the offices of Chang Yi. Chang Yi went back [to Ch'in] and once more became Ch'in's Prime Minister (317 B.C.). Three years later (314 B.C.), Wei once more abandoned Ch'in and made alliances. Ch'in attacked Wei and took Ch'ü-wo. The next year (313 B.C.), Wei served Ch'in again.

Ch'in wanted to attack Ch'i, but Ch'i and Ch'u had formed an alliance, thus Chang Yi went to Ch'u to serve as its Prime Minister.[31] When King Huai 懷 of Ch'u (r. 328-299 B.C.) heard that Chang Yi was coming, he cleared a high-class guesthouse for him and personally saw him to his lodgings.

"Ours is a remote and rustic country. What will you instruct us in, sir?"

Yi advised the King of Ch'u:[32] "If you are able to heed your servant, Great King, and close your borders and break off relations with Ch'i, I beg to offer the six-hundred *li* [on a side] of Shang and Wu, and to have a daughter of Ch'in sent as your slave in charge of brooms and dustpans. Ch'in having married off a daughter and Ch'u having taken a wife, we will be brotherly states for a long time to come. This way you can weaken Ch'i in the north and benefit from Ch'in in the west. No other plan would be as advantageous as this."

The King of Ch'u was delighted and granted his request. The assembled vassals all offered him their congratulations, Ch'en Chen 陳軫 alone offered him his condolences.

The King of Ch'u was angry. "Without raising our forces or sending out troops, We have acquired a territory of six-hundred *li*. The assembled vassals all offered us congratulations, why do you alone offer condolences?"

Ch'en Chen replied, "Not so. As your servant sees it, the territory of Shang and Wu cannot be gained but Ch'i and Ch'in will ally. If Ch'i and Ch'in ally, calamity will come to us."

The King of Ch'u said, "Have you an argument?"

Ch'en Chen replied, "That Ch'in values Ch'u is because [Ch'u] has Ch'i [on its side]. If we now close our borders and break relations with Ch'i, then Ch'u will be isolated. What does Ch'in covet from an isolated country that it would give six-hundred *li* [on a side] of territory in Shang and Wu? Once Chang Yi arrives in Ch'in, he is sure to betray you, Your Majesty. Thus we will have broken relations with Ch'i to the north, and made trouble with Ch'in to the west; the troops of both states are sure to fall upon us in concert. In laying plans for Your Majesty it would be better to ally secretly while publicly breaking with Ch'i and send a man to accompany Chang Yi. If they give us the land, it is still not too late to break with Ch'i. If they do not give us the land, we will lay plans with our secret allies."

The King of Ch'u said, "We hope that you might shut your mouth and speak no more, Ch'en Tzu. You may thus assist us in acquiring territory."

He then gave the prime minister's seal to Chang Yi and showered him with lavish gifts. After this he closed the borders, abrogated his agreement with Ch'i, and sent a general to [*2288*] accompany Chang Yi.

When Chang Yi arrived in Ch'in, he pretended to lose his grip on his reins and fall from his carriage. He did not attend court for three months. When the King of Ch'u heard this, he said, "Does Yi think that We have not yet completely broken with Ch'i?" He then

---

[31] According to *Shih chi*, 5:207 and 15:733, Chang Yi became Prime Minister of Ch'u in 313 B.C.

[32] Other versions of the following dialogue appear in *Shih chi*, 40:1723-4, and in *Chan-kuo ts'e* (3:15a-17a, SPTK).

sent a bravo to Sung, where he borrowed Sung's tally, went north and cursed the King of Ch'i.[33] The King of Ch'i was furious. He broke the tally and submitted to Ch'in. When Ch'in and Ch'i had established relations, Chang Yi then appeared at court and told Ch'u's envoy, "I have a fief of six *li* [on a side] which I hope to present to your Great King."

The envoy of Ch'u said, "I received instructions from my king that [you would present us] with six-hundred *li* [on a side] of land at Shang and Wu. I have heard nothing about six *li* [on a side]." He returned and reported to the King of Ch'u.

The King of Ch'u was furious and raised troops to attack Ch'in. Ch'en Chen said, "May I open my mouth and speak? To attack is not as good as ceding land to bribe Ch'in, then joining forces with it to attack Ch'i. Thus we have granted territory to Ch'in, but have obtained compensation from Ch'i, and Your Majesty's state can still be preserved."

The King of Ch'u did not listen. In the end he raised troops and had general Ch'ü Kai 屈丐 assault Ch'in. Ch'in and Ch'i jointly attacked Ch'u. They cut off eighty thousand heads, killed Ch'ü Kai, then took the lands of Tan-yang 丹陽 and Han-chung 漢中.[34] Ch'u raised more troops and launched a surprise attack on Ch'in. When they reached Lan-t'ien 藍田[35] there was a great battle. Ch'u was crushed. After this, Ch'u made peace with Ch'in by ceding two walled cities.

Ch'in threatened Ch'u. It wanted to obtain the territory of Ch'ien-chung 黔中, and offered the land outside the Wu 武 Pass in exchange for it.[36]

The King of Ch'u said, "I don't want to exchange land. I want to have Chang Yi. Then I will present you with Ch'ien-chung."

The King of Ch'in wanted to dispatch Chang Yi, but could not bring himself to say it. Chang Yi then asked to go. King Hui said, "This King of Ch'u is angry with you for failing [to give him] the land of Shang-wu. He will vent his resentment on you."

Chang Yi said, "Ch'in is strong and Ch'u is weak. Your servant gets on well with Chin Shang 靳尚. Shang serves the queen of Ch'u, Cheng Hsiu 鄭袖, and whatever Hsiu says, [the king] will obey. Moreover, I go on a mission to Ch'u bearing the tally of Ch'in. [*2289*] How would Ch'u dare kill me? If he does kill me, and because of this Ch'in obtains Ch'ien-chung, this is your servant's most fervent wish." He then went on the mission to Ch'u.

King Huai of Ch'u imprisoned Chang Yi upon his arrival and prepared to kill him. Chin Shang told Cheng Hsiu, "Did you know that you are going lose His Majesty's favor, my lady?"[37]

"Why?" said Cheng Hsiu.

---

[33] This story also appears in *Shih chi,* 40:1724. For the use of tallies in diplomatic missions, see n. 89 of our translation of Chapter 69. As for "borrowing" a tally from Sung, Hu San-hsing 胡三省 (1230-1302), in his annotations on the *Tzu-chih t'ung-chien* 資治通鑑 (3:91, *SPPY*), suggests that the Ch'u emissary had to borrow a tally from Sung because Ch'u and Ch'i no longer had diplomatic relations.

[34] There were two places called Tan-yang. Here it probably refers to the area north of the Tan River 丹水, which flows through modern Shensi and Hopei provinces (T'an Ch'i-hsiang, 1:43-4). For the location of Han-chung, see n. 4 to our translation of Chapter 69. According to *Shih chi,* 5:207, 15:733, and 40:1724, these events took place in 312 B.C.

[35] Ancient Lan-t'ien was about 5 miles west of modern Lan-t'ien in Shensi (T'an Ch'i-hsiang, 1:43-4).

[36] Ch'ien-chung included the area of southwestern Hupei, northwestern Hunan, northeastern Kueichow and the basin of the Ch'ien River 黔江 in Szechwan (T'an Ch'i-hsiang, 1:45-6). The Wu Pass was about 10 miles south of modern Shang-nan 商南 County in Shensi (T'an Ch'i-hsiang, 1:43-4). According to *Shih chi,* 40:1724, Ch'in offered this exchange in 311 B.C.

[37] Similar narratives of Chin Shang's efforts to save Chang Yi appear in *Shih chi* (40:1725), and *Chan-kuo ts'e* (5:16b-17b, *SPTK*).

Chin Shang said, "The King of Ch'in loves Chang Yi dearly, but [the King of Ch'u] does not wish to release him. Now [the King of Ch'in] is going to bribe Ch'u with the six counties of Shang-yung 上庸,[38] present Ch'u with a beautiful woman, and send the best singers in his palace as her attendants. The King of Ch'u will value the land and exalt Ch'in, so the Ch'in woman is sure to gain favor and you [are sure to be] dismissed, my lady. It would be better if you speak up for [Chang Yi] and have the king release him."

After this, Cheng Hsiu spoke to King Huai day and night. "Every vassal serves his ruler. Now our land has not been presented to Ch'in, but Ch'in has sent Chang Yi here. They have great respect for you, Your Majesty. If you act contrary to propriety and kill Chang Yi, Ch'in is sure to be enraged and attack Ch'u. I ask permission for my children and myself to move south of the Chiang so that we will not be humiliated by Ch'in." King Hui regretted his actions, pardoned Chang Yi, and treated him with great pomp as before.

After Chang Yi had been released, but before he had left, he heard that Su Ch'in had died.[39] He then advised the King of Ch'u:[40] "Ch'in's territory covers half the world, its troops are the equal of the states of the four quarters. Cloaked by redoubts, girded by the Ho River, its four barriers are its fastnesses. It has more than one-million knights of the palace guard,[41] a thousand chariots, ten-thousand cavalrymen and grain heaped in mounds and hills. Its laws and ordinances clear, its troops are calm before difficulties and rejoice before death. Its ruler is perspicacious and thus stern, its generals wise and thus martial. It has not yet sent out its armored troops; if it but sends them out, it will roll up the redoubts of Mount Ch'ang 常山 like a mat and is sure to break the world's spine.[42] The last of the world to submit will be first to perish. As for those who make alliances, this is no different from driving a flock of sheep to attack a fierce tiger. It is obvious that sheep and tiger are no match. If Your Majesty now does not side with the tiger but with the flock of sheep, I personally find [*2290*] Your Majesty's planning in error.

"The mightiest state in the world, if not Ch'in, must be Ch'u, and if not Ch'u, must be Ch'in. Both states are locked in contention, and the situation is such that both cannot survive. If you do not side with Ch'in, Great King, Ch'in will send down its armored troops to seize Yi-yang, and [the road to] Han's Shang-ti 上地 will be cut off. When it subdues Ho-tung 河東 and takes Ch'eng-kao 成皋,[43] Han is sure to enter Ch'in as its vassal, and Liang will see which way the wind is blowing. Ch'in will attack Ch'u's west, Han and Liang will attack it's north; how could your altars of soil and grain not be in danger?

"As for these alliances, they assemble a flock of weaklings and attack the mightiest. They fail to estimate their adversary, and rashly give battle. Their states are poor, yet they

---

[38] Shang-yung was about 25 miles southwest of modern Chu-hsi 竹溪 county in Hupei (T'an Ch'i-hsiang, 1:45-6).

[39] There are many problems associated with the date of Su Ch'in's death. For a summary, see n. 78 of our translation of Chapter 69.

[40] A parallel to this speech appears in *Chan-kuo ts'e* (5:18a-21a, *SPTK*).

[41] *Hu-pen* 虎賁 Knights were the Palace Guard during the Chou era (see Hsü Lien-ta, pp. 575-6 and Legge, 3:549-550).

[42] We follow Wang Nien-sun (4:18a-b) and Wang Shu-min's (70:2243) interpretation of the phrase *sui wu* 雖無.
Prior to the Han dynasty Mount Ch'ang was known as Mount Heng 恆山. Its name was changed to Ch'ang in the Han dynasty because Emperor Hsiao-wen's *praenomen* was Heng and *heng* was therefore tabooed (see Ch'en Yüan 陳垣, *Shih wei chü li* 史諱舉例 [Peking: Chung-hua, 1962], 8:130).

[43] Shang-ti was also known as Shang-tang 上黨. It covered the area of modern Wu-hsiang 武鄉 and Ch'ang-chih 長治 in Shansi (T'an Ch'i-hsiang, 1:35-6).
Ho-tung was the area east of the Yellow River in modern Shansi province (T'an Ch'i-hsiang, 1:35-6).
Ch'eng-kao was about 10 miles west of modern Ying-yang 榮陽 in Honan (T'an Ch'i-hsiang, 1:35-6).

mobilize their troops time and again. This is a policy of destruction. Your servant has heard that 'If your troops are not his equal, do not challenge him to battle; if your stores are not his equal, do not engage him in stalemate.' These advocates of alliance, with specious arguments and empty speech, exalt the ruler's principles and speak of advantages but not disadvantages; when catastrophe comes from Ch'in, it will be too late to stop. This is why I hope you might plan thoroughly, Great King.

    "Ch'in has Pa and Shu in the west. If a great vessel full of grain starts from the Min 汶[44] Mountains and floats down the Chiang River, it is over three-thousand *li* to Ch'u. With a two-hulled vessel to carry troops, each vessel can carry fifty men and provisions for three months. When it sets sail on the river, it can travel over three-hundred *li* in a day. Though it is many *li* it does not require the strength of horses and oxen, and in less than ten days, they will arrive at Han 扞 Pass.[45] When Han Pass sounds the alarm, from east of the border the walled cities will be guarded, and Ch'ien-chung and Wu 巫 Commandery[46] will no longer be yours, Your Majesty. If Ch'in's armored troops march out of Wu-kuan, face south and launch an attack, [Ch'u's] northern territory will be cut off. If Ch'in's troops launch an attack on Ch'u, danger and hardship will come within three months, but if Ch'u waits for help from the feudal lords, it will take more than half a year. [*2291*] The situation is such that [help] cannot arrive in time. Relying on the help of weak countries and forgetting the catastrophe that may come from mighty Ch'in, this is why your servant is troubled for you, Great King.

    "Your Majesty once fought with the men of Wu and won three battles out of five,[47] but your battlefield troops were used up. You held your newly acquired walled cities,[48] but your surviving people suffered. Your servant has heard that 'a great achievement is easily endangered; a worn out people will resent their sovereign.' Guarding an easily endangered achievement, while affronting mighty Ch'in, your servant personally finds this dangerous indeed for you, Great King.

    "Moreover, the reason why Ch'in has not sent its troops out of Han-ku [Pass] to attack Ch'i and Chao for the past fifteen years is that it plots with the intention of swallowing the world.[49] Ch'u once had difficulties with Ch'in, and they fought at Han-chung. The men of Ch'u did not gain victory. More than seventy of its jade-baton holders and ranking marquises died, and it lost Han-chung. The King of Ch'u was enraged, levied troops, and launched a surprise attack against Ch'in. They fought at Lan-t'ien. This is what people call a struggle between two tigers. No plan would be more dangerous than for Ch'in and Ch'u to wear each other out while Han and Wei remain intact and control the aftermath. I hope that you might calculate carefully, Great King.

    [2292] "If Ch'in sends down its troops to attack Wey's Yang-chin, it is sure to completely lock the pass to the bosom of the world. If you, Great King, mobilize all your troops and attack Sung, it will not be more than several months before Sung can be taken. Take

---

[44] Usually written 岷. These mountains lie in northern Szechwan (T'an Ch'i-hsiang, 1:43-4).

[45] Han-kuan was about 30 miles east of modern Feng-chieh 奉節 County in Szechwan (T'an Ch'i-hsiang, 1:45-6).

[46] A commandery covering the region around Wu-shan 巫山 in modern Szechwan (T'an Ch'i-hsiang, 1:43-44).

[47] According to *Shih chi,* 15:689, Wu was destroyed by the state of Yüeh in 473 B.C. Yü Ch'ang (quoted in Ho Chien-chang, p. 519, n. 47) suggests that Wu in fact refers to Yüeh, and that the old name of an occupied state could be used to refer to the power which annexed it. Unfortunately, there are still no records of fighting between Ch'u and Yüeh after the reign of King Wei 威 of Ch'u (339-329 B.C.; see also *Shih chi,* 41:1751).

[48] Hsin-ch'eng 新城 may refer to the place Hsin-ch'eng (see n. 8 above), but in the context it more likely means "newly acquired cities."

[49] Ch'in actually attacked Chao in 316, 315 and 313 B.C. (*Shih chi,* 5:207 and 15:732-3). Liang Yü-sheng (29:1252) therefore suggests that this statement is only intended to apply to Ch'i.

Sung, point eastward, and the twelve feudal lords on the banks of the Ssu 泗 will all belong to Your Majesty.[50]

"Su Ch'in, who sought to strengthen the entire world through treaties and alliances, was once enfeoffed as Lord of Wu-an 武安 and made Prime Minister of Yen, secretly plotted with the King of Yen to attack and crush Ch'i and divide its land. He then pretended to have committed a crime and fled the state to Ch'i. The King of Ch'i took him in and made him Prime Minister. After two years had passed, he discovered [the plot]. The King of Ch'i was enraged and had Su Ch'in's body torn to pieces by chariots in the marketplace.[51] To hope to govern the world and unify the feudal lords with one deceitful, dishonest Su Ch'in, that this could never succeed is clear indeed!

"Now Ch'in and Ch'u share a common border and are naturally close states by their topography. If you can truly heed your servant, Great King, I will have the Heir of Ch'in sent to Ch'u as a hostage and the Heir of Ch'u sent to Ch'in as a hostage. I will ask to have a woman of Ch'in become Your Majesty's dustpan-and-broom slave, and offer a city of ten-thousand houses as her bath-town. We will be brotherly states for a long time to come and will not attack each other for as long as you live. Your servant feels that there is no other plan as advantageous as this."

After this, the King of Ch'u, feeling indebted to Chang Yi and heavy [in heart] about giving up Ch'ien-chung to Ch'in, wanted to grant his request. Ch'ü Yüan 屈原[52] said, "Earlier you were deceived by Chang Yi, Great King. When Chang Yi arrived, your servant thought that you would boil him alive. If you cannot bear to kill him now, you must not listen to his pernicious advice again."

King Huai said, "If We grant Chang Yi's request and gain Ch'ien-chung, this is a marvelous profit. It would not be acceptable to renege afterwards." Thus in the end he granted Chang Yi's request and allied with Ch'in.

[2293] Chang Yi then left Ch'u for Han. He advised the King of Han:[53] "The land of Han is a precipitous and dangerous mountain abode. Of the five grains, it grows only beans and barley. The people's food is mostly cooked beans or bean-leaf broth. If there is no harvest for a year, its people will not have their fill of rice dregs and husks. Its territory is no more than 900 li [on a side] and it has had no provisions for two years. I would estimate that your troops, Great King, total no more than 300,000, and that includes slaves and porters. If we exclude those who guard the watchtowers and forts, the troops available are no more than 200,000. Ch'in has more than 1,000,000 armored troops, 1,000 chariots, and 10,000 cavalrymen. Its Tiger Racing Knights who dash forward without helmets, drawing their bows[54] and brandishing their halberds, simply cannot be calculated. The number of its armored

---

[50] The Ssu River is in central Shantung (T'an Ch'i-hsiang, 1:39-40). *Shih chi,* 46:1900 refers to *Ssu-shang chu-hou Tsou Lu chih chün* 泗上諸侯鄒魯之君 "the feudal lords on the banks of the Ssu, Tsou and Lu." "So-yin" suggests that these are "states such as Chu 邾, Chü 莒, Sung 宋, and Lu 魯" (Chu was the name during the Spring and Autumn period for the state later known as Tsou). Ho Chien-chang (p. 263 n. 16) suggests that the twelve states included: Tsou 鄒, Lu 魯, Ch'en 陳, Ts'ai 蔡, Sung 宋, Wey 衛, T'eng 滕, Hsüeh 薛, Pi 費, Jen 任, T'an 郯, and P'i 邳.

[51] This contradicts *Shih chi* Chapter 69, in which the King of Ch'i did not become aware of Su Ch'in's plot until after his death, and had Su Ch'in's corpse torn apart as a scheme to draw out Su Ch'in's assassin (*Shih chi,* 69:2265).

[52] For a biography of Ch'ü Yüan, see *Shih chi* Chapter 84.

[53] There is a parallel text for this speech in *Chan-kuo ts'e* (8:11b-13b, *SPTK*).

[54] "So-yin" glosses *kuan yi* 貫頤 as *liang shou p'eng yi* 兩手捧頤 "cupping the face with both hands." As Crump, p. 466, notes, this makes no sense. Wang Nien-sun (3.8b-9a) suggests that *kuan* means *wan* 彎 "to bend a bow" while *yi* is a kind of bow.

cavalrymen, the fine horses of Ch'in, with forelegs thrust forward and rear legs stretched back, from hoof to hoof measuring three *hsün* as they soar through the air, are beyond counting. The knights from East of the Mount join battle after girding armor and donning helmets; the men of Ch'in charge the enemy casting off their armor, barefoot and stripped to the waist, a human head dangling in their left hands, a live captive clutched in their right. These soldiers of Ch'in and the soldiers from East of the Mount are like Meng Fen 孟賁 and a coward; pushing against each other with all their weight and strength, they are like Wu Huo 烏獲 and an infant.[55] To attack a weak and recalcitrant state by throwing into battle soldiers like Meng Fen and Wu Huo is no different from dropping a weight of a 1000 *chün* on bird's eggs; there are sure to be no survivors.

[2294] "Your assembled vassals and the feudal lords do not consider the small size of their lands, but heed the candied words and fine speech of the advocates of alliance. Forming cabals and covering up for each other, they proclaim, 'Listen to my plan, and you may rule mightily over the world.' Ignoring the long-term interests of the altars of grain and soil and following shortsighted advice, nothing could surpass the error into which they have led the rulers of states.

"If you do not serve Ch'in, Great King, Ch'in will send down its armored troops, seize Yi-yang, cut off Han's Shang-ti, take Ch'eng-kao and Ying-yang 滎陽[56] in the east, and the palace of Hung-t'ai 鴻臺 and the garden of Sang-lin 桑林[57] will belong to Your Majesty no more. When it fortifies Ch'eng-kao and cuts off Shang-ti, Your Majesty's country will be partitioned. If you serve Ch'in first, you are secure; if not, you are in peril. If you create catastrophe yet seek fortune in return, if you plan shallowly, yet incur deep resentment, if you oppose Ch'in and side with Ch'u, though you might hope to avoid destruction, it is not possible.

"Thus in planning for you, Great King, nothing can compare with serving Ch'in. There is nothing Ch'in wants more than to weaken Ch'u, and there is no country more able to weaken Ch'u than Han. It is not that Han could ever be stronger than Ch'u, but the lie of its land has made it so. If Your Majesty now faced west and served Ch'in by attacking Ch'u, the King of Ch'in would be sure to rejoice. Avail yourself of their land by attacking Ch'u, shift misfortune [to Ch'u] and please Ch'in, there is no plan more advantageous than this." The King of Han heeded Chang Yi's plan.

Chang Yi returned to report, and King Hui of Ch'in gave him a fief of five towns and granted him the title Lord of Wu-hsin 武信.[58] He sent Chang Yi east to advise King Min 湣 (r. *323-284 B.C.) of Ch'i.[59]

"The mightiest states of the world cannot surpass Ch'i. Its great vassals and its royal kin are numerous and prosperous. Yet in planning for you, Great King, all offer only short-term advice, and ignore the welfare of future generations. The advocates of alliance, when advising you, Great King, are sure to say, 'To the west of Ch'i lies mighty Chao, to its south Han and Liang. Ch'i is a country with the sea at its back. Its territory is wide and its people numerous, its troops strong and its soldiers courageous. Even if there were a hundred

---

[55] Both Meng Fen and Wu Huo were famous for their strength (see *Shih chi,* 5:209).

[56] Ying-yang was about 5 miles northwest of modern Ying-yang city in Honan (T'an Ch'i-hsiang, 1:36).

[57] These palaces (or resort areas) remain otherwise unidentified.

[58] We have been unable to locate Wu-hsin.

[59] According to Yang K'uan, *Chan-kuo shih,* the correct dates for King Min were 300-284 B.C. Since Chang Yi supposedly died in 309 B.C. (see below), this would make the following speech anachronistic. Commentators generally get around this difficulty by supposing that it was actually addressed to King Min's predecessor, King Hsüan. A parallel to this speech appears in *Chan-kuo ts'e* (4:25a-26b, *SPTK*).

Ch'in's, they could do nothing to Ch'i.' You thought their advice worthy, Great King, but did not take stock of the facts. These advocates of alliance form cabals and factions and all think alliances acceptable.

"Your servant has heard [*2295*] that Ch'i and Lu fought three battles and Lu won three victories; mortal danger to their state followed in the aftermath. Though in name a victor in battle, Lu in fact incurred destruction.[60] Why was this? Ch'i was a great state and Lu a small one. Today Ch'in and Ch'i are like Ch'i and Lu. Ch'in and Chao fought on the banks of the Ho and Chang Rivers.[61] They fought twice and Chao triumphed over Ch'in twice. Then they fought at the foot of P'u-wu 番吾.[62] They fought twice and [Chao] triumphed over Ch'in again. After four battles, Chao's fallen soldiers numbered in the hundreds of thousands and Han-tan alone survived. Though in name a victor in battle, their state was already defeated. Why was this? Ch'in was mighty and Chao weak.

"Now Ch'in and Ch'u have married [each other's] daughters and presented [each other with] wives, and the two have become brother states. Han has presented Yi-yang, Liang has offered Ho-wai 河外,[63] Chao has paid homage at Min-ch'ih 澠池 and serves Ch'in by ceding Ho-chien 河間.[64] If you do not serve Ch'in, Great King, Ch'in will force Han and Liang to attack Ch'i's southern territories, it will mobilize all of Chao's troops, cross the Ch'ing River 清河, march to the pass of Po 博,[65] and Lin-tzu 臨淄 and Chi-mo 即墨[66] will no longer belong to Your Majesty. Once your state is attacked, though you might want to serve Ch'in, it will not be possible. For these reasons, I hope you will weigh matters carefully, Great King."

The King of Ch'i said, "Ch'i is remote and rustic, lying in seclusion by the East Sea 東海,[67] and I had not until now heard of the long-term interests of the altars of grain and soil." He then granted Chang Yi's [request].

Chang Yi left and advised the King of Chao in the west.[68] "The King of our humble manor Ch'in sends his envoy to offer this foolish plan to you, Great King. You led the world to repel Ch'in, and the troops of Ch'in did not dare to venture out of the Han-ku Pass for fifteen years. Your Majesty reached throughout East of the Mount, Great King; our humble manor was filled was fear, and groveled in panic. We mended our armor, sharpened our weapons, polished our chariots and cavalry, and drilled our horsemen and archers. We toiled [*2296*] in our fields, stored up our grains, and guarded our borders, living in worry, dwelling in fear, not daring even to tremble, lest you take it into your mind to tax us with our errors, Great King.

"Your strength, Great King, is sufficient to take Pa and Shu, annex Han-chung, surround the two Chou's, carry off the Nine Cauldrons, and hold the Pai-ma 白馬 Ford.[69]

---

[60] The state of Lu was not actually destroyed by Ch'u until 235 B.C. (see *Shih chi*, 33:1547).

[61] See n. 26 to our translation of *Shih chi* Chapter 69.

[62] See n. 26 to our translation of *Shih chi* Chapter 69.

[63] Ho-wai usually refers to the area of Wei south of the Yellow River. Ch'ien Mu (*Ti-ming k'ao*, p. 92) suggests this refers to the cities of Chüan, Yen and Suan-tsao mentioned above (see n. 29).

[64] The only record of a meeting between Ch'in and Chao at Min-ch'ih is in 279 B.C. (*Shih chi*, 15:742; see also our translation of Chapter 81). This is far too late to be what Chang Yi refers to here. Ho-chien was the area located between the two ancient branches of the Yellow River; it was also the name of a city in this area, just southeast of modern Hsien-hsien 獻縣 in Hopei (T'an Ch'i-hsiang, 1:38).

[65] The Ch'ing River and the Po Pass were both on Ch'i's western border with the state of Chao. See n. 39 of our translation of Chapter 69.

[66] Lin-tzu was the capital of the state of Ch'i. It was located a few miles northwest of modern Lin-tzu in Shantung. Chi-mo was about 25 miles northwest of modern Chi-mo in Shantung (T'an Ch'i-hsiang, 1:39-40).

[67] Now known as the Huang-hai 黄海, or Yellow Sea (T'an Ch'i-hsiang, 1:39-40).

[68] A parallel speech appears in *Chan-kuo ts'e* (6:14b-16b, *SPTK*).

[69] The Pai-ma Ford over the Yellow River was about 5 miles northwest of modern Hua-hsien 滑縣 in Shantung

Though Ch'in is remote and far away, its heart has burned and its anger smoldered for long indeed. Today Ch'in has troops in worn out armor and blunted weapons camped at Min-ch'ih; it intends to ford the Ho River, cross the Chang River, seize P'u-wu and meet you at the foot of the walls of Han-tan. We hope that you might join us in battle on the first day of the cycle; thus we rectify the affairs of Chow 紂 of Yin.[70] We respectfully send our envoy to inform your attendants of this first.

"All those you have entrusted to make alliances for you, Great King, have relied on Su Ch'in. Su Ch'in bewitched and confused the feudal lords, made right into wrong and wrong into right, attempted to subvert Ch'i and caused himself to be ripped to pieces by chariots in the marketplace. That the world cannot be unified is clear indeed! Today Ch'u and Ch'in have become brother states and Han and Liang call themselves the Vassals of the Eastern Barrier, while Ch'i has presented territories with fish and salt. This amounts to severing Chao's right arm. To fight with the right arm severed, to lose one's allies and live alone, even if you have not chosen such peril, how can you avoid it?

"Today Ch'in will dispatch three generals. One will block the Wu road, inform Ch'i, have it levy a force, ford the Ch'ing River and camp east of Han-tan. One will camp at Ch'eng-kao and drive troops of Han and Liang to Ho-wai. One will camp at Min-ch'ih. It will attack Chao with four states bound as one. If Chao is defeated, its land is sure to be partitioned four ways. Thus I dare not conceal our intentions or cover the facts, but inform your attendants of all this beforehand. If your servant were to lay plans for you, Great King, it would be best to meet the King of Ch'in at Min-ch'ih, see him face to face, speak with him person to person, and ask him to hold his troops, to not attack. I would hope that you might lay your plans, Great King."

[2297] The King of Chao said, "In the time of the late king, the Lord of Feng-yang 奉陽[71] monopolized authority and arrogated power; he deceived the late king and acted at his whim, holding the threads of all matters in his hand. We lived with Our tutor and did not take part in planning affairs of state. When the late king abandoned his assembled vassals, We were tender in years and new to the duties of the ancestral sacrifices. In Our heart, We did indeed have our doubts on this matter, thinking that to join in alliance and not to serve Ch'in were not in the state's long-term interest. We are thus willing to alter our intentions and reconsider, to cede lands as an apology for our former faults, and serve Ch'in. We were just about to arrange for a carriage to rush out when We happened to hear the Envoy's enlightened instructions." The King of Chao granted Chang Yi's request and Chang Yi then left.

He went north to Yen and advised King Chao 昭 of Yen (r. 311-279 B.C.).[72] "There is no state you are closer to than Chao, Great King. In ancient times, Viscount Hsiang 襄 of Chao[73] made his elder sister the wife of the King of Tai 代.[74] He intended to annex Tai and

(T'an Ch'i-hsiang, 1:36).

[70] Chow, the last emperor of the Yin Dynasty, was an infamous tyrant. King Wu 武 of the Chou dynasty defeated and killed him on the first day of the Chinese sixty-day cycle (see *Shih chi*, 3:108 and our translation of that chapter). Obviously, the King of Chao is being compared to Chow.

[71] For further information on the Lord of Feng-yang, see n. 8 of our translation of Chapter 69. If Ssu-ma Ch'ien is correct in identifying the Lord of Feng-yang as the younger brother of Marquis Su 肅 of Chao (r. 349-326 B.C.), then the "late king" referred to above is presumably Marquis Su and the speech is addressed to Marquis Su's successor, King Wu-ling 武靈 (r. 325-299 B.C.). If scholars such as Ch'ien Mu are correct in identifying the Lord of Feng-yang as an associate of King Wu-ling, however, then the speech would have to be addressed to King Wu-ling's successor, King Hui-wen 惠文 (r. 298-266 B.C.). Since Hui-wen ascended the throne after Chang Yi's death in 309 B.C., that would make this entire speech anachronistic.

[72] The following speech also appears in *Chan-kuo ts'e* (9:14b-16a, *SPTK*).

[73] Viscount Hsiang (r. 457-425 B.C.) was the ruler of one of the most powerful clans of the ancient state of

arranged to meet the King of Tai at the fort of Kou-chu 句注.[75] He then ordered his artisans to make a bronze dipper and lengthen its handle so that it could be used to strike a man. He drank with the King of Tai and secretly told his cook, 'When he is in his cups, pour some hot porridge with the dipper, then reverse it and strike him down.' When [the King of Tai] was in his cups, [the cook] brought in some hot porridge. The cook came forward and poured out the porridge, then reversed the dipper, struck the King of Tai and killed him. The king's brains spattered the ground. When [Viscount Hsiang's] sister heard this, she sharpened her hairpin and stabbed herself. Thus even today we still have Mount Mo-chien 摩笄.[76] There is no one in the world who has not heard of the death of the King of Tai.

[2298] "The King of Chao's cruelty and lack of fraternal feelings you cannot have failed to observe, Great King. Do you still think the King of Chao approachable? Chao levied troops, attacked Yen and twice besieged the capital of Yen, seizing Your Majesty. You ceded ten towns as a ransom, Great King.[77] Now the King of Chao has already gone to pay homage at Min-ch'ih and serves Ch'in by offering Ho-chien. If you do not serve Ch'in, Ch'in will send down its armored troops to Yün-chung 雲中 and Chiu-yüan 九原,[78] drive Chao to attack Yen, and the Yi River 易水 and the Long Wall 長城[79] will no longer be yours, Great King.

"Chao is like a commandery or county of Ch'in; it does not dare to rashly muster its forces for attacks and expeditions. If you now serve Ch'in, Your Majesty, the King of Ch'in is sure to rejoice, and Chao will not dare to move rashly. Thus Yen will have mighty Ch'in's support to the west and without Ch'i and Chao's menace to the south. For these reasons, I would hope that you might carefully weigh matters, Great King."

The King of Yen said, "We live in an outlying land among the Man and Yi. Though they may be full-grown men, they are no more than children, and their speech is unworthy of taking note of in correcting our plans. Today we are fortunate enough to receive instruction from our honored guest; we ask permission to face west and serve Ch'in, presenting five walled cities at the foot of Mount Heng 恆山."[80] The King of Yen heeded Chang Yi.

[Chang] Yi returned to report. Before he reached Hsien-yang, King Hui of Ch'in died (311 B.C.) and King Wu was enthroned. From the time he had been installed as Heir, King Wu had disliked Chang Yi. When he ascended the throne, the assembled vassals slandered Chang Yi: "[Chang Yi is] faithless. He sells his state left and right to gain appreciation. If Ch'in must employ him once more, we fear we will be the laughingstock of the world." When

Chin. It was Viscount Hsiang, together with the leaders of the clans of Wei and Han, who, after defeating their rival, Chih Po 智伯, in 453 B.C., in effect partitioned Chin into three states. The incident described below is also mentioned in *Shih chi*, 43:1793. According to *Shih chi*, 15:694, it took place in 457 B.C.

[74] Tai was an ancient state located in the area of modern Wei-hsien 蔚縣 in Hopei (T'an Ch'i-hsiang, 1:28).

[75] This was a hill northwest of modern Tai-hsien 代縣 in Hopei (T'an Ch'i-hsiang, 1:37-8).

[76] Mo-chien shan, "Mount Sharpened Hairpin," is about 20 miles southeast of modern Hsüan-hua 宣化 in Hopei (T'an Ch'i-hsiang, 1:41-2).

Ho Chien-chang (p. 1096, n. 10) cites two other instances in which people were beaten to death with a dipper.

[77] The King of Chao referred to here is apparently King Wu-ling. However, there are no records in the "Nien-piao" of any conflicts between Chao and Yen from the time of Chao Hsiang-tzu through the reign of King Chao of Yen.

[78] Yün-chung was the area around modern T'o-k'o-t'o 托克托 in the Inner Mongolian Autonomous Region. Chiu-yüan was about 5 miles west of modern Pao-t'ou 包頭 in the same region (T'an Ch'i-hsiang, 1:37-8).

[79] The Yi River ran south of Yi-hsien 易縣 in Hopei (T'an Ch'i-hsiang, 1:37-8). Most states built extensive defensive bulwarks on frontier areas next to aggressive neighbors. Yen's "Long Wall" was on its northern border, and a large portion of it followed the Yi River.

[80] This is Mount Ch'ang (see n. 41 above). Since the word *heng* was tabooed in Ssu-ma Ch'ien's time, Wang Shu-min (70:2254) believes that later copyists or editors changed *ch'ang* to *heng* in this narrative.

the feudal lords heard there was bad blood between Chang Yi and King Wu, they all rebelled against the counter-alliance and once more joined in alliances.

[2299] In the first year of King Wu of Ch'in (310 B.C.), the assembled vassals denounced Chang Yi day and night without ceasing; on top of this, a rebuke came from Ch'i.[81] Chang Yi feared he would be punished. He thus told King Wu of Ch'in, "I have a foolish plan I hope to offer."

The king said, "What would you undertake?"

He replied, "In laying plans for our altars of grain and soil, only when there is a great revolt in the east can you have more land ceded to you, Your Majesty. I have heard that the King of Ch'i loathes me fiercely, and that wherever I might be, he is sure to muster his forces and attack. I thus beg to retire to Liang. Ch'i is sure to levy troops and attack Liang. When the troops of Ch'i and Liang are locked in battle at the foot of the capital's walls, and neither is able to flee, Your Majesty may seize the opportunity to launch an attack on Han and invade San-ch'uan. Send your troops out of Han-ku and instead of launching an attack, confront Chou with them. Their sacrificial vessels are sure to arrive. Control the Son of Heaven and hold his maps and registers, this is a task fit for a king."

The King of Ch'in thought his plan good. He then prepared thirty leather-armored chariots and sent Yi to Liang. As expected, Ch'i mustered its forces and attacked it. King Ai 哀 of Liang (i.e., Wei, r. 318-296 B.C.) was frightened. Chang Yi said, "Do not fret, Your Majesty, I ask your permission to have the Ch'i troops withdraw." He sent his houseman Feng Hsi 馮喜 to Ch'u. [Feng Hsi] borrowed [the tallies of] an envoy, and set off for Ch'i.

He told the King of Ch'i, "Your Majesty loathes Chang Yi fiercely, yet how much you have increased Ch'in's reliance on him!"

The King of Ch'i said, "We loathe Yi, and wherever Yi might be, We will muster our forces and attack it. How have We caused Yi to be relied upon?"

He replied, "It is thus that Your Majesty has caused Yi to be relied upon. When Yi departed, he made an agreement with the King of Ch'in: 'In laying plans for you, Your Majesty, only when there is a great revolt in the east, can Your Majesty have more land ceded to yourself. The King of Ch'i now loathes me fiercely, and wherever I might be, he is sure to muster his forces and attack it. I thus beg to retire to Liang. Ch'i is sure to levy troops and attack Liang. When the troops of Ch'i and Liang are locked in battle at the foot of the capital's walls, and neither is able to flee, Your Majesty may seize the opportunity to launch an attack on Han and invade San-ch'uan. Send your troops out of Han-ku and instead of launching an attack, confront Chou with them. Their sacrificial vessels are sure to arrive. Control the Son of Heaven and hold the maps and registers, this is a task fit for a king.'

"The King of Ch'in thought his plan good. He therefore provided thirty leather-armored chariots and escorted Yi to Liang. Now Yi has entered Liang and Your Majesty has attacked it as expected. Thus Your Majesty exhausts your own state within, and attacks an ally without, increases the enemies neighboring you, confronting only yourself, and raises the creditability of [Chang] Yi with the King of Ch'in. This is what I meant when I said you have made Yi relied upon."

The King of Ch'i said, "Well put." He then had his troops raise their siege.

Chang Yi served as Wei's Prime Minister for one year and died in Wei.[82]

---

[81] A parallel to the following narrative appears in *Chan-kuo ts'e* (4:26b-27b, *SPTK*).

[82] According to *Shih chi*, 5:209 and 15:734, Chang Yi died in 309 B.C. Ch'ien Mu, *Chu-tzu*, pp. 381-2, argues that he actually died in 310 B.C.

Ch'en Chen

[2300] Ch'en Chen was a traveling persuader. He and Chang Yi both served King Hui of Ch'in. Both were powerful nobles and contended for favor. Chang Yi denounced Ch'en Chen before the King of Ch'in.[83]

"Chen carries precious gifts and travels on urgent missions between Ch'in and Ch'u in order to build ties for the state. Now Ch'u is on no better terms with Ch'in, but is on excellent terms with Chen. Chen has done much for himself but little for Your Majesty. Moreover, Chen intends to leave Ch'in and go to Ch'u. Haven't you heard this, Your Majesty?"

The king told Ch'en Chen, "I have heard that you intend to leave Ch'in and go to Ch'u. Is this true?"

"Yes," said Chen.

The king said, "Then what Yi said is true."

Chen said, "It's not just Yi who knows this. Every man walking the streets knows it. In ancient times, Tzu Hsü was loyal to his lord and the world contended for his services as vassal. Tseng Shen[84] was filial towards his parents and the world hoped to have him as son. Thus, when male or female slaves up for sale are sold without leaving the gate of their village lane, these are fine slaves indeed. When a divorced woman is married again in her own county township, this is a fine wife indeed. If I were now disloyal to My Lord, how could Ch'u think I would be loyal? A loyal man cast aside, where should I turn to if not to Ch'u?" The king thought his words rang true, and thus treated him well.

He stayed in Ch'in for one year. Eventually King Hui of Ch'in made Chang Yi Prime Minister and Ch'en Chen fled to Ch'u.[85] Ch'u had no high opinion of him, but sent Ch'en Chen on a mission to Ch'in.[86] When he passed through Liang, he attempted to gain audience with the *Hsi-shou* 犀首.[87] The *Hsi-shou* refused to grant him an audience.

Chen said, "I have come on business. If you will not see me, Master, I will be on my way; it will not wait for another day."

The *Hsi-shou* granted him an audience.

[2301] Ch'en Chen said, "Why are you fond of drinking, Master?"

The *Hsi-shou* said, "I have nothing to do."

[Ch'en Chen] said, "I ask your permission to fill your plate. May I?"

"How would you do that?"

"T'ien Hsü 田需[88] has arranged for the feudal lords to join in alliance, but the King of Ch'u is suspicious and does not trust him. Tell the King [of Liang], 'Your servant is an old acquaintance of the kings of Yen and Chao, and they have several times sent men here to say, "If you have nothing to do, why not come see us." I wish to inform Your Majesty of my journey.' If the king grants your request, I beg you not to take too many carriages. Take thirty carriages, place them in your yard, and openly announce that you are going to Yen and Chao."

[83] A parallel to the following dialogue also appears in *Chan-kuo ts'e* (13:10a-10b, *SPTK*).
[84] See *Shih chi*, 67:2205.
[85] A parallel to the following narrative also appears in *Chan-kuo ts'e* (7:18b-19b, *SPTK*).
[86] The *Chan-kuo ts'e* text reads Ch'i for of Ch'in.
[87] According to "Chi-chieh," *Hsi-shou* was a Wei military title. In both *Shih chi* and *Chan-kuo ts'e*, however, this title usually refers to Kung-sun Yen, who apparently once received it.
[88] T'ien Hsü was a Prime Minister of Wei (*Shih chi*, 44:1851). The *Chan-kuo ts'e* text reads Li Ts'ung 李從, who is otherwise unknown. The *Chan-kuo ts'e* text also has the King of Wei, rather than the King of Ch'in, send Ch'en Chen to Ch'u.

When [Liang's] guests from Yen and Chao heard of this, they sped back by carriage to inform their kings, who sent men to receive the *Hsi-shou*. When the King of Ch'u heard this, he was enraged.

"T'ien Hsü wants to conclude a treaty of alliance with Us, but the *Hsi-shou* is going to Yen and Chao. He has deceived Us!" Enraged, he refused to hear anything further of the matter.

When Ch'i heard that the *Hsi-shou* was going north, he sent a man to entrust him with some matters. The *Hsi-shou* then set out and the ministerial matters of three states were all decided by the *Hsi-shou*. Ch'en Chen then went to Ch'in.

Han and Wei attacked each other.[89] After one year there was no resolution. King Hui of Ch'in wanted to stop them and asked his courtiers. Some of the courtiers said it would be advantageous to stop them, while others said it would advantageous not to stop them. King Hui was unable to reach a decision. Ch'en Chen happened to arrive just then in Ch'in.

King Hui said, "Now that you have left Us and gone to Ch'u, sir, do you miss Us or not?"

Ch'en Chen replied, "Has Your Majesty heard the story of the Yüeh native, Chuang Hsi 莊舄?"

The king said, "I have not."

"Chuang Hsi, a native of Yüeh, served in Ch'u as a Jade-baton Holder. After a short while, he fell ill. The King of Ch'u said, 'Chuang Hsi was a humble rustic of old Yüeh. Now that he serves Ch'u as a Jade-baton Holder, both prominent and rich, does he still miss Yüeh?" An attendant[90] said, "Whenever a man misses his place of birth, he will show it when he is ill. If he misses Yüeh, he will speak with a Yüeh accent. If he does not miss Yüeh, he will speak with a Ch'u accent.' [The king] sent a man to listen to him, and he still spoke with a Yüeh accent.' Although your servant has been cast aside and driven to Ch'u, how could I help but speak with a Ch'in accent."

King Hui said, "Well put. Now Han and Wei attack each other and a year has passed without a settlement. Some have told Us it would be advantageous to stop them, others say it would be advantageous not to stop them. We cannot [*2302*] decide on this. We hope that when you are not planning for your ruler, sir, you might plan for Us."

Ch'en Chen replied, "Has anyone ever told Your Majesty the story of Chuang Tzu 莊子 of Pien 卞 killing tigers?[91] Chuang Tzu wanted to kill some tigers, but a slave boy at his inn stopped him, saying, 'Both tigers are going to eat the ox. Once they find that it tastes good they are sure to seize it. If they seize it, they are sure to fight. If they fight, the bigger one will be injured and the smaller one will die. Go after the injured one and kill it, and in one stroke you are sure to gain a name for [killing] a pair of tigers.' Chuang Tzu of Pien thought that he was right, so he stood and waited. After a short while, both tigers fought as expected. The bigger one was injured and the smaller one was killed. Chuang Tzu went after the injured one and killed it, and in one stroke he did indeed gain merit for [killing] a pair of tigers.

"Now Han and Wei attack each other, and a year has passed without a settlement. Thus it is certain that the bigger one will be injured and the smaller one destroyed. If one then goes after the injured one and attacks it, one will get two results with one stroke. This is

---

[89] A parallel to this dialogue also appears in *Chan-kuo ts'e* (3:17a-18a, *SPTK*). A major difference in the *Chan-kuo ts'e* version is that the two countries at war are Ch'i and Ch'u, rather than Han and Wei.

[90] *Chung-hsieh* 中謝. We follow "So-yin's" suggestion in translating this title.

[91] This figure is variously known as Pien Chuang-tzu, Kuan Chuang-tzu 管莊子 and Kuan Chuang-tzu 館莊子 in different sources. For further discussion, see Wang Shu-min, 70:2260-1.

similar to Chuang Tzu killing the tigers. What difference will it make whether it is My Lord or Your Majesty [who does this]?"

King Hui said, "Well put." In the end he did not stop [the conflict]. The bigger country was injured as expected while the smaller country was destroyed. Ch'in mustered its forces, launched an attack and won a decisive victory. This was Ch'en Chen's plan.

Kung-sun Yen

The *Hsi-shou* was a native of Wei's Yin-chin 陰晉.[92] His *praenomen* was Yen 衍 and his *cognomen* Kung-sun 公孫. He and Chang Yi were not on good terms.

[2303] Chang Yi went to Wei on behalf of Ch'in and the King of Wei made Chang Yi Prime Minister (322 B.C.). The *Hsi-shou* thought this to his disadvantage.[93] He thus had a man tell Kung-shu 公叔 of Han,[94] "Chang Yi has already allied Ch'in and Wei. He now says, 'Let Wei attack Nan-yang and Ch'in attack San-ch'uan.' The reason the King of Wei honors Chang Yi is that he wants to obtain Han's land. In a short while, Han's Nan-yang will have been taken. Why not entrust it to me, sir, and allow me to gain some merit for it? Then the alliance of Ch'in and Wei can be laid to rest. Thus Wei is sure to take measures against Ch'in and abandon Chang Yi, to buy Han's allegiance and to make me minister."

Kung-shu thought this to his advantage, so he entrusted him [with Nan-yang] and let the *Hsi-shou* gain merit. The *Hsi-shou* did indeed become Wei's Prime Minister and Chang Yi left.

The Lord of Yi-ch'ü 義渠 went to pay homage at the court of Wei.[95] The *Hsi-shou* had heard Chang Yi had become Ch'in's Prime Minister again, and envied him. The *Hsi-shou* then told the Lord of Yi-ch'ü, "[Yi-ch'ü] is far away and we may not be able to meet again. I beg to inform you of matters. If the middle states are at peace, Ch'in is free to roast and plunder, burn and destroy your lordship's state. If they are not at peace, Ch'in will send urgent missions and lavish gifts to serve your state."

After this, the five middle states attacked Ch'in.[96] It happened that Ch'en Chen told the King of Ch'in, "The Lord of Yi-ch'ü is a worthy lord among the barbarians. It would be better to assuage his ambitions by rewarding him."

The King of Ch'in said, "Excellent." He then gave the Lord of Yi-ch'ü a thousand rolls of embroidered silk and a hundred women.

The ruler of Yi-ch'ü summoned his vassals and consulted them. "Is this what Kung-sun Yen was talking about?" He then raised troops, launched a surprise attack on Ch'in, and crushed the men of Ch'in at the foot of Li-po 李伯.[97]

---

[92] Yin-chin was a few miles east of modern Hua-yang 華陽 in Shensi (T'an Ch'i-hsiang, 1:35-6).

[93] A parallel to this narrative also appears in *Chan-kuo ts'e* (7:14b-15a, *SPTK*).

[94] Kung Shu is usually identified as Han Chiu 韓咎, one of the sons of King Hsiang of Han, who at some point served as Prime Minister of Han. The Ch'ing scholar Yü Ch'ang (quoted in Ho Chien-chang, p. 1027, n. 5) also identifies Kung-shu with Po-ying 伯嬰, who is identified elsewhere (*Shih chi*, 45:1872) as the Heir of King Hsiang of Han. This is speculative; it is possible these were two different men.

[95] A parallel to the following narrative appears in *Chan-kuo ts'e* (3:12a-12b, *SPTK*). The inhabitants of Yi-ch'ü were Jung 戎, a non-Chinese tribe (see *Shih chi*, 110:2885 and n. 10 to our translation of *Shih chi* Chapter 4 above). Yi-ch'ü was 15 miles southeast of modern Ch'ing-yang 慶陽 in Shensi (T'an Ch'i-hsiang 1:44).

[96] According to *Shih chi*, 5:207 and 15:731, this occurred in 318 B.C.

[97] In *Chan-kuo ts'e*, 伯 is written 帛. Li-po was apparently a place name, but there is no consensus on where it was (see Ch'ien Mu, *Ti-ming k'ao*, p. 243).

[2304] After Chang Yi had died, the *Hsi-shou* entered Ch'in and became Prime Minister. He once hung the ministerial seals of five states from his belt and was master of the treaties of alliance.

His Honor the Grand Scribe says: "The Three Chin 三晉 produced many designers of exigent and expedient plans. Those who spoke of alliances and coalitions in order to strengthen Ch'in were almost all natives of the Three Chin. Chang Yi's actions were more excessive even than Su Ch'in's, but the world denounced Su Ch'in, because he died first and Chang Yi upheld his theories and established his doctrine of coalition by exposing Su Ch'in's shortcomings. In short, this pair were truly men capable of ruining a country!"

TRANSLATORS' NOTE

Chang Yi, along with Su Ch'in, has been cited by Western scholars as one of the many "fictional" characters portrayed in the *Shih chi*. Unlike Su Ch'in, however, we find references to Chang Yi in the works of men who must have been almost his contemporaries, such as the *Meng Tzu* (see Yang Po-chün, *Meng Tzu i-chu*, p. 140; Legge, *Mencius,* v. 2, p. 264), and *Hsün Tzu* (see *Hsün Tzu*, 9:1b, *SPPY*) and *Lü-shih ch'un-ch'iu* (15:11b-12a, *SPPY*). This does not mean that we must accept all that is found about Chang Yi in the *Shih chi* and other texts as completely accurate. Instead, while accepting the historicity of Chang Yi, we have attempted to point out the anachronistic elements in the biography in the notes.

The juxtaposition of the Grand Scribe's accounts of Su Ch'in and Chang Yi invites comparison. Indeed, the chapters are structured similarly: after the native place and early studies, we find both men met adversity; then there is a series of speeches by these great rhetoricians; finally we have their deaths. While these memoirs primarily provided an opportunity to illustrate the arts of the persuader (both chapters contain a number of parallels to the extant Chan-kuo ts'e), and while Ssu-ma Ch'ien concludes that both Chang Yi and Su Ch'in "were truly men capable of ruining a country," there are some distinctions between these two accounts which suggest Ssu-ma Ch'ien found Chang Yi more distasteful. We see this first in the troubles both men encounters early in their careers. Su Ch'in's distress comes from his impoverishment: he shows shame, returns to his studies, and emerges successful. Chang Yi, however, although suspected (falsely it turns out) of stealing a jade disc and demeaned by the beating he received, shows no remorse. It is almost as if this unjustified punishment allows Chang Yi to treat all others in an unjustified manner (witness his dealings with several states, most noticeably Ch'u). Even in their demise, although Su Ch'in is assassinated and Chang Yi presumably dies a natural death, these differences are present. Chang Yi died in a new position having been expelled from Ch'i, whereas Su Ch'in was killed because he enjoyed too much favor with his lord.

BIBLIOGRAPHY

I. Translations

Erich Haenisch. *Der Herr von Sin-ling, Reden aus dem Chan-kuo ts'e und Biographien aus dem Shi-ki*. Stuttgart: Reclam, 1965, pp. 35-41 (partial).
Mizusawa Toshitada 水澤利忠. *Shiki* 史記. V. 8. *Retsuden (ichi)* 列傳 (一). Tokyo: Meiji Shoten, 1990, pp. 305-63.
Ōgawa Tamaki 小川環樹, trans. *Shiki retsuden* 史記列傳. Rpt. Tokyo: Chikuma Shobō, 1986 (1969), pp. 64-76.

II. Studies

Yang Tsung-yüan 楊宗元. "Kuei-ku Tzu shu-k'ao chi 'Su Ch'in, Chang Yi lieh-chuan' shu-cheng" 鬼谷子書考及蘇秦張儀列傳疏證. M.A. thesis, Chinese Cultural College, 1962.

Shu-li Tzu and Kan Mao, Memoir 11

Shu-li Tzu

[71:2307] Shu-li Tzu's 樗里子 (d. 300 B.C.) *praenomen* was Chi 疾.[1] He was a younger brother of King Hui 惠 of Ch'in (r. 337-311 B.C.). He and King Hui had different mothers. [Shu-li Tzu's] mother was a daughter of Han. Shu-li Tzu was eloquent[2] and had many clever schemes, and the people of Ch'in called him a "sack of schemes."

In his eighth year (330 B.C.), King Hui of Ch'in ennobled Shu-li Tzu as a Veteran of the Left[3] and sent him to lead an attack on Ch'ü-wo 曲沃.[4] He drove out all of its inhabitants and took their city. The land was annexed by Ch'in.

In his twenty-fifth year (313 B.C.), King Hui of Ch'in made Shu-li Tzu commander of the attack on Chao. He captured the Chao commander Chuang Pao 莊豹[5] and seized Lin 藺.[6]

The next year (312 B.C.), he helped Wei Chang 魏章 attack Ch'u. They defeated the Ch'u commander Ch'ü Kai 屈丐 [*2308*] and took [Ch'u's] territory of Han-chung 漢中.[7] Ch'in enfeoffed Shu-li Tzu and he was entitled Lord of Yen 嚴.[8]

When King Hui of Ch'in expired (311 B.C.), the Heir, King Wu 武 (r. 310-307 B.C.), was enthroned. [King Wu] expelled Chang Yi[9] and Wei Chang and made Shu-li Tzu and Kan Mao the left and right chancellors (309 B.C.).[10] Ch'in sent Kan Mao to attack Han, and he

---

[1] As a member of the royal family of Ch'in, his *cognomen* was Ying 嬴. As Ssu-ma Ch'ien informs us later in this biography, he was called Shu-li Tzu (literally, "the man from the lane with ailanthus trees") because his residence was in a lane with ailanthus trees. Based on this biography, Ch'eng En-tse 程恩澤 (d. 1837) claims to have located this lane in northwest Sian (see *Kuo-ts'e ti-ming k'ao* 國策地名考, in *Yüeh-ya T'ang ts'ung-shu* 粵雅堂叢書 [Taipei: Yi-wen, n.d.], 2:21b-22a).

[2] In modern Chinese, 滑稽, pronounced *hua-chi,* means humorous or comical. However, "So-yin" notes that it should be pronounced *ku-chi* 骨雞 here. There are three different theories on the original meanings of the characters: 1) both *ku* and *chi* mean "to confuse," 2) *ku-chi* was a kind of wine container from which wine flowed continuously (see "So-yin"), 3) *ku* is the overflowing of water while *chi* means *chi* 計 (plans, schemes or plots-- see "Cheng-yi"). Nevertheless, it is commonly agreed that the extended meaning of the term is "eloquent" or "eloquence."

[3] *Yu-keng* 右更.

[4] There were two Ch'ü-wo during the Warring States Period--that referred to here was about 10 miles southwest of modern San-men hsia 三門峽 in Honan (see T'an Ch'i-hsiang, 1:35-6).

There is another record of Shu-li Tzu commanding an attack against Ch'ü-wo in the eleventh year of King Hui of Ch'in (314 B.C.). Liang Yü-sheng (29:1257) would therefore amend the text here to read "the eleventh year." It seems, however, that Ch'ü-wo was the object of several attacks by Ch'in. These are recorded for the eighth, ninth, and eleventh years of King Hui's reign (see *Shih chi,* 5:206-7, 15:729 and 44:1848-50). In none of these instances is the name of the Ch'in commander recorded, but we see no reason why Shu-li Tzu could not have commanded two of these attacks, in which case there is no need to change the date here.

[5] In *Shih chi*, 15:732 and 43:1808 he is called Chao Pao 趙豹, while *Shih chi,* 5:207 tells us he was a Chao commander called Chuang 莊. *Tzu-chih t'ung-chien* 資治通鑑, therefore, suggests that Chuang was his *cognomen* and Pao his *praenomen* (see *Tzu-chih t'ung-chien* [Peking: Chung-hua, 1963], 3:90).

[6] West of modern Li-shih 離石 in Shansi (see Wang Li-ch'i, 71:1755).

[7] This was an area that covered the southern part of modern Shansi and northern part of Hopei (see T'an Ch'i-hsiang, 1:43-4).

[8] Ch'ien Mu (*Ti-ming k'ao,* p. 907) believes that Yen was Yen-tao 嚴道 and locates it in modern Yung-ching 榮經 County in Shensi.

[9] See his biography in *Shih chi* Chapter 70.

seized Yi-yang 宜陽 (307 B.C.).[11] [Ch'in] sent Shu-li Tzu into Chou 周 with one-hundred chariots . Chou welcomed him with troops and was very deferential.

The King of Ch'u was angry and rebuked Chou for exalting the Ch'in guest. Yu T'eng 游騰 advised the King of Ch'u on behalf of Chou: "When the Earl of Chih 智[12] attacked Ch'iu-yu 仇猶,[13] he gave Ch'iu-yu a wide wagon and then followed it with troops and Ch'iu-yu thus perished.[14] Why? Because it had taken no precautions. When Duke Huan 桓 of Ch'i (r. 685-643 B.C.) attacked Ts'ai, it was termed 'punishing Ch'u,' but in fact it was a surprise attack on Ts'ai.[15]

"Now Ch'in is a state of tigers and wolves. When it sent Shu-li Tzu into Chou with a hundred chariots, Chou looked upon him with Ch'iu-yu and Ts'ai [in mind]. Thus it had long pikes placed before him and stout crossbows behind him; in name they were Chi's guards, but in fact they imprisoned him. How could Chou not worry for its altars of soil and grain? It feared that once [Chou] had perished, it would cause you trouble, Great King."

The King of Ch'u was finally pleased.[16]

[2309] When King Wu of Ch'in died (307 B.C.) and King Chao 昭 (r. 306-251 B.C.) was enthroned, Shu-li Tzu was even more venerated and exalted.

In the first year of King Chao (306 B.C.), Shu-li Tzu led an attack on P'u 蒲.[17] The Governor of P'u was frightened and called on Hu Yen 胡衍.[18] On behalf of P'u, Hu Yen told Shu-li Tzu, "In attacking P'u, My Lord, are you doing it for Ch'in, or for Wei 魏? If you are doing it for Wei, that is fine, but if you are doing it for Ch'in, then it is not profitable. Wey 衛 is Wey because of P'u. If you now attack P'u and P'u becomes a part of Ch'in, Wey is sure to yield and follow it.[19] Wei lost the area beyond Ho-hsi [to Ch'in] but hadn't the means to retake it; this was because its soldiers were weak. Now if you cause Wey to be annexed by Wei, Wei is sure to become mighty. The day Wei becomes mighty, the lands beyond Ho-hsi are sure to be in danger. Moreover, when the King of Ch'in examines your affairs and finds that you have harmed Ch'in and benefited Wei, he is sure to find fault with you, My Lord."

Shu-li Tzu said, "What's to be done?"

Hu Yen said, "Let P'u be and do not attack; your servant will try to go in and speak on your behalf; thus the King of Wey will owe you a favor."

Shu-li Tzu said, "Excellent."

Hu Yen entered P'u and told its governor, "Shu-li knows that P'u is exhausted and says that he is determined to seize P'u. But I can make him let P'u be and not attack it."

---

[10] Later in this biography it is made clear that Shu-li Tzu was Chancellor of the Right and Kan Mao Chancellor of the Left.

[11] About 15 miles west of modern Yi-yang 宜陽 in Honan (T'an Ch'i-hsiang, 1:35-6).

[12] The Earl of Chih was a powerful member of the nobility of the state of Chin. According to Shih chi, 15:696, he died in 453 B.C.

[13] Written as 厹由 in *Chan-kuo ts'e* (1:5a, *SPTK*) and 仇由 in "Shuo-lin" 說林 of *Han Fei Tzu* (8:4b-5a, *SPPY*), Ch'iu-yu was a small country neighboring Ch'in near modern Yü-hsien 盂縣 in Shansi (see T'an Ch'i-hsiang, 1:22-3).

[14] A fuller account of this story is recorded in *Han Fei Tzu* (8:4a-5b, *SPPY*). The "wide wagon" was used to transport a large bell which the Earl of Chih claimed he wanted to present to the ruler of Ch'iu-yu .

[15] See *Shih chi*, 62:2133.

[16] An almost identical account of Chou's reception of Shu-li Tzu and Yu T'eng's speech is found in *Chan-kuo ts'e* (1:5a-b, *SPTK*).

[17] Modern Ch'ang-yüan 長垣 County in Honan (see T'an Ch'i-hsiang, 1:35-6).

[18] A parallel text of this speech appears in *Chan-kuo ts'e* (10:7b-8b, *SPTK*).

[19] The Shih chi text reads 今伐浦入於魏, 衛必折而從之. We follow Wang Nien-sun (3:18b-19b) and Wang Shu-min (71:2271) and amend this to 今伐浦, 浦入於魏, 衛必折而入於魏.

The Governor of P'u was frightened, knelt and touched his forehead to the ground twice, and said, "I hope I might ask you [to handle this matter]."

He then presented three-hundred catties of gold [to Hu Yen] and said, "If the Ch'in troops withdraw, I will be sure to put in a good word for you with the Lord of Wey, and have you face south." Thus Hu Yen received gold from P'u and enhanced his position in Wey. After this, [Shu-li Tzu] lifted [the siege of] P'u and left. On his way back, he attacked P'i-shih 皮氏,²⁰ but P'i-shih did not surrender and he left it, too.

[2310] In the seventh year of King Chao (300 B.C.), Shu-li Tzu died. He was buried east of Illustrious-terrace 章臺 [Palace]²¹ and south of the Wei 渭 [River]. [Before he died,] he said, "One-hundred years from now, there will be palaces of the Son of Heaven flanking my tomb." The residence of Shu-li Tzu Chi was located at Shu-li of Yin 陰 Township south of the Wei and west of the temple of King Chao, thus the common people called him Shu-li Tzu. By the time Han arose, the Ch'ang-lo 長樂 Palace lay to its east and the Wei-yang 未央 Palace lay to its west, while the Armory 武庫 lay directly in front of his tomb. The men of Ch'in had a saying that went, "For strength, there was Jen Pi 任鄙,²² for schemes, there was Shu-li."

Kan Mao

Kan Mao 甘茂 was a native of Hsia-ts'ai 下蔡.²³ He served Master Shih Chü 史舉²⁴ of Hsia-ts'ai [as a disciple] and studied the paths of the hundred schools. He sought an audience with King Hui of Ch'in through Chang Yi and Shu-li Tzu. [*2311*] King Hui granted him an audience, was pleased with him, and put him in command of aiding Wei Chang in overrunning and pacifying the territory of Han-chung (312 B.C.).

When King Hui died, King Wu was enthroned. Chang Yi and Wei Chang left and went east to Wei. The Marquis of Shu 蜀, Hui 煇, and his minister Chuang 壯 rebelled.²⁵

---

²⁰ Just west of modern Ho-chin 河津 in Shansi (T'an Ch'i-hsiang, 1:35-6).

²¹ See n. 147 to our translation of *Shih chi* Chapter 6 above.

²² We know little about Jen Pi. According to *Shih chi*, 5:209, King Chao's father, King Wu, was fond of sports and feats of strength. He employed a number of "strong men" (*li-shih* 力士). among them Jen Pi, who eventually reaced high position. According to *Shih chi*, 15:740, Jen Pi died in 288 B.C.

²³ Modern Feng-t'ai 鳳台 County in Anhwei (T'an Ch'i-hsiang, 1:45-6).

²⁴ Master Shih Chü appears in several pre-Ch'in texts including the *Chan-kuo ts'e* (5:27b, *SPTK*) where he is identified as a gatekeeper of Hsia-ts'ai and criticized as someone who could neither govern nor manage his household well (see also Wang Li-ch'i, *Jen-piao*, p. 332).

²⁵ The Marquis of Shu, Hui was a Noble Scion of Ch'in who had been enfeoffed in Shu; Chuang was surnamed Ch'en 陳 (see "So-yin").

The chronology here conflicts with *Shih chi*, 5:207 and 15:732-6 which date relevant events as follows:

316 B.C. Ch'in attacked Shu and annexed it.

314 B.C. (*Shih chi*, 15:733 says 313 B.C.) the Noble Scion Yu T'ung 繇通 was enfeoffed with Shu

311 B.C. Ch'en Chuang, Minister of Shu, rebelled and killed the Marquis of Shu (Noble Scion T'ung)

310 B.C. Ch'in executed Ch'en Chuang

309 B.C. Kan Mao became Chancellor

301 B.C. Noble Scion Hui, Marquis of Shu, rebelled. Ssu-ma Ts'o 司馬錯 pacified Shu and killed the Marquis of Shu

According to these sources, Noble Scion Hui did not rebel until 301 B.C.. Moreover, it was Ssu-ma Ts'o (not Kan Mao) who put down Hui's rebellion. It seems likely, therefore, that Kan Mao was involved in surpressing only Ch'en Chuang's uprising and that Hui 煇 is an error or interpolation here. Without Hui the line would

Ch'in sent Kan Mao to pacify Shu.[26] Upon his return, [Ch'in] appointed Kan Mao Chancellor of the Left while Shu-li Tzu was appointed Chancellor of the Right (309 B.C.).

In his third year (308 B.C.), King Wu of Ch'in said to Kan Mao, "If only I could ride in my carriage all the way to the San-ch'uan 三川[27] and peer into the House of Chou,[28] I could die yet remain immortal."

Kan Mao said, "I ask permission to go to Wei and ally with them to attack Han, and to have Hsiang Shou 向壽 accompany me."[29]

When Kan Mao reached Wei, he told Hsiang Shou, "You return, sir, and tell the king that Wei has heeded me, but that I hope he will not attack. If matters succeed, all the merit will be counted as yours."

Hsiang Shou returned and told the king. The king met Kan Mao at Hsi-jang 息壤.[30] When Kan Mao arrived, the king asked his reason [for delaying the attack on Han].

He replied, "Yi-yang is a great county; Shang-tang 上黨[31] and Nan-yang 南陽[32] have long kept stores there. In name a county, it is in fact a commandery. If Your Majesty now puts several defiles behind him, then travels a thousand *li* to attack it, this will be difficult.

"Long ago, Tseng Shen was lodging at Pi 費[33] when a man from Lu[34] with the same *cognomen* and *praenomen* as Tseng Shen killed a man. A man told his mother, 'Tseng Shen has killed a man.' His mother calmly continued weaving. A short while later, another man again told her, 'Tseng Sheng has killed a man.' His mother still calmly continued weaving. A short while later, yet another man told her, 'Tseng Shen has killed a man.' His mother threw down the shuttle, got off the loom, climbed over the wall and fled. Even with Tseng Shen's virtue and his mother's trust in him, when three people cast doubt on him, his mother was frightened. Now your servant's virtue is not equal to Tseng Shen's virtue, nor is Your Majesty's trust in me the equal of Tseng Shen's mother's trust in Tseng Shen, while those who cast doubt on me are not just three men. Your servant fears that you will throw down the shuttle, Great King. Earlier, when Chang Yi annexed the lands of Pa 巴 and Shu[35] in the west (316 B.C.), opened the lands beyond Hsi Ho in the north (330 B.C.), and took Shang-yung 上庸[36] in the south, the world did not think Chang Tzu meritorious, but thought the late king worthy.

read: "The Marquis of Shu, the Minister Chuang, rebelled" 蜀侯相壯反. Thus, all three *Shih chi* accounts could be reconciled.

[26] Shu approximated middle and western modern Szechwan.

[27] A region surrounding modern Loyang in Honan (T'an Ch'i-hsiang, 1:35-6).

[28] As Pao Piao 鮑彪 (*fl.* 1147) observes in his annotation to an identical paragraph in *Chan-kuo ts'e*, this is a euphemism meaning to occupy Chou (see 3:20b-21a, *SPTK*).

[29] In *Chan-kuo ts'e* (3:21a, *SPTK*) this line reads, "The King ordered Hsiang Shou to accompany him" 王令向壽輔行. Ho Chien-chang (p. 130) points out that Hsiang Shou was the king's favorite and suggests he was appointed as Kan Mao's aide so that he could spy on him. This is more consistent with the rest of the story and *erh* 而 here may be a corrupted form of *wang* 王.

[30] "Cheng-yi" notes that this was a town of Ch'in; its exact location is not known.

[31] An area around modern Ch'ang-chih 長治 City in southeastern Shansi (T'an Ch'i-hsiang, 1:35-6).

[32] Surrounding modern Nan-yang City in southwestern Honan (T'an Ch'i-hsiang, 1:35-6).

[33] According to Pao Piao, this was a town in Lu (see *Chan-kuo ts'e*, 3:21a, *SPTK*). T'an Ch'i-hsiang (1:39-40) located it about 5 miles northwest of modern Pi-hsien 費縣 in Shantung.

[34] In *Chan-kuo ts'e* (3:22a, *SPTK*) this man is said to be from Pi.

[35] The small state of Pa spanned the eastern part of modern Szechwan and western Hunan (T'an Ch'i-hsiang, 1:43-4). See Chapter 70 for the background to Ch'in's annexation of Shu and Pao. In Chapter 70, however, Chang Yi is depicted as an opponent of an attack on Shu and Pa.

[36] Shang-yung was about 25 miles southeast of modern Chu-hsi 竹溪 in Hupei (T'an Ch'i-hsiang, 1:45-6). Takigawa (71:11) suggests that Chang Yi's capture of Shang-yung refers to Ch'in's capture of Han-chung in 312

[2312] "Marquis Wen 文 of Wei (r. *424-387 B.C.) had Yüeh Yang 樂羊 lead an attack on Chung-shan 中山;[37] after three years he seized it. When Yüeh Yang returned and recounted his merit, Marquis Wen showed him a box-full of slanderous letters. Yüeh Yang
knelt down, touched his forehead to the ground twice, and said, 'This [victory] was not because of your servant's merit, but because of My Lord and ruler's strength.'

"Now I am a vassal serving in a foreign state. If these two men Shu-li Tzu and Kung-
sun Shih 公孫奭[38] protect Han,[39] and criticize [the attack], Your Majesty is sure to heed them;
then Your Majesty would have deceived the King of Wei, while I would have earned the rancor of [Han's minister] Kung-chung Ch'ih 公仲侈."[40]

The king said, "We will not heed them. We ask permission to make a covenant with
you, sir." In the end he sent the Chancellor, Kan Mao, to command troops in an attack on Yi-
yang. Five months passed without Yi-yang's capture, and Shu-li Tzu and Kung-sun Shih, as
expected, argued against [the siege]. King Wu summoned Kan Mao, intending to recall the
troops.

Kan Mao said, "There was Hsi-jang."

The king said, "There was."

He then raised all his forces and sent Kan Mao to attack. [Kan Mao] cut off 60,000
heads and seized Yi-yang (307 B.C.).[41] King Hsiang 襄 of Han (r. 311-296 B.C.) sent Kung-
chung Ch'ih in to apologize and make peace with Ch'in.

[2313] Eventually King Wu went to Chou, and expired in there.[42] His younger brother
was enthroned, and was known as King Chao. The king's mother, the Queen Dowager Hsüan
宣, was a native of Ch'u. King Huai 懷 of Ch'u (r. 328-299 B.C.) resented Han's failure to
help when Ch'in had previously defeated Ch'u at Tan-yang 丹陽 (312 B.C.),[43] and he besieged
Han's Yung-shih 雍氏[44] with his troops. Han sent Kung-chung Ch'ih to inform Ch'in of its
plight. King Chao of Ch'in, being newly enthroned, and the Queen Dowager, being a native
of Ch'u, did not want to help. Kung-chung sought the offices of Kan Mao, and Mao spoke to

B.C., since Shang-yung was located in Han-chung.

[37] Chung-shan was a state located in modern Hopei with its capital at modern Ting-hsien 定縣 (T'an Ch'i-
hsiang, 1:37-8). See Chapter 80 for details Yüeh Yang and his capture of Chung-shan.

[38] His name is given as Kung-sun Yen 公孫衍 in *Chan-kuo ts'e* (3:21b, *SPTK*). Ho Chien-chang (pp. 131-2) argues that Kung-sun Shih and Kung-sun Yen were the same person.

[39] As noted above, Shu-li Tzu's mother came from Han. Ho Chien-chang (p. 132) points out that Kung-sun
Shih's mother was from Han too. We read *chia* 挾 as "to protect." Another reading would be "to hold," *chia
Han* meaning "to hold onto [their relationships with] Han."

[40] Kung-chung Ch'ih was apparently at one time the Prime Minister of Han. See n. 46 below for further
details.

[41] A slightly different version of King Wu's ambition for the Chou throne and Kan Mao's attack of Yi-yang is
found in *Chan-kuo ts'e* (3:21a-22b, *SPTK*).

[42] Both *Shih chi*, 5:209 and 43:1805 record that King Wu died while trying to lift the caldrons (*ting* 鼎) in the
Chou court.

[43] Tan-yang was about 30 miles west of modern Nei-hsiang 內鄉 in Honan (T'an Ch'i-hsiang, 1:43-4). This is
apparently a reference to Ch'u's defeat at the hands of Ch'in in 312 B.C. (see n. 285 to our translation of Chapter
5 above).

[44] Yung-shih was about 10 miles northeast of Yü-hsien 禹縣 in Honan (T'an Ch'i-hsiang, 1:35-6). The date of
Ch'u's attack on Yung-shih is extremely unclear. It seems that Ssu-ma Ch'ien puts it in 307 B.C. here, since this
record comes after the death of King Wu and before the attack on P'i-shih in 306 B.C. He also seems to follow
this dating in Chapter 4, but not in Chapter 5, where Ch'u's attack on Han follows (somewhat more logically) immediately after Ch'u's defeat at the hands of Ch'in in 312 B.C. A number of authors have suggested that there
were two or even three battles at Yung-shih. A longer version of this anecdote appears in *Chan-kuo ts'e*, 8: 27a,
SPTK.

King Chao of Ch'in on behalf of Han: "Kung-chung recently obtained Ch'in's help, thus he dared to resist Ch'u. Now Yung-shih is under siege; if the forces of Ch'in do not descend through the Yao 崤 Pass,[45] Kung-chung [Ch'ih] will bow his head [in shame] and refuse to appear in court, and Kung-shu 公叔[46] will join his country in alliance with Ch'u in the south. Once Ch'u and Han have become one, the royal clan of Wei will not dare not to heed them and the conditions for an attack on Ch'in will be complete. I wonder then whether is it more advantageous to sit and wait for an attack, or to launch an attack."

"Well put," said the King of Ch'in. He then sent troops down through the Yao Pass to rescue Han. Ch'u's troops left.

Ch'in sent Hsiang Shou to pacify Yi-yang and sent Shu-li Tzu and Kan Mao to attack Wei's P'i-shih (306 B.C.). Hsiang Shou was the Queen Dowager Hsüan's maternal relative and grew up together with King Chao, thus he was made use of. When Hsiang Shou went to Ch'u. Ch'u, having heard that Ch'in esteemed Hsiang Shou, treated him lavishly. Hsiang Shou held Yi-yang for Ch'in, and prepared to attack Han. Kung-chung [Ch'ih] of Han sent Su Tai 蘇代[47] to speak to Hsiang Shou: "When cornered, a beast can overturn a chariot. You defeated Han, Master, and humiliated Kung-chung. Kung-chung pulled his state together and once more served Ch'in, thinking himself sure to be enfeoffed. Now you give the territory of Chieh-k'ou 解口[48] to Ch'u and enfeoff its Vice Premier[49] with Tu-yang 杜陽;[50] if Ch'in and Ch'u ally and once more attack Han, Han is sure to perish. If Han perishes, Kung-chung himself will lead his personal followers to ambush you in Ch'in. I would hope you might consider this carefully, Master."

Hsiang Shou said, "My alliance of Ch'in with Ch'u is not aimed at Han. Explain this for me [*2314*] to Kung-chung, sir. Tell him that Ch'in and Han can form an alliance."

Su Tai replied, "I beg to explain something to *you*, Master. People say that if one esteems the things that others are esteemed for, one may himself become esteemed. The king's love for and closeness to you, Master, is not equal to [his love for and closeness to] Kung-sun Shih; his opinion of your wisdom and ability is not equal to [his opinion of] Kan Mao. Now neither of these two are allowed to involve themselves closely in the affairs of Ch'in; and yet you are allowed to make decisions of state together with the king. Why? They have given cause for mistrust. Kung-sun Shih is a partisan of Han and Kan Mao a partisan of Wei, thus the king does not trust them. Now Ch'in and Ch'u are contending for power and you have become a partisan of Ch'u, Master. This is the same path as Kung-sun Shih and Kan Mao; how do you differ from them? Men all say Ch'u is capricious, and yet you are bound to forget this; this is leaving yourself open to blame. It would be better for you to plan with the king

---

[45] Located in western Honan near San-men Hsia 三門峽 City (see T'an Ch'i-hsiang, 1:22-3).

[46] The identities of the two high-ranking Han officials, Kung-chung and Kung-shu, are very unclear. They were probably members of the Han royal family, perhaps even sons of the king. Apparently the king appointed them both to high office at the same time, and as a result they became bitter rivals. The point of the passage above is that if Ch'in refuses to help Kung-chung, who has gone to the trouble of seeking its assistance, not only will its potential ally Kung-chung be humiliated, his rival Kung-shu will go to Ch'in's enemy for help. It is unclear what is meant by the reference to Kung-chung having recently obtained Ch'in's help.

[47] Su Tai was a younger brother of Su Ch'in 蘇秦; see his biography in *Shih chi,* Chapter 69. There is a parallel text for the following anecdote in *Chan-kuo ts'e,* 8:14b-15b, *SPTK.*

[48] Chieh-k'ou was located just southeast of modern Loyang in Honan (T'an Ch'i-hsiang, 1:35-6). In *Chan-kuo ts'e,* we have Chieh-chung 解中. The two place names are possibly scribal variants (see Ho Chien-chang, p. 995).

[49] *Hsiao Ling-yin* 小令尹.

[50] About 5 miles northwest of Lin-yu 麟游 County in Shensi (T'an Ch'i-hsiang, 1:43-4). In *Chan-kuo ts'e,* it is Kuei-yang 桂陽 (8:14b, *SPTK*).

against [Ch'u's] capriciousness, Master, and to treat Han well in preparation against Ch'u; in this way you will have no worries. The clan of Han are sure to first follow with their state after Kung-sun Shih and then to entrust their state to Kan Mao. Han is your foe, Master. Yet now if you speak of preparing against Ch'u by befriending Han, this is a case of '[one who] in recommending those outside the family, does not avoid his foe.'"[51]

Hsiang Shou said, "Very well, I really desire the alliance of Han."

[Su Tai] replied, "Kan Mao has promised Wu-sui 武遂[52] to Kung-chung and the return of the commoners of Yi-yang. Now you want to buy [Kung-chung Chih's] support without doing anything; this is quite difficult."

Hsiang Shou asked, "What then? I cannot after all obtain Wu-sui [to give Han]."

[Su Tai] replied, "Why not use Ch'in's auspices to seek Ying-ch'uan 潁川 from Ch'u on behalf of Han, Master? This was the land that Han depended on.[53] If you seek it and obtain it, it will mean your orders are effective in Ch'u and Han will owe you a favor for [Ch'u's] land. If you seek it and do not obtain it, it will mean unsettled resentment between Han and Ch'u and both will run to Ch'in [for support]. Ch'in and Ch'u are contending for power; to buy Han's support by casually putting Ch'u at fault, this is to Ch'in's benefit."

Hsiang Shou said, "How is this to be done?"

[Su Tai] replied, "This would be an excellent thing [for you]. Kan Mao wants to gain Ch'i's support through Wei's auspices, while Kung-sun Shih wants to gain Ch'i's support through Han's auspices. Now you may take the occupation of Yi-yang as your merit, secure it by buying the support of Ch'u and Han, and denounce the crimes of Ch'i and Wei; thus Kung-sun Shih and Kan Mao will have no affairs to tend."[54]

[2316] Kan Mao eventually told King Chao of Ch'in to return Wu-sui to Han. Hsiang Shou and Kung-sun Shih argued, but were unable to prevail. Following this Hsiang Shou and Kung-sun Shih harbored resentment and slandered Kan Mao. Mao was afraid; he broke off the attack on Wei's P'u-pan and fled (306 B.C.). Shu-li Tzu came to terms with Wei and withdrew the troops.

When Kan Mao fled from Ch'in to Ch'i, he met Su Tai.[55] Tai was going on a mission for Ch'i to Ch'in. Kan Mao said, "I offended Ch'in and, fleeing out of fear, have no place to hide my tracks. I have heard there was a poor man's daughter making cloth together with a wealthy man's daughter. The poor man's daughter said, 'I do not have the means to buy candles, but fortunately you have an excess of candlelight, mistress; if you might lend me your

---

[51] This saying comes from *Lü-shih ch'un-ch'iu* (1:11a, *SPPY*) where Confucius praises the impartiality of Ch'i Huang-yang 祁黃羊, who "in recommending someone [to office] from those outside his family, did not avoid his enemy; in recommending someone from among people in his family, did not avoid his own son" 外舉不避讎, 內舉不避子.

[52] Wu-sui was on the north side of the Yellow River about 50 miles northwest of modern Loyang (T'an Ch'i-hsiang, 1:35). According to *Shih chi*, 5:209, it was taken by Ch'in at the same time that Yi-yang was taken. Having been seized by Kan Mao, it was not in Hsiang Shou's power to offer it to Han, hence Hsiang Shou's remark below.

[53] Located near modern Yü-hsien 禹縣 in Honan (Wang Li-ch'i, 71:1759 and Ch'ien Mu, *Ti-ming k'ao*, p. 440). It was originally a Han territory and is therefore referred to here as Han's *chi-ti* 寄地, the land that [Han] depended on.

[54] This passage also has a parallel in the *Chan-kuo ts'e* (8:14b, *SPTK*). The shift from Su Tai's plan for alienating Ch'u and Ch'in to his explanation of how this will benefit Hsiang Shou personally is not particularly clear, and our translation is tentative. The idea seems to be that if Hsiang Shou can undercut Han's support for Kung-sun Shih and Wei's support for Kan Mao, he can retain control of the rich area around Yi-yang and eventually depose his two rivals by sabotaging their schemes to ally with Ch'i.

[55] There is a parallel text for the following anecdote in *Chan-kuo ts'e*, 3:27b-328a, *SPTK*.

excess radiance, it would not reduce your light, yet would allow me to share in its benefit.'
Now I am hard-pressed, while you hold a key post [in Ch'i] and are about to go on a mission
to Ch'in. My wife and children are there, I would hope you might bathe them in your excess
radiance."

Su Tai promised, then completed his mission to Ch'in. When it was finished, he therefore said to the King of Ch'in, "Kan Mao is not an ordinary knight. During his stay in Ch'in,
he held high positions for the reigns of several Ch'in kings. From Yao 崤 to Kuei-ku,[56] he
knows clearly the land's topography, precipitous and level. If this fellow, under Ch'i's auspices, were to plot to turn Han and Wei against Ch'in, it would not be to Ch'in's benefit."

[2317] The King of Ch'in said, "Then what's to be done?"

Su Tai said, "It would be better for Your Majesty to welcome him back by making his
welcoming gift a more exalted one and by making his salary a more lavish one; if he comes,
confine him to Kuei-ku and do not let him out for the rest of his life."

The King of Ch'in said, "An excellent idea." He then granted [Kan Mao] the title of
Senior Excellency[57] and sent a man carrying the Prime Minister's seal to escort him back from
Ch'i.

Kan Mao did not go. Su Tai told King Min 湣 of Ch'i (r. *323-284 B.C.), "Kan Mao
is a worthy man. Now Ch'in grants him the title of Senior Excellency and sends a man carrying the Prime Minister's seal to escort him back. Kan Mao is grateful for Your Majesty's
grants; he would like to become Your Majesty's vassal, and thus has declined and will not go.
Now what will Your Majesty reward him with?"

The King of Ch'i replied, "Well said." He then gave him the title of Senior Excellency, and asked him to stay. Ch'in then sought favor with Ch'i by exempting Kan Mao's
family from conscription.[58]

Ch'i sent Kan Mao to Ch'u. King Huai of Ch'u and Ch'in were on good terms because
of their recent nuptial ties,[59] and when Ch'in heard that Kan Mao was in Ch'u, it sent a man to
tell the King of Ch'u, "We hope that you might send Kan Mao to Ch'in."

The King of Ch'u asked Fan Hsüan 范蜎[60] "We want to install a Prime Minister in
Ch'in. Who might do?"

[Fan Hsüan] replied, "Your servant's wisdom is not sufficient to know the answer."

The King of Ch'u said, "We want to install Kan Mao as Prime Minister. Will he do?"

[Fan Hsüan] replied, "He will not do. This fellow Shih Chü was a gatekeeper at Hsia-
ts'ai. In great matters, he did not act to serve his lord, and in lesser matters, he did not manage his own household. He was known in his time for his base compromising and his lack of
integrity; yet Kan Mao served him [as a disciple] and got along well with him. Thus when
Kan Mao served men with the perspicacity of King Hui, the acumen of King Wu, and the perspicuity of Chang Yi, he [still] held [*2318*] ten posts without giving offense. Mao is truly a
worthy man, but will not do as Prime Minister in Ch'in. A worthy Prime Minister in Ch'in
would not be to Ch'u's benefit.

---

[56] See n. 2 to our translation of *Shih chi* Chapter 69 above.

[57] *Shang-ch'ing* 上卿 (Hsü Lien-ta, p. 74).

[58] There are substantial differences in the *Shih chi* and *Chan-kuo ts'e* versions of the story of the weaving girls.
This story is also recorded in *Lieh-nü chuan* 列女傳 where the two women are called Hsü Wu 徐吾 and Li Wu
李吾. The *Lieh-nü chuan* version is closer to the *Chan-kuo ts'e* version (6:13a-b, *SPPY*).

[59] According to *Shih chi*, 15:735, Ch'in escorted a Ch'u bride to Ch'in in 305 B.C. (presumably T'ang Pa Tzu
唐八子, the wife of King Chao, who had just taken the throne in Ch'in).

[60] He is known alternatively as Fan Huan 環, Fan Hsün 蠉 and Kan Hsiang 干象 in different sources. A parallel text for the following anecdote appears in *Chan-kuo ts'e*, 5.27b-28a, *SPTK*.

"Moreover, Your Majesty earlier employed Shao Hua 召滑 in Yüeh and he secretly instigated the insurrection of Chang Yi 章義.[61] Yüeh's state was in turmoil, thus Ch'u built barriers to the south at Li-men 厲門[62] and made Chiang-tung 江東[63] its commandery. By my calculation, the reason Your Majesty's achievements were such was because Yüeh was in turmoil, while Ch'u was well-governed.

"Now Your Majesty knew enough to employ this against Yüeh but forgets to employ it against Ch'in. Your servant believes this to be a great mistake on Your Majesty's part. Thus if Your Majesty intends to install a Prime Minister in Ch'in, there is no one more suitable than Hsiang Shou.[64] Hsiang Shou is a close relative of the King of Ch'in; in youth they shared clothing, in maturity they share a chariot; thus [the king] has entrusted him with many tasks. If Your Majesty is set on installing Hsiang Shou as Prime Minister in Ch'in, this is to the state of Ch'u's advantage."

[King Huai] then sent an envoy to ask that Ch'in install Hsiang Shou as Prime Minister in Ch'in. Eventually Ch'in made Hsiang Shou Prime Minister and Kan Mao in the end was not able to enter Ch'in again. He died in Wei.

Kan Mao had a grandson named Kan Lo 甘羅.

Kan Lo

[2319] Kan Lo was the grandson of Kan Mao. After Mao died, when Kan Lo was twelve years old, he served Ch'in's Prime Minister, Marquis Wen-hsin 文信, Lü Pu-wei 呂不韋.[65]

The First Emperor of Ch'in sent the Lord of Kang-ch'eng 剛成, Ts'ai Tse 蔡澤,[66] to Yen. After three years, Hsi 喜, King of Yen (r. 254-221 B.C.) sent his Heir Tan 丹 to Ch'in as a hostage. Ch'in sent Chang T'ang 張唐 to serve as Prime Minister of Yen, hoping to attack Chao together with Yen and thus to broaden its territory in Ho-chien 河間.[67]

Chang T'ang told the Lord of Wen-hsin, "Your servant once attacked [the state of] Chao for King Chao of Ch'in. Chao harbored resentment against me and said, 'A hundred *li* [on a side] of land to the one who can capture T'ang.' If I go to Yen now, I must pass through Chao, thus I cannot go."

[61] The original reads *nei hsing Chang Yi chih nan* 內行章義之難. "So-yin" notes that *Chan-kuo ts'e* reads *nei Kou-chang chih nan* 內句章之難, close to the extant version of *Chan-kuo ts'e* (5:28a, *SPTK*) which reads *nei Kou-chang*. *Mei chih nan* 內句章昧之難. According to Pao Piao, Kou-chang was a place in K'uai-chi 會稽 while Mei was a person named T'ang Mei 唐昧. *Mei chih nan* will then refer to the disaster in which Ch'i, Wei and Han joined in attack of Ch'u and killed T'ang Mei. However, as Yü Ch'ang has noticed, the attack of Ch'u by Ch'i, Wei and Han took place in 301 B.C., four years after this dialogue took place. Ho Chien-chang (p. 506) cites a number of involved explications of this text which attempt to resolve (unsuccessfully, in our opinion) the *Shih chi* and *Chan-kuo ts'e* versions.
We follow Wang Li-ch'i (71:1760) who argues that *Chang Yi* was the name of a rebel in Yüeh.
[62] Near modern P'ing-lo 平樂 in Kwangsi (T'an Ch'i-hsiang, 1:45-6). Ch'ien Mu takes this to be Lai-hu 瀨湖, which he locates northwest of Li-yang 溧陽 in Kiangsu (*Ti-ming k'ao*, p. 588).
[63] Stretching from south of modern Wu-hu 蕪湖 City to south of Shanghai (T'an Ch'i-hsiang, 1:45-6).
[64] *Chan-kuo ts'e* has Kung-sun Ho instead of Hsiang Shou here (5:27b, *SPTK*). In the context of this memoir, Hsiang Shou may be more appropriate here since similar observations about him were made earlier.
[65] See his biography in *Shih chi* Chapter 85.
[66] See his biography in *Shih chi* Chapter 79.
[67] About 5 miles southwest of modern Hsien-hsien 獻縣 in Hopei (T'an Ch'i-hsiang, 1:37-8).

The Lord of Wen-hsin was not happy, but had no way to force him. Kan Lo said, "Why is My Lord the Marquis so unhappy?"

The Lord of Wen-hsin said, "It has been three years since I sent the Lord of Kang-ch'eng, Ts'ai Tse, to serve Yen. Yen's Heir Tan has already come as a hostage. When I myself asked His Excellency Chang to serve as Prime Minister of Yen, he refused to go."

Kan Lo said, "Allow me to make him go."

The Lord of Wen-hsin shouted, "Be off with you! I myself asked him and he refused. How can *you* make him go?"

Kan Lo said, "The great Hsiang T'uo 項橐 was only seven years old when he became Confucius's teacher.[68] Your servant is already twelve years old this year. Give me a chance, My Lord; why shout at me so hastily?"

After this, Kan Lo saw His Excellency Chang [T'ang]. "How does Your Excellency's merit compare with that of the Lord of Wu-an 武安?"[69]

His Excellency said, "The Lord of Wu-an defeated mighty Ch'u in the south, awed Yen and Chao in the north, fought and triumphed, attacked and conquered, crushed cities and leveled towns, I know not how many times. My merit is not equal to his."

Kan Lo said, "When the Marquis of Ying 應[70] was employed in Ch'in, how did his monopoly on power compare with that of Marquis Wen-hsin?"

Minister Chang said, "The Marquis of Ying's monopoly was not equal to that of Marquis Wen-hsin."

Kan Lo said, "Are you certain that his monopoly was not equal to that of Marquis Wen-hsin?"

"I am."

Kan Lo said, "The Marquis of Ying wanted to attack Chao and the Lord of Wu-an opposed him. [The Lord of Wu-an] went seven *li* from Hsien-yang and was put to death at the Tu 杜 Relay-station (257 B.C.).[71] Now Marquis Wen-hsin himself has asked Your Excellency to serve as Prime Minister of Yen, and you refuse to go. I wonder where *you* will die."

Chang T'ang said, "Allow me to go, child." He packed and prepared for his journey.

[2320] When a date had been set for their journey, Kan Lo told Marquis Wen-hsin, "If you will lend me five chariots, I ask permission to first inform Chao on behalf of Chang T'ang."

Marquis Wen-hsin then entered [the palace] and spoke to the First Emperor. "Kan Lo, the grandson of Kan Mao of old, is only a youth, but as the descendant of a famous family, the feudal lords have all heard of him. Recently, Chang T'ang intended to refuse to set out on the pretext of illness. Kan Lo persuaded him to set out. He now begs to first inform Chao, and I ask for permission to dispatch him."

The First Emperor summoned [Kan Lo] to an audience, then sent him to Chao. King Hsiang of Chao 趙襄王 (r. 244-236 B.C.) welcomed Kan Lo in the suburbs. Kan Lo advised the King of Chao.

"Has Your Majesty heard that Yen's Heir Tan has entered Ch'in as a hostage?"

"I have heard that."

"Have you heard that Chang T'ang is to serve as Prime Minister of Yen?"

---

[68] This legend of Hsiang Tuo's being Confucius teacher is seen in various sources later than the *Shih chi* (for a summary, see Wang Shu-min, 71:2283).

[69] This was Pai Ch'i 白起. For his biography see *Shih chi* Chapter 73.

[70] This was Fan Sui 范睢. For his biography see *Shih chi,* Chapter 79.

[71] Between ancient Hsien-yang and the modern city of the same name in Shensi (T'an Ch'i-hsiang, 1:43-4).

"I have heard that."

"Yen's Heir Tan[72] having entered Ch'in, Yen will not deceive Ch'in. Chang T'ang having become Yen's Prime Minister, Ch'in will not deceive Yen. If Yen and Ch'in do not deceive each other and attack Chao, this will be perilous indeed. There is only one reason that Yen and Ch'in do not deceive each other: they intend to attack Chao and broaden [their territories in] Ho-chien. It would be better for Your Majesty to grant me five cities so as to broaden [Ch'in's territory in] Ho-chien and to ask [Ch'in] to return the Heir of Yen, then to attack feeble Yen with mighty Chao."

The King of Chao at once personally ceded five cities to broaden [Ch'in's holdings in] Ho-chien. Ch'in returned Yen's Heir (232 B.C.). Chao attacked Yen, took thirty cities at Shang-ku 上谷[73] and let Ch'in have eleven of them.[74]

[2321] When Kan Lo returned to report to Ch'in, Ch'in enfeoffed Kan Lo as a Senior Excellency, and also granted him Kan Mao's original residences and fields.

His Honor the Grand Scribe says: "When Shu-li Tzu gained high rank as flesh and blood [of the Ch'in royal family], this was only the normal way of things, but the men of Ch'in praise his schemes, thus I have incorporated several of them here. Kan Mao rose from the alleys of Hsia-ts'ai, manifested his name among the feudal lords and was highly regarded by mighty Ch'i and Ch'u. Kan Lo was young in years, but proposed a unique plan and his name was acclaimed by posterity. Although they were not gentlemen of earnest behavior, they were at least strategists of the Warring States. As Ch'in's might grew, the world rushed to schemes and treacheries all the more."

---

[72] He engaged Ching K'o 荆軻 to assassinate the First Emperor of Ch'in in 227 B.C., see *Shih chi,* 86:2526-38.

[73] The area covering northwest modern Hopei (see T'an Ch'i-hsiang, 1:41-2).

[74] The original reads *shih-yi* 十一. *Chan-kuo ts'e* (3:78b, *SPTK*) reads *shih-yi* 什一, "one tenth."

For an almost identical account of the story of Kan Lo, see *Chan-kuo ts'e* (3:77a-78b, *SPTK*).

TRANSLATORS' NOTE

Scholars have argued that Ssu-ma Ch'ien linked his accounts of Shu-li Tzu and Kan Mao because they held the equal rank of Chancellor. Yet the key to this chapter seems to be the Grand Scribe's observations in his comments: "As Ch'in's might grew the world rushed to schemes and treacheries all the more!" In the several long speeches by Shu-li Tzu, Hu Yen and even Su Tai (whose biography is in the preceding chapter), we find resonances of *Shih chi* Chapters 69 and 70 here, as these three chapters portray the role of the lesser spokesmen (in comparison to Su Ch'in and Chang Yi) who advocated "schemes and treachery"--Su Tai, Shu-li Tzu, Hu Yen, Kan Mao, Hsiang Shou, and Kan Lo.

BIBLIOGRAPHY

I. Translations

Mizusawa Toshitada 水澤利忠. *Shiki* 史記. V. 8. *Retsuden (ichi)* 列傳 (一). Tokyo: Meiji Shoten, 1990, pp. 364-91.
Ōgawa Tamaki 小川環樹, trans. *Shiki retsuden* 史記列傳. Rpt. Tokyo: Chikuma Shobō, 1986 (1969). pp. 77-83.
Watson, Burton. *Records of the Grand Historian: Qin Dynasty.* V. 3. Hong Kong and New York: The Research Centre for Translation, The Chinese University of Hong Kong and Columbia University Press, 1993, pp. 101-112.

II. Studies

Chu Yüan 朱瑗. "*Shih chi* "Shu-li Tzu, Kan Mao lieh-chuan' shu-cheng" 史記樗里子甘茂列傳疏證, *Kuo-li Pien-yi-kuan kuan-k'an,* 1.4 (December 1972), 101-58.

The Marquis of Jang, Memoir 12

[72:2323] Wei Jan 魏冄, the Marquis of Jang 穰,[1] was the younger brother of the Queen Dowager Hsüan 宣, the mother of King Chao 昭 of Ch'in (r. 306-251 B.C.). His ancestors were natives of Ch'u with the *cognomen* Mi 芈. When King Wu 武 of Ch'in died (307 B.C.), he had no sons and his younger brother was enthroned as King Chao.[2] The former title of King Chao's mother was Mi Pa Tzu 芈八子.[3] When King Chao took the throne, Mi Pa Tzu was titled the Queen Dowager Hsüan. The Queen Dowager Hsüan was not King Wu's mother. King Wu's mother was titled Queen Hui-wen 惠文 and died before King Wu. The Queen Dowager Hsüan had two younger brothers. Her oldest younger brother by a different father was the Marquis of Jang. He had the *cognomen* of the Wei clan and his *praenomen* was Jan. Her younger brother by the same father was Mi Jung 芈戎; he became the Lord of Hua-yang 華陽.[4] King Chao's younger brothers by the same mother were called the Lord of Kao-ling 高陵 and the Lord of Ching-yang 涇陽.[5] Wei Jan was the worthiest [of these men].

[Wei Jan] held office and wielded power from the time of Kings Hui 惠 (r. 336-311 B.C.) and Wu (r. 310-307 B.C.). When King Wu died, his younger brothers all struggled to become king. It was only Wei Jan's power that enabled King Chao to become king. When King Chao ascended the throne (306 B.C.), he made [Wei] Jan General and had him defend [Ch'in's capital] Hsien-yang 咸陽. [Wei Jan] put down the revolt of the Lord of Chi 季[6] and expelled King Wu's queen. She left the country and went to Wei. He destroyed those brothers of King Chao with whom he did not get along and his power shook the state of Ch'in.[7] During King Chao's minority, the Queen Dowager Hsüan ruled by herself, and she entrusted Wei Jan with the reins of government.[8]

---

[1] Jang was located in the modern Teng 鄧 County in Honan (Ch'ien Mu, *Ti-ming k'ao*, p. 360).

[2] See *Shih chi*, 5:210 for a detailed account of King Chao's enthronement.

[3] Pa Tzu 八子 was a title (see Pan Ku, *Han shu*, 97a:3935). Yen Shih-ku's 顏師古 (581-645) *Han shu* commentary suggests that the "eight" in this title might be the rank or salary of these concubines.

[4] Both "So-yin" and "Cheng-yi" suggest that Hua-yang was located in territory originally belonging to Han. According to T'an Ch'i-hsiang (1:36), this Hua-yang was about 10 miles north of modern Hsin-cheng 新鄭 in Honan (this is the Hua-yang referred to in the battle with Mang Mao mentioned below). It is hard to understand how a member of the Ch'in nobility could have a fief in the heart of the state of Han, so close to its capital. It seems more likely that this Hua-yang refers to the area south of Mount Hua, in modern Shang-hsien 商縣 in Shansi.

[5] "So-yin" gives the name of the Lord of Kao-ling as Hsien 顯 and the name of the Lord of Ching-yang as K'uai 悝. This is certainly an error, and Wang Shu-min (72:2287-8) follows Liang Yü-sheng in suggesting that the Lord of Kao-ling was the Noble Scion K'uai and the Lord of Ching-yang was the Noble Scion Fu 巿, as "So-yin" itself states in other places (*Shih chi*, 5:210 and 5:214).

According to T'an Ch'i-hsiang (1:44), Ching-yang and Kao-ling were 5 to 10 miles north and northeast of Ch'in's capital of Hsien-yang respectively; Hsien-yang was about 5 miles north of modern Sian 西安 in Shensi.

[6] I.e., Noble Scion Chuang 壯 (see *Shih chi*, 5:210 and Ma Fei-pai, p. 119), one of King Hui's sons.

[7] This revolt is mentioned in *Shih chi*, 5:210, under the second year of King Chao of Ch'in (305 B.C.): "In the second year a comet appeared. Chief of Staff Chuang 壯 [the Lord of Chi] and the great vassals, feudal lords, and noble scions revolted and were all executed. Queen Hui-wen was also involved; in no case could any of them be allowed to die a normal death. The Queen Dowager Tao-wu was sent back to Wei." In *Shih chi*, 15:735, under the Ch'in entry for 305 B.C., it also states, "A comet appeared. The Lord of Sang 桑 created strife and was punished." "Chi-chieh" (*Shih chi*, 72:2324) quotes *Shih chi* Chapter 15 as saying 'the Lord of Chi,' so that the reading 'Lord of Sang' in the current edition may be a textual error. "So-yin" quotes the *Chu-shu chi-nien* 竹書紀年 as saying: "There was civil strife in Ch'in. They killed their Queen Dowager, the Noble Scion Yung 雍, and the Noble Scion Chuang 壯."

There is obviously a contradiction in *Shih chi*, since *Shih chi* Chapter 5 states that King Hui's queen was

[2324] In the seventh year of King Chao (300 B.C.), Shu-li Tzu 樗里子 died and [Wei Jan] sent the Lord of Ching-yang to Ch'i as a hostage.[9]

Lou Huan 樓緩, a native of Chao, came to Ch'in as Prime Minister.[10] This was to Chao's detriment, and Chao sent Ch'iu Yeh 仇液 to Ch'in to ask that Wei Jan serve as the Prime Minister of Ch'in.[11] When Ch'iu Yeh was about to set out, one of his retainers, Master Sung 宋, told Yeh, "If Ch'in does not heed you, Master, Lou Huan is certain to bear resentment against you. You would be better off telling Lou Huan 'For your sake, sir, I will not press Ch'in.' When the King of Ch'in sees that Chao's request to make Wei Jan minister is not being pressed, he might not listen to you. If you speak and do not succeed, Lou Tzu will owe you a favor. If you do succeed, Wei Jan will of course owe you a favor."

After this, Ch'iu Yeh followed his advice. Ch'in did indeed remove Lou Huan and Wei Jan became Prime Minister of Ch'in.

[2325] [Wei Jan] prepared to execute Lü Li 呂禮. Li fled to Ch'i.[12]

---

killed after King Wu's death, while this biography claims she died before King Wu. If we follow the *Chu-shu chi-nien*, King Hui's queen was executed following the Noble Scion Chuang's failed revolt. As Ma Fei-pai notes (p. 119), the biggest losers in this revolt seem to have been Queen Hui-wen, her offspring, and their families, while the winners were all relatives of Mi Pa Tzu.

[8] According to *Shih chi*, 5:210, King Chao had his "capping ceremony" in the third year of his reign. Assuming that he was twenty when he was capped (the usual age), this would mean he was eighteen *sui* when he took the throne.

[9] *Shih chi*, 5:210 says that the Lord of Ching-yang went to Ch'i in the sixth year of King Chao, not the seventh.

Shu-li Tzu was King Chao's paternal uncle. He was a chancellor at the time of his death. See *Shih chi* Chapter 71 for his biography.

[10] According to *Shih chi*, 5:210, Lou Huan became chancellor of Ch'in in 297 B.C., following Hsüeh Wen's dismissal (Hsüeh Wen was the Lord of Meng-ch'ang, T'ien Wen; his biography is in Chapter 75) and was himself dismissed in 295 B.C. *Shih chi*, 15:737-8 does not record Lou Huan's appointment, but does record that Lou Huan was relieved of this office in Chao's twelfth year (295 B.C.), which agrees with *Shih chi*, 5:210. Prior to his service in Ch'in, Lou seems to have been an advisor to King Wu-ling 武靈 of Chao (r. 325-299 B.C.), and is mentioned in *Shih chi*, 43:1806 as approving of King Wu-ling's decision to adopt "Hu attire" in 307 B.C. *Shih chi*, 43:1811 states that the next year King Wu-ling sent Lou Huan to Ch'in, presumably as an ambassador. He apparently returned to Chao after his dismissal as Prime Minister, since he figures in the debates over how to handle Chao's defeat at Ch'ang-p'ing in 260 B.C. (*Shih chi*, 76:2373-4). If this is accurate, Lou must have been very young when King Wu-ling consulted with him or very old when he returned to Chao in King Hsiao-ch'eng's era.

[11] A version of this anecdote also appears in *Chan-kuo ts'e* (6:27b, *SPTK*). There are textual variants for the name of the Chao ambassador and his advisor, and the *Shih chi* version is more complete than the *Chan-kuo ts'e* version.

The statement that Lou came to Ch'in to serve as minister is confusing. Apparently Lou did not come to Ch'in in this year, but had resided there for several years before he became minister. The practice of one state "recommending" someone as prime minister to another state had several connotations (see Hsu Cho-yun, *Ancient China in Transition* [Stanford: Stanford University Press, 1965], pp. 39-52). What is unusual in this case is that Chao is depicted as reluctant to have a native of Chao become Prime Minister in Ch'in, when usually the opposite was true. If we examine the background to this event, however, we find that Lou Huan had been sent to Ch'in by King Wu-ling of Chao, so presumably Wu-ling and Lou Huan had good relations. King Wu-ling was then murdered by the partisans of his son, King Hui-wen of Chao, in 295 B.C., the same year that Lou Huan was relieved of his post as Prime Minister, at the request of Chao. Perhaps King Hui-wen feared that Ch'in might respond to his own complicity in his father's death if Lou Huan continued as Ch'in's Prime Minister, and hence took steps to have him removed from office.

[12] See Ma Fei-pai's *Ch'in chi-shih*, vol. 1, pp. 286-7 for a brief summary of the fragmentary references in various texts to Lü Li. Lü Li's flight from Ch'in is also mentioned in *Shih chi*, 5:212, under the thirteenth year of King Chao (294 B.C.): "the Full Grand Man Lü Li left Ch'in and fled to Wei." Lü Li appears again in *Shih chi*, 75:2357-8. The background of this incident is very obscure, as is its relation with the Ch'in and Ch'i kings' decision to declare themselves "emperors."

In the fourteenth year of King Chao (293 B.C.), Wei Jan recommended Pai Ch'i 白起 to replace Hsiang Shou 向壽 as commander of the attack on Han and Wei.[13] [Pai Ch'i] defeated them at Yi-ch'üeh 伊闕,[14] cut off 240,000 heads and captured the Wei general Kung-sun Hsi 公孫喜.

The next year (292 B.C.), [Pai Ch'i] took Ch'u's [cities] Yüan 宛 and She 葉.[15] Wei Jan pleaded illness and was relieved of his position as Prime Minister.[16] The Foreign Excellency Shou Chu 壽燭 was made Prime Minister.

The next year (291 B.C.), [Shou] Chu was removed and Jan made Prime Minister again. [The king] then enfeoffed Wei Jan in Jang, and in addition gave him a fief in T'ao 陶.[17] He was titled Marquis of Jang.[18]

In the fourth year after he was enfeoffed (288 B.C.), the Marquis of Jang led an attack on Wei for Ch'in. Wei presented four-hundred *li* [on a side] of the land of Ho-tung 河東.[19] He also took Wei's territory of Ho-nei 河內 and over sixty cities, great and small.[20]

In the nineteenth year of King Chao (288 B.C.), [the King of] Ch'in declared himself the Western Emperor and [the King of] Ch'i declared himself the Eastern Emperor. After more than a month Lü Li came [back to Ch'in] and Ch'i and Ch'in both restored their emperors to kings. Wei Jan again became Prime Minister of Ch'in.[21] He was removed in the sixth year after this (283 B.C.).

---

[13] Pai Ch'i was the most important Ch'in general of this period and a protege of Wei Jan. See Chapter 73 for Pai Ch'i's biography. Hsiang Shou was a maternal relative of King Chao. He is mentioned several times in Chapter 71. According to *Shih chi*, 5:212, this attack on Han and Wei began in 294 B.C.

[14] Yi-ch'üeh was a mountain located about 10 miles south of modern Lo-yang 洛陽.

[15] There are a number of problems involved with Pai Ch'i's actions for this year. See n. 10 and 11 of our translation of Chapter 73 for a more detailed discussion.

[16] *Shih chi*, 5:212 dates this a year later, in 291 B.C.

[17] T'ao was located just northwest of modern Ting-t'ao 定陶 in Shantung (T'an Ch'i-hsiang, 1:39). This is puzzling, since T'ao was located in the state of Sung, close to its border with the state of Wey, but hundreds of miles from Ch'in. We know of no explanation for how Wei Jan received a fief in another country. Wei Jan did have the royal surname of the state of Wei, which at this time had great influence over its weaker neighbors, Wey and Sung. If Wei Jan had some marital connection with Wei, he could perhaps have used this connection to obtain territory there.

[18] In the *Shih chi*, 5:210 entry for 295 B.C. recording Wei Jan's appointment as Prime Minister, he is already referred to as Marquis of Jang. This might be an anachronism, but the *Shih chi*, 5:212 entry for 291 B.C. states that the king enfeoffed Wei Jan in T'ao and does not mention Jang. This should probably be viewed then as a contradiction between *Shih chi* Chapter 5 and this chapter.

[19] Ho-tung refers to the territory of Wei east of the Yellow River and largely west of the Fen River, in the southwest corner of modern Shansi province. This is where the former capital of Wei, An-yi, was located (see n. 237 to our translation of *Shih chi* Chapter 5 above).

As we have noted in the "Note on Chronology" at the beginning of to this volume, and in the footnotes to Chapter 66, the *Shih chi* sometimes uses a counting system beginning with one rather than zero. We tentatively suggest that is the case in this chapter as well. We continue to use the notation of *Shih chi* Chapter 66 by translating these dates as "in the x year after . . . ." *Shih chi*, 15:739 and 44:1853 claim that Wei surrendered its Ho-tung territory in 290 B.C.

[20] Ho-nei refers to the area of the state of Wei north of the Yellow River. *Shih chi*, 5:212 mentions an attack on Ho-nei in 289 B.C. but it seems certain the whole area of Ho-nei could not have been taken at this early point (see Wang Shu-min, 72:2291 for a discussion).

The capture of "sixty cities great and small" occurred in 289 B.C., according to *Shih chi*, 15:737 and 44:1853.

[21] The biography states that in 291 B.C. Wei Jan became Prime Minister. If he also became Prime Minister in 288 B.C., he presumably was relieved of the post sometime in the intervening years, but there is no record of this in *Shih chi*.

In the second year after he was removed, he again served as the Ch'in Prime Minister (282 B.C.).[22]

In the fourth year after this (279 B.C.), he sent Pai Ch'i to seize Ch'u's Ying 郢.[23] Ch'in established its Nan-chün 南郡 Commandery and enfeoffed Pai Ch'i as the Lord of Wu-an 武安.[24] Pai Ch'i was appointed and promoted by the Marquis of Jang. They got along well. After this, the Marquis of Jang's wealth was greater than that of the royal house.[25]

In the thirty-second year of King Chao (275 B.C.), when the Marquis of Jang was Minister of State, he led troops to attack Wei, put Mang Mao 芒卯[26] to flight, invaded Pei-chai 北宅,[27] and surrounded [Wei's capital] Ta Liang 大梁.[28] The Liang Grand Master Hsü Chia 須賈 spoke before the Marquis of Jang.[29]

"Your servant heard Wei's senior officials tell Wei's king: 'Long ago, King Hui 惠 of Liang (r. *370-335 B.C.) attacked Chao and triumphed at San-liang 三梁,[30] seizing [Chao's capital] Han-tan 邯鄲.[31] The Chao clan did not cede territory and Han-tan was later returned [to them]. The men of Ch'i attacked Wey and took its old capital,[32] killing Tzu-liang 子良.[33] The men of Wey did not cede territory and their old lands later came back to Wey. The reason the states of Wey and Chao remained whole, their troops remained strong, and their land was not taken by the feudal lords was that Wey and Chao were able to endure hardship and took cession of land seriously. Sung and Chung-shan were attacked and ceded land several times, and through this their states soon perished.

[2326] "'Your servants feel that Wey and Chao may be taken as models and Sung and Chung-shan may be taken as examples. Ch'in is a greedy and vicious state, close to none. Nibbling away at the clan of Wei, it has finished off the state of Chin.[34] It triumphed over Pao

---

[22] According to *Shih chi,* 5:213 and 15:741, Wei Jan became Prime Minister again in 281 B.C.

[23] See n. 70 to our translation of Chapter 69 above.

[24] For details of Pai Ch'i's expedition against Ch'u, see our translation of Chapter 73. The attack began in 279 B.C., Ying was taken in 278 B.C., and Pai Ch'i was enfeoffed in the same year.

[25] The dates at which Wei Jan held or resigned the position of Prime Minister to Ch'in are unclear. For three different views, see Wang Shu-min (72:2291-2), Ma Fei-pai, p. 181, and Lin Chien-ming 林劍鳴, *Ch'in-shih kao* 秦史稿 (Shanghai: Shang-hai Jen-min Ch'u-pan-she, 1981), p. 275, n. 23.

[26] Mang Mao held various posts in Wei. Other sources write his name as Meng Mao 孟卯.

[27] This is generally identified with the later name Chai-yang 宅陽, located about 10 miles north of modern Chengchow 鄭州 in Honan (T'an Ch'i-hsiang, 1:35-36).

[28] The circumstances of this siege are not well established (see n. 35 below).

[29] The following speech by Hsü Chia appears in both the current edition of *Chan-kuo ts'e* (7:45a-48a, *SPTK*) and *Chan-kuo tsung-heng-chia shu*, pp. 51-57).

[30] "So-yin" and "Chi-chieh" both claim that San-liang should read Nan-liang 南梁, but according to T'an Ch'i-hsiang (1:36), Nan-liang was on the Ju 汝 River near modern Honan province's Lin-ju 臨汝, over 100 miles southwest of Ta Liang. This is an impossible location for an attack on Chao, which was north of Wei. T'an Ch'i-hsiang (1:41) apparently identifies San-liang with Shao-liang 勺梁, about 15 miles southwest of modern Pao-ting 保定 in Hopei. The editors of *Chan-kuo tsung-heng-chia shu* (see n. 29 above) accept the Ch'ing scholar Chang Ch'i's 張琦 (1765-1833) suggestion that *san* 三 may be an error for *ch'ü* 曲, noting that Ch'ü-liang was located in modern Yung-nien 永年 County in Hopei.

[31] According to *Shih chi,* 15:722, Wei captured Han-tan in 353 B.C. and returned it to Chao in 351 B.C.

[32] The old capital of Wey was Ch'u-ch'iu 楚丘 ("So-yin," 72:2327), located in modern Shantung province, just east of Ts'ao-hsien 曹縣 (T'an Ch'i-hsiang, 1:39).

[33] Both *Chan-kuo tsung-heng-chia shu* and *Chan-kuo ts'e* have Yen 燕 and Tzu-chih 子之 instead of "Wey" and "Tzu-liang." We have not been able to find any other references to a "Tzu-liang" from Wey. Tzu-chih was the Prime Minister of Yen, who persuaded the King of Yen to yield the throne to him, provoking a civil war which led to an invasion by the state of Ch'i. For further details, see our translation of Chapter 69.

[34] "So-yin" states that "the state of Chin" here refers to a specific area of Wei: Ho-tung, Ho-hsi, and Ho-nei. It

Tzu 暴子 in battle and we ceded eight counties.³⁵ Before being given all the land, its troops issued forth again. When could Ch'in ever be satisfied? Now they have further put Mang Mao to flight and invaded Pei-chai. It isn't that they dare to attack Liang; they threaten Your Majesty with this, seeking to be ceded yet more land. Your Majesty must not listen. If Your Majesty turns your back on Ch'u and Chao and comes to terms with Ch'in, Ch'u and Chao will be furious and leave Your Majesty, competing with you in serving Ch'in. Ch'in is certain to accept them. If Ch'in, using the soldiers of Ch'u and Chao, attacks Liang again, even if you sought to avoid destruction, you would be unable to. We hope that Your Majesty makes certain not to come to terms with Ch'in. If Your Majesty does wish to come to terms, then cede little and have hostages. Otherwise, you are certain to be cheated.'

"This is what your servant heard in Wei. I hope that Your Lordship will keep this in mind when considering matters. The *Documents of Chou* says, '[Heaven's] mandate does not last forever.' This means that good fortune cannot be counted on. In triumphing over Pao Tzu in battle and being ceded eight counties, this was not because of the quality of your forces, nor the polish of your planning. Heaven's favor counted the most. Now you have further put Mang Mao to flight and invaded Pei-chai in your attack on Ta Liang. This is taking Heaven's favor for granted. Wise men do not do this.

"Your servant has heard that the clan of Wei has assembled every man in their counties who can bear armor to garrison Ta Liang. Your servant believes there are not less than 300,000. With 300,000 men guarding the seven-*jen* walls of Liang, your servant believes even if T'ang 湯 and Wu 武 were to live again, they could not easily attack it.³⁶ To lightly turn your back on the troops of Ch'u and Chao, scale seven-*jen* walls, battle a force of 300,000, and be certain of taking it, this is something that your servant believes has never existed from the time Heaven and Earth first separated until today. If you attack and do not take the city, the troops of Ch'in are sure to be worn out and your manor of T'ao is sure to fall. This would be throwing away your previous achievements.

"Now the clan of Wei is at a loss [on what to do]; you can conclude this matter by taking a little land. I would hope that Your Lordship took this little land from Wei as quickly as possible, before the troops of Chao and Ch'u arrive in Liang. Wei is at a loss [on what to do], and if it is able to gain advantage³⁷ by ceding a little territory, it is sure to desire this, in which case Your Lordship will obtain what *you* desire. Chao and Ch'u will be angry that Wei acted before them and will be sure to compete in serving Ch'in. This will end the alliance and Your Lordship will afterwards be able to choose among them.

"Why then must Your Lordship gain land with arms?³⁸ The state of Chin was ceded [to you], even though the troops of Ch'in did not attack it; Wei had no choice but to present

---

may be that *kuo* here does not mean "state" but "great cities."

³⁵ *Chan-kuo ts'e* has Kao-tzu 睪子, apparently an error for Pao-tzu. This is a reference to the Han general Pao Yüan 暴鳶 sent by Han to assist Wei. Since the text below also says that Wei Jan defeated Pao a year after this speech supposedly took place, Ssu-ma Ch'ien seems to suggest that Pao and Wei Jan fought twice, with Wei ceding eight counties after the first defeat (in 275 B.C.) and three counties after the second (in 274 B.C.). In addition, the beginning of this narrative states above that Wei Jan "put Mang Mao to flight" in 275 B.C., and below says that Mang Mao was defeated again at Hua-yang in 273 B.C. Such overlapping circumstances seem unusual, and it may be that this speech should simply be dated to 273 B.C., after Mang Mao's defeat at Hua-yang. This is in fact the dating that both the *Chan-kuo ts'e* and *Chan-kuo tsung-heng-chia shu* texts use, placing the entire speech after Mang Mao's defeat at Hua-yang.

³⁶ T'ang was the founder of the Shang dynasty and King Wu was the founder of the Chou dynasty (see our translations of *Shih chi* Chapters 3 and 4).

³⁷ The *Chan-kuo ts'e* and *Chan-kuo tsung-heng-chia shu* texts both read *ho* 和 instead of *li* 利.

³⁸ There are a number of problems with this paragraph. Our translation remains tentative.

Chiang 絳 and An-yi 安邑.[39] Now further open a second road to T'ao, and you may almost encompass old Sung; Wey will have no choice but to present Shan-fu 單父.[40] The troops of Ch'in can remain intact and you will be master of the situation. What could you seek that you would not obtain? What could you attempt that would not succeed? I hope that Your Lordship will consider this carefully and not take a perilous path."

The Marquis of Jang said "Excellent," and ended the siege of Liang.

[2328] The next year (274 B.C.), Wei betrayed Ch'in and allied itself with Ch'i. Ch'in sent the Marquis of Jang to punish Wei. He cut off 40,000 heads and put the Wei general Pao Yüan 暴鳶 to flight, gaining three of Wei's counties. The Marquis of Jang's fief was increased.

The next year (273 B.C.), the Marquis of Jang together with Pai Ch'i and the Foreign Excellency Hu Yang 胡陽[41] again attacked Chao, Han, and Wei, defeating Mang Mao at the foot of Hua-yang 華陽 and cutting off 100,000 heads. They seized Wei's Chüan 卷, Ts'ai-yang 蔡陽, Ch'ang-she 長社 and the Chao clan's Kuan-chin 觀津.[42]

They prepared to give Kuan-chin to Chao and reinforce Chao with troops to strike Ch'i. King Hsiang of Ch'i was afraid, and sent Su Tai 蘇代 to deliver a secret letter to the Marquis of Jang on behalf of Ch'i which read:[43]

> Your servant has heard those coming and going say that Ch'in is going to give Chao 40,000 more armored troops to attack Ch'i with. Your servant assured our humble manor's king, 'The King of Ch'in is perspicacious and skilled in his plans. The Marquis of Jang is wise and experienced in affairs. They surely will not give Chao reinforcements of 40,000 armored men to attack Ch'i with.
>
> Why is this? When the Three Chin join as allies, they are the bitter foes of Ch'in. They have betrayed it a hundred times, deceived it a hundred times, yet they do not feel that they have been unfaithful, or that they have acted wrongly. Now you

---

[39] Chiang was approximately 5 miles northeast of modern Hou-ma 侯馬 city in Shansi. An-yi was approximately 3 miles northwest of Hsia-hsien 夏縣 in Shansi (T'an Ch'i-hsiang, 1:35).

[40] Located at modern Ts'ao-hsien 曹縣. in Shantung (T'an Ch'i-hsiang, 1:39). "Cheng-yi" suggests that by obtaining Chiang and An-yi, Wei Jan had already gained a northern route to T'ao. By obtaining Shan-fu, he could also have a southern route. Wey was so completely dominated by Wei that it would certainly have been appropriate for Wei Jan to demand Wey's territory from Wei; the largest difficulty with this suggestion is that Shan-fu was not just south of T'ao, but also considerably farther east.

[41] According to the *Chan-kuo ts'e* (6:47b, *SPTK*), Hu Yang (written Hu Shang 傷 in *Shih chi*, 5:213) was a native of Wey (following the interpretation of Ma Fei-pai, *Ch'in chi-shih*, p. 242). In addition to this attack, he also led a failed attack on Han in 271 or 270 B.C. (see our translation of Chapter 81).

[42] Ts'ai-yang was located about 5 miles north of modern Shang-ts'ai 上蔡 in Honan (T'an Ch'i-hsiang, 1:45; note that Ts'ai-yang apparently belonged to Ch'u, rather than Wei). Ch'ang-she was close to the border of Han and Wei, about 5 miles northeast of modern Chang-ko 長葛 in Honan. Chüan was about 10 miles west of modern Yüan-yang 原陽, also in Honan (T'an Ch'i-hsiang, 1:36). Kuan-chin was located a few miles east of modern Wu-yi 武邑 in Hopei (T'an Ch'i-hsiang, 1:38). It is hard to understand how Ch'in could have taken places as far apart as Ts'ai-yang and Kuan-chin as the result of one battle. Perhaps Kuan-tse 觀澤 (located just south of modern Ch'ing-feng 清豐 in Honan) is intended, rather than Kuan-chin This would at least reduce the distance between these cities. The Ch'in annal ("Pien-nien chi," p. 10, n. 22) presents a slightly different chronology, with some of these cities taken in 274 B.C., rather than 273 B.C. In addition, rather than Ts'ai-yang, it mentions Ts'ai (another name for Ts'ai-yang) and Chung-yang 中陽 (located west of modern Chung-mou 中牟 in Honan).

[43] A version of this letter also appears in *Chan-kuo ts'e* (3:33b-35b, *SPTK*). The *Chan-kuo ts'e* version is preceded by a summary of events which does not match those in this biography very well (suggesting rather a date some thirty years before). See Su Tai's biography in Chapter 69.

fatten Chao by destroying Ch'i. Chao is Ch'in's bitter foe, and this is not to Ch'in's benefit. This is my first point.

The strategists of Ch'in are to sure to say "We will destroy Ch'i and wear out Chin and Ch'u. Afterwards we can ensure victory over Chin and Ch'u." Ch'i is a worn out state. To attack Ch'i with the entire world is like lancing an ulcerating boil with a thousand-*chün* crossbow. It is sure to die. How could this wear out Chin and Ch'u? This is my second point.

If Ch'in sends out few troops, then Chin and Ch'u will not trust it. If Ch'in sends out many troops, then Chin and Ch'u will be controlled by Ch'in. Ch'i will be afraid, and will not turn to Ch'in; instead, it is sure to turn to Chin and Ch'u. This is my third point.

If Ch'in cedes Ch'i to tempt Chin and Ch'u, and Chin and Ch'u fortify it and hold it with troops, Ch'in will itself be threatened.[44] This is my fourth point.

This is Chin and Ch'u playing Ch'in against Ch'i and Ch'i against Ch'in. How could Chin and Ch'u be so wise and Ch'in and Ch'i so foolish? This is my fifth point.

Thus if [Ch'in] obtains An-yi, and then treats [Ch'i] well, it is sure to suffer no troubles.[45] If Ch'in has An-yi, the clan of Han is certain to lose Shang-tang 上黨. Which is to [Ch'in's] advantage: to seize the belly and guts of the world,[46] or to send out troops and fear that they will not return?

[2329] Thus your servant said, "The King of Ch'in is perspicacious and skilled in his plans. The Marquis of Jang is wise and experienced in affairs. They will surely not give Chao reinforcements of 40,000 armored men to attack Ch'i with."

After this, the Marquis of Jang did not proceed, but led his troops back.

In the thirty-sixth year of King Chao (270 B.C.), the Minister of State, the Marquis of Jang said to the Foreign Excellency Tsao 竈 that he wanted to punish Ch'i and seize Kang 剛 and Shou 壽 to enlarge his manor of T'ao.[47] At this, a native of Wei, Fan Sui 范睢, who called himself Venerable Chang Lu 張祿,[48] criticized the Marquis of Jang's expedition against Ch'i because it would mean leaping over the Three Chin to attack Ch'i. He thus took this opportunity to speak before King Chao of Ch'in and King Chao then made use of Fan Sui. Fan Sui said that the Queen Dowager Hsüan was monopolizing power, that the Marquis of Jang was arrogating authority over the feudal lords, and that the Lord of Ching-yang and the Lord of Kao-ling and their like were too extravagant, and wealthier than the royal house. At this King Chao of Ch'in awoke [to his situation], and relieved the Minister of State, ordering the Lord of Ching-yang and the others to go out through the pass and take up their fiefs. When the Marquis of Jang went out through the pass, his wagons numbered more than one thousand.[49]

[44] *Chan-kuo ts'e* says, "If Ch'i cedes land to strengthen Chin and Ch'u, they will be at peace. If Ch'i takes up arms and blunts its swords for them, then Ch'in will itself be attacked."

[45] The *Shih chi* text reads 故得安邑，以善事之，亦必無患矣. It is unclear what the *chih* 之 refers to here. We supply Ch'i as the object because of the *Chan-kuo ts'e* text, which reads 秦得安邑，善齊以安之，亦必無患矣.

[46] The *Chan-kuo ts'e* text reads "the Three Chin" instead of "world."

[47] Kang and Shou were located in modern Shantung, Shou a few miles south of modern Tung-p'ing 東平 and Kang 10 miles north of modern Ning-yang 寧陽 (T'an Ch'i-hsiang, 1:39), both between 60 and 100 miles east of Wei Jan's fief of T'ao. *Shih chi*, 15:74 says Ch'in attacked Ch'i at Kang and Shou in 270 B.C. (*Shih chi*, 5:213 records this attack in 271 B.C., but the Ch'in annals ("Pien-nien chi," p. 5) confirms the date of 270 B.C.

[48] See Fan Sui's biography in Chapter 79.

[49] A *tzu* 輜 "wagon" was a two-wheeled cart with cloth or leather top and walls on all four sides; some apparently also had tailboards (*ti* 軧). They were primarily used to transport supplies, but sometimes carried disabled or injured officers (see for instance our translation of *Shih chi* Chapter 65).

The Marquis of Jang died at T'ao and was buried there. Ch'in later took back T'ao and made it into a commandery.

[2330] His Honor the Grand Scribe says: "The Marquis of Jang was King Chao's own maternal uncle and it was through the Marquis of Jang's achievements that Ch'in increased its lands to the east and weakened the feudal lords, once proclaiming itself emperor of the world, so that the world faced west and made obeisance. When his rank had reached its pinnacle and his wealth was overflowing, one man spoke out and his position was broken, his power stripped from him, so that he died of frustration. How much more was this so for 'a vassal serving in a foreign state!'"[50]

According to *Shih chi*, 5:213, Wei Jan went to his fief in the ninth month of 265 B.C. Perhaps not coincidentally, this event took place just prior to the death of his half-sister, the Queen Dowager Hsüan (or perhaps in 264 B.C., after the Queen Dowager's death). The date of Wei Jan's death is not recorded.

[50] "Vassal serving in a foreign state" is the way Kan Mao frequently referred to himself (see Chapter 71). Here it probably refers not just to Kan Mao, but to the numerous foreigners who served in Ch'in. After Wei Jan's banishment from the capital, it was generally felt outside Ch'in (and perhaps inside as well) that he had been harshly and even unjustly treated (see for instance *Shih chi*, 44:1857). It is typical of Ssu-ma Ch'ien, however, that he should reserve his final expression of sympathy for men such as Kan Mao.

TRANSLATORS' NOTE

The relationship between this chapter and the memoir of Shu-li Chi and Kan Mao (*Shih chi* Chapter 71) is very close. In these two chapters Ssu-ma offers his vision of the great ministers who laid the foundations of Ch'in's triumph over the other six states of China. Shu-li Tzu was King Chao's paternal uncle, the younger brother of King Hui, a member of the Ch'in royal house. Wei Jan was a maternal uncle of the King of Ch'in. Kan Mao was completely unrelated to the ruling family, having risen from obscurity to serve as one of the highest officials in Ch'in. These were the three great factions of Ch'in and we suggest that Ssu-ma Ch'ien's accounts of them were intended more as illustrative of the groups rather than these particular men.

This biography can also be read as a supplement to both the more detailed account of the Marquis in *Shih chi* Chapter 79, "Fan Sui and Ts'ai Tse," and to Su Tai's biography (Chapter 69), and its rhetorical style--the bulk of the text consists of a persuasion given by Hsü Chia and the letter in the form of a persuasion delivered by Su Tai--also reflects these two memoirs.

BIBLIOGRAPHY

Translations

Mizusawa Toshitada 水澤利忠. *Shiki* 史記. V. 8. *Retsuden (ichi)* 列傳 (一). Tokyo: Meiji Shoten, 1990, pp. 392-408.

Ōgawa Tamaki 小川環樹, trans. *Shiki retsuden* 史記列傳. Rpt. Tokyo: Chikuma Shobō, 1986 (1969). pp. 84-87.

Watson, Burton. *Records of the Grand Historian: Qin Dynasty*. V. 3. Hong Kong and New York: The Research Centre for Translation, The Chinese University of Hong Kong and Columbia University Press, 1993, pp. 113-119.

Studies.

Fujita Katsuhisa 藤田勝久. "*Shiki* 'Jōkō retsuden' ni kansuru ichi kōsatsu 史記穰侯列傳に關する一考察," in *Tōhōgaku,* 71(1985), 18-34.

Pai Ch'i and Wang Chien, Memoir 13

Pai Ch'i

[73:2331] Pai Ch'i 白起 was a native of Mei 郿.[1] Skilled at commanding troops, he served King Chao 昭 of Ch'in (r. 306-251 B.C.).

In the thirteenth year of King Chao (294 B.C.), Pai Ch'i was a Left Chief of Staff.[2] He led an attack against Han's Hsin-ch'eng 新城.[3] The Marquis of Jang 穰 was the Prime Minister of Ch'in that year. He promoted Jen Pi 任鄙, making him governor of Han-chung 漢中.[4]

The next year (293 B.C.), Pai Ch'i became a Left Veteran[5] and attacked Han and Wei at Yi-ch'üeh 伊闕, cutting off 240,000 heads. He also captured their general Kung-sun Hsi 公孫喜 and seized five walled cities.[6]

Pai Ch'i was promoted to Commandant of the State.[7] He crossed the Ho River and took Han's [land] east of An-yi 安邑 to the Kan 乾 River.[8]

The next year (292 B.C.), Pai Ch'i became a Grand Excellent Achiever.[9] He attacked Wei, seized it, and took sixty-one walled cities, great and small.[10]

The next year (291 B.C.), [Pai] Ch'i and the Foreign Excellency Ts'o 錯 attacked Yüan-ch'eng 垣城 and seized it.[11]

---

[1] Mei was located just south of modern Mei-hsien 郿縣 in Shansi province (T'an Ch'i-hsiang, 1:43). This was in the northern part of of Ch'in, west of its capital, Hsien-yang.

[2] *Tso Shu-chang* 左庶長. There were two types of "rank" (*chüeh* 爵) in Ch'in. One was equivalent to the system used in other states, and included the five steps *kung* 公, *hou* 侯, *po* 伯, *tzu* 子, and *nan* 男. The other type of rank was a twenty-step hierarchy, which assigned a rank to virtually every person in the state. This system, supposedly introduced by the Lord of Shang (see his biography in Chapter 68), was important for the various rights it conferred, including conscription and tax status. The *Tso Shu-chang* was the tenth of the twenty ranks. The various ranks Pai Ch'i receives throughout his biography thus mark his advance up the hierarchy, until he is finally demoted to the bottom of the system, "the ranks of knights," for his defiance of King Chao of Ch'in (see n. 33 below).

[3] Hsin-ch'eng was the name often given to a newly captured city, so that Ch'ien Mu (*Ti-ming k'ao*, pp. 308-310) lists seven different cities with this name. According to Ch'ien Mu, this is the same Hsin-ch'eng mentioned in Chapter 70, n. 9. It was about two miles southwest of modern Yi-ch'uan 伊川 in Honan province (T'an Ch'i-hsiang, 1:35-6).

[4] Han-chung was the name of a Ch'in commandery established in 312 B.C., located to the south of modern Shensi province's Ch'in-ling 秦嶺 mountains. For Jen Pi, see n. 22 of our translation of Chapter 71. *Shih chi* Chapter 15 does not record Pai Ch'i's attack on Hsin-ch'eng. *Shih chi*, 5:212, records that "The Left Veteran (*Tso-keng* 左更) Pai Ch'i attacked Hsin-ch'eng" in 294 B.C. This differs from the biography, which says Pai Ch'i at this time was a Left Chief of Staff.

[5] *Tso keng* 左更. This was the twelfth rank in the Ch'in hierarchy (see n. 2 above).

[6] This was a continuation of Ch'in's attack on Han, begun the previous year. See our translation of *Shih chi*, 72:2325 for further details.

[7] *Kuo-wei* 國尉 (see Chang Cheng-lang, p. 639).

[8] "Chi-chieh" suggests that the Kan River was northeast of modern Wen-hsi 溫喜 in Shansi. Ch'ien Mu (*Ti-ming k'ao*, p. 455) suggests it was somewhat farther east, south of Yi-ch'eng 翼城 in Shansi. An-yi (just northwest of modern Hsia-hsien 夏縣 in Shansi) belonged to Wei. "So-yin" says that while An-yi belonged to Wei, the land east of it belonged to Han. Our translation attempts to interpret this passage according to "So-yin."

[9] *Ta Liang-tsao* 大良造. This was the second rank in the Ch'in hierarchy (see n. 2 above).

[10] *Shih chi* Chapter 5 and the Ch'in annal ("Pien-nien chi," p. 4) agree that there was an attack on Wei in this year, but according to *Shih chi*, 15:737 and 44:1853, Ch'in captured "61 cities great and small" from Wei in 289 B.C., while *Shih chi* Chapter 72 to places this event in 288 B.C. (see our translation of *Shih chi*, 72:2325).

[11] Yüan-ch'eng was located about 10 miles southeast of Yüan-ch'ü 垣曲 in modern Shansi. *Shih chi*, 5:212,

Five years later (286 B.C.), Pai Ch'i attacked Chao and seized Kuang-lang Ch'eng 光狼城.[12]

Seven years later (279 B.C.), Pai Ch'i attacked Ch'u and seized five cities [including] Yen 鄢 and Teng 鄧.[13]

The next year (278 B.C.), he attacked Ch'u, seized Ying 郢, burned Yi-ling 夷陵, then went east until he reached Ching-ling 竟陵.[14] The King of Ch'u abandoned Ying and fled east, moving to Ch'en 陳.[15] Ch'in made Ying its Nan-chün 南郡 [Commandery}.[16]

Pai Ch'i was promoted to Lord of Wu-an 武安. The Lord of Wu-an then took Ch'u and established Wu 巫 and Ch'ien-chung 黔中 commanderies.[17]

In the thirty-fourth year of King Chao (273 B.C.), Pai Ch'i attacked Wei, seized Hua-yang 華陽, put Mang Mao 芒卯 to flight, and captured the Three Chin commander, cutting off 130,000 heads. He fought with the Chao general Chia Yen 賈偃, and drowned 20,000 of [Chia Yen's] men in the Ho River.[18]

In the forty-third year of King Chao (264 B.C.), Pai Ch'i attacked Han at Hsing Ch'eng 陘城, seized five walled cities and cut off 50,000 heads.[19]

In the forty-fourth year (263 B.C.), Pai Ch'i attacked the road from Nan-yang 南陽 through the T'ai-hang 太行 [mountains] and severed it.[20].

---

says that Pai Ch'i attacked Wei, took Huan, then gave it back again, all in 292 B.C. The Ch'in annal ("Pien-nien chi," p. 4) says that Ch'in attacked Yüan and Chih 枳 in 290 B.C.

[12] Kuang-lang Ch'eng was about 5 miles west of modern Kao-p'ing 高平 in Shansi. *Shih chi,* 5:213, 15:741, and 43:1820 all place this attack in 280 B.C.

[13] *Shih chi,* 5:213, 15:742, and 40:1735 all state that these cities were captured in 279 B.C. The Ch'in annal, however, records an attack by Ch'in on Teng in 280 B.C ("Pien-nien chi," p. 4, and also n. 17, p. 9). For a discussion of the location of these cities and the question of the Ch'u capital, see n. 70 to our translation of Chapter 69.

There is an interesting description of Pai Ch'i's capture of Yen in the *Shui-ching chu* 水經注 of Li Tao-yüan 酈道元 (*Shui-ching chu chiao* 水經注校, Wang Kuo-wei 王國維, ed. [Shanghai: Shang-hai Jen-min Ch'u-pan-she, 1981], p. 908): "Long ago when Pai Ch'i attacked Ch'u, he led in the waters of the West Mountain valleys . . . the waters swept through the city from west to east . . . they washed away the northeast corner of the city wall, and hundreds of thousands of the populace were swept away and died in the waters. The whole east of the city stank, and the pool formed was thus called 'Stinking Pool.'"

[14] For the location of Ying, see n. 70 of our translation of Chapter 69. Yi-ling was just south of modern Yi-ch'ang 宜昌 city in Hupei province (T'an Ch'i-hsiang, 1:45). According to *Shih chi,* 40:1735, Yi-ling was the location of the Ch'u kings' tombs. Ching-ling was just west of modern Ch'ien-chiang 潛江 in Hupei (T'an Ch'i-hsiang, 1:46).

[15] Ch'en was located near modern Huai-yang 淮陽 in Honan.

[16] According to *Shih chi,* 5:213, 15:742, and 40:1735, the capture of Ying and destruction of Yi-ling took place in 278 B.C.

[17] *Shih chi,* 5:213, 15:742, and 40:1735 all claim that Ch'in took Ch'u's Wu and Ch'ien-chung commanderies in 277 B.C., a year after the fall of Ying. *Shih chi* Chapter 5 gives 278 B.C. as the year of Pai Ch'i's enfeoffment, while *Shih chi* Chapter 15 has 277 B.C. According to *Shih chi* Chapter 5, the governor of Shu, Jo 若, rather than Pai Ch'i, took Wu and Ch'ien-chung.

[18] Regarding the battle at Hua-yang, *Shih chi,* 15:743-4 and 44:1854 both agree with Pai Ch'i's biography. *Shih chi,* 5:213 places it in 274 B.C. According to the Ch'in annal, however, *Shih chi* Chapter 5 has conflated events from 274 and 273 B.C., and it confirms a Ch'in attack on Hua-yang in 273 B.C. ("Pien-nien chi," p. 5). None of these accounts mention Chia Yen, who appears nowhere else in *Shih chi* or *Chan-kuo ts'e.*

[19] Hsing-ch'eng was located about 10 miles north of modern Hou-ma 侯馬 in Shansi. *Shih chi,* 5:213 records the number of cities captured as nine, rather than five.

[20] Nan-yang was a heavily populated area of the state of Han, located between the T'ai-hang Mountains and the Yellow River. The road through these mountains connected Han with its northern territories in the area referred to as Shang-tang.

[2332] In the forty-fifth year (262 B.C.), he attacked Han's Yeh-wang 野王.²¹ Yeh-wang surrendered to Ch'in and Shang-tang 上黨 was cut off.²² Its governor Feng T'ing 馮亭 consulted with his subjects.

"The road to Cheng 鄭²³ is severed, we can no longer be subjects of Han. The soldiers of Ch'in grow closer every day, but Han cannot respond. It would be better to turn over Shang-tang to Chao. If Chao accepts it, Ch'in will be angered and is sure to attack Chao. When Chao is menaced by [*2333*] soldiers, it is sure to ally with Han. When Han and Chao are one, they can resist Ch'in."

He then sent a messenger to inform Chao. King Hsiao-ch'eng 孝成 of Chao (r. 265-245 B.C.) laid his plans with the Lord of P'ing-yang 平陽 and the Lord of P'ing-yüan 平原.²⁴ The Lord of P'ing-yang said, "It would be better not to accept it. If we do, our woes will be greater than our gain." The Lord of P'ing-yüan said, "If we may obtain a commandery without troubles, it would be to our advantage to accept it." Chao accepted it and enfeoffed Feng T'ing as the Lord of Hua-yang 華陽.²⁵

In the forty-sixth year (261 B.C.), Ch'in attacked Han at Kou-shih 緱氏²⁶ and Lin 藺, and seized them.²⁷

In the forty-seventh year (260 B.C.), Ch'in sent the Left Chief of Staff, Wang Ho 王齕,²⁸ to attack Han. He took Shang-tang. The subjects of Shang-tang fled to Chao. Chao camped its army at Ch'ang-p'ing 長平 to hold down the subjects of Shang-tang.²⁹

---

²¹ Yeh-wang was located at modern Shen-yang 沁陽 in Shansi.

²² *Shih chi,* 5:213 records that "In the forty-fifth year [of King Chao, 262 B.C.], Pen, a Full Grand Man, attacked Han and took ten cities."

Shih chi, 15:746, in the Ch'in entry under 262 B.C., records that "(We) attacked Han and seized ten walled cities." It does not mention Yeh-wang or the other events here. This is perhaps a separate attack on Han, not related to Pai Ch'i's. The Ch'in annal confirms a 262 B.C. attack on Yeh-wang ("Pien-nien chi," p. 5).

²³ Cheng was the capital of Han.

²⁴ The Lord of P'ing-yüan was King Hsiao-ch'eng of Chao's paternal uncle, Chao Sheng 趙勝. See his biography in Chapter 76. The Lord of P'ing-yang apparently was a maternal uncle. He is sometimes referred to as Chao Pao 趙豹 (Pao was his *praenomen*).

²⁵ Hua-yang here refers to the area of Mount Heng 恆 (T'an Ch'i-hsiang, 1:38). The most detailed account of the debate in Chao on whether to accept Shang-tang occurs in *Shih chi,* 43:1824-1826. Interestingly, this debate is not mentioned at all in Chapter 76, the biography of the Lord of P'ing-yüan, perhaps because of Ssu-ma Ch'ien's belief that the faults of important men should not be mentioned in their biographies, but shown instead in other places. Certainly Ssu-ma felt that the Lord of P'ing-yüan was in error when he said that Chao should accept Shang-tang, as his comments at the end of the Lord of P'ing-yüan's biography show. Nor did he feel kindly toward Feng T'ing's attempt to involve Chao in a war with Ch'in.

²⁶ About 25 miles southeast of Loyang in Honan (T'an Ch'i-hsiang, 1:36).

²⁷ Located about 10 miles west of Li-shih 離石 near the Yellow River in west-central Shansi (T'an Ch'i-hsiang, 1:37). Lin was apparently part of Chao, rather than Han.

Shih chi Chapter 15 does not mention this event. In the Chao entry under 261 B.C., it records that "[Chao] sent Lien P'o to resist Ch'in at Ch'ang-p'ing." This differs from the section below, which places this in 260 B.C. The Ch'in annal mentions an attack on a "T'ing" ("Pien-nien chi," p. 5) and the commentators speculate that this was Feng T'ing.

²⁸ "So-yin" (*Shih chi,* 6:224) says that Wang Ho was the same person as Wang Yi 王齮. a Ch'in general who died in 218 B.C. (*Shih chi,* 6:224). In *Shih chi,* 5:219 and 15:750 these two names are confused.

²⁹ Ch'ang-p'ing was located about 5 miles north of modern Kao-p'ing 高平, in Shansi province (T'an Ch'i-hsiang, 1:35-36).

An-chü 按據 seems to mean not that Chao was protecting Shang-tang from Ch'in, but rather that it was preventing Shang-tang's inhabitants from fleeing, perhaps because of problems the refugees were causing in Chao or to prevent the area from becoming depopulated and thus losing its economic value.

In the fourth month, [Wang] Ho attacked Chao. Chao made Lien P'o 廉頗 general.[30] The soldiers and officers of Chao's army encountered advance forces of Ch'in, and the advance forces cut down Chao's Adjutant General[31] Chia 茄.[32]

In the sixth month, [Ch'in] defeated the Chao army, capturing two forts and four commandants.

In the seventh month the Chao army built earthworks and barricades and held to them. Ch'in attacked their earthworks, took two commandants, broke their formations and seized the western earthworks and barricades. Lien P'o fortified his barricades against Ch'in. Ch'in challenged him to battle several times, but the Chao soldiers would not come out.

The King of Chao several times thought Lien P'o was giving way. The Ch'in Prime Minister, the Marquis of Ying 應,[33] also [*2334*] sent a man to spread a thousand catties of gold in Chao creating agents for Ch'in. [These agents] said, "Ch'in's only fear is that the son of [the Lord of] *Ma-fu* 馬服,[34] Chao K'uo 趙括, will be made general. Lien P'o gives way easily and will soon surrender."

The King of Chao was already angry that Lien P'o's troops had suffered many losses and been defeated several times. In addition, they now fortified their barricades and did not dare to fight. In addition, [the king] heard the rumors of the Ch'in agents. As a result, he sent Chao K'uo to replace Lien P'o as commander of the counter-attack against Ch'in.

When Ch'in heard that *Ma Fu*'s son was to be [Chao's] general, it secretly sent the Lord of Wu-an, Pai Ch'i, as senior general,[35] and made Wang Ho the commanding assistant general,[36] then told the army that those who dared leak word that the Lord of Wu-an was now commanding would be beheaded.

When Chao K'uo arrived, he sent out troops to attack the Ch'in army. The Ch'in army feigned defeat and fled, extending two ambushes to attack Chao. The Chao army pursued victory, chasing Ch'in up to the Ch'in barricades. They could not break into the barricades which the Ch'in troops defended, and the Ch'in ambushing troops, 25,000 men, cut off the Chao army's rear, while another army of 5,000 mounted soldiers cut them off from the Chao barricades, cutting the Chao army into two and severing their supply lines. Ch'in then sent light infantry to attack them. Having taken the bad end of the fighting, Chao's army built more barricades and held closely to them, waiting for aid to arrive.

When the King of Ch'in heard that Chao's supply lines were cut, he came himself to Ho-nei 河內,[37] granted the people each a rank of nobility,[38] and sent all those over fifteen years old to Ch'ang-p'ing to pin down Chao's relief and supplies.

[2335] By the ninth month, the Chao soldiers had been without food for forty-six days, and were all secretly killing and eating each other inside [their barricades]. They came out and attacked the Ch'in fortifications, attempting to escape. They formed four squads and attacked four or five times but could not escape. Their general Chao K'uo sent out his best

---

[30] See Lien P'o's biography in Chapter 81.

[31] *Pi-chiang* 裨將.

[32] Otherwise unknown.

[33] The Marquis of Ying was Fan Sui 范睢. See his biography in Chapter 79.

[34] The Lord of Ma-fu was Chao She 趙奢. See his biography in Chapter 81.

[35] *Shang chiang-chün* 上將軍.

[36] *Wei pei-chiang* 尉裨將.

[37] Ho-nei refers to the area north of the Yellow River stretching from modern Wu-chih 武陟 in Honan northeast towards the border of modern Hopei for about 50 miles; it was about 40 miles south of Han-tan and later became a Ch'in commandery (T'an Ch'i-hsiang 1:36 and II:9).

[38] The Ch'in twenty-step hierarchy assigned a rank to virtually every person in the state--see also n. 2 above.

soldiers and entered the fray himself. The Ch'in army shot him dead. Chao K'uo's army was defeated and 400,000 soldiers surrendered to the Lord of Wu-an.

The Lord of Wu-an laid his plans. "When Ch'in previously took Shang-tang, the subjects of Shang-tang were unwilling to become Ch'in's [subjects] and turned to Chao. The soldiers of Chao are treacherous and inconstant. If I do not kill them all, I fear they may rebel." Using deceit, he massacred them all, leaving 240 of the youngest to return to Chao. From the beginning to the end [of the war], he captured or cut off the heads of 450,000 men. The men of Chao were deeply shaken.[39]

In the tenth month of the forty-eighth year (260 B.C.),[40] Ch'in again pacified Shang-tang Commandery. Ch'in divided its army into two. Wang Ho attacked P'i-lao 皮牢[41] and took it. Ssu-ma Keng 司馬梗 pacified T'ai-yüan 太原.[42] Han and Chao were afraid, and sent Su Tai 蘇代[43] with rich gifts to speak to Ch'in's Prime Minister, the Marquis of Ying.[44]

"Has the Lord of Wu-an captured the son of the [Lord of] Ma-fu?"

"Yes."

"Has he surrounded Han-tan?"

"Yes."

"If Chao perishes, then the King of Ch'in will be king [of the world], and the Lord of Wu-an will be one of his Three Masters.[45] The walled cities that the Lord of Wu-an has attacked, defeated, and captured for Ch'in number over seventy. To the south he pacified Yen 鄢, Ying 郢, and Han-chung 漢中, to the north he captured Chao K'uo's army. Even the accomplishments of Chou 周, Shao 召, and Lü Wang 呂望 did not surpass this.[46] If Chao perishes now, and the King of Ch'in become king [of the world], then the Lord of Wu-an is sure to become one of his Three Masters. Can your lordship serve as his subordinate? Even if you did not wish to serve as his subordinate, you are sure to have no choice.

"When Ch'in attacked Han, besieged Hsing-ch'iu 邢丘,[47] [*2336*] and pressed Shang-tang, the subjects of Shang-tang all turned to Chao. For a long time now, the world has been unwilling to be subjects of Ch'in. If Chao perishes, its northern lands will go to Yen, its eastern lands to Ch'i, its southern lands to Han and Wei, and the subjects your lordship gains will be few indeed. It would thus be better to take advantage of the situation to gain territory from them, rather than allow the Lord of Wu-an to gain this merit."

After this, the Marquis of Ying spoke to the King of Ch'in. "The soldiers of Ch'in are weary. I ask that you allow Han and Chao to make peace by ceding land, and rest your

---

[39] *Shih chi*, 15:747, in the Ch'in entry for 260 B.C., records that "Pai Ch'i defeated Chao at Ch'ang-ping and killed 450,000 soldiers." The Chao entry records that "[Chao] sent Chao K'uo to replace Lien P'o as general. Pai Ch'i defeated K'uo's 450,000."

[40] See the Translators' Note on this date.

[41] P'i-lao was located about 10 miles northwest of modern Yi-ch'eng 翼城 in Shansi (T'an Ch'i-hsiang, 1:35).

[42] T'ai-yüan was a large area around modern T'ai-yüan in Shansi.

Ssu-ma Keng is otherwise unknown.

[43] The brother of the famous statesman, Su Ch'in; see his biography in Chapter 69.

[44] A dialogue similar to the one following also appears in the *Chan-kuo ts'e* (3:54b, *SPTK*), where it is addressed to the Marquis of Ying by an unnamed interlocutor.

[45] The Three Masters (*san-kung* 三公) were the three highest officers of government (Hsü Lien-ta, p. 28).

[46] Chou refers to the Duke of Chou, Tan 旦. Shao refers to the Duke of Shao, Shih 奭. Lü Wang refers to the T'ai-kung 太公 Wang. These were three of the most important advisors to the founder of the Chou dynasty, King Wu 武. See our translation of Chapter 4 for further details.

[47] Hsing-ch'iu was about 5 miles west of modern Wen-hsien 溫縣 in Honan. Wang Nien-sun (4:21.b-22b) argues that Hsing-ch'iu is an error for Hsing 陘, and refers this to Ch'in's capture of Hsing Ch'eng, mentioned above, in 264 B.C.

officers and men." The king followed his suggestion, and made peace in return for Yüan-yung 垣雍⁴⁸ from Han and six walled cities from Chao. In the first month (of 259 B.C.),⁴⁹ they all withdrew their troops. The Lord of Wu-an heard of this, and afterwards there was bad blood between him and the Marquis of Ying.

In the ninth month, Ch'in again mobilized its troops and sent the Full Grand Man⁵⁰ Wang Ling 王陵 to attack Chao at Han-tan.⁵¹ The Lord of Wu-an was sick at the time and unable to travel.

In the first month of the forty ninth year (258 B.C.), Ling attacked Han-tan, and Ch'in mobilized more troops to support Ling. Ling's troops lost five companies.⁵² The Lord of Wu-an having recovered from his illness, the King of Ch'in wished to send the Lord of Wu-an to replace Ling as general.

The Lord of Wu-an said, "Han-tan is not in fact easy to attack. Moreover, the reinforcements of the feudal lords arrive every day, and these lords have held a grudge against Ch'in for a long time now. Even though Ch'in broke the army at Ch'ang-p'ing, [*2337*] over half of Ch'in's infantry died and Ch'in is empty inside. With Ch'in traveling far, crossing the Ho River and mountains, struggling for a great city of another state, and with Chao answering inside and the feudal lords attacking on the outside, the defeat of Ch'in's army is certain. This will not do."

The King of Ch'in commanded [Pai] himself, but he would not go. He then sent the Marquis of Ying to plead with him. The Lord of Wu-an in the end declined and was unwilling to go, claiming illness.

The King of Ch'in sent Wang Ho to replace Ling as general, and for eight or nine months he besieged Han-tan, but was unable to take it. Ch'u sent the Lord of Ch'un-shen 春申 and the Noble Scion of Wei,⁵³ leading several hundred thousand troops, to attack the Ch'in army and the Ch'in army suffered many casualties.⁵⁴ The Lord of Wu-an proclaimed, "Ch'in did not listen to my advice, and now what has happened!"

The King of Ch'in heard of this and, enraged, forcibly summoned the Lord of Wu-an. The Lord of Wu-an then claimed he was seriously ill. The Marquis of Ying asked him [to go], but he did not get up. [Ch'in] then degraded the Lord of Wu-an to the ranks of knights and transported him to Yin-mi 陰密.⁵⁵ The Lord of Wu-an was sick and could not travel. For three months, the feudal lords pressed the attack against Ch'in's army and the Ch'in army retreated several times, messengers arriving daily. The King of Ch'in then sent a man to dispatch Pai Ch'i, forbidding him to remain in Hsien-yang. When the Lord of Wu-an left, he went out the West gate of Hsien-yang for ten *li*, till he reached the Tu 杜 Relay-station.⁵⁶

---

⁴⁸ Yüan-yung was about 10 miles west of modern Yüan-yang 原陽 in Honan (T'an Ch'i-hsiang, 1:36).

⁴⁹ See the Translators' Note on this date.

⁵⁰ *Wu Tai-fu* 五大夫. This was the ninth rank of the Ch'in hierarchy.

⁵¹ *Shih chi*, 5:214 records that Wang Ling led an attack on Chao in the tenth month.

⁵² *Hsiao* 校.

⁵³ The Lord of Ch'un-shen's biography is in Chapter 78. The biography of the Noble Scion of Wei (the Lord of Hsin-ling) is in Chapter 77.

⁵⁴ For a fuller account of these events, see Chapters 76 and 77.

⁵⁵ Yin-mi was located about 10 miles southwest of modern Ling-t'ai 靈臺, in Shensi, approximately 90 miles northwest of Ch'in's capital, Hsien-yang (T'an Ch'i-hsiang, 1:43). The phrase *mien Wu-an chün wei shih-wu* 免武安君為士伍 has several interpretations. "Cheng-yi" quotes Ju Shun 如淳 (189-265) and Yen Shih-ku 顏師古 (581-645) as saying that *shih-wu* was a term for those who were stripped of their rank because of an offense. Robin Yates, "Social Status in the Ch'in: Evidence from the Yün-meng Legal Documents, Part One: Commoners," *HJAS*, 47(1987), 197-237, suggests that *shih-wu* simply meant "commoners."

⁵⁶ *Yu* 邮.

The King of Ch'in consulted the Marquis of Ying and his assembled vassals.
"When Pai Ch'i was transported, he was still discontent and refused to acknowledge his error, continuing to speak out."

The King of Ch'in sent a messenger to present him with a sword to resolve matters himself. The Lord of Wu-an lifted the sword and prepared to cut his throat: "How have I offended Heaven that I should come to this?"

He paused for a long time.

"I do indeed deserve death. In the battle of Ch'ang-p'ing, the Chao soldiers who surrendered numbered hundreds of thousands, but I deceived them and massacred them all. This is worthy of death."

He then killed himself.[57]

The Lord of Wu-an's death came in the eleventh month of the fiftieth year of King Chao of Ch'in (258 B.C.).[58] Having died even though he had not committed an offense, the people of Ch'in pitied him and the county towns all made sacrifices for him.

Wang Chien

[2338] Wang Chien 王翦 was a native of P'in-yang's 頻陽 Tung 東 District.[59] In his youth he delighted in arms and served the First Emperor of Ch'in.

In the eleventh year of the First Emperor (236 B.C.), Chien led an attack against Chao at O-yü 閼與.[60] He defeated [Chao] and took nine walled cities.

In the eighteenth year (229 B.C.), Chien led an attack against Chao. After over a year, he seized Chao. The King of Chao surrendered and all of Chao's territory was made into commanderies.[61]

The next year (227 B.C.),[62] Yen sent Ching K'o 荊軻 to perpetrate a crime in Ch'in and the King of Ch'in sent Wang Chien to attack Yen.[63] The King of Yen, Hsi 喜, fled to Liao-tung 遼東 and Chien pacified Yen's Chi 薊 before returning.[64]

---

[57] Another account (*Chan-kuo ts'e* [3:77b-78b, *SPTK*]), citing a speech by Kan Lo 甘羅, claims that Pai Ch'i was strangled: "The Marquis of Ying wanted to lead an expedition against Chao. Pai Ch'i opposed him and seven miles outside of Hsien-yang he was strangled to death." This speech also appears in *Shih chi*, 71:2319, which reads *li ssu* 立死 instead of *chiao erh sha chih* 絞而殺之 in the *Chan-kuo ts'e*.

[58] On this date, see the Translators' Note at the end of this chapter.

[59] P'in-yang was a county located about five miles southeast of modern T'ung-ch'uan 銅川 in Shensi province (T'an Ch'i-hsiang, 1:44).

[60] O-yü was located at modern Shansi province's Ho-shun 和順 (T'an Ch'i-hsiang, 1:30). In 270 B.C., it was the scene of one of the last great defeats for the state of Ch'in (see our translation of the biography of Chao She in Chapter 81), a defeat that Ch'in was no doubt eager to avenge. According to *Shih chi*, 6:231, however, Wang Chien's attack on O-yü was part of a much larger operation, and Wang Chien was only one of a number of generals who took part in this operation.

[61] For a more detailed description of the fall of Chao and the circumstances leading up to it, see our translations of Chapters 6 and 81.

[62] Notice that "next year" here is calculated after the "over a year" mentioned in the last entry, so that this year is actually 227 B.C., not 228 B.C.

[63] In 227 B.C. the Heir of Yen sent Ching K'o to assassinate the King of Ch'in. See our translation of Chapter 86.

[64] Chi, the capital of the state of Yen, was located at modern Peking. *Shih chi,* 6:233 states that Ch'in sent two generals, Wang Chien and Hsin Sheng 辛勝, against Yen.

Ch'in sent Chien's son Wang Pen 賁 to defeat Ching 荆 (= Ch'u), and the soldiers of Ching were defeated. He further defeated Wei. The King of Wei surrendered and [Wang Pen] pacified Wei's territory.[65]

[2339] The First Emperor of Ch'in had already destroyed the Three Chin, put the King of Yen to flight and defeated the forces of Ching several times.[66] The Ch'in general Li Hsin 李信 was young, strong, and brave. With several thousand troops he had driven Yen's Heir Tan 丹 into the Yen 衍 River, finally capturing Tan. The First Emperor thought him worthy and brave.

After this the First Emperor asked Li Hsin, "I want to attack and seize Ching. In your estimate, how many men do we need to use?" Li Hsin said, "No more than 200,000."

The First Emperor asked Wang Chien. Wang Chien said, "No less than 600,000 will do."

The First Emperor said, "General Wang is old. How cowardly he is! General Li is resolute and courageous, his opinion is the correct one." He then sent Li Hsin and Meng T'ien 蒙恬 leading 200,000 south to attack Ching.[67]

Wang Chien's advice being ignored, he took the occasion to announce that he was ill and would retire in his old age to P'in-yang.

Li Hsin attacked P'ing-yü 平輿 and Meng T'ien attacked Ch'in 寝, crushing the army of Ching.[68] Hsin went on to attack Yen 鄢 and Ying 郢. He defeated them and led his army west, where he met with Meng T'ien at Ch'eng-fu 城父.[69] The men of Ching took the occasion to follow him, going three days and three nights without pitching camp and crushed Li Hsin's army, overrunning two barricades and killing seven chief commandants.[70] The Ch'in army fled.

[2340] When the First Emperor heard this, he was furious and hurried off personally to P'in-yang, where he held audience with Wang Chien and apologized. "We did not use your plan and Li Hsin did indeed humiliate the army of Ch'in. Now We have heard that the Ching soldiers advance further west every day. Although you are sick, General, could you really bring yourself to abandon Us?"

---

[65] *Shih chi,* 15:755-6, under the Ch'in entry for 226 B.C., records that "Wang Pen assaulted Ch'u." The Ch'u entry for the same year records that "Ch'in completely defeated us and seized ten walled cities." The Ch'in entry for 225 B.C. records that "Wang Pen assaulted Wei, captured its King Chia and seized all its territory." Thus these events did not take place in the same year.

[66] Of the three Chin states, Han was destroyed in 230 B.C., the King of Chao was captured in 228 B.C., and Wei, as just noted, was destroyed in 225 B.C. However, a noble scion of Chao named Chia 嘉 escaped from Chao and declared himself the King of Tai 代 in the same year that the King of Chao was captured. This man was not defeated by Ch'in until 222 B.C. The "flight" of the King of Yen refers to his forced moved to Liao-tung, as mentioned above. It is not clear what the "several" defeats inflicted on Ch'u were. The only one recorded in *Shih chi* Chapter 15 for this period was Wang Pen's attack in 226 B.C.

[67] See Meng T'ien's biography in Chapter 88. There is some question as to whether this was actually Meng T'ien, or his father, Meng Wu 蒙武 (see Wang Shu-min, 73:2308).

[68] P'ing-yü was located just north of modern P'ing-yü, about 150 miles southeast of Cheng-chou in Honan province. Ch'in was about 30 miles east of modern P'ing-yü (T'an Ch'i-hsiang, 1:45).

[69] There were two Ch'eng-fu's at this time. The commentators ("So-yin" "Cheng-yi" and Ch'ien Mu, *Ti-ming k'ao,* p. 367) all agree this should refer to the Ch'eng-fu which was just northwest of modern P'ing-ting Shan 平頂山 in Honan. The statement that Li Hsin attacked Yen and Ying and then went west to meet Meng T'ien at Ch'eng-fu is very puzzling, since Ch'eng-fu was east of Yen and Ying (or perhaps Yen-ying, a single place; see n. 68 of our translation of Chapter 69). Perhaps Yen-ying refers to Ying-ch'en 郢陳, another former capital of Ch'u which was east of Ch'eng-fu, or perhaps it is an error for Yen-ling 鄢陵 (see also Wang Shu-min, 73:2309).

[70] *Tu-wei* 都尉.

Wang Chien refused. "Your aged servant is worn out and contrary. I suggest that you choose some other worthy general, Great King."

The First Emperor refused. "Stop! Speak no more, General!"

Wang Chien said, "If you must make use of your servant, Great King, no less than 600,000 men will do."

The First Emperor said, "We shall listen only to your advice, General."

Wang Chien then took charge of 600,000 men and the First Emperor himself accompanied them to the banks of the Pa 灞.[71] When Wang Chien set out, he asked for many rich fields and houses, gardens and pools.

The First Emperor said, "Go, General! Why fear poverty?"

Wang Chien said, "In leading troops for you, Great King, your servant has achieved merit but never been enfeoffed as a noble. Thus since you have now turned to your servant, Great King, your servant takes this opportunity to ask for some gardens and pools as his descendants' property." The First Emperor burst out laughing.

After reaching the pass, Wang Chien sent a messenger to ask for more fertile fields five times. Someone said, "You go too far in your demands for property, General."

"Not so," said Wang Chien. "The King of Ch'in is harsh and distrustful. He has now emptied the state of Ch'in of its finest soldiers and entrusted them completely to me. If I did not ask for many fields and houses as my descendants' property in order to strengthen myself, would I not merely give the King of Ch'in cause to doubt me?"

[2341] Wang Chien did indeed replace Li Hsin in the attack against Ching. When Ching heard that Wang Chien had come with reinforcements, they summoned every soldier in the state to resist Ch'in.

When Wang Chien arrived, he reinforced his barricades and held to them, refusing to give battle. The soldiers of Ching came out several times to challenge them to battle, but they would not come out. Wang Chien rested and bathed his soldiers every day, feeding them well and eating with the men himself.

After a while, Wang Chien sent a man to ask if the army was amusing itself.

He replied, "They are pitching stones and wrestling."[72]

Wang Chien said, "Our forces will serve now."

Ching challenged them to battle several times, but Ch'in's troops did not come out, so Ching led its troops east. Chien took the opportunity to mobilize his troops and chase them. He had his bravest troops assault and defeat the Ching army. When they reached south of Ch'i 蘄,[73] they killed the Ching general Hsiang Yen 項燕[74] and the Ching troops finally fled in defeat. Ch'in followed up on its victory by securing the walled cities and towns of Ching.

Over a year later, they captured the Ching King Fu-ch'u 負芻 and pacified the territory of Ching, making it into commanderies and counties.[75] Following this, [Wang Chien and

---

[71] The Pa River joined the Wei 渭 from the south a few miles east of Ch'in's capital at Hsien-yang (T'an Ch'i-hsiang, 1:44).

[72] "Pitching stones" perhaps refers to the game of pitch-pot. Our translation of ch'ao-chü 超距 as "wrestling" follows Wang Nien-sun's suggestion. For a further discussion, see Wang Shu-min, 73:2311.

[73] Ch'i was located just south of modern Su-chou 宿州 in Anhwei (T'an Ch'i-hsiang, 1:45).

[74] Hsiang Yen was the last of Ch'u's great generals. His leadership of the Ch'u resistance against Ch'in made him so popular that when Ch'en Sheng 陳勝 (see his biography in Chapter 48) began his revolt against Ch'in, he proclaimed his chief assistant, Wu Kuang 吳廣, to be Hsiang Yen (Shih chi, 48:1950). Hsiang Liang 項梁, another of the leaders of the revolt against Ch'in, was supposedly the son of Hsiang Yen (Shih chi, 7:295).

[75] Shih chi, 15:756, for the Ch'in entry for 224 B.C, records that "Wang Chien and Meng Wu assaulted and broke Ch'u's army, killing their general Hsiang Yen." Under the Ch'in entry for 223 B.C., it records that "Wang Chien and Meng Wu broke Ch'u and captured its king, Fu Ch'u." This confirms the memoir's claim that the

Meng Wu] mounted an expedition south against the lords of the Hundred Yüeh 百越.[76] Wang Chien's son Wang Pen, together with Li Hsin, conquered and pacified the territory of Yen and Ch'i.[77]

In his twenty-sixth year (221 B.C.), the First Emperor conquered the world. The Wang and Meng families achieved the most merit and their names were passed on to later generations.

By the time of the Second Emperor (209-207 B.C.), Wang Chien and his son Pen were both already dead and the Meng family had been destroyed.[78] When Ch'en Sheng 陳勝 rebelled against Ch'in, Ch'in sent Wang Chien's grandson Wang Li 王離 to crush Chao. He besieged the King of Chao and Chang Erh 張耳 at Chü-lu-ch'eng 鉅鹿城.[79]

Someone said, "Wang Li is a famous general of Ch'in. Leading the troops of mighty Ch'in to attack the newly created Chao, he is certain to take them."

A stranger said, "Not so. Those who serve as generals for the third generation are certain to go down in defeat. Why are they certain to go down? Because they killed and attacked many and their descendants will suffer the evil fortune that comes from this. Wang Li is already a general of the third generation."

Before long had passed, Hsiang Yü 項羽 had rescued Chao, crushed the Ch'in troops, and captured Wang Li. Wang Li's troops then surrendered to the feudal lords.

[2342] His Honor the Grand Scribe says: "A country saying goes, 'a foot sometimes comes up short and an inch sometimes comes out long.' Pai Ch'i anticipated his foes and matched their stratagems. He produced surprises without end and his name shook the world, but he was unable to save himself from the attack of the Marquis of Ying. Wang Chien was a general of Ch'in and pacified the six states. At the time, Chien was Commander-in-Chief and the First Emperor treated him like a teacher, but he was unable to assist Ch'in in establishing its virtue or consolidating its roots. He bowed to his master's will, seeking only to please him and in the end died. When his grandson Wang Li was captured by Hsiang Yü, it was only to be expected. They both came up short."

---

campaign lasted more than a year. *Shih chi,* 6:234, however, records a different sequence of events. See our translation of Chapter 6 for details.

[76] "Pai-yüeh" refers to a number of non-Chinese tribes living over a wide area of southern China.

[77] *Shih chi,* 15:757, in the Ch'in entry for 222 B.C., records that "Wang Pen assaulted Yen and captured its king, Hsi. (He) further assaulted and captured the King of Tai, Chia." In the Ch'in entry for 221 B.C., it records that "Wang Pen assaulted Ch'i and captured the king, Chien." Thus these events extended over a two year period.

[78] See Chapter 88 for the fall of the Meng family.

[79] This siege occurred in 208 B.C. See *Shih chi,* 89:2579 for a more detailed account.

TRANSLATORS' NOTE

This is the first of two chapters devoted to famous generals of the state of Ch'in, the second being that on Meng T'ien and his brother Meng Yi (*Shih chi* Chapter 88). The reasons for separating these two chapters appear to have been largely chronological. Pai Ch'i served King Chao of Ch'in and Wang Chien served the First Emperor of Ch'in. Meng T'ien served the First Emperor as well, but Ssu-ma Ch'ien perhaps distinguished between them on the basis of the role they played in Ch'in history. Wang Chien's most important victories paved the way for the establishment of the Ch'in empire, and it appears Wang died not long after this occurred. Meng T'ien, on the other hand, participated in such great public works as the construction of the Straight Road and the Long Wall during the reign of the First Emperor, before he was eventually killed by the Second Emperor. Ssu-ma Ch'ien thus places him with other figures such as Li Ssu and Lü Pu-wei. The implication is that these men were all at fault for their role in the shaping or conduct of policies which brought about the fall of Ch'in.

Even though history would thus seem to demand a more positive assessment of Pai Ch'i and Wang Chien, Ssu-ma Ch'ien cannot find it in himself to praise them. Pai Ch'i receives the same treatment that figures such as Wei Jan do. In a ruthless age, he was just not ruthless enough. Wang Chien, on the other hand, is able to avoid such a fate through wily manipulation of his ruler, yet is condemned by Ssu-ma Ch'ien as a sycophant. Having demonstrated that he had the talent to avoid death in the maze of Ch'in politics, he is found guilty of failing to put this talent to a better use than simply preserving his own life. To Ssu-ma Ch'ien, the short-sightedness of Wang Chien is seen most clearly in the fall of his descendants less than a generation later.

The dates we give for the battle of Ch'ang-p'ing and the siege of Han-tan depend on our understanding of the Ch'in calendar. According to *Shih chi*, 6:237, when the First Emperor of Ch'in declared himself Emperor, he changed the calendar so that the beginning of the year (*sui-shou* 歲首) fell in the tenth month. What this meant was that the year of the king's reign was calculated from the beginning of the tenth lunar month, rather than from the beginning of the first lunar month. This practice is clearly reflected in the *Shih chi*'s records of the First Emperor's reign (for examples, see Huang P'ei-jung 黃沛榮, *Chou shu Chou Yüeh p'ien chu-ch'eng te shih-tai chi yu-kuan san-cheng wen-t'i te yen-chiu* 周書周月篇著成的時代及有關三正問題的研究 [Taipei: Kuo-li T'ai-wan Ta-hsüeh wen-shih ts'ung-k'an, 1972], p. 89). With the discovery of the Ch'in annals at Shui-hu-ti (see Huang Sheng-chang, "Yün-meng Ch'in-chien pien-nien-chi ch'u-pu yen-chiu" *K'ao-ku hsüeh-pao* [1977.1], 1-21), it is also now generally accepted that the practice of using the tenth month as the *sui-shou* did not begin in Ch'in with the First Emperor's assumption of the title of "Emperor" but was a more ancient custom (for an opposing view, however, see B. J. Mansvelt Beck, "The First Emperor's Taboo Character and the Three Day Reign of King Xiaowen: Two Moot Points Raised by the Qin Chronicle Unearthed in Shuihudi in 1975," *TP*, 73 [1987], 68-85). The dates in Chapter 73 support the use of a year beginning with the tenth month during the reign of King Chao.

First, the long sequence of events leading up to the defeat of Chao's army is explicitly said to begin in King Chao's 47th year, when Wang Ho attacks Han. In the fourth month, the state of Chao intervenes and Wang Ho attacks Chao. In the sixth month, Ch'in defeats Chao. In the seventh month, Chao builds fortifications and changes its general. In the ninth month, Chao is completely defeated, its army surrenders, and is subsequently massacred.

The next date we are given is the tenth month of King Chao's *48th* year. If the standard calendar were being used here, this event would have to be dated thirteen months after the defeat of Chao at Ch'ang-p'ing, which clearly took place in the ninth month of Chao's 47th year. It is difficult to understand why such a long time should elapse before Ch'in decided to follow up on its tremendous victory. This point already suggests that the *sui-shou* was in the tenth month.

The sequel to Chao's defeat at Ch'ang-p'ing is that the Marquis of Ying comes to an agreement with Chao in order to prevent Pai Ch'i from gaining too much credit for his victory over Chao. King Chao of Ch'in accepts the agreement and Ch'in's troops are withdrawn in "the first month." Since the last date before this was the tenth month of Chao's 48th year, if the standard calendar is being followed here, this first month should mark the beginning of King Chao's 49th year. The agreement falls through and in the ninth month of what was apparently King Chao's 49th year, Ch'in mobilizes its troops again, and sends its general Wang Ling to attack Chao's capital Han-tan. Pai Ch'i is "sick" and does not participate.

The next date given reveals the contradiction here; the *Shih chi* explicitly states that in the first month of Chao's *49th* year, Ling arrives at Han-tan and begins his attack. This renders the entire preceding paragraph anachronistic, since it apparently took place in the ninth month of Chao's 49th year. Yet the events described are not anachronistic, but represent a logical sequence of events.

If Ch'in's *sui-shou* was in the tenth month, this would remove both the question of Ch'in's long delay in coming to terms with Chao after defeating it at Ch'ang-p'ing and the anachronism of the ninth month of Chao's 49th year being recorded before the first month. The corrected sequence of events would run as follows: Chao's troops were annihilated in the ninth, or last month of Chao's 47th year. In the next month, the tenth month, which was the first month of Chao's 48th year, Ch'in and Chao came to an agreement. In the first month of the calendar, which was the fourth month of Chao's 48th year, Ch'in withdrew its troops. In the ninth month of the calendar, the last month of Chao's 48th year, the agreement fell through, and Ch'in sent Wang Ling to attack Han-tan. In the first month of the calendar, which was the fourth month of Chao's 49th year, Wang Ling reached Han-tan after a journey lasting three to four months, about what we might expect for an army of several hundred thousand traveling on foot, and besieged the city.

BIBLIOGRAPHY

Translations

Mizusawa Toshitada 水澤利忠. *Shiki* 史記. V. 8. *Retsuden (ichi)* 列傳 (一). Tokyo: Meiji Shoten, 1990, pp. 409-31.
Ōgawa Tamaki 小川環樹, trans. *Shiki retsuden* 史記列傳. Rpt. Tokyo: Chikuma Shobō, 1986 (1969). pp. 88-92.
Watson, Burton. *Records of the Grand Historian: Qin Dynasty*. V. 3. Hong Kong and New York: The Research Centre for Translation, The Chinese University of Hong Kong and Columbia University Press, 1993, pp. 121-130.

No important **Studies**.

Mencius and Excellency Hsün, Memoir 14

[74:2343] His Honor the Grand Scribe says: "Whenever I read the works of Master Meng and reach King Hui 惠 of Liang's (r. *370-335 B.C.) question 'How can you profit my state?'[1] I never fail to put the book aside and sigh. Alas, 'profit' is truly the beginning of disorder. That 'our Master seldom spoke of profit'[2] was because he was constantly on guard against its source. Thus he said, 'To act based on profit brings resentment.'[3] From the Son of Heaven to common men, how do the flaws of desire for profit differ?"

Mencius

Meng K'o 孟軻[4] was a native of Tsou 騶.[5] He received instruction from a disciple of Master Ssu 子思.[6] After he had mastered the Way, he went abroad and served King Hsüan 宣 of Ch'i (r. *342-324 B.C.). King Hsüan was unable to use him and he went to Liang. King Hui of Liang did not think his speech fruitful. He was thought of as impractical and removed from the reality of events.[7]

At this time Ch'in employed the Lord of Shang 商[8] to enrich the state and strengthen its forces, Ch'u and Wei used Wu Ch'i 吳起[9] to win battles and weaken their enemies, King Wei 威 (r. *378-343 B.C.) and King Hsüan of Ch'i used people like Sun Tzu 孫子[10] and T'ien Chi 田忌[11] and the feudal lords faced east and paid homage to Ch'i. The world was caught up in alliances and counter-alliances[12] and thought attacks and expeditions worthy affairs. Yet Meng K'o laid out the virtues of T'ang 唐 [Yao], Yeu 虞 [Shun], and the Three Dynasties. Thus wherever he went he did not fit in. He retired and together with disciples such as Wan Chang 萬章[13] discussed the *Odes* and *Documents* and laid out the ideas of Confucius, composing *Meng Tzu* in seven *p'ien*.

After Mencius, there were men like the Masters Tsou 騶子.

[1] *Meng Tzu* 1/1A/1. The "Hereditary House of Wei" (*Shih chi*, 44:1847) has a substantially different version of this conversation. We believe the text here is clearly an instance of Ssu-ma Ch'ien paraphrasing his sources using a more modern idiom.

[2] *Lun yü*, 9/1.

[3] *Lun yü*, 4/12.

[4] We follow Western convention and refer to Meng Tzu as "Mencius" throughout. K'o was his *praenomen*, Tzu Yü 子輿 his *cognomen* (cf. "Cheng-yi").

For additional biographical information on Mencius see D. C. Lau, *Mencius*, Appendices 1 and 2.

[5] A city in the state of Lu, just south of modern Tsou County in Shantung (T'an Ch'i-hsiang, 1:39).

[6] "So-yin" argues that the word *jen* 人 (part of *men-jen* 門人, "disciple") here is an error. Without *jen* the sentence would read "He received instruction at the gate of Master Ssu" [i.e., with Master Ssu himself]. Since Master Ssu was supposedly Confucius's grandson, the chronology involved is highly unlikely.

[7] Ssu-ma Ch'ien erroneously places Mencius's stay in Ch'i prior to his stay in Wei. For a detailed discussion, see D.C. Lau, *Mencius*, pp. 9-10. Wang Shu-min (74:2315) suggests that the edition of *Meng Tzu* which Ssu-ma Ch'ien saw differed from the extant versions.

[8] See his biography in *Shih chi* Chapter 68.

[9] See his biography in *Shih chi* Chapter 65.

[10] See his biography in *Shih chi* Chapter 65.

[11] Cf. *Shih chi*, 48:1892.

[12] See the Translators' Note for Chapter 69 above.

[13] See Wang Li-ch'i, *Jen-piao*, p. 338 and *Meng Tzu, passim*.

Master Tsou

[2344] There were three "Master Tsou's" 騶子 in Ch'i. The first of these was Tsou Chi 騶忌,[14] who sought favor with King Wei by plucking his zither.[15] He rose to the government of the state, was enfeoffed as the Marquis of Ch'eng 成, and received the prime minister's seal. He was prior to Mencius.

The next of these was Tsou Yen 騶衍 (305-240 B.C.),[16] who was after Mencius. Tsou Yen saw that those who possessed states had become even more dissolute and were unable to exalt virtue, while those who possessed great refinement had put their virtue in order and extended it to the black-haired common folk.[17] He therefore carefully observed the growth and decay of the *yin* and *yang* and wrote of the strange and uncanny in essays like "Chung-shih" 終始 (Ends and Beginnings) and "Ta-sheng" 大聖 (The Great Sage)[18] in over 100,000 characters.

His words were transcendent and unconventional. He was sure to first illustrate them through small things, extending these to larger things, reaching finally to infinity. He first narrated what was current, then reached back to The Huang-ti, from whom all scholars derive their methodology, and [narrated] the rise and fall of many generations.[19] Accordingly, he recorded a system for interpreting omens,[20] and inferred [from it] far back to before the birth of Heaven and Earth into darkness too remote to trace [otherwise].[21]

He first ranked the famous mountains and the great rivers of the Central Region, the birds and beasts of the deep valleys, the things produced by water and earth, and the species and objects people held precious. Based on these he went on to things which were beyond the seas and which man could not behold. He described from the splitting of Heaven and Earth the ways the Five Essences revolve,[22] how during each era there was a government appropriate to [each revolution], and how human response to the heavenly omens should also be appropriate to [each revolution]. He thought that the Central Region which scholars spoke of occupied just one of the eighty-one parts of the world. The Central Region he called "the Sacred Township of the Red County."[23] The "Sacred Township of the Red County" itself

---

[14] See Wang Li-ch'i, *Jen-piao,* p. 462.

[15] See the detailed account on *Shih chi,* 46:1889.

[16] These dates are those of Ch'ien Mu (*Chu-tzu,* p. 619); on Tsou Yen, see "Tsou Yen k'ao" 考, *ibid.,* pp. 438-41, Wang Li-ch'i, *Jen-piao,* pp. 328-9, and Knoblock, pp. 64-5.

[17] This passage parallels closely the Grand Scribe's comments to "Ssu-ma Hsiang-ju, Memoir 57" (*Shih chi,* 117:3073): 大雅言王公大人而德逮黎庶. One interpretation (see Lo Chi-tsu 羅繼祖, "*Shih chi* 'Meng Tzu Hsün Ch'in lieh-chuan' chiao-shih" 史記孟子荀卿列傳校釋, *Chung-kuo li-shih wen-hsien yen-chiu chi-k'an* 中國歷史文獻研究集刊, 1, p. 86) is that "Wang-k'ung ta-jen" 王公大人 refers to King Wen 文 and Kung Liu 公劉 (see our translation of *Shih chih* Chapter 4).

Wing-tsit Chan, *A Sourcebook in Chinese Philosophy* (Princeton: Princeton University Press, 1963), p. 247, n. 12 believes that *ta-ya* 大雅 here refers merely to "a real gentleman," similar to our "those who possessed great refinement" Other readings (including the Chung-hua editors) believe it refers to the "Ta-ya" section of the *Odes,* perhaps specifically Mao #240 (Legge, 4:446f).

[18] In the "Yi-wen chih" 藝文志 (Bibliographic Treatise) of the *Han shu* (30:1733) two no longer extant works, *Tsou Tzu* 鄒子 in 49 sections and *Tsou Tzu chung-shih* 鄒子終始 in 56 sections are attributed to Tsou Yen. "Ends and Beginnings" and "The Great Sage" were probably two of these sections.

[19] We omit the *ta* 大 in *ta ping shih sheng shuai* 大並世盛衰 following Wang Shu-min (74:2717).

[20] For examples of Tsou Yen's interpreting omens from a number of classical texts, see Ho Hsin 何新, "Tsou Yen k'ao" 騶衍考, *Chu-shen te ch'i-yüan* 諸神的起原 (Peking: San-lien, 1986), pp. 319-324.

[21] Following Wang Li-chi's reading (74:1786) of *yüan* 原 as a verb here.

[22] See our translation of *Shih chi,* 5:237 above and *Shih chi,* 26:1259: "Thereafter the Warring States struggled with each other . . . at this time only Tsou Yen understood the revolutions of the Five Essences."

contained nine lands, the nine which Yü ordered, but these could not be counted as "lands."
Outside the Central Region there were nine places like the "Sacred Township of the Red
County" and these were what he called the "nine lands." There was a small ocean around
each of them and men and animals could not travel between them, each located as if placed in
the midst of a sphere. There were nine places like these and then a great ocean surrounding
them. Heaven and Earth met there. His methods were all like this. But in summing up his
intents, he was sure to turn to humanity, righteousness, frugality, and the six relationships of
lord and vassal, superior and inferior.[24] In the beginning he was wild, that was all.[25] When
kings, nobles, and great men first saw his method, they were amazed and turned to his teaching, but afterwards were not able to carry it out.

[2345] Thus Master Tsou was honored in Ch'i.[26] When he went to Liang, King Hui
met him in the suburbs, [condescending to treat him] on an equal footing as would normal host
and guest.[27] When he went to Chao, the Lord of P'ing-yüan [escorted him in] walking sideways and dusted off his mat.[28] When he went to Yen, King Chao 昭 (r. 311-279 B.C.) went
before him holding a broom and asked to be ranked among the seats of his disciples and receive instruction. [King Chao] built Chieh-shih 碣石 Residence[29] where he went and attended
on Tsou Yen as Master.[30] He wrote *Chu yün* 主運 (The Dominant Cosmic Influence).[31] Such
was the respect and honor he received when he traveled among the feudal lords, different indeed from Confucius, who grew pale [from hunger] in Ch'en and Ts'ai,[32] and Meng K'o
[Mencius], who was hard pressed in Ch'i and Liang!

Thus when King Wu [of Chou] punished Chow [of Yin] with humanity and
righteousness and became king.[33] Po Yi refused to eat Chou's grain despite his hunger.[34]

[23] The word *chou* 州 had several meanings: 1) a river islet, 2) an administrative unit containing 2,500 families,
3) a much larger area, usually translated simply as "region" or "land." Tsou Yen here seems to be using this ambiguity to imply that what must have seemed like the vast area that China occupied at the time was in reality very
small. Thus for the first occurrence of *chou* here, either the first or second meaning would be appropriate (since
Tsou claimed China was surrounded by water). We have chosen the second meaning, translated as "township" by
Hucker (p. 178, #1332), to emphasize the contrast with "region."

[24] I.e., those between father and mother, elder and younger brothers, and wife and children--see also n. 25 to
Chapter 62 above.

[25] See the comments on Ssu-ma Hsiang-ju 司馬相如 (179-117 B.C.) in *Shih chi*, 117:3073: "相如雖多虛辭濫
說，然其要歸引之節儉."

[26] Where he, along with 76 others including Ch'un-yü K'un, T'ien P'ien, Chieh Yü 接予, Shen Tao and Huan
Yüan, were members of the Chi-hsia 稷下 Academy (see *Shih chi*, 46:1895).

[27] In 336 B.C. Tsou Yen, along with Mencius and Chun-yü K'un, answered King Hui's appeal for worthy men
to come to him (see *Shih chi*, 44:1847).

[28] In *Shih chi*, 76:2370 we read: "When Tsou Yen passed through Chao and spoke of the Supreme Way, [the
Lord of P'ing-yüan] demoted Kung-sun Lung."

Ts'e-hsing 側行, "walking sideways" or "stepping aside," showed respect (see also *Shih chi*, 77:2382).
"Dusting off the mat" was also a typical form of polite behavior--see the Heir of Yen's reception of T'ien Kuang
田光 (*Shih chi*, 86:2530): "The Heir welcomed him, and, walking backwards, led him [to his place], knelt
down, bent over, and dusted off the mat."

[29] About 10 miles southwest of modern Peking according to the "Cheng-yi" (see T'an Ch'i-hsiang, V:48).

[30] On King Chao's reception of Tsou Yen (along with Yüeh Yi 樂毅 and Chü Hsin 劇辛), see *Shih chi*, 34:1558
and the other versions of the story cited in Wang Shu-min (74:2318).

[31] This no longer extant work is also mentioned on *Shih chi*, 28:1369. This translation of the title is that of F.
W. Mote (in Mote's translation of Kung-chuan Hsiao, *A History of Chinese Political Thought, Volume 1: From
the Beginnings to the Sixth Century A.D.* [Princeton: Princeton University Press, 1979], p. 62. There is an excellent discussion of Yin-Yang thought and Tsou Yen's role in it in *ibid.*, pp. 61-5. On his writings in general see
Ch'ien Mu, *Chu-tzu*, pp. 441-3.

[32] See *Shih chi*, 47:1909.

When Duke Ling 靈 of Wey (r. 534-492 B.C.) asked about military formations, Confucius did not answer.[35] When King Hui of Liang sought counsel on his desire to attack Chao, Mencius described the Great King's[36] departure from Pin 邠.[37] Was this because they intended to flatter worldly men or placate them promiscuously? Take a square stick and try to put it in a round hole; will it go in? Some say Yi Yin 伊尹 carried his cauldrons and urged T'ang 湯 on to kingship,[38] Pai-li Hsi 百里奚 fed cows by a cart and through him Duke Mu 繆 became Hegemon.[39] In rising, first placate him and then lead him onto the Great Way. As for Tsou Yen, although his teachings were not reliable, perhaps he too had the same intentions as the men with cows and cauldrons.

[2346] Starting from Tsou Yen and the teachers by [the] Chi [Gate], men like Ch'un-yü K'un 淳于髡, Shen Tao 慎到, Huan Yüan 環淵, Master Chieh 接子, T'ien P'ien 田駢 and Tsou Shih 騶奭, all composed books teaching on matters of [political] order and disorder with which they sought favor from the rulers of the time. There are too many to discuss them all.

Ch'un-yü K'un

[2347] Ch'un-yü K'un 淳于髡[40] was a native of Ch'i. He had broad learning and a strong memory, and did not follow any school in his studies. In his remonstrances and persuasions, he admired the conduct of Yen Ying 晏嬰,[41] but worked hardest at deducing intent and observing expressions.

A retainer presented K'un to King Hui of Liang. King Hui barred his retainers and sat alone [with him]. He granted audience to him twice, but [K'un] never said a word. King Hui wondered at this and complained to his retainer. "When you spoke of Master Ch'un-yü, you said Kuan [Chung][42] and Yen [Ying] were not his equal. Yet when he appeared before Us,

---

[33] See *Shih chi* Chapter 4.

[34] See *Shih chi*, 61:2123: "When King Wu had quelled the disorders of Yin, the world took Chou 周 as its leader; but Po Yi and Shu Ch'i were ashamed to. Their principles would not allow them to eat the grain of Chou, so they hid on Mount Shou-yang 首陽山, where they plucked ferns to eat. When their hunger had brought them to the verge of death, they made a song . . . ."

[35] See *Lun yü*, 15/1: "Duke Ling of Wey asked Confucius about military formations. Confucius replied, 'Matters of the sacrificial table and vessel, I have heard about. Matters of the army I have not studied.' The next day he left."

[36] I.e., Ku-kung Tan-fu 古公亶父 (see *Shih chi*, Chapter 4).

[37] In the current version of *Meng Tzu*, the only reference to the Great King's departure from Pin is in 1A/14-15, where the interlocutor is Duke Wen of T'eng, who asks Master Meng how to avoid being attacked by neighboring states. There is no reference in *Meng Tzu* to Liang attacking Chao.

[38] See *Shih chi*, 3:93: "Yi Yin's praenomen was O-heng 阿衡. O-heng wanted to see T'ang but had no way to do so. Therefore, he made himself a betrothal servant from the Yu-hsi 有莘 Clan, carrying a tripod and a cutting board; by means of gastronomy he persuaded T'ang to realize the way of the king."

[39] See *Shih chi*, 5:186ff.

[40] A much less complimentary account of Ch'un-yü K'un is given in *Shih chi*, 126:3197ff., where he appears as a dwarf adopted by his wife's family (a very shameful position in Chinese society). The two other subjects of this chapter are both *yu* 優 or musicians. These often served in positions similar to European court jesters. The anecdotes in *Shih chi* Chapter 126 relating to Ch'un-yü all concern his service with King Wei of Ch'i (r. 356-320 B.C.). This would place him earlier than the other "teachers under Chi," who were supported primarily by King Hsuan (r. 319-301 B.C.), but would have made it possible for him to meet King Hui of Liang, who reigned from 368-319 B.C. See also Ch'ien Mu, *Chu-tzu*, pp. 359-62.

[41] See his biography in *Shih chi*, Chapter 62.

[42] See Kuan Chung's biography in *Shih chi* Chapter 62.

We obtained nothing. Can it be We are not worth speaking to? Why is this?" The retainer told this to K'un. K'un said, "Of course. When I saw the king the first time, his mind was on the chase. When I saw him again, the king's mind was on music and song. Thus I was silent." The retainer reported this to the king. The king was astounded. "Alas, Master Ch'un-yü is indeed a sage! When Master Ch'un-yü came the first time, someone had presented a fine horse. We had not yet seen it when the Master arrived. When the Master came the next time, someone had presented a singer. Before We had time to listen, the master arrived again. Although We barred our courtiers, Our private thoughts were indeed on this. It is true." When Ch'un-yü K'un appeared before the king again, he spoke for three days and three nights without fatigue. King Hui wished to honor him with the position of a minister. K'un refused and left. Thus [the king] set him off in a "safe wagon"[43] hitched to four horses, with bundles of fabric, jade rings, and one-hundred *yi* of gold. He did not take office for the rest of his life.

Shen Tao

Shen Tao 慎到 (*c.* 350-*c.* 275 B.C.) was a native of Chao.[44] T'ien P'ien 田駢 (*c.* 350-*c.* 275 B.C.)[45] and Master Chieh (*c.* 350-*c.* 275 B.C.) 接子[46] were natives of Ch'i. Huan Yüan 環淵 (*c.* 360-*c.* 280 B.C.) was a native of Ch'u.[47] They all studied the doctrines of the Huang-Lao Way and its virtue, which they expanded and developed.[48] Shen Tao wrote twelve dissertations on them, Huan Yüan wrote *Shang hsia* 上下 (Superiority and Inferiority) [in response] to them,[49] and T'ien P'ien and Master Chieh all had discussions of them.[50] Tsou Shih 騶奭[51] was one of the Tsou's of Ch'i, and often adopted Tsou Yen's doctrines in his writing.[52] The King of Ch'i sang their praises and from Ch'un-yü K'un on down called them all "[high-]ranking Grand Masters,"[53] and built houses for them by the great thoroughfares, honoring them with high gates and great roofs. [*2348*] He gathered together[54] the retainers of the feudal lords, showing that Ch'i could summon the worthiest men in the world.

[43] A cart allowing the rider to sit. Most carts in the Warring States period were meant to stand in. Supposedly, "safe carts" were reserved for the use of aged ministers and women (see *Chou Li* 周禮, "Ch'un-kuan" 春官, "Chin-che" 巾車, 27:1b, *SPPY*).

[44] Shen Tao's dates are based on Ch'ien Mu, *Chu-tzu*, p. 618. See also his "Shen Tao k'ao" 考, *ibid.*, pp. 425-8, Wang Li-ch'i, *Jen-piao*, pp. 577-8, Knoblock, p. 61, and the lengthy discussion of this account in Paul M. Thompson, *The Shen Tzu Fragments* (Oxford: Oxford University Press, 1979), pp. 127-8.

[45] His dates are from Ch'ien Mu, *Chu-tzu*, p. 618. For other sources on T'ien P'ien, see Mukai Tetsuo 向井哲夫, "Den Ben shisō ni tsuite" 田駢の思想について, *Tōhōgaku*, 74(July 1987), 15-29; see also "T'ien P'ien k'ao" 考, *ibid.*, pp. 429-30, Wang Li-ch'i, *Jen-piao*, p. 462, and Knoblock, p. 61.

[46] Chieh Tzu's (also written as 捷子) dates are based on Ch'ien Mu, *Chu-tzu*, p. 618. See also his "Chieh Tzu k'ao" 考, *ibid.*, pp. 428-9 and Wang Li-ch'i, *Jen-piao*, pp. 461-2,

[47] Also known as Yüan Yüan 蜎淵 (see Wang Li-ch'i, *Jen-piao*, p. 541 and Ch'ien Mu, *Chu-tzu*, pp. 448-9). Other than his membership in the Chi-hsia coterie (*Shih chi*, 46:1895), little is known of him.

[48] For a discussion of "Huang-Lao" see n. 26 in *Shih chi* Chapter 63 above.

[49] Probably based on Lao Tzu's discussion of these terms, *shang* 上 and *hsia* 下.

[50] As recorded in the "Bibliographic Treatise" of the *Han shu* their writings remaining in the Han dynasty were: Shen Tzu in 42 *p'ien* 篇 (listed under Fa-chia 法家, *Han shu*, 30:1735), Chieh Tzu in 2 *p'ien*, Yuan Tzu in 13, and T'ien Tzu in 25 (all under Tao-chia 道家, *Han shu*, 30:1730-1).

[51] See Ch'ien Mu, *Chu-tzu*, pp. 440-1.

[52] See the record of his remaining works in 12 *p'ien* listed as Yin-Yang chia in *Han shu*, 30:1733.

[53] "Ranking Grand Masters" (*Lieh Tai-fu* 列大夫) apparently refers to honorary positions with no administrative or political functions. This does not conform with "Hereditary House of T'ien Ching Chung-wan" (*Shih chi*, 46:1895) where it states Tsou Yen and the others were made "Senior Grand Master" (*Shang Tai-fu* 上大夫).

Excellency Hsün

Excellency Hsün 荀卿 was a native of Chao.[55] He arrived at Ch'i to study when he was already 50 years old.[56] The doctrines of Tsou Yen were circumlocutory and grandiose. As for [Tsou] Shih, his writings were comprehensive, but difficult to implement. After associating with Ch'un-yü K'un for a long time, one could often obtain good advice. Thus the men of Ch'i depicted them as "[Tsou] Yen the Empyrean Talker," "[Tsou] Shih the Dragon Carver," and "[Ch'un-yü] K'un the Oil Can."[57] T'ien P'ien and the others all died in the reign of King Hsiang 襄 (r. 283-265 B.C.) and Excellency Hsün was then the oldest teacher there. Ch'i still filled vacancies among the "[high-]ranking Grand Masters" and Excellency Hsün was Libationer[58] three times. Someone in Ch'i slandered Excellency Hsün. Excellency Hsün went to Ch'u and the Lord of Ch'un-shen[59] made him Prefect of Lan-ling 蘭陵.[60] The Lord of Ch'un-shen died (238 B.C.), and Excellency Hsün was dismissed. He thus came to take residence in Lan-ling. Li Ssu 李斯 was once his disciple and not long after became Prime Minister of Ch'in.[61]

Excellency Hsün loathed the government of his troubled time, with lost states and disorderly rulers one following the other, refusing to follow the Great Way and instead laboring at sorcery and spells and believing in omens; he was contemptuous of scholars arguing over minutiae, such as people like Chuang Chou disordering convention with smooth talk. Thus he discoursed on the advantages and disadvantages of the Confucian, Mohist,[62] and Taoist ways of conduct, writing several tens of thousands of characters,[63] and expired. He was then buried in Lan-ling.

---

[54] Reading *lan* 攬 for *lan* 覽.

[55] Our translation of the name Hsün Ch'ing takes *ch'ing* as a polite title, not a *tzu* or actual post. Some suggest that this is just a phonetic loan for *k'uang* 況, which is also recorded as Hsün Tzu's *praenomen*.

See also "Biography: The Early Years" and "Biography: The Later Years," in Knoblock, pp. 3-35.

[56] There is controversy over whether the text here should read *shih-wu* 十五 "fifty" or *wu-shih* 五十 "fifteen." If it originally read "fifteen," this does not fit in with the word *shih* 始, an adverb usually implying that an action occurred later than expected. If the text read "fifty," Hsün Tzu must have been an old man indeed when he died.

Wang Shu-min (74:2324-5) suggests that *shih* is the same as *yi* 巳 which would then imply Minister Hsün came earlier than expected, so that he feels no compunction in altering "fifty" to "fifteen." For a fuller discussion of Hsun Tzu's chronology, see John H. Knoblock, "The Chronology of Xunzi's Works," *Early China* 8, (1982-3), 29-52.

[57] There epithets all seem to have two edges. "Empyrean Talker" may suggest the lack of practicality in Yen's discourse as much as its grand scope. Similarly, while to carve a dragon is a considerable skill, it has little utilitarian purpose. "The Oil Can" (literally *Chih-ku kuo K'un* 炙轂過, "A Box [for Oil] to Make Wheels Turn" suggests Ch'un-yü K'un had the potential to perform a useful service ("one could often obtain good advice"), but did not think in larger, theoretical terms.

[58] *Chi-chiu* 祭酒. See also Ch'ien Mu, *Chu-tzu*, pp. 437-8.

[59] See biography in *Shih chi* Chapter 78.

[60] This occurred in 255 B.C. (see Knoblock, p. 28). "Cheng-yi" believes Lan-ling may have been near modern Lin-Yi 臨沂 County in southeastern Shantung (T'an Ch'i-hsiang, V:45).

[61] According to the biography of Li Ssu (*Shih chi*, 87:2546), Li Ssu served Ch'in more than twenty years before he became prime minister.

[62] Ssu-ma Ch'ien's claim that Hsün Tzu's philosophy incorporated elements of Mohist thought may refer to Hsün Tzu's apparent interest in logic and terminology.

[63] See Knoblock, pp. 105ff.

Kung-sun Lung

[2349] Chao also had Kung-sun Lung 公孫龍 (*c.* 320-*c.* 250 B.C.)[64] who disputed on hardness and white and similarity and difference,[65] and the doctrines of Master Chü 劇子 (*c.* 290-*c.* 242 B.C.).[66] Wei had Li K'uei 李悝 (*c.* 455-*c.* 395 B.C.),[67] who taught the full use of the earth's strength.[68] Ch'u had Master Shih 尸子 (*c.* 390-*c.* 330 B.C.)[69] and Ch'ang Lu 長盧,[70] and Master Hsü 吁子[71] of O 阿.[72] From Mencius to Master Hsü, many of our generation have their works, thus I have not included any of their transmitted teachings.

Mo Ti

[2350] Probably Mo Ti 墨翟 (*c.* 480-*c.* 390 B.C.)[73] was a Grand Master of Sung, skilled at defense and practicing frugality.[74] Some say he lived at the same time as Confucius, others after him.

---

[64] Dates are those of Ch'ien Mu, *Chu-tzu,* p. 619. See also Wang Li-ch'i, *Jen-piao,* p. 579 and Knoblock, pp. 62-3.

[65] *Kung-sun Lung Tzu* in 14 *p'ien* is listed in the *Han shu,* 30:1736. See also A. C. Graham, The Composition of the *Gongsuen Long tzyy," AM, NS* 5(1957), 147-83, "The 'Hard and White' Disputation of the Chinese Sophists," *BSOAS,* 30(1967), 358-68, and "Kung-sun Lung's Essay on Meaning and Things," *JOS,* 2(1955), 282-301.

[66] Dates according to Ch'ien Mu, *Chu-tzu,* p. 620; see also *ibid.,* p. 480 and Wang Li-ch'i, *Jen-piao,* p. 774. Chu was killed by the Chao general P'ang Huan in 242 B.C. (see n. 44 to our translation of Chapter 81 and *Shih chi,* 15:751).

[67] Dates after Ch'ien Mu, *Chu-tzu,* p. 616. Also known as Li K'o 李/里克, he served as minister to Marquis Wen 文 of Wei (r. 445-396 B.C.). See also Wang Li-ch'i, *Jen-piao,* p. 324 and n. 37 to our translation of *Shih chi* Chapter 65 above.

[68] See *Shih chi,* 30:1441: 魏用李克,盡地力,為彊君. *Han shu* lists a *Li K'o* in 7 *p'ien* under the Ju 儒 Chia section (30:1724) and a *Li Tzu* 李子--by Li K'uei--in 32 *p'ien* under the Fa 法 Chia (30:1735)

[69] Dates according to Ch'ien Mu, *Chu-tzu,* p. 617. Master Shih or Shih Chiao 佼 was Shang Yang's teacher and fled to Shu 蜀 with the death of his famous pupil (*Han shu,* 30:1741 n.). see also Wang Li-ch'i, *Jen-piao,* p. 461 and Ch'ien Mu, *Chu-tzu,* pp. 272-3. His works are also recorded in the *Han shu (ibid.)* in 20 *p'ien.*

[70] There is a *Ch'ang Lu Tzu* in the *Han shu* bibliography (30:1730) in 9 *p'ien* (Tao Chia). On Ch'ang Lu see Wang Shu-min (74:2330-1) and Ch'ien Mu, *Chu-tzu,* p. 500.

[71] See Wang Shu-min, 74:2331. Also known as Mi Tzu 芈子 and Yü Tzu 芋子. A *Mi Tzu* in 18 *p'ien* is listed in the *Han shu* bibliography (30:1725). See also Ch'ien Mu, *Chu-tzu,* p. 498.

[72] "So-yin" identifies O as Tung-O 東阿, about 65 miles southwest of modern Tsinan in Shantung (T'an Ch'i-hsiang, 1:39). But this was Ch'i at the time, not Ch'u (see also Wang Shu-min's discussion of this problem, 74:2331).

[73] Dates according to Ch'ien Mu, *Chu-tzu,* p. 616. Wang Li-ch'i, Jen-piao, pp. 312-3. Ch'ien Mu, Chu-tzu, has a number of passages devoted to Mo Ti, see especially pp. 89-96. See also Knoblock, pp. 57-8

[74] See the bibliographic treatise in the *Han shu* (30:1738) *Mo Tzu* is listed in 71 *p'ien.*

TRANSLATORS' NOTE

Despite its title, this chapter treats the various masters of schools of thought (*chu-tzu* 諸子) during the Warring States era in an arrangement which somewhat mirrors that of Memoir 7, "Confucius's Disciples." The Grand Scribe's comments coming here at the beginning of the chapter (as in chapters 49, 61 and 124) further indicates that this chapter was meant to convey more general meaning (as, for example, Chapter 61 has been read as the "preface" to the memoirs), probably, as the title suggests, to place the various other schools under a Confucian banner.

Placed strategically behind a series of chapters devoted to those rhetoricians and "thinkers" who masterminded Ch'in's rise (Chang Yi and the Lord of Shang, for example), chapters which were followed by memoirs devoted to those more active leaders who put the plans and ideas of the persuaders and Legalist philosophers into effect and directly guided Ch'in's success (such as Pai Ch'i), this memoir may also be read as an introduction to the intellectual background of the Four Lords, since several of the men discussed above were involved in advising these four leaders who were essentially the last bastions against Ch'in's gradual dominance.

Kung-ch'uan Hsiao (in his *A History of Chinese Political Thought,* F. W. Mote, trans. [Princeton: Princeton University Press, 1979], p. 64) argues that Ssu-ma Ch'ien saw a similarity of principle in Mencius and Tsou Yen. In Hsiao's interpretation Tsou Yen was trying to adapt Confucian principles to the competition of the competing doctrines of his era. If he is correct, Ssu-ma Ch'ien could also have linked Mencius, Tsou Yen, and Hsün Tzu as the major transmitters of the Master's teachings. At the same time he used Mencius and Tsou to illustrate his dismay that humanity and righteousness (which both advocated) were so difficult to apply.

BIBLIOGRAPHY

I. Translations

Chan, Wing-tsit. *A Source Book on Chinese Philosophy.* Princeton: Princeton University Press, 1963, pp. 246-8 (Tsou Yen).

Dubs, H. H. "Sün-tzu," *The Moulder of Ancient Confucianism.* London, 1927, pp. 26-28.

Fung Yu-lan. *A History of Chinese Philosophy.* Derk Bodde, trans. 2v.; Princeton: Princeton Univesity Press, 1952-53, v. 1, p. 132 (Ch'un-yü K'un, Ch'en Tao, Huan Yüan, T'ien P'ien, Chia-tzu).

Kou Pao-koh. *Deux sophistes chinois, Houei Che et Kong-souen Long.* Paris, 1953, p. 7 (Kong-souen Long).

Needham, Joseph. *Science and Civilization in China.* V. 2, *History of Scientific Thought.* Cambridge: Cambridge University Press, 1955, pp. 232-3 (Tsou Yen).

Ōgawa Tamaki 小川環樹, trans. *Shiki retsuden* 史記列傳. Rpt. Tokyo: Chikuma Shobō, 1986 (1969). pp. 93-97.

Ware, James R. *The Sayings of Mencius, A New Translation.* New York, 1960, pp. 10-11 (Mencius).

II. Studies

Chu Hsüan 朱玄. "*Shih chi* 'Meng Hsün lieh-chuan' shu-cheng" 史記孟荀列傳疏證. *[Shih-Ta] Kuo-wen Yen-chiu-so chi-k'an* 師大國文研究所季刊, 10 (1966), 69-216.

Ichiguro Shunitsu 石黑俊逸. "*Shiki* 'Mōshi Junkei retsuden' no kōsei" 史記孟子荀子列傳の構成, *Shingaku kenkyū*, 12(1956), 1-4.

Kang Chou 岡周. "Tu 'Meng Hsun lieh-chuan' hou te chi-yi yi t'i-yao" 讀孟荀列傳後的稽疑及提要, *Chung-fa Ta-hsüeh yüeh-k'an* 中法大學月刊, v. 10, no. 4 (February 1937).

Knoblock, John. *Xunzi, A Translation and Study of the Complete Works.* 2v. Stanford: Stanford University Press, 1988 and 1991.

Lau, D. C. "The Dating of Events in the Life of Mencius" and "Early Traditions about Mencius," in Lau's *Mencius.* London: Penguin, 1970, pp. 205-213 and 214-219, respectively.

Li Shu-yi 李叔毅. "Tu *Shih chi* 'Meng Hsün lieh-chuan'" 讀史記孟荀列傳, *Ku-chi cheng-li yen-chiu hsüeh-k'an* 古籍整理研究學刊, 1985.4

T'an Chieh-fu 譚戒甫. "*Shih chi* 'Meng Tzu Hsün Ch'ing lieh-chuan chiao-shih" 史記孟子荀卿列傳校釋, *Chung-kuo li-shih wen-hsien yen-chiu chi-k'an* 中國歷史文獻研究集刊, 1(1982), 84-96.

Thompson, Paul M. *The Shen Tzu Fragments.* Oxford: Oxford University Press, 1979.

The Lord of Meng-ch'ang, Memoir 15

[75:2351] The Lord of Meng-ch'ang's 孟嘗[1] *praenomen* was Wen 文; his *cognomen* was T'ien 田. Wen's father was T'ien Ying 田嬰, the Lord of Ching-kuo 靖郭.[2] T'ien Ying was a younger son of King Wei 威 of Ch'i (r. *378-343 B.C.),[3] and a younger half-brother of King Hsüan 宣 of Ch'i (r. *342-324 B.C.) by a concubine.[4] T'ien Ying held office and wielded power from the time of King Wei. He was a commander, together with the Marquis of Ch'eng 成 Tsou Chi 鄒忌,[5] and T'ien Chi 田忌, in the rescue of Han and expedition against Wei.[6]

The Marquis of Ch'eng and T'ien Chi struggled for favor and the Marquis of Ch'eng traduced T'ien Chi. T'ien Chi was afraid and attacked a border-town of Ch'i. He did not succeed and fled the state.[7] When King Wei expired, King Hsüan ascended the throne; knowing that the Marquis of Ch'eng had slandered T'ien Chi, he summoned T'ien Chi to serve again as a commander.[8]

[1] "Chi-chieh" and "So-yin" (*Shih chi* 75:2358) both identify Meng-ch'ang with the city of Ch'ang 嘗, located a few miles east of modern Mount Wei 微 in Shantung (T'an Ch'i-hsiang 1:39).

[2] Ching-kuo was located a few miles northeast of Mount Wei near Meng-ch'ang 孟嘗 (see Ch'ien Mu, *Ti-ming k'ao*, p. 279).

[3] Ssu-ma Ch'ien was in error on the dates of King Wei and King Hsüan, as discussed in the "Note on Chronology" at the beginning of this volume. Moreover, since this chapter is centered upon these two reigns, most of the dates are also erroneous. According to the revised chronology of Yang K'uan (in his *Chan-kuo shih*), the correct reign dates are 356-320 B.C. for King Wei and 319-301 B.C. for King Hsüan. Thus the dates in the text, preceded by an asterisk, are those of Ssu-ma Ch'ien. Those in the notes are Yang's.

[4] If T'ien Ying were King Hsüan's *younger* brother, this would be hard to reconcile with the chronology proposed by Yang K'uan. It appears that he was not. *Chan-kuo ts'e* (*SPTK*, 4:21b) relates a story in which an advisor, speaking to King Hsüan, claims he told T'ien Ying to remove King Hsüan from the position of Heir and name another man as successor. When King Hsüan learns how T'ien Ying wept and refused, he is moved and says, "I was young and had no idea of this." The same story occurs in *Lü-shih ch'un-ch'iu* (9:6a-b, *SPPY*), 371-4. Thus there is at least one tradition predating *Shih chi* in which T'ien Ying is older than King Hsüan.

[5] See his biography in *Shih chi* Chapter 74.

[6] Yang K'uan (p. 258) gives the date 342 B.C. for this event, but does not explain his reasons. Haenisch, *Gestalten*, p. 1, gives 341 B.C. Liang Yü-sheng (40:1274) claims this refers to Ch'i's attack on Wei in 353 B.C. (See *Shih chi*, 15:722, 44:1845, 46:1892, and *Chan-kuo ts'e* [4:1b, *SPTK*]. There are two problems with this: 1) the attack on Wei was supposed to be in support of Chao, not Han. Liang recognizes this and says that Han is a textual error for Chao. 2) Even if we grant Liang's emendation, in none of the other accounts of this attack is T'ien Ying mentioned leading troops.

[7] *Shih chi*, 15:724 and 46:1893 place this in 344 B.C. *Shih chi*, 46:1893 gives a slightly different version of this story in which T'ien Ying attacks the Ch'i capital in an attempt to capture Tsou Chi. This at least has a point. Otherwise, it is not clear why T'ien Ying would attack a border-town if he were merely afraid of being slandered by Tsou Chi.

[8] If Yang Kuan's chronology is correct, we encounter the first of many anachronisms here. It can be interpreted in at least two different ways. According to the next sentence, T'ien Chi must have been summoned back by King Hsüan in the first year of his reign. We could assume that Ssu-ma Ch'ien had a textual source which actually stated this, in which case we would simply use the corrected dates of King Hsüan to determine the time of this event. If Ssu-ma Ch'ien did *not* see a text which stated that King Hsüan summoned Tien Chi in his first year, however, we must consider other means by which he could have dated this incident. The most likely way to have done this would be by deciding on a date relative to other events which he had already dated. He then indicated his indirectly determined dating by stating that it occurred in what he believed was the first year of the reign of King Hsüan. In the latter case, the actual *date* may be correct, but the reign years, which must have been provided by Ssu-ma Ch'ien himself, are at fault. We believe that Ssu-ma Ch'ien determined most of the dates in this chapter by indirect means. Thus the actual dates that Ssu-ma Ch'ien indicates are his best guesses, but because of the errors in his chronology of the state of Ch'i, the reign years that he uses to indicate events are incorrect for the first half of the chapter. In this particular case, his erroneous chronology has led him to state a cause and effect

In the second year of King Hsüan (341 B.C.), T'ien Chi, together with Sun Pin 孫臏 and T'ien Ying, led an attack against Wei, defeated it at Ma-ling 馬陵, captured the Wei Heir Shen 申, and killed Wei's general P'ang Chüan 龐涓.[9]

In the seventh year of King Hsüan (336 B.C.),[10] T'ien Ying was sent on a mission to Han and Wei. Han and Wei submitted to Ch'i.[11] Ying participated in the meeting of Marquis Chao 昭 of Han (r. *358-333 B.C.) and King Hui 惠 of Wei (r. *370-335 B.C.) with King Hsüan south of Tung-o 東阿, where they swore allegiance before leaving.[12]

The next year (335 B.C.), [the King of Ch'i] met again with King Hui of Liang [i. e., Wei] at Chüan 甄. King Hui of Liang died this year.[13]

In the ninth year of King Hsüan (334 B.C.), T'ien Ying became the Prime Minister of Ch'i.[14] King Hsüan of Ch'i and King Hsiang 襄 of Wei (r. *334-319 B.C.) met at Hsü-chou 徐州, where they recognized each other as kings.[15] King Wei 威 of Ch'u (r. 339-328 B.C.) heard this and was angry with T'ien Ying.[16]

The next year (333 B.C.), Ch'u led an expedition against the army of Ch'i and defeated it at Hsü-chou. [Ch'u] sent a man to expel T'ien Ying [from Ch'i]. T'ien Ying sent Chang Ch'ou 張丑 to speak with King Wei of Ch'u and King Wei then desisted.[17]

relationship between the ascension of King Hsüan and the return of T'ien Chi to Ch'i. If we accept Yang Kuan's chronology, and also accept the fact that T'ien Chi was exiled from Ch'i and returned in 342 B.C., this cannot be correct, since King Wei did not die in this year and therefore King Hsüan could not recall T'ien Chi.

[9] For details of this famous battle, see the biography of Sun Pin in *Shih chi* Chapter 65. According to Yang Kuan's chronology , 341 B.C. was the sixteenth year of King Wei.

[10] According to Yang Kuan's chronology, 336 B.C. was the twenty-first year of King Wei.

[11] *Chan-kuo ts'e* (4:6b, *SPTK*) seems to refer to this diplomatic mission when it says, "Ch'i then mobilized its soldiers and assaulted Wei, completely defeating it at Ma-ling. Wei was defeated and Han weakened, and through the offices of T'ien Ying the lords of Han and Wei faced north and paid homage to the Marquis of Ch'i." One edition of the *Chan-kuo ts'e* does not have the words "T'ien Ying."

[12] According to Yang Kuan's chronology, this meeting must have been between King Wei of Ch'i and King Hui of Wei. "So-yin" notes that the *Chu-shu chi-nien* also said the Ch'i king at this meeting was King Wei (this passage does not occur in the current *SPPY* edition of *Chu-shu chi-nien* [B:28a]).

Shih chi, 15:727 and 44:1894 both specify the location of this meeting as P'ing-o 平阿, not Tung-o 東阿. "So-yin" says that the *Chu-shu chi-nien* also reads P'ing-o (once again the current *SPPY* edition of *Chu-shu chi-nien* [B:28a] does not mention either place in this year). The difficulty is that P'ing-o was in Ch'u, while Tung-o was at least in Ch'i. Wang Shu-min (75:2336) accepts the P'ing-o reading and suggests that King Hsüan had travelled to P'ing-o for some reason.

Ssu-ma Ch'ien was also in error on King Hui of Wei's dates, as discussed in the introduction to this volume. According to Yang Kuan's chronology, King Hui's correct reign dates are 369-319 B.C.

[13] According to Yang K'uan's chronology this is incorrect. King Hui did not die at this time, but began a new reign period the next year, probably to commemorate his assumption of the title of king.

[14] This event is not mentioned in *Shih chi* Chapters 15 or 46. According to Yang Kuan's chronology , 334 B.C. was the twenty-third year of King Wei.

[15] According to Yang Kuan's chronology , this meeting was between King Hui of Wei and King Wei of Ch'i, not between King Hsiang of Wei and King Hsüan of Ch'i.

[16] Liang Yü-sheng (40:1275) complains that this doesn't make sense. "Was he angry when he heard that T'ien Wen had been made Prime Minister, or angry when he heard that Ch'i and Wei recognized each other as kings?" Wang Shu-min (75:2336) suggests that the King of Ch'u was angry at the role T'ien Ying played in Ch'i and Wei's decision to recognize each other as kings. As discussed in n. 17 immediately below, there may have been other reasons for the King of Ch'u's displeasure with T'ien Ying.

[17] *Shih chi,* 40:1721 gives the following anecdote: "In the seventh year (of King Wei of Ch'u), T'ien Ying, the father of Ch'i's Lord of Meng-ch'ang, took advantage of Ch'u. King Wei of Ch'u led an expedition against Ch'i, defeated it at Hsu-chou, and ordered it to expel T'ien Ying. T'ien Ying was afraid. Chang Ch'ou falsely spoke to the King of Ch'u. 'The reason that Your Majesty triumphed in battle at Hsü-chou was that T'ien P'an Tzu 田盼子 was not employed. P'an Tzu has merit for the state and the families of the hundred cognomens will exert

T'ien Ying served as Prime Minister of Ch'i for eleven years (334-323 B.C.?). When King Hsüan died, King Min took the throne (323 B.C.).[18] In the third year after his ascension (321 B.C.), he enfeoffed T'ien Ying at Hsüeh 薛.[19]

[2352] Earlier, T'ien Ying had over forty sons. One of his low-born concubines had a son named Wen. Wen was born on the fifth day of the fifth month. Ying told Wen's mother, "Do not raise this one." Wen's mother raised him in secret.[20]

When he was grown, his mother arranged an audience for her son with T'ien Ying through his brothers. T'ien Ying was angry at Wen's mother. "I told you to get rid of this child. Why have you dared to raise him?"

Wen knelt and bowed and said, "For what reason would Your Lordship not raise a child born in the fifth month?"

Ying replied, "When a child born in the fifth month grows as tall as the door frame, he will harm his father and mother."

Wen said, "When a man is born, is his fate determined by heaven, or by a door frame?" Ying was silent.

"If his fate must be determined by heaven, what is there for Your Lordship to fear? If his fate must be determined by a door frame, you need only raise the height of your door frame until none can reach it."

"Enough, sir," said Ying.

[2353] After some time had passed, Wen seized a moment of leisure to ask his father Ying, "What is the son of your son?"

"A grandson."

"What is the grandson of your grandson?"

"A great, great grandson."

"What is the grandson of your great, great grandson?"

"I do not know."

---

themselves for him. Master Ying does not get along well with him, and employed Shen Chi 申紀. This Shen Chi, the great vassals will not follow him and the the families of the hundred cognomens will not exert themselves for him, thus Your Majesty triumphed over him. Now Your Majesty expels Master Ying. With Master Ying expelled, Master P'an is sure to be employed. If he can re-invigorate his knights and foot soldiers and meet Your Majesty with them again, this would surely be to Your Majesty's disadvantage.' The King of Ch'u thereafter did not expel [T'ien Ying]."

The same story appears in *Chan-kuo ts'e* (4:7b, *SPTK*) with minor variations. Hsü Kuang (quoted in "Chi-chieh," *Shih chi*, 40:1721) claims that Ch'u was angry with T'ien Ying because he had been encouraging the state of Yüeh to attack Ch'u. This suggestion is based on events described in *Shih chi*, 41:1748-51. Interestingly, the Ch'i king mentioned in *Shih chi* Chapter 41 is King Wei, not King Hsüan. This supports Yang Kuan's chronology. Chang Ch'ou appears several times in *Chan-kuo ts'e*, usually in connection with T'ien Ying, but apparently also as an advisor in Wei.

[18] According to Yang Kuan's chronology , 324 B.C. was the thirty-third year of King Wei.

[19] This event is also recorded in *Shih chi*, 15:731 and 46:1896. According to Yang Kuan's chronology , 321 B.C. was the thirty-sixth year of King Wei. If this is correct, then King Min could not have enfeoffed T'ien Wen.

Hsüeh was located near modern Hsü-chou 徐州 not far from Mount Wei (see n. 1 above and T'an Ch'i-hsiang 1:39).

Haenisch (*Gestalten*, p. 2) demarcates the section above as the "Introduction" to this biography.

[20] The reasons for not keeping a child who was born on this date are not clear. This superstition is mentioned in both Wang Ch'ung's 王充 (29-91 A.D.) *Lun-heng* 論衡 and Ying Shao's 應劭 (*fl.* 200 A.D.) *Feng-su t'ung* 風俗通. Wang Shu-min (75:2338) suggests that the written forms for "five" 五 (*ngagx*) and "offend" 忤 (*ngagh*) were similar. They were certainly homophonous. Ogawa (p. 99, n. 6) speculates that this belief involves offense to the door gods. Other theories point to this day as the apex of the *yang* force, a time likely to produce fiery and impetuous offspring, see Bodde, *Festivals*, pp. 309-11.

Wen said, "Your Lordship has wielded power and served as Prime Minister of Ch'i for the reigns of three kings now.[21] Ch'i has not grown larger, but the wealth of Your Lordship's own family has grown to ten-thousand *chin,* and there is not a worthy man to be seen among your gate attendants. I have heard that within the gates of a general there are sure to be more generals and within the gates of a minister there are sure to be more ministers. Now [the women of] Your Lordship's back palaces tread on damask silk gauze, while your knights have no plain-cloth jackets.[22] Your slaves have grain and meat left over, while your knights do not have their fill of rice dregs and husks. Yet Your Lordship still heaps up more stores, hoping to bequeath them to I don't know what man, and forgets that the affairs of government decline day by day. I wonder at this."

Only then did Ying treat Wen with due propriety, making him master of the household and attendant to guests and retainers. The guests and retainers to be presented increased daily, and Wen's renown spread among the feudal lords. The feudal lords all sent envoys requesting that the Duke of Hsüeh T'ien Ying make Wen his Heir. Ying consented. When Ying died, his title was Lord of Ching-kuo and Wen did indeed take his place in Hsüeh.[23] He was known as the Lord of Meng-ch'ang.

The Lord of Meng-ch'ang lived in Hsüeh and recruited guests and retainers from the feudal lords, even wanted men and those who had committed offenses. They all turned to the Lord of Meng-ch'ang. The Lord of Meng-ch'ang set aside his own income to care for them lavishly. Thus he swayed the knights of the world.

[2354] All of his thousands of household-retainers were treated exactly the same as Wen, without distinction in rank. When the Lord of Meng-ch'ang entertained his retainers and sat talking with them, there were always attendant scribes behind a screen, charged with recording their lord's conversations with his guests and his queries about their relatives and homes. When the retainers left, the Lord of Meng-ch'ang had already sent messengers to present greetings and offer gifts to their relatives.

The Lord of Meng-ch'ang once accompanied his retainers at an evening meal. One man blocked off the torch light. A retainer became angry, thinking the food unequal, and leaving off his meal asked to be excused. The Lord of Meng-ch'ang got up and took his own food over to compare it. The retainer was ashamed and cut his throat. After this, knights turned to him in great numbers. The Lord of Meng-ch'ang did not choose among his guests, but treated them all well. Each man thought that the Lord of Meng-ch'ang favored him.

King Chao of Ch'in (306-251 B.C.) heard of [T'ien Wen's] worth. He first sent the Lord of Ching-yang 涇陽 as a hostage to Ch'i in order to seek an audience with the Lord of Meng-ch'ang.[24]

The Lord of Meng-ch'ang decided to enter Ch'in. None of his guests wished him to go. They admonished him, but he would not listen. Su Tai 蘇代[25] told him, "This morning when I was coming from outside I saw a wooden mortuary figure and a clay mortuary figure talking to each other. The wooden figure said, 'When it rains, you will dissolve.' The clay

---

[21] By Ssu-ma Ch'ien's accounting, these must be Kings Wei, Hsüan, and Min. According to Yang Kuan's chronology, T'ien Ying could not have served under three kings.

[22] Reading *tuan* 短 as *shu* 裋.

[23] Wang Shu-min (75:2339), following Ts'ui Shih 崔適 (1852-1924), argues that *shih* 謚 here does not mean 'posthumous title' (which "the Lord of Ching-kuo" does not appear to be), but is equivalent to *hao* 號, "fief title."

[24] The Lord of Ching-yang was King Chao of Ch'in's younger brother. See n. 2 in Chapter 73 above. *Shih chi,* 15:736-7 says the Lord of Ching-yang arrived as a hostage in Ch'i in 300 B.C. and returned to Ch'in the next year.

[25] See his biography in *Shih chi* Chapter 69.

figure said, 'I was born from the earth and when I dissolve I will return to the earth. If it rains today, it will wash you away and there is no knowing where you will come to rest.' Now Ch'in is a land of tigers and wolves, yet My Lord wishes to go there. If you are unable to return, can you avoid being mocked by the clay figure?"

The Lord of Meng-ch'ang then gave up his plan.[26]

In the twenty-fifth year of King Min of Ch'i (299 B.C.), the Lord of Meng-ch'ang was finally sent on a mission into Ch'in and King Chao of Ch'in made the Lord of Meng-ch'ang Prime Minister of Ch'in.[27]

Someone advised King Chao of Ch'in: "The Lord of Meng-ch'ang is worthy and is moreover a [member of the royal] clan of Ch'i. Now that he is Prime Minister of Ch'in, he is sure to put Ch'i first and Ch'in last. Ch'in is in danger." After this, King Chao of Ch'in imprisoned the Lord of Meng-ch'ang. He decided to kill him.[28]

The Lord of Meng-ch'ang sent a man to a favorite concubine of King Chao, seeking his release. The favorite concubine said, "Your handmaid slave hopes to obtain My Lord's white fox-coat."[29] At that time, the Lord of Meng-ch'ang had a white fox-coat worth a thousand *chin*. There wasn't a match for it in the world. When he had entered Ch'in, he presented it to King Chao, and now had no other fur coats. The Lord of Meng-ch'ang was dismayed. He asked all his retainers, but none was able to reply.

[2355] In the lowest seat there was one who could act like a dog and commit robberies. He said, "Your servant can get the white fox-coat." That night he acted like a dog[30] and entered the vault of the Ch'in palace. He took the white fox-coat which [T'ien Wen] had presented and returned with it [to T'ien Wen]. [T'ien Wen] presented it to King Chao's favorite concubine. The concubine spoke up for [the Lord of Meng-ch'ang] to King Chao and King Chao released the Lord of Meng-ch'ang.

When the Lord of Meng-ch'ang was able to leave, he hastened away, changing his border pass and switching names to get through the pass. He arrived at Han-ku Pass at midnight. King Chao of Ch'in afterwards regretted releasing the Lord of Meng-ch'ang. When [the king] sought him, [Wen] was already gone. [The king] immediately sent men to pursue him in a fast carriage. The Lord of Meng-ch'ang reached the pass. The law of the pass was that visitors were allowed through only when the cock crowed. The Lord of Meng-ch'ang feared that his pursuers would catch up with him. There was a retainer in a low seat who could imitate a cock crowing. When he did so, the cocks crowed together, the pass was opened, and they were allowed through.[31] The length of a meal later, pursuers from Ch'in did indeed reach the Pass, but only after the Lord of Meng-ch'ang had left. They turned around and went back.

[26] A very similar speech appears in *Chan-kuo ts'e* (4:31b, *SPTK*), but in one edition it is credited to Su Ch'in (Ho Chien-chang, p. 358). *Feng-su t'ung-yi* 風俗通義 (8:3a-b, *SPPY*) also quotes this speech as uttered by Su Ch'in.

[27] According to Yang Kuan's chronology, 299 B.C was the second year of King Min. *Shih chi*, 5:210 says T'ien Wen's term as Prime Minister in Ch'in was in the ninth and tenth years of King Chao of Ch'in, or 298-7 B.C. All other *Shih chi* references to T'ien Wen's service in Ch'in, however, place it from 299-8 B.C.

While it seems fairly safe to conclude that T'ien Wen did serve as Ch'in's Prime Minister for a brief period, there are certainly folklore elements in the following story, such as the cocks tricked into crowing early, the thief acting like a dog, the bribe to the king's favorite, and so forth. Interestingly, this story does not occur in *Chan-kuo ts'e*.

[28] Taking *chih ch'ou* 止囚 as a compound (Wang Shu-min 75:2342). *Shih chi*, 15:737 mentions that in 298 B.C., the year that T'ien Wen left Ch'in, Ch'i, Wei, and Han attacked Ch'in. This perhaps explains why King Chao became concerned about T'ien Wen's loyalty.

[29] *Hu-pai* 狐白 is the white fur under a fox's front legs (*yeh* 腋).

[30] Haenisch understands this passage (*Gestalten*, p. 4, n. 5) as "crept in disguised as a dog."

[31] As Wang Shu-min (75:2343) points out, the motif of cocks being tricked into crowing early also occurs in

When the Lord of Meng-ch'ang had first ranked these two men among his retainers, all his retainers had been ashamed. When the Lord of Meng-ch'ang encountered troubles in Ch'in, it was these two men who finally extricated him. After this, his retainers all yielded to them.[32]

When the Lord of Meng-ch'ang passed through Chao, the Lord of P'ing-yüan treated him as a guest. The men of Chao had heard that the Lord of Meng-ch'ang was worthy and came out to see him. They all laughed. "We thought at first the Duke of Hsüeh would be of stalwart build. Now that we see him, he's just a tiny little fellow." The Lord of Meng-ch'ang heard this and was furious. The retainers traveling with him dismounted and hacked, beat, and killed hundreds of people, laying waste to the entire county before leaving.[33]

King Min of Ch'i berated himself for sending away the Lord of Meng-ch'ang. When the Lord of Meng-ch'ang returned, he made him Prime Minister of Ch'i and entrusted him with the reins of government.

[2356] The Lord of Meng-ch'ang harbored resentment for Ch'in. He intended to borrow troops and provisions from West Chou and to join with Han and Wei, for whom he had Ch'i attack Ch'u, to attack Ch'in. Su Tai advised him on behalf of West Chou:[34] "Your Lordship attacked Ch'u with the troops of Ch'i on behalf of Han and Wei for nine years. You took the land north of Yuan 宛 and She 葉 and strengthened Han and Wei.[35] Now you will further attack Ch'in to expand their territory. When Han and Wei have no worries over Ch'u to the south and no trouble with Ch'in to the west, then Ch'i will be in peril indeed! Han and Wei are sure to regard Ch'i lightly and fear Ch'in. Your servant sees this as perilous for Your Lordship.

"Your Lordship would do better to order our humble manor[36] to form a close alliance with Ch'in, while Your Lordship neither attacks nor borrows soldiers or provisions. When Your Lordship faces Han-ku Pass and does not attack, order our humble manor to tell King Chao of Ch'in Your Lordship's situation, saying 'The Duke of Hsüeh will never break Ch'in in order to strengthen Han and Wei. In attacking Ch'in, he wants Your Majesty to order the King of Ch'u to cede its eastern states,[37] granting them to Ch'i. Ch'in should then make peace by freeing King Huai of Ch'u.'

"Let Your Lordship order our humble manor to grant this to Ch'in. If Ch'in is able to escape harm without granting Ch'u's eastern states, Ch'in is sure to wish this. When the King of Ch'u is freed, he is sure to be grateful to Ch'i. Ch'i will be even stronger when it obtains the eastern states and Hsüeh then will be without worry for generation after generation. Ch'in will not be weakened too much and with it located to the west of the Three Chin, the Three Chin are sure to respect Ch'i."

---

later versions of the story of Heir Tan of Yen; it is not found, however, in the *Shih chi* or *Chan-kuo ts'e* account of Tan.

[32] According to *Shih chi*, 15:737, T'ien Wen stayed in Ch'in for only a year. He returned to Ch'i and became Prime Minister in 298 B.C.

[33] This highly derogatory story does not appear in the *Chan-kuo ts'e*. It's inclusion here suggests Ssu-ma Ch'ien did not hold a high opinion of T'ien Wen. There is further evidence of this later in this chapter.

[34] The following speech also appears in *Chan-kuo ts'e*, (1:6b, *SPTY*), attributed there to a Han Ch'ing 韓慶, rather than Su Tai.

[35] According to *Shih chi*, 15:736, Ch'in, Ch'i, Han, and Wei attacked Ch'u in 301 B.C., and defeated Ch'u's general T'ang Mo 唐眛 at Ch'ung-ch'iu 重丘. This may be the incident referred to. The "nine years" in the previous sentence is obscure.

[36] A polite reference to the Western Chou court.

[37] "So-yin" claims this refers to Ch'u's Hsü-yi 徐夷.

The Duke of Hsüeh said "Excellent." He ordered Han and Wei to restore relations with Ch'in, prevented the three states from attacking, and did not borrow soldiers or provisions from West Chou.

At this time, King Huai of Ch'u (328-298 B.C.) had entered Ch'in and Ch'in held him there, thus it was planned to free him. Ch'in did not, however, free King Huai of Ch'u as a result [of Su Tai's plan].[38]

When the Lord of Meng-ch'ang was Prime Minister of Ch'i, his attendant Wei Tzu 魏子 collected income from his manors for him. He went three times and did not bring back income once.

[2357] The Lord of Meng-ch'ang questioned him. He answered, "There was a worthy man whom I lent it to without consulting you, thus I have not brought back the income." The Lord of Meng-ch'ang was angry and demoted Master Wei.

After several years passed, someone slandered the Lord of Meng-ch'ang to King Min, saying "The Lord of Meng-ch'ang is going to revolt." When T'ien Chia 田甲 kidnapped King Min, King Min suspected the Lord of Meng-ch'ang. The Lord of Meng-ch'ang fled.[39]

When the worthy man whom Master Wei had lent the grain to heard this, he submitted a memorial saying that the Lord of Meng-ch'ang had not rebelled and offering his life as a guarantee, cut his throat in front of the palace gate to clear the Lord of Meng-ch'ang. Shocked, King Min followed up and investigated. The Lord of Meng-ch'ang had indeed never plotted to rebel. He then recalled the Lord of Meng-ch'ang. The Lord of Meng-ch'ang then pleaded illness and retired to Hsüeh. King Min consented.

Later, the exiled Ch'in general Lü Li 呂禮 became Prime Minister of Ch'i.[40] He wanted to entrap Su Tai. Tai said to the Lord of Meng-ch'ang, "Chou Tsui 周最 was the most loyal to Ch'i. The reason the King of Ch'i exiled him and made Lü Li Prime Minister, following the advice of Ch'in Fu 親弗, was that he wanted to win over Ch'in.[41]

"If Ch'i and Ch'in ally, then Ch'in Fu and Lü Li will become important men. If they exercise power, Ch'i and Ch'in are sure to treat you lightly, My Lord. It would be better to immediately send troops rushing north to Chao in order to make allies of Wei and Ch'in. Take Chou Tsui in to show your own generosity and restore trust in the King of Ch'i, further preventing changes in the world. If Ch'i is without Ch'in, the world will flock to Ch'i. Ch'in Fu is sure to flee. Who then will manage the state for the King of Ch'i?"

[38] Chronologically, this is suspect if we assume that Su Tai's speech came in the same year that King Huai died.

[39] *Shih chi,* 15:738 gives the date for this event as 294 B.C., in the thirtieth year of King Min. By Yang Kuan's chronology this should be the seventh year of King Min.

T'ien was the royal surname, but there is no other mention of a T'ien Chia elsewhere in *Shih chi* or *Chan-kuo ts'e.* Chia is sometimes used in the sense of 'so and so.' Perhaps here it means 'one of the T'iens?'

The story of Wei Tzu is strikingly similar to the story below involving Feng Hsü.

[40] Yang K'uan (p. 262) dates this in 294 B.C.

[41] Chou Tsui appears as an advisor to the King of Chou in *Shih chi,* 4:167 (in 270 B.C.), trying to persuade Ch'in not to attack Chou. "So-yin" describes him as "a Noble Scion of Chou." In another entry dated 257 B.C. a 'guest' makes a speech advising Chou to keep on good terms with both Ch'in and Ch'i, in which he says, "If Ch'i becomes great, there is still Chou Chu (=Tsui) to ally us with Ch'i." He also appears in *Shih chi,* 6:279 as one of a long list of diplomats. ("So-yin" describes him as "a Noble Scion of Chou who held office in Ch'in.")

Chou Tsui's loyalty to Ch'i is mentioned in *Chan-kuo ts'e* (2:7a, *SPTK*). On the other hand, disreputable dealings are proposed by Chou Tsui to Lü Li in another story in *Chan-kuo ts'e* (2:10b, *SPTK*). There are numerous fragments of this very complex story involving Su Tai, Lü Li, Ch'in Fu, Chou Tsui, T'ien Wen and Wei Jan in the East and West Chou sections of *Chan-kuo ts'e,* but most of them are very short and very corrupt. *Shih chi* offers only this partial version of the story and many details are left unclear. The following speech by Su Tai occurs in *Chan-kuo ts'e* (2:14b, *SPTK*), without the attribution to Su Tai. Ch'in Fu in the *Chan-kuo ts'e* speech is Chu Fu 祝弗 and other details also differ.

The Lord of Meng-ch'ang followed his plan. Lü Li hated the Lord of Meng-ch'ang. [*2358*] The Lord of Meng-ch'ang was afraid. He sent a letter to the Prime Minister of Ch'in, the Marquis of Jang, Wei Jan 魏冉.[42]

> I've heard that Ch'in wants to ally with Ch'i through the offices of Lü Li. Ch'i is the strongest state in the world. You will thus lose prestige, sir. If Ch'i and Ch'in ally and face down the Three Chin, Lü Li is sure to be Prime Minister of both [Ch'i and Ch'in]. Thus your alliance with Ch'i adds to Lü Li's prestige. If Ch'i is spared by the world's troops, her hatred of you will be deep, sir.
> "You would do better to advise the King of Ch'in to lead an expedition against Ch'i.[43] If Ch'i is defeated, I will ask permission to enfeoff you with what [Ch'in] obtains. If Ch'i is defeated, Ch'in will fear the strength of Chin and Ch'in is sure to honor you in order to obtain alliance with Chin. The states of Chin, exhausted by Ch'i, will fear Ch'in and Chin will also be sure to honor you in order to obtain alliance with Ch'in. In that case, you can take the merit of breaking Ch'i and take the importance of carrying Chin. In that case you can break Ch'i, consolidate your fief while Ch'in and Chin both honor you. If Ch'i is not broken and Lü Li is employed again, you will be hard pressed indeed, sir."

After this, the Marquis of Jang spoke to King Chao about leading an expedition against Ch'i and Lü Li fled.

After King Min of Ch'i destroyed Sung,[44] he became more and more arrogant and wanted to remove the Lord of Meng-ch'ang. The Lord of Meng-ch'ang was afraid and went to Wei. King Chao 昭 of Wei (295-277 B.C.) made him Prime Minister.[45] He allied to the west with Ch'in and Chao, and together with Yen led an expedition against Ch'i and defeated it.[46] King Min of Ch'i fled to Chü 莒, where he died. King Hsiang 襄 of Ch'i (283-265 B.C.) took the throne and the Lord of Meng-ch'ang became independent among the feudal lords, subordinate to no state. New to the throne, King Hsiang of Ch'i feared the Lord of Meng-ch'ang and allied with him, once again becoming close with the Duke of Hsüeh.

---

[42] Lü Li was apparently a personal enemy of Wei Jan (see Wei Jan's biography in chapter 72 of the *Shih chi*). A very similar text appears in *Chan-kuo ts'e* (3:29b, *SPTK*), but there T'ien Wen is supposedly arguing on behalf of Wei. According to *Shih chi*, T'ien Wen became Prime Minister of Wei after Ch'i took Sung, so it is possible that this letter is out of sequence here. If it is not, Ssu-ma Ch'ien seems to be saying that T'ien Wen's conduct was not particularly loyal to Ch'i. Liang Yü-sheng (40:1276-7) finds the implication that T'ien Wen was plotting with Ch'in against Ch'i offensive, but this cannot serve as an argument against the timing of this letter. T'ien Wen's loyalty to Ch'i should be judged by the timing of the letter, not the other way round. As we pointed out above, Ssu-ma Ch'ien is certainly not fond of T'ien Wen, who comes out by far the worst of the 'Four Lords' (see also Chapters 76-78) under his pen.

[43] *Chan-kuo ts'e* version reads "advise the King of Ch'in to order our humble manor to speed up the matter of the attack on Ch'i." The *Chan-kuo ts'e* commentator Pao Piao thinks 'humble manor' refers to T'ien Wen's fief, Hsüeh. It seems more likely, however, that it refers to Wei, where presumably T'ien Wen was serving as Prime Minister.

[44] In 286 B.C., according to *Shih chi*, 15:740.

[45] Liang Yü-sheng (40:1277) argues T'ien Wen never actually became Prime Minister of Wei, but as Wang Shu-min (75:2347-8) points out, there are two passages in earlier texts (in *Han Fei Tzu* and *Chan-kuo ts'e*), which state T'ien Wen held this position.

[46] According to *Shih chi* 15:741, this happened in 284 B.C. Details of the Five States' invasion of Ch'i are given in *Shih chi* Chapters 80 and 82. King Hsiang took the throne in 283 B.C. Following this event, the *Shih chi* chronology and Yang Kuan's chronology are in harmony again.

When [T'ien] Wen died, he was titled Lord of Meng-ch'ang.[47] His sons fought over the throne and Ch'i and Wei together destroyed Hsüeh. Meng-ch'ang's line ended and he had no posterity.[48]

[2359] Earlier, Feng Huan 馮驩 heard that the Lord of Meng-ch'ang delighted in guests and went to see him wearing straw sandals.[49] The Lord of Meng-ch'ang said, "You have troubled yourself to come a great distance, Venerable Sir. What do you have to teach me?"

Feng Huan said, "I heard that My Lord was fond of knights and have come to live with you because of my poverty."

The Lord of Meng-ch'ang put him in the Transient's Hostel for ten days. The Lord of Meng-ch'ang asked the Master of Hostels:[50] "What has my guest been doing?"

He replied, "Master Feng Huan is quite poor. All he has is a sword with its hilt wrapped in straw.[51] He taps his sword and sings, 'Long blade let's go home, for food there's no fish.'"

The Lord of Meng-ch'ang transferred him to the Favored Hostel and fed him fish. Five days later, he again asked the Master of Hostels.

He replied, "Your guest again taps his sword and sings 'Long blade let's go home, when we go out we've no carriage.'"

The Lord of Meng-ch'ang transferred him to the Substitute's Hostel and gave him a carriage to travel in.

In five days, the Lord of Meng-ch'ang again asked the Master of Hostels. The Master of Hostels answered, "The Venerable Sir once again taps his sword and sings 'Long blade let's go home, we've nothing for a house.'" The Lord of Meng-ch'ang was annoyed.[52]

A year passed and Feng Huan offered no advice. At that time, the Lord of Meng-ch'ang was the Prime Minister of Ch'i, enfeoffed with ten thousand households at Hsüeh. He had three thousand household-retainers and the income from his manors was not enough to provide for his [*2360*] retainers. He sent someone to lend money in Hsüeh. There was no harvest for more than a year and many of those who had borrowed from him were unable to pay him their interest. The provisions for his guests would soon be inadequate.

This worried the Lord of Meng-ch'ang and he asked his advisors, "Who can be sent to collect the debts in Hsüeh?" The Master of Hostels said, "Master Feng, the guest in the Substitute's Hostel, has the appearance and bearing of great perspicuity. He's an older man and has no other abilities. Perhaps you can have him collect the debts."

The Lord of Meng-ch'ang had Feng Huan brought in and made his request. "My guests have ignored my lack of worth and favored me with their presence to the number of

---

[47] See n. 23 above.

[48] *Shih chi* gives no date for the death of T'ien Wen. From the events in which T'ien Wen was involved, he seems to have been the oldest of the 'four great princes.' There is only one derogatory story linking him with the Lord of P'ing-yuan. It is not clear how much credibility this has. The Lord of Hsin-ling, the Lord of P'ing-yuan, and the Lord of Ch'un-shen, however, were undoubtedly contemporaries and there are several stories describing their meetings.

[49] A sign of poverty. See n. 15 in our translation of Chapter 76.

[50] *Chuan-she chang* 傳舍長.

[51] Another sign of poverty. The most common hilt insets were apparently wood, while the more elaborate ones were made of ivory.

[52] Compare this with the *Chan-kuo ts'e* (4:37a, *SPTK*) version: "(T'ien Wen's) attendants disliked him (Feng Huan). They thought his greed knew no bounds. The Lord of Meng-ch'ang asked, "Does Master Feng have relatives?" They answered, "He has an aged mother." The Lord of Meng-ch'ang sent a man to take care of her food and expenses, so that she wouldn't lack. After this, Feng Huan did not sing again." Here we find T'ien Wen portrayed in a negative light in the *Shih chi* version of a common story.

over three thousand men. The income from my cities is not sufficient to care for them, thus I lent out money at interest in Hsüeh. Hsüeh has had no harvest for a year and the people have not given much in the way of interest. I fear that my guests' food will not be sufficient and hope that you can collect from them, Venerable Sir."

"I shall comply," said Feng Huan. He took his leave and set off. When he reached Hsüeh, he summoned those who had taken the Lord of Meng-ch'ang's money to a meeting. The interest came out to one hundred thousand coins. He had quantities of wine brewed, bought fat cows, and summoned all of the debtors, both those who could pay the interest and those who could not, and had them all bring their tallies for an accounting. When they had all arrived for the meeting, he killed a cow and set out wine every day. After they were in their cups, he took out the tallies and matched them. For those who could pay the interest, he set a date. For those who were poor and could not pay interest, he took their tallies and burned them.

"The reason the Lord of Meng-ch'ang lent out money was that the people had nothing with which to pursue their occupations. The reason he asked for interest was that he had nothing with which to support his guests. For those wealthy enough we have now set dates. For those too poor, we have burned the tallies and given up the money. Force yourselves to drink and eat, gentlemen. With a lord such as this, you must not turn your back on him."

All seated rose, then touched their heads to the ground twice.

When the Lord of Meng-ch'ang heard that Feng Huan had burned the tallies, he was furious and sent a messenger to summon Huan. When Huan arrived, the Lord of Meng-ch'ang said, "I have three thousand household-retainers, that is why I lent money in Hsüeh. My manors are few, and moreover almost none of the peasants paid their interest on time. I feared that my guests' food would be inadequate, that is why I asked you to collect debts for me, Venerable Sir. Now I've heard that when you got the money, you provided many cattle and much wine with it, then burned the tallies. Why was that?"

Feng Huan said, "It is so. If I had not provided cattle and wine, I could not have gathered them all and would have been unable to know if they had enough or not. [*2361*] For those who had enough I set dates. For those who did not, even if you watch over them and collect from them for ten years, the interest will just grow larger and larger. When they are desperate and flee because of this, you will have to write it off yourself. If they are desperate, they will never repay it. The superior will then be a ruler who loves profit and not his people. The inferior will have the name of abandoning his ruler and reneging on his obligations. This is not how to encourage the people or build Your Lordship's reputation. I've burned useless tallies for worthless debts and written off empty profits that were unobtainable, brought the people of Hsüeh closer and made a name for My Lord. What do you find puzzling about all this?" The Lord of Meng-ch'ang clapped his hands and apologized.

Misled by the slanders of Ch'in and Ch'u, the King of Ch'i thought that the Lord of Meng-ch'ang's reputation was higher than his own and that he was usurping the powers of state. He therefore dismissed the Lord of Meng-ch'ang. When the guests discovered that the Lord of Meng-ch'ang had been dismissed, they all left.[53]

Feng Huan said, "If you would lend your servant a carriage in which I could enter Ch'in, I am sure of making you an important man in the state and increasing your manors even more. How will this do?"

The Lord of Meng-ch'ang prepared a carriage and gifts and dispatched him. Feng

---

[53] This dismissal and reinstatement does not fit what we know of T'ien Wen's chronology.

Huan went west and spoke to the King of Ch'in.[54]

"Of the wandering knights of the world, leaning over their carriage rails, pulling their reins, and entering west into Ch'in, not one does not desire to strengthen Ch'in and weaken Ch'i. Of those leaning over their carriage rails, pulling their reins, and entering east into Ch'i, not one does not desire to strengthen Ch'i and weaken Ch'in. These must be dominant and submissive states. The one whose power will stand no equal shall be dominant. The one who becomes dominant will win the world."

The King of Ch'in rose off his heels and asked him, "What may be done to prevent Ch'in from becoming the submissive one?"

Feng Huan said, "Do you know then of Ch'i's dismissal of the Lord of Meng-ch'ang?"

The King of Ch'in said, "I have heard this."

Feng Huan said, "It was the Lord of Meng-ch'ang who made Ch'i the world's most important state. Now the King of Ch'i has dismissed him because of slander. His heart is resentful and he is sure to betray Ch'i. If he betrays Ch'i and enters Ch'in, presenting to Ch'in the affairs of Ch'i and the facts of men and business, even the territory of Ch'i can be gained, not just mere dominance! Your Majesty should quickly send a messenger bearing gifts to secretly welcome the Lord of Meng-ch'ang. Do not lose this opportunity. If it happens that Ch'i wakes up and employs the Lord of Meng-ch'ang again, then where dominance and submission will fall cannot be known."

The King of Ch'in was delighted and sent ten carriages and one-hundred *yi* of gold to welcome the Lord of Meng-ch'ang. Feng Huan took leave, going first. When he arrived in Ch'i, he spoke to the king.

"Of the wandering knights of the world, leaning over their carriage rails, pulling their reins, and entering east into Ch'i, not one does not desire to strengthen Ch'i and weaken Ch'in. Of those leaning over their carriage rails, pulling their reins and entering west into Ch'in, not one does not desire to strengthen Ch'in and weaken Ch'i. Ch'in and Ch'in are dominant and submissive states. If Ch'in is strong then Ch'i is weak. The circumstances are such that they cannot both be dominant.

"Your servant has now privately heard that Ch'in has sent a messenger with ten carriages carrying one hundred *yi* of gold to welcome the Lord of Meng-ch'ang. [*2362*] If the Lord of Meng-ch'ang does not go west then that is the end of it. If he goes west as Prime Minister to Ch'in, the world will turn to him. Ch'in will be dominant and Ch'i submissive. As the submissive one, Lin-tzu and Chi-mo are in danger.

"Why not restore the Lord of Meng-ch'ang before the Ch'in messenger arrives, your Majesty, and give him yet more manors as an apology? The Lord of Meng-ch'ang is sure to be pleased and accept them. Although Ch'in is a powerful state, how can it invite the prime minister of another [state]? Thus you can deflect Ch'in's design and sever its strategy for hegemony and strength."

The King of Ch'i said, "Excellent!" then sent a man to the border to watch for the messenger of Ch'in. As soon as the Ch'in messenger's carriage entered Ch'i's borders, the Ch'i messenger raced back to inform him. The king summoned the Lord of Meng-ch'ang and restored his position as Prime Minister. He gave him his old estates and increased these by a thousand households. The messenger of Ch'in heard the Lord of Meng-ch'ang had resumed his post of Prime Minister of Ch'i, turned his carriage around, and left.

When the King of Ch'i dismissed the Lord of Meng-ch'ang, his guests all left. When he was later summoned and restored to his post, Feng Huan came out to welcome him back.

---

[54] The *Chan-kuo ts'e* version of this story has Feng Huan go to Wei rather than Ch'in.

Before arriving, the Lord of Meng-ch'ang let out a great sigh. "I once delighted in guests. In my treatment of them I never dared to forget one thing, and had three thousand household-retainers, as you know, Venerable Sir. As soon as they saw I had been dismissed, my guests all turned against me and left. Not one looked back. Now that I have been restored to my post thanks to you, Venerable Sir, what face do these guest have to see me again? If there is one who does see me again, I will surely spit in his face and humiliate him."

Feng Huan pulled on his reins, dismounted, and knelt and bowed. The Lord of Meng-ch'ang dismounted from his carriage and raised him up.

"Is this in apology for my retainers, Venerable Sir?"

Feng Huan said, "It is not in apology for your retainers, but because of My Lord's slip of the tongue. Some things are sure to arrive, and some matters are necessarily so. Do you understand this, My Lord?"

The Lord of Meng-ch'ang said, "I am foolish and do not understand what you mean."

"That which lives is sure to meet death. This is a thing which is sure to arrive. The rich and noble have many knights, the poor and base have few friends. This is a matter which is necessarily so. My lord, haven't you seen those rushing to market? When dawn breaks, they fight to enter the gates, shoulder to shoulder. After the sun has begun to set, those passing the market drop their shoulders and don't look back. It's not that they love the market in the morning and despise it at dusk, but that the things which they wanted are no longer there.

"When you lost your post, My Lord, your guests all left. It is not worth harboring resentment against knights or pointlessly cutting off the paths of guests because of this. I hope that My Lord will treat his guests as before."

The Lord of Meng-ch'ang knelt and bowed twice. "I respectfully obey your commands. Having heard your words, Venerable Sir, I dare not but accept your instructions."

[2363] His Honor the Grand Scribe says: "I once passed through Hsüeh and the youths of its villages were hot-tempered and violent, quite different from those of Tsou 鄒 and Lu 魯. I asked why and they said, 'The Lord of Meng-ch'ang attracted the families of perhaps sixty thousand highwaymen and criminals to Hsüeh.' The stories of our age say that the Lord of Meng-ch'ang was quite pleased with himself for his generosity to his retainers. His reputation was not a hollow one."

TRANSLATORS' NOTE

This chapter focuses on the first of the Four Lords, the Lord of Meng-ch'ang and his retainers. Retainers and their relationship to their lords is a sub-theme of this and the following three chapters (see also n. 2 to our translation of *Shih chi* Chapter 76). Ssu-ma Ch'ien expresses what he believes to have been a selfish nature in the Lord of Meng-ch'ang not only in his treatment of his retainers, but even in his government service. His letter to Ch'in encouraging it to attack his own state so that he might personally profit is the ultimate statement on that selfishness and this is reflected in the Grand Scribe's comment that the Lord "was quite pleased with himself for his generosity to his retainers." The contrast between his reasons for supporting retainers and those of the Lord of Hsin-ling (Chapter 77) will become apparent in the chapters which follow.

Despite the purposes for the Lord of Meng-ch'ang's seeking retainers, in the accounts of his own birth and the difficulties he faced as a boy, his miraculous escape from Ch'in, and his gradual discovery of the merits of Feng Huan, Ssu-ma Ch'ien returns from a style dominated by speeches in previous chapters to effective dramatic and narrative scenes. Even the structure of this chapter suggests the hand of a skilled editor in the front and back frames of which depict the a person initially scorned and finally seen for his talents (T'ien Ying's recognition of his son's worth and Meng-ch'ang's discovery Feng Huan's talent).

On a larger scale, this chapter follows those on the the rhetoricians who plied their speeches among the various states seeking to win hegemony for their lords, and those of the Ch'in generals who sought similar success on the battlefields, to begin the story of the Four Lords (continuing through Chapter 78) who opposed Ch'in and slowed its conquest of the Six States East of the Mount.

Dates are again a problem here, since the events of this memoir stride one of the fault lines in the differences between the *Shih chi*'s chronology and that revised by modern scholars--the history of the state of Ch'i in the late fourth century B.C. We have adopted Yang K'uan's 楊寬 chronology in our notes. If Yang's chronology is correct, Ssu-ma Ch'ien has either systematically altered the reigns and years given in the materials which were used to compose this chapter, or the materials from which this chapter was drawn were composed after the chronology was already confused. The former seems more likely, since these materials must have come from miscellaneous sources which were unlikely to all have the same mistake.

BIBLIOGRAPHY

I. Translations

Dolby, William and John Scott, trans. *Sima Qian, War-Lords, Translated with Twelve Other Stories from His Historical Records.* Edinburgh: Southside, 1974, pp. 69-86.

Franke, Herbert and Wolfgang Bauer. *Die Goldene Truhe.* Munich, 1962, pp. 15-19 (partial).

Haenisch, Erich. "Gestalten aus der Zeit der chinesischen Hegemoniekämpfe: Übersetzungen aus Sze-ma Ts'ien's Historischen Denkwürdigkeiten," *Abhandlungen für die Kunde des Morgenlandes,* XXXIV.2. Wiesbaden: Harrassowitz, 1962, pp. 1-13.

Nyitray, Vivian-Lee. "Mirrors of Virtue: Four 'Shih chi' Biographies." Unpublished Ph. D. dissertation, Stanford University, 1990.

Ōgawa Tamaki 小川環樹, trans. *Shiki retsuden* 史記列傳. Rpt. Tokyo: Chikuma Shobō,
    1986 (1969). pp. 98-105.
Yang Hsien-yi and Gladys Yang. *Records of the Historian.* Rpt. Hong Kong: The Commer-
    cial Press, 1985, pp. 76-88.

II. Studies

Ch'en Han-nien 陳瀚年. "Lun *Shih chi* Meng-ch'ang Chün, P'ing-yüan Chün, Ch'un-shen
    Chün, Hsin-ling Chün" 論史記孟嘗君平原君春申君信陵君, *Kuo-hsüeh ts'ung-k'an*
    國學叢刊, 10 (September 1942).
Nieh Kan-kung 聶紺弩. "Tu 'Tu Meng-ch'ang Chün chuan'" 讀讀孟嘗君傳, *Chung-kuo She-
    hui K'o-hsüeh Yüan Yen-chiu Yüan hsüeh-pao* 中國社會科學院研究院學報, 71.6
    (December 1985), 27 and 30.
Nyitray, *op. cit.*

The Lord of P'ing-yüan and Excellency Yü, Memoir 16

The Lord of P'ing-yüan

[76:2365] Chao Sheng 趙勝, the Lord of P'ing-yüan 平原, was one of the Noble Scions of Chao.[1] Among the Scions, Sheng was the most worthy. He delighted in guests,[2] and guests arrived by the thousands. The Lord of P'ing-yüan served as Prime Minister to King Hui-wen 惠文 (r. 298-266 B.C.) and King Hsiao-ch'eng 孝成 (r. 265-245 B.C.) of Chao. He left the Prime Minister's position three times and was restored to his post three times.[3] He was invested with East Wu-ch'eng 東武城.[4]

The belvederes of the Lord of P'ing-yüan's residence faced the houses of the common folk. Among the houses of the common folk there was a cripple who limped as he went to draw water from the well. A beauty of the Lord of P'ing-yüan, looking down from the top of the tower, saw him and burst out laughing. The next day the cripple went to the gate of the Lord of P'ing-yüan's house and made a request.

"Your servant has heard that My Lord's fondness of knights is such that they consider it nothing to travel a thousand miles to come here. This is through My Lord's ability to treat

---

[1] According to *Shih chi*, 77:2379, Chao Sheng was the younger brother of King Hui-wen of Chao. *Chan-kuo ts'e* (6:69a, *SPTK*) also quotes a speech by a Chao emissary in which Chao Sheng is referred to as King Hui-wen's brother-german.

P'ing-yüan was about 10 miles southwest of modern P'ing-yüan, Shantung (Tan Ch'i-hsiang 1:39-40).

[2] The words *pin* 賓 and *k'o* 客, are usually treated as synonyms, both meaning "guests," and they often occur together as a compound. There is a slight difference between them, however, with *pin* closest to English "guest" and *k'o* carrying the additional sense of someone living outside his native land or village. A further distinction which seems to follow from this is that the host generally refers to his visitor as *pin* and the visitor refers to himself as *k'o*. By the Warring States period, there had also evolved the institution of *shih-k'o* 食客, "kept retainers" or "household-retainers." These were quite distinct from guests: they were dependent on their "host's" largess for their livelihood, and seem to have been comparable to the "household knights" of medieval Europe. With the evolution of this new institution, the single word *k'o* was often used by itself to indicate this relationship. In order to distinguish these various senses in the translation, we use "guest" to translate both *pin* and *pin-k'o*, and "retainer" to translate *k'o* (occasionally "protege" might be more appropriate, but we have tried to be as consistent as possible). Other terms that imply a more official function for these retainers include "attendant before the gate," our translation of the term *men-hsia* 門下. These differed from "guests" in that these men were apparently required to attend their host's court functions. The *she-jen* 舍人 "houseman" apparently had other duties as well as attending court. For a fuller discussion of the position of "guests" in the pre-Ch'in to Han period, see T'ung-tsu Ch'u, *Han Social Structure* (Seattle: University of Washington Press), pp. 127-135.

[3] Liang Yü-sheng (30:1279) attempts to reconstruct the three dismissals and comes up with the following chronology: According to *Shih chi* 15:737 and 746, the Lord of P'ing-yüan became Chao's Prime Minister in the first year of King Hui-wen of Chao (298 B.C.) and in the first year of King Hsiao-ch'eng of Chao (265 B.C.). Liang claims that King Hui-wen once "presented Yüeh Yi with the Minister of State's seal" and that King Hsiao-ch'eng ceded Chao's territory east of the Chi river to Ch'i in order to obtain the services of T'ien Tan as general of Chao, after which T'ien remained in Chao as Prime Minister. As evidence that Yüeh Yi and T'ien Tan did serve as Chao's Prime Minister for some period of time, he notes that *Shih chi* 43:1816 says "the minister of state Yüeh Yi led the troops of Chao, Ch'in, Han, Wei, and Yen to attack Ch'i" in the 14th year of King Hui-wen (285 B.C.). According to *Shih chi*, 43:1824, in 265 B.C., T'ien Tan supposedly attacked Yen, while in 264 B.C., "T'ien Tan became Prime Minister." This would imply that Chao Sheng was restored to the Prime Minister's position for only a year or so at the beginning of King Hsiao-ch'eng's reign, after which he was dismissed in favor of T'ien Tan. As for Chao Sheng's third "restoration" to the Prime Minister's post, Liang concludes that this must simply have been omitted. Another possibility is that "three times" is used here to suggest the vagaries of a mercurial political career (cf. *Shih chi*, 119:3100 and *Kuo-yü* [18:5b, *SPPY*]).

[4] Eastern Wu-ch'eng was located in modern Wu-ch'eng county in Shantung (Ch'ien Mu, *Ti-ming k'ao*, 233).

knights nobly and concubines meanly. Your servant is cursed with an infirmity, yet My Lord's rear-palace women looked down and laughed at me. I beg to have the head of the one who laughed at me." The Lord of P'ing-yüan smiled and answered, "So be it." After the cripple had left, he laughed and said, "It seems this whelp actually wanted to kill my beauty because of a laugh. This is really too much!" In the end he did not kill the woman.

After more than a year had passed, his guests, gate attendants, and housemen gradually packed up and left, until more than half were gone. The Lord of P'ing-yüan wondered at it: "I have not once dared to treat you with less than due propriety, gentlemen. Why is it then that so many have gone?"

[2366] One of his gate attendants gate came forward and replied, "Because My Lord did not kill the one who laughed at the cripple, they felt that you loved belles and scorned knights, thus the knights left." At this, the Lord of P'ing-yüan cut off the head of the beauty who laughed at the cripple and went up to the gate of the cripple himself, presenting the head to him with his apologies. After this, his gate attendants gradually came back. At this time, Ch'i had [the Lord of] Meng-ch'ang 孟嘗, Wei had [the Lord of] Hsin-ling 信陵 and Ch'u had [the Lord of] Ch'un-shen 春申. Thus they competed in their attempts to sway and serve knights.

When Ch'in besieged Han-tan,[5] Chao sent the Lord of P'ing-yüan to seek aid by allying with Ch'u.[6] He arranged to go with twenty of his bravest, strongest household-retainers and gate attendants, men with both civil and martial prowess.

The Lord of P'ing-yüan said, "If we can attain victory through the civil arts that would be best. If we cannot attain victory through the civil arts, then we will swear a blood oath outside the great hall. We must obtain certain alliance before we return. I will not seek knights outside, but choose among my household-retainers. There are sufficient there."

He obtained nineteen men. None of the rest were worth choosing, and he was unable to fill the number of twenty. Among his attendants there was one Mao Sui 毛遂 who came forward and introduced himself to the Lord of P'ing-yüan. "I have heard that My Lord will join in alliance with Ch'u and has arranged to go with twenty household-retainers and attendants before the gate, that you will not seek these outside your household, and that you are short one man. I hope that My Lord might take me to fill the number [of twenty]."

"How many years has it been since your were placed among my gate attendants?" asked the Lord of P'ing-yüan.

"It has been three years since I was place here," said Mao Sui.

"A worthy knight in this world can be compared to a nail placed in a sack. The tip immediately shows. It has been three years since you were placed here among my gate attendants. My attendants have had no occasion to speak of you and I have had no occasion to hear of you. You must have nothing to speak *of*, Venerable Sir. You are no capable, Venerable Sir. You shall stay here, Venerable Sir!"

Mao Sui said, "Your servant merely asks to be placed in the sack today. If he could have been placed in the sack earlier, he would have burst out entirely, not just shown his tip."

[2367] The Lord of P'ing-yüan finally took Mao Sui with him. The other nineteen men looked at each other and smiled, but no one spoke. When Mao Sui arrived with them at Ch'u, he debated with the other nineteen, and they all conceded to him.

---

[5] Han-tan was the capital of Chao. The siege of Han-tan lasted for over a year, thus different dates are given in various sources for various events during the siege. According to Yang K'uan (pp. 711-712), the first attacks on Han-tan were in 259 B.C., and the final lifting of the siege occurred in 257 B.C.

[6] *Shih chi*, 43:1827 gives the date of this mission as the eighth year of King Hsiao-ch'eng (258 B.C.).

The Lord of P'ing-yüan, to ally with Ch'u, spoke of the advantages and disadvantages of alliance. He spoke from sunrise and at noon it was still not decided. The other nineteen men said to Mao Sui, "Go up, Venerable Sir."

Mao Sui put his hand on his sword, went up the steps without pausing,[7] and said to the Lord of P'ing-yüan, "The advantages and disadvantages of alliance can be put in two sentences and decided on. Why is it then that you have spoken of alliance since sunrise and not yet decided at noon?"

The King of Ch'u said to the Lord of P'ing-yüan, "Who is this retainer?"

The Lord of P'ing-yüan answered, "This is one of my housemen."

The King of Ch'u shouted at Mao. "Why don't you go down? I am speaking with Your Lord. Who do you think you are?"

Mao Sui put his hand on his sword and stepped forward. "Your Majesty shouts at me because you have the forces of Ch'u behind you. But within ten paces you cannot rely on the forces of Ch'u. Your life hangs in my hands. My Lord is before you, what do you mean by shouting at me?

"Moreover, I've heard that T'ang became ruler of the world with 70 *li* of land, and King Wen made vassals of the feudal lords with 100 *li* of earth. Was this merely because their soldiers were numerous? It was because they were truly able to make use of their potential and exert their authority. Now the lands of Ch'u are 5000 *li* [on a side] and those who hold halberds number 1,000,000. These are the resources of a Hegemon King. With Ch'u's might, there should be one in the world who can withstand her. Yet Pai Ch'i, a mere whelp, commanding a host of less than 100,000, marshalled his forces and fought with Ch'u.[8] After the first battle, he took Yen and Ying.[9] After the second battle he burned Yi-ling 夷陵.[10] After the third battle, he defiled Your Majesty's ancestors. This is a grudge which cannot be settled in a hundred generations. Chao is ashamed for you, and yet Your Majesty doesn't know enough to resent [your disgrace]. We would join in alliance for the sake of Ch'u, not for the sake of Chao. My Lord is before you, what do you mean by shouting at me?"

The King of Ch'u said, "Yes, yes. It is just as you have said, Venerable Sir. We will respectfully present our altars of the soil and grain and with these ally with you."

Mao Sui said, "Shall alliance be sworn?"

"It shall," said the King of Ch'u.

Mao Sui said to the King of Ch'u's courtiers, "Bring in the blood of a chicken, a dog, and a horse."[11]

[2368] Mao Sui held up the bronze platter with both hands and kneeling down, presented it to the King of Ch'u, saying, "Your Majesty should smear the blood on your lips to swear alliance. Next shall be My Lord, and next myself." Thus they swore alliance in the hall.

Holding the platter with his left hand, Mao Sui beckoned to the other nineteen with his right. "Smear this blood on your lips among yourselves in the courtyard. You gentlemen are

[7] Etiquette required those ascending the throne steps to have both feet together on each step before going on to the next one. Mao is walking up the steps in the normal way.

[8] Pai Ch'i's attacks on Ch'u occurred in 279-278 B.C. (see our translation of *Shih chi* Chapter 73).

[9] Yen was a previous capital of Ch'u and Ying the then-current capital of Ch'u. Some scholars believe that Yen and Ying should be one place, Yen-ying, but in *Shih chi* 73:2331, it states that Pai took Yen in 279 B.C. and Ying in 278 B.C. (see also n. 69 to our translation of *Shih chi* Chapter 69).

[10] Yi-ling was the location of the Ch'u kings ancestral tombs located (according to T'an Ch'i-hsiang, 2:11) just south of modern Yi-ch'ang 宜昌 City in Hupei.

[11] See n. 37 to our translation of Chapter 69 above.

mere mediocrities, [the sort of whom] it is said 'they accomplish matters through the offices of others."

Having sworn alliance, the Lord of P'ing-yüan returned home. When he reached Chao he said, "I will not dare to take the measure of a knight again. I have done this for as many as a thousand men, or at least hundreds, and I thought that I could not misjudge any man in the world. Yet today with Venerable Mao, I misjudged him. As soon as Venerable Mao arrived in Ch'u, he made the prestige of Chao greater than that of the Nine Cauldrons and the Great Lü Bells.[12] Venerable Mao, with his three inch tongue, was mightier than a force of a million. I will not dare to take the measure of a knight again." After this he made Mao Sui his Senior Retainer.

The Lord of P'ing-yüan having returned to Chao, Ch'u sent the Lord of Ch'un-shen to lead troops to the aid of Chao. Wei's Lord of Hsin-ling also seized the army of Chin Pi 晉鄙[13] under false pretenses and went to the aid of Chao. None of these had arrived however, and Ch'in pressed the siege of Han-tan.

[2369] Han-tan was in dire straits and about to surrender. The Lord of P'ing-yüan was deeply dismayed. The son of the officer in charge of Han-tan's relay station, Li T'ung 李同,[14] advised the Lord of P'ing-yüan.

"Is My Lord not afraid that Chao will fall?"

The Lord of P'ing-yüan said, "If Chao falls, I will become a slave, why would I not fear this?"

Li T'ung said, "The people of Han-tan now use human bones for kitchen kindling and exchange their children to eat. They can be said to have reached dire straits indeed! Yet My Lord's rear-palace women number in the hundreds. Your handmaids and concubines wear damask silk gauze and have meat and grain left over, while the common people's coarse cloth clothing is ragged and their rice dregs and husks are not enough to fill them. The people are fatigued and their weapons exhausted. Some sharpen wood into spears and arrows and yet My Lord's vessels and utensils, bells and chimes are untouched. If Ch'in takes Chao, where will you be able to get these? If Chao survives, why fear you will have to do without? If you could order your women, from your wife on down, to be assigned among the knights and foot soldiers, putting them to work by dividing the labor, and expend every object in your home to care for the knights, the knights in their suffering may easily be moved to gratitude."

The Lord of P'ing-yüan followed his advice and obtained three-thousand knights willing to die for him. Li T'ung led the three thousand into battle with the Ch'in army and because of them the Ch'in army retreated thirty *li*. Just then the rescue forces from Ch'u and Wei arrived, the Ch'in soldiers departed, and Han-tan was saved. Li T'ung died in battle and his father was enfeoffed as the Marquis of Li.

Excellency Yü wanted to request a fief for the Lord of P'ing-yüan because [the Lord of P'ing-yüan caused] the Lord of Hsin-ling to save Han-tan. Kung-sun Lung 公孫龍 heard of this and hitched up his carriage that night to see the Lord of P'ing-yüan. "I've heard that Excellency Yü wants to request a fief for you because [you caused] the Lord of Hsin-ling to save Han-tan. Is this true?"

"Yes," said the Lord of P'ing-yüan.

---

[12] Sacrificial vessels and ritual bells in the Chou state's ancestral temple.

[13] A general of the state of Wei. See our translation of *Shih chi* Chapter 77 for this incident.

[14] Ssu-ma Ch'ien's father's name was *T'an* 談 and he usually observes a taboo on this character replacing it where it is part of a name with the word *t'ung* 同. The Li T'ung mentioned here appears as Li T'an in other Han dynasty works, suggesting that the name in the original anecdote was in fact T'an.

"This will never do. That the king raised up Your Lordship to be Prime Minister of Chao was not because [men with] your intellect or ability were not to be found in Chao. That he ceded East Wu-ch'eng as your fief was not because he thought you had merit and other men of the state lacked accomplishments. Rather, it was because you were kin. When Your Lordship received the Prime Minister's seal, you did not decline, saying you were incapable, and when the king awarded you land, you did not claim that you had no merit; this too was because you were kin. Now you would seek enfeoffment for the Lord of Hsin-ling's rescue of Han-tan. This would be a kinsman receiving a city, with his merit calculated as that of a commoner of the state. This will certainly not do. Moreover, Excellency Yü will have two options.

[2370] "If his scheme succeeds, he will lay claim on you with the right half of the tally [to your fief]. If his scheme fails, you will owe him a favor for nothing. My Lord must not heed him."

The Lord of P'ing-yüan did not heed Excellency Yü's advice.

The Lord of P'ing-yüan died in the fifteenth year of King Hsiao-ch'eng of Chao (251 B.C.).[15] His descendants inherited the title and finally fell with Chao. The Lord of P'ing-yüan treated Kung-sun Lung very well. Kung-sun Lung was skilled in disputing on "the white and hard." When Tsou Yen 鄒衍 passed through Chao and spoke of the supreme way, [the Lord of P'ing-yüan] demoted Kung-sun Lung.[16]

Excellency Yü

Excellency Yü 虞 was a knight who traveled about offering advice. He advised King Hsiao-ch'eng of Chao wearing straw sandals and carrying a bamboo umbrella over his shoulder.[17] The first time he met with the king, he received one-hundred *yi* of gold and a pair of white-jade rings. The second time they met, he was made a Senior Excellency of Chao, thus he was called Excellency Yü.[18]

[2371] Ch'in and Chao fought at Ch'ang-p'ing 長平.[19] Chao was no match for Ch'in and lost a Chief Commandant.[20] The King of Chao summoned Lou Ch'ang 樓昌[21] and

---

[15] "So-yin" says that both *Shih chi* Chapters 15 and 43 give the fourteenth year of Hsiao-ch'eng as the date of Chao Sheng's death. *Shih chi*, 43:1827 does in fact say Chao Sheng died in the fourteenth year, but *Shih chi*, 15:749 says he died in the fifteenth year. Wang Shu-min (76:2362) suggests that perhaps a T'ang edition of *Shih chi* Chapter 15 recorded his death in the fourteenth year. Curiously, the "So-yin" commentary for *Shih chi*, 43:1828 says *Shih chi* Chapter 15 gives the fifteenth year for Chao Sheng's death, contradicting its own statement here.

[16] For brief notices of Kung-sun Lung and Tsou Yen, and the philosophical concepts of "hard and white," see our translation of Chapter 74.

[17] The straw sandals and umbrella mentioned here are intended to present Excellency Yü as a rustic peasant. The "travelling rhetoricians" who flourished at this time are often presented in the literature as poverty-stricken or holding extremely low social positions. The straw sandals were naturally worn mostly by the poorest members of society. The "bamboo umbrella" mentioned was apparently similar to the *li* 笠 still worn by Chinese farmers today (which are often quite large), except that it had a stick attached to it.

[18] "Excellency Yü" is also mentioned in *Han Fei Tzu*, where he is referred to as Yü Ch'ing 虞慶. "Chi-chieh" says that the Chin-dynasty commentator Chiao Chou 譙周 (199-270) claimed Yü was the name of the city he was enfeoffed with. Takigawa (76:12) argues that Yü must have been his *nomen*, since he was author of a work called *Yü-shih ch'un-ch'iu* 虞氏春秋.

[19] Ch'ang-p'ing was located about 5 miles northwest of modern Kao-p'ing 高平, Shansi (Tan Ch'i-hsiang 1:35-6). According to traditional historians, this was one of the greatest battles of Chinese antiquity. Yang K'uan

Excellency Yü. "Our army fights but is no match and now we have lost a commander. If We were to don armor and charge the enemy, how would that be?"

Lou Ch'ang said, "It would be of no use. It would be better to send a high-ranking emissary and come to terms."

Excellency Yü said, "When Ch'ang speaks of coming to terms, he must mean that if we do not come to terms, our army is sure to be destroyed, yet setting terms is up to Ch'in. In Your Majesty's judgment of Ch'in, do they want to destroy the army of Chao or not?"

The king said, "Ch'in spares no pains in its efforts. It certainly wishes to destroy our army."

Excellency Yü said, "If Your Majesty heeds your servant, you will send out an emissary with great treasures to attach yourself to Ch'u and Wei. Ch'u and Wei will want to obtain Your Majesty's treasures and are certain to accept our emissary. When Chao's emissary enters Ch'u and Wei, Ch'in is sure to suspect that the world is joining in alliance against it, and is sure to fear this. If we do this then terms can be reached."

The King of Chao did not listen. He agreed with the Lord of P'ing-yang 平陽[22] that terms should be reached and sent Cheng Chu 鄭朱[23] into Ch'in. Ch'in accepted him.

The King of Chao summoned Excellency Yü. "We sent the Lord of P'ing-yang to come to terms with Ch'in. Ch'in has already accepted Cheng Chu. What do you think of this?"

Excellency Yü said, "Your Majesty will not be able to come to terms and the army is sure to be destroyed. The emissaries of the world are all in Ch'in to congratulate them on their victory in battle. Cheng Chu is a high noble. When he enters Ch'in, the King of Ch'in and the Marquis of Ying 應[24] are sure to make much of his importance, displaying him for the world to see. Ch'u and Wei will believe that Chao is coming to terms and are certain to refuse to rescue Your Majesty. When Ch'in knows that the world will not rescue Your Majesty, then terms cannot be reached."

The Marquis of Ying did indeed display Cheng Chu before the world's emissaries who had come to congratulate Ch'in on its victory in battle and in the end was unwilling to come to terms. [Chao] suffered a great defeat at Ch'ang-p'ing and was besieged at Han-tan, becoming the laughing stock of the world.

[2372] After Ch'in abandoned its siege of Han-tan, the King of Chao paid homage and had Chao Shih 趙郝[25] arrange with Ch'in to award it six counties to make peace.[26] Excellency

(p. 711) gives 260 B.C. as the date of this battle. See our translations of Chapters 73 and 81 for more details of the battle.

[20] *Tu-wei* 都尉.

[21] A parallel to the following anecdote appears in *Chan-kuo ts'e* (6:58a, *SPTK*). Apparently a general of Chao, he is mentioned once in the *Shih chi* (43:1821) as leading troops in an unsuccessful attack on Wei.

[22] "Chi-chieh" (*Shih chi*, 43:1821) identifies the Lord of P'ing-yang was Chao Pao 趙豹. According to *Chan-kuo ts'e* (6:58a, *SPTK*), King Hui-wen, the Lord of P'ing-yüan, and Chao Pao were all brothers-german.

[23] Cheng Chu appears in the same *Chan-kuo ts'e* anecdote mentioned in n. 21 above., but is otherwise unknown.

[24] The Marquis of Ying was Fan Sui (see our translation of Chapter 79 for his biography).

[25] This may be the same person as Ch'iu Shih 仇郝, mentioned in several *Chan-kuo ts'e* anecdotes, and perhaps also the Ch'iu Yeh 仇液 in *Shih chi* Chapter 72.

[26] The following two anecdotes are combined into one in *Chan-kuo ts'e* (6:58b-62b, *SPTK*) with substantial differences. While *Shih chi* divides Excellency Yü's opposition in the two anecdotes between Chao Shih and Lou Huan, *Chan-kuo ts'e* makes Lou Huan his antagonist in both. *Shih chi* sets both the anecdotes after Ch'in's unsuccessful siege of Han-tan, while *Chan-kuo ts'e* places them after Chao's defeat at Ch'ang-p'ing. The *Chan-kuo ts'e* commentator Pao Piao 鮑彪 (*fl.* 1160) claims that the *Chan-kuo ts'e* version is superior, but it seems unlikely. To follow the *Chan-kuo ts'e* version would mean dispensing with the siege of Han-tan, at least as a consequence of

Yü told the King of Chao, "When Ch'in attacked Your Majesty, was it because they were weary that they returned home, or does Your Majesty think that they still had the strength to press forward, but refrained from attacking for love of you?"

The king said, "Ch'in spared no pains in its efforts to attack us. It is certain that they were weary and so returned home."

Excellency Yü said, "Ch'in attacked what their strength was unable to take, grew weary and returned home. Now Your Majesty presents them with what their strength was unable to take as a parting gift. This is helping Ch'in to attack yourself. When Ch'in attacks Your Majesty next year, you will be beyond salvation."

The king told Chao Shih what Excellency Yü had said. Chao Shih replied, "Is Excellency Yü truly able to assess the strength of Ch'in? If he truly knows that Ch'in is unable to press us and we do not give this scrap of land no bigger than a catapult stone, if Ch'in were then to attack Your Majesty next year, could you avoid ceding the heart of Chao in order to come to terms?"

The king said, "I will let you decide whether or not to cede this land. Can you be sure then of preventing Ch'in from attacking us again next year?"

Chao Shih said, "This is not something which your servant would dare to undertake. In other days, the Three Chin all had good relations with Ch'in. Now Ch'in is on good terms with Han and Wei and attacks Your Majesty. It must be that Your Majesty has not served Ch'in to a degree equal to that of Han and Wei. Now I can break off this attack brought on by your betrayal of an ally, open the passes and pass on our goods to Ch'in, equaling the relations of Han and Wei [with Ch'in]. If, by next year, Your Majesty has again provoked an attack from Ch'in, this must be because Your Majesty has fallen behind Han and Wei in serving Ch'in. This is not something which your servant would dare to undertake."

The king told this to Excellency Yü. Excellency Yü replied, "This fellow Shih says, 'If terms are not reached, when Ch'in attacks Your Majesty again next year, could you avoid ceding the heart of Chao in order to come to terms?' Yet if we come to terms now, Shih still cannot say for certain that Ch'in will not attack again. Then even though we cede six counties, what good will it be! Next year when they attack again, we will also cede what their strength is unable to take in order to come to terms. This is a policy of self-extermination. It would be better not to come to terms. Although Ch'in is 'skilled in attack,' it was not able to take six counties. Although Chao was 'unable to defend,' in the end it did not lose six counties. If Ch'in becomes weary and returns home, its troops are certain to be exhausted. If we can buy the world's [help] with our six cities and attack the exhausted Ch'in [troops] with them, what we lose to the world we gain in repayment from Ch'in. Our state will then still have some benefit. How is that compared to ceding territory for no good reason, [*2373*] weakening ourselves and strengthening Ch'in?"

"Now Shih says, 'Ch'in has good relations with Han and Wei and attacks Chao.[27] It must be that Your Majesty does not serve Ch'in as well as Han and Wei.' If Your Majesty were to serve up six cities every year to Ch'in, you would run out of cities for no purpose. Next year when Ch'in again demands that you cede territory, will Your Majesty give it to them? If you don't, you are throwing away your previous merit and inviting disaster from Ch'in. If you do, you will have no land with which to supply them. The saying goes, 'The strong are skilled at attack, the weak unable to defend themselves.' Now if we sit and obey Ch'in, Ch'in's soldiers will not be exhausted and they will obtain much land. This is

Chao's defeat at Ch'ang-p'ing.

[27] The sixteen characters which follow here (and in the *Po-na* [76:8a] edition and *Chien-pen* [76:7a-b]) are an interpolation and we have omitted them in our translation (see Wang Nien-sun, 4:28a-b).

strengthening Ch'in and weakening Chao. To cede land from an ever-weaker Chao to an ever-stronger Ch'in, it would certainly be in their interests to continue. Moreover, Your Majesty's territories can be exhausted, but Ch'in's demands will never end. To meet endless demands with exhaustible territory is certain to mean the end of Chao."

The King of Chao had not settled his plans when Lou Huan 樓緩 came from Ch'in.[28] The king discussed his plans with Lou Huan. "Which would be more auspicious, to give Ch'in land or not to?"

Lou Huan declined to speak. "This is not something which your servant could know."

The king said, "Even so, try speaking your private thoughts."

Lou Huan replied, "Has Your Majesty heard then of Kung-fu Wen-po's 公甫文伯 mother?[29] Kung-fu Wen-po was in office in Lu, where he died of an illness. There were two women who killed themselves in their rooms because of his death. When his mother heard of this, she would not wail for him. Her Personal Attendant[30] said, "Who ever heard of losing a son and not wailing for him?" His mother said, "Confucius was a worthy man. When he was expelled from Lu, this fellow would not go with him. Now that he has died, two of his ladies have killed themselves for him. It must be that he treated his betters lightly and his ladies dearly." For a mother to speak so, she must be a worthy mother. For a wife to speak so, she could not but be regarded as a jealous wife. Thus although the speech might be the same, when those who speak are different, the intention changes. Now your servant has just come from Ch'in. If I were to say don't give Ch'in the land, it would be an unwise plan. If I were to say give the land, I fear that Your Majesty would think I was speaking on Ch'in's behalf. If your servant were planning for Your Majesty, I would say it would be better to give it."

The king said, "So be it."

[2374] When Excellency Yü heard this, he went in to see the king and said, "This is specious advice, Your Majesty must be sure not to give this land!"

Lou Huan heard this and went to see the king. The king again told Lou Huan what Excellency Yü had said.

Lou Huan replied, "That is not so. Excellency Yü has grasped the first point, but not the second. Now that Ch'in and Chao are locked in struggle, the whole world rejoices. Why? They are saying, 'We will side with the stronger and take advantage of the weaker.' Now that the troops of Chao are pressed by Ch'in, the emissaries of the world offering congratulations on victory in battle will all be in Ch'in. Thus it would be better to quickly cede territory and make peace, in order to confuse the rest of the world and console the hearts of Ch'in. Otherwise, the world will use the anger of Ch'in and seize the exhaustion of Chao to split it up like a melon. When Chao is about to be lost, how can we take steps against Ch'in? Thus I say that Excellency Yü has grasped the first point but not the second. I hope that Your Majesty might make your decision based on this, without further planning."

When Excellency Yü heard this, he went to see the king and said, "Dangerous indeed are Lou Tzu's efforts for Ch'in! This will lead the world to suspect Chao even more deeply, and in what way will it console the heart of Ch'in? Why does he not speak of the weakness this would display before the world? Moreover, when your servant said do not give the land, I did not mean simply never to give it. Ch'in has demanded six cities from Your Majesty. Now Your Majesty should present Ch'i with six cities. Ch'i is a mortal enemy of Ch'in. To gain Your Majesty's six cities and join together with us in striking at Ch'in in the west, Ch'i

---

[28] Lou Huan had previously served as Prime Minister of Ch'in (see also our translation of *Shih chi,* 72:2324).

[29] On Kung-fu Wen-po see *Tso chuan* (Yang, *Tso chuan,* Ting 5 and Ai 3, pp. 447 and 470 respectively) and Wang Li-ch'i, *Jen-piao,* p. 310.

[30] *Hsiang-shih* 相室.

would follow Your Majesty before the speech could be presented. If this were done, Your Majesty's loss to Ch'i would be more than regained from Ch'in. Ch'i and Chao's deep grudge could be repaid, while showing the world Your Majesty's ability in action. Let word of this leak out, Your Majesty, and before the troops get a peek at the border, your servant will see great gifts from Ch'in arriving in Chao, seeking to come to terms with Your Majesty rather than the other way around. When Ch'in comes asking for terms and Han and Wei hear of it, they will be sure to hold Your Majesty in great honor. Holding Your Majesty in great honor, they are sure to bring out great treasures to present to Your Majesty. Thus with one stroke Your Majesty can make ties with three states and turn the tables on Ch'in."

The King of Chao said, "Excellent." He then sent Excellency Yü east to see the King of Ch'i, and consulted on a plan against Ch'in. Before Excellency Yü had returned, the emissaries of Ch'in were already in Chao. When Lou Huan heard this, he fled. After this Chao enfeoffed Excellency Yü with a city.

[2375] Not long after, Wei asked for an alliance. King Hsiao-ch'eng of Chao summoned Excellency Yü for consultations. When he passed the Lord of P'ing-yüan, the Lord said, "I hope that you will speak for alliance." Excellency Yü entered and saw the king.[31]

The king said, "Wei has asked for an alliance."

He replied, "Wei has made a mistake."

The king said, "We thus did not grant their request."

He replied, "Your Majesty has made a mistake."

The king said, "Wei asked for an alliance and you say that Wei has made a mistake. I did not accede to this and you say that I've made a mistake too. Do you mean that alliance is unacceptable or not?"

He replied, "Your servant has heard that if a small state conducts affairs in concert with a great state when there is benefit, the great state will receive the good fortune and when there is failure, the small state will receive the misfortune. Now Wei as a small state asks for its misfortune, and Your Majesty as a ruler of great state declines your good fortune. Thus your servant said that Your Majesty has made a mistake and Wei has too. My own opinion is that alliance would be to our advantage."

The king said, "Excellent." He then joined in alliance with Wei.

When Excellency Yü, for the sake of Wei Ch'i 魏齊,[32] gave up the fief of a ten-thousand-household marquis and the seal of a minister, he traveled in secret with Wei Ch'i until they had at last left Chao and were hard pressed in Liang [i.e., Wei]. After Wei Ch'i had died, things went badly with Excellency Yü, so he composed a book which for earlier times utilized the *Spring and Autumn* [*Annals*] and for later times viewed the events of near generations. It included "Chieh-yi" 節義 (Standards and Principles), "Ch'eng-hao" 稱號 (Titles and Terms), "Ch'uai-mo" 揣摩 (Second-guessing), "Cheng-mou" 政謀 (Political Consultations),

---

[31] In the *Chan-kuo ts'e* version of this story (6:72a, *SPTK*), Wei attempts to gain alliance by having the Lord of P'ing-yüan present its case, but the King of Chao refuses the Lord of P'ing-yüan's presentation three times. By omitting this part of the story, the *Shih chi* version robs the Lord of P'ing-yüan's appearance here of any meaning. Possibly in rewriting the story, Ssu-ma Ch'ien neglected to excise this passage, or perhaps a sentence has dropped out of the current *Shih chi* text.

[32] Wei Ch'i was once the Prime Minister of Ch'i. He beat his underling, Fan Sui, for an offense. When Fan became Prime Minister of Ch'in, he demanded that Ch'i send him Wei Ch'i. Wei Ch'i fled to Chao, where he enlisted the help of Excellency Yü. When the King of Chao appeared ready to obey Ch'in's demand for Wei Ch'i, Excellency Yü fled with Wei Ch'i to Wei where he hoped to take refuge under the Lord of Hsin-ling. When the latter did not immediately welcome him, Wei Ch'i committed suicide (see also our translation of *Shih chi* Chapter 79 below).

altogether in eight *p'ien*. With this he criticized the merits and faults of statecraft. The ages have transmitted it as *Yü-shih ch'un-ch'iu* 虞氏春秋 (The Spring and Autumn of Yü).[33]

[2376] His Honor the Grand Scribe says: "The Lord of P'ing-yüan was elegant indeed, a fine gentleman in a foul age, but he did not see things in the broadest light. A country saying goes, "Profit makes wise men fools." The Lord of P'ing-yüan was tempted by Feng T'ing's 馮亭 pernicious advice and caused Chao to lose over 400,000 soldiers at Ch'ang-p'ing and almost lose Han-tan.[34]

Excellency Yü anticipated events and deduced men's emotions. In drawing up policies for Chao, how skilled was his draftsmanship! But when he could not bear [to ignore] Wei Ch'i, and in the end was hard pressed in Ta Liang, even an incompetent man would have known this was a bad choice, much less a worthy man. But if Excellency Yü had not known the depths of sorrow he would not have been able to compose his book and reveal himself to later generations.

---

[33] This text is now lost. Some scholars have suggested that fragmentary texts found with the Ma-wang-tui silk manuscripts may be identified with this book.

[34] Feng T'ing was the governor of Shang-tang, a major city of the state of Han. See our translation of *Shih chi* Chapter 73 and also 43:1825 for further details involving Feng T'ing. "Chi-chieh" (*Shih chi,* 76:2376) quotes Chiao Chou 譙周 (199-270) as saying, "the fall of the Ch'ang-p'ing troops was the fault of the King of Chao for believing an enemy spy and changing generals. Why blame the Lord of P'ing-yüan for accepting Feng T'ing?" In fact, however, Ssu-ma Ch'ien clearly blames Chao Sheng for his failure to perceive Feng T'ing's attempt to deliberately lure Chao into a war with Ch'in in order to provide support for Han.

TRANSLATORS' NOTE

This text is the second of the depictions of the Four Lords. In addition to the Lord of P'ing-yüan, it also treats a knight, Excellency Yü, who had advised the Lord. The two sections differ considerably.

The former resembles Chapter 75 in the vivid narratives of the crippled retainer and Mao Sui. But, although the Lord of P'ing-yüan was as unsuccessful as the Lord of Meng-ch'ang, his failure seems due more to his failure to "see things in the broadest light" rather than the to the self-serving disposition Ssu-ma Ch'ien found in the Lord of Meng-ch'ang.

In Excellency Yü we gain a better understanding of one of the types of men who were sought as retainers. Yü is obviously not a warrior. In his loyalty and his perception of other men's strengths, he provided someone from a tawdry era in Chinese history whom Ssu-ma Ch'ien could sympathize. Ssu-ma Ch'ien also praises Yü's skill in strategy, condemning him merely for a "bad choice." The motivations for Yü's composition of his *Spring and Autumn* are, moreover, those attributed to many writers in the *Shih chi,* and may even have been shared by Ssu-ma Ch'ien himself.

This chapter may also be read as paired with that of Pai Ch'i and Wang Chien (Chapter 73). In Chapter 73 we see the triumph of Ch'in at Ch'ang-p'ing; here we have a description of the various events from the losing Chao point of view.

BIBLIOGRAPHY

I. Translations

Dolby, William and John Scott, trans. *Sima Qian, War-Lords, Translated with Twelve Other Stories from His Historical Records.* Edinburgh: Southside, 1974, pp. 87-102.
Haenisch, Erich. "Gestalten aus der Zeit der chinesischen Hegemoniekämpfe: Übersetzungen aus Sze-ma Ts'ien's Historischen Denkwürdigkeiten," *Abhandlungen für die Kunde des Morgenlandes,* XXXIV.2. Wiesbaden: Harrassowitz, 1962, pp. 14-26.
Nyitray, Vivian-Lee. "Mirrors of Virtue: Four 'Shih chi' Biographies." Unpublished Ph. D. dissertation, Stanford University, 1990.
Ōgawa Tamaki 小川環樹, trans. *Shiki retsuden* 史記列傳. Rpt. Tokyo: Chikuma Shobō, 1986 (1969). pp. 106-12.

II. Studies

Fu Yi 傅義. "Tu *Shih chi* 'P'ing-yüan Chun lieh-chuan'" 讀史記平原君列傳, *Yü-wen hsüeh-hsi*, 1956.8.
Nyitray, *op. cit.*

The Noble Scion of Wei, Memoir 17

[77:2377] The Noble Scion of Wei, Wu-chi 無忌, was a younger son of King Chao 昭 of Wei (r. 295-277 B.C.) and a younger half-brother of King An-hsi 安釐 of Wei (r. 276-243 B.C.). When King Chao passed away, King An-hsi ascended the throne and enfeoffed the Noble Scion as the Lord of Hsin-ling 信陵.¹ At the time, Fan Sui 范睢² had fled from Wei and become Prime Minister of Ch'in. Because of his resentment against Wei Ch'i 魏齊, Ch'in's troops besieged [the capital of Wei] Ta Liang 大梁, crushed Wei's army at the foot of Hua-yang 華陽,³ and put Mang Mou 芒卯 to flight.⁴ The King of Wei and the Noble Scion were dismayed.

The Noble Scion was by nature kindly and humbled himself before knights; worthy or unworthy, he treated all knights with humility and courtesy, rather than daring to treat them with arrogance because of his wealth and rank. Because of this, knights for thousands of *li* around competed in turning to him, and he attracted three-thousand household-retainers. At the time, the Noble Scion's worthiness and the number of his retainers was such that the feudal lords did not dare send troops or plot against Wei for over ten years.⁵

The Noble Scion was playing *liu-po*⁶ with the King of Wei, when the northern border sent word that beacons had been raised, signaling that "Invaders from Chao are coming, and will soon cross the border." The King of Wei put down his game-piece and prepared to summon his great vassals for consultations.

The Noble Scion stopped the King. "The King of Chao is only hunting in the fields, not invading." He resumed playing *liu-po* as before. The King was frightened, and his mind was not on the game. After a short time had passed, word came from the north again, saying, "The King of Chao is only hunting, not invading." The King of Wei was astounded and said, "How did you know this, Noble Scion?"

The Noble Scion said, "There is one of your servant's retainers who can learn many details of the King of Chao's secret affairs; my retainer constantly reports to me whatever the King of Chao is doing, and this is how your servant knew."

After this, the King of Wei feared the Noble Scion's worth and ability, and did not dare entrust the Noble Scion with [*2378*] the reins of state.

There was a hermit in Wei called Hou Ying 侯嬴. He was seventy years old, his household was poor, and he served as watchman at the Yi-men 夷門 Gate of Ta Liang. When the Noble Scion heard of him, he went to pay his respects, intending to present lavish gifts.

¹ Ch'ien Mu (*Ti-ming k'ao*, p. 172) believes that Hsin-ling was located at Ko-hsiang 葛鄉 in Ning-ling 寧陵 of Honan. Hsia Ch'iung-ying 夏瓊英 (Wang Li-ch'i, 77:1823) thinks it was west of Ning-ling. According to *Shih chi*, 15:742, Wei Wu-chi was enfeoffed at Hsin-ling in 276 B.C., the first year of King An-hsi's reign.

² See his biography in *Shih chi* Chapter 79. According to that account, Fan Sui was accused of revealing Wei's state secrets to Ch'i and was humiliated and tortured by Wei's Prime Minister, Wei Ch'i 魏齊. Fan managed to escape to Ch'in and after an audience with King Chao 昭 of Ch'in (r. 306-251 B.C.), became Ch'in's Prime Minister, after which he swore to take revenge against Wei Ch'i.

³ A mountain located about 10 miles southeast of modern Cheng-chou 鄭州, Honan (Tan Ch'i-hsiang, 1:35-6).

⁴ Ch'in besieged Ta Liang in 275 B.C. and defeated Wei at Hua-yang in 273 B.C. (*Shih chi*, 15:743). Mang Mou was the Wei commander in the latter battle (see *Shih chi*, 15:743-44, 44:1854, and 73:2331-37). According to *Shih chi*, 79:2412, Fan Sui became Prime Minister of Ch'in in 266 B.C. The sequence of events in this first paragraph is thus anachronistic.

⁵ That is, except Ch'in. *Shih chi*, 15:742-5 records that between 276 and 266 B.C., the decade after Wei Wu-chi was enfeoffed as the Lord of Hsin-ling, Ch'in attacked Wei several times: in 275 B.C. it besieged Ta Liang, in 268 B.C. it took Hui-ch'eng 懷城, and two years after it took Lin-ch'iu 廩丘.

⁶ See n. 65 to our translation of *Shih chi* Chapter 69.

[Hou Ying] refused to accept. "Your servant has cultivated himself and kept his conduct pure for decades; he will never accept the Noble Scion's money because of his poverty as a gate watchman."

After this, the Noble Scion set out wine and assembled many guests. The guests having taken their places, the Noble Scion, leading horsemen and carriages, went to escort the Scholar Hou of Yi-men himself, with the left side of his carriage vacant.[7] Scholar Hou straightened his worn clothing and cap and mounted directly onto the position of honor in the carriage carrying the Noble Scion without yielding, intending in this way to scrutinize the Noble Scion. The Noble Scion held the reins even more deferentially. Scholar Hou told the Noble Scion, "I have a retainer among the marketplace butchers. I hope that you might trouble your carriages and horsemen to call on him."

The Noble Scion drove the carriage into the marketplace and Scholar Hou dismounted to see his retainer, Chu Hai 朱亥; watching out of the corner of his eyes, he deliberately stood there for some time talking with his retainer, secretly observing the Noble Scion. The Noble Scion's countenance became even more amicable. At the time, the generals, ministers, and royalty of Wei and their guests filled his hall, waiting for the Noble Scion to present the wine, the tradesmen watched the Noble Scion holding the reins, and the attendant horsemen all cursed Scholar Hou under their breath. When Scholar Hou saw that the Noble Scion's countenance had not changed, he took leave of his retainer and mounted the carriage. When they reached his house, the Noble Scion led Scholar Hou in, put him in the seat of honor, and introduced him to each of the guests. The guests were all astonished. When they were all in their cups, the Noble Scion rose and made a toast before Scholar Hou.

Scholar Hou then told the Noble Scion, "Today I have done enough for you, Noble Scion. I, Ying, am a gate-keeper at Yi-men Gate, yet the Noble Scion personally troubled his carriages and horsemen, escorting me himself to this host of men and this sea of mats. Inappropriate though it was to call on me, the Noble Scion insisted on calling. Thus it was that I determined to make a name for the Noble Scion, and had the Noble Scion's carriage and horsemen stand so long in the marketplace, calling on my retainer while observing the Noble Scion. The Noble Scion was even more deferential. The tradesmen all thought me a small man and the Noble Scion a man of honor who humbled himself before knights." [*2379*] At this the banquet ended and Scholar Hou became Senior Retainer.

Scholar Hou told the Noble Scion, "The butcher I called on, Chu Hai, is a worthy man, yet none in the world could appreciate him, and he thus retired among the butchers."

The Noble Scion went several times to pay his respects, but Chu Hai deliberately neglected to return the courtesy. The Noble Scion wondered at this.

In the twentieth year of King An-hsi of Wei (258 B.C.), King Chao of Ch'in 秦昭王 (r. 306-251 B.C.), having crushed Chao's Ch'ang-p'ing 長平 army,[8] dispatched more troops to besiege Han-tan 邯鄲.[9] The Noble Scion's elder sister was Lady of the Lord of P'ing-yüan,[10] younger brother of King Hui-wen of Chao; [she] sent letters again and again to the King of Wei and the Noble Scion asking for help from Wei. The King of Wei sent General Chin Pi 晉鄙 to lead 100,000 troops to the aid of Chao. The King of Ch'in sent an envoy to tell the King of Wei: "We are attacking Chao and it will fall any day now. If one of the feudal lords dares to help it, after seizing Chao we will be sure to move troops to attack him first."

---

[7] The left seat was the seat of honor (Takigawa, 77:5).

[8] Various aspects of this important battle are narrated throughout the *Shih chi*. See particularly chapters 73, 76, and 81.

[9] The capital of Chao, located near modern Han-tan in Hopei (Tan Ch'i-hsiang, 1:37-8).

[10] See his biography in *Shih chi* Chapter 76.

The King of Wei was afraid and sent a man to stop Chin Pi and have him remain encamped at Yeh 鄴.[11] In name aiding Chao, in fact he grasped both ends of the situation and
watched. The caps and carriage canopies of the messengers of the Lord of P'ing-yüan followed one after another to Wei, rebuking the Noble Scion of Wei:

"The reason that I [the Lord of P'ing-yüan] bound myself through marriage with the
Noble Scion was because I thought that the Noble Scion's lofty principles would enable him to
hasten to those in difficult straits. Now Han-tan might surrender any day to Ch'in, yet Wei's
aid has not arrived; where is the Noble Scion's hastening to those in difficult straits? Moreover, though the Noble Scion may think little enough of me to abandon me, allowing me to surrender to Ch'in, does he feel no love for his elder sister?"

The Noble Scion was dismayed by this, begging the King of Wei again and again,
while his guests and rhetoricians persuaded the king with myriad arguments. The King of Wei
feared Ch'in and heeded the Noble Scion not at all. The Noble Scion, realizing that he would
never be able to gain [help] from the king and determined that he would not survive himself
while allowing Chao to perish, invited his guests, gathered more than a hundred chariots and
horsemen, and prepared to confront the army of Ch'in with his retainers and die together with
Chao.

[2380] When [the Noble Scion's] retinue passed through Yi-men Gate, he saw Scholar
Hou, and told him of why he was preparing to die against the Ch'in troops. He bid farewell
and set out. Scholar Hou said, "Do your best, Noble Scion; your aged vassal cannot follow."

After the Noble Scion had proceeded several *li,* he became displeased. "My treatment
of Scholar Hou has been adequate in every respect, the entire world has heard of it. Now that
I am about to die, Scholar Hou hasn't a single sentence or half a phrase to see me off; could it
be that I have failed in some way?"

He led the carriages back again and asked Scholar Hou. Scholar Hou laughed and
said, "Your servant knew that you would return, Noble Scion. The Noble Scion delights in
knights, and his name is renowned throughout the world. Now that you have difficulty, you
have no better plan than to confront the army of Ch'in; one might compare this to throwing
meat to a hungry tiger. What merit is there in this? What use has your patronage been? Thus
you treated me generously, Noble Scion, so when you departed and I did not see you off, I
knew that you would resent this and return."

The Noble Scion knelt, bowed twice and questioned him. Scholar Hou dismissed the
others and spoke privately with him. "I have heard that Chin Pi's military tally is always kept
in the king's bedchamber, and Consort Ju 如 is now highest in his favor; going in and out of
the king's bedchamber, it is within her means to steal it. I have also heard that Consort Ju's
father was killed by a man and that Consort Ju nursed [her hatred] for three years, and from
the king on down sought [someone] to repay her father's foe, but she was unable to do so.
Consort Ju wept for you, Noble Scion, and you sent your retainer to cut off her foe's head,
presenting it to Consort Ju with your respects. Consort Ju's willingness to die for you, Noble
Scion, is such that she would refuse no request; it is only that there has been no way for her to
do this. If you only once open your mouth, Noble Scion, and ask Consort Ju, Consort Ju is
sure to give her word, and you may then obtain the tiger tally, seize Chin Pi's army, aid Chao
in the north, and repel Ch'in in the west; this is an expedition worthy of the Five Hegemons."

The Noble Scion followed his plan and asked Consort Ju. Consort Ju did indeed steal
Chin Pi's military tally and give it to the Noble Scion.

---

[11] South of modern Lin-chang 臨漳 in Honan (Ch'ien Mu, *Ti-ming k'ao*, p. 426).

The Noble Scion set out. Scholar Hou said, "'In the interest of the state, when a commander is abroad, there will be orders from his ruler he will not accept.'[12] Even though you match his tally, Noble Scion, Chin Pi may not give you the troops, but instead send back a request [for confirmation]; your task is then sure to be endangered. Your servant's retainer Chu Hai can go with you, Noble Scion. This man is a knight of great strength. If Chin Pi heeds you, that would be best; if he does not heed you, you may have [Chu Hai] strike him down."

[2381] At this the Noble Scion wept. Scholar Hou asked, "Are you afraid to die, Noble Scion? Why weep?"

The Noble Scion said, "Chin Pi is a blustering veteran general; when I go, I fear he will not listen, and I will certainly have to kill him; it was for this I wept. I would never fear death!"

After this, the Noble Scion went to make his request of Chu Hai. Chu Hai laughed and said, "I am only a butcher brandishing a chopper in the marketplace, yet the Noble Scion personally inquired after me again and again. The reason I did not return your courtesy was because I thought petty propriety useless. Now that the Noble Scion is in dire straits, this is the moment I shall serve him with my life." He went with the Noble Scion.

The Noble Scion called on Scholar Hou and thanked him. Scholar Hou said, "I should accompany you, but I am aged and unable to. Let me see you off [with the promise] that I shall count the days your journey should take, then face north the day the Noble Scion arrives at Chin Pi's camp cut my throat." The Noble Scion then set out.

When he reached Yeh, the Noble Scion falsely claimed that the King of Wei had ordered him to replace Chin Pi. Chin Pi joined the tallies; he was suspicious, and raising his hand and gazing at the Noble Scion said, "I am now in command of a host of one hundred thousand camped on the border. This is the state's weightiest appointment, yet you come in a single chariot to replace me. How can this be?" He decided not to heed them.

Chu Hai had hidden a forty-catty iron hammer in his sleeve. He hammered Chin Pi to death and the Noble Scion took command of Chin Pi's army. He drilled the troops and sent out a command to the army. "If father and son are both in the army, the father shall return home; if elder and younger brothers are both in the army, the elder brother shall return home; if there are only sons without brothers, they shall return home to care [for their parents]." He obtained eighty-thousand picked men and led his troops forward to attack the army of Ch'in. The army of Ch'in lifted the siege and left, and thus Han-tan was saved and Chao preserved.

The King of Chao and the Lord of P'ing-yüan greeted the Noble Scion at the city limits themselves, and the Lord of P'ing-yüan, carrying a quiver with arrows on his back,[13] went in front and led the way for the Noble Scion. The King of Chao knelt, bowed twice, and said, "Of the worthy men since ancient times, there is none who can match the Noble Scion." At the time, the Lord of P'ing-yüan did not dare compare himself.

After the Noble Scion parted with Scholar Hou and reached [Chin Pi's] camp, Scholar Hou did indeed face north and cut his throat.

[2382] The King of Wei was angry with the Noble Scion for stealing his military tally and killing Chin Pi under false pretenses, and the Noble Scion realized this. After repelling Ch'in and preserving Chao, the Noble Scion sent a general to lead his army back to Wei, while the Noble Scion and his retainers remained in Chao. King Hsiao-ch'eng of Chao,

---

[12] Cf. our translation of *Shih chi*, 65:2158 and n. 10 to that chapter.

[13] Hsia Ch'iung-ying (Wang Li-ch'i, 77:1826) notes that this is a very formal way of welcoming someone important. In *Shih chi*, 117:3047, local officials of Szechwan met Ssu-ma Hsiang-ju, who was serving as a special messenger of the emperor, carrying crossbows and arrows on their backs (*fu nu shih* 負弩矢) as they led him on his way.

indebted to the Noble Scion for seizing Chin Pi's troops under false pretenses and preserving Chao, planned with the Lord of P'ing-yüan to invest the Noble Scion with five towns. When the Noble Scion heard of it, his attitude became proud and pompous and his countenance became smug. One of his retainers advised the Noble Scion: "There are things that one must not forget, and there are other things that one must forget. If a man does you a favor, Noble Scion, you must not forget this. If you do someone a favor, Noble Scion, I would hope that you might forget this. Moreover, in feigning an order from the King of Wei to seize Chin Pi's troops and help Chao, you have earned merit in Chao, Noble Scion, but you have not been a loyal vassal of Wei. Yet now you take pride in yourself and grow smug over [your actions]. This is not what I personally would choose for you to do, Noble Scion.[14]"

At this, the Noble Scion immediately began to reproach himself as if there were no place to hide his shame. The King of Chao swept the steps [of the hall] and greeted him himself. Acting in the role of host, he led the Noble Scion to the west steps. The Noble Scion stepped aside, declined the honor, and ascended by the east steps.[15] He spoke of his offenses and faults, of his betrayal of Wei and his lack of merit in Chao. The King of Chao accompanied him drinking until dusk, but fearing that the Noble Scion would decline and withdraw, he did not have the heart to mention the offer of five cities.

The Noble Scion eventually remained in Chao. The King of Chao made Hao 鄗[16] the bath-town[17] of the Noble Scion, while Wei offered Hsin-ling to the Noble Scion again as his fief. The Noble Scion remained in Chao.

The Noble Scion had heard that Chao had hermits named Master Mao 毛, who concealed himself among the gamblers and Master Hsüeh 薛, who concealed himself among the wine-sellers. The Noble Scion wished to see these two men, but the two concealed themselves and refused to see the Noble Scion. The Noble Scion heard of their whereabouts and went there in disguise and on foot in order to make their acquaintance. They got along very well. When the Lord of P'ing-yüan heard this, he said to his Lady, "I first heard that my Lady's younger brother the Noble Scion was without a match in the world. Now I hear that he foolishly associates with gamblers and wine-sellers. The Noble Scion is himself just a fool!"

The Lady told this to the Noble Scion. The Noble Scion [*2383*] bade farewell to the Lady and departed. "I first heard that the Lord of P'ing-yüan was worthy, thus to please the Lord of P'ing-yüan I turned my back on the King of Wei and aided Chao. [But] the way the Lord of P'ing-yüan seeks associates is nothing but an act of extravagance, he does not search for [talented] knights. When I lived in Ta Liang, I often heard these two men were worthy, and when I arrived in Chao, I feared that I would not be able to meet them. I feared that *they*

[14] This conversation is also recorded in *Chan-kuo ts'e* (7:61b, *SPTK*), where the name of the retainer is given as T'ang Chü 唐且.

[15] The "Ch'ü-li" 曲禮 chapter of *Li chi* 禮記 describes the etiquette of meeting as follows: "The host takes the east steps while the guest takes the west steps. If the guest is lower in rank, he takes the steps of the host [as if to follow him up them]." 主人就東階，客就西階，客若降等，則就主人之階 (see *Li-chi chu-shu* 禮記注疏, 1:6b, *SPPY*, and James Legge, trans. *Li-chi--Book of Rites*, New York: University Books, 1967, p. 72). Apparently, by taking the east steps, the Noble Scion showed that he did not dare presume to rank equal to the King of Chao.

[16] About 5 miles east of modern Kao-yi 高邑 in Hopei (T'an Ch'i-hsiang, 1:37-8).

[17] *T'ang-mu yi* 湯沐邑. The "Wang chih" 王制 chapter of *Li chi* 禮記 describes this as follows: "In order for the chiefs of regions to see the Son of Heaven at court, they are all [allowed] a bath-town in the Son of Heaven's domain, like his top officers" 方伯為朝天子，皆有湯沐之邑於天子之縣內，視元土. Cheng Hsüan 鄭玄 (127-200) notes that they were supposed to be the places for the feudal lords to fast before they saw the Son of Heaven (see *Li chi chu-shu* 禮記注疏, 4:19b, *SPPY*; see also James Legge, trans., *Li-chi*, p. 247). Wang Li-ch'i (77:1827) observes that during the Warring States era, a bath-town referred to temporary fiefs that the feudal lords granted to important officials.

would be unwilling to associate with one such as I. If the Lord of P'ing-yüan thinks this shameful, *he* is not worth associating with."

He packed and prepared to leave. The Lady told the Lord of P'ing-yüan all of this. The Lord of P'ing-yüan took off his cap and apologized, insisting that the Noble Scion stay. When the Lord of P'ing-yüan's gate attendants heard of this, half of them left the Lord of P'ing-yüan and turned to the Noble Scion, the finest knights in the world turned again to the Noble Scion, and the Noble Scion thus swayed the Lord of P'ing-yüan's retainers.

The Noble Scion remained in Chao for ten years without returning home. When Ch'in heard that the Noble Scion was in Chao, it sent out troops to attack Wei in the east day and night. The King of Wei was troubled by this and sent a messenger to invite the Noble Scion [back to Wei]. The Noble Scion feared the King was angry with him, and he warned his gate attendants: "Anyone who dares to admit an envoy of the King of Wei will die." His guests had turned their backs on Wei and gone to Chao [with him], and none dared to urge the Noble Scion [to return].

Master Mao and Master Hsüeh went to see the Noble Scion. "The reason that you carry weight in Chao and that your name is renowned among the feudal lords, Noble Scion, is only because there is a Wei. Now Ch'in attacks Wei, and Wei is in dire straits, yet you feel no concern, Noble Scion; if Ch'in crushes Ta Liang and levels the late king's ancestral temple, how will you be able to face the world?"

Before they had finished speaking, the Noble Scion immediately turned pale and informed his charioteer [he would] go back to the aid of Wei. When the King of Wei saw the Noble Scion, they both wept and the king gave the seal of the Commander-in-Chief to the Noble Scion. The Noble Scion thus became his commander. In the thirtieth year of King An-hsi of Wei (247 B.C.), the Noble Scion dispatched messengers [*2384*] to inform all of the feudal lords. When the feudal lords heard that the Noble Scion had become commander, each one dispatched their generals leading troops to aid Wei. The Noble Scion led the troops of five states on to defeat the army of Ch'in beyond the Ho and put Meng Ao 蒙驁[18] to flight. Following up on their victory, he drove the army of Ch'in to Han-ku 函谷 Pass.[19] He bottled up Ch'in's troops there and the army of Ch'in did not dare to come through [the Pass]. At the time, the Noble Scion's power shook the world, and the retainers of the feudal lords presented their arts of war. The Noble Scion gave titles to all [their works], and thus these are commonly called *Wei Kung-tzu ping-fa* 魏公子兵法 (The Noble Scion of Wei's Arts of War).[20]

The King of Ch'in was troubled. He spent ten-thousand catties of gold in Wei seeking a retainer of Chin Pi and had him slander the Noble Scion to the King of Wei: "The Noble Scion fled abroad ten years ago, yet now he has become Wei's commander. The generals of the feudal lords all belong to him and the feudal lords hear only of the Noble Scion of Wei, they hear nothing of the King of Wei. The Noble Scion is preparing to seize this time to secure a position facing south as king. The feudal lords fear the Noble Scion's power and intend to enthrone him."

Ch'in sent counter-agents several times to pretend to congratulate the Noble Scion, inquiring whether or not he had been enthroned as the King of Wei yet. The King of Wei, hearing this slander daily, could not help but believe it, and afterward did indeed send a man to replace the Noble Scion as commander. The Noble Scion, realizing that he had been

---

[18] The grandfather of Meng T'ien 蒙恬 (*Shih chi,* 88:2565).

[19] About 20 miles southwest of modern San-men hsia City 三門峽, in Shensi (T'an Ch'i-hsiang, 1:35-6).

[20] The "Yi-wen chih" chapter of *Han shu* lists a book entitled *Wei Kung-tzu* 魏公子 in twenty-one chapters (see *Han shu* 30:1758); it is no longer extant.

dismissed a second time because of slander, excused himself from court attendance because of an illness, and stayed up night after night with his retainers, drinking strong wine and frequently taking the company of women. He drank and indulged himself day and night for four years and in the end died from an illness caused by wine.[21] That same year King An-hsi of Wei also passed away.

When the King of Ch'in heard that the Noble Scion had died, he sent Meng Ao to attack Wei. [Meng Ao] seized twenty cities (242 B.C.) and for the first time established [Ch'in's] Tung 東 Commandery.[22] After this, Ch'in gradually nibbled away at Wei,[23] and in eighteen years (225 B.C.), captured the King of Wei[24] and butchered [the inhabitants of] Ta Liang.

[2385] In his youth, when Emperor Kao-tsu 高祖 [of Han] (r. 206-195 B.C.) was still a commoner, he often heard how worthy the the Noble Scion was. After ascending the Son of Heaven's throne, whenever he visited Ta Liang he always made sacrifices to the Noble Scion. In his twelfth year (195 B.C.), Kao-tsu returned there from attacking Ch'ing Pu 黥布[25] and established five households as gravekeepers for the Noble Scion, to make sacrifices to the him generation after generation in all four seasons of the year.

His Honor the Grand Scribe says: "I visited the ruins of Ta Liang and asked about the place called Yi-men Gate. Yi-men was the city wall's east gate. Among the other Noble Scions of the world, there were also some who delighted in knights, but when the Lord of Hsinling sought the friendship of the recluses of the cliffs and caves, and never found it shameful to associate with the lowly, he did so with good reason. That his fame ranked first among the feudal states was not in vain. Emperor Kao-tsu often passed by [his grave] and ordered the people to reverently offer sacrifices without cease."

---

[21] According to *Shih chi,* 15:751, Wei Wu-chi died in 243 B.C.

[22] Covering the eastern part of modern Honan and the western part of Shantung (T'an Ch'i-hsiang, 1:35-6).

[23] This refers to Ch'in's seizure of Wei territory in 242, 241, 240 and 238 B.C., during the reign of King Ching-min 景愍 of Wei (r. 242-228; see *Shih chi,* 14:1863).

[24] This was Chia 假, King of Wei (r. 227-225 B.C.), King Ching-min's son.

[25] *Ching* was the punishment of tattooing. Ching Pu was the nickname given to the Han general Ying Pu 英布 because he had received such punishment (see his biography in *Shih chi* Chapter 91).

TRANSLATORS' NOTE

This is the third of four chapters in sequence which depict the more famous of the lords--known as "the Four Lords"--opposing Ch'in during the final years of its unification of the empire. Unlike the accounts of the other three lords, however, Ssu-ma Ch'ien lauds the Noble Scion of Wei (even the chapter name--the Noble Scion's title was Lord of Hsin-ling, but the Grand Scribe refers to him by the prestigious rank of "Noble Scion") for his comprehension of what it should mean to "delight in retainers."

Nevertheless, this chapter (like those preceding) recount the eventual defeat of one of the Six States by Ch'in, in this case Wei. But this defeat is accomplished despite the Noble Scion's efforts, not because of them. Unlike the other lords in whose retinues able men sometimes went unrecognized while good counsel sometimes fell on deaf ears, the Noble Scion of Wei actively sought such advisors and advice even among tradesmen and recluses. The openings of the three chapters invite comparison. Whereas in the preceding two chapters an archetypal anecdote revealing the lord's failure to recognize a loyal and capable retainer begin the text, Ssu-ma Ch'ien shows us in this memoir the prescience of the Noble Scion in the description of the *liu-po* game. This prescience allows him to act with deference toward Chu Hai, a man of mean circumstances who has no apparent use to the Noble Scion. The reader, not the lord, may prove imperceptive here, but he is soon enlightened when Chu Hai's talents and courage allow the Noble Scion to rescue Chao.

BIBLIOGRAPHY

I. Translations

Dolby, William and John Scott. *Sima Qian, War-Lords, Translated with Twelve Other Stories from His Historical Records.* Edinburgh: Southside, 1974, pp. 102-115.

Haenisch, Erich. "Gestalten aus der Zeit der chinesischen Hegemoniekämpfe: Übersetzungen aus Sze-ma Ts'ien's Historischen Denkwürdigkeiten," *Abhandlungen für die Kunde des Morgenlandes,* XXXIV.2. Wiesbaden: Harrassowitz, 1962, pp. 27-37.

_____. *Der Herr von Sin-ling, Reden aus dem Chan-kuo ts'e und Biographien aus dem Shi-ki.* Stuttgart: Reclam, 1965, pp. 58-70.

Nyitray, Vivian-Lee. "Mirrors of Virtue: Four 'Shih chi' Biographies." Unpublished Ph. D. dissertation, Stanford University, 1990.

Ōgawa Tamaki 小川環樹, trans. *Shiki retsuden* 史記列傳. Rpt. Tokyo: Chikuma Shobō, 1986 (1969), pp. 73-118.

Yang Hsien-yi and Gladys Yang. *Records of the Historian.* Rpt. Hong Kong: The Commercial Press, 1985, pp. 118-27.

II. Studies

Lu Ting-hsiang 陸鼎祥. "Hsin-ling Chün 'ch'ieh-fu chiu-Chao' te chi-ke wen-t'i" 信陵君竊符救趙的幾個問題, *Yü-wen hsüeh-k'an* 語文學刊, 1985.

Naitō Shigenobu 內藤戊申. "Shinryōkun" 信陵君, *Ritsumeikan bungaku,* 1967, 735-56.

Wu Yu 吳璵. "*Shih chi* Wei Kung-tzu chuan p'ing-hsi" 史記魏公子傳評析, *Ku-tien wen-hsüeh,* 1 (1979), 33-46.

The Lord of Ch'un-shen, Memoir 18

[78:2387] The Lord of Ch'un-shen 春申[1] was a native of Ch'u. His *praenomen* was Hsieh 歇 and his *cognomen* Huang 黄. He studied at many schools and was widely read. He took service with King Ch'ing-hsiang 頃襄 of Ch'u (r. 298-263 B.C.). King Ch'ing-hsiang thought Hsieh skilled in debate, and sent him on a mission to Ch'in.

King Chao 昭 of Ch'in (r. 306-251 B.C.) sent Pai Ch'i 白起[2] to attack Han and Wei. He defeated them at Hua-yang 華陽,[3] capturing Wei's general Mang Mao 芒卯.[4] Han and Wei submitted and served Ch'in.[5] King Chao of Ch'in then ordered Pai Ch'i to lead an expedition against Ch'u with the troops of Han and Wei. They had not yet departed, however, and it was at this point that the Ambassador of Ch'u, Huang Hsieh, arrived and heard of Ch'in's plan.

Prior to this, Ch'in had also sent Pai Ch'i to attack Ch'u. He took the commanderies of Wu 巫 and Ch'ien-chung 黔中, captured Yen 鄢 and Ying 郢,[6] and reached as far east as Ching-ling 竟陵.[7] King Ch'ing-hsiang of Ch'u moved his seat of government east to Ch'en-hsien 陳縣.[8]

Huang Hsieh had seen King Huai of Ch'u lured into entering Ch'in to pay homage, then tricked and held in Ch'in until his death.[9] King Ch'ing-hsiang was King Huai's son, and Ch'in held him lightly. Thus Huang Hsieh feared that with one great mobilization of its troops, Ch'in would wipe out Ch'u. He therefore sent a letter advising King Chao of Ch'in:[10]

> None in the world are stronger than Ch'in and Ch'u. Now I have heard that you wish to lead an expedition against Ch'u, Great King. This is like two tigers fighting with each other. 'If two tigers fight, even a slow dog can catch them when they're worn out.' [*2388*] It would be better to cultivate Ch'u. Your servant asks permission to explain the reasons.
>
> Your servant has heard that when things reach their acme, they fall back. So it is with winter and summer. When safety is greatest there is danger. So it is with game pieces piled up.[11] The territory of your great state now encompasses two corners of the world. From the birth of man until now, a land of ten-thousand chariots has never held such an expanse. For three generations, the late emperors King Wen and King Chuang, and Your Majesty,[12] Ch'in has not forgotten its desire to extend its land to

[1] Ch'ien Mu (*Ti-ming k'ao*, p. 386) believes that Ch'un-shen was located near modern Feng-t'ai 鳳臺 County, on the north bank of the Huai River about 20 miles west of Huai-nan 淮南 City in Anhwei (see also T'an Ch'i-hsiang, 8:18).

[2] See his biography in *Shih chi* Chapter 73.

[3] See n. 3 to our translation of *Shih chi* Chapter 77 above.

[4] See n. 4 to our translation of *Shih chi* Chapter 77 above.

[5] For dating and details of this event, see *Shih chi* Chapter 73.

[6] On Ch'ien-chung see See n. 68 to our translation of *Shih chi* Chapter 69 above; on Yen and Ying see n. 70 to our translation of Chapter 69.

[7] See n. 14 to our translation of *Shih chi* Chapter 73 above.

[8] Dating and details of this event are discussed in *Shih chi* Chapter 73.

[9] See our translation of *Shih chi* Chapter 84 for details of this event.

[10] The following speech and part of the prologue which precedes it appear in *Chan-kuo ts'e* (3:36b-41b, *SPTK*).

[11] On this game see n. 65 to our translation of Shih chi Chapter 69 above. It is not clear why (or how) game pieces were stacked.

[12] There are a number of anachronisms in this letter. If, as seems likely, the reference to these kings as *hsien-ti* 先帝 "the late emperors" is an attempt to honor the First Emperor's ancestors, this would mark the recipient of this letter as the First Emperor himself. The two Ch'in kings listed here, Wen and Chuang, could only be Kings Hsiao-wen 孝文 (r. 250 B.C.) and Chuang-hsiang 莊襄 (r. 249-247 B.C.), the First Emperor's father and grand-

Ch'i or its goal of breaking the alliances.[13] Your Majesty sent Sheng Ch'iao 盛橋 to guard affairs in Han[14] and Sheng Ch'iao presented its land to Ch'in. Thus you did not use your armored troops nor extend your might, yet obtained a territory of a hundred *li* [on a side]. Your Majesty can be termed able indeed.

Your Majesty mobilized your armored troops and attacked Wei, blocking the gates of [its capital] Ta Liang, taking Ho-nei, capturing Yen 燕, Suan-tsao 酸棗, Hsü 虛, and T'ao 桃, and invading Hsing 邢.[15] The troops of Wei gathered like clouds without daring to resist. Your Majesty's accomplishments are numerous indeed.

Your Majesty rested your warriors, gave repose to your troops, then two years later mobilized them again and went on to annex P'u 蒲, Yen 衍, Shou 首, and Yüan 垣,[16] until you looked down on Jen 仁 and P'ing-ch'iu 平丘.[17] Huang 黃 and Chi-yang 濟陽[18] ringed their walls with defenders and the royal clan of Wei submitted. Your Majesty further took the lands north of P'u 濮 and Mo 磨,[19] cutting the waist of Ch'i and Han, and breaking the back of Ch'u and Chao. The world joined in fives and gathered in sixes, but none dared to come to the rescue. Your Majesty's authority is complete indeed!

[2389] "If Your Majesty is able to hold to your accomplishments and guard your authority, subdue your desire to attack and annex, and enrich your nature with kindness and justice, the future will hold no worries at all. The Three Kings will not be worthy enough to rank you as the fourth, nor the Five Hegemons worthy enough to rank you as the sixth.

If Your Majesty takes pride in the masses of your soldiers, or relies on the strength of your weapons and armor, if you use the awe you inspired in your destruction of Wei to make vassals of the world's rulers through brute force, Your servant fears that the future will hold many worries. The *Odes* say,

> There are none that don't have a beginning,
> there are few able to bring things to an end.[20]

father. Several of the military events referred to in the letter also seem to be from the First Emperor's reign. Ssu-ma Ch'ien's ascription of this letter to Huang Hsieh is therefore questionable, though some commentators would amend the text rather than accept this.

[13] Takigawa's text differs from Chung-hua, having *wang* 忘 instead of *wang* 妄. We follow Takigawa here.

[14] The *Chan-kuo ts'e* commentator Pao Piao suggests *shou* 守 means *tai* 待 "to await matters." Takigawa (78:4) believes it means "to watch over and urge." Others argue it means that Ch'in made Sheng a sort of caretaker prime minister, governing Yen in Ch'in's interest. Liang Yü-sheng (30:1282) suggests that Sheng Ch'iao was Ch'eng Ch'iao 成蟜, the younger brother of the First Emperor (he was also known as the Lord of Ch'ang-an 長安, see *Shih chi*, 6:224).

[15] The account in *Shih chi*, 6:224 mentions most of these locations; T'an Ch'i-hsiang (2:8) believes T'ao was a town about 15 miles east of modern Tung-p'ing 東平 in Shantung; Wang Li-ch'i (78:1835n) identifies Hsing with Hsing-ch'iu 邢丘 (which he locates east of Wen 溫 County in modern Honan) and notes that Yen refers not to the state of Yen but to a county which was northeast of modern Yen-chin 延津 in Honan.

[16] According to Wang Li-ch'i (78:1835-6n.), P'u, Yen, Shou and Huan were towns near modern Ch'ang-yüan 長垣, Chengchow, Sui 睢 County, and Huan-ch'ü 垣曲 County, all in what is now Honan.

[17] Jen's location is unknown; P'ing-ch'iu was a county east of modern Feng-ch'iu 封丘, according to Wang Li-ch'i (78:1836n).

[18] Wang Li-ch'i (78:1836n) locates the city of Huang and the county of Chi-yang west and northeast of modern Lan-k'ao 蘭考 County in Honan.

[19] P'u was a county in modern Feng-ch'iu County, Mo a place overlooking Chin-p'u 近濮 County, all in Honan (Wang Li-ch'i, 78:1836n.).

[20] Mao #255, Legge, 4:505.

The *Changes* says, "When the fox fords the river, it must wet its tail."[21] Both of these speak of the ease of beginning something and the difficulty of ending it. How can one know this is so?

In days past, The Chih 智 saw the profit of leading an expedition against Chao, but did not know of the disaster to come at Yü-tz'u 榆次.[22] Wu saw the advantages of attacking Ch'i but did not know of the defeat to come at Kan-sui 干隧.[23]

These two states were not without great accomplishments, but they fell prey to the desire for profit beforehand, and so were ripe for disaster after. When Wu trusted Yüeh, he went on to attack Ch'i. After conquering the men of Ch'i at Ai-ling 艾陵, he returned to become the King of Yüeh's captive at the mouth of the three rivers.[24] When The Chih trusted Han and Wei, he went on to attack Chao, assaulting the city of Chin-yang 晉陽. [*2390*] With victory days away, Han and Wei rebelled and killed Yao, Earl of Chih, at the foot of the Tso-t'ai 鑿臺 (Chiseled Terrace).[25] Your Majesty is annoyed today that Ch'u has not been laid waste, and has forgotten that laying waste to Ch'u will strengthen Han and Wei. Your servant is concerned for Your Majesty's sake, and would not make such a choice. A song says:[26]

> When Great Wu made quarters far away,
> he did not ford.

Viewed in this way, the state of Ch'u is your ally and your neighboring states are your enemies. The *Odes* say:

> Hop, hop the swift rabbit,
> he meets a dog and is caught.
> When someone else is making plans,
> I anticipate and measure him.[27]

Your Majesty has now decided halfway down the road to trust Han and Wei's good intentions. This is just what Wu did in trusting Yüeh.

[2391] Your servant has heard that 'Enemies cannot be given loans and opportunities cannot be lost.' Your servant fears Han and Wei will speak humbly for fear of trouble but will in fact deceive your great state. Why is this? Your Majesty has not earned gratitude from Han and Wei, accumulating it over the ages; instead you have won their hatred, and piled it up for generations. Ten generations of Han and Wei's fathers and sons, older and younger brothers, have died at the hands of Ch'in, one after another. Their states were torn apart, their altars ruined, and their clan temples laid waste. Their bellies were cut out and their bowels slashed, their necks broken and their cheeks pierced. Their heads and bodies were sundered, their bones exposed on the grassy plains, and their skulls lay helter-skelter, stretching all the way to the borders of Ch'in. Their fathers and sons, their old and weak, became crowds of slaves with necks roped and hands bound, following one another down the road. The souls and anima of their dead are alone and sorrowful, without sacrificial blood to eat.

---

[21] *Yi-ching chu-shu* 易經注疏 (6:13b, *SPPY*) [Hexagram #64].

[22] Yü-tz'u was about 5 miles east of the modern city of the same name in Shansi province (T'an Ch'i-hsiang, 1:38).

[23] See n. 56 to our translation of *Shih chi* Chapter 69 above.

[24] See our translation of *Shih chi* Chapter 66 above.

[25] On the Earl of Chih's defeat see also *Shih chi*, 39:1685-6. The Tso-t'ai was just south of Yü-tz'u (T'an Ch'i-hsiang, 1:38).

[26] Or possibly a lost poem of the *Odes*.

[27] Mao #198, Legge, 4:342. In the current text of the *Odes*, these two couplets are reversed.

Their living are without livelihoods, their clans are scattered and exiled as slaves, both men and women, filling the lands between the seas! Thus as long as Han and Wei have not perished, they are a threat to Ch'in's altars of grain and soil, yet Your Majesty now uses them in an attack on Ch'u. Is this not a profound mistake?

Moreover, when Your Majesty attacks Ch'u, how will you send out your troops? Would you ask passage from your foes Han and Wei? From the day your soldiers set forth, you must worry that they will not return. This is like aiding your enemies Han and Wei with your own troops. If you do not ask passage from your foes Han and Wei, you must attack the right [west] side of the Sui 隧 River.[28] The right side of the Sui River is broad streams and great rivers, mountain forests and gullies and valleys, a land that will feed no one. Even if you could hold it, it would not be the same as gaining territory. [*2392*] Your Majesty would have the hollow reputation of destroying Ch'u, but not the reality of gaining territory.

Moreover, on the day Your Majesty attacks Ch'u, the four states[29] are certain to call up all their troops in response to you. When the troops of Ch'in and Ch'u are locked in combat, the royal clan of Wei will come out and attack Liu 留, Fang-yü 方與, Chih 銍, Hu-ling 湖陵, Tang 碭, Hsiao 蕭, and Hsiang 湘,[30] completely taking old Sung. When the men of Ch'i face south and attack Ch'u, the banks of the Ssu 泗[31] are sure to fall. This is flat plain on every side, a rich and fertile land, yet you would let Ch'i tattack it alone. Your Majesty will break Ch'u, fatten the central states of Han and Wei , and strengthen Ch'i. The strength of Han and Wei alone will be enough for Ch'in to reckon with. To the south, Ch'i will have the Ssu River as its border, to the east it will carry the sea, to the north lean on the Ho River, and from then on it need fear nothing further. None of the states of the world will be stronger than Ch'i and Wei. If Ch'i and Wei gain territory, protect their profits, and carefully instruct their lower officials, after one year they might be unable to become emperor, but they will be more than able to prevent *you* from becoming emperor, Your Majesty.

With the breadth of Your Majesty's lands, the masses of your troops, and the strength of your weapons and armor, to declare war on Ch'u and make it your enemy, to cause Han and Wei to confer the eminence of the emperor's title on Ch'i, this is Your Majesty's miscalculation. Your servant is concerned for Your Majesty; it would be better to cultivate Ch'u.

Faced with Ch'in and Ch'u united into one, Han can only fold its hands. [*2393*] With the heights of the Eastern Mountains as your collar, and the advantage of the Ho River's bend as your belt, Han is sure to become a 'marquis within the pass.'[32] If Your Majesty then garrisons [Han's capital] Cheng 鄭 with one hundred

---

[28] Referring to the river near modern Sui-chou City in Hupei (T'an Ch'i-hsiang, 2:7; see also Wang Li-ch'i's comments, 78:1837n.).

[29] Ch'i, Chao, Han, and Wei.

[30] According to Wang Li-ch'i (78:1837n.) Liu was a city located southeast of modern P'ei 沛 County in Kiangsu; Fang-yü was a town west of T'ai 台 County in Shantung, Chih a place west of Su-chou 宿州 in modern Anhwei, Hu-ling a place southeast of modern Yü-t'ai 魚台 County in Shantung, Tang a town south of Tang-shan 碭山 County in Anhwei, Hsiao the name of a statelet northwest of modern Hsiao 蕭 County in Anhwei, and Hsiang the name of a place northwest of Huai-pei 淮北 City in Anhwei.

[31] According to T'an Ch'i-hsiang (2:8) the Ssu flowed from what is now central Shantung through Hu-ling (see above) and then southeast to join with the Huai River near the modern city of Hung-tse 洪澤 in Chekiang.

[32] Substituting the the *Chan-kuo ts'e* reading of *chin* 襟 for *shih* 施 in the phrase 施以山東之險, and the *Chan-kuo ts'e* 河曲之利 rather than the *Shih chi's* 曲河之利. The translation is based on a forced reading for *yi* 以. It might be better to take this as an instrumental phrase, in which case the translation would be 'collar [Han] with the heights of the eastern mountains, belt [Han] with the advantage of the curve of the Ho River, and Han will be a 'marquis within the pass.' In either case, Huang Hsieh is urging the king to make better use of his geographical advantages to pressure Han, rather than military force.

A 'marquis within the pass' was a titular rank which carried no grant of land with it.

thousand men, Liang's 梁 [i.e., Wei] blood will run cold, Hsü 許 and Yen-ling 鄢陵[33] will ring their walls with defenders, and passage from Shang-ts'ai 上蔡 to Shao-ling 召陵[34] will be severed. In that case, Wei too will become a 'marquis within the pass.' If Your Majesty just cultivates Ch'u, these two lords of 10,000 chariots within the pass will seize land from Ch'i, and you can take Ch'i's right [west] territory with your hands folded. Once Your Majesty's territory cuts between the two seas, constricting the world at the waist, Yen and Chao will not have Ch'i and Ch'u, and Ch'i and Ch'u will not have Yen and Chao. Your menace can then shake Yen and Chao, straight up to Ch'i and Ch'u and these four states will submit without any pains at all.

"Excellent!" said King Chao. He then halted Pai Ch'i and apologized to Han and Wei. He sent out a messenger with gifts to Ch'u and agreed to become its ally.

Huang Hsieh received the agreement and returned to Ch'u. Ch'u sent Hsieh and the Heir Wan 完 as hostages to Ch'in. Ch'in kept them for several years.

King Ch'ing-hsiang of Ch'u became sick. The Heir was not allowed to return. Ch'u's Heir and Ch'in's Prime Minister, the Marquis of Ying 應,[35] were on good terms. Huang Hsieh thus advised the Marquis of Ying: "Are you truly on good terms with Ch'u's Heir, Minister of State?"

"I am," said the Marquis of Ying.

"The King of Ch'u will most likely not recover from this illness. Ch'in would do best to return his Heir. If the Heir becomes king, he is certain to serve Ch'in well and to owe you, Minister of State, a favor beyond repayment. [*2394*] This would ingratiate you with an ally and enable you to store up ten-thousand chariots. If you do not return him, then he is just a commoner in [Ch'in's capital] Hsien-yang. Ch'u will choose another Heir, who will certainly not serve Ch'in. To lose an ally and break peace with [a state with] ten-thousand chariots is no scheme at all. I hope that you will consider this carefully, Minister of State."

The Marquis of Ying informed the King of Ch'in. The King of Ch'in said, "Have the Ch'u Heir's tutor go first and ask about the King of Ch'u's illness. After he returns, we will make further plans."

Huang Hsieh analyzed the situation for Ch'u's Heir. "In detaining you, Heir, Ch'in wishes to seek profit. Your strength is not yet sufficient to profit Ch'in, and this worries me sorely. The Lord of Yang-wen's 陽文[36] two sons are both in the palace. If the king suddenly meets the great fate and you are not there, a son of the Lord of Yang-wen is sure to become the successor, and you will never have a chance to make offerings at the clan temple. It would be better to flee Ch'in and leave the country together with the ambassador. Your servant asks permission to remain and die in your place."

The Ch'u Heir took Huang's advice, changed his clothing and left through the border pass as the Ch'u ambassador's chariot driver. Huang Hsieh kept to the Heir's quarters, constantly pleading illness [for the Heir]. When he decided the Heir was already long gone, and Ch'in could not pursue him, Huang Hsieh told King Chao of Ch'in in person, "Ch'u's Heir has already returned. He is far out of the country by now. I deserve to die. I hope that you will grant me death by my own hand." King Chao was enraged. He wanted to allow Hsieh to kill himself. The Marquis of Ying said, "Hsieh is acting as a vassal should, offering to die for

---

[33] According to Wang Li-ch'i (78:1837n.) Hsü was a city near modern Hsü-ch'ang 許昌 and Yen-ling a place northwest of modern Yen-ling County, both in what is now Honan.

[34] Wang Li-ch'i (78:1837n.) locates the city of Shang-ts'ai near southeast of the modern county by the same name in Honan and that of Shao-ling just east of Yen-ch'eng 郾城 County in the same modern province.

[35] I.e., Fan Sui (see his biography in *Shih chi* chapter 79).

[36] Wang Li-ch'i believes he was a brother of King Ch'ing-hsiang (78:1838n.).

his ruler. When the Heir becomes king, he is sure to employ Hsieh. It would be better to send him back without punishing him. By doing so, we ingratiate ourselves with Ch'u." Ch'in followed this advice and dispatched Huang Hsieh.

Three months after Hsieh arrived in Ch'u, King Ch'ing-hsiang of Ch'u died. The Heir Wan took the throne. He became King K'ao-lieh 考烈 (r. 262-238 B.C.). In the first year of King K'ao-lieh (262 B.C.), Huang Hsieh was made Prime Minister. He was enfeoffed as the Lord of Ch'un-shen, and granted twelve counties in the territory north of the Huai 淮 River.

Fifteen years later, Huang Hsieh said to the King of Ch'u, "The territory north of the Huai borders Ch'i. Military affairs are urgent there. I ask that it be made a commandery for convenience." He then presented his twelve counties north of the Huai and asked for a fief in Chiang-tung 江東.[37] King K'ao-lieh granted his request. The Lord of Ch'un-shen then built a walled city at the old ruins of Wu 吳, and made his capital there.

[2395] At the time when the Lord of Ch'un-shen became Prime Minister of Ch'u, Ch'i had the Lord of Meng-ch'ang, Chao had the Lord of P'ing-yüan, and Wei had the Lord of Hsin-ling, competing in humbling themselves before knights and attracting retainers, moving men and winning hearts to support their states and wield their power.[38]

When the Lord of Ch'un-shen had been Prime Minister of Ch'u for four years, Ch'in broke Chao's army of 400,000 at Ch'ang-p'ing (259 B.C.).[39] In the fifth year (258 B.C.), they besieged Han-tan. Han-tan told Ch'u of its straits. Ch'u sent the Lord of Ch'un-shen leading soldiers to rescue them. The soldiers of Ch'in left and the Lord of Ch'un-shen returned.

When the Lord of Ch'un-shen had been Prime Minister of Ch'u for eight years, he led an expedition for Ch'u north against Lu, destroying it.[40] He made His Excellency Hsün[41] the prefect of Lan-ling. At this point, Ch'u had again become strong.

Chao's Lord of P'ing-yüan send a messenger to the Lord of Ch'un-shen. The Lord of Ch'un-shen housed him in the upper hostel. The Chao emissary wanted to boast before Ch'u. He made a tortoise shell hair pin and scabbards decorated with pearls and jade and asked to present them to the Lord of Ch'un-shen's retainers. Of the Lord of Ch'un-shen's three-thousand some retainers, the seniors all came to see the Chao emissary wearing pearl sandals. The Chao emissary was utterly humiliated.

When the Lord of Ch'un-shen had been Prime Minister for fourteen years (249 B.C.), King Chuang-hsiang 莊襄 of Ch'in (r. 249-247 B.C.) took the throne and made Lü Pu-wei 呂不韋[42] his Prime Minister, enfeoffing him as Marquis of Wen-hsin 文信. He took East Chou.

When the Lord of Ch'un-shen had been Prime Minister for twenty-two years (241 B.C.), the feudal lords, fearing that there would never be an end to Ch'in's attacks and expeditions, united in alliance and mounted an expedition west against Ch'in. The King of Ch'u was head of the alliance and the Lord of Ch'un-shen wielded all power. When they reached the

---

[37] The region bordering the Yangtze on the south from modern Wu-hu 蕪湖 City in Anhwei to the delta (Wang Li-ch'i, 78:1837n.).

[38] See the biographies of these rulers in *Shih chi* Chapters 75, 76, and 77 above. As noted in *Shih chi* Chapter 75, the Lord of Meng-ch'ang was probably slightly earlier than the other three great princes. When Huang Hsieh became Prime Minister in 262 B.C., the Lord of Meng-ch'ang had almost certainly died.

[39] The defeat at Ch'ang-p'ing and the beginning of the siege of Han-tan both began in 260 B.C. according to *Shih chi*, 73:2332-35 and 15:747.

[40] *Shih chi*, 15:748 says Ch'u took Lu in 255 B.C. and enfeoffed its lord with Chü 莒, but Ch'u's destruction of Lu is dated six years later, in 249 B.C. (*Shih chi*, 15:749).

[41] I. e. Hsün Tzu (see his biography in Shih chi Chapter 74).

[42] See his biography in *Shih chi* Chapter 85.

Han-ku Pass, Ch'in sent troops out to attack them and the soldiers of the feudal lords all fled in defeat. King K'ao-lieh of Ch'u blamed the Lord of Ch'un-shen for this and because of it the Lord of Ch'un-shen became more and more alienated from the king.

A foreigner named Chu Ying 朱英, a native of Kuan-chin 觀津,[43] told the Lord of Ch'un-shen, "The people all think that Ch'u is strong and that My Lord leads it weakly. As for me, I do not think so.

[2396] "In the time of the late king, Ch'in was well treated for twenty years and did not attack Ch'u. Why was this? For Ch'in to cross Meng 澠 Defile[44] and attack Ch'u would have been difficult; for it to borrow passage through the two Chous and attack Ch'u with its back to Han and Wei would have been impossible. Now, however, matters are different. Wei could perish between dawn and dusk. It cannot cling to Hsü 許 and Yen-ling 鄢陵; it would be best to allow Wei to cede them to Ch'in. The soldiers of Ch'in are 160 *li* from Ch'en 陳. Your servant foresees struggle day and night between Ch'in and Ch'u."

After this, Ch'u left Ch'en and moved to Shou-ch'un 壽春.[45] Ch'in transported the King of Wey to Yeh-wang 野王,[46] and established its Tung 東 Commandery.[47] Following this, the Lord of Ch'un-shen took up residence at his fief at Wu and carried out the duties of Prime Minister.

King K'ao-lieh of Ch'u had no sons.[48] The Lord of Ch'un-shen was troubled by this. He sought out fertile women and presented many of these to the king, but in the end there were no children.

Li Yüan 李園, a native of Chao, brought in his younger sister, hoping to present her to the King of Ch'u. When he heard that the king was not fruitful, he was afraid that his sister would not gain favor. Li Yüan sought to serve the Lord of Ch'un-shen as an attendant. After a while, he reported that he was returning home, then deliberately missed the date appointed for his return. When he reported on his return, the Lord of Ch'un-shen asked him about the circumstances. He replied, "The King of Ch'i sent a messenger to seek Your servant's younger sister. I was drinking with the messenger and thereby missed the appointment."

"Has she been promised?" asked the Lord of Ch'un-shen.

"Not yet," he replied.

"May I see her?" said the Lord of Ch'un-shen.

"Of course."

Li Yüan then presented his younger sister and she was soon favored by the Lord of Ch'un-shen. When she found she was pregnant, Li Yüan plotted with his sister.

Yüan's sister seized a moment of leisure to speak to the Lord of Ch'un-shen. "The King of Ch'u's favor to My Lord has been greater than that to his own brothers. You have been Prime Minister of Ch'u for twenty some years now, but the king has no sons. After the king's hundred years, his brother will take the throne in turn. When Ch'u has a new lord, all will then ennoble their old intimates, and how will you be able to hold on to favor, My Lord?

[43] According to Wang Li-ch'i (78:1839n.) this city was located southeast of modern Wu-yi 武邑 County in Hopei.

[44] Wang Li-ch'i (78:1839n.) locates Meng Defile near modern P'ing-ching 平靖 Pass, southeast of Hsin-yang 信陽 County in Honan.

[45] According to *Shih chi* 15:752, Ch'u moved its capital to Shou-ch'un (according to Wang Li-ch'i [78:1839n.] it was located southwest of modern Shou 壽 County in Anhwei) and the King of Wey moved to Yeh-wang in 241 B.C.

[46] A city about 30 miles northeast of modern Lo-yang in Honan (T'an Ch'i-hsiang, 2:9).

[47] Wang Li-ch'i (78:1839n.) believes this occupied the northeastern part of modern Honan and the western part of modern Shantung with its capital southwest of modern P'u-yang 濮陽 County in Honan.

[48] A parallel to this section appears in *Chan-kuo ts'e* (5:45a-48a, *SPTK*).

[2397] "Not only is there this, but My Lord has wielded power from a noble position for many years and often failed to treat the king's brothers with due propriety. If a brother is in fact enthroned, disaster will soon strike you. How then will you hold on to the Prime Minister's seal and your fief in Chiang-tung?

"Your handmaid has discovered she is pregnant but no one knows this. I have not been long in your favor. If through My Lord's eminence you could present me to the King of Ch'u, the king is certain to favor me. If, through Heaven's help, I have a male child, then your son would be king and all of Ch'u could be yours. How does this compare with facing a death sentence?"

The Lord of Ch'un-shen wholeheartedly approved. He sent Li Yüan's sister to a closely watched hostel,[49] and spoke of her to the King of Ch'u. The King of Ch'u summoned her in and favored her. She later gave birth to a male child. He was made Heir and Li Yüan's sister became queen. The King of Ch'u ennobled Li Yüan and Yüan held power.

Having presented his sister, his sister having become queen and her son having become the Heir, Li Yüan feared that the Lord of Ch'un-shen would reveal matters and become even more arrogant. He secretly cultivated fighters, planning to kill the Lord of Ch'un-shen to silence him, but many in the state already knew of the affair.

When the Lord of Ch'un-shen had been Prime Minister for twenty-five years, King K'ao-lieh of Ch'u became ill. Chu Ying told the Lord of Ch'un-shen, "Life has unexpected fortune, but also unexpected disasters. My Lord lives in an unpredictable age and serves an unpredictable master. How then can you expect to do without an unpredictable man?"

The Lord of Ch'un-shen said, "What do you mean by unexpected fortune?"

"My Lord has served as Prime Minister of Ch'u for over twenty years now. Although your title is Prime Minister, you are in fact King of Ch'u. Now the King of Ch'u is sick. He could pass away between dawn and dusk, but My Lord is minister to a young master, enabling you to stand in his place and rule the state like Yi Yin and the Duke of Chou. When the king is grown, you can return the government. On the other hand, you might immediately face south, call yourself 'the orphan' and hold the state of Ch'u. This is what is called unexpected fortune."

The Lord of Ch'un-shen said, "What do you mean by unexpected disaster?"

"Li Yüan does not rule the state yet he is My Lord's equal. He controls no soldiers and yet has cultivated fighters for a long time now. When the King of Ch'u passes away, Li Yüan is sure to enter first, seize power and kill My Lord in order to silence you. This is what is called unexpected disaster."

The Lord of Ch'un-shen said, "What do you mean by an unpredictable man?"

"My Lord should make me a palace attendant.[50] When the King of Ch'u passes away, Li Yüan is sure to enter first, and I will kill him for My Lord. This is what is called an unpredictable man."

The Lord of Ch'un-shen said, "Abandon this idea, sir. Li Yüan is a weak man. Moreover, I have treated him well. How could he go to such extremes?" Chu Ying realized that his advice would not [*2398*] be taken. Fearing disaster would touch him too, he fled.

Seventeen days later, King K'ao-lieh of Ch'u passed away. Li Yüan did indeed enter first and concealed his fighters inside the portcullis. When the Lord of Ch'un-shen entered through the portcullis, Yüan's fighters trapped and stabbed the Lord of Ch'un-shen, cut off his head, and threw it out of the portcullis. Afterwards, he sent functionaries to destroy all of the Lord of Ch'un-shen's family. The child which Li Yüan's sister had conceived when she was

---

[49] Our rendering of chin-she 謹舍 follows Ho Chien-chang (p. 595, n. 31).
[50] Lang-chung 郎中.

first favored by the Lord of Ch'un-shen and gave birth to after she was presented to the king succeeded to the throne. This was King Yu 幽 of Ch'u (r. 237-228 B.C.).

This year was the ninth year of the ascension of the First Emperor of Ch'in (238 B.C.). Lao Ai 嫪毐 also rebelled in Ch'in.[51] When he was discovered, his three clans were exterminated and Lü Pu-wei was dismissed.

[2399] His Honor the Grand Scribe says: "When I went to Ch'u, I saw the Lord of Ch'un-shen's old city. Its palaces and mansions were splendid indeed! In earlier days, when the Lord of Ch'un-shen advised King Chao of Ch'in and sent the Heir of Ch'u home at the risk of his life, how brilliant his wisdom was! Later, when he was overcome by Li Yüan, he was aged. The saying goes: 'Cut lose when it's time, or you'll suffer for it later.' So might one say when the Lord of Ch'un-shen lost Chu Ying."

---

[51] See *Shih-chi*, 6:227 and our translation of Chapter 6 above.

TRANSLATORS' NOTE

This is the final biography of the Four-Lords' series. It agains views development in the third century from a provincial persepctive--here the state of Ch'u. Although Huang Hsieh's career surpasses that of his three fellow lords and he is shown to excell as both a persuasive advisor and a courageous general, his life is ultimately unsuccessful. He fails in part because--like two of his fellow lords--he did not fully appreciate a retainer (Chu Ying). Ssuma Ch'ien in his comments suggests that it was senility that caused the Lord of Ch'un-shen's downfall. But the curious reference to the parallel of the licentious Lao Ai and his clans in Ch'in in the final lines of this memoir may also be read as the Grand Scribe's condemnation of Huang Hsieh's most heinous act, his relationship with Li Yüan's sister and the deception of his lord.

BIBLIOGRAPHY

I. Translations

William Dolby and John Scott, trans. *Sima Qian, War-Lords, Translated with Twelve Other Stories from His Historical Records*. Edinburgh: Southside, 1974, pp. 115-28.
Haenisch, Erich. "Gestalten aus der Zeit der chinesischen Hegemoniekämpfe: Übersetzungen aus Sze-ma Ts'ien's Historischen Denkwürdigkeiten," *Abhandlungen für die Kunde des Morgenlandes*, XXXIV.2. Wiesbaden: Harrassowitz, 1962, pp. 38-49.
Nyitray, Vivian-Lee. "Mirrors of Virtue: Four 'Shih chi' Biographies." Unpublished Ph. D. dissertation, Stanford University, 1990.
Ōgawa Tamaki 小川環樹, trans. *Shiki retsuden* 史記列傳. Rpt. Tokyo: Chikuma Shobō, 1986 (1969), pp. 118-24.

II. Studies

Ch'en Han-nien 陳瀚年. "Lun *Shih chi* Meng-ch'ang Chün, P'ing-yüan Chün, Ch'un-shen Chün, Hsin-ling Chün" 論史記孟嘗君平原君春申君信陵君, *Kuo-hsüeh ts'ung-k'an* 國學叢刊, 10 (September 1942).
Fujita Katsuhisa 藤田勝久. "Shiki 'Shunshin Kun retsuden' no henshū katei" 史記春申君列傳の編集過程, *Tōhōgaku,* 77(Jan. 1989), 40-55.
Nyitray, *op. cit.*

Fan Sui and Ts'ai Tse, Memoir 19

[79:2401] Fan Sui 范睢 was a native of Wei. His *agnomen* was Shu 叔.[1] He traveled about giving advice to the feudal lords and wanted to serve the King of Wei, but since his family was poor and he had no way to pay his own expenses, he first served a Regular Grand Master[2] named Hsü Chia 須賈.[3]

Hsü Chia was sent by King Chao 昭 of Wei (r. 295-277 B.C.) as an envoy to Ch'i and Fan Sui accompanied him. After they had stayed there several months, they still had received no reply. King Hsiang 襄 of Ch'i (r. 283-265 B.C.) learned that Sui had skill in debate and sent someone to offer him ten catties of gold, some beef and some wine, but Sui refused to accept them. When Hsü Chia learned of it, he was incensed, thinking that Sui must have told some state secrets of Wei to Ch'i to receive this kind of gift, so he ordered Sui to accept the beef and wine, but to return the gold.

After they returned to Wei, Hsü Chia still harbored anger against Fan Sui and told the Prime Minister of Wei what had happened. The Prime Minister of Wei was a Noble Scion, known as Wei Ch'i 魏齊.[4] Wei Ch'i became incensed and had his housemen beat Fan Sui with heavy sticks until his ribs were broken and his teeth knocked out. Sui pretended to be dead, so they wrapped him in a mat and put him in the privy. Guests who were drunk then took turns urinating on him, purposely and publicly demeaning him as a warning to keep others from careless talk.

From inside the mat Fan Sui said to the attendant, "If you can get me out of here, I will reward you handsomely." The attendant then asked if he might throw out the corpse in the mat. Wei Ch'i was drunk and said, "You may!" Thus Fan Sui escaped. Later, Wei Ch'i changed his mind and again sent people to look for him. A native of Wei, Cheng An-p'ing 鄭安平,[5] learned of this and carried [*2402*] Fan Sui off into hiding. [Fan Sui] changed his name to Chang Lu 張祿.[6]

At this time King Chao 昭 of Ch'in (r. 306-251 B.C.) sent the Internuncio[7] Wang Chi 王稽 to Wei. Cheng An-p'ing disguised himself as a soldier and was assigned to attend Wang Chi. Wang Chi asked him, "Among the worthy men of Wei, are there any who might go west with me?"

"In my hamlet there is a Venerable Chang Lu. He would like to see you, to speak of affairs of the world. This man has enemies and cannot show himself during the day."

"Bring him tonight!" Wang Chi replied.

Cheng An-p'ing and Chang Lu went to see Wang Chi that night. Before they finished speaking Wang Chi understood that Fan Sui was a worthy man and said to him, "Venerable Sir, please wait for me south of San-t'ing."[8] And, after making secret arrangements with Fan, he left.

---

[1] Some editions read Chü 雎 for Sui 睢. Wang Shu-min (79:2399) provides a detailed explanation in support of Sui which we follow.

[2] *Chung Tai-fu* 中大夫.

[3] On Hsü Chia see *Shih chi*, 72:2325 and our n. 28 to the translation of Chapter 72 above.

[4] See our n. 31 to the translation of *Shih chi* Chapter 76 above.

[5] Cheng later became a general in Ch'in, participated in the siege of Han-tan in 257 B.C. (*Shih chi*, 15:757), and was enfeoffed as the Lord of Wu-yang 武陽.

[6] Watson, *Qin*, p. 132 understands Cheng An-p'ing to be the subject of this passage, translating the sentence as follows: "Cheng An-p'ing . . . spirited Fan Chu into hiding and kept him in concealed, changing Fan Chu's name to Chang Lu."

[7] *Yeh-che* 謁者.

After Wang Chi took his leave from Wei, he passed [the agreed upon place], took Fan into his chariot, and returned to Ch'in. When they reached Hu 湖 [County]⁹ they saw a chariot and outriders approaching from the west. Fan Sui asked, "Who is approaching over there?"

Wang [*2403*] said, "That is the Prime Minister of Ch'in, the Marquis of Jang 穰,¹⁰ on an inspection tour of the eastern counties."

"I have heard," Fan Sui said, "That the Marquis of Jang single-handedly controls Ch'in and he detests the foreigners from the feudal states. This time I am afraid that he will insult me. I would rather hide in the chariot for the time being."

After a short while the Marquis of Jang indeed arrived and stopped to inquire after Wang Chi's health. Thus he stood in his chariot¹¹ and said, "What's new East of the Pass?"

"Nothing."

Again he said to Wang Chi, "Lord Receptionist, you didn't find one of those 'persuaders' to bring back with you, did you? They are useless, only bringing disorder to other people's countries!"

Wang Chi said, "I wouldn't dare to." Then he took his leave and left.

Fan Sui said, "I had heard the Marquis of Jang was an intelligent man, but slow in understanding things; just now he suspected there was someone in the chariot, but forgot to search it." At this he got out of the chariot and left, saying, "This time he is certain to think of it."

After [Wang Chi] had gone a little over five miles, [Jang] indeed sent his outriders back to search the chariot, and they left off only after [making sure] there were no foreigners. Wang Chi then entered Hsien-yang together with Fan Sui.

After he had reported on his mission, he took advantage [of the audience] to say, "There is a Venerable Chang Lu from Wei who is one of the greatest orators in the world. He said to me, 'The King of Ch'in's state is more perilous than a pile of eggs,¹² and only if he can employ me can he assure its stability. But I cannot transmit this in writing.' Therefore, I have brought him along." The King of Ch'in did not believe this, but gave Fan lodging and simple meals. Fan Sui waited for more than a year for the king's orders.

[2404] At this time King Chao had already reigned for thirty-six years (271 B.C.).¹³ In the south he had seized Yen and Ying in Ch'u, and King Huai 懷 of Ch'u (r. 328-299 B.C.) had died in prison in Ch'in (296 B.C.).¹⁴ To the east of Ch'in he had defeated Ch'i. King

---

⁸ The "So-yin" identifies San-t'ing 三亭 as Three Pavilions located at the border of Wei (with Ch'in). "Cheng-yi" identifies this as a hill (lookout?), a reading followed by Wang Li-ch'i (79:1847).

⁹ East of Hua Mountain and west of Han-ku Pass in modern Shansi near Ling-pao 靈寶 (T'an Ch'i-hsiang, 1:44).

¹⁰ See his biography in *Shih chi* Chapter 72.

¹¹ It would have been proper to get down from his chariot to speak to Wang Chi; this is an indication of the Marquis of Jang's arrogance.

¹² "Cheng-yi" cites a story in which Duke Ling 靈 of Chin (r. 620-607 B.C.) was building a nine-tiered terrace at considerable expenditure. When he had warned his retainers not to criticize him regarding this matter, one of them, Hsün Hsi 荀息, asked for an audience. The Duke received him with an arrow nocked in a drawn bow but Hsün said, "I don't dare to remonstrate. I can pile up twelve pitch-pot pieces [the nature of this game is uncertain, but the pieces were similar to checkers] and place nine eggs atop them."

When Hsün had piled the eggs atop the pieces, the Duke felt it was very precarious, but Hsün pointed out this was no where near as dangerous as the situation Chin was then in as a result of the money and manpower occupied in building the terrace.

¹³ Wang Li-ch'i (79:1848n.) notes that the events in Ch'u, Ch'i and San-Chin which are next depicted took place around the thirty-sixth year of King Chao's reign, but not necessarily in that year.

¹⁴ See *Shih chi,* 15:737 and *Shih chi,* 84:2484.

Min 湣 [of Ch'i (r. *323-284 B.C.)][15] once declared himself emperor, but later abandoned [this title]. King Chao had [also] several times pressed the Three Chin. He detested the world's persuaders and trusted none of them.

The Marquis of Jang and the Lord of Hua-yang were the younger brothers of King Chao's mother, the Queen Dowager Hsüan;[16] the Lord of Ching-yang and the Lord of Kao-ling were both younger brothers of King Chao by the same mother.[17]

When the Marquis of Jang became Prime Minister, the three men alternated as commanders and received fiefs; because of the Queen Dowager, the private wealth of their households exceeded that of the royal house. When the Marquis of Jang was commander for Ch'in, in order to expand his fief at T'ao he wanted to cross Han and Wei to attack Kang and Shou in Ch'i. Fan Sui thereupon submitted a memorial which read:[18]

Your subject has heard that an enlightened ruler in setting up his government never fails to reward those with merit in battle, never fails to give positions to those of talent. Those who have labored the most should have the most generous emolument, those whose merit in battle was greatest should have the most exalted rank, those who can rule the masses should have the highest official posts. Therefore, the untalented do not dare to take office nor can the talented hide themselves. If you consider what I say to be proper, put it into action and improve the Way of ruling; if you consider it improper, then there is no point in keeping me further.

The saying goes, "The mediocre ruler rewards those whom he loves and punishes those whom he hates; the enlightened ruler is not like this--if he gives rewards, they will only be granted to those with merit and if he punishes, it will only be someone who has been found guilty of an offense."

Now since my neck can't stand up to a chopping block and ax and my waist can't fend off a battle-ax or war-ax, how would I dare to offer dubious matters before Your Majesty? Although you may consider me a base man and thus treat me with contempt, shouldn't you respect the loyalty of those who presented me?

[2405] Moreover, I have heard that in the Chou court there was the Chih-o 砥砨 Jade, in Sung they had the piece called Chieh-lu 結綠, in Liang one named Hsüan-li 縣藜, and in Ch'u the Ho-p'u 和朴.[19] These four treasures were all produced from the earth and were all overlooked by able craftsmen, yet came to be the most famous artifacts in the world. This being the case, could it not be that even among those rejected by sage kings there are some capable of bringing riches to the state?

I have heard that those skilled at bringing riches to their households take from [the wealth of] the state, those who are skilled at bringing riches to their states, take from [the wealth of] the feudal lords. When the world has an enlightened ruler, the feudal lords will not be able to monopolize riches. Why is this?[20] Because they would be taking from the [ruler's] glory. An able doctor knows if a sick man will live or die, and an sage ruler can discern those events which will bring him success or failure. If something is profitable, he will try it out; if it is harmful, he will abandon it; if it is doubtful, he will give it a try. Even if Shun and Yü were reborn, they could not do otherwise. I cannot record in this letter my most profound suggestions, and my shallower suggestions are not worth heeding. Perhaps you think that either I am ignorant and can not measure Your Majesty's mind or that he who spoke for me is

[15] See *Shih chi*, 46:1895ff.

[16] A daughter of the Ch'u nobility and a former consort of King Hui-wen 惠文 of Ch'u (r. 337-311 B.C.). King Chao held her in special favor--and she exercised considerable political influence on him--from when he was nineteen until the forty-first year of his reign (266 B.C.) when Fan Sui became Prime Minister.

[17] All of these figures, and the following events, are introduced in *Shih chi* Chapter 72.

[18] A parallel version of this memorial can be found in *Chan-kuo ts'e* (3:42b-44a, *SPTK*).

[19] On the Ho-p'u jade, see our translation of *Shih chi* Chapter 81.

[20] Watson (*Qin*, p. 134) follows a different reading here.

of low rank [and his recommendation to employ me] cannot be taken. If this is not the case, I beseech you to find a moment in your leisure time to grant me audience. If even one of my suggestions is without positive results, then I will gladly suffer the ax and chopping block.

Thereupon King Chao of Ch'in was delighted, apologized to Wang Chi, and had him send a fast carriage to summon Fan Sui.

[2406] As a result Fan Sui was able to gain an audience in the "detached palace."[21] He pretended not to recognize the Unending Lane[22] and entered it. As the king was approaching, the eunuchs angrily drove him out, saying, "The king has arrived!" Fan Sui feigned [surprise]: "How could Ch'in have a king? There is only the Queen Dowager and the Marquis of Jang!" He hoped to thereby incite King Chao. When the king arrived, he heard Fan arguing with the eunuchs and then received him and said by way of apology, "I should have long before been here to receive your instructions in person, but during the Yi-ch'ü 義渠 Affair,[23] I have had to attend the Queen Mother day and night. Now the Yi-ch'ü Affair has been resolved and I can receive your instructions. I humbly acknowledge my lack of social graces, and now would respectfully conduct the rituals appropriate to host and guest." Fan Sui declined. On this day all of the assembled vassals who saw Fan Sui's audience showed respect and amazement.[24]

The King of Ch'in caused his retainers to retire so that the palace was completely empty. Then he rose from his haunches[25] and asked, "Won't you be kind enough to instruct me, Venerable Sir?"

"Of course, of course," Fan Sui replied.

After a short time, the king again rose from his haunches and asked, "Will I not have the benefit of your instructions, Venerable Sir?"

"Of course, of course."

So it went three times. Then the King of Ch'in rose from his haunches and said, "On what matters will I have the benefit of your instructions after all, Venerable Sir?"

"I would not dare to act so," Fan Sui replied. "I have heard that when Lü Shang 呂尚 met King Wen in ancient times,[26] he was only a fisherman fishing on the banks of the Wei River. This being the case, their relationship was [still] not close. After Lü advised him, King Wen appointed him Grand Tutor[27] and took him back in his own chariot and then his advice became more profound! Therefore, King Wen received the meritorious service of Lü Shang and finally became king of the world. If prior to that King Wen had not become close with Lü Shang and had not discussed matters deeply with him, Chou would have never have had the virtue of a Son of Heaven and [kings] Wen and Wu would have had no one to help them complete their tasks necessary to become king. Now your servant is but a vassal serving abroad and my relationship with Your Majesty is not close; yet the matters I hope to lay before you are all matters of how to reform your rule, how to handle your flesh-and-blood

---

[21] See "Cheng-yi."

[22] A road in the women's quarters in the palace.

[23] Yi-ch'ü was a tribe of the Western Jung. The Queen Dowager carried on an affair with the King of the Jung and bore him two children, then had him killed at the Kan-ch'üan Palace near the capital. Thereafter, King Chao sent an army to attack the Yi-ch'ü (see *Shih chi*, 110:2285).

[24] A parallel version of part of this preface and the following lengthy persuasions by Fan Sui can be found in *Chan-kuo ts'e* (3:44a-48a, *SPTK*).

[25] With no chairs one sat or knelt on the mat. From his kneeling position the king raised himself up from his haunches as a sign of respect when addressing Fan Sui.

[26] See our translation of *Shih chi*, 4:120 above.

[27] *T'ai Shih* 太師.

relatives. I hope to present my loyal advice, [*2407*] but I am not yet sure of Your Majesty's intent. This is the reason why I dared not respond though you asked me three times. It was not fear that kept me from speaking. I understand that what I say before you today may cause me to be executed tomorrow, but I dare not shirk my duty. If you, Great King, apply my words, then death would not trouble me, exile would not worry me, lacquering my body [to form sores] as if leprous, or letting my hair down as if mad would not shame me.

"Moreover, even those as sage as the Five Emperors[28] die, even those as humane as the Three Kings die,[29] even those as worthy as the Five Hegemons[30] die, even those as strong as Wu Huo 烏獲 and Jen 任鄙,[31] as courageous as Ch'eng Ching 成荊, Meng Pen 孟賁,[32] Prince Ch'ing-chi 慶忌,[33] and Hsia Yü 夏育[34] die. Dying is that which man cannot avoid. If by making use of this inevitable circumstance I can be of some small assistance to Ch'in, this would be my greatest wish--how could I be troubled by it? Wu Tzu Hsü got out through Chao 昭 Pass in a sack, traveling by night and hiding by day till he reached the Ling 陵 River. With nothing to eat he crawled along on his hands and knees, struck his head on the ground and stripped to the waist, drummed on his belly and played the flute; [thus] he begged for food in the market of Wu, yet finally he raised up Wu and made Ho-lu 闔廬 [King of Wu (r. 514-496 B.C.)] the Hegemon.[35] If I were able to exhaust my plans as did Wu Tzu Hsü, even if imprisonment were added to my lot, so that for the rest of my life I would not see you again, but as a result of my words were put into action, what more would trouble me? The Viscount of Chi 箕 and Chieh-yü 接輿 lacquered their bodies [to form sores] as if leprous and let their hair down as if mad, but without any benefit to their lords.[36] If by following the Viscount of Chi's actions I could be of assistance to a ruler whom I deem worthy, this would be my great honor. What shame is there in this? My only fear is that after I have died, the world will see how I died completely loyal and because of it close their mouths or stay their feet from Ch'in. Above, Honorable Sir, you fear the Queen Dowager's sternness and below you are deluded by the poses of depraved vassals. Sequestered deep in the palace, never free from the arms of your wet-nurse, your entire life you have been misled so that there is no one who can make clear to you what depravity is. This can result at the greatest in the overthrow of the ancestral temples, and at the very least in a situation where your isolation imperils you. These are the things that I fear most! As for the matter of humiliation or the sorrow of death or exile, I don't dare to stand in fear of them. If I were to die but Ch'in were well ruled, my death would be worth more than my life!"

The King of Ch'in rose up from his haunches and said, "What are you saying, Venerable Sir? The state of Ch'in is remote and distant and I am ignorant and unworthy, yet you deign to come here and honor Us with your presence, Venerable Sir. This must be Heaven

---

[28] Five mythical rulers of the earliest period (see our translation of *Shih chi* Chapter 1 above).

[29] King Yü 禹 of the Hsia, King T'ang 湯 of the Shang and either King Wu 武 or King Wen 文 of the Chou..

[30] There were several schemes of identification of these five leaders, see Sydney Rosen, "Changing Conceptions of the Hegemon in Pre-Ch'in China," in *Ancient China: Studies in Early Civilization,* ed. by David T. Roy and Tsuen-hsuin Tsien (Hong Kong: Chinese University Press, 1978), pp. 100-14.

[31] See n. 306 and 307 to our translation of *Shih chi* Chapter 5 above.

[32] See n. 55 to our translation of *Shih chi* Chapter 70 above.

[33] Son of Liao 僚, King of Wu (r. 526-515 B.C.; see Wang Li-ch'i, 79:1851n.).

[34] A brave from the state of Wey (Wang Li-ch'i, 79:1851n.); nothing about either Hsia or Prince Ch'ing-chi's deaths are known.

[35] On these events concerning Wu Tzu Hsü see our translation of *Shih chi* Chapter 66.

[36] The Viscount of Chi was the uncle of King Wu of Chou who had been imprisoned by King Chow of Yin because he had admonished Chow (see *Shih chi,* 3:108); Chieh Yü was a recluse from the state of Ch'u who pretended to be mad to avoid political involvement (see *Shih chi,* 47:1933).

troubling you on Our behalf to preserve the ancestral temple of Our former kings. That we are able to receive you commands, Venerable Sir, this must be Heaven granting its favor to Our former kings and refusing to abandon their orphan. How can you say things like this! In all affairs small or larger, from the Queen Dowager on high to the great vassals below, I want you to instruct me in them all and to have no doubts about me!" Fan Sui bowed and the king returned [*2408*] his bow.

Fan Sui said, "In the Great King's state barriers of the four quarters are its fastnesses: to the north is the Kan-ch'üan 甘泉 and the Ku-k'ou 谷口,[37] the south is belted by the Ching and Wei rivers, to the right [i.e., west[38]] are the Lung 隴 and Shu 蜀 mountains,[39] and to the left [east] the [Han-ku] Pass and the Slope[40]; with a million shock troops, a thousand war-chariots, if it is to your advantage, you can emerge and attack, if not you can reenter and defend yourself. These are territories fit for a king! The populace shun quarrels among private persons and are enboldened in battles for the state. These are people fit for a king! Your Majesty has both of these at the same time. Ruling the feudal lords with troops as brave [as Ch'in's], with chariots and horsemen as numerous [as Ch'in's], this might be compared to releasing Blackie of Han to catch a crippled rabbit.[41] The status of Hegemon could be attained, but your assembled vassals are not fit for their posts. As of today you have sealed the pass for fifteen years, not daring to have your armies peek east of the mountains. This [*2409*] is because the advice the Marquis of Jang has given Ch'in was not given loyally and the Great King's plans have contained errors."

Rising from his haunches the king replied, "I would like to hear about these erroneous plans."[42]

But since many of the king's retainers were eavesdropping, Fan Sui was afraid and didn't dare to speak of the domestic affairs; first he spoke of foreign affairs to see how the king would react.

He then moved forward and said, "The Marquis of Jang's plan to cross over Han and Wei to attack Kang and Shou in Ch'i is not good.[43] If you send too few troops they will be insufficient to harm Ch'i, if you send too many that will do injury to Ch'in. I suppose Your Majesty's plan is to send a small army and dispatch all the troops of Han and Wei, but this is not appropriate. Now when you see that your ally is disaffected, you cross over other men's states and attack it. Will this do? This plan is filled with holes. Long ago when King Min 湣 of Ch'i (r. *323-284 B.C.) attacked Ch'u to the south, he smashed their armies and killed their generals, then opened up one-thousand miles [on a side] of territory, and yet he didn't gain even an inch of land from it. This was not because he didn't want to gain territory, but because circumstances did not allow him to keep it. The other feudal lords saw that Ch'i was exhausted and its lord and minister at odds, so they raised armies to attack Ch'i and crushed it. Its officers humiliated and its weapons blunted, they all faulted their king, asking, 'Who made

---

[37] Both mountains: the first 20 miles north of modern Ch'un-hua 淳化 in Shensi and the second on the Ching 涇 River about the same distance northwest of Hsien-yang (T'an Ch'i-hsiang, 1:44).

[38] Ancient Chinese maps were arranged so that south was at the top, west to the right, east to the left, and north at the bottom.

[39] The Lung divide the modern provinces of Shensi and Kansu and the Shu are now known as the Ch'ung 崇 Mountains in west-central Szechwan (Wang Li-ch'i, 79:1851n.).

[40] Referring to the strategic "slope" extending from Mount Hsiao 崤 eastward (modern T'ung-kuan 東關 County in Shensi to Hsin-an 新安 County in Honan (Wang Li-ch'i, 79:1851n.).

[41] Blackie of Han was a hound known for his hunting prowess.

[42] This format reflects the source--the Chao-kuo ts'e--here.

[43] See our translation of *Shih chi*, 72:2329 and n. 47 on these events.

this plan?' The king replied, 'Wen Tzu 文子[44] made it.' At that the great vassals rebelled and Wen Tzu had to flee. Thus the reason for Ch'i's great defeat was that by attacking Ch'u it fattened Han and Wei. This is what is known as 'lending weapons to thieves and offering provisions to bandits.'[45] You would do better to ally yourself with distant states and attack those nearer, so that if you take an inch, it will be Your Majesty's inch, if you take a foot, it will be Your Majesty's foot. If you now abandon this and attack a distant state, surely this would be a mistake? In ancient times the state of Chung-shan, though it had an area of over one-hundred miles [on a side], was swallowed by Chao alone.[46] Its merit achieved, its name established, benefits then attached to it and no one in the world was able to harm it. Now Han and Wei are located among the central states and are the hinges of the world. If Your Majesty wants to be Hegemon, you must ally yourself with the central states and make yourself the hinge of the world, thus you may awe Ch'u and Chao. If Ch'u is mighty, ally with Chao. If Chao is mighty, ally with Ch'u. If you ally with both Ch'u and Chao, Ch'i is sure to be afraid. If Ch'i is afraid, [*2410*] it is sure to seek to serve Ch'in with humble words and lavish gifts.[47] Once you are allied with Ch'i, Han and Wei may be taken captive."

"I have wanted to get close to Wei for a long time," the king said, "yet Wei has proved a fickle state and it has not been possible. Please tell me how to get close to Wei!"

"Your Majesty should serve it with humble speech and lavish gifts. If this fails, then cede some of your territory and offer it. If this fails, then raise your army and attack them."

"We have respectfully listened to your instructions," said the king.

Thus he made Fan Sui a Foreign Excellency and consulted him on military affairs. In the end he followed Fan Sui's advice and sent the Full Grand Man Wan 綰, to attack Wei and take Huai 懷.[48] After two years, they took Hsing-ch'iu 邢丘.[49]

The Foreign Excellency Fan Sui once more advised King Chao: "The physical features of Ch'in and Han are interlaced like a piece of embroidery. For Ch'in, Han's existence is like a tree with wood grubs or a man with a disease of the heart. If the world doesn't change much, this wouldn't be of much consequence. But if the situation does change, who could harm Ch'in more than Han! Your Majesty should buy Han's allegiance [with a bribe of territory]."

"I would certainly like to buy Han's allegiance," the king said, "but if Han will not heed me, what should I do?"

"How could Han not heed you?" Fan responded. "If you send out your troops and attack Ying-yang 滎陽, then the roads to Kung 鞏 and Ch'eng-kao 成皋 will be blocked. Then cut the T'ai-hang 太行 Road in the north and the forces at Shang-tang 上黨 will be bottled up. As soon as Your Majesty raises his army and attacks Ying-yang, their state will be cut into three.[50] When Han sees it is sure to perish, how could they not heed you. If Han does heed you, you can begin to consider the matter of becoming Hegemon."

[44] I.e., T'ien Wen 田文, the Lord of Meng-ch'ang (see "So-yin").

[45] Fan Sui also uses this maxim in the parallel account in *Chan-kuo ts'e* (3:47a, *SPTK*); see also n. 44 to our translation of Chapter 87 below.

[46] According to *Shih chi*, 15:738, Chao, in concert with Ch'i and Yen, destroyed Chung-shan in 295 B.C.

[47] "Lavish gifts" normally referred to silk, jade, pi, leather and gold.

[48] Located a few miles north of the Yellow River southwest of the modern county of Wu-chih 武陟 in Honan (T'an Ch'i-hsiang, 1:36).

[49] A city about ten miles southwest of Huai (see preceding note).

[50] The Ch'in armies would apparently be moving from Huai and Hsing-ch'iu which they had recently taken. Huai and Hsing-ch'iu are both located just north of the Yellow River across from the modern city of Ying-yang 滎陽 (Honan). If the Ch'in army drove from Hsing-ch'iu to Ying-yang (which was less than 10 miles northeast of the modern city by the same name), it would cut off Ch'eng-kao (about ten miles due west of Ying-yang) and

"Excellent," said the king. Thereupon he prepared to send an envoy to Han.

[2411] Fan Sui daily became closer [to the king] and after being employed as advisor for a few more years he subsequently asked for an opportunity to advise the king,[51] and said, "When I was living east of the mountains, I heard that Ch'i had a T'ien Wen 田文,[52] but I never heard it had a king. I heard that Ch'in had a Queen Dowager, a Marquis Jang, a Lord Hua-yang, a Lord Kao-ling and a Lord Ching-yang, but I never heard it had a king. One who wields the sole authority of a state is a king; he who can accord benefit or harm is a king; he who holds the power of life and death is a king. Now the Queen Dowager wields this authority without even giving you a glance, the Marquis of Jang sends envoys abroad without reporting [to you], Lords Hua-yang, Ching-yang and the others openly apply the law as they please, and Lord Kao-ling hires and dismisses men without requesting your permission.

A state with *four* persons as exalted as these must be imperiled. Living under four such exalted persons is that which is called being without a king. How could your authority not be undermined? How could orders ever come from you? Your servant has heard those skilled in governing a state consolidate their power at home and strengthen their authority abroad. The envoys of Marquis Jang have usurped the royal prerogatives, have made decisions on behalf of the feudal lords; splitting tallies with the rest of the world, they have punished enemies and attacked other states, and none dare but heed them. If victory is won in battle, or if territory is seized in attacks, the fruits of these are turned over to T'ao 陶.[53] When the state is exhausted, it must heed the feudal lords. When battle ends in defeat, then the ill will of the common people and the adversity [of defeat] are turned over to the state. The song[54] says:

When the fruit on the tree multiplies, it breaks the branches,
By breaking the branches, it damages the trunk.
To enlarge a manor imperils the state,
Through revering vassals the ruler is demeaned.

When Ts'ui Chu 崔杼 and Nao Ch'ih 淖齒 were administering Ch'i, [the former] shot his king in the thigh [while the latter] lashed his king's tendons and hung him from the beam of a temple so that overnight he died.[55] When Li Tui 李兌 was administering Chao he

Kung (near the modern county of Kung, some thirty miles to the west-southwest). The T'ai-hang Mountains form the border between the modern provinces of Hopei and Shansi. Shang-tang is a region forty miles west of these mountains which runs north from modern Hsiang-yüan 襄垣 (Shansi). Cutting off the road to the T'ai-hang Mountains would leave Han divided into Shang-tang in the north, Cheng 鄭 (modern Hsin-Cheng 新鄭) in the southeast, and Yi-yang 宜陽 (near the modern city of the same name in Honan) in the west (see T'an Ch'i-hsiang, 1:36).

[51] There is a parallel to the following speech in *Chan-kuo ts'e* (3:48b-50a, *SPTK*).

[52] I.e., the Lord of Meng-ch'ang (see his biography in *Shih chi* Chapter 75).

[53] The Marquis of Jang's fief (see n. 17 to our translation of *Shih chi* Chapter 72 above).

[54] This song also appears in the *Chan-kuo ts'e* passage following this speech (3:50b, *SPTK*) where it is accorded the status of folk wisdom.

[55] Ts'ui Chu was a high-ranking official of the state of Ch'i during a period in which Ch'i's government was unstable. Duke Chuang 莊 (553-548 B.C.) had relations with Ts'ui's wife and was generally licentious, so Ts'ui laid a trap for him and, when the Duke tried to escape by climbing a wall, he was shot and killed (see *Shih chi*, 32:1500-1).

Nao Ch'ih was sent by Ch'u to assist King Min of Ch'i when the latter was under attack by Yen's general Yüeh Yi 樂毅. King Min made him his minister, but in 284 B.C. Nao killed the king and partitioned Ch'i with Yen (see *Shih chi*, 46:1900-1). The method of the king's demise is not specified elsewhere in *Shih chi*. However, in *Chan-kuo ts'e* [3:50a in a parallel to the persuasion given here and 5:40a (*SPTK*) in a speech by Sun Tzu] there

imprisoned the Ruler's Father at Sha-ch'iu 沙丘 for one-hundred days until he starved to death.[56] Now I have heard that the Queen Dowager of Ch'in and the Marquis of Jang have wielded power and [the Lords of] Kao-ling, Hua-yang and Ch'ing-yang assist them. If finally there is no King of Ch'in, this will indeed be a situation similar to those of Nao Ch'ih and Li Tui. As for the reasons why the [rulers of the] Three Eras[57] lost their states, their rulers completely entrusted the reins of government, indulged in wine, horses [*2412*] and hunts, and did not attend to the affairs of state. Those to whom they entrusted government were envious of worth and jealous of ability, dominated those below and hid things from those above, in order to reach their own selfish goals. They did not plan with their ruler in mind, and their rulers did not realize this, thus they lost their states. Now from those who merely have some official rank on up to the highest officers and back down even to Your Majesty's attendants, they are all the Minister of State's men. When I see how isolated you are at court, I fear that after your reign of a myriad ages someone other than one of your descendants will possess the state of Ch'in."

When King Chao heard this he was terrified, but replied, "Well said!" Then he deposed the Queen Dowager and drove the Marquis of Jang and the Lords of Kao-ling, Hua-yang, and Ching-yang beyond the Pass. The King of Ch'in then appointed Fan Sui as the Prime Minister. He took back Marquis Jang's seal of office and sent him back to T'ao. Then he accordingly had government officials supply carts and oxen, over a thousand teams, to move [his goods]. When Marquis Jang reached the Pass and the pass inspector examined his precious vessels, his precious vessels and rare curios were more numerous than those of the royal house.

Ch'in invested Fan Sui with Ying 應[58] and titled him the Marquis of Ying. This was the forty-first year of King Chao of Ch'in's reign (266 B.C.).

[2413] After Fan Sui became Prime Minister of Ch'in, Ch'in called him Chang Lu. But Wei did not know this and thought that Fan Sui had died long before. When Wei heard that Ch'in was about to mount a campaign east against Han and Wei, Wei dispatched Hsü Chia to Ch'in. Fan Sui heard of this and went incognito in tattered clothes and by backways to Hsü Chia's hostel to see him. Hsü Chia saw him and said in surprise, "Well, Fan Shu 范叔,[59] you haven't met with misfortune after all!"

"So it would seem," Fan Sui said.

Hsü Chia smiled and said, "Have you been offering advice in Ch'in, Fan Shu?"

---

are two accounts of this gruesome death. *Chan-kuo ts'e* (4:50b-51b, *SPTK*) also includes an account which says King Min died in a public execution.

[56] The most detailed account of this story appears in *Shih chi*, 43:1812-16: King Wu-ling 武靈 of Chao (r. 325-299 B.C.) decided to abdicate, taking for himself the title Chu-fu 主父 "the Ruler's Father" and enthroning his younger son the Noble Scion Ho 何 as his successor (King Hui-wen 惠文, r. 298-266 B.C.) in 298 B.C. This displeased one of his older sons, Noble Scion Chang 章, who finally (four years later) attacked King Hui-wen and the Chu-fu when they were vacationing at a pleasure palace at Sha-ch'iu (according to T'an Ch'i-hsiang, 1:38, located just southeast of modern Hopei province's Chü-lu 巨鹿) in 295 B.C. Another son of Wu-ling, Noble Scion Ch'eng 成, and Ch'eng's advisor Li Tui 李兌 came to Hui-wen's rescue, and Chang fled to the Chu-fu's palace. The Chu-fu felt that Chang had indeed been treated unjustly when his younger brother became king and at one point thought of partitioning Chao and making Chang king of the area known as Tai 代. Apparently acting in order to protect King Hui-wen's interests, Ch'eng and Li Tui besieged the Chu-fu's palace, and after Chang's death refused to allow the Chu-fu to leave, so that he finally starved to death in his palace.

[57] The Three States were Hsia, Shang (or Yin), and Chou.

[58] Less than 10 miles south of modern Pao-feng 寶豐 in Honan, located on what was then the Sha 沙 River (see T'an Ch'i-hsiang, 1:36).

[59] Shu was Fan Sui's *agnomen*.

"No. In days past I offended the Prime Minister of Wei, thus I fled here. How could I dare to offer advice!?"

"What are you doing now?" Hsü Chia asked.

"Working as a hired hand," Fan said.

Hsü Chia felt pity for him and had Fan stay to eat and drink with him. "That you have come to such straits!" Then he took one of his thick silk robes and presented it to Fan Sui.

Hsü Chia accordingly asked him, "Do you know Ch'in's Prime Minister, Lord Chang? I understand he has the king's favor and all the affairs of the world are decided by the Lord Prime Minister. Now whether my mission is successful depends on Lord Chang. My boy, do you know anyone who is familiar with the Lord Prime Minister?"

"My master," Fan said, "Knows him well, but even I can see him. Let me arrange an audience with Lord Chang for you!"

"My horses are sick and my axle is broken," Hsü said. "Unless I have a large carriage and a team of four horses I certainly can not set out."

"Allow me to borrow a large carriage and a team of four horses from my master for you."

Fan went back to get a large carriage and a team of four horses and drove it for Hsü Chia into the residence of the Prime Minister of Ch'in. Within the residence all those who recognized Fan Sui moved to the side to make way. Hsü Chia found this strange. When they reached the gate of the Prime Minister's home Fan said to Hsü Chia, "Wait for me! I'll go in first and announce your arrival to the Lord Prime Minister."

Hsü Chia waited before the gate; after holding the reins for a long time, he asked the gate attendant: "Why doesn't Fan Shu [*2414*] come out?"

"There's no Fan Shu here," the gatekeeper answered.

"The one who brought me here a little while ago."

"That was Venerable Chang, our Prime Minister!" the gatekeeper replied.

Hsü Chia was astounded. Realizing he had been deceived, he bared his torso and knelt down,[60] offering apologies for his offense through the attendant. Then, sitting midst a splendor of curtains and surrounded by a host of attendants, Fan Sui saw him. Hsü Chia touched his forehead to the ground and proclaimed his offenses worthy of death: "I never expected you raise yourself to the highest ranks.[61] From now on I'll not read the books of the world or meddle in its politics. My offense calls for the boiling cauldron! Allow me to retire to the lands of the Hu 胡 and Mo 貊![62] My fate is in your hands!"

"How many offenses do you have?" Fan Sui said.

"If I plucked out a hair as I tallied each of them there would not be enough on my head," he said.

"You have only three offenses," Fan Sui said. "Long ago during the time of King Chao 昭 of Ch'u (r. 515-489 B.C.), Shen Pao-hsü 申包胥[63] drove off the army of Wu for Ch'u and the King of Ch'u enfeoffed him with five-thousand households in Ching 荆. Shen refused to accept it, because [his efforts on Ch'u's behalf were due to the fact that] his [ancestral] graves were located in Ching. Now the graves of my ancestors are also in Wei and you earlier maligned me to Wei Ch'i because you thought I had traitorous designs in Ch'i. This

---

[60] To demonstrate he awaited punishment.

[61] See n. 47 to our translation of *Shih chi* Chapter 61 above.

[62] Barbarians to the north and west of lands settled by the Chinese at this time.

[63] An official of Ch'u enfeoffed with a city in Shen; in 505 B.C. he enlisted the assistance of troops from Ch'in to repulse Wu (see our translation of *Shih chi*, 66:2176-7 and 5:197 above).

was your first offense. When Wei Ch'i disgraced me in the privy, you did not stop him. This was your second offense. Then you took your turn while drunk to urinate on me. How could you have been so hardhearted? This was your third offense. The reason you will be spared death, Master, is because of a kindly given thick silk gown and an old friend's heart. Because of these I shall spare you." Hsü Chia thanked him and the audience was ended. [Fan Sui] entered and told King Chao of this and had him dismiss Hsü Chia and send him back.

When Hsü Chia came to take leave of Fan Sui, Fan had a great feast prepared, inviting all the envoys of the other feudal lords. As they sat together in the hall, they partook of a plethora of food and drink. But he had Hsü Chia seated outside in the courtyard at the foot of the hall and placed fodder and beans before him, ordering two tattooed convicts to hold him on either side and to force him to eat them like a horse. Then he reproved him, "Tell the King of Wei for me to bring Wei Ch'i's head here at once! Otherwise, I will slaughter everyone in Ta Liang."

When Hsü Chia had returned, he reported this to Wei Ch'i. Wei Ch'i was frightened, fled to Chao and went into hiding in the Lord of P'ing-yüan's residence.

After Fan Sui became Prime Minister, Wang Chi said to him,[64] "There are three matters we can not anticipate and three we can do nothing about. The first thing we cannot anticipate is if the palace carriage will be hitched late one day.[65] The second thing we cannot anticipate is if you were to suddenly abandon your hostels and houses.[66] The third thing we cannot anticipate is if I might suddenly be used to fill in a ditch.[67] If the palace carriage is hitched late, though you might feel sorry for me, nothing can be done about it. If you suddenly abandon your hostels and houses, although you might feel sorry for me, [*2415*] nothing indeed can be done about it. If I were suddenly used to fill in a ditch, no matter how much you might feel sorry for me, nothing indeed can be done about it."

Fan Sui was upset and went to speak of this to the king: "Only a man as loyal as Wang Chi could have brought me through the Han-ku Pass; only a man as worthy and sagely as you, Great King, could have ennobled me. Now my position has reached that of Prime Minister and my rank is that of a [High] Ranking Marquis, while Wang Chi's position is still only a Receptionist, not that which he hoped for when he brought me to you." King Chao summoned Wang Chi and appointed him Governor of Ho-tung 河東[68] and exempted him from submitting annual reports for three years.[69] Fan also recommended Cheng An-p'ing and King Chao made him a general. He then distributed all the wealth of his household to repay those whom he had encountered when in distress. Even the kindness of a single meal had to be rewarded, even the enmity of an angry look had to be repaid.

When Fan Sui had been Prime Minister of Ch'in for two years, in the forty-second year of King Chao of Ch'in (264 B.C.), he mounted a campaign eastward against Shao-ch'ü 少曲[70] and Kao-p'ing 高平[71] in Han and seized them.

---

[64] This conversation all takes place in the context of Wei Chi's resentment that Fan Sui seems to have forgotten all that Wei did for him and has not yet recommended him to King Chao.

[65] The palace carriage brings the king to early morning court. For it to be late would suggest a problem with the king and it is in fact a standard euphemism for the death of a ruler.

[66] I.e., a polite euphemism for "to die."

[67] Once again a euphemism for to die (in the case of a commoner).

[68] A commandery east of the Yellow River after it bends northward from its confluence with the Wei River (in modern Shensi; see T'an Ch'i-hsiang, 1:35); Ho-tung was established after Wei ceded its capital city of An-i 安邑 to Ch'in and moved east to Ta Liang.

[69] These reports were filed by emissaries from the commanderies each winter and designed to keep the court informed about major events and developments in the provinces (see "Chi-chieh").

When King Chao of Ch'in learned that Wei Ch'i was in the residence of the Lord of P'ing-yüan, he felt he had to seek revenge for Fan Sui; feigning friendship, he send a letter to the Lord of P'ing-yüan saying: "We have heard of Your Lordship's high principles and would like to establish a friendship between us man to man. If you would favor Us with a visit, We would hope to drink with you for ten days."

The Lord of P'ing-yüan feared Ch'in and moreover believed the king's letter, [*2416*] so he entered Ch'in and saw King Chao. After the King and the Lord had drunk for several days, King Chao told the Lord of Ping-yüan, "Long ago King Wen of Chou obtained Lü Shang as his 'Grandfather,' and Duke Huan of Ch'i obtained Kuan Yi-wu as his 'Uncle' Chung;[72] now Lord Fan is my 'Uncle' Shu.[73] Lord Fan's enemy is now in your home and I hope you might send an envoy back to fetch his head. If not, I will not let you go out through the Pass."

The Lord of P'ing-yüan said, "Those friends one makes when one is high ranked are for the time when one is in a lowly situation. Those friends one makes when one is wealthy are for the time when one is impoverished. Now Wei Ch'i is my friend. Even if he were at my house, I certainly could not put him out. But he isn't even at my residence."

King Chao of Ch'in then sent a letter to the King of Chao which read:

> Your younger brother[74] is in Ch'in, while the enemy of Lord Fan, Wei Ch'i, is in Lord P'ing-yüan's home. Let Your Majesty send someone to quickly fetch me his head! Otherwise, I shall call up my troops and attack Chao and moreover will not allow your brother to leave through the Pass.

King Hsiao-ch'eng 孝成 of Chao (r. 265-245 B.C.) then sent soldiers to surround the Lord of P'ing-yüan's house. When matters became desperate, Wei Ch'i fled by night to see the Prime Minister of Chao, His Excellency Yü.[75] Excellency Yü, figuring that in the end the King of Chao could never be persuaded, untied his seal of office and fled with Wei Ch'i over back roads. Realizing that they could reach none of the other feudal states quickly, they fled back to Ta Liang, hoping that through the office of the Lord of Hsin-ling[76] they might flee to Ch'u. When the Lord of Hsin-ling learned of this, fearing Ch'in, he vacillated and would not see them, asking, "What sort of man is Excellency Yü?" At the time Hou Ying 侯嬴[77] was at his side and said, "A man is indeed difficult to know and knowing a man can be indeed be a difficult matter! When Excellency Yü first came to see the King of Chao, wearing straw sandals and carrying a bamboo umbrella over his shoulder,[78] he received a pair of white-jade discs[79]

---

[70] A region east of modern Chi-yüan 濟源 City in Honan (T'an Ch'i-hsiang, 1:36).

[71] A city (also known as Hsiang 向) about fifteen miles southeast of modern Chi-yüan just north of the Yellow River (T'an Ch'i-hsiang, 1:36).

[72] On Lü Shang see our translation of *Shih chi,* 4:120 and *Shih chi,* 32:1477 above; on Kuan Yi-wu, see our translation of *Shih chi* Chapter 62.

[73] These are puns. T'ai-kung 太公 is an abbreviation for T'ai-kung Wang 太公望, a title applied to Lü Shang 呂尚 which literally means " Our Grandfather's Hope" (see n. 49 to our translation of *Shih chi* Chapter 4 above). Chung Fu 仲父 was perhaps a title as well, but literally it means "Elder Paternal Ucle." Shu 叔 was Fan Sui's *agnomen,* but Shu Fu 叔父 literally means "Younger Paternal Uncle."

[74] He was actually his uncle, see n. 1 in our translation of Chapter 76.

[75] See his biography in *Shih chi* Chapter 76.

[76] See his biography in *Shih chi* Chapter 77 .

[77] The Lord of Hsin-ling's most trusted advisor, see our translation of *Shih chi* Chapter 77.

[78] See n. 17 to our translation of Chapter 76 above.

[79] *Pi* 璧 were jade discs with a circular hole in the center. Their shape imitated heaven and they were used in

and one-hundred *yi* of gold. When the king saw him the second time, he was made Senior Excellency. The third time, he received the seal of the office of the prime minister and was enfeoffed as a marquis with ten-thousand households. At that time the whole world strove to know him."

"When Wei Ch'i, in dire straits, went to call on Excellency Yü, Excellency Yü, without concern for his high rank and salary, untied his seal of office as prime minister, abandoned his fief of ten-thousand households and fled over back roads. Anxious on behalf of a knight in distress, he turns to Your Lordship and you now say, 'What sort of man is he?' A man is indeed difficult to know and knowing a man can indeed be a difficult matter!"

Lord of Hsin-ling was greatly ashamed and went by carriage beyond the city limits to welcome them. When Wei Ch'i heard that the Lord of Hsin-ling was at first troubled about seeing them, he was angry and slit his throat. The King of Chao heard this and at last got his head and presented it to Ch'in. Then King Chao of Ch'in allowed the Lord of Ping-yüan to return to Chao.

[2417] In the forty-third year of King Chao (263 B.C.), Ch'in attacked Fen-hsing 汾陘[80] in Han and took it, accordingly building a city wall around Kuang-wu 廣武 on the River.[81]

In the fifth year after this (259 B.C.),[82] King Chao, employing a plan of the Marquis of Ying sent in a counter-agent to deceive Chao. Because of him, Chao ordered [the Lord of] Ma-fu's 馬服[83] son to replace Lien P'o 廉頗[84] as commander. Ch'in crushed Chao at Ch'ang-p'ing 長平[85] and then laid siege to Han-tan.[86] Not long after[87] Fan Sui had a quarrel with the Lord of Wu-an 武安, Pai Ch'i 白起; he spoke up bluntly [and Ch'in] killed [Pai Ch'i] (257 B.C.).

Fan Sui recommended Cheng An-p'ing and [Ch'in] sent him to strike at Chao. Cheng An-p'ing was surrounded by the Chao armies and, when the situation became critical, surrendered with twenty-thousand men to Chao. The Marquis of Ying, seated on a straw mat, asked for punishment. According to the law of Ch'in, when one person recommended another, and the person recommended failed, both were guilty of the same offense. Therefore, because of the Marquis of Ying's crime, his three clans[88] should have been taken into custody. The King of Chao was afraid of discomforting the Marquis of Ying, and thus sent out an order throughout the capital saying, "Whoever dares to speak of the Cheng An-p'ing affair will be guilty of

sacrifices to heaven (by the ruler) or to the ruler (by the feudal lords).

[80] The "So-yin" suggests Fen and Hsing are two locations both on the Western border of Han and T'an Ch'i-hsiang (1:35) does list two walled cities by these names a each a few miles from the modern city of Hou-ma 侯馬 in Shansi; but this could also refer to a gorge on the Fen River.

[81] Kuang-wu was a city a few miles south of the Yellow River at the extreme eastern border of Han (about 5 miles northeast of modern Ying-yang in Honan, see T'an Ch'i-hsiang, 1:36). It was located between the cities of Ying-yang and Ch'eng-kao which Ch'in had earlier annexed. Fortification of the city was probably necessary because retaliation by Han was expected.

[82] "In the fifth year after this" is puzzling. It seems Ssu-ma Ch'ien is using the counting system discussed in "Chronology" in the front-matter, but even so this date seems incorrect since the battle of Ch'ang-p'ing took place in 260 B.C. (see our translation of *Shih chi* Chapter 73).

[83] Son of Chao She 趙奢, Chao K'uo 括.

[84] See his biography in *Shih chi* Chapter 81.

[85] About 10 miles north of modern Kao-p'ing 高平 in a "high plateau" along the Tan River 丹 in Shansi. It was about equidistant between the eastern border of Ch'in and Han-tan (see T'an Ch'i-hsiang, 1:36).

[86] Han-tan was the capital of Chao, nearly coterminous with the modern city of the same name.

[87] The events next described took place the following year, 257 B.C. (see *Shih chi*, 73:73:2331-8).

[88] His parents, his brothers, and his wife. Other explanations claim that the families of his father, mother and wife should have been arrested.

the same crime as he!" And he increased generously the daily allotment of food for the Minister of State, The Marquis of Ying, to put his concerns to rest. Two years later (255 B.C.), while Wang Chi was serving as Governor of Ho-tung, he colluded with the other feudal lords and was sentenced according to the law to be executed. And the Marquis of Ying grew daily more uncomfortable.[89]

While holding court one day King Chao sighed. The Marquis of Ying came forward and said, "I have heard that 'When the ruler is troubled, the minister is disgraced, when the ruler is disgraced, the minister deserves to die.' Now the Great King sits troubled in his court and I venture to ask for [*2418*] punishment." King Chao said, "I have heard that Ch'u's iron swords are sharp, but its singers and jesters unskilled. With iron swords sharp, its knights are courageous; with singers and jesters unskilled, their thoughts are far reaching.[90] With far-reaching thoughts leading courageous knights, I fear Ch'u has designs on Ch'in. If the materials are not at hand, one cannot respond to sudden developments. Now the Lord of Wu-an has died and Cheng An-p'ing and others have proved traitors. Within we have no excellent commanders and without are many enemy nations. For this I am troubled." The King hoped thereby to rouse the Marquis of Ying. The Marquis took fright and could not come up with a plan. When Ts'ai Tse heard of this, he went to enter Ch'in.

Ts'ai Tse

Ts'ai Tse 蔡澤 was a native of Yen. He had traveled about studying and seeking office from many feudal lords, great and small, without success. Then he went to consult T'ang Chü 唐舉,[91] the physiognomist, saying, "I have heard, Venerable Sir, that you examined Li Tui and said to him, 'Within one-hundred days you will hold the reins of power.' Is it true?"

"It is," he replied.

"What about me?" Ts'ai asked.

T'ang Chü looked at him carefully and answered with a smile, "You have a forceful nose,[92] gigantic shoulders, a prominent forehead, eyebrows which join across the bridge of your nose, and bowed legs. I have heard that a sage is ill formed.[93] Similar to you, sir?" Ts'ai Tse knew T'ang Chü was joking and so he said, "Wealth and status are that which I am fated for. What I don't know is whether I shall have a long life. This I would like to hear from you." T'ang Chü said, "You have forty-three years to go." Ts'ai Tse thanked him with a smile and left, saying to his driver, "To eat fine millet and fatty meat, to jump and race swift horses, to wear a golden seal of office at my chest, a purple cord at my waist, to bow before my ruler, and to eat the meat of the rich and noble, forty-three years will be enough!" [Then] he left to go to Chao, but was driven out. He went to Han and Wei, but his pot and rice-steamer were stolen along the road. When he heard that Cheng An-p'ing and Wang Chi, whom had been recommended by the Marquis of Ying, had both committed serious crimes against Ch'in and that the Marquis had been shamed, Ts'ai Tse headed west into Ch'in.[94]

---

[89] According to *Shih chi*, 15:748, Wang Chi was executed in 255 B.C. According to the Ch'in Annals (*Pien-nien chi*, p. 6), Fan Sui was executed in the same year

[90] Since they have no distractions in Ch'u, they plot conquest beyond their borders.

[91] A noted physiognomist from Wei (see Wang Li-ch'i, 79:1857).

[92] Reading the variant *chieh* 偈 for *ho* 曷 as noted in "Chi-chieh."

[93] We follow "Cheng-yi" (see also Takigawa, 79:35). Another reading would be "a sage does not go to a physiognomist."

[94] Another version of the following conversation appears in *Chan-kuo ts'e* (3:70b-74b, *SPTK*).

[2419] Just before he was to see King Chao, he sent someone to make the following announcement to incite the Marquis of Ying: "This visitor from Yen, Ts'ai Tse, is the world's most elegant, eloquent and wise knight. Once he has audience with the King of Ch'in, the king will certainly press you and strip you of your position."

The Marquis of Ying said, "I am well versed in the hundred schools of thought, as well as all the historical events of the Three Dynasties and the reigns of the Five Emperors. I can refute any speaker no matter how eloquent. How could he embarrass me or seize my position?" And thus he sent to summon Ts'ai Tse.

When Ts'ai Tse entered, he merely bowed [to the Marquis]. The Marquis of Ying was already displeased, and when he saw furthermore how arrogant he was, he rebuked him, "Can it be true that you have proclaimed that you intend to replace me as Prime Minister of Ch'in?"

"That is correct!"

"May I ask how?"

"Alas, how can you be so slow? Just as the four seasons change, what has reached completion gives way to the new. In life to have strong limbs, quick hands and feet, [*2420*] sharp ears and eyes, and a heart sage and wise, is this not the desire of a true knight?"

"It is!" said the Marquis of Ying.

Ts'ai Tse said, "To be imbued with humanity and hold to one's principles, to follow the Way and to spread virtue, to succeed in the world so that the world bears one good will and respectful love, and exalts one as lord and king, is this not the hope of the eloquent and wise?"

"It is," the Marquis said.

Ts'ai Tse continued, "To have rank and wealth, fame and honor, to complete and order the myriad things, causing each to be in its proper place, to be endowed with long life and to live out all one's years without suffering premature death, to have the world carry on one's line and guard one's legacy, passing it on without end, to have purity in name and fact and grace flowing for a thousand *li*, to have generation after generation praise one without end, beginning and ending with Heaven and Earth, is this not the mark of the Way and its Virtue and what the sage calls an auspicious and excellent matter?"

"It is," said the Marquis.

Ts'ai Tse said, "The Lord of Shang 商 (c. 390-338 B.C.) of Ch'in, Wu Ch'i 吳起 (d. 381 B.C.) of Ch'u, or Grand Master Chung 種 of Yüeh, was their final end also something to be desired?"[95]

The Marquis of Ying realized that Ts'ai Tse was trying to trap him through this kind of argument, so he purposely twisted logic and replied, "What would be wrong with this? When Kung-sun Yang [The Lord of Shang] served Duke Hsiao[96] he brought his life to a close without duplicitous thoughts. He exhausted himself for the public good and turned his back on

---

[95] The Lord of Shang served Duke Hsiao 孝 of Ch'in (r. 361-338 B.C.) for years, but on the Duke's death was branded a rebel, killed and his corpse torn apart by chariots at King Hui-wen 惠文 of Ch'in's orders in 338 B.C. (see our translation of *Shih chi*, 68:2337 above).

Wu Ch'i served King Tao 悼 of Ch'u (r. 401-381 B.C.) and incurred the wrath of Ch'u's powerful families; after King Tao died he threw himself on the king's body and was stabbed and shot by a mob (see our translation of *Shih chi*, 65:2168 above).

Wen Chung 文種 (*agnomen* Shao-ch'in 少禽) was a trusted advisor to Kou-chien 句踐, the King of Yüeh (r. 497-465 B.C.--see also n. 57 to our translation of *Shih chi*, Chapter 66 above). Kou-chien eventually turned against him, gave him a sword, and order him to take his own life (in 472 B.C., see *Wu Yüeh ch'un-ch'iu*, 10:9b, *SPPY*).

[96] See also n. 95 above.

selfish thoughts. He set out knives and saws to restrain depravity and evil and attained good order by establishing faith in rewards and punishments. He bared his belly and heart, displayed his nature and qualities, suffered resentment and blame, deceived his old friend, seized the Noble Scion of Wei, Ang 卬,[97] secured Ch'in's altars of soil and grain, benefited the populace, and in the end, captured commanders, defeated enemies, and extended the borders a thousand *li,* all for Ch'in."

"When Wu Ch'i served King Tao 悼 (r. 401-381 B.C.) he prevented selfish interest from harming public good, he prevented slander from concealing the loyal. In words he did not seek casual agreement, in actions he did not seek casual acceptance. He did not change his path because of peril. In pursuing his principles he did not avoid hardships. Instead, to make his ruler Hegemon and to strengthen the state, he did not decline disaster and calamity. When Grand Master Chung served the King of Yüeh, though his ruler was trapped and humiliated, he remained completely loyal, without lapse. Those his ruler was dethroned, he exhausted his ability without swerving, achieved merit without arrogance, achieved rank and wealth, without pride or slackness. Gentlemen such as these three are indeed the epitome of principle, the model of loyalty. Thus the superior gentleman will die for his principles and looks on death as a return home. Living in humiliation cannot compare to dying in glory. The knight as a matter of course will sacrifice his life to achieve fame. He thinks only of the dictates of his principles. Though death comes, he has no regrets. What would be wrong with this?"

[2421] "If the ruler is sagacious and his vassals worthy, this is the world's great good fortune," said Ts'ai Tse. "If the lord is intelligent and his vassals upright, this is the state's good fortune. If the father is kind and the son filial, the husband faithful and the wife chaste, this is the family's good fortune."

"Thus Pi-kan 比干 was loyal, but could not save Yin,[98] [Wu] Tzu Hsü 伍子胥 was wise, but could not preserve Wu,[99] and Shen Sheng 申生 was filial, but the state of Chin suffered strife.[100] They all had loyal vassals and filial sons, but their states and houses suffered destruction and strife. Why was this? There were neither intelligent lords nor worthy fathers to heed them. Thus the world viewed the lords and fathers as objects of scorn and pitied the vassals and sons. Now the Lord of Shang, Wu Ch'i, and Grand Master Chung were vassals; they were in the right, their lords, in the wrong. Thus the world speaks of these three men as those who achieved merit but won no gratitude, rather than admiring them for dying unappreciated. But if one must wait for death to establish one's loyalty and make one's name, not even Viscount of Wei 微 would be considered humane, not even Confucius would be considered sagely, not even Kuan Chung 管仲 would be considered great![101] A man who would establish merit surely must hope to achieve *complete* success. If one can keep one's name and one's life intact, this is best. If one's name becomes a model through the loss of one's life, this is next. But to preserve one's life in shame, this is the worst." At this the Marquis of Ying expressed his agreement.

---

[97] See our translation of *Shih chi,* 68:2232-33 for details of the Lord of Shang's deception of Noble Scion Ang.

[98] Pi-kan was loyal in that he dared to warn King Chow 紂, the last sovereign of the Yin dynasty, of his indiscretions; for his temerity he was put to death (see our translation of *Shih chi,* 3:107-8 above).

[99] See our translation of *Shih chi* Chapter 65.

[100] Shen Sheng was the son of Duke Hsien 獻 of Chin (r. 676-651 B.C.) and his chosen successor. Though loyal to his father, he was slandered and forced to commit suicide (see Yang, *Tso chuan,* Hsi 10, p. 334). Since his father did not appoint another successor, after his death Chin was thrown into chaos as his brothers fought for power (see also n. 83 to our translation of *Shih chi* Chapter 5 above).

[101] On the Viscount of Wei see our translation of *Shih chi,* 3:105 and 108-9. There is a biography of Confucius in *Shih chi,* Chapter 47 and one for Kuan Chung in Chapter 62.

After a short time had passed, Ts'ai Tse took advantage of a moment of leisure to say: "As vassals, the Lord of Shang, Wu Ch'i and Grand Master Chung exhausted their advice, achieved merit, and thus are worthy of emulation. Hung Yao 閎夭[102] in his service to King Wen and the Duke of Chou in his support of King Ch'eng 成 (r. *c.* 1067-1031 B.C.), were they not also loyal and sage? In evaluating the relationship between lord and vassal, were the the Lord of Shang, Wu Ch'i and Grand Master Chung more worthy of emulation than Hung Yao and the Duke of Chou?"

"The Lord of Shang, Wu Ch'i and Grand Master Chung were not their equals," the Marquis of Ying said.

"Then in that case how does My Lord's ruler compare in mercy and humanity, in employing the loyal, in exalting old friends, in worth and wisdom, in his ability to grow as close as glue and lacquer to gentlemen possessing the Way, in his principled refusal to turn his back on meritorious vassals, how does he compare with Duke Hsiao [of Ch'in], [King] Tao of Ch'u, or the King of Yüeh?"

"I do not know how he compares," the Marquis said.

"Your current ruler's trust in his loyal vassals cannot surpass that of Duke Hsiao, King Tao, or the King of Yüeh," Ts'ai Tse said. "In laying out clever schemes, My Lord, in being able to guard against peril and to polish administration for your ruler, in bringing order from strife and strengthening armies, in fending off disaster and turning back difficulties, in expanding territory and sowing grains, in enriching the state and providing for the royal house, in strengthening the ruler, in exalting the altars of soil and grain, in honoring the ancestral temple, so that the world does not dare to deceive or transgress against one's ruler and the ruler's [*2422*] majesty covers and rocks all within the seas, while one's own merit is illustrious for over ten-thousand *li,* and one's fame and glory are passed on to a thousand generations, how do you, My Lord, compare to the Lord of Shang, Wu Ch'i or Grand Master Chung?"

"I am not their equal," the Marquis of Ying said.

Ts'ai Tse said, "Your current ruler's trust in his loyal vassals and his refusal to forget old friends does not surpass that of Duke Hsiao, King Tao and Kou-chien, and My Lord's merit and achievements, love and trust, intimacy and favor are not equal to that of the Lord of Shang, Wu Ch'i and Grand Master Chung. Yet My Lord' emolument and position are the acme of nobility and the wealth of your personal household surpasses all three of them. Now if you decline to retire, I fear that the disaster which will befall you shall be worse than that which befell them and privately feel apprehension on My Lordship's behalf. As the saying goes, 'The sun at noon must sink, the moon when full must shrink.' When matters reach their acme they must decline, this is Heaven and Earth's constant rule. To advance and retreat, to expand and contract, changing with the times, this is sage's constant Way. Thus [Confucius said], "When a state has the Way, then may you hold office; when a state is without it, then you should go into reclusion."[103] The sage said, "When a flying dragon is in heaven,[104] it brings profit to meet a great man."[105] "Wealth and nobility gained by doing what is not right are to me like the floating clouds."[106] Now you have avenged the wrongs done you, repaid your debts of gratitude and reached your aspirations, yet you have not made any change in your plans. This is not what I would personally chose on your behalf, My Lord!"

[102] An aide to King Wen of Chou. When the king was being held by King Chow, Hung Yao sent the latter beautiful women and fine horses to gain King Wen's freedom (see *Shih chi,* 4:106).

[103] *Lun yü,* 8/13.

[104] I.e., when the ruler is a sage .

[105] This text is from the first hexagram of the *Yi ching* (*Chou Yi cheng-yi* [1:3b, *SPPY*]).

[106] *Lun yü,* 7/15; "floating clouds" are a symbol here of something insubstantial or worthless.

"It is not that the kingfisher, swan, rhinoceros and elephant put themselves in positions close to death, but that they are lured by the bait. It is not that Su Ch'in 蘇秦[107] and the Earl of Chih 智[108] did not possess wits enough to avoid shame and keep far from death, but that they were lured by an insatiable greed for profit. Thus the sage establishes a social norm to regulate desire, takes from the people in strict measure, employs them in the proper season, and uses them for a limited term. Thus his ambitions are not overweening and his behavior is not overbearing. He treads the Way without swerving, thus the world accepts him without hesitation. Long ago Duke Huan 桓 of Ch'i (r. 685-643 B.C.) called the feudal lords together nine times,[109] and at one stroke rectified the world, [yet] at the assembly at Kuei-ch'iu 葵丘 because of his arrogance the nine states turned their backs on him.[110] The troops of Fu-ch'ai 夫差, King of Wu were without peer in the world, but because his prowess and might led him to treat the feudal lords with contempt, humiliating Ch'i and Chin, he lost his life and his state.[111] Hsia Yü 夏育[112] and Grand Scribe Chiao 噭[113] could cow armies with their shouting and bellowing, but they died at the hands of common men. Such are the disasters brought on by going to extremes without regard for Way or Principle, failing to dwell in humility or to retire with frugality.

"The Lord of Shang clarified the laws and ordinances and cut off the sources of evil for Duke Hsiao of Ch'in, gave due reward to the worthy and due punishment to offenders, equalized scales and standardized measures, adjusted "the light and heavy,"[114] and removed the raised paths and boundary balks,[115] thus securing the populace in their tasks, and unifying social conventions. He encouraged the commoners to till and farm, to make use of the soil, each household was not to pursue a secondary occupation, but to labor in the fields, to store up their harvest, and to practice matters of battle and drill. Thus when they mobilized their troops, their territory expanded, when they rested their troops, their state prospered. Thus Ch'in is without peer within the world. He struck awe into the feudal lords, fulfilling the State of Ch'in's goal. His merit accomplished, he was torn apart by chariots!"

"Ch'u had thousands of *li* [on a side] of territory and a million halberd-bearing troops, yet Pai Ch'i led a force of several tens of thousands in battle against [*2423*] Ch'u, and in the first battle captured Yen 鄢 and Ying 郢, burning Yi-ling 夷陵; in the second battle he annexed Han 漢 and Shu in the south. Then crossing Han 韓 and Wei and attacking mighty Chao, to the north he killed Ma-fu 馬服 and butchered his host of more than 400,000, annihilating them at the foot of Ch'ang-p'ing. Blood ran in rivers and the sound of screams thundered. He then advanced and besieged Han-tan, putting the imperial goal within Ch'in's grasp. Ch'u and Chao were the world's mightiest states and Ch'in's bitter foes. Yet after

---

[107] See his biography in *Shih chi* Chapter 69.

[108] See n. 242 to our translation of *Shih chi* Chapter 4 above.

[109] See *Shih chi,* 62:2131.

[110] This meeting took place in 651 B.C. about 50 miles east of modern Kai-feng in Honan (according to T'an Ch'i-hsiang, 1:25). The states of Ch'i, Lu, Sung, Wei, Cheng, Hsü, and Ts'ao, among others, took part (see *Shih chi,* 5:187 and n. 99 to our translation of Chapter 5).

[111] See our translation of *Shih chi* Chapter 66 above.

[112] Our information on Hsia Yü is based entirely on "So-yin." Also known at Fen Yü 賁育, he was killed by a certain T'ien Po 田博. Of his talent for shouting, nothing is known aside from this passage.

[113] The "So-yin" cites Kao Yu and provides some information on Chiao--namely that he was not the same Grand Scribe Chiao who lived during King Hsiang 襄 of Ch'i's reign (283-265 B.C.), but gives no information on Chiao's ability to wage war.

[114] See n. 52 to our translation of *Shih chi* Chapter 62 above.

[115] See also n. 28 to our translation of *Shih chi* Chapter 68.

this, Ch'u and Chao groveled in fear, not daring to attack Ch'in. Such was the power of Pai Ch'i![116] He personally conquered more than 70 cities. His merit accomplished, he was granted a sword and death at the Tu 杜 Relay-station.[117]

"On behalf of King Tao of Ch'u, Wu Ch'i established laws, humbled and diminished the might and authority of the great vassals, fired the incompetent, dismissed the useless, removed unnecessary official posts, cut off the pleading of special interests, unified the social conventions of the state of Ch'u, barred wandering and transient commoners, turning out tillers and warriors of the highest caliber; to the south he took the Yang-yüeh 楊越[118] and to the north he annexed Ch'en and Ts'ai. He broke their alliances and shattered their counteralliances, closing the mouths of wandering persuaders; he barred factions, thus disciplining the populace. He secured the government of the state of Ch'u; its military might shook the world and its majesty subdued the feudal lords. His merit accomplished, he was dismembered.

"Grand Master Chung made circumspect and far-sighted plans for the King of Yüeh, rescued him at K'uai-chi, turned destruction into salvation, and made disgrace into glory. He cultivated the wastelands and filled the cities, he expanded its territory and cultivated grains, leading the men of the four quarters. Mobilizing the strength of superior and inferior, he aided Kou-chien in his worthiness, wreaked vengeance on Fu-ch'ai and in the end seized powerful Wu, establishing Yüeh's hegemony. His merit already clear and certain, Kou-chien in the end betrayed and killed him.

"When their merit was accomplished these four men did not step aside and disaster befell them. This is what is meant by stretching out and not being able to pull back, setting out and not being able to return.

"Fan Li 范蠡[119] knew this, rose above the world [of politics] and lived a long life as His Honor Chu 朱 of T'ao 陶. Haven't you seen the *liu-po*[120] players? Sometimes they stack large amounts on one throw, sometimes they split up their wager into smaller amounts for smaller gain. This you know well. Now as Prime Minister of Ch'in you draw up plans without leaving your mat and make strategy without leaving the corridors of the court, you control the other feudal lords from your seat, wield San-ch'uan 三川 to your benefit, thus securing Yi-yang 宜陽.[121] You cut off the redoubt of Yang-ch'ang 羊腸, blocked the road to T'ai-hang 太行, and severed the paths to Fan 范 and Chung-hang 中行,[122] and the Six States were unable to join in alliance [against Ch'in]. Your plank roads extend a thousand *li*, reaching to Shu and Han, and cause the entire world to fear Ch'in. Ch'in's desires are achieved. My Lord's merits have reached their limit. This is the time for Ch'in to 'split up their wager into smaller amounts for smaller gain.' This being the case, if you do not now retire, you will be a Lord of Shang, a Magistrate of Pai 白,[123] a Wu Ch'i, a Grand Master Chung.

"I have heard that 'If you take water as a mirror, you will learn the features of your face, if you take other men as a mirror you may learn of fortune and disgrace.' And in the *Book of*

[116] On these events see our translation of *Shih chi* Chapter 73.

[117] See our translation of *Shih chi*, 73:2337 and 71:2139 and n. 71 to our translation of Chapter 71.

[118] One of the Yüeh tribes in middle and lower Yangtze Valley (see Wang Li-ch'i, 79:1861n. and also *Shih chi*, 65:2168 and n. 60 to our translation of Chapter 65).

[119] See n. 406 to our translation of *Shih chi* Chapter 6.

[120] On this game see n. 65 to our translation of Chapter 69 above.

[121] Ch'in took Yi-yang in 309 B.C. (see *Shih chi*, 71:2308 and n. 12 to our translation of Chapter 71).

[122] On Yang-ch'ang and T'ai-hang, see n. 51 and 67 (respectively) to our translation of *Shih chi* Chapter 65 above. Fan and Chung-hang were statelets taken by the Three Chin (see Wang Li-ch'i, 79:1861n.) and here stand metonymically for those three states.

[123] See our translation of his biography in *Shih chi*, 61:2181-83.

Documents it is written that 'One cannot dwell long in a state of success.'[124] Which of the disasters that befell these four men would you chose, My Lord? Why not take this opportunity to return the prime minister's seal, yield to a worthy man and turn the seal over to him, retire and [*2424*] dwell on the cliffs gazing on the rivers? You may be sure of the integrity of a Po Yi 伯夷,[125] and, after a long life as the Marquis of Ying, [your descendants] may call themselves 'the lonely one' for generation after generation. You are sure to have the humility of a Hsü Yu 許由[126] and a Chi Tzu 季 of Yen-ling 延陵,[127] and the longevity of a [Wang Tzu] Ch'iao 喬[128] and Sung 松.[129] How does this compare with ending in disaster? Which of these would you choose, My Lord? If you endure, unable to part, if you hesitate unable to decide, you are sure to suffer the disaster of the four men! The *Book of Changes* says: 'The dragon on high will have its regrets!'[130] This refers to those who climb high and cannot come down, this is what is meant by stretching out and not being able to pull back, setting out and not being able to return. I hope that you might lay your plans carefully, My Lord.

"Well put," said the Marquis of Ying. 'I have heard that a man who cannot check his desires will lose what he desires. One dissatisfied with what he possesses will lose his possessions.'[131] Since you have been kind enough to instruct me, Venerable Sir, I shall respectfully accept your command." Then he led Ts'ai Tse to his seat and made him a senior retainer.

A few days later the marquis went to court and told King Chao: "There is a traveler newly arrived from east of the pass who is called Ts'ai Tse. He is a rhetorician and so well versed in both the affairs of the Three Kings [*2425*] and the Five Hegemons and the changes of the mundane world that he can be entrusted with the government of the state of Ch'in. I have seen a great number of men, but none measure up to him. I myself am not his equal. I venture to inform you of this!"

King Chao of Ch'in summoned [Ts'ai Tse] to an audience and, after speaking with him, was so pleased by him that he appointed him Foreign Excellency. The Marquis of Ying, using the pretext of illness, asked to return the prime minister's seal. King Chao urged him to continue, but the Marquis of Ying insisted he was too ill. When Fan Sui resigned as Prime Minister, King Chao, still pleased with Ts'ai Tse's plans, appointed him Prime Minister of Ch'in and annexed the [Royal] House of Chou to the east (255 B.C.).

After Ts'ai Tse had been in office for several months, someone denounced him and, fearing that he would be executed, he returned his seal of office on the pretext of being ill and was titled Lord Kang-ch'eng 綱成. He lived in Ch'in for more than ten years, serving King Chao, King Hsiao-wen 孝文 (r. 250 B.C.), and King Chuang-hsiang 莊襄 (r. 249-247). Finally he served the First Emperor as the envoy to Yen and after three years, Yen sent its Heir, Tan 丹, to Ch'in as a hostage.

---

[124] Not in extant version of the *Book of Documents*.

[125] See our translation of *Shih chi* Chapter 61.

[126] See n. 9 of our translation of Chapter 61 above.

[127] Chi Cha 季札, the fourth son of Shou-meng 壽夢, King of Wu (r. 585-561 B.C.). The king wanted to yield his throne to him, but he declined in favor of his brother and was later enfeoffed at Yen-ling (modern Ch'ang-chou 常州 City in Kiangsu [Wang Li-ch'i, 79:1861n.]).

[128] According to legend, he was Heir to King Ling 靈 of Chou (r. 571-545 B.C.) and eventually became an immortal (see Wang Li-ch'i, 79:1861n).

[129] Ch'ih Sung Tzu 赤松子, also a legendary immortal (*Ibid.*).

[130] *Chou Yi cheng-yi,* 1:3b, *SPPY*; this is an admonition against arrogance among those in high positions.

[131] The Chung-hua editors follow Wang Nien-sun's (4:35a) emendation here, reversing the positions of *tsu* 足 and *chih* 知 in this sentence. The revised lines rhyme.

His Honor the Grand Scribe says: "Han Tzu 韓子 proclaimed, 'Those with long sleeves can dance, those with much money are skilled in trade.'[132] These are words we can put trust in! Fan Sui and Ts'ai Tse were typical rhetoricians, but they traveled about advising the feudal lords until their heads were gray and yet met no success. It was not that their plans were drafted poorly, but because the strength of those for whom they made them was too small. When these two men entered Ch'in in their travels, they won the highest posts in the land, one after the other, and their merit was displayed before the entire world. This was naturally owing to the [relative] power of mighty states and weak states. But men also have their luck, and there were many worthy men such as these two, who were unable to attain their ambitions. One cannot even begin to enumerate them. But if these two men had not encountered adversity, how could they ever have been inspired to such heights?!"

---

[132] In *Han Fei Tzu* this is identified as a folk maxim (19:17b, *SPPY*).

TRANSLATORS' NOTE

This is a multi-dimensional text.   First, it clearly continues the *leitmotif* of Ssu-ma Ch'ien's Warring States' *lieh-chuan*--speeches, schemes and treachery.   But here, although both Fan and Ts'ai achieve success through their schemes, the two protagonists are never treacherous (the only treachery is that of Hsü Chia).   They are linked more by Ts'ai's succeeding Fan as chancellor of Ch'in than by parallels in their lives.

The account of Fan Sui is one of the most carefully structured among the pre-Han biographies.   It is framed by the ignominy Fan suffered at Wei Chi's hands and by Fan's eventual revenge.   In this, it stands in contrast to Chapter 66 where revenge became an all-consuming passion for Wu Tzu-hsu and the others depicted there.   The general impression we have of Fan, however, is of a man who thinks on his feet, as portrayed in his escapes--so vividly told-- from Wei Chi and the Lord of Jang.

Ts'ai Tse's biography also begins with an episode which, like the disgrace Fan Sui endured, seems to predict an outcome.   But here the detailed prognostication of the forty-three years remaining to Ts'ai is left unfulfilled--at least for the reader of this account.   Ts'ai's skills are much closer to the conventional persuader and he is a man solely dependent on his eloquence.

A final comparison may be inferred from the success these two "foreign ministers" had in Ch'in, namely that to the most notorious of the pre-Han persuaders, Li Ssu (see Chapter 87).   Fan Sui realized that his time had ended when Ts'ai Tse spoke before him; Ts'ai Tse prudently stepped down from his position to live out his years in Ch'in.   The restraint and self awareness of these acts are in sharp contrast to the megalomania and greed of Li Ssu.

BIBLIOGRAPHY

I. Translations

Ōgawa Tamaki 小川環樹, trans.   *Shiki retsuden* 史記列傳.   Rpt. Tokyo: Chikuma Shobō, 1986 (1969), pp. 124-38.
Watson, Burton.   *Records of the Grand Historian: Qin Dynasty.*   V. 3.   Hong Kong and New York: The Research Centre for Translation, The Chinese University of Hong Kong and Columbia University Press, 1993, pp. 131-157.
Yang Hsien-yi and Gladys Yang.   *Records of the Historian.*   Rpt. Hong Kong: The Commercial Press, 1985, pp. 94-117.

II. Studies

No important studies.

Yüeh Yi, Memoir 20

[80:2427] Yüeh Yi's 樂毅 ancestor was Yüeh Yang 樂羊.[1] Yüeh Yang was a commander of Marquis Wen 文 of Wei (r. *424-387 B.C.).[2] He attacked and took [the state of] Chung-shan 中山.[3] Marquis Wen of Wei invested Yüeh Yang with Ling-shou 靈壽.[4] When Yüeh Yang died, he was buried in Ling-shou. Following this, his descendants took up residence there. Chung-shan was restored, then destroyed again in the time of King Wu-ling 武靈 of Chao (r. 325-299 B.C.). Among the descendants of the Yüeh clan was Yüeh Yi.

Yüeh Yi was worthy and delighted in arms. The men of Chao gave him a post. After the rebellion against King Wu-ling at Sha-ch'iu 沙丘,[5] he left Chao and went to Wei. [Yüeh Yi] heard that Ch'i had used the rebellion of Tzu-chih 子之 to crush Yen,[6] that King Chao 昭 of Yen (r. 311-279 B.C.) bore resentment against Ch'i, not forgetting for even a day to repay Ch'i, but that the state of Yen was small and isolated, too weak to conquer Ch'i, so that [King Chao] humbled himself and deferred to knights, attracting worthy men by first treating Kuo Wei 郭隗 with ceremony.[7] It was after this that Yüeh Yi went to Yen on a mission for King Chao 昭 of Wei (r. 295-277 B.C.). The King of Yen received him with the ceremony due a guest. Yüeh Yi declined [his hospitality], then laid down his pledge and became his vassal. King Chao of Yen made him a Junior Excellency[8] [and he held this post] for some time.

[2428] At the time, King Min 湣 of Ch'i (r. *323-284 B.C.)[9] was mighty. He defeated the Ch'u Prime Minister T'ang Mo 唐眛 to the south at Ch'ung-ch'iu 重丘[10] and shattered the Three Chin to the west at Kuan-chin 觀津.[11] He then attacked Ch'in together with the Three

---

[1] Yüeh Yang is also mentioned in *Shih chi* 44:1840, and 71:2312.

[2] According to Yang K'uan (pp. 247-52), Marquis Wen's reign dates were 445-396 B.C.

[3] The best source for textual references to the state of Chung-shan is Wang Hsien-ch'ien's 王先謙 (1842-1918) *Hsien-yü Chung-shan kuo-shih piao* 鮮虞中山國事表 (published in *Wang Yi-wu so-k'o shu* 王益吾所刻書 [Changsha, 1883]). Due to recent archaeological discoveries, we now know a great deal about this state. For a summary of these finds see Li Xueqin, *Eastern Chou Civilization*, translated by K. C. Chang (New Haven: Yale University Press, 1985), pp. 93-108.

[4] Located just northwest of modern Ling-shou in Shansi province (T'an Ch'i-hsiang, 1:37-38).

[5] See n. 54 to our translation of *Shih chi* Chapter 79.

[6] For further details of this event, see our translation of *Shih chi* Chapter 69. The most detailed description of this event in the *Shih chi* appears in 34:1555-57. Summarizing briefly, Tzu-chih, the Prime Minister of Yen, persuaded the King of Yen, K'uai 噲, to yield the throne to him in 316 B.C. Ch'i took advantage of the political confusion this caused to attack and conquer Yen in 314 B.C. Yen finally expelled the forces of Ch'i and enthroned a son of K'uai as King Chao in 312 B.C.

[7] Dialogues between King Chao and Kuo Wei appear in *Shih chi*, 34:1558, and *Chan-kuo ts'e* (9:16a-17b, SPTK). The latter version is somewhat longer.

[8] *Ya-ch'ing* 亞卿.

[9] As noted in the front matter to this volume, Ssu-ma Ch'ien's records of the state of Ch'i, among others, were incorrect at several points. According to Yang K'uan (pp. 263-65), , the standard we have adopted, the correct reign dates for King Min of Ch'i are 300-284 B.C. Thus the events attributed here to King Min actually took place in the reign of his predecessor, King Hsüan.

According to *Shih chi*, 15:736, Ch'in, Han, Wei, and Ch'i attacked Ch'u in 301 B.C. This is not completely consistent with *Shih chi* Chapter 5 (see our translation of *Shih chi*, 5:210 above). Contrary to Kierman (p. 63, n. 13), this date *is* consistent with the the record in *Shih chi* Chapter 46. T'ang Mei is unknown except for this incident, but in the other chapters which mention it, he is referred to as a general rather than prime minister.

[10] Ch'ung-ch'iu was located about 5 miles northeast of modern Mi-yang 泌陽 in Honan (Ch'ien Mu, *Ti-ming k'ao*, p. 376)

[11] Kuan-chin was located about 5 miles east of modern Wu-yi 武邑 in Shantung (T'an Ch'i-hsiang, 1:38). According to *Shih chi* 15:732, Ch'i attacked Chao in 317 B.C. In several other places in the *Shih chi*, however, this

Chin, helped Chao destroy Chung-shan, defeated Sung and expanded his territory by over a thousand *li* [squared].[12] He competed with King Chao of Ch'in for the honor of [the title of] Emperor,[13] then shortly afterward restored [his title of king]. The feudal lords all wanted to turn their backs on Ch'in and submit to Ch'i, [but] King Min was arrogant and the populace could not bear [his exactions]. It was then that King Chao of Yen asked about attacking Ch'i.

Yüeh Yi replied, "Ch'i is the remnant legacy of a hegemon state. Its territory is large and its people numerous. It would not be easy to attack it alone. If Your Majesty insists on attacking, it would be better [to attack] with Chao, Ch'u, and Wei." [The king] sent Yüeh Yi to ally with King Hui-wen 惠文 of Chao (r. 298-266 B.C.), sent other missions to recruit Ch'u and Wei, and had Chao tempt Ch'in with the profits of an expedition against Ch'i.[14] The feudal lords hated King Min's arrogance and cruelty and raced to join in alliance and attack Ch'i with Yen. When Yüeh Yi returned to report, King Chao of Yen mobilized all his troops and made Yüeh Yi Senior General. King Hui-wen of Chao presented Yüeh Yi with the Minister of State's seal. Yüeh Yi, with combined command of the troops of Chao, Ch'u, Han, Wei and Yen, attacked Ch'i. He defeated Ch'i west of the Chi 濟 River. The feudal lords' troops broke off and returned; only the Yen army's Yüeh Yi pursued Ch'i's army all the way to [Ch'i's capital] Lin-tzu 臨菑.[15]

When King Min of Ch'i was defeated west of the Chi river, he fled and took refuge in Chü 莒. Yüeh Yi stayed alone and garrisoned Ch'i. Ch'i defended itself from its walled cities. Yüeh Yi attacked and entered Lin-tzu, seizing all of Ch'i's treasure, money, goods, and sacrificial vessels, and transported them to Yen.

[2429] King Chao of Yen was delighted and personally traveled to the banks of the Chi River. He entertained the army, gave out awards, and feasted the knights, enfeoffing Yüeh Yi at Ch'ang-kuo 昌國.[16] His title was Lord of Ch'ang-kuo. Afterwards, King Chao of Yen packed up the goods of Ch'i and returned home with them. He sent Yüeh Yi leading troops to further pacify the cities of Ch'i which had not surrendered.

Yüeh Yi remained and patrolled Ch'i for five years,[17] subduing over seventy of the walled cities of Ch'i; all were made into commanderies and counties and incorporated into Yen. Only Chü and Chi-mo 即墨 did not submit. It was at this point that King Chao of Yen died and his son took the throne as King Hui 惠 of Yen (r. 278-272 B.C.). At some time after he had become Heir, King Hui was displeased with Yüeh Yi. When [King Hui] took the throne, T'ien Tan 田單 of Ch'i heard of this and sent a counter-agent to Yen.

"The cities of Ch'i which have not surrendered number only two. The reason they were not captured long ago, we have heard, is that there is bad blood between Yüeh Yi and

---

battle is said to have taken place at Kuan-tse 觀澤, rather than Kuan-chin (Kuan-tse was located just south of modern Ch'ing-feng 清豐 in Honan [T'an Ch'i-hsiang, 1:36]).

[12] According to *Shih chi*, 15:737-40, Wei, Han, and Ch'i attacked Ch'in in 298 B.C. (this is not a complete list of the participants in this attack, see our translation of *Shih chi* Chapter 5 for further details), Ch'i and Chao destroyed Chung-shan in 295 B.C., and Ch'i destroyed Sung in 286 B.C.

[13] According to *Shih chi*, 15:739, King Min declared himself emperor in 288 B.C., then restored his title of king two months later.

[14] The Chung-hua edition has added the word *shui* 說 here, probably based on the suggestion of Wang Nien-sun (4:35a).

[15] According to *Shih chi*, 15:740, six states (Ch'in is the one not mentioned in the text of this chapter) attacked Ch'i in 284 B.C. Kierman (p. 66, n. 22) states that *Shih chi* Chapter 43 gives the date as 285 B.C., but this is incorrect. *Shih chi* 43:1816 gives the date as the fifteenth year of King Hui-wen of Chao, which was 284 B.C.

[16] Just south of the modern city of Tzu-po 淄博 in Shantung (T'an Ch'i-hsiang, 1:39).

[17] Perhaps 283-279 B.C.

the new King of Yen. [Yüeh Yi] intends to remain in Ch'i together with his troops, face south, and rule over Ch'i. Ch'i fears only the arrival of another general."

King Hui of Yen had already suspected Yüeh Yi, and after receiving this agent sent Chi Chieh 騎劫 to replace [Yüeh Yi] as general, summoning Yüeh Yi. Yüeh Yi knew that King Hui of Yen's replacement of him was not well intentioned. Fearing execution, he surrendered to Chao in the west. Chao invested Yüeh Yi with Kuan-chin. His title was Lord of Wang-chu 望諸.[18] [Chao] thus warned Yen and Ch'i by honoring Yüeh Yi.

[2430] T'ien Tan of Ch'i afterwards fought with Chi Chieh and by setting a trap fooled the Yen army, following which he defeated Chi Chieh below the walls of Chi-mo. He fought Yen again and again, drove it back north to the banks of the Ho River, retook all the walled cities of Ch'i, met King Hsiang 襄 (of Ch'i, r. 283-265 B.C.) at Chü, and escorted him into Lin-tzu.[19]

King Hui of Yen afterwards regretted sending Chi Chieh to replace Yüeh Yi, thus destroying his army, losing his general, and forfeiting Ch'i. He also resented Yüeh Yi's surrendering to Chao and feared that Chao would employ Yüeh Yi, taking advantage of Yen's exhaustion to attack Yen. King Hui of Yen sent a man to rebuke Yüeh Yi and also to apologize to him.

"Our late king entrusted the entire state to you General, and you took Ch'i for Yen, repaying our late king's foe. No one in the world was not thunder-struck. How could We dare to forget your accomplishments for even a day, General! When the late king abandoned his assembled vassals, We had just ascended the throne and our advisors misled us. When we sent Chi Chieh to replace you, General, it was because you had endured privation for so long outside the state. It was for this reason we recalled you General, so that you might rest and advise Us on affairs. You misunderstood, General, that this was due to bad blood between you and I, and you then abandoned Yen and turned to Chao. If you would make plans for yourself, General, that is proper, but how will you repay our late king's treatment of you?"

Yüeh Yi sent a letter answering King Hui of Yen.

Your servant is clumsy and in carrying out Your Majesty's orders was unable to put the minds of your advisors at ease. Fearing to damage our late king's [reputation for] perspicacity and to harm your [reputation for] principled behavior, Honored Sir, I thus fled to Chao. Now you have sent a man to enumerate my crimes for me, Honored Sir. Your servant fears that your attendants do not see why the late king cared for and favored me, nor do they understand my motives in serving him. Thus I presume to write in reply.

[2431] Your servant has heard that a worthy and sagely lord does not provide care for his kin with official salaries. Those with many accomplishments he rewards, those whose abilities meet his needs he employs. Thus one who observes ability and then awards office is a lord capable of succeeding in his deeds. One who can evaluate

[18] "So-yin" says that Wang-chu was the name of a marsh originally belonging to the state of Ch'i. Ch'ien Mu, Ti-ming k'ao, p. 111, suggests that Wang-chu may have been the name of a marsh located near Yüeh Yi's fief.

[19] These events are also narrated in Shih chi Chapters 15 and 82, but there is a minor inconsistency in Shih chi, 15:742. The first year of King Hui of Yen is recorded as 278 B.C., but the Ch'i entry for 279 B.C., the last year of King Chao's reign, states, "We killed Yen's Chi Chieh." This would seem to imply that Yüeh Yi was replaced by King Chao, not King Hui. One possible explanation for this discrepancy is that King Chao of Yen died in 279 B.C. and the actions described in the text took place in the same year, after his death. The general practice seems to have been that the first year of a new king was calculated beginning from the first new year after the former king's death. This was not always done consistently, however, and such inconsistencies are undoubtedly responsible for many apparent anachronisms (see Lin Chien-ming's 林劍鳴 Ch'in-shih kao 秦史稿 [Shanghai: Jen-min Ch'u-pan-she, 1981], p. 6 for a brief discussion of this important problem).

behavior and then form bonds is a knight capable of establishing great fame. Your servant, in humbly observing the actions of our late king, saw that his heart surpassed those of the rulers of our generation. Thus I borrowed [an ambassador's] tally from Wei and was able to observe Yen at first hand. The late king advanced me by error, placing me among his guests and elevating me above his assembled vassals. Without consulting with the royal family, he made me a Junior Excellency. Your servant did not realize [his own shortcomings], but thinking that if he were fortunate he could avoid offense in receiving instructions, accepted his order and did not decline.

The late king instructed me, 'I have accumulated grudges and a deep anger against Ch'i, so that I would not consider how unimportant and weak Yen is, but desire to take on Ch'i.'

I said, 'Ch'i is the remaining legacy of a Hegemon's state, where excellent things of the past clustered.[20] It is practiced in arms and accustomed to battle. If you wish to lead an expedition against it, Your Majesty, you must consult with the world against Ch'i. In consulting with the world, it would be best to join with Chao. Moreover, the lands of Huai-pei 淮北 and of Sung are what Ch'u and Wei desire. If Chao consents and you can unite these four states to attack it, Ch'i can be crushed.' Our late king agreed. He supplied the tally of an ambassador and sent me south on a mission to Chao. When I returned and reported, he mobilized his troops and struck Ch'i. Through the way of Heaven and the inspiration of our late king, the lands north of the Ho followed our late king and assembled on the banks of the Chi 濟. The armies on the banks of the Chi received the command to attack Ch'i and routed the men of Ch'i. The light infantry and crack troops drove headlong to the capital. The King of Ch'i fled, running to Chü, and survived with only his life. His pearls, jade, money, treasures, carts, armor and precious vessels were all captured and sent to Yen. The vessels of Ch'i were laid out at Ning-t'ai 寧臺 and the Great Lü 呂 Bells were set up at Yüan-ying 元英, while Yen's old cauldrons were returned to the Mo-shih 磨室[21] and what they planted on Chi-ch'iu 薊丘 were bamboos from the Wen 汶 River.[22] From the time of the Five Hegemons[23] until now, none can match the achievements of our late king. Our late king felt satisfied in his ambitions. He thus split his territory and enfeoffed me, allowing me to compare with the feudal lord of a small state. Your servant did not realize [his own shortcomings], but thinking that if he were fortunate he could avoid offense in receiving instructions, accepted his order and did not decline.

[2432] Your servant has heard that a worthy and enlightened lord's achievements do not fall once they are accomplished, thus they are recorded in the annals. A foresighted knight's name does not suffer once it is made, thus he is praised by later generations. As for our late king, he repaid his grudge, wiped out his shame,

---

[20] *Sheng* 勝 here means "excellent" or "superior." The *Chan-kuo ts'e* version of this letter reads *tsou-sheng chih yi-shih* 騶勝之遺事. Thus *Tsui* 最 here is similar to *tsou* (=*chü* 聚)--"to assemble" or "cluster, cf. *Chung-wen Ta Tz'u-tien*, #14632).

[21] According to "Cheng-yi," Ning-t'ai, Yüan-ying, and Mo-shih (Li-shih 歷室 in the *Chan-kuo ts'e* text) were all palaces belonging to the King of Yen. T'an Ch'i-hsiang (1:41) locates the Li-shih just west of ancient Chi 薊, the site of modern Peking.

The *ta lü* were probably ceremonial bells. A set of bells kept in the Chou dynasties' temples were known as the *Ta lü* (see n. 12 to our translation of *Shih chi* Chapter 76), and Ch'i, apparently aspiring to a position equal to the Chou dynasty's, also made a set of bells which it called *Ta lü* (see *Lü-shih ch'un-ch'iu chi-shih* 集釋, Hsü Wei-yü 許維遹, comp. [Taipei: Shih-chieh Shu-chü, 1988], p. 223).

"Yen's old cauldrons" were presumably sacrificial vessels carried off by Ch'i after its invasion of Yen in 314 B.C.

[22] Chi-ch'iu may have been the hills surrounding the Yen capital, Chi. Wen was a river in Ch'i. We follow "So-yin" and a number of other commentators (see Wang Shu-min, 80:2440) in our understanding of this line.

[23] See n. 12 to our translation of *Shih chi* Chapter 68 above.

destroyed a mighty state of ten thousand chariots, and took eight hundred years of accumulated wealth. On the day he abandoned his assembled vassals, his posthumous teachings did not decline. His vassals holding the reins of government and wielding power polished the laws and regulations, distinguished the children of wives and concubines, and his measures extended to commoners and serfs. All of these may serve as a lesson to later generations.

Your servant has heard that those skilled at creating are not necessarily skilled at completing. Those skilled at beginnings are not necessarily skilled at endings. Long ago, Wu Tzu Hsü's advice was followed by Ho-lu and the King of Wu left his mark as far away as Ying. Fu-ch'ai thought him wrong, granted him a leather bag and floated him down the Chiang.[24] The King of Wu did not realize that elders' judgments can establish merit and thus drowned Wu Tzu Hsü without regret. Wu Tzu Hsü did not see beforehand that these [two] rulers' capacity was not equal, thus he entered the Chiang without changing his mind.

[2433] To heighten the luster of the late king's deeds by escaping death and fulfilling achievement, this is your servant's foremost plan. To tarnish our late king's name by falling prey to slander and libel, this is what your servant fears most. Though faced with the gravest of charges, principle would not allow me to utilize my good fortune [in finding haven in Chao] for [unprincipled] profit.[25]

Your servant has heard that when their friendships ended, the gentleman of old did not speak ill [of former friends]. When a loyal vassal left his state, he did not clear his name. Although your servant is clumsy, he has received instruction several times from gentlemen. I fear that the royal attendants will believe the speeches of your courtiers, without taking account of the actions which led to our parting of ways, thus I have presumed to offer this letter for your inspection. I hope that My Lord the King will take due note of it.

[2434] After this, the King of Yen made Yüeh Yi's son Yüeh Chien 樂閒 Lord of Ch'ang-kuo again and Yüeh Yi in his travels once more entered Yen. Yen and Chao made him a Foreign Excellency. Yüeh Yi died in Chao.

Yüeh Chien and Yüeh Ch'eng

[2435] Yüeh Chien 樂閒 lived in Yen for over thirty years. The King of Yen, Hsi 喜, (r. 254-222 B.C.) accepted the plan of his Prime Minister, Li Fu 栗腹, prepared to attack Chao, and questioned the Lord of Ch'ang-kuo, Yüeh Chien.

Yüeh Chien said, "Chao is a state that has done battle against the four quarters. Its people are accustomed to fighting. To attack it will not do."

The King of Yen did not heed him and attacked Chao. Chao sent Lien P'o to counter-attack. He crushed Li Fu's army at Hao 鄗,[26] capturing Li Fu and Yüeh Ch'eng 樂乘. Yüeh Ch'eng was a clansman of Yüeh Chien. After this, Yüeh Chien fled to Chao and Chao besieged Yen. Yen ceded much territory to make peace with Chao, and Chao ended the siege and left.[27]

---

[24] For details, see Wu Tzu Hsü's biography in *Shih chi* Chapter 66.

[25] Yüeh Yi is telling King Hui in a very polite way that even if Chao tried to force him, he would not attack Yen.

[26] A few miles east of modern Kao-yi 高邑 in Hopei (T'an Ch'i-hsiang, 1:38).

[27] According to *Shih chi*, 15:749, Yen attacked Chao in 251 B.C. For a more detailed account of Yen's attack,

The King of Yen regretted that he had not employed Yüeh Chien. After Yüeh Chien was in Chao, the king sent a letter to him.[28]

> In the time of Chow 紂, Chi Tzu 箕子 was not employed, but he remonstrated without wearying, hoping that Chow would listen. Shang Jung 商容 could not get through [to Chow], and allowed himself to be humiliated, hoping Chow would change.[29] Afterwards when the will of the commoners was not able to reach into [the court], and [jailors] on their own freed prisoners, these two gentlemen retired from the world. Thus Chow had to bear the blame for his cruelty and violence, while these two gentlemen did not lose the name of loyal and enlightened. Why was this? Because of the completeness of their concern and sorrow. Although We are foolish, We are not as violent as Chow. Although the people of Yen are disorderly, they are not as bad as the people of Yin. Now we have had words in our house, and without finishing matters you speak of it to our neighbors. Neither of these would We choose for you.

Yüeh Chien and Yüeh Ch'eng resented Yen's failure to follow their advice, and the two in the end stayed in Chao. Chao enfeoffed Yüeh Ch'eng as the Lord of Wu-hsiang 武襄.[30]

[2436] The next year, Yüeh Ch'eng and Lien P'o besieged Yen on behalf of Chao. Yen made peace with rich gifts and they ended the siege.[31] Five years later, King Hsiao-ch'eng 孝成 of Chao (r. 265-245 B.C.) died. King Hsiang 襄 (of Chao, r. 244-236 B.C.) had Yüeh Ch'eng replace Lien P'o. Lien P'o attacked Yüeh Ch'eng. Yüeh Ch'eng fled and Lien P'o fled to Wei.[32] Sixteen years later Ch'in destroyed Chao.[33]

More than twenty years later, the Emperor Kao 高 (of Han, r. 202-195 B.C.) passed through Chao and asked, "Did Yüeh Yi have descendants?" "There is Yüeh Shu 樂叔." Emperor Kao enfeoffed him as Excellency Yüeh. His title was Lord Hua-ch'eng 華成. Lord Hua-ch'eng was Yüeh Yi's grandson. The Yüeh clan also had Master Yüeh Hsia 樂瑕 and Master Yüeh Chü 樂巨. When Chao was about to be destroyed by Chin, they fled to Kao-mi 高密[34] in Ch'i. Master Yüeh Chü was skilled in the study of the doctrines of the Huang-Lao [School].[35] He was well-known in Ch'i, and was called a worthy teacher.

His Honor the Grand Scribe says: "Long ago when K'uai T'ung 蒯通[36] of Ch'i and Chu-fu Yen 主父偃 (206-127 B.C.)[37] read Yüeh Yi's letter replying to the King of Yen, they

---

see *Shih chi* 34:1559. There is some confusion about Yüeh Ch'eng's allegiance in this period. According to *Shih chi,* 43:1827, Yüeh Ch'eng served as a general for Chao in 256 B.C., the same year in which Yen attacked Chao.

[28] A longer and quite different version of this letter appears in *Chan-kuo ts'e* (9:38a-40b, *SPTK*).

[29] Chow was the last ruler of the Shang dynasty (also known as the Yin dynasty). For more detailed notes on Chow, Shang Jung, and Chi Tzu, see our translation of Chapter 3.

[30] We have been unable to locate any place called Wu-hsiang. "So-yin" suggests that this title meant "Ending Violence" and did not refer to a place. According to *Shih chi,* 43:1828, Yeh Ch'eng was enfeoffed in 250 B.C.

[31] According to *Shih chi,* 43:1828, this occurred in 249 B.C. This presents a problem, since the next sentence says that King Hsiao-ch'eng died five years later, but all sources agree that Hsiao-ch'eng died in 245 B.C.

[32] According to *Shih chi,* 43:1829, Lien P'o was replaced after he successfully attacked the state of Wei in 245 B.C. It is unclear why he was replaced. See our translation of Chapter 81 for another version of these events.

[33] Ch'in's destruction of Chao probably refers to the capture of Chao's capital Han-tan and the King of Chao, Ch'ien 遷 which *Shih chi,* 15:755 dates to 228 B.C. This adds up to either seventeen or eighteen years later, depending on which counting system is used (see also "Chronology" in the front-matter).

[34] About 10 miles west-southwest of modern Kao-mi in Shantung (T'an Ch'i-hsiang, 1:40).

[35] See n. 30 to our translation of Chapter 63 above.

[36] K'uai T'ung is a political persuader from Ch'i in *Shih chi* Chapter 92 where he attempts, unsuccessfully, to

did not once but put down the letter and weep. Master Yüeh Chü studied the [doctrines of] the Huang-Lao [School]. The patriarch [of his school] was called "the old man by the river."[38] None know where he came from. "The old man by the river" taught Scholar An-ch'i 安期生.[39] Scholar An-ch'i taught Master Mao Hsi 毛翕. Master Mao Yi taught Master Yüeh Hsia. Master Yüeh Hsia taught Master Yüeh Chü. Master Yüeh Chü taught Master Ko 蓋.[40] Master Ko taught in Ch'i at Kao-mi and Chiao-hsi 膠西.[41] He was Minister of State Ts'ao's 曹 teacher.[42]"

convince Han Hsin 韓信 to turn against Liu Pang. Wang Li-ch'i (80:1878n.) observes that he was actually from Fan-yang 范陽 (modern Ting-hsing 定興 District in Hopei) but had studied in Ch'i. Wang Li-ch'i also claims K'uai changed his *praenomen* to avoid the tabooed-conflict with Emperor Wu's *praenomen,* but it seems unlikely that K'uai, who was giving advice to Han Hsin in the early third century B.C., would have changed his name over sixty years later! Yang Chia-lo (p. 817n.), moreover, gives his dates as 275-195 B.C. Perhaps there are two individuals with the same name, one who lived during Emperor Wu's time and one who lived several generations earlier. This would also fit the claim that K'uai T'ung and Chu-fu Yen read the letter together, since Chu-fu Yen clearly lived during the reign of Emperor Wu.

[37] See his biography in *Shih chi* Chapter 112.

[38] Yang Chia-lo (p. 817, n. 62) believes this may have been Chan Ho 詹何 (330-251 B.C., according to Yang). Wang Li-ch'i (80:1878n.) says he was a late Warring States figure, also known as "Ho-shang Kung" 河上公, whose name is unknown.

[39] A native of Lang-ya 瑯琊 (modern Chiao-nan 膠南 District in Shantung) who made his living selling drugs (see Wang Li-ch'i, 80:1878n.).

[40] A Taoist in the early years of the Han (see Wang Li-ch'i, 80:1878n.).

[41] Ch'ien Mu (*Ti-ming k'ao,* p. 286) argues that Kao-mi was the capital of the statelet known as Chiao-hsi.

[42] I.e., Ts'ao Ts'an 參, see *Shih chi,* 54:2021.

TRANSLATORS' NOTE

The events of this chapter are in large part repeated in *Shih chi* Chapters 81 and 82 ("Lien P'o and Lin Hsiang-ju" and "T'ien Tan"), but the focus here is on Yüeh Yi and his descendants. After the Grand Scribe has depicted the Four Lords and their use of retainers, here we have a retainer who, when properly used, brought great success to his ruler. The emphasis is not on exciting detail or dialogue (as in "Fan Sui and Ts'ai Tse"), but rather on the letter Yüeh Yi sent to King Hui when the latter tried to entice him back to Yen.

The latter part of the chapter marks an attempt to chronicle the achievements of the main figure's descendants, a feature which became standard feature in biographies of later official histories.

BIBLIOGRAPHY

I. Translations

Kierman, Frank A., Jr. *Ssu-ma Ch'ien's Historiographical Attitude as Reflected in Four Late Warring States Biographies*. Wiesbaden: Harrassowitz, 1962, pp. 20-25.

Ōgawa Tamaki 小川環樹, trans. *Shiki retsuden* 史記列傳. Rpt. Tokyo: Chikuma Shobō, 1986 (1969), pp. 138-42.

Panasjuk, V. *Syma Czjan', Izbrannoe*. Moscow, 1956, pp. 147-55.

II. Studies

Kierman, *op. cit.*

Lien P'o and Lin Hsiang-ju, Memoir 21

[81:2439] Lien P'o 廉頗 was an able general of Chao.[1] In the sixteenth year of King Hui-wen 惠文 of Chao (283 B.C. [r. 298-266 B.C.]), Lien P'o led Chao's attack on Ch'i. He crushed Ch'i's army, took Yang-chin 陽晉,[2] and was made Senior Excellency. He was renowned among the feudal lords for his bravery.

Lin Hsiang-ju 藺相如 was a native of Chao. He was a houseman of Mou Hsien 繆賢, Chao's Prefect of Eunuchs.[3]

During the time of King Hui-wen, Chao acquired Ch'u's Jade of the Ho Clan.[4] King Chao 昭 of Ch'in (r. 306-251 B.C.) heard of this and sent a messenger to deliver a letter to the King of Chao, saying that he wished to offer fifteen walled cities in exchange for the jade. The King of Chao took counsel with his Commander-in-Chief[5] Lien P'o and his great vassals.

"If we give it to Ch'in, we most likely will not obtain Ch'in's cities, but will only be cheated. If we do not give it, then we must fear the arrival of Ch'in's soldiers." With their plans unsettled, they sought someone to send their response to Ch'in, but could find no one.

Prefect of Eunuchs Mou Hsien said, "Your servant's houseman Lin Hsiang-ju could undertake this mission."

The king asked, "How do you know that he could?"

[Mou Hsien] replied, "I once committed an offense and planned in secret to flee to Yen. My Houseman Hsiang-ju stopped me, saying 'How do you know the King of Yen?'

"I said, 'I once went to a border meeting with the King of Yen in our king's entourage. The King of Yen privately squeezed my hand and said, "I hope to become a friend." This is how I know him, and why I wish to go there.'

"Hsiang-ju told me, 'Chao is strong and Yen weak, and my lord moreover favored by the King of Chao; this is why the King of Yen wanted to make my lord's acquaintance. Yet now my lord would flee Chao and run to Yen. Yen fears Chao; under such circumstances it certainly would not dare to keep you, my lord, but [*2440*] would send you back in bonds to Chao. It would be better for my lord to strip to the waist, kneel before the ax and chopping block, and ask for punishment. Then if fortune is with you, you will escape.'

"I followed his plan and by good fortune you pardoned me, Great King. Your servant personally considers him a brave knight, gifted with wisdom and cunning, fit to undertake this mission."

After this, the King of Chao summoned him to an audience. He asked Lin Hsiang-ju, "The King of Ch'in offers to exchange fifteen walled cities for Our jade. Can We give it to him, or not?"

Hsiang-ju said, "Ch'in is mighty and Chao is weak, you must grant his request."

The king said, "If he takes my jade, but gives us no cities, what then?"

Hsiang-ju said, "If Ch'in seeks the jade with its cities and Chao does not accede, the fault lies with Chao. If Chao gives Ch'in the jade and Ch'in does not give Chao the cities, the fault lies with Ch'in. In weighing these two measures, it would be better to accede, and lay the fault on Ch'in."

The king said, "Who could undertake this mission?"

---

[1] Lien P'o is mentioned twice in *Chan-kuo ts'e* (6:47b and 9:38a, *SPTK*). Lin Hsiang-ju, on the other hand, does not appear in *Chan-kuo ts'e* at all.

[2] A few miles west of modern Yün Ch'eng 鄆成 in Shantung (T'an Ch'i-hsiang, 1:39).

[3] *Huan-che ling* 宦者令.

[4] *Ho-shih pi* 和氏璧.

[5] *Ta chiang-chün* 大將軍.

Hsiang-ju said, "If Your Majesty is certain there is no one else, your servant is willing to accept the jade and undertake this mission. If the cities are granted to Chao, the jade will remain in Ch'in; if the cities are not granted, allow your servant to return to Chao with the jade intact."

The King of Chao dispatched Hsiang-ju, bearing the jade, west into Ch'in. The King of Ch'in granted Hsiang-ju an audience seated on the Illustrious Terrace.[6] Hsiang-ju presented the jade to the King of Ch'in with both hands. The King of Ch'in was delighted and passed it around to his Beauties and courtiers. His courtiers all shouted "Long live the King!"

Hsiang-ju saw that the King of Ch'in had no intention of giving Chao the cities owed it. He came forward. "The jade has a flaw. Allow me to show it to Your Majesty."

The king handed him the jade. Holding the jade, Hsiang-ju retreated and stood with his back to a pillar. His hair bristling against his hat in rage, he told the King of Ch'in, "You wanted to acquire the jade, Great King, so you sent a man to bring your letter to the King of Chao. The King of Chao summoned all of his assembled vassals in consultation, and they all said, 'Ch'in is greedy. It relies on its might and seeks the jade with empty words. To receive cities in return for it, we fear this will not be the case.' Their advice was not to give Ch'in the jade.

"Your servant felt, 'Commoners dressed in cloth do not cheat each other in their trans-actions; how much more should this be so for a Great State! Moreover, to offend mighty Ch'in for the sake of one jade, this is unacceptable.'

"The King of Chao then fasted and purified himself for five days and sent Your servant bearing the jade to make obeisance and deliver his letter in your court. Why did he do this? To renew his respect by exalting the majesty of your Great State [Ch'in].

"Yet after arriving, Your Majesty grants me audience in one of your pleasure pavil-ions, with protocol and ceremonies arrogant in the extreme, and having received the jade, you mock me by passing it among your Beauties.

"It seems to me that Your Majesty has no intention of giving the King of Chao the cit-ies owed him. Thus I have reclaimed the jade. If you must press me, Great King, my head and the jade will both shatter against this pillar!"

Holding the jade, Hsiang-ju looked at the pillar out of the corner of his eye, preparing to strike it [with the jade]. The King of Ch'in feared that he would break the jade. He apolo-gized and pleaded, summoned the officials to display the maps, and pointed: "The fifteen cities from here on will be given to Chao."

Hsiang-ju concluded that the King of Ch'in was merely pretending to offer Chao the cities with this ruse and that in fact they could never be acquired. He told the King of Ch'in, "The jade of the Ho Clan is a treasure that the entire world has transmitted with reverence. The King of Chao [*2441*] was afraid and did not dare refuse to offer it. When the King of Chao sent off the jade, he fasted and purified himself for five days. Now you too should fast and purify yourself for five days, Great King, then hold the Chiu-pin 九賓 Ceremony[7] in your court, and then your servant would dare to offer up the jade."

---

[6] The Chang-t'ai 章臺 was a "pleasure palace" rather than an official residence. This incident perhaps harks back to the humiliation inflicted on the King of Ch'u, who, when tricked into entering Ch'in, was forced to pay homage to the Ch'in king at the Illustrious Terrace, treating him as a vassal, rather than an equal (*Shih chi*, 40:1728). The motif of forcing the feudal lords to pay homage at the Illustrious Terrace also appears in a number of speeches made by various sophists to the Ch'in king. The Illustrious Terrace was south of the Ch'in capital (see *Shih chi*, 6:239).

[7] Kierman (pp. 83-4, n. 8) has a long note on this discussing the merits of the three theories by which *chiu-pin* is understood.

The King of Ch'in concluded that the jade could never be taken by force and agreed to fast for five days, housing Hsiang-ju in the Kuang-ch'eng 廣成 Hostel.[8]

Hsiang-ju concluded that even though the King of Ch'in was fasting, he was sure to break his agreement and not to give the cities that were owed. He had his follower dress in coarse cloth, conceal the jade, and flee by a back road, returning the jade to Chao.

After the King of Ch'in had fasted for five days, he held the Chiu-pin Ceremony in his court, and led in the Emissary of Chao, Lin Hsiang-ju.

When Hsiang-ju arrived, he told the King of Ch'in, "Out of the twenty odd lords of Ch'in since Duke Mu 穆 (r. 659-621 B.C.), not one has honored his agreements and oaths. Your servant truly feared he would be cheated by Your Majesty and thus betray Chao. That is why I had a man take the jade back; he reached Chao by the back roads.

"Ch'in is strong and Chao weak. When Your Majesty sent an embassy of one[9] to Chao, Chao would have instantly come with the jade. Now, as mighty as Ch'in is, it first cedes fifteen cities to Chao; how would Chao dare keep the jade and offend you, Great King? Your servant knows the penalty for deceiving the Great King is death. Your servant asks to receive the punishment of cauldron and boiling water; consider it well with your assembled vassals, Great King!"

The King of Ch'in and his assembled vassals looked at each other, hissing in astonished fury. Some of the courtiers wanted to lead Hsiang-ju away, but the King of Ch'in said, "If We kill Hsiang-ju now, We still cannot acquire the jade, and it would ruin the good relations between Ch'in and Chao. It would be better to treat him with great civility instead, then send him back to Chao. How *would* the King of Chao dare to deceive Ch'in for the sake of a jade?" In the end he granted Hsiang-ju an audience in his court, completed the ceremonies, and sent him back.

After Hsiang-ju had returned, the King of Chao thought him a worthy grand master, who in his mission had escaped humiliation by the feudal lords, and appointed Hsiang-ju Senior Grand Master. Ch'in neither gave the cities to Chao, nor did Chao ever give Ch'in the jade.

[2442] Afterwards, Ch'in attacked Chao and took Shih-ch'eng 石城.[10] The next year it attacked Chao again and killed twenty thousand men.[11]

The King of Ch'in sent a messenger to tell the King of Chao that he wanted to hold a friendly meeting with the king at Mien-ch'ih 澠池,[12] past Hsi Ho 西河.[13] The King of Chao was afraid of Ch'in and wanted to refuse to go. Lien P'o and Lin Hsiang-ju's counsel was that, "If the king does not go, it will show that Chao is weak and cowardly." The King of Chao went, and Hsiang-ju accompanied him. Lien P'o escorted them to the border. He bid farewell to the king.

---

[8] This translation follows Wang Shu-min's emendation (81:2248). The location of this hostel is unknown; we know of it only through this story.

[9] The original reads *yi chieh chih shih* 一介之使. A *chieh* 介 was a 'secondary guest' at a banquet (See *Yi li*儀禮 [4:8b, *SPPY*], Cheng Hsüan's commentary); in this context, however, it means an unaccompanied (hence unimportant or minor) official.

[10] About 10 miles southwest of modern Shih-chia-chuang 石家庄 in Hopei (T'an Ch'i-hsiang, 1:38). According to *Shih chi*, 15:741, Ch'in took Shih-ch'eng in 281 B.C.

[11] According to *Shih chi*, 15:742, Ch'in killed thirty thousand Chao troops rather than twenty thousand.

[12] About 50 miles west of modern Loyang (near modern Mien-ch'ih) in Honan (T'an Ch'i-hsiang, 1:35).

[13] Hsi Ho was that portion of the Yellow River which flowed south dividing modern Shensi from Shansi (T'an Ch'i-hsiang, 1:37).

According to *Shih chi*, 15:742, the meeting took place in 279 B.C.

"For Your Majesty's travels, I estimate that the length of the road, the conclusion of the ceremonies at the meeting, and your return should not require more than thirty days. If you do not return in thirty days, I ask permission to enthrone the Heir as king, thereby frustrating the ambitions of Ch'in." The king granted his request and met with the King of Ch'in at Mien-ch'ih.

The King of Ch'in drank until he was intoxicated. "We have heard that the King of Chao is fond of music. Might you play the zither?"

The King of Chao strummed the zither. The Ch'in attendant scribe came forward and wrote, "In such and such a year, month and day, the King of Ch'in met to drink with the King of Chao and commanded the King of Chao to strum the zither."

Lin Hsiang-ju came forward. "The King of Chao has heard that the King of Ch'in is skilled at playing Ch'in tunes. We ask permission to present a clay pot drum to the King of Ch'in for our mutual pleasure."

The King of Ch'in was angry and refused. Hsiang-ju came forward and presented the pot, kneeling to beg the King of Ch'in. The King of Ch'in was unwilling to strike the pot. Hsiang-ju said, "Within the space of the five paces [between us], I ask permission to splash you with my throat's blood!" His courtiers prepared to cut Hsiang-ju down. Hsiang-ju opened his eyes wide and shouted at them. The courtiers retreated in confusion.

The King of Ch'in was discomfited and tapped once on the pot. Hsiang-ju turned around and summoned the Chao attendant scribe to write, "On such and such a year, month, and day, the King of Ch'in played the pot for the King of Chao."

The assembled vassals of Ch'in said, "We ask for fifteen of Chao's walled cities as a gift to the King of Ch'in."

Hsiang-ju responded, "We ask for [Ch'in's capital] Hsien-yang as a gift to the King of Chao."

The King of Ch'in finished his wine, still unable to triumph over Chao. Chao had assembled massive forces in preparation for Ch'in, and Ch'in did not dare move.

[2443] After concluding the meeting and returning home, Hsiang-ju was appointed Senior Excellency because his merit was great. His seat was to the right of Lien P'o's.[14]

Lien P'o said, "I have served as Chao's commander; I have earned great merit attacking walled cities and fighting in the fields. Lin Hsiang-ju has labored only with his tongue and mouth, and his seat is in front of mine. Moreover this Hsiang-ju was once a commoner! I am shamed; I cannot bear to be a subordinate to him."

He announced [to all], "When I see Hsiang-ju, I will be sure to insult him."

Hsiang-ju heard this and was unwilling to meet with him. Whenever court was held, Hsiang-ju always claimed illness, since he did not want to argue over ranking with Lien P'o. A short while after, Hsiang-ju came out [of his house] and saw Lien P'o in the distance. Hsiang-ju turned his cart aside and hid.

At this, his retainers protested: "The only reason your servants left their families and took service with your lordship is because we admired your high principles. Now your lordship holds the same rank as as Lien P'o, but Lord Lien openly utters insults and you timidly hide from him, palpitating in fear! Even the commonest of men would be ashamed to do this, how much more a commander or minister? Your servants are unworthy, allow us to take leave and depart."

Hsiang-ju detained them. "How do you gentlemen think General Lien compares with the King of Ch'in?"

"He is not his equal."

[14] Right indicates Lin Hsiang-ju had precedence over Lien P'o.

"As awesome as the King of Ch'in was, I shouted at him in his own court, and insulted his assembled vassals. I may be a plug, but would I fear a mere General Lien? But I thought this: the sole reason mighty Ch'in does not dare to bring its arms to bear against Chao is the presence of the pair of us. When a pair of tigers fight, the circumstances are such that one of them cannot live. The reason I acted as I have is because I place the needs of my state and house first and my private grudges last."

Lien P'o heard this. He stripped to the waist, put a switch of thorns on his back, and through the offices of a guest arrived at Lin Hsiang-ju's gate to acknowledge his offense. "This lowly country bumpkin did not know how great your compassion was, General." In the end they became friends and swore to die together.

[2444] This year (277 B.C.) Lien P'o attacked Ch'i to the east and defeated one of its armies.

Two years later, Lien P'o again attacked Ch'i at Chi 幾 and seized it.[15]

Three years later, Lien P'o attacked Wei's Fang-ling 防陵 and An-yang 安陽 and seized them.[16]

Four years later Lin Hsiang-ju led an attack on Ch'i. He reached P'ing-yi 平邑 before he stopped.[17]

The next year Chao She 趙奢 defeated the army of Ch'in below the walls of O-yü 閼與.[18]

Chao She was a tax officer of Chao. He collected taxes, but the household of the Lord of P'ing-yüan 平原 was unwilling to pay them. Chao She handled them according to the law and killed nine of those who managed affairs for the Lord of P'ing-yüan. Angered, the Lord of P'ing-yüan was about to kill She. Chao She advised him.

"My lord's rank is that of Noble Scion. If I spare my lord's household today and do not uphold the public good, the laws will decline. If the laws decline, the state will weaken. If the state weakens, the feudal lords will bring their arms to bear on us. If the feudal lords bring their arms to bear on us, that will be the end of Chao. Where then will my lord find wealth such as this?

"If someone with your prestigious status, My Lord, could preserve the public good and observe the laws, then those above [*2445*] and below will be regulated. If those above and below are regulated, then the state will be made strong. If the state is made strong, then Chao will be made secure. As a nobleman with royal kinship, how could you ever be held in contempt by the world?"

---

[15] Chi was located just south of modern Tung-yueh 東樂 in extreme southeastern Hopei on the east bank of the Yellow River in its course at that time (T'an Ch'i-hsiang, 1:38).

According to *Shih chi,* 43:1821, this occurred in 276 B.C., which would make it three years after the meeting at Mien-ch'ih, rather than two years. *Shih chi* Chapter 43 says this city belonged to Wei, rather than Ch'i. It also says that prior to Lien P'o's attack, another Chao general attacked Chi but failed to take it, which would presumably account for the word "again" here.

[16] According to *Shih chi,* 43:1821, Lien P'o took the Wei cities of Fang-tzu 房子 and An-yang in 275 B.C., one year after the previous entry, rather than three years. In "Chi-chieh," Hsü Kuang also says that another text reads Fang-tzu for Fang-ling. T'an Ch'i-hsiang (1:36) has located Fang-ling a few miles southwest of An-yang in modern Honan. An-yang is close to the modern city of the same name.

[17] Near modern Tung-yüeh (Hopei) a few miles south of Chi (see n. 13 and T'an Ch'i-hsiang, 1:38).

According to *Shih chi,* 15:744, Lin Hsiang-ju attacked Ch'i in 271 B.C.

[18] Near modern Ho-shun 和順 in Shansi. Han Chao-ch'i (p. 289, n. 47) claims it belonged to Han at this time, but it was near the Chao border (T'an Ch'i-hsiang, 1:37).

The Lord of P'ing-yüan thought him a worthy man. He spoke of him to the king. The king employed him in the management of the state's taxes. The state's taxes were put in perfect order. The people were enriched and the treasury and storage vaults were filled.

Ch'in attacked Han. It camped its army at O-yü.[19] The king summoned Lien P'o and asked him, "Can we save [Han],[20] or not?" He replied, "The road is long, craggy, and narrow. It would be hard to save them." He then summoned Yüeh Ch'eng and asked him. Yüeh Ch'eng's reply was the same as Lien P'o's. He then summoned Chao She. Chao She replied, "The road is long, craggy, and narrow. One might compare it to two rats struggling in a hole. The bravest general will win." The king finally ordered Chao She to lead the rescue [of Han].

When the troops had left Han-tan thirty *li* behind, he commanded the army, "Anyone who advises me on military matters will die."

The army of Ch'in was encamped west of Wu-an 武安.[21] When the Ch'in army sounded its drums and drilled its troops, every house and roof tile in Wu-an shook. One of the [Chao] army scouts said they should go to the rescue of Wu-an immediately. Chao She beheaded him on the spot. He secured his fortifications, where he remained twenty-eight days without moving, then raised his fortifications even higher. A Ch'in agent entered. Chao She gave him a fine meal and sent him off. The Ch'in agent reported this to the Ch'in general.

The Ch'in general was delighted: "This fellow goes thirty *li* outside of his state's capital, stops his army, and builds bunkers! O-yü is no longer Chao's land."

Having sent off the Ch'in spy, Chao She rolled up his armor and rushed for Wu-an. They arrived in two days and one night. He ordered his best archers to encamp fifty *li* from O-yü. When the barricades were finished, the men of Ch'in heard about it and came with all their troops.

The officer Hsü Li 許歷 asked permission to advise Chao She on military strategy. Chao She said, "Bring him in."

Hsü Li said, "The men of Ch'in did not expect the host of Chao to reach here. They come now with their spirits at their zenith. My commander must concentrate his formations in preparation for them, otherwise defeat is certain."

Chao She said, "Allow me to accept your command."

Hsü Li said, "Allow me to receive the punishment of ax and chopping block."

Chao She said, "I must delay the order until [we have returned to] Han-tan."

Hsü Li asked permission to advise him again: "The first to occupy the summit of the north hill will gain victory, the last to arrive will suffer defeat."

Chao She agreed and immediately sent ten-thousand men rushing towards it. The Ch'in troops arrived last and were unable to ascend the hill. Chao She sent out his troops to attack them and crushed the Ch'in army. The Ch'in army raised the siege and retreated. Thus [Chao She] raised the siege of O-yü and returned.

[2446] King Hui-wen of Chao granted She the title of Lord of Ma-fu 馬服[22] and made Hsü Li Commandant of the State.[23] After this, Chao She shared the same ranking with Lien P'o and Lin Hsiang-ju.

Four years after (266 B.C.), King Hui-wen of Chao expired and his son, King Hsiao-ch'eng 孝成 (r. 265-245 B.C.) was enthroned. In his seventh year (259 B.C.),[24] the forces of

---

[19] There are other versions of how the battle of O-yü came about, see *Chan-kuo ts'e*, 6:47b, *SPTK*.

[20] Depending on how the background of this incident is interpreted, this could be either Han or O-yü.

[21] Near modern Wu-an about 20 miles northwest of the Chao capital of Han-tan 邯鄲 (near modern Han-tan) in Hopei (T'an Ch'i-hsiang, 1:38). Wu-an would then be about 60 miles southeast of O-yü.

[22] Ma-fu is a mountain located a few miles northwest of modern Han-tan in Hopei (T'an Ch'i-hsiang, 1:38).

[23] *Kuo-wei* 國尉.

Ch'in and Chao locked horns at Ch'ang-p'ing 長平.[25] At the time, Chao She was already dead, while Lin Hsiang-ju lay seriously ill. Chao sent Lien P'o to lead the attack on Ch'in. Ch'in defeated the Chao army several times. The Chao army consolidated its fortifications and refused to give battle. Ch'in challenged them to battle several times, but Lien P'o was unwilling.

The King of Chao trusted a Ch'in agent. The Ch'in agent said, "Of all the things Ch'in would dislike, it only fears that Chao K'uo 趙括, son of Chao She, Lord of Ma-fu, will become commander." The King of Chao then made K'uo commander in place of Lien P'o.

Lin Hsiang-ju said, "Your Majesty is sending K'uo because of his reputation; this is like gluing the tuning bridges to strum a zither.[26] K'uo can only recite his father's writings and instructions; he knows nothing about adapting to the changes of battle." The king did not listen, but promptly made him commander.

[2447] Chao K'uo had studied the arts of war since youth. When he spoke of military affairs, he thought no one in the world could equal him. He once discussed military affairs with his father She, and She could not confound him, but still refused to call him a good [strategist]. K'uo's mother asked She his reasons. She said, "The battlefield is a place of death, yet K'uo speaks lightly of it. If Chao does not make K'uo its commander, that's the end of it. If they must needs make him commander, it's K'uo who will defeat Chao's army."

When K'uo was going to set out, his mother sent a letter to the king:

> You cannot send K'uo as commander.

"For what reason?" asked the king.

She replied, "When I first served his father, he was already a general at the time, but the men he served food to with his own hands numbered in the dozens; the men he befriended numbered in the hundreds; the rewards Your Majesty and the royal house bestowed on him, he gave every last bit of to his army officers, knights, and grand masters. From the day he received his appointment [as general], he never asked about household affairs.

"As soon as K'uo became commander, he faced east to receive homage and not one of his army's officers dared to look him in the face. The cash and silk Your Majesty bestowed on him he stored at his house, and looked every day for conveniently located fields and houses; if they were worth buying, he bought them. How does Your Majesty think he compares with his father? Father and son have different characters; I would hope Your Majesty might not dispatch him."

The king said, "Give it up, mother! I have already decided."

K'uo's mother then said, "If Your Majesty does send him and he does not meet your expectations, might your handmaid be spared from his punishment?" The king granted her request.

Chao K'uo having replaced Lien P'o, he changed all standing orders and replaced army officers. When the Ch'in general Pai Ch'i heard this, he unleashed a surprise attack; pretending to flee in defeat, he severed their supply routes, cutting their army in two. The officers and foot-soldiers all lost confidence. After more than forty days, the army was starving.

---

[24] The date for this battle is given elsewhere in the *Shih chi* (73:2333, for example) as 260 B.C. See the discussion of this problem in the Translators' Note to *Shih chi* Chapter 73.

[25] Near modern Kao-p'ing 高平 in Shansi on a direct line between Chao and Ch'in, some 100 miles southwest of Han-tan (T'an Ch'i-hsiang, 1:36).

[26] The *se* 瑟 zither did not have tuning pegs, but used movable wooden bridges under each string to tune it. If the bridges were glued to the sounding board, the instrument could not be tuned.

Chao K'uo sent out crack troops and engaged the enemy himself. The Ch'in army shot and killed Chao K'uo. K'uo's army was defeated and hundreds of thousands of troops surrendered to Ch'in. Ch'in massacred them all. From beginning to end, Chao's losses totaled 450,000.

The next year, Ch'in's troops followed up by besieging Han-tan; after more than a year, [Han-tan] was almost done for. It was only through the arrival of rescuing troops from Ch'u and Wei that the siege of Han-tan was broken. Because K'uo's mother had spoken beforehand, the King of Chao did not execute her.

Five years after the siege of of Han-tan was raised, Yen adopted the plan of Li Fu 栗腹. "The adult men of Chao were exhausted at Ch'ang-p'ing, and their orphans have not yet reached manhood." They raised their troops and attacked Chao. Chao sent [*2448*] Lien P'o to lead its attack; he crushed the Yen army at Hao 鄗, killed Li Fu, and besieged Yen. Yen ceded five walled cities and sued for peace; only then did Chao accept. Chao enfeoffed Lien P'o with Wei-wen 尉文,[27] made him Lord of Hsin-p'ing 信平[28] and Acting Minister of State.[29]

When Lien P'o returned after being relieved at Ch'ang-p'ing and had lost all his power, his old retainers all left. When he was reinstated as commander, his retainers returned. Lien P'o said, "Retire, my retainers!" The retainers said, "Alas! How is it your lordship has not seen it yet! The world's transactions follow the way of the marketplace.[30] When your lordship has power, we follow you; when your lordship has no power, we leave. This is only natural; what is there to resent?"[31]

Six years later, Chao sent Lien P'o to attack Wei's Fan-yang 繁陽.[32] He took it.

King Hsiao-ch'eng of Chao expired and his son King Tao-hsiang 悼襄 was enthroned. He sent Yüeh Ch'eng[33] to replace Lien P'o. Lien P'o was furious and attacked Yüeh Ch'eng; Yüeh Ch'eng fled. Lien P'o then fled to Wei's [capital] Ta Liang.[34]

The next year Chao made Li Mu 李牧 general and attacked Yen, taking Wu-sui 武遂[35] and Fang-ch'eng 方城.[36]

During his long stay in Liang, Wei was unable to trust or employ Lien P'o. Chao was troubled several times by the soldiers of Ch'in. The King of Chao hoped to regain Lien P'o and Lien P'o hoped to be re-employed by Chao. The King of Chao sent an emissary to see if Lien P'o could still be employed. Lien P'o's enemy Kuo K'ai 郭開[37] gave the emissary much additional cash to have him denigrate Lien P'o. After the Chao emissary saw Lien P'o, at one

---

[27] Ch'ien Mu (*Ti-ming k'ao*, p. 500) believes Wei-wen to be located in Wei-chou 蔚州 (modern P'ing-yao 平遙 County in Shansi).

[28] Ch'ien Mu (*Ti-ming k'ao*, p. 734) believes that Hsin 信 should be written Hsin 新; Hsin-p'ing 新平 was located in modern Huai-yang 淮陽 County in Honan.

[29] *Chia-hsiang* 假相. Li Fu is mentioned as a Yen general in *Chan-kuo ts'e* (4:52a, *SPTK*). This incident is also described in *Chan-kuo ts'e* (9:38a, *SPTK*), and in *Shih chi*, 80:2435.

[30] Perhaps there is a deliberate ambiguity here, *chiao* 交 being used both in the sense of "making friends" and "doing business."

[31] This is strikingly similar to the advice the Lord of Meng-ch'ang received from his retainer Feng Hsüan, see our translation of Chapter 75.

[32] A few miles north of modern Nei-huang 內黃 in Honan on the east bank of the Yellow River (T'an Ch'i-hsiang, 1:36).

[33] See the translation of Chapter 80 for a brief notice on Yüeh Ch'eng.

[34] For another description of this incident see *Shih chi*, 80:2435.

[35] About 15 miles north of modern Pao-Ting 保定 in Hopei (T'an Ch'i-hsiang, 1:38).

[36] About 30 miles south of modern Peking (T'an Ch'i-hsiang, 1:41).

[37] Kuo K'ai appears later in this chapter as a Ch'in agent.

sitting Lien P'o ate a *tou* of rice, ten *chin* of meat, threw on his armor, and mounted his horse to show that he could still be employed.

The Chao emissary returned and reported to the king: "Although General Lien is old, he still has a fine appetite, but [*2449*] as he sat with your servant, he had to relieve himself three times in a short span." The king decided Lien P'o was old, and did not summon him.

Ch'u heard that Lien P'o was in Wei, and secretly sent a man to welcome him to Ch'u. After Lien P'o became a commander for Ch'u he earned no merit.

"I long to command men of Chao," he said.

Lien P'o finally died in [the capital of Ch'u] Shou-ch'un 壽春.

Li Mu

Li Mu 李牧 was an able general from Chao's northern border. He once resided at Yen-men 鴈門 in Tai 代,[38] in preparation against the Hsiung-nu. He appointed his officers according to what was appropriate and sent all the market tax to the tent-headquarters[39] as funds for the officers and soldiers. He killed several cattle every day to feed his warriors, practiced marksmanship and horsemanship, attended to the signal fires, and sent out many spies and agents, richly rewarding his warriors. He had one standing order: "When the Hsiung-nu come to raid, immediately enter and hold your fortifications. Anyone who dares to capture a prisoner will be beheaded." Every time the Hsiung-nu invaded, the signal fires were tended, and [the troops] immediately entered and held to their fortifications, not daring to fight.

Things went on like this for several years, and he lost no men. The Hsiung-nu, however, considered Li Mu a coward. Even the Chao border troops thought their general was a coward. The King of Chao rebuked Li Mu; Li Mu continued as before. The King of Chao angrily summoned him and sent another man to replace him as general.

[2450] For over a year, every time the Hsiung-nu invaded, [the Chao troops] came out and fought. When they came out and fought, they frequently had the worst of it and the border area could not be used for farming or grazing. [The king] asked Li Mu to return. Li Mu bolted his gate and would not come out, stubbornly claiming he was sick. The King of Chao forced him to come out and sent him to command the troops.

Mu said, "If Your Majesty must employ me, I will only dare accept your command if I act as before." The king granted his request. When Li Mu arrived, he reinstated his old standing orders. The Hsiung-nu gained nothing for several years, but still considered him a coward.

The border warriors were rewarded daily but never made use of; they all longed for a fight. After this, [Li Mu] prepared the fastest chariots and obtained 1300, reviewed the horsemen and obtained 13,000, plus 50,000 "hundred-cash" warriors,[40] and 100,000 bowmen, all of whom he drilled in preparation for battle. Then he let out vast numbers of livestock; people filled the moors. The Hsiung-nu invaded with a few men and he pretended to be defeated, throwing them a few thousand men. The Khan heard this and led all his troops in a huge invasion. Li Mu laid out numerous clever formations, spread out left and right columns and attacked them, crushing the hundred-thousand Hsiung-nu horsemen. He annihilated the Tan-lan 襜襤, broke the Tung-hu 東胡, subjugated the Lin-hu 林胡, and the Khan fled to another

---

[38] Tai was a commandery located along the modern Shansi-Hopei border. Yen-men was a mountain range about 50 miles northeast of modern Ta-t'ung 大同 City in Shansi (T'an Ch'i-hsiang, 1:38).

[39] This is the earliest reference we have found to the famous *mu-fu*.

[40] Those border warriors who were "rewarded daily."

state.[41] For more than a dozen years after, the Hsiung-nu did not dare to approach the walled border cities of Chao.

In the first year of King Tao-hsiang 悼襄 of Chao (244 B.C. [r. 244-236 B.C.]), Lien P'o having fled to Wei, Chao sent Li Mu to attack Yen. He took Wu-sui and Fang-ch'eng.[42]

Two years later, P'ang Hsüan 龐煖 broke the army of Yen [*2451*] and killed Chü Hsin 劇辛.[43]

Seven years later, Ch'in defeated and killed the Chao general Hu Tse 扈輒 at Wu-sui and cut off 100,000 heads.[44] Chao made Li Mu commander-in-chief. He attacked the Ch'in army at Yi-an 宜安, crushed the Ch'in army and put the Ch'in general Huan Ch'i 桓齮 to flight.[45] [Chao] enfeoffed Li Mu as the Lord of Wu-an 武安.

Three years later, Ch'in attacked P'u-wu 番吾.[46] Li Mu attacked and defeated the Ch'in army, and held off Han and Wei to the south.

In the seventh year of Ch'ien 遷, King of Chao (229 B.C. [r. 235-228 B.C.]), Ch'in sent Wang Chien 王翦 to attack Chao.[47] Chao sent Li Mu and Ssu-ma Shang 司馬尚 to resist him. Ch'in gave the King of Chao's trusted vassal Kuo K'ai much cash to act as a subversive agent, and suggest that Li Mu and Ssu-ma Shang wanted to rebel.

The King of Chao sent Chao Ts'ung 趙蔥 and the Ch'i general Yen Chü 顏聚 to replace Li Mu. Li Mu refused to accept the orders. Chao sent a man to secretly arrest Li Mu, and when he was captured, beheaded him, and stripped Ssu-ma Shang of his post.[48]

Three months after, Wang Chien launched a furious attack against Chao, killed Chao Ts'ung, crushed his army, and captured Ch'ien, King of Chao, and his general Yen Chü, finally destroying Chao.

His Honor the Grand Scribe says, "To face death knowing full well one must die, surely this is courage! But as for dying itself, that is no difficult matter; it is using one's death to good purpose that is difficult!. When Lin Hsiang-ju took the jade and glanced back at the pillar, when he shouted at the attendants of the King of Ch'in, he faced, [*2452*] at the most, execution, yet others would have failed to act from fear or cowardice. When Hsiang-ju showed his spirit, he inspired awe in enemy states; when he retreated and yielded to Lien P'o, his reputation became outweighed Mount T'ai. Using wisdom and courage to good purpose-- he might be said to have done both at once."

---

[41] According to Wang Li-ch'i (81:1890n.) the Tan-lan operated north of Tai Commandery, the Tung Hu in the west of modern Liang-ning, and the Lin-hu from Shansi north into the Inner Mongolian Autonomous Region.

[42] According to *Shih chi*, 15:751, although King Tao-hsiang's reign began in 244 B.C., Chao took Wu-sui and Fang-ch'eng in 243 B.C., the next year.

[43] P'ang was a Chao general; Chü had switched allegiances from Chao to Yen which he served as a general. According to *Shih chi*, 15:751, Chü Hsin died in 242 B.C. See also *Shih chi*, 34:1560.

[44] According to both Shih chi 15:753 and *Shih chi*, 43:1831, this occurred in 234 B.C., a date which cannot be reconciled with the "seven years" figure here.

[45] According to *Shih chi*, 43:1832, Li Mu defeated Ch'in in 233 B.C. and was enfeoffed the same year. *Shih chi*, 15:754, however, says that Ch'in's general Huan Ch'i "pacified P'ing-yang, Wu-ch'eng and Yi-an."

[46] P'u-wu was located about 20 miles south of Han-tan (see T'an Ch'i-hsiang, 1:38 and n. 26 to our translation of *Shih chi* Chapter 69).

Shih chi, 43:1832 says that this occurred in 232 B.C., which is not consistent with the statement "three years later." *Shih chi*, 15:754 says that Ch'in *captured* P'u-wu in 232 B.C., flatly contradicting the account here.

[47] With the exception of the date and a few minor variations, this section is identical with *Chan-kuo ts'e*, 6:85a (*SPTK*).

[48] *Chan-kuo ts'e* (6:81b, *SPTK*) gives a different version of Li Mu's death, in which he is allowed to commit suicide.

TRANSLATORS' NOTE

This is an essay on the major civil and military leaders of Chao: Lin Hsiang-ju, representing the civil, and Lien P'o, Chao She, Chao K'uo, and Li Mu, the martial. It is also a dissertation on defensive strategy, civil and martial. Lin Hsiang-ju pretended to fear Lien P'o so that he would not cause internecine strife in Chao thereby aiding Ch'in. Chao She fought Ch'in only out of a defensive position. Li Mu bided his time so much that the Hsiung-nu, his own men and his king all believed him to be a coward, but in the end won a decisive victory over rivals who had come to take him for granted. The only offensive leader here is Chao K'uo and the loss of his life and that of nearly half a million of his soldiers only reinforces the merits of the defensive.

The chapters is also distinguished by vivid and detailed accounts of skirmishes and battles, such as Lin Hsiang-ju's duel with the drunken King of Ch'in at Mien-ch'ih and the preparations for the battle to relieve O-yü. Other seemingly small details such as the letter Chao K'uo's mother sent to warn the king of her own son's ineptitude or the aging Lien P'o's attempt to impress the emissary from Chao by gorging himself on food and drink and then arraying himself for battle add to the realistic tone of the narrative.

BIBLIOGRAPHY

I. Translations

Kierman, Frank A., Jr. *Ssu-ma Ch'ien's Historiographical Attitude as Reflected in Four Late Warring States Biographies.* Wiesbaden: Harrassowitz, 1962, pp. 26-36.

Ōgawa Tamaki 小川環樹, trans. *Shiki retsuden* 史記列傳. Rpt. Tokyo: Chikuma Shobō, 1986 (1969), pp. 143-150.

Panasjuk, V. *Syma Czjan', Izbrannoe.* Moscow, 1956, pp. 156-78.

Yang Hsien-yi and Gladys Yang. *Records of the Historian.* Rpt. Hong Kong: The Commercial Press, pp. 139-51.

II. Studies

Chan Hsü-tso 詹緒佐. *"Shih chi* 'Lien Lin lieh-chuan' chu-shih, piao-tien chih-yi" 史記廉藺列傳注釋標點質疑, *Hsüeh yü-wen* , 1986.3.

Kierman, *op. cit.*

T'ien Tan, Memoir 22

[82:2453] T'ien Tan 田單 was a distant relative of the T'iens of Ch'i 齊.[1] During the time of King Min 湣 (r. *323-284 B.C.), Tan was a market clerk[2] in Lin-tzu, but he remained unrecognized. When the state of Yen sent Yüeh Yi[3] to campaign to crush Ch'i,[4] King Min of Ch'i fled,[5] shortly after setting up defenses in the walled city of Chü 莒.[6] As the Yen host pushed deep into Ch'i to subdue it,[7] T'ien Tan fled to An-p'ing 安平,[8] ordered his clansmen to cut off the ends of their carriage axles, and cover them with iron caps. Shortly after, the Yen army attacked An-p'ing. When the city walls had been breached, the men of Ch'i ran, struggling [to be first] on the roads; as their caps broke off, their chariots collapsed, and they were taken captive by Yen. Only the clansmen of T'ien Tan, because of their iron hubcaps, were able to get away, setting up defenses to the east at Chi-mo 即墨.[9] Yen then caused all the other cities of Ch'i to surrender; only Chü and Chi-mo did not submit. When the Yen army heard that the King of Ch'i was in Chü, it regrouped to attack it.[10] After Nao Ch'ih 淖齒 slew King Min in Chü,[11] [the people of the city] put up a resolute defense and held off the Yen army for several years without submitting. Yen led their troops eastward to lay siege to Chi-mo; the grand master of Chi-mo came out to battle with them but was defeated and died. Those within the city walls joined together to choose T'ien Tan [to replace him]: "In the battle of An-p'ing, T'ien Tan's clansmen were able to get away unscathed because of their iron hubcaps; he is well versed in military strategy." They made him [their] general and held off Yen from Chi-mo.

[1] The T'ien clan originated in the state of Ch'en 陳. Ch'en Wan 完, a member of the Ch'en royal family, fled to Ch'i in 669 B.C. (see *Shih chi*, 46:1880). His descendants quickly rose to power in Ch'i, and in 386 B.C. Ch'en Ho 何 deposed the King of Ch'i and declared himself king.

It appears that the clan kept their surname for at least part of their reign in Ch'i, contrary to Ssu-ma Ch'ien's claim in *Shih chi* Chapter 46, since all references to the family found so far in bronze inscriptions and in many Warring States texts (such as *Meng Tzu*) refer to them as "Ch'en." It is only in fairly late texts that they are referred to as T'ien.

[2] *Shih-yüan* 市掾 (see Chang Cheng-lang, p. 376).

[3] See his biography in *Shih chi* Chapter 80.

[4] An account of this campaign, which originally involved armies from Chao, Ch'u, Han and Wei (these troops withdrew after an initial victory over Ch'i just west of the Chi 濟 River), can be found in the biography of Yüeh Yi (*Shih chi*, 80:2428-9). After this battle Yüeh Yi took Ch'i's capital of Lin-tzu and carried its treasures back to King Chao. The king then ordered him to return to Ch'i and take the other walled cities; within five years he had captured all but two.

[5] These events took place in 284 B.C. (see *Shih chi*, 15:740).

[6] Chü was originally a separate state which was absorbed by Ch'i; it is located in the southeastern part of modern Shantung (T'an Ch'i-hsiang 1:40).

[7] Taking seventy cities as he moved forward, see our translation of *Shih chi* Chapter 80 above.

[8] An-p'ing was a city just a few miles northeast of Lin-tzu (T'an Ch'i-hsiang, 1:39).

[9] Chi-mo is in modern east-central Shantung, about 50 miles north of Tsingtao (T'an Ch'i-hsiang, 1:40).

[10] The troops had been spread throughout Ch'i taking its cities one by one.

[11] This story, as recounted in *Shih chi*, 46:1900-1, tells that in the fortieth year [of King Min (*284 B.C., according to the chronology of the *Shih chi*)], Yen, Ch'in, Ch'u and the Three Chin joined together to invade Ch'i. King Min fled Ch'i and went to Wei, but his rudeness and arrogance made him unwelcome first in Wei and then in Tsou and Lu. Finally he went to Ch'u. Ch'u sent Nao Ch'ih with an army to relieve Ch'i. Nao eventually became a minister in Ch'i, killed King Min and surrendered parts of Ch'i to Yen. Nao Ch'ih himself was finally killed by a mob of Ch'i citizens (see also *Chan-kuo ts'e*, 3:48b and 4:50b, *SPTK*).

[2454] Shortly thereafter, King Chao 昭 of Yen (r. 311-279 B.C.) passed away and King Hui 惠 (r. 278-272 B.C.) was enthroned.[12] There was bad blood between him and Yüeh Yi.[13] T'ien Tan heard of it and released a counter-agent[14] to Yen who spread a rumor: "The King of Ch'i has died, only two walled cities remain which have not been captured.[15] Yüeh Yi fears execution and will not venture to return. Ostensibly attacking Ch'i, he actually wants to gather the troops, face south and become the King of Ch'i. Since the people of Ch'i do not yet support him, he puts off attacking Chi-mo and bides his time. The people of Ch'i only fear that with the arrival of another general Chi-mo will be destroyed!" The King of Yen considered this to be so and sent Chi Chieh 騎劫[16] to replace Yüeh Yi.

Yüeh Yi accordingly went over to Chao and the men of Yen, officers and soldiers, were indignant. And T'ien Tan then ordered that the people within the city walls must sacrifice to their ancestors in their courtyards whenever they ate. The flying birds all hovered and swooped inside the city walls, before descending to eat [the sacrificial offerings]. The men of Yen marveled over it. T'ien Tan accordingly proclaimed: "A deity is coming down to instruct me." Then he issued an order to the people within the city walls: "There will be a divine man to serve as my teacher." One of the foot soldiers said, "May I serve as your teacher?" Because of this [question], he turned and ran. T'ien Tan stood up, led him back, sat him facing east,[17] and served him as was appropriate for a teacher. The soldier said, "I have deceived your lordship. I actually have no abilities." "Say no more!" T'ien Tan replied. Then he treated him as his teacher. Whenever he issued a command, he referred to the divine teacher.

He then announced, "My only fear is that the Yen army might cut off the noses of those Ch'i soldiers they have taken captive and place them in the front ranks when they give us battle; [if so] Chi-mo will be defeated." The men of Yen heard this and did as he had said. When the people within the city walls saw that all those from Ch'i who had surrendered had

---

[12] Scholars have noted that parallels for most of the *Shih chi* passages on T'ien Tan can be found in the *Chan-kuo ts'e*, and Chu Tsu-keng (3:1762) has identified two more episodes in the *T'ai-p'ing yü-lan* which occur in the *Shih chi* and were originally part of the *Chan-kuo ts'e*.

[13] Enmity since he had been Crown Prince, see *Shih chi* 34:1558 and 80:2429.

[14] *Fan-chien* 反間. Whether this is a Yen agent who had been captured or a subject of Ch'i is not clear. Fritz Jäger, "Das 82. Kapitel des Schi-gi," *Sino-Japonica, Festschrift André Wedemeyer zum 80. Geburtstag* (Leipzig: Otto Harrassowitz, 1956), p. 110, n. 11, has a long discussion of the expression which is common in the *Chan-kuo ts'e*. He notes that the term is found in *Sun Tzu* (13:6b, *SPPY*) as one of the five types of spies. Lionel Giles, in his translation (*Sun Tzu on the Art of War* [London 1910], p. 164), renders it "converted spies," to bring across the idea that these men were originally spies of an enemy who were then "converted" to work for the state they had originally intended to ruin. But Wang Shu-min (in a personal communication) argues that *fan* 反 merely means that he spread subversive talk (*fan-yü* 反語).

[15] *Shih chi,* 34:1558 says three cities continued to resist--Chi-mo, Chü, and Liao 聊. The latter, located over sixty miles west-southwest of modern Tsinan (Shantung) near the modern city of the same name, was just south of the course of the Yellow River as it flowed at that time (T'an Ch'i-hsiang 1:39). Possibly because Liao was on the "western front" of the warfare between Yen and Ch'i it was overlooked in this account where the focus was the resistance by the "eastern front" cities of Chi-mo and Chü.

[16] *Shih chi,* 15:742 and 34:1558 claim he was killed in this battle.

[17] On *Shih chi* 81:1447 Chao K'uo 趙括 faces east after he has become general to assert his authority. Takigawa again (81:17) quotes Ku Yen-wu 顧炎武 (1613-1682): "When the ancients sat down, they considered that [the seat] facing east was the place of honor. Therefore, in sacrifices in the ancestral temples, the place of the original ancestor is facing east. Also in the positions of social relationships, a guest likewise faces east and the host west . . . ." The clearest statement of this practice in the *Shih chi,* however, may be seen in Hsiang Yü's "seating [Wang] Ling's 王陵 mother facing east," hoping to bring Wang Ling over to his side (*Shih chi,* 56:2059).

lost their noses, they grew angry and more determined to hold out, only fearing that they would be taken captive. Tan released another agent to say: "I am afraid that the men of Yen might dig up our grave mounds outside the city walls and disgrace our ancestors. My heart turns cold at the thought!" The army of Yen dug up all of the grave tumuli and burned the corpses. The people of Chi-mo watched from the city walls. They all wept. Everyone ached to go out to give battle and their anger grew tenfold.[18]

[2455] T'ien Tan, knowing his troops were ready to be put to use, carried planks and shovels to share the work with his troops;[19] he placed his wives and concubines among the rank and file, he distributed food and drink to feed the soldiers. He ordered all his armored troops to hide, and sent the old, the infirm, the women, and the children up onto the city walls [in defensive positions]. He dispatched an envoy to negotiate surrender to Yen and the Yen army all shouted huzzahs. T'ien Tan also collected the people's gold, obtaining more than one-thousand *yi*,[20] which he ordered the wealthy of Chi-mo to send to the Yen general,[21] saying: "If Chi-mo surrenders, we ask that you neither plunder the women nor the homes of our clans, but leave us in peace!" The Yen general was greatly pleased and granted their request. From this time on the Yen army became more and more negligent.

T'ien Tan then searched everywhere within the city walls, obtaining more than one-thousand head of cattle, outfitted them in red silk, painted them as multi-colored dragons, tied knives to their horns, poured animal fat onto reeds tied to their tails, and lit the ends. Having cut several dozen holes through the city walls, he loosed the cattle [through them] at night; five thousand stalwart troops followed in their wake. As the cattle felt their tails burning, in their fury they rushed towards the Yen army, and the Yen army became terrified in the dark of night. The torches on the cattle's tails blazing brilliantly, the Yen army saw only dragon-like shapes when it looked at [the cattle]; all whom the cattle ran into were killed or wounded. [Then] the five-thousand men, with bits in their mouths [to silence them], attacked [the Yen army], others from within the city walls followed them drumming and shouting; the old and the infirm all struck on bronze vessels to cause a din, a din which shook heaven and earth. The Yen army was terrified and fled in defeat. The men of Ch'i then cut down their general, Chi Chieh. As the Yen army fled in disorder, the men of Ch'i chased and drove the fleeing [soldiers]. Every walled city that they passed rebelled against Yen and came over to T'ien Tan; the number of his soldiers swelled daily and he took full advantage of their victories. Yen's losses mounted daily until they finally reached the banks of the Ho. Ch'i's seventy-odd walled cities were all restored to Ch'i. King Hsiang 襄 (r. 283-265 B.C.) was escorted from Chü and entered Lin-tzu to preside over the government.

The King of Ch'i enfeoffed T'ien Tan, titling him the Lord of An-p'ing.

His Honor the Grand Scribe says: "Battles are fought according to standard strategies, [but] won by clever stratagems.[22] Those who are skilled at it can come up with clever stratagems without end. Clever stratagems and standard strategies in turn give birth to one another and like a ring have no starting point.[23] At the beginning [the troops] are like a [quiet] maiden

---

[18] We follow two variants--which occur in several editions--noted by Wang Shu-min (82:2468) in the final sentence of this passage: *ch'i* 其 for *chü* 俱 and *chieh* 皆 for *tzu* 自. The present text does not make sense.

[19] The work here could be that of repairing and shoring up the city walls or that of tunneling under the city walls to allow the cattle to rush out (see below).

[20] *Yi* 溢 here is a loan for *yi* 鎰 each of which equals twenty or twenty-four *liang* 兩 of gold.

[21] The wealthy sent it themselves to avoid the appearance of another ruse by T'ien Tan.

[22] *Cheng* 正 and *ch'i* 奇, here "standard strategies" and "clever stratagems," are general philosophical terms of traditional Chinese military science.

to whom the enemy opens its door. Later they are as [fast as] fleeing hares, so that the enemy has no time to resist.[24] Might this not be said of T'ien Tan?![25]"

Earlier,[26] when Nao Ch'ih killed King Min, the people of Chü sought King Min's son, Fa-chang 法章, and found him in the house of the Grand Scribe Chiao 嫩.

When he was working as a gardener, Chiao's daughter fell in love with him [*2457*] and treated him well. Later Fa-chang told her in confidence of his situation; she then had relations with him.[27] The people of Chü in common accord enthroned Fa-chang as King [Hsiang] of Ch'i, and resisted Yen from Chü. The daughter of the Grand Scribe's clan became his queen and was referred to as "Our Ruler's Queen."

When the Yen [army] had first entered Ch'i, they heard of a worthy man [named] Wang Chu 王蠋[28] who lived in Hua-yi 畫邑[29] and issued an order to their troops because of Wang Chu: "Do not go within thirty *li* of Hua-yi!" A little later they sent an envoy to say to Wang Chu: "The men of Ch'i highly value your righteousness. We will make you a general and enfeoff you with ten-thousand households." Chu adamantly declined the offer. The man from Yen said, "If you don't accept, we will lead our armies and put Hua-yi to the sword!" Wang Chu replied, "A loyal vassal does not serve two lords and a virtuous women does not take a second husband. The King of Ch'i did not heed my admonitions, so I retired to till the countryside. My country having been destroyed, I can not go on living. Now you go a step further, coercing me through military force to be your general: this is assisting Chieh in his tyranny![30] I would surely rather be boiled alive than to live without righteousness!" Then he put a rope around his neck, tied it to the branch of a tree, threw himself down, broke his neck and died. The grand masters of Ch'i who had fled heard this and said, "Wang Chu was a commoner, yet in his righteousness he would not face north [accepting allegiance] to Yen. How could those who hold positions and take salary do so?" Then they all assembled and went to Chü, sought out [King Min's] sons, and enthroned [one] as King Hsiang.

---

[23] There is a parallel to these two lines in *Sun Tzu* (5:6b, *SPPY*).

[24] These two lines have been variously interpreted (see Jäger, *op. cit.*, p. 113 and Kierman, p. 39). Our interpretation is related to the Chinese maxim 靜如處女, 動如脫兔 used to describe the way a warrior should act: "[When biding his time], to be as quiet as a maiden, [when attacking], to move like a fleeing hare." A parallel passage can be found in the *Sun Tzu* (11:39b, *SPPY*).

[25] This expression occurs often in the *Shih chi*; see also *Lun yü*, 1/15.

[26] Although passages begun by *ch'u* 初 often have been added or interpolated from a text other than the main source, Liang Yü-sheng (82:1296) argues that the problem may have resulted from a misplaced bamboo strip. Wang Shu-min notes (in a letter) that Ssu-ma Ch'ien used two types of commentary: one to provide sources and the second--like this chapter--to provide supplementary material.

[27] Other versions of this story can be found in *Shih chi*, 46:1901 (more detailed) and in the *Chan-kuo ts'e* (4:50b, *SPTK*). Some scholars are bothered by the title "Our Ruler's Queen" 君王后. It supposedly came about because Chiao's daughter was called "Lady Hou" 后氏 and would have been referred to as "Wang-hou Hou" 王后后 as queen (see Chavannes 5:274, n. 1).

[28] A similar account of this episode appears in the *Shuo yüan* (4:8b-9a, *SPPY*).

[29] Located a few miles west of modern Lin-tzu (T'an Ch'i-hsiang 1:39).

[30] On Emperor Chieh 桀 see our translation of *Shih chi* Chapter 2. This resembles a set expression in common use today: "to assist Chou in his tyranny" 助紂為虐.

TRANSLATORS' NOTE

This chapter is similar to *Shih chi* Chapters 64 and 65 ("Marshal Jang-chü" and "Sun Tzu and Wu Ch'i") in which a single incident or several incidents characterize the military skills of a famous general. The focal point of the "biography" is, of course, the famous nocturnal charge of the T'ien Tan's little army from within the walls of Chi-mo led by oxen adorned with painted dragons, at the same time illuminated and goaded by burning bunches of faggots which had been tied to their tails. It is this account which has made the chapter a popular selection of anthologists.

This is one of the shortest *lieh-chuan* and would be even briefer but for the lengthy "comments" of the Grand Scribe. Here two other stories related to the defense of Ch'i against Yen are presented: that of Fa-chang, King Min's son who succeeded him as King Hsiang, and the brave Wang Chu who tried to exert his countrymen with his death. Some critics believe that these stories are interpolations; others argue that the Grand Scribe used his comments for two purposes, to evaluate his biographies and to augment them.

BIBLIOGRAPHY

I. Translations

Kierman, Frank A, Jr. *Ssu-ma Ch'ien's Historiographical Attitude as Reflected in Four Late Warring States Biographies.* Wiesbaden: Harrassowitz, 1962, pp. 37-40.

Jäger, Fritz. "Das 82. Kapitel des Schi-gi," *Sino-Japonica, Festschrift André Wedemeyer zum 80. Geburtstag.* Leipzig: Otto Harrassowitz, 1956, pp. 107-117.

Ōgawa Tamaki 小川環樹, trans. *Shiki retsuden* 史記列傳. Rpt. Tokyo: Chikuma Shobō, 1986 (1969), pp. 150-52.

Watson, Burton. *Records of the Historian. Chapters from the Shih chi of Ssu-ma Ch'ien.* Rpt. New York: Columbia University Press, 1969, pp. 30-35.

II. Studies

Kierman, *op. cit.*

Lu Chung Lien and Tsou Yang, Memoir 23

Lu Chung Lien

[83:2459] Lu Chung Lien 魯仲連 (*c.* 305-245 B.C.)[1] was a native of Ch'i. He loved grandiose and extraordinary schemes, but was unwilling to serve as an official or to hold a post, delighting only in holding to his high principles.

He traveled to Chao. In the time of King Hsiao-ch'eng 孝成 of Chao (r. 265-245 B.C.), the King of Ch'in sent Pai Ch'i to defeat Chao's army at Ch'ang-p'ing, from beginning to end [killing] over 400,000.[2] The soldiers of Ch'in subsequently besieged Han-tan 邯鄲 to the east. The King of Chao was afraid, and none of the rescuing troops of the feudal lords dared to attack the Ch'in army.[3]

King An-li 安釐 of Wei (r. 276-243 B.C.) sent General Chin Pi 晉鄙[4] to rescue Chao;[5] he was afraid of Ch'in, stopped at Tang-yin 蕩陰[6] and proceeded no farther. The King of Wei sent the Foreign General[7] Hsin-yüan Yen 新垣衍[8] by a back road into Han-tan and through the offices of the Lord of P'ing-yüan 平原[9] informed the King of Chao, "The cause for Ch'in's swift siege of Chao lies in its struggle previously over the title of emperor with King Min 湣 of Ch'i (r. *323-284 B.C.), which [King Min] shortly afterward relinquished. Now Ch'i grows weaker and weaker, and as of today only Ch'in dominates the world. It is not that he has his heart set on Han-tan; his intent is to regain the title of Emperor. If Chao can send out an emissary [*2460*] to honor King Chao of Ch'in as Emperor, Ch'in is sure to be pleased, withdraw his troops and leave." The Lord of P'ing-yüan hesitated and could reach no decision.

At this time, Lu Chung Lien happened to be traveling through Chao, and when Ch'in besieged Chao, he heard that the Wei general wanted to have Chao honor Ch'in as Emperor. He saw the Lord of P'ing-yüan and said, "How are affairs to be settled?"

The Lord of P'ing-yüan said, "How would I, Sheng, dare to speak on affairs! Before this, we lost an army of 400,000 beyond our borders, and now within our borders we are besieged at Han-tan, unable to drive [Ch'in] away. The King of Wei has sent his Foreign General Hsin-yüan Yen to have Chao confer the title of emperor on Ch'in, and the fellow is here today. How would I, Sheng, dare to speak on affairs!"

Lu Chung Lien said, "I thought at first that My Lord was one of the worthiest Noble Scions in the world; now, after this, I know that My Lord is not. Where is Liang's retainer, Hsin-yüan Yen? Let me chastise him and send him back for My Lord."

---

[1] Lu Chung Lien also appears in the *Chan-kuo ts'e*. He is sometimes known as Lu Lien 魯連. Chung may have been an *agnomen*.

These dates are based on Ch'ien Mu, *Chu-tzu*, p. 619.

[2] On this battle see Pai Ch'i's biography in *Shih chi* Chapter 72.

[3] See *Shih chi* Chapter 81.

[4] He appears in *Shih chi*, 76:2368 and several times in Chapter 77.

[5] See the parallel passage in *Chan-kuo ts'e* (6:62b, *SPTK*).

[6] Located near modern Tang-yin in Honan about 50 miles south of Han-tan and some 70 miles north of the Wei capital (T'an Ch'i-hsiang, I:36).

[7] *K'o-chiang* 客將.

[8] "So-yin" says he had been a general for Liang.

[9] See his biography in *Shih chi* Chapter 76.

The Lord of P'ing-yüan said, "Allow me to act as your intermediary and present him to you, Venerable Sir." The Lord of P'ing-yüan then saw Hsin-yüan Yen and said, "There is a Venerable Lu Chung Lien of an eastern state here now. Allow me to act as your intermediary and introduce him to you, General."

Hsin-yüan Yen said, "I have heard that Venerable Lu Chung Lien is a high-principled knight of the state of Ch'i. As a vassal, I, Yen, am duty-bound to carry out my mission. I do not wish to see Venerable Lu Chung Lien."

The Lord of P'ing-yüan said, "I have already revealed [your presence]." Hsin-yüan Yen [then] agreed [to see Lu Chung Lien].

Lu Chung Lien saw Hsin-yüan Yen and was silent. Hsin-yüan Yen said, "When I look at those living in this besieged city, it seems to me that every one of them has a favor to ask of the Lord of P'ing-yüan. Yet viewing your jade visage today, Venerable Sir, it seems to me that you are not one of them. Why do you linger in this besieged city and not depart?"

Lu Chung Lien said, "The world thinks [*2461*] of Pao Chiao 鮑焦[10] as a man who died through his lack of tolerance, but they are all wrong. The masses did not understand and thought he acted for personal reasons. This Ch'in is a land that casts aside propriety and principle, and exalts merit that is measured in human heads. Its king handles its knights by trickery; he handles its commoners as slaves. If he should wantonly assume the title of emperor, or even worse, assume rule over the world, I would have no choice left but to drown myself in the East Ocean; I could not bear to be his subject. The reason I wish to see you, General, is to help Chao."

[2462] Hsin-yüan Yen said, "How would you help it, Venerable Sir?"

Lu Chung Lien said, "I will have Liang and Yen help it; Ch'i and Ch'u then must help it."

Hsin-yüan Yen said, "As for Yen, I too would ask for alliance with them. As for Liang, I am a native of Liang. How can you make Liang help?"

Lu Lien said, "It is only that Liang has not seen the harm of Ch'in's assuming the title of emperor; if Liang is made to see the harm of Ch'in's assuming the title of emperor, it is sure to help Chao."

Hsin-yüan Yen said, "What is the harm of Ch'in's assuming the title of emperor?"

Lu Lien said, "Long ago, King Wei 威 of Ch'i (r. *378-343 B.C.) conducted himself both humanely and justly. He led the feudal lords of all the world to pay homage at Chou's court. Chou was poor and humble; none of the feudal lords wished to pay homage. Ch'i alone made them pay homage.

"More than a year later, King Lieh 烈 (r. 375-369 B.C.) of Chou died. Ch'i came late. Chou angrily sent a funeral notice to Ch'i: 'The sky falls down and the earth cracks when the Son of Heaven leaves his mat.[11] The vassal of the Eastern Barriers [T'ien] Yin 田因 of Ch'i[12] arrived late; let him be beheaded.' King Wei of Ch'i's neck bulged in anger: "Huh! Your mother was a slave-woman!" In the end he was the laughingstock of the whole world. Thus while the Chou king was alive, he paid homage at his court, and when the Chou king died, he shouted at him. He could not bear his demands, but the Son of Heaven is naturally so; there is nothing worth puzzling about here."

---

[10] Wang Shu-min (83:2474-5) collects the sources on Pao Chiao (see also Wang Li-ch'i, *Jen-piao,* p. 321). Alluding to him suggested that the person under discussion was a man of principles. Thus the point of this paragraph is Lu Chung Lien is "lingering in the besieged city" out of principle, not for any personal motive.

[11] A euphemism for death.

[12] T'ien Yin was King Wei of Ch'i.

Hsin-yüan Yen said, "Can it be you haven't seen porter-slaves, Venerable Sir? Ten men following one man; can it really be that their strength does not surpass his or their wits are not his equal? They fear him."

Lu Chung Lien said, "Woe! Does Liang compare itself to the porter of Ch'in?"

Hsin-yüan Yen said, "Yes."

Lu Chung Lien said, "Then I will have the King of Ch'in [*2463*] boil the King of Liang and make him into mincemeat."

Hsin-yüan Yen scowled in displeasure: "Hah! This talk of yours is too much, Venerable Sir. And how can you have the King of Ch'in boil the King of Liang?"

Lu Chung Lien said, "I assure you I can. I will explain it. Long ago, the Marquis of Chiu 九, the Marquis of O 鄂, and King Wen 文 were the Three Masters of Chow [the last ruler of the Yin Dynasty]. The Marquis of Chiu had a child who was beautiful. He offered her to Chow; Chow thought her ugly and made the Marquis of Chiu into a mincemeat. The Marquis of O reproached Chow strongly, defended Chiu quick-wittedly, and [Chow] made the Marquis of O into strips of dried meat. King Wen heard this and sighed deeply, so [Chow] locked him in the storehouse of Yu-li 羑里 for a hundred days, hoping to make him die.[13] Why did these men all call themselves king and wind up receiving the punishment of meat strips and mincemeat?

"King Min of Ch'i went to Lu. Yi-wei Tzu 夷維子 held his horsewhip and followed. He said to the men of Lu, 'How will you entertain Our Lord?'

"The men of Lu said, 'We will entertain your lord with ten T'ai-lao 太牢 sacrifices.'[14]

"Yi-wei Tzu said, 'Where do you find rituals such as these to entertain Our Lord? This lord of ours is the Son of Heaven! When the Son of Heaven makes his tour of inspection, the feudal lords yield their dwellings and surrender their keys; holding mats and tables, they observe the feast from the courtyard at the foot of the hall; when the Son of Heaven has finished his meal, they retire and await court.'

"The men of Lu put their keys [into their locks] and refused to admit King Min. Unable to enter Lu, [King Min] decided to go to Hsüeh, and asked safe passage through Tsou. At that time, the Lord of Tsou had died. King Min wanted to pay his respects, and Yi-wei Tzu told the Orphan of Tsou, 'When the Son of Heaven pays his respects, the host must turn the coffin around, so that the south side faces north and only then will the Son of Heaven face south and pay his respects.[15]

"The assembled vassals of Tsou said, 'If it must be done this way, we will fall on our swords and die.'

"Of course, he did not dare enter Tsou.

"The vassals of Tsou and Lu did not obtain the largesse [of the King of Chou] when they were alive, nor his funeral gifts when they died. Yet when [Ch'i] demanded to be treated as a Son of Heaven in Tsou and Lu, the vassals of Tsou and Lu would not allow him into their states.

[13] See *Shih chi*, 3:106 for an account of these events.

[14] *T'ai-lao* 太牢 was a sacrifice intended for the lords involving three kinds of meat: beef, mutton and pork (there were corresponding sacrifices for the grand masters [*tai-fu* 大夫], with mutton and pork, and the patricians [*shih* 士], with pork only--see *Ta Tai Li-chi*, 5:9a-b, *SPPY* and *A Concordance to the Daidai Liji*, D. C. Lau, ed. [Hong Kong: The Commercial Press, 1992], p. 35).

[15] The head of the body was usually north, so that he would be facing south if he were standing. To face south was the sign of a ruler and arranging the corpse in this position was a sign of respect. Yi-wei-tzu is demanding that Tsou degrade its ruler, as if the corpse were attending an audience with the King of Ch'i, who claims that as the Son of Heaven he must always face south.

"Ch'in is a state of ten-thousand chariots. Liang is also a state of ten-thousand chariots. Both hold states of ten-thousand chariots, both call themselves kings; now seeing [Ch'in's] victory after one battle, [Liang] wishes to follow after him and call him Emperor. This is treating the great vassals of the Three Chin as less than the slaves of Tsou and Lu.

"Moreover, if Ch'in is allowed to call himself Emperor, he will soon replace the great vassals of the feudal lords. He will remove those he finds unworthy and send in those he thinks worthy; he will remove those he dislikes and send in those he likes. He will send in [Ch'in's] women and nagging slave-women as the consorts and concubines of the feudal lords, and they will live in the palaces of Liang. How will the King of Liang ever know peace again? How will you, General, ever regain your old favor?"

[2464] Hsin-yüan Yen rose, made obeisance twice, and apologized. "At first I thought you an incompetent fool, Venerable Sir. Now I know you are the world's greatest knight. Allow me to [*2465*] leave, I will not dare speak again of making Ch'in emperor."

When the Ch'in commander heard this, he retreated fifty *li*. At the same time, Wu-chi 無忌, the Noble Scion of Wei,[16] seized Chin Pi's army and came to Chao's rescue. He attacked the Ch'in army and the Ch'in army subsequently withdrew and left.

After this, the Lord of P'ing-yüan wanted to enfeoff Lu Lien. Lu Lien refused three times and in the end remained unwilling to accept. The Lord of P'ing-yüan laid out wine; after he was in his cups, he rose and stepped forward, presenting one-thousand chin as a gift to Lu Lien. Lu Lien smiled: "What I value in the knights of the world is how they avert troubles, resolve dilemmas, and cut tangled knots for others without ever receiving anything for it. If they received something for it, that would be a transaction of shopkeepers and traveling peddlers; *I* could not bear to do so." He then bid farewell to the Lord of P'ing-yüan, departed, and never sought audience again.

Twenty-odd years after this,[17] a general of Yen attacked and subdued Liao Ch'eng 聊城.[18] Someone in Liao Ch'eng slandered the general to Yen. The Yen general was afraid he would be executed; he defended Liao Ch'eng, but didn't dare return to Yen. T'ien Tan 田單[19] of Ch'i attacked Liao Ch'eng for over a year. He lost many officers and soldiers but Liao Ch'eng would not submit. Lu Lien wrote a letter, tied it to an arrow, and shot it into the city. It was addressed to the Yen general. The letter read:

> I have heard the wise man does not turn his back on opportunity and cast aside profit; the brave knight does not destroy his reputation by retreating before death; the loyal vassal does not put himself first and his lord last. If you act now from one morning's anger, and ignore the King of Yen's lack of vassals, this is not loyalty. If you are killed and Liao Ch'eng is lost, and you fail to inspire awe in Ch'i, this is not courage. If your achievements are ruined, and your name destroyed, in later ages they will never be spoken of; this is not wisdom. Men with these three faults, the rulers of our age will not accept as vassals, and the speculators will not record: thus the clever

---

[16] See his biography in *Shih chi* Chapter 77.

[17] There is some controversy containing the frame for the letter. "Twenty-odd years after" the battle at Ch'ang-p'ing (259 B.C.) would be the mid-230s and since T'ien Tan had been active in the 270s, he would have been a very old man at best (cf. "Chi-chieh" and "So-yin"). Moreover, the anonymity of the Yen general combined with the motif of his there being "bad blood" between himself and the King of Yen (as with another near contemporary general of Yen, Yüeh Yi 樂毅--cf. *Shih chi*, 80:2429), suggests the frame may be a rhetorical construction allowing the letter to fit into this "biography" of Tsou Yang.

[18] A few miles northwest of modern Liao-ch'eng in northwest Shantung just south of the Yellow River in its course at that time (T'an Ch'i-hsiang, I:39).

[19] See his biography in *Shih chi* Chapter 82.

man does not make more than one plan and the brave knight does not retreat before death. [*2466*] Death or life, honor or shame, nobility or baseness, high rank or low; this moment will not come again. I beg you to lay your plans carefully, Venerable Sir, and not fall into base ways.

Now Ch'u has attacked Ch'i at Nan-yang 南陽[20] and Wei has attacked [Ch'i at] P'ing-lu 平陸,[21] but Ch'i has no intention of turning south. Ch'i thinks the loss of Nan-yang would bring small harm, unequal to the great profit of gaining [Liao Ch'eng in] Chi-pei 濟北;[22] thus they have laid their plans and will act accordingly. Moreover, when Ch'in sends down its troops, Wei will not dare to face east; when counter-alliance with Ch'in is completed, then Ch'u's situation will be perilous. Ch'i will cast off Nan-yang, it will abandon its western territory [at P'ing-lu], and it will secure Chi-pei; it will hold to its plan. Ch'i has resolved to have Liao Ch'eng, do not plan otherwise, Venerable Sir. Now Ch'u and Wei are both retreating from Ch'i and assistance from Yen will not arrive. With all the troops of Ch'i [besieging you], and without the rest of the world plotting against Ch'i, I foresee that you have no chance, Venerable Sir, of enduring the exhaustion of holding Liao Ch'eng for a year.

Moreover, the state of Yen is in chaos; plans of king and vassal have failed, and superior and inferior are at a loss; Li Fu 栗腹 with his army of a hundred thousand has been defeated abroad,[23] and Yen, a state with ten-thousand chariots, has been besieged by Chao. Its territory diminished, its ruler hard pressed, it has become the laughingstock of the world. The state exhausted and disasters multiplying, the common people are losing their allegiance.

Today you have held off the troops of a reunited Ch'i with the commoners of an exhausted Liao; this is a defense worthy of Mo Ti 墨翟.[24] Eating human flesh and burning bones for kindling, your knights still have no thought of revolt; these are troops worthy of Sun Pin 孫臏.[25] You can face the world. Even so, in planning for you, Venerable Sir, it would be better to keep your chariots and armor intact, for with these you can repay Yen. Returning to Yen with chariots and armor intact, the King of Yen is sure to be pleased. Returning to their state with their lives intact, the knights and commoners will look on you as if looking on their fathers and mothers, your acquaintances will throw up their arms and speak of you for generations and your achievements can be made brilliant. Above you can support a lone ruler, controlling his assembled vassals, below you can care for the populace, and give the speculators materials [for their writings]. Correct the state and change its customs; thus you might secure your achievements and reputation. On the other hand, you might cast aside Yen, abandon the world's [accolades], and make ties east with Ch'i. Split off land and secure a fief, with wealth comparable to that of T'ao 陶 and Wei 衛,[26] and your descendants calling themselves "the orphan" for generation after generation, surviving as long as Ch'i itself. This is yet another plan. Both these plans will make your name

---

[20] Referring to the area south of the Chi 濟 River between modern Tung-p'ing 東平 and T'ai-an 泰安 in western Shantung (T'an Ch'i-hsiang, I:39).

[21] Just south of Nan-yang and a few miles north of modern Wen-shang 汶上 in Shantung (T'an Ch'i-hsiang, I:39).

[22] Presumably the area north of the Chi River which flows northeast to the sea through modern Shantung about 50 miles south of its present border (cf. T'an Ch'i-hsiang, I:39).

[23] Another Yen general who attacked Chao in 251 B.C. but was defeated by Lien Po 廉頗, see *Shih chi*, 81:2447-8.

[24] Mo Ti, usually referred to as Mo Tzu, was famous for his skill in defending besieged cities; see the comments by Ssu-ma Ch'ien at the end of *Shih chi* Chapter 74.

[25] See his biography in *Shih chi* Chapter 65.

[26] Referring to two Prime Ministers of Ch'in: Wei Jan 魏冉, who was enfeoffed with T'ao, and Shang Yang 商鞅, whose family ruled Wei (see *Shih chi* Chapters 71 and 68, respectively).

prominent and your advantage considerable. I would hope that you measure them carefully and decide on one.

[2467] Moreover, I have heard that those who cling to petty standards of conduct cannot achieve honorable names. Those who dislike small shames cannot establish great achievements. Long ago, Kuan Yi-wu shot Duke Huan and hit [*2468*] his belt buckle. This was treason. He abandoned the Noble Scion Chiu and was unable to die for him. This was cowardice. He was bound in ropes, manacled and chained. This was humiliation.[27] For these three actions, the rulers of his time would not accept him as vassal, the villages and hamlets would not allow him passage. In the past if Venerable Kuan had been imprisoned and not emerged, had died without returning to Ch'i, he could not have escaped a reputation as a humiliated man with base actions. Slave men and women would have been ashamed to share the same name with him; how much more the common men of his time? Yet Venerable Kuan was not ashamed that he lay in ropes and bonds; he was ashamed that the world was not in order. He was not ashamed that he did not die for the Noble Scion Chiu, but that he did not inspire awe in the feudal lords. Thus he had the error of all three of these actions and made the first of the Five Hegemons, with a name towering above the world and a glory that illuminated the neighboring states. Ts'ao Tzu 曹子 was a commander of Lu; he fought three times and was defeated three times, losing a territory of five-hundred *li* [on a side].[28] If, in times past, Ts'ao Tzu had not paused in his plans, if he had refused to turn in his tracks, or had cut his throat and died, then his reputation could not but be that of a captured general who led his army to defeat. Ts'ao Tzu cast aside the shame of three defeats and retreated to consult with the Lord of Lu. Duke Huan had the world pay homage to him, and gathered the feudal lords. Ts'ao Tzu pressed his single blade against Duke Huan's heart on top of the sacrificial altar; [Ts'ao's] color did not change, his language was not perverse, and in the space of one day he restored the losses of three battles. The world was shaken, the feudal lords astounded, and Wu and Yüeh were filled with awe.

These two knights were not unable to achieve a petty integrity or petty standards; they thought that killing themselves, destroying their bodies, cutting off their lines, annihilating their posterity, and failing to establish their merit and fame was lacking in wisdom. Thus they cast off the resentment inspired by anger, and established fame that lasted for the rest of their lives. They abandoned the standards dictated by anger and shame, and secured merit that lasted for generations. Thus their legacies compare with those of the three kings and their fame will perish with heaven and earth. I beg you to choose one of these [plans] and carry it out, Venerable Sir.

[2469] The Yen general saw Lu Lien's letter, and wept for three days, hesitating, unable to reach a decision. He wanted to return to Yen, but there was already bad blood [between the king and himself], and he feared execution; he wanted to surrender to Ch'i, but had killed and captured many in Ch'i, and feared that after his surrender he would be humiliated. He sighed sadly and said, "I would rather cut myself down than be cut down by another." Then he killed himself. Liao Ch'eng was thrown into confusion, and T'ien Tan put Liao Ch'eng to the slaughter. He returned and spoke of Lu Lien [to the king] intending to ennoble him. Lu Lien fled into hiding by the seashore. "I would rather be poor and humble, mock the world and do as I will, than be rich and noble, but oppressed by others."

---

[27] For these three incidents, see the biography of Kuan Chung in *Shih chi* Chapter 62.
[28] On Ts'ao Tzu see *Shih chi*, 86:2515-6.

Tsou Yang

Tsou Yang 鄒陽 (*c.* 206-129 B.C.)[29] was a native of Ch'i. He traveled to Liang, and struck up acquaintanceships with Venerable Chuang Chi 莊忌 (*c.* 188-105 B.C.), a native of former Wu, , Scholar Mei [Sheng] 枚乘 (d. 140 B.C.) of Huai-yin 淮陰,[30] and their followers. He presented a memorial and secured a place between Yang Sheng 羊勝 (d. 148 B.C.) and Kung-sun Kuei 公孫詭 (d. 148 B.C.). Sheng and the others were jealous of Tsou Yang and denounced him to King Hsiao 孝 of Liang (r. 168-144 B.C.).[31] King Hsiao angrily sent him down to his functionaries, and decided to kill him. Tsou Yang, a sojourner abroad, seized because of slander, fearing death and bound in ropes, submitted a memorial from prison.

[2470] Your servant has heard that loyalty is always repaid, trust is never doubted. Your servant once thought it so: just empty words! Long ago when Ching K'o 荆軻 admired [Heir] Tan 丹 of Yen's principles, a white rainbow pierced the sun, yet the Heir was worried.[32] When Venerable Wei 衛 planned affairs [after the battle] of Ch'ang-p'ing 長平 for Ch'in, Venus eclipsed the Pleiades, yet King Chao 昭 was doubtful.[33] These men's essence moved Heaven and Earth, and their fidelity was unrecognized by their rulers. Is it not sad! Now your servant has exhausted his advice and used up his sincerity discussing all that he hoped you might know. Yet he was not understood by Your attendants and finally was sent to the functionaries for interrogation and distrusted by the world; this is a case where if Ching K'o and Venerable Wei were to arise once more, Yen and Ch'in would still not come to their senses. I would hope that Your Majesty might carefully inquire into this.

[2471] Long ago Pien Ho 卞和 submitted a treasure and the King of Ch'u had his foot mutilated.[34] Li Ssu 李斯 exhausted his advice and Hu Hai 胡亥 inflicted the

[29] Tsou Yang (biography in *Han shu*, 51:2338-58) served both the King of Wu, Liu P'i 劉濞 (r. 195-154 B.C., see his biography in *Shih chi* Chapter 106) and King Hsiao of Liang and is best known for this letter and one submitted to the King of Wu.

[30] See his biography in *Han shu* Chapter 51.

[31] Liu Wu 劉武 was the son of Emperor Wen 文 (r. 180-157 B.C.) and the younger brother of Emperor Ching 景 (r. 157-141 B.C.); see also *Shih chi*, 58:2081-7.

[32] See the account of Ching K'o and Heir Tan of Yen in *Shih chi* Chapter 86. After Ching K'o had agreed to try to assassinate the King of Ch'in, a white rainbow pierced the sun (cf. *Chan-kuo ts'e* [7:67a, *SPTK*] where the same phenomenon occurred after Nieh Cheng 聶政 killed Han K'uei 韓傀 [cf. *Shih chi* Chapter 86] and the Heir Yen vacillated in his resolve to send Ching K'o. See also Wang Shu-min, 83:2488 for lost *Chan-kuo ts'e* passages which associate this strange phenomenon with Ching K'o.

[33] According to "Chi-chieh," after Pai Ch'i 白起 defeated the Chao armies at Ch'ang-p'ing (see *Shih chi,* Chapter 72), he sent Venerable Wei back to Ch'in to persuade King Chao 昭 to provide him with more troops and supplies to complete the destruction of Chao. Fan Sui 范睢 ("So-yin" says it was Wei Jan 魏冄) opposed the plan and it was thwarted. Although there is no corroborating source for this story, in another *Chan-kuo ts'e* passage (beginning on 3:56a, *SPTK*) Fan Sui attempts to convince Pai Ch'i to attack Chao, but Pai argues that Ch'in lost its advantage when it did not immediately follow up the initial victory at Ch'ang-p'ing to destroy Chao.

There are various interpretations of the image of Venus eclipsing the Pleiades. Venus, the brightest of the planets, would have obscured the seven relatively dim stars in the Pleiades when it moved too near. Since T'ai-po 太白 (Venus) was associated with the West, and since Ch'in was more powerful, it seems to represent Ch'in. The Pleiades may (as in the "Chi-chieh") represent the divisions of Chao territory outside the capital--i.e., a positive omen for Ch'in. The point of this line and that about Ching K'o above is despite good omens neither of these rulers were completely supportive.

[34] Pien Ho was a native of Ch'u who presented a piece of rough jade to two successive kings of Ch'u. Each believed the piece was undistinguished and, believing Pien was trying to deceive them, had a foot mutilated in punishment (there are two versions involving different kings--see *Han Fei Tzu* [4:11a-b, *SPPY*] and *Huai-nan Tzu*

ultimate penalty.[35]   This was why the Viscount of Chi 箕子 feigned madness[36] and Chieh-yü 接輿 fled the world;[37] they feared to meet with this evil fate. I hope that you might carefully examine the intentions of Pien Ho and Li Ssu, Great King, and put behind you the judgments of the King of Ch'u and Hu-hai, so that you do not give the Viscount of Chi and Chieh-yü cause to mock your servant. Your servant has heard that Pi-kan's 比干 heart was cut out[38] and Tzu Hsü 子胥 [put] in a wineskin.[39] At first I did not believe it, now I know it was so. I would hope that Your Majesty might carefully inquire into this and confer a bit of pity on me.

The adage goes, "There are those whose heads have turned white together, yet are like strangers, and those whose carriage canopies have bumped on the road yet are like old acquaintances." Why is this? It is through knowing and failing to know. Thus long ago Fan Wu-ch'i 樊於期 fled from Ch'in to Yen, and served Tan's plan by lending Ching K'o his head;[40] Wang She 王奢 left Ch'i for Wei, then repulsed Ch'i and preserved Wei by facing the city wall and cutting his throat.[41] Wang She and Fan Wu-ch'i were not strangers to Ch'i and Ch'in, and old acquaintances of Yen and Wei; the reason why they left their two states and died for two [different] sovereigns was that these sovereigns' actions met their ideals and they admired Yen and Wei's principles without end.

This was why Su Ch'in 蘇秦 gave the world no cause to trust him but played a Venerable Wei 尾 for Yen,[42] and Pai Kuei 白圭 lost six cities in battle, but took Chung-shan for Wei.[43] Why was this? Their rulers truly [*2472*] gave these two cause to think they knew them.

Su Ch'in served as Prime Minister of Yen. The men of Yen denounced him to the King, and the King grasped his sword in anger and feted him with stallion meat.[44] Pai Kuei gained fame in Chung-shan. The men of Chung-shan denounced him to Marquis Wen 文 of Wei, and Marquis Wen cast him a jade ring which glowed in the dark.[45] Why was this? The two rulers and their vassals held each other in mutual trust, bearing their hearts and exposing their innermost thoughts. How could they be moved by cheap phrases!

[2473] Thus a woman is envied when she is taken into the palace, regardless of whether she is beautiful or ugly; a knight is the object of jealousy when he is taken into the court, regardless of whether he is talented or mediocre.

[6:4a, *SPPY*]).

[35] See our translation of *Shih chi* Chapter 87.

[36] See this story in our translation of *Shih chi* Chapter 3.

[37] See *Lun yü,* 18/5.

[38] See *Shih chi,* 38:1610 and our translation of Chapter 3.

[39] See n. 62 to our translation of *Shih chi* Chapter 66.

[40] See our translation of *Shih chi* Chapter 86 and *Chan-kuo ts'e* (9:41b, *SPTK*).

[41] According to "Chi-chieh," Wang She was a native of Ch'i who fled to Wei. Later, when Ch'i attacked Wei, he ascended the wall, avowed his intention not to involve Ch'i in a war with Wei, and cut his throat.

[42] Su Ch'in's loyalty to Yen is compared to the Venerable Wei (see *Chuang Tzu,* 9:21b, *SPPY*) who made an engagement to meet a woman under a bridge and, when she failed to appear, remained their as the water rose, wrapping his arms around a pillar and dying. This comparison is also made on *Shih chi,* 69:2265, but in the following passage it is made clear that in the end Su Ch'in was no more loyal to Yen than he had been to other states.

[43] In *Hsin hsü* (3:9a, *SPTK*) Pai Kuei is said to have lost six cities while commander of Chung-shan. The king was about to kill him, so he fled to Wei. *Lü-shih ch'un-ch'iu* (16:3a-b, *SPPY*) claims he refused an appointment from the King of Chung-shan and left for Wei voluntarily (see also Wang Li-ch'i, *Jen-piao,* p. 328).

[44] In *Shih chi* 69:2464-5 Su Ch'in is able to refute slanderous claims to the King of Yen. But there is no mention of the king then feasting him. *Chan-kuo ts'e* (9:4b-5a, *SPTK*) is similar. See also Wang Shu-min, 83:2491.

[45] Apparently made from a particular type of luminescent jade, see *Chan-kuo ts'e* (5:21a, *SPTK*).

Long ago Ssu-ma Hsi's 司馬喜 leg was cut off in Sung, and in the end he became Prime Minister of Chung-shan.[46] Fan Sui's 范睢 ribs were fractured and teeth broken, and in the end he became Marquis of Ying 應.[47] These two men both carried out the most necessary of plans, abandoning the most partial of ties, and held to the most lonely of posts. Thus they could not be spared by jealous men. This is why Shen-t'u Ti 申屠狄 drowned himself in the Ho[48] and Hsü Yen 徐衍 put a rock on his back and entered the sea.[49] [Though it meant they were] unable to secure a place in their age, their principles prevented them from gaining favor through insincere means or forming cliques at court to move their ruler's heart.

Thus Pai-li Hsi 百里奚 begged for food on the roadside, and Duke Mu 穆 entrusted him with the government;[50] Ning Ch'i 甯戚 fed cattle walking beside carts and Duke Huan 桓 entrusted him with the state.[51] Did these two men borrow posts from their courts, or borrow praise from their courtiers before these two rulers employed them? Their hearts were in accord and their actions were united; closer than glue or lacquer, even their own brothers could not estrange them; how could they be misled by the mouths of the multitudes?

Thus to heed just one side will produce treachery; to entrust just one man will ensure strife. Long ago Lu heeded the advice of Chi Sun 季孫 and drove off Confucius 孔丘;[52] Sung believed Tzu-han's 子罕 plan and imprisoned Mo Ti 墨翟.[53] With all their skill in argument, Confucius and Mo could not avoid slander and two states were thus endangered. Why was this? The mouths of the multitudes can smelt metal, a pile of lies can melt bone.

This is why Ch'in employed the Jung native Yu Yü 由余 and gained hegemony over the Central States;[54] Ch'i employed the Yüeh native Meng 蒙 and he made [Dukes] Wei 威 and Hsüan 宣 mighty.[55] Were these two states bound by convention, dragged down by their age, entangled by obsequious phrases? They listened impartially and observed broadly and their names are displayed for the ages. Thus if hearts are united, then the tribes of Hu and Yüeh can become brothers; such was the case of Yu Yü and the Yüeh native Meng; if they are not united, then flesh and blood will expel each other instead of accepting each other; such was the case of Chu 朱 and Hsiang 象, Kuan 管 and Ts'ai 蔡.[56] If a ruler of men today could truly make use of the principles of Ch'i and Ch'in, and put the listening of Sung and Lu behind him, the Five

[46] The only mention of Ssu-ma Hsi's amputation is in this text (see Wang Li-ch'i, Jen-piao, p. 444).

[47] See our translation of Shih chi Chapter 79.

[48] According to Chuang Tzu (9:6b, SPPY), Shen-t'u Ti should be a man of the early Shang dynasty. But as Kuo Hsiang 郭象 (d. 312) points out in his commentary, Shen-t'u Ti had spoken about Wu Tzu Hsü's death and probably lived during the Warring States Era. See also Wang Shu-min, 83:2292-4.

[49] "So-yin" says this story can be found in Chuang Tzu, but it is not in extant editions (see also Wang Shu-min, 83:2494).

[50] See Shih chi, 5:186.

[51] See "Chi-chieh." The story can also be found in Lü-shih ch'un-ch'iu (19:18a-b, SPPY), Yen-tzu ch'un-ch'iu (4:2a, SPPY) and Huai-nan Tzu (12:6a-b, SPPY) where he is called Ning Yüeh 甯越.

[52] See Shih chi, 47:1918.

[53] We have not found this story in other sources.

[54] See Shih chi, 5:192-3.

[55] In the Han shu version of this text (51:2346) is it Tzu Tsang 子臧 instead of Meng. Wang Hsien-ch'ien 王先謙 (1842-1918) comments that it was Tzu Tsang who was a prince of Yüeh and then fled to Ch'i (cf. Shih chi, 31:1450), but we have not been able to locate an account of his achievements for these dukes.

[56] Chu is Tan Chu 丹朱, the son of Emperor Yao, whom he passed over in choosing a successor (see Shih chi, 1:30); Hsiang is the younger brother of Emperor Shun who tried to kill Shun (see Shih chi, 1:32); Kuan is Kuan Shu Hsien 管叔鮮 and Ts'ai is Ts'ai Shu Tu 蔡叔度, sons of King Wen of Chou who rebelled against Chou in opposition to the Duke of Chou, their elder brother (see Shih chi, 4:132 and 35:1563-5).

Hegemons would not be worth speaking of; the [legacy of the] Three Kings would be easy to achieve.

[2474] This is why when the Sage king awakens, he casts off the heart of Tzu-chih 子之 and is able not to take pleasure in the worthiness of a T'ien Ch'ang 田常;[57] he enfeoffs the posterity of Pi-kan and tends the grave [*2475*] of the pregnant woman,[58] thus his merit and legacy are attained to again throughout the world. Why is this? He desires good without end.

Duke Wen 文 of Chin was close to his foe and his might brought him hegemony over the feudal lords;[59] Duke Huan of Ch'i made use of his foe and completely rectified the world.[60] Why was this? They were diligent in their mercy and humanity, and they sincerely cultivated these in their hearts, instead of embroidering them out of empty words.

As for Ch'in's making use of Shang Yang's 商鞅 laws, to the east it weakened Han and Wei, and its troops were the mightiest in the world, but in the end it had him torn in half by carts;[61] Yüeh used the counsel of Grand Master Chung 大夫種, captured powerful Wu and was hegemon over the Central States, but in the end executed him.[62] This is why Sun Shu Ao 孫叔敖 left the prime minister's post three times without regret,[63] and Wu-ling Tzu Chung 於陵子仲 resigned the Three Masters, tending gardens for others.[64]

If today a ruler of men were truly able to put aside his arrogant attitude, to clasp to his bosom a sense of indebtedness, to open his mind and viscera, to reveal his true nature, to drop his foul humors, to practice good deeds, and to follow this consistently through thick and thin, without partiality toward his knights, then Chieh's 桀 dog could be made to bark at Yao 堯,[65] and [Bandit] Chih's 蹠 attendants could be made to stab Yu 由.[66] How much more would this be so if he were backed with the authority of ten-thousand chariots and borrowed the resources of a sage king? In such a case, how could Ching K'o's liquidation of his seven clans[67] and Yao Li's 要離 burning of his wife and children be worth speaking of![68]

[2476] Your servant has heard if the Bright-moon Pearl or a glowing jade ring were tossed from the dark to a man on the road, he would put his hand to his sword and glare at those around him. Why is this? It arrived before him without notice. A

---

[57] Tzu-chih and T'ien Ch'ang are prototypical usurpers, see *Shih chi,* 34:1555-7 and *Shih chi,* 32:1508-12 and 46:1883-4, respectively.

[58] "So-yin" raises questions about the validity of these claims. Chow Hsin ripped apart pregnant women according to the Shang shu (*Shang shu ching chu-shu* 尚書經注疏, 11:5a) and King Wu of Chou raised a tumulus over the grave of Pi-kan (*Shang shu ching chu-shu,* 11:24b), but references to both Pi-kan's children and a grave for a pregnant woman are unknown.

[59] See *Shih chi,* 39:1656 and 1661-2.

[60] See *Shih chi,* 62:2131-5 and 32:1485-6.

[61] See *Shih chi,* 68:2227-40.

[62] See *Shih chi,* 41:1746-7.

[63] See *Shih chi,* 119:3100.

[64] *Meng Tzu* (3B/10) records that Ch'en 陳 Chung Tzu's elder brother was a high-ranking official in Ch'i. Chung Tzu did not approve of his conduct and went into retirement at Wu-ling in Ch'u, calling himself "Wu-ling Chung Tzu." When the King of Ch'u sought to employ him, he fled with his family, finally tending garden.

[65] Meaning that servants will do anything for their master if they have been treated well. On Chieh, see *Shih chi,* 2:88. Cf. also *Chan-kuo ts'e* (4:57a, SPTK).

[66] I.e., Hsü Yu, see *Shih chi,* 61:2121.

[67] "Chi-chieh" tells us that when Ching K'o failed in his attempt to assassinate the King of Ch'in, his clansmen we executed.

[68] Yao Li let Ho-lü burn his wife and children to win the trust of Ch'ing Chi 慶忌 so that he could assassinate him (see *Wu-Yüeh ch'un-ch'iu,* 4:4b-6a, SPPY).

twisted tree with gnarled roots, bent and bulging with not one straight twig may become the vessel of a ten-thousand chariot state. Why is this? Because it was first polished by [the ruler's] attendants. Thus when something arrives without notice, even though one might be giving away the Marquis of Sui's 隨 pearl[69] or a glowing jade ring, one will acquire resentment and be accorded no gratitude. When men speak of one beforehand, one can establish such merit with a wilted tree and a shriveled stump that none will forget it. Though the world's knights, dressed in plain cloth, living afar, and dwelling in poverty, might have inherited the political arts of Yao and Shun 舜, or possess the perspicuity of Yi 伊 [Yin] and Kuan 管 [Chung], or harbor the ambitions of Lung-feng 龍逢[70] and Pi-kan, though they might intend to exhaust their advice for the lords of their age, if their gnarled roots have never been polished, when they exhaust their most refined thoughts, or wish to lay out their loyalty and fidelity, and assist the ruler in his rule, the ruler is sure to take the path of putting his hand on his sword and glaring about him. This will prevent men in plain cloth from gaining even the resources of a wilted tree and shriveled stump.

[2477] This is why when a sage king controls the world and masters conventions, he shapes them alone on his potter's wheel, without being entangled by base disorderly speech, without being swayed by the mouths of the multitudinous masses. Thus when the First Emperor of Ch'in employed the words of his Household Headmaster, Venerable Meng Chia 蒙嘉,[71] and believed the speech of Ching K'o, a dagger appeared from concealment; King Wen 文 of Chou hunted by the Ching 涇 and Wei 渭, and returned carrying Lü Shang 呂尚, thus becoming king of the world.[72] Thus Ch'in trusted his attendants and was wounded, Chou utilized the circling of crows and became king.[73] Why was this? Through his ability to surpass twisted and bent speech and give free reign to opinions outside the commonplace, gazing alone at the bright and silvery way.

Today the rulers of men are sunk in the phrases of sycophants, caught in the coils of [those behind] curtains and skirts, and pasture the unrestrained knight with the stallions and cattle; this is why Pao Chiao 鮑焦 bore anger at his age and did not linger over the pleasures of wealth and nobility.[74]

[2478] Your servant has heard those who enter court richly attired do not soil their principles with advantage; those who polish their names and titles do not wound their conduct through desire. Thus the county was named Sheng mu 勝母 (Victorious over Mother) and Tseng Tzu 曾子 refused to enter it;[75] the town was called Chao-ko 朝歌 (Morning Song) and Mo Tzu 墨子 turned his carriage around.[76] Now to hope to bring the world's broad and unbound knights under the control of the mighty and powerful, so that they are ruled by nobility with power and high position, and thus turn their faces and soil their actions in order to serve sycophants and to seek intimacy with

[69] This is the "Bright-moon Pearl" referred to in the paragraph above. The Sui treasure was a great pearl that had been presented to a Marquis of Sui (a small state in modern Sui County in Hupei) by a large snake in return for the marquis nursing its wounds (see Kao Yu's 高誘 [fl. 205-212 A.D.] commentary in the Huai-nan Tzu, 6:3b, SPPY and Knechtges, 1:122, n. to line 192).

[70] I.e., Kuan Lung-feng 關龍逢, a loyal servant of Chieh of the Hsia dynasty, who was killed by his king (see Hsün Tzu, 15:2a and 20:5a, SPPY).

[71] See Shih chi, 86:2534.

[72] See Shih chi, 31:1477-9.

[73] "Ch'in" here is the First Emperor; Chou is King Wen who used the sign of a heavenly fire entering his domicile and turning into ch'ih wu 赤烏 "crimson crows" (cf. Shih chi, 28:1366) to assist him in becoming king.

[74] See n. 10 above.

[75] See Huai-nan Tzu, 16:12a, SPPY.

[76] Mo Tzu apparently did not like the name since it had been the name of the capital of the lascivious tyrant Chow-hsin (see our translations of Shih chi Chapters 4 and 5 above).

courtiers, then the knights will lie down and die in caves or dig their graves in the moors; how could they be willing to rush to the foot of your palace tower and exhaust their fealty and fidelity!

When the letter was presented to King Hsiao of Liang, King Hsiao sent a man to free him, and eventually made him Senior Retainer.[77]

[2479] His Honor the Grand Scribe says, "Although Lu Lien's views did not accord with the Great Principles, I grant him much for vigorously laying out his ideas from the ranks of men in plain cloth, unfettered by the feudal lords, and talking and speaking before the men of his generation, beating back the authority of men in the highest positions. Although Tsou Yang's phrases were not suitably humble, his metaphors and comparisons are enough to move men, and he too may be called straightforward and unbending. Thus I have appended them to these memoirs."

[77] *Shang-k'o* 上客.

TRANSLATORS' NOTE

Ssu-ma Ch'ien's decision to put Lu Chung Lien and Tsou Yang into the same biography has generated severe criticism found. Separated by over two-hundred years, living in totally different milieus, and with few apparent similarities in their personalities, later historians have generally failed to see what connections Ssu-ma could find between the two.

The most important similarity between them, if we may judge from Ssu-ma Ch'ien's concluding remarks, was their refusal to bow down to authority, or to abase themselves before those holding higher social rank.   In this respect, both men do seem to have held similar views, though Tsou Yang's refusal to address King Hsiao of Liang in a suitably humble tone is perhaps less obvious to Western readers. To Chinese readers, however, his vigorous disputation and unrestrained polemic has occasioned both condemnation and admiration.   Tsou Yang's strange letter to King Hsiao--unusual not in the number of allusions, but in the obscurity of their reference--has also appeared in Tsou Yang's biography in the *Han shu,* and in the Six Dynasties anthology *Wen Hsüan* 文選.

Scholars have also called the two episodes which make up the "biography" of Lu Chung Lien (the first occurred in 257 B.C. and the second sometime after 279 B.C.) into question. But Ch'ien Mu, having reviewed all the evidence, finds it reliable (see Bibliography below). There is one translation of Lu Chung Lien's biography, by Frank A. Kierman, Jr. In addition, both of the stories related here appear in almost identical form in the *Chan-kuo Ts'e* and have been translated by Crump.

BIBLIOGRAPHY

I. Translations

Kierman, Frank A. Kierman, Jr. *Ssu-ma Ch'ien's Historiographical Attitude as Reflected in Four Late Warring States Biographies.* Wiesbaden: Harrassowitz, 1962, pp. 41-7 (Lu Chung Lien).

Ōgawa Tamaki 小川環樹. *Shiki retsuden* 史記列傳. Rpt. Tokyo: Chikuma Shobō, 1986 (1969), pp. 153-161.

von Zach, Erwin. *Die Chinesische Anthologie.* 2v. Cambridge: Harvard University Press, 1952, v. 2, pp. 722-7 (Tsou Yang's letter from the *Wen Hsüan*).

II. Studies

Ch'en Han-nien 陳瀚年. *"Shih chi* 'Lu Chung Lien lieh-chuan' shu-hou (Erh-p'ien)" 史記魯仲連列傳書後〔二篇〕, *Kuo-hsüeh ts'ung-k'an* , 10 (September 1942).

Ch'ien Mu 錢穆. *Hsien Ch'in chu-tzu hsi-nien* 先秦諸子繫年. 2v. Rpt. Peking: Chung-hua Shu-chü, 1985, v. 2, pp. 472-7.

Kierman, Frank A., Jr. "Lu Chung Lien and the *Lu Lien Tzu,*" in *Transition and Permanence: Chinese History and Culture.* David C. Buxbaum and Frederick W. Mote, eds. Hong Kong: Cathay Press, 1972, pp. 269-74.

Ch'ü Yüan and Scholar Chia, Memoir 24

Ch'ü Yüan

[84:2481] Ch'ü Yüan's 屈原 *praenomen* was P'ing 平.[1] He had the same *cognomen* as the Ch'u [royal family].[2] He was Under-secretary[3] to King Huai 懷 of Ch'u (r. 328-299 B.C., d. 296 B.C.). His knowledge was broad, his memory strong, he clearly understood how to bring order to chaos, and he was practiced in rhetorical arts. At court, he planned and discussed affairs of state with the king, so as to issue orders and commands [for him]. Outside court, he would receive guests and converse with the feudal lords. The king made much use of him.[4]

The Grand Master Shang-kuan[5] held the same rank as he.[6] He strove for favor and was secretly envious of his abilities. King Huai had Ch'ü Yüan draw up laws;[7] he was writing a draft, but it was not finished. The Grand Master Shang-kuan saw it and wanted to take it. Ch'ü P'ing did not give [it to him]. Then [the Grand Master] slandered him: "When the king has Ch'ü P'ing draw up a decree, everyone knows [the contents of] it.[8] Every time a decree is

---

[1] In the opening lines of "Li sao" 離騷 (*Ch'u-tz'u pu-chu* 楚辭補注, 1:4a, *SPPY*) Ch'ü Yüan gives his own *praenomen* as "Cheng-tse" 正則 and his *agnomen* as "Ling-chün" 靈均. David Hawkes (*The Songs of the South* [Rpt. Harmondsworth: Penguin, 1985], p. 82n) renders these names "True Exemplar" and "Divine Balance" respectively, and, after noting the traditional explanation that they were literary names which are semantically related to P'ing and Yüan (see also Wang Shu-min, 84:2503), suggests that these names were pseudonyms "chosen in reference to the 'correct,' 'balanced' state of the heavens at the time of the poet's nativity" (according to the "Li sao").

[2] Ch'ü was the *nomen*--not the *cognomen*--of one of the three collateral branches of the Ch'u royal clan. The royal *cognomen* and that of Ch'ü P'ing was Mi 芈 (see also *Shih chi* 40:1690ff.).

[3] *Tso-t'u* 左徒. "Cheng-yi" claims that this position was approximate to that of Left or Right Reminder (左右拾遺) during the T'ang. But this was relatively minor position, and, as the following sentences make clear, Ch'ü Yüan held a high post. We know this, too, from *Shih chi*, 40:1735 which tells us that Huang Hsieh 黃歇 moved from *Tso-t'u* to *Ling-yin* 令尹, Ch'u's equivalent of prime minister or premier (as we translate it). Therefore, given the duties depicted in this paragraph it would seem Ch'ü held a position much like that of "secretary." Since in pre-Ch'in times "Tso" was beneath "Yu" 右, we have opted to call his post "Under-secretary" (see Miao Wen-yüan, pp. 82-3).

[4] Hawkes, *op. cit.*, p. 55, renders this line: "The king held his services in high esteem."

[5] There are several explanations of Shang-kuan Tai-fu 上官大夫. One identifies him as Chin Shang 靳尚. However, Liang Yü-sheng (31:1304) observes that, according to the *Chan-kuo ts'e* (5:17b, *SPPY*), Chin Shang was killed by Chang Mao 張旄 during King Huai's reign. Therefore, since Shang-kuan Tai-fu appears later in this chapter after the king's death in 296 B.C., we read Shang-kuan as a *nomen* for an otherwise unidentified Grand Master. Hawkes, *op. cit.*, p. 55, n. 19, understands it as a title, but Miao Wen-yüan lists no such title in the section of Ch'u officials (pp. 64-108).

[6] Hawkes (*op. cit.*, p. 55) renders this expression "equal in rank and office."

[7] Hawkes (*op. cit.*, p. 55, n. 20) believes that this passage--in part because of the use of Ch'ü P'ing's *nomen* Yüan and in part because it is a non-sequitur--has been "interpolated" here. But his assumption is based upon the concept that there is a third, unknown source which Ssu-ma Ch'ien utilized (see Translators' Note).

The non-sequitur argument--why would the Grand Master attempt to take the law from Ch'ü Yüan. if the King had ordered Ch'ü to do it--has been raised and answered by a host of scholars. Ch'en Tzu-lung's 陳子龍 explanation that the Grand Master only wanted to look at the law to enable him in making other political designs is typical (Takigawa, 84:1527C).

[8] An alternative reading of *chung mo pu-chih* 眾莫不知 would be that "everyone knows this," i.e., knows that it is the king and not Ch'ü Yüan should get the merit for these decrees. This interpretation fits the sort of flattery one might expect of a slanderer.

issued, P'ing boasts of his merit and thinks 'None but I am capable of doing [this].'" The king was angry and distanced himself from Ch'ü P'ing.⁹

[2482] Ch'ü P'ing was distressed

that the king listened without understanding,
that his vision was blocked by flattery and slandering,
that depravity obstructed the just,
that the upright won no trust.¹⁰

This filled with sorrow and gloom, he composed "Li sao" 離騷.¹¹

"Li sao" means "Encountering Sorrow." Heaven is the origin of humankind. Fathers and mothers are the root of humankind. When humans despair, they return to their roots. For this reason, those who have been driven to the limits of exhaustion by toil and suffering, who push themselves to exhaustion, always cry out to heaven. Those who endure the grief and sorrow caused by sickness and pain, always call out to their fathers and mothers.¹²

Ch'ü P'ing walked the straight and narrow path and served his lord with utmost loyalty and intelligence; when slanderers divided them,¹³ he can be said to have despaired. Faithful and yet doubted, loyal but defamed, could he have failed to be resentful? It was this resentment, perhaps, which gave rise to Ch'ü P'ing's composition "Encountering Sorrow."

"The Airs of the States" are sensual without lasciviousness, "The Lesser Elegantiae" give voice to resentment without disorder. As for "Encountering Sorrow," it can be said to combine the two.

In early times he speaks of Ti K'u 帝嚳, in later times he talks of [Duke] Huan 桓 of Ch'i, between the two he tells of T'ang 湯 and Wu 武,¹⁴ in this way criticizing contemporary affairs. Revealing the breadth and height of the Way and its virtue, and the principles of order and chaos--he manifests all of these. His style is concise, his language subtle, his aspirations pure, his actions honest. His topics are small but his intentions grandiose; the things he brings forth are near at hand, but their significance is far reaching. His aspirations are pure: for this reason the things he mentions are fragrant. His behavior is honest: for this reason he won't allow himself to be distanced [from King Huai] for his whole life.¹⁵ He bathed in muck and mire, shed the filth of standing water like a chrysalis, thereby to float beyond the dust, without

⁹ In the "Chieh-shih" 節士 chapter of Liu Hsiang's *Hsin hsü,* 7:10a-11a [*SPTK*]) the king was estranged because of a diplomatic row which also resulted in Ch'ü P'ing's banishment.

¹⁰ These four lines are rhymed in the original. The final line literally reads: "that the upright could not win acceptance."

¹¹ See also Liang Yü-sheng (31:1302) on the time the "Li sao" was composed.

¹² Hawkes (*op. cit.,* p. 55, n. 21) argues that this paragraph has been taken from Liu An's 劉安 (d. 122 B.C.) commentary to the "Li-sao" ("Li-sao chuan" 離騷傳) which has been partially preserved in commentaries to the *Ch'u-tz'u* 楚辭 (see also Wang Shu-min, 84:2514).

¹³ Hawkes, *op. cit.,* p. 57, reads "only to have this slanderer standing between him and the man he served" for 讒人閒之； we read *chien* 閒 as "to put some space between, to divide."

¹⁴ Ti K'u was on of China's earliest rulers (see our translation of *Shih chi,* 1:13 above); Duke Huan became a Hegemon with the help of Kuan Chung (see our translation of *Shih chi* Chapter 62); T'ang was the first ruler of the Yin dynasty (see our translation of *Shih chi* Chapter 3) and Wu the founder of the Chou dynasty (see our translation of Chapter 4).

¹⁵ We follow here the revised Chung-hua punctuation in the overall slightly revised 1972 impression of the original edition: 故死而不容自疏．濯淖汙泥之中. According to the parsing in the original 1959 edition the lines would read: 故死而不容．自疏濯淖汙泥之中--"For this reason his whole life he did not win acceptance. He distanced himself from muck and mire, shed off the filth to float beyond the dust . . . ." We feel there is an attempt at creating a parallelism in the 1959-edition reading that cannot be sustained by the syntax.

taking on the stains of this world. In his purity he went through the mud unsullied. If we look closely at his aspirations, they could even contend with the sun and moon for glory.

[2483] Ch'ü P'ing was demoted and sometime later Ch'in wanted to attack Ch'i. Ch'i was allied with Ch'u. King Hui[-wen] 惠 [(文) of Ch'in (r. 337-311 B.C.)] was troubled by this and ordered Chang Yi 張儀[16] to pretend to forsake Ch'in, to make lavish gifts, to present his pledge, and to serve Ch'u.[17] [Chang Yi] said, "Ch'in loathes Ch'i. Ch'i is allied with Ch'u. If Ch'u truly can break off with Ch'i, Ch'in would be willing to present it with 600 *li* [on a side] of territory between Shang 上 and Wu 於."[18]

King Huai of Ch'u was greedy and trusted Chang Yi; he broke relations with Ch'i. He sent an envoy to Ch'in to receive the territory. Chang Yi lied to him: "I agreed on six *li* [on a side] with your king. I haven't heard anything about six hundred." The Ch'u envoy left angrily and returned to report to King Huai.

King Huai was angry, raising a great force to attack Ch'in. Ch'in sent out troops to attack them. They crushed the forces of Ch'u between the Tan 丹 and the Hsi 浙 [rivers],[19] cut off 80,000 heads, and captured the Ch'u commander, Ch'ü Kai 屈丐,[20] then took Ch'u's territory of Han-chung 漢中.[21] King Huai then sent out all the troops in the state to strike deep into Ch'in. They fought at Lan-t'ien 藍田.[22] Wei[23] heard of it and launched a surprise attack on Ch'u reaching as far as Teng 鄧.[24] The troops of Ch'u were frightened and returned from Ch'in. Ch'i was so angry that it did not go to Ch'u's rescue. Ch'u was in dire straits.

[2484] The next year [311 B.C.] Ch'in ceded the territory of Han-chung and to Ch'u to make peace.[25] The King of Ch'u said, "I don't want to have territory. I want to have Chang Yi and take sweet revenge on him." Chang Yi heard this and said, "If a single Yi is worth the territory of Han-chung, your servant asks permission to go to Ch'u." When he got to Ch'u he once more made lavish gifts to the man holding power, the vassal Chin Shang, in order to present cunning arguments to the King's favorite consort, Cheng Hsiu 鄭袖.[26] King Huai was so persuaded by Cheng Hsiu that he again released Chang Yi. At this time Ch'ü P'ing, having been alienated from the king no longer held his [high] position. He was sent as an envoy to

---

[16] See his biography in *Shih chi* Chapter 70.

[17] According to *Shih chi*, 15:733, Chang Yi came to Ch'u to become Prime Minister in 313 B.C. Hawkes translates this sentence rather freely (*op. cit.*, p. 56): "Qi was an ally of Chu, and King Hui of Qin, feeling uneasy about this alliance, commissioned Zhang Yi to leave Qin with costly presents with which he was to pretend to pledge his services to Chu."

[18] Located between modern Hsi-chia 西峽 and Nei-hsiang 內鄉 in southern Honan (T'an Ch'i-hsiang, 1:44).

[19] As Liang Yü-sheng points out (31:1303) Ssu-ma Ch'ien's other accounts of this battle are usually said to have occurred in Tan-yang 丹陽, i.e., the region on the north side of the Tan River (see *Shih chi*, 5:207, 40:1724, 45:1872, 70:2288, and 71:2313). But according to T'an Ch'i-hsiang (1:44) this is the region between the Tan and Hsi rivers.

[20] On this battle which took place in 312 B.C. see our translation of *Shih chi*, 5:207 above.

[21] See n. 4 to our translation of *Shih chi* Chapter 69 above.

[22] See n. 35 to our translation of Chapter 70 above.

[23] *Shih chi*, 40:1724 says both Han and Wei which attacked. Liang Yü-sheng (31:1304) argues that it was only Han.

[24] Located about 100 miles south of modern Kaifeng in Honan (T'an Ch'i-hsiang, 1:45-46).

[25] According to *Shih-chi*, 70:2288, Ch'in wanted to exchange lands beyond Wu 武 Pass (the Pass was located 20 miles southeast of modern Shang-nan 商南 in Shensi near the intersection of Shensi, Honan and Hupei--essentially these lands outside the pass were Shang and Wu [see n. 18 above]) for Ch'ien-chung 黔中 (according to T'an Ch'i-hsiang, 1:45, a commandery in what is now northwestern Hunan), but King Huai of Ch'u was willing to give up the land simply to have Chang Yi sent back to him.

[26] She was the primary wife of the king (see *Shih chi*, 40:1725).

Ch'i, but returned[27] to admonish King Huai: "Why didn't you kill Chang Yi?" King Huai had second thoughts and had Chang Yi pursued, but it was too late.

After this the feudal lords attacked Ch'u in concert, crushing it[s army] and killing its general, T'ang Mo 唐眛.[28]

At that time,[29] King Chao 昭 of Ch'in (r. 306-251 B.C.), who had marital ties with Ch'u,[30] wanted to meet with King Huai. King Huai wanted to go, but Ch'ü P'ing said, "Ch'in is a country of tigers and wolves and cannot be trusted. It would be better not to go."[31] King Huai's youngest son, Tzu Lan 子蘭, urged the king to go: "How can you put an end to our happy relations with Ch'in?" In the end King Huai went. When he entered Wu 武 Pass[32] troops hidden by Ch'in cut off his retreat and they then detained King Huai, seeking territorial concessions. King Huai was angry and would not agree. He fled to Chao, but Chao would not receive him. They sent him back to Ch'in. He finally died in Ch'in and his body was returned for burial.[33]

His eldest son, King Ch'ing-hsiang 頃襄 (r. 298-263 B.C.) was enthroned. He made his younger brother, Tzu Lan, the Premier. The people of Ch'u blamed Tzu Lan for urging King Huai to go to Ch'in and his failure to return.

[2485] Ch'ü P'ing hated him. Though exiled, he still longed for Ch'u's capital and felt a strong attachment to King Huai. He never lost his desire to return.[34] He hoped that his lord would awaken completely and convention would be reformed completely. His desire to maintain his lord, to revive the state, and to reverse [the course of recent events] he expressed three times in one scroll.[35] Yet in the end nothing could be done. Thus he was unable to return. Thus he finally realized that King Huai could never be awakened.[36]

The lords of men, whether foolish, intelligent, worthy or unworthy, all want to find loyal men to act on their behalf, to employ worthy men to assist them. But states fall and lineages are ruined one after another and a state ruled by a sagely lord has not appeared for generations. This is because the men they call loyal are disloyal and the men they call worthy are unworthy. Because King Huai could not recognize the duty of a loyal vassal, he was deluded at home by Cheng Hsiu and deceived abroad by Chang Yi. He distanced himself from Ch'ü P'ing and trusted Grand Master Shang-kuan and the Premier, Tzu Lan.[37] His weapons were blunted and his territories whittled away, he lost six commanderies and died abroad in Ch'in, becoming the laughingstock of the world. This was the misfortune of not being able to recognize men. *The Book of Changes* reads[38]:

---

[27] According to *Shih-chi,* 40:1725 Ch'ü Yüan remained in Ch'i and sent an envoy back.

[28] Ch'in, Han, Wei and Ch'i attacked Ch'u in 301 B.C. (*Shih chi,* 15:736) and defeated T'ang Mo, the Ch'u general, at Chung-ch'iu 重丘 (about 50 miles east of modern Nan-yang 南陽 in Honan [T'an Ch'i-hsiang, 1:45]).

[29] Although King Chao perhaps began to initially take an interest in bringing King Huai to Ch'in in 301 B.C. ("at the same time"), King Huai did not actually go to Ch'in until 298 B.C. (see *Shih chi,* 15:735).

[30] According to *Shih chi,* 15:735, this marriage took place in 305 B.C.

[31] "So-yin" observes that it was Chao Chü 昭雎 in *Shih chi* Chapter 40 (40:1726) who urged the king not to go in a very similar speech.

[32] See n. 25 above.

[33] He died (*Shih chi,* 15:737) in 296 B.C.

[34] Or "to have King Huai return."

[35] This piece is variously identified as the "Chao hun" 招魂 (Summoning the Soul) or the "Li-sao."

[36] This seems to be the Grand Scribe's personal comment.

[37] This is anachronistic--Tzu Lan was made Premier first under King Huai's successor.

[38] A similar passage occurs under Hexagram 48 (*Chou Yi cheng-yi,* 5:10a, *SPPY*). The purified well symbolizes a pure vassal whom the king does not employ.

Not to drink when the well has been dredged,[39]
Causes my heart sorrow.
It can be drawn.
If the king is perspicacious,
All can receive blessings from it.

If the king is not perspicacious, how could there be good fortune?

The Premier was enraged when he heard this.[40] In the end he had the Grand Master Shang-kuan relate Ch'ü Yüan's shortcomings to King Ch'ing-hsiang. The king was angered and banished Ch'ü Yüan.

[2486] When Ch'ü Yüan arrived at the banks of the Chiang,[41] he let down his hair and walked singing along the water's edge. His face was filled with distress, his form withered and wizened. A fisherman saw him and asked: "Aren't you Grand Master of the Three Gates[42]? What has brought you to this?"

Ch'ü Yüan said, "The whole world is muddied, only I am pure. All men are drunk and only I am sober. For this reason I was exiled."

The fishermen said, "The sagely man is not encumbered by things but can move with the world. If the whole world is muddied, why not follow its current and float on its waves? If all men are drunk, why not dine on their dregs and sip their sweet wines? Why hold a fine jade to your bosom and another in your hand and get yourself banished?"

Ch'ü Yüan said, "I have heard it said that one who has just washed his hair should brush his cap, one who has just bathed should beat [the dust from] his clothes. What man could then accept the smudges of the material world on the pure brightness of his body? I would rather throw myself into the long river and be buried in the belly of a river fish. How then can I suffer the world's dust on my brightest whiteness?"

Then he wrote the rhapsody "Huai sha" 懷沙 (Embracing Sands)[43] which goes:

[2487] In the bountiful early summer,[44]
        When flowers and trees are flourishing,
        My heart was wounded with an eternal sadness,
        And I rushed to the southern lands.
5   I look about, but all seems remote,
        In a vacant silence, an isolated quiet.
        Pent-up sadness and repressed pain
        Long enough have I met with grief.
        I followed my emotions in search for my goals,
10   Though wrong, I restrained myself.

---

[39] On the symbolic significance of dredging wells, see Bodde, *Festivals*, pp. 294-5.

[40] The three sentences are considered to be out of place here. There are two problems: (1) the antecedent of the pronoun *chih* 之 is unclear here (our "this") and (2) Ch'ü Yüan has already been banished above. An argument based on traditional scholars and summarized by Chin Jung-hua 金榮華 (*"Shih chi 'Ch'ü Yüan lieh-chuan'* shu-cheng" 史記屈元列傳疏證, *Shih-ta Kuo-wen Yen-chiu-so chi-k'an* 師大國文研究所集刊, 9 [June 1965], 629-30) would place these three sentences above, following the line "Ch'ü P'ing hated him."

[41] See also the parallel passage in *Ch'u-tz'u pu-chu,* 7:1b-3a, *SPPY.*

[42] *San-lü Tai-fu* 三閭大夫, see also Tung Yüeh, p. 77.

[43] See also the text in the *Ch'u-tz'u pu-chu,* 4:18b-22b, *SPPY.*

[44] *Meng* 孟 refers to the first month of a season, in this case summer. But the first month of the lunar summer normally falls in late spring or early summer of the solar calendar. Hawkes' "late summer" (*op. cit.,* p. 170) is thus perhaps an error for "late spring."

Let others trim the square to fit the round,
My own standards will not be replaced.
To change one's first intent or alter one's origins[45]
Is what the gentleman decries.
15   I made clear my boundaries and reminded myself to toe the line,
My original standards will not be changed.
Upright in character, reliant in nature,[46]
Are those which the great man commends.
If a skilled carpenter doesn't make a cut,
20   Who can know if it's crooked or straight?
When a black pattern is put in a dark place,
The blind will say it is obscure.
Though Li Lou 離婁 needs only to open his eyes a crack [to see something],[47]
The purblind think that he cannot see clearly.
25   They change white into black,
Confuse up and down.
The *feng* and *huang*[48] are in a cage,
While fowl and pheasant soar freely about.
Jade and stones are mixed together,
30   Leveled and weighed as one.
The faction [opposing me] is narrow-sighted and jealous,
And don't understand the things I value.
[2488] I bore a heavy weight, carried many things,
And sank immobilized without crossing.
35   A fine jade to my bosom, another in my hand,[49]
I was at wits' end and unable to show them.
The dogs in the city bark in chorus,
Bark at that which they feel is strange.
They condemn the lofty and suspect the outstanding,
40   As is their common manner.
Indifferent to my appearance,
There is substance within,
But people do not recognize my extraordinary elegance.
Lumber and timber and bark in piles and heaps,
45   With no one recognizing that I had them.
I doubled my humanity, increased my righteousness twofold,
Through respect and sincerity I made them even more abundant.
As I could not meet [men like] Shun,
Who could understand my natural confidence?
50   Since antiquity [two such men] have generally not been paired,
[2489] But how could we know why?
T'ang and Yü are remote from us,
So distant I can not look to them.
I must curb my grudge and replace my hatred,
55   Restrain my mind and strengthen myself.

---

[45] Following Wen I-to's 聞一多 suggestion to read *pien* 變 "alter" for *pen* 本 (see Chin Jung-hua, *op. cit.,* p. 26).

[46] *Ch'u-tz'u pu-chu* (4:19b, *SPPY*) reads: *nei hou chih cheng hsi* 內厚質正兮 here.

[47] A man with legendarily powerful vision (see *Meng Tzu,* 4/1/1, Legge, 2:288).

[48] *Feng* 鳳 and *huang* 凰 are often translated as phoenixes (male and female--see also Jean-Pierre Diény, "Le Fenghuang et le Phénix," *Cahiers d'Extrême-Asie,* 5(1989-90), 1-13).

[49] Jade is here a symbol of purity.

I have met grief without changing,
I hope my resolution will be a model.
Moving forward along the road north, I stop,[50]
The sun dims as it is about to set.
60   I will contain[51] my troubles and find joy in my grief,
Bringing an end to them in death.

Epilogue:

The vast waters of the Yüan 沅 and Hsiang 湘,
Rush along separately.[52]
The long road is dark and covered,
65   The way is distant and desolate.
Repeatedly I chanted my unending sorrow,[53]
[2490] Continuously sighing and melancholy.
No one in the world having recognized me,
It is not possible to speak of human hearts.
70   The feelings I embrace, the nature I embody,
Are unmatched in the world.
Po Le 伯樂 having passed on,[54]
How will a courser be put through his paces?
Each man's life has its allotted span,
75   Every one has been arranged.
I calm my mind and broaden my goals,
What remains for me to fear?
Repeatedly injured and accordingly mournful
I am continuously sighing.
80   As the world is topsy-turvy and did not recognize me,
It is not possible to speak of heart.
I know that death is inevitable,
And I hope I will not begrudge it.
Openly I hereby declare to all gentlemen,
85   That I will be the exemplar for you!

Then he placed a rock in [the folds of] his robe, threw himself into the Mi-lo 汨羅[55] and died.

[2491] After Ch'ü Yüan had died, there were [writers] like Sung Yü 宋玉, T'ang Le 唐勒, and Ching Ts'o 景差, all known for their fondness for writing and their rhapsodies. Though they all modeled themselves on [the style in which] Ch'ü Yüan naturally expressed veiled criticism, in the end none ventured to employ his straightforward admonitions. After this Ch'u daily went downhill, to the point that in several decades it was annihilated by Ch'in.

---

[50] Ch'ü Yuan had been heading south, but he is apparently returning northward towards the capital here.

[51] *Ch'u-tz'u pu-chu* (4:21b, *SPPY*) has *shu* 舒 "release" for *han* 含 "contain."

[52] Looking south and west from the point of view of Lake Tung-t'ing, the Yüan and the Hsiang flow into the Lake "separately." Wen I-to (cited Chin Jung-hua, *op. cit.*, p. 33) thinks that Hsiang was a local word for "river" in Ch'u, but that interpretation makes it difficult to see how a single river, the Yüan, could flow "separately."

[53] This line and the following three do not occur in the current text of the *Ch'u-tz'u*.

[54] Po Le was a noted trainer and judge of horses who appears in anecdotes in a several early texts (see *Chan-kuo ts'e*, 5:44a-45a, *SPTK*, for example), often as the one person who could perceive the merits of a fine horse who had been mistreated by others (some scholars believe there were two Po Le's, one a trainer and one an arbiter of the equine.

[55] According to "So-yin" the Mi was a river in the county of Lo (near the modern town of Mi-lo about 60 miles south of Yüeh-yang 岳陽 City in Hunan [T'an Ch'i-hsiang, 1:29]).

More than one hundred years after Ch'ü Yüan sank into the Mi-lo, there was Scholar Chia of the Han [dynasty] who was the Grand Tutor to the King [Kung 恭 (r. 186-179 B.C.)] of Ch'ang-sha 長沙.[56]   As he crossed the Hsiang River, he threw his piece mourning Ch'ü Yüan into it.[57]

Scholar Chia

Scholar Chia's 賈 *praenomen* was Yi 誼 and he was a native of Lo-yang.[58]   In his eighteenth year, he was well known in his commandery because of his ability to recite the *Book of Odes* and compose literature.   When Commandant of Justice Wu 吳 was made Governor of Ho-nan 河南,[59] he heard of Chia's talent, appointed him to head a department, and favored him highly.   When Emperor Hsiao Wen 孝文 (r. 180-157 B.C.) was first enthroned, he heard that the administration of the Governor of Honan, His Honor Wu, was the best in the world.   Thus, since he was from the same city as Li Ssu 李斯[60] and had studied and served with him, he was summoned to be the Commandant of Justice.   The Commandant of Justice then told [the Emperor] that although Scholar Chia was young, he had mastered the writings of the various masters and the hundred schools.   Emperor Wen summoned him to be an Erudite.

[2492] At the time Scholar Chia was just over twenty, the youngest [among the Erudites].   Each time the text of an edict came under discussion, all of the older gentlemen were unable to speak, but Scholar Chia responded for them to each query in a way that each of them would have liked to express it.   His fellow scholars understood from this that he had ability and that they could not measure up to him.   Emperor Hsiao Wen delighted in him and promoted him several grades at a time so that in the space of one year he had reached Grand Master of the Palace.[61]

Scholar Chia thought that since it had been more than twenty years from the rise of the Han to the reign of Emperor Hsiao Wen and the world was at peace, it was certainly due time to change the calendar, to replace the colors of the vestments and vehicles, to codify the legal system, to fix official titles, and to restore the rites and music.   Thus he drafted a proposal concerning these matters of ceremony and law [suggesting that] in color yellow should be given priority, in numbers, five, that [new] official titles should be made, and the Ch'in laws should be completely revised.   When Emperor Hsiao Wen had first acceded to the throne, he humbly declined because he had no time.   But the ideas behind everything that was revised in the laws and [the plan] to return the high ranking lords to their lands[62] all came from Scholar Chia.   Then the Son of Heaven asked for discussion of his intention to appoint Scholar Chia to high office.   The Marquis of Chiang 絳, the Marquis of Kuan 灌, and the Marquis of Tung-yang 東陽, Feng Ching 馮敬,[63] and their group were jealous of him and maligned Scholar

---

[56] This was a particularly discouraging posting, first because the King of Ch'ang-sha was the great-great-grandson of Wu Jui 吳芮, one of Han Kao-tsu's lieutenants, and thus not a member of the royal family, and second because Ch'ang-sha (located surrounding modern Ch'ang-sha in Hunan, see T'an Ch'i-hsiang, 2:22) was a pestilent backwater.

[57] See below.

[58] He lived from 200-168 B.C. See also the account of Chia Yi in *Han shu* (48:2221-66).

[59] A commandery located south and west of modern Loyang (Wang Li-ch'i, 84:1926n.).

[60] See his biography in *Shih chi* Chapter 87.

[61] *T'ai-chung Tai-fu* 太中大夫.

[62] These lords (high-ranking marquis) had been given fiefs, but preferred to live in the capital where they could seek influence at court.

Chia, "[This] fellow from Lo-yang is young and has just begun to study, yet he alone wants to monopolize power and has thrown all affairs into disorder." After this the Song of Heaven became more distant from him, did not employ his suggestions, and at last made Scholar Chia Grand Tutor to the King of Ch'ang-sha.

Scholar Chia took his leave and departed. Hearing that Ch'ang-sha was low-lying and wet, believing that he would not be able to live to a ripe old age [there] and departing as a result of banishment, he felt he had failed in all his goals. As he crossed the Hsiang River, he wrote a rhapsody to condole Ch'ü Yüan which ran[64]:

[2493] With reverence I receive beauteous favor [from the king]
   and await punishment [because of my position] at Ch'ang-sha.
   I have heard tell of Ch'ü Yüan
   Who drowned himself in the Mi-lo River.
5   I have come here to trouble the Hsiang current
   to respectfully lament you, Sir,
   You encountered an era of no restraint,
   And thus you lost your life.
   Woe is me!
10   The times you met were inopportune,
   Luan and *feng* birds[65] hunched down and hid away,
   While owls[66] soared on high!
   The mediocre were honored and distinguished,
   The slanderer and flatterer had their way.
15   The worthy and the sage were dragged backwards
   The square and the upright were turned upside down.
   Your age called Po Yi covetous,
   Said Bandit Chih was honest![67]
   The Mo-yeh sword[68] was called dull,
20   While a lead knife was termed sharp!
   Alas, you were unable to express
   That you had no guilt!
   Contrary to expectation they cast aside the Chou tripods
   To treasure an empty gourd.
25   They harnessed a hackneyed ox,
   And hitched a team of lame donkeys,
   While the thoroughbred, his ears drooping,
   pulled a salt-wagon.
   A ceremonial cap made to line hempen slippers
30   This situation you could not withstand for long!
   Oh, how miserable, Sir,
   Only you encountered this calamity!

---

[63] The Marquis of Chiang was Chou Po 周勃 (see *Shih chi*, 57:2065), Marquis Kuan was Kuan Ying 灌嬰 (see *Shih chi*, 95:2667), the Marquis Wu 武 of Tung-yang was Chang Hsiang-ju 張相如 (see *Shih chi*, 10:429), and Feng Ching was Grand Master of the Imperial Scribes at the time (see *Shih chi*, 22:1127 and 118:3077).

[64] See also the translation by David Knechtges, "Two Han Dynasty *Fu* on Ch'ü Yüan: Chia I's *Tiao Ch'ü Yüan* and Yang Hsiung's *Fan-sao*," *Parerga*, 1(1968), 5-43.

[65] On the *feng*, see n. 48 above; the *luan* 鸞 is sometimes translated as simurgh. Both are auspicious birds.

[66] An inauspicious bird, see the text of the biography below.

[67] On Po Yi and Bandit Chih see our translation of *Shih chi* Chapter 61.

[68] A precious sword from made by a Grand Master from the state of Wu named Mo-yeh (see "So-yin").

[2494] Coda:
        It is all over! No one in the state understands us!
        Alone in our grief, to whom could we speak?
35   The *feng* whirls and mounts on high
        He will surely retire and go far away.
        I take the divine dragon of the profound pool as a model,
        Hiding deep and unseen to cherish himself.
        I turn my back on the crocodile and otter and dwell in hiding;
40   We were not following ants, leeches and earthworms.
        What we valued was the divine virtue of the sage,
        Remaining aloof from the filthy world and keeping himself intact.
        If the thoroughbred were bridled and leashed
        How would he differ from a dog or a sheep?
45   It was through disorder that you encountered this trouble.
        It was all your fault!
        You could have looked around the nine lands and served as prime minister,
        Why did you have to long for your home capital?
        The *feng* and *huang* soar a thousand *jen*,
50   When they observe virtue shining, they land there.
        Where they see the dangerous signs of [too] little virtue
        They flap their wings faster [*2495*] and leave it.
        How can a sluice or a ditch one *hsün*-wide
        Accommodate a boat-swallowing leviathan?
55   [Even] sturgeons that cross the rivers and lakes
        Will certainly be controlled by mole-crickets and ants.[69]

[2496] After Chia had been Grand Tutor for the King of Ch'ang-sha for three years, an owl flew into Scholar Chia's residence and perched near his seat. The people of Ch'u called owls "*fu*." Scholar Chia already felt that as he was banished to live in Ch'ang-sha and as Ch'ang-sha was low-lying and wet, he would not be able to live to a ripe old age, and he was distressed by it. Thus he wrote a rhapsody to console himself which read:[70]

[2497] In the *ts'an-yen* year,[71] the fourth month, the first of summer,
        On the *keng-tzu* 庚子 day as the sun set, an owl alighted in my residence.
        Perched in the corner near my seat, its appearance completely at ease.
        That this strange being came and alighted,
        I found most strange.
        I lay open a text and consulted about it;
        The divining straws told what was determined:
5   "When a wild fowl enters a residence,
        The master shall to go away!"
        I should like to ask the owl,
        "If I should leave, where should I go?
        If you bring good luck, please tell me!
10   If bad, let me know what misfortune!

[69] See the parallel passage in *Chuang Tzu* (8:2a, *SPPY*).

[70] See James Robert Hightower's translation, "Chia Yi's 'Owl Fu,'" *AM, N.S.,* 7(1959), 125-30. Besides this version, there are also texts of this rhapsody in *Han shu* (48:2226-29) and *Wen hsüan* (13:16a-19b [Taipei: Hua-cheng Shu-chü, 1982).

[71] The original text reads the *tan-o* 單閼 year, but we have emended the date following Hightower, *op. cit.,* p. 129, n. 3.

Is it determined to be fast or slow?
Tell me when it is due!"
Then the owl sighed,
Raised its head and flapped its wings,
15   Without being able to utter a word,
It responded with this idea:
[2498] All things are in flux,
And naturally do not stop.
Like a whirlpool they move along,
20   Now forward, then back.
Body and spirit continue to regenerate one another,
Transformed and shed.
Profound and infinite,
How can words describe it?
25   Disaster is that on which fortune is based,
Fortune is that in which disaster hides.[72]
Sorrow and joy live within the same gate,
Good luck and bad come from the same domain.
Though Wu was mighty and great
30   Fu-ch'ai was defeated because of it.[73]
When Yüeh took refuge on K'uai-chi,
Kou Chien held sway over all the world.[74]
Li Ssu traveled abroad and achieved success,
But finally suffered the Five Punishments.[75]
35   After Fu Yüeh had been in bonds,
He served Wu-ting as minister.[76]
Disaster and fortune
Are no different than two strands of a rope.
Fate can not be explained--
40   Who can know its end?
"When water is deflected it fails to moisten,
When arrows are deflected they go far [from the target]."[77]
All things revolve and collide,
Shaking as they refract each other.
45   Clouds rise and rain falls,
Mixing together they throw each other in disorder.
The Great Potter's wheel turns forth all things,
Around and around endlessly.
We can not take part in Heaven's intentions,
50   Or participate in the Way's plans.
Sooner or later is determined by fate--
How can one discern when his time is come?
[2499] Furthermore, Heaven and earth are the furnace,
The creator is the smith,
55   *Yin* and *yang* the charcoal,

[72] Cf. *Lao Tzu*, Section 58.

[73] I.e., defeat comes from might and greatness. On Wu's defeat by Yüeh see *Shih chi* Chapter 41.

[74] Again a paradox since Kou Chien was driven up Mount K'uai-chi by the invading armies of Fu-ch'ai's state of Wu (see *Shih chi* Chapter 31).

[75] "Five punishments" are *pars pro toto* for the legal system; see Li's biography in *Shih chi* Chapter 87.

[76] See *Shih chi*, 3:102 and our translation above.

[77] See Hightower, *op. cit.*, p. 130, n. 11 for a different reading.

The myriad things the bronze.[78]
Coming together, breaking apart, growing, shrinking,
Where are [*2500*] the norms?
A thousand changes, then thousand transformations,
60   There will never be an end.
Unexpectedly you were made into a human being,
What use is there to cling to this?
If you are transformed into the otherworld,
What need is there to worry?
65   Those with a little knowledge are partial to themselves,
Despising that world and exalting this.
Those who are enlightened take a broader view,
And whatever form they take is all right.
'The greedy man sacrifices himself for wealth,
70   the ardent knight for a name.
He who blusters dies for power,
and the common masses cling to life.'
Those fellows driven from within or without,
Some hasten west, some east.
75   The Great Man will not be bent,
A million changes are all the same to him.
The restrained man is tied by custom,
Fenced in as if restrained in prison.
The Perfect Man has divorced himself from physical objects,
80   And only keeps company with the Way.
The man of the masses is muddled,
And stores good and bad in his mind.[79]
The True Man is dispassionate,
And only dwells with the Way.
85   He casts off knowledge and leaves the human body,[80]
Transcends and loses his self;
In this vastness where all is uncertain,
He soars off with the Way.
Riding the current, he moves along,
90   When he encounters a sand bar, he stops.
He lets go of his body, entrusts it to fate,
Does not partially hoard it as his own.
He lets his life seem to float,
His death be like taking a rest.
95   He is as tranquil as the silence of a deep pool,
He bobs like a boat untied.
He doesn't overvalue himself because he is alive,
He nourishes his emptiness and floats.
The Man of Virtue has no attachments,
100   He understands his fate without worry.
Small problems, tiny obstructions,

---

[78] See *Chuang Tzu*, 3:18a, *SPPY*.

[79] "Chi-chieh" reads *yi* 億 for *yi* 意: "Stores a million 'good' and 'bads' in his mind," i.e., tries to have too many pre-judgments.

[80] Hightower (*op. cit.*, p. 129) begins here to read most of the subsequent text in the imperative, as an admonition to the reader; but the text continues to depict the "True Man" (*Chen-jen* 真人) until it reaches the "Man of Virtue" in the closing lines.

How can they cause him doubt?

[2502] A little over a year later, Scholar Chia was summoned to an audience. Emperor Hsiao Wen had just received sacrificial viands and was seated in the Hsüan 宣 Hall.[81] The sovereign, since matters of ghosts and spirits were on his mind, asked about their origins. [*2503*] Scholar Chia accordingly spoke in detail about why spirits exist. For half the night Emperor [Hsiao] Wen was on the edge of his mat. When Scholar Chia had finished, the emperor said, "I had not seen Scholar Chia for a long time and felt I had gone beyond him. Now I see I am not up to him." After a short time, he appointed Scholar Chia Grand Tutor to King Huai 懷 of Liang (r. 178-154 B.C.). King Huai of Liang was Emperor Wen's youngest son; [the emperor] loved him and he was fond of books, so the emperor had Scholar Chia tutor him.

Emperor Wen further enfeoffed four of the sons of King Li 厲 of Huai-nan (r. 196-154 B.C.)[82] as [high-]ranking marquis. Scholar Chia admonished him, considered that trouble would arise form this. Scholar Chia many times submitted memorials. He said that some of the kings had combined several commanderies, and, as this was not [in accord with] ancient regulations, should have their territory gradually reduced. But Emperor Wen did not listen.

A few years later, King Huai fell from his horse while riding and died without a successor. Scholar Chia was grieved that as a tutor he had not been up to form, so he wept for more than a year and also died. When Scholar Chia died, he was thirty three.

When [Emperor] Hsiao Wen passed away, Emperor Hsiao Wu 孝武 (r. 141-87 B.C.)[83] was enthroned and he brought two of Scholar Chia's grandsons into service as governors. Chia Chia 賈嘉 was most fond of study[84] and continued the family line, and corresponded with me. When it came to the time of [Emperor] Hsiao Chao 孝昭 (r. 87-74 B.C.),[85] he was ranked as one of the Nine Ministers.[86]

His Honor the Grand Scribe says: "When I read 'Encountering Sorrow,' 'T'ien-wen' 天問 (Heaven Questioned), 'Summoning the Soul,' and 'Ai ying' 哀郢 (A Lament for Ying), I was moved by Ch'ü Yüan's resolve. Whenever I go to Ch'ang-sha and see the place where Ch'ü Yüan sunk into the depths, I weep and wish that I might have seen what sort of man he was. When I saw how Scholar Chia lamented for him, on the other hand, I wondered how a man with Ch'ü Yüan's talents, who could not have failed to find a welcome in any of the states if he had chosen to consort with the feudal lords, brought himself to such a pass. When I read 'The Rhapsody on the Owl' which equates life and death, makes light of leaving or taking political position, I was dumbfounded and dazed!"

---

[81] The main hall in the Wei-yang 未央 Palace northwest of modern Sian (see Wang Li-ch'i, 84:1930n.).

[82] Liu Ch'ang 劉長, Kao-tsu's youngest son, who because of his pride, violent nature, and misbehavior was exiled to Pa-Shu in 174 B.C. and died en route (see *Shih chi* Chapter 118).

[83] This final passage seems to be an interpolation. The reference to Emperor Wu during his reign should be *chin-shang* 今上, "the present sovereign" (Hsiao Wu was a posthumous title--see also Liang Yü-sheng, 31:1307).

[84] He was a specialist in the *Spring and Autumn Annals* and the *Book of Documents* (see *Shih chi*, 121:3125 and T'ang Yen, pp. 102 and 448).

[85] Further support that this paragraph is an interpolation.

[86] *Chiu-ch'ing* 九卿, see Chang Cheng-lang, p. 11.

TRANSLATORS' NOTE

The sources for Ch'ü Yüan's life are essentially the works attributed to him in the *Ch'u tz'u* (especially the "Li sao" and its commentaries) and this biography. However, since this biography is based in part on the other sources, some scholars have labeled the entire procedure tautological and questioned whether Ch'ü Yüan actually existed (David Hawkes called his biography "a footnote" to the "Li sao").

But there is no question that Ssu-ma Ch'ien believes Ch'ü Yüan lived. And since this biography presents information not attributable to the "Li sao" and unlikely to have come from its commentaries, it is itself an important piece of evidence in support of that theory.

In the most recent edition of his *Songs of the South,* Hawkes has posited an unknown and no longer extant source for much of the material on Ch'ü Yüan in this memoir. He argues that many of the inconsistencies in this biography arise from problems Ssu-ma Ch'ien had accommodating this hypothetical text with the other texts and data he had. Although the inconsistencies can be explained in other fashions, such as by re-arranging portions of the text (see n. 40 above), Hawkes' hypothesis that divisions in the text suggest multiple sources is significant.

Scholars have also argued that Ch'ü Yüan's biography was cobbled together to serve as a foil for that of Chia Yi. But it is more likely that Ch'ü Yüan's is the basic text here, since the surrounding biographies in the *Shih chi* (Lu Chung-lien, Tsou Yang and Lü Pu-wei) were individuals from the pre-Ch'in era (see Takigawa, 84:1-2, headnote). Chia Yi's biography was added to that of Ch'ü Yüan because of the similarity of their lives.

BIBLIOGRAPHY

I. Translations

Bönner, Theodor. "Übersetzung des zweiten Teiles der 24. Biographies Seu-mà Ts'ien's (Kià-i.), mit Kommentar." Ph. D. dissertation, Friedrich Wilhelm's Universität, Berlin, 1908.

Hawkes, David. *The Songs of the South, An Anthology of Ancient Chinese Poems by Qu Yuan and Other Poets.* Rpt. Harmondsworth: Penguin Books, 1985.
    The translation of Ch'ü Yüan's biography (pp. 55-60) here--unlike the Songs themselves--has been revised considerably from the 1959 Oxford University Press edition.

Hightower, James Robert. "Chia Yi's 'Owl Fu,'" *AM, N.S.,* 7(1959), 125-30.

Knechtges, David. "Two Han Dynasty *Fu* on Ch'ü Yüan: Chia I's *Tiao Ch'ü Yüan* and Yang Hsiung's *Fan-sao,*" *Parerga,* 1 (1968), 5-43. Contains a translation of "Tiao Ch'ü Yüan," pp. 10-16.

Ōgawa Tamaki 小川環樹, trans. *Shiki retsuden* 史記列傳. Rpt. Tokyo: Chikuma Shobō, 1986 (1969), pp. 162-70.

Watson, Burton. *Records of the Grand Historian.* New York: Columbia University Press, 1961, 1:499-516.

II. Studies

Chiang Liang-fu 姜亮夫. "*Shih chi* 'Ch'ü Yüan lieh-chuan' shu-cheng" 史記屈原列傳疏證, in Chiang's *Ch'ü Yüan fu chiao-chu* 屈原賦校註. Peking: Chung-hua, 1972, pp. 1-26.

Chin Jung-hua 金榮華. "*Shih chi* 'Ch'ü Yüan lieh-chuan' shu-cheng" 史記屈元列傳疏證, *Shih-ta Kuo-wen yen-chiu-so chi-k'an* 師大國文研究所集刊, 9 (June 1965), 615-636.

Fu Yi 傅義. "Tu 'Ch'ü Yüan lieh-chuan'" 讀屈原列傳, *Yü-wen hsüeh-hsi* 語文學習, 1956, No. 10.

Hawkes, David. *The Songs of the South, An Anthology of Ancient Chinese Poems by Qu Yuan and Other Poets*. Rpt. Harmondsworth: Penguin Books, 1985.

_____. Review of *A Madman of Ch'u: The Chinese Myth of Loyalty and Dissent*, by Laurence A. Schneider, *CLEAR*, 4.2(July 1982), 245-7.

Miao K'o-hsiu 苗可秀. "*Shih chi* 'Ch'ü Yüan Chia Sheng lieh chuan shu-cheng" 史記屈原賈生列傳疏證, *Tung-pei ts'ung-chien* 東北叢鐫, No. 16.

Schneider, Laurence A. *A Madman of Ch'u: The Chinese Myth of Loyalty and Dissent*. Berkeley and Los Angeles: University of California Press, 1980.

Sun Tso-yün 孫作雲. "Tu *Shih chi* 'Ch'ü Yüan lieh-chuan'" 讀史記屈元列傳, *Shih-hsüeh yüeh-k'an* 史學月刊, 1959, No. 9.

Wen, I-fan 溫一凡. "Tu 'Ch'ü Yüan lieh-chuan'" 讀屈原列傳, *Chiang-hsi Ta-hsüeh Hsüeh-pao* 江西大學學報, 1978.3.

Lü Pu-wei, Memoir 25[1]

[2505] Lü Pu-wei 呂不韋 was a great merchant from Yang-ti 陽翟.[2] He came and went, buying cheap and selling dear, and his household accumulated thousands of *chin.*.

In the fortieth year (267 B.C.) of King Chao 昭 of Ch'in (r. 306-251 B.C.), the Heir died. In his forty-second year (265 B.C.), the son next in rank, the Lord of An-kuo 安國,[3] was installed as Heir. The Lord of An-kuo had more than twenty sons. The Lord of An-kuo had a consort whom he deeply loved; he installed her as his principal wife,[4] with the title of the Lady of Hua-yang 華陽.[5] The Lady of Hua-yang had no sons. The middle son of the Lord of An-kuo was named Tzu Ch'u 子楚;[6] Tzu Ch'u's mother was Madame Hsia 夏; she did not find favor [with the Lord of An-kuo]. Tzu Ch'u became Ch'in's hostage prince in Chao 趙. Ch'in attacked Chao several times, and Chao did not accord Tzu Ch'u much courtesy.

[2506] As a grandson of the royal family by a secondary wife and a hostage among the feudal lords, Tzu Ch'u's equipage and allowance were not lavish. He lived in straitened circumstances, unable to enjoy himself. When Lü Pu-wei was doing business at Han-tan 邯鄲, he saw [Tzu Ch'u] and was much taken: "Here is a rare commodity for me to claim."

He then went to see Tzu Ch'u and said, "I can widen your house's gate, sir."

Tzu Ch'u laughed and said, "Widen your own house's gate, My Lord, before you widen mine."

Lü Pu-wei said, "You don't understand, sir; my gate depends on yours for its widening."

Tzu Ch'u realized what he meant, led him in, sat with him and spoke frankly.

Lü Pu-wei said, "Now that the King of Ch'in is old, the Lord of An-kuo has become Heir. I have privately heard that the Lord of An-kuo loves and favors the Lady of Hua-yang, that the Lady of Hua-yang has no sons, and that only the Lady of Hua-yang can install [the Lord of An-kuo's] principal son and successor. Now you, sir, have more than twenty brothers; you are a junior son, you are not much favored, and you have long been hostage among the feudal lords. If the Great King dies and the Lord of An-kuo is enthroned as king,

---

[1] The story of Lü Pu-wei (290-235 B.C.) also appears in *Chan-kuo ts'e* (3:75a-77b, *SPTK*). The *Shih chi* and *Chan-kuo ts'e* versions differ sharply. Comparisons of the two can be found in Ch'ien Mu, *Chu-tzu* (p. 492), Derk Bodde, "Biography of Lü Pu-wei" in his *Statesman* (pp. 14-5) and T'ien Feng-t'ai 田鳳台, *Lü-shih ch'un-ch'iu t'an-wei* 呂氏春秋探微 (Taipei: Hsüeh-sheng, 1986, pp. 31-5). In the translation, we shall note, where appropriate, some of the most significant differences between the *Chan-kuo ts'e* and *Shih chi* versions.

[2] Yang-ti was located at modern Yü-hsien 禹縣, Honan province (see T'an Ch'i-hsiang, 1:35-6). In *Chan-kuo ts'e*, Lü Pu-wei is said to be a native of P'u-yang 濮陽 (about six miles southwest of modern P'u-yang). In the preface to his commentary on the *Lü-shih ch'un-ch'iu*, Kao Yu 高誘 (*fl.* A.D. 205-212), apparently trying to reconcile the two sources, says that Lü Pu-wei was a native of P'u-yang, who became a wealthy merchant at Yang-ti (see *Lü-shih ch'un-ch'iu*, 1:1a, *SPPY*).

[3] Ch'ien Mu, *Ti-ming k'ao*, pp. 601-602 and 695-696 lists two places called An-kuo, both of which were apparently in modern Hopei province and hence seem unlikely locations for a Ch'in fiefdom. As in the case of Lü Pu-wei, and perhaps Pai Ch'i, An-kuo may be a descriptive title ("Lord who Secures the State") rather than a location.

[4] *Cheng fu-jen* 正夫人.

[5] This Hua-yang is probably the same area as the fief of Mi Jung, the Lord of Hua-yang; see n. 4 to our translation of Chapter 72.

[6] According to *Chan-kuo ts'e*, his name was originally Yi-jen 異人. He was renamed by the Lady of Hua-yang when, following Lü Pu-wei's advice, he dressed in Ch'u clothing and went to seek the lady's support. The lady was from Ch'u.

you could not hope to compete for the status of Heir with the eldest son[7] or all the other sons who appear before [the Lord and Lady] day and night."

Tzu Ch'u said, "True. What's to be done?"

Lü Pu-wei said, "You are poor and live abroad; you do not have the means to send gifts to your parents or attract retainers. Though I am poor, allow me to travel west with a thousand *chin*, serve the Lord of An-kuo and the Lady of Hua-yang, and install you as the principal son."

Tzu Ch'u bowed his head and said, "If it really happens as you plan, My Lord, allow me to divide the state of Ch'in and share it with you."

[2507] Lü Pu-wei then gave five-hundred *chin* to Tzu Ch'u as an allowance to attract retainers, and with five-hundred more *chin* bought rare objects and curios. He himself carried these west to Ch'in. He sought an audience with the elder sister of the Lady of Hua-yang[8] and offered all of his goods to the Lady of Hua-yang. He took the occasion to mention that Tzu Ch'u was worthy and wise, that he had attracted retainers from throughout the world, and that he often said "I revere Her Ladyship as I do Heaven;[9] day and night I weep, thinking of the Heir and his Lady."

The Lady was delighted. Lü Pu-wei then had her elder sister advise the Lady: "I have heard that if one obtains service with a man through her beauty, when her beauty fades, his love will slacken. Now that Your Ladyship serves the Heir, you have great favor, but no sons. Why not use this opportunity to ally youself as quickly as you can with a worthy and filial son among the Noble Scions, install him as the principle son, and treat him as your own son. While your husband still lives, you will be doubly respected, and after your husband has lived out his hundred years,[10] the one whom you have taken as son will become king and you will never lose your influence. This is what is meant by 'a single comment that is equal to ten thousand [*2508*] generations of profit.' If you do not put down roots while you are blossoming, when your beauty fades his love will slacken, and even if you wished to offer a single suggestion, could you still do so? Tzu Ch'u, now, is worthy; realizing that he is a junior son, that by rank he cannot become the principle son, and that his mother is not favored, he binds himself to Your Ladyship. If Your Ladyship could take this opportunity to raise him up as the principle son and successor, Your Ladyship would have favor in Ch'in for the rest of your life."

The Lady of Hua-yang agreed. Taking advantage of a moment when the Heir was at leisure, she calmly remarked that Tzu Ch'u, the hostage at Chao, was most worthy and that those coming and going all praised him. She then began to weep and snivel. "Your handmaid has the good fortune to occupy your rear palace, but the misfortune to be without sons. I hope that you might install Tzu Ch'u as your principle son and successor so that I may then entrust myself to his care."[11]

---

[7] *Chan-kuo ts'e* gives his name as Tzu-hsi 子傒.

[8] In *Chan-kuo ts'e*, Lü Pu-wei went to see the Lord of Yang-ch'üan 陽泉君, the younger brother of the Lady of Hua-yang.

[9] Compare this with the following quote from the ritual manual *Yi li* 儀禮: "The father is the son's Heaven; the husband is the wife's Heaven" 父者子之天, 夫者妻之天 (*Yi li*, 11:8b, *SPPY*). A similar metaphor is also found in *Shih chi*, 97:2694: "A man fit to be king reveres the people as Heaven; the people revere food as Heaven." 王者以民人為天, 民人以食為天.

[10] *Pai-nien chih-hou* 百年之後, literally "after one-hundred years," is a euphemism for death.

[11] In *Chan-kuo ts'e*, it was the Lord of Yang-ch'üan who went to persuade his sister to make Tzu Ch'u the heir after Lü Pu-wei reminded him of the precarious position he would be in if the current Heir, Tzu-hsi, whom the-Lord of Yang-ch'üan surpassed in wealth and influence, ascended the throne. As Ch'ien Mu notices, in *Chan-kuo ts'e*, Lü Pu-wei went to see the Lord of Yang-ch'üan when the Lord of An-kuo had already been enthroned as

The Lord of An-kuo consented, gave the Lady a carved jade tally, and swore that Tzu Ch'u would be his principle son and successor. The Lord of An-kuo and the Lady then sent lavish presents to Tzu Ch'u, and asked Lü Pu-wei to be his mentor. Tzu Ch'u's fame thus grew among the feudal lords.

Lü Pu-wei married one of the ladies of Han-tan, one of the most beautiful and skilled dancers. He took up residence with her and found she was pregnant. When Tzu Ch'u was drinking with Lü Pu-wei, he saw her and was much taken. He took the occasion to make a toast and asked for her. Lü Pu-wei was angry. Mindful of how he had already beggared himself for the sake of Tzu Ch'u, and of his desire to make a rare catch, he finally presented his lady.[12] His lady concealed the fact that she was pregnant, and after a long period,[13] she gave birth to a son, Cheng 政.[14] Tzu Ch'u then installed the lady as his principle wife.

[2509] In the fiftieth year of King Chao of Ch'in (257 B.C.), [Ch'in] sent Wang Yi 王齮[15] to besiege Han-tan.[16] He pressed the attack and Chao prepared to kill Tzu Ch'u. Tzu Ch'u took counsel with Lü Pu-wei, and they passed out six-hundred catties of gold to the officers guarding Tzu Ch'u. He managed to escape, fled to the Ch'in army and thus managed to return to Ch'in.[17] Chao prepared to kill Tzu Ch'u's wife and son. Tzu Ch'u's woman was the daughter of a powerful family of Chao; she managed to hide and thus mother and child managed to survive.

In his fifty-sixth year, King Chao of Ch'in passed away. His Heir, the Lord of An-kuo, was enthroned as king, the Lady of Hua-yang became Queen and Tzu Ch'u became Heir. Chao sent Tzu Ch'u's lady and son Cheng back to Ch'in.

One year after the King of Ch'in was enthroned, he passed away. His posthumous title was King Hsiao-wen 孝文 (r. 250 B.C.).[18] The Heir Tzu Ch'u was enthroned in his place. He was known as King Chuang-hsiang 莊襄. The Lady of Hua-yang, whom King Chuang-hsiang had taken as his mother, became the Queen Dowager Hua-yang, and his real mother, Madame Hsia, was honored as the Queen Dowager Hsia.

In his first year, King Chuang-hsiang made Lü Pu-wei Chancellor and enfeoffed him as the Marquis Wen-hsin 文信, with a hundred-thousand households at Lo-yang 雒陽 in Ho-nan 河南 for his provisions.[19]

King Hsiao-wen (see Ch'ien Mu, *Chu-tzu*, p. 492).

[12] This entire episode is lacking in the *Chan-kuo ts'e* text.

[13] The meaning of the phrase *ta-ch'i* 大期 "long period" is disputed. "Chi-chieh" suggests that this was a period of twelve months, implying that Cheng was Lü Pu-wei's son. Liang Yü-sheng (31:1308) disputes this and notes that in the *Tso chuan*, the term *ta-ch'i* means "ten months." He argues that Ssu-ma Ch'ien is implying that Cheng was indeed Tzu Ch'u's son, and speculates that Lü Pu-wei himself spread rumors that Cheng was his son in order to gain higher status. Derk Bodde (*Statesman*, p. 18) suggests that the *Shih chi* text was altered by Han scholars in order to denigrate the First Emperor. For a summary of traditional views on whether Lü Pu-wei was the First Emperor's father, see Ch'ien Mu, *Chu-tzu*, pp. 491-2.

[14] This was the *praenomen* of the future First Emperor; he was called this because he was born in the first month (*cheng-yüeh* 正月). See Wang Shu-min, 5:188.

[15] All other sources say that Wang Ho 齕 led this attack. See n. 28 to our translation of Chapter 73.

[16] This attack began in 258 B.C. and lasted for over a year. See our translation of Chapter 73 for a detailed account.

[17] In *Chan-kuo ts'e*, it was the Lady of Hua-yang, by that time already Queen, who demanded the return of Tzu Ch'u. Chao, persuaded by Lü Pu-wei, complied.

[18] In fact, he was on the throne for only three days. See *Shih chi*, 5:219. Despite the fact that Hsiao-wen died almost immediately after taking the throne, the first year of King Chuang-hsiang's reign did not begin until one year after Hsiao-wen's death.

[19] This is anachronistic. Ho-nan was the name of a commandery established after Ch'in unified China.

Three years after he ascended the throne, King Chuang-hsiang passed away and his Heir Cheng was enthroned as king. He honored Lü Pu-wei as Minister of State and called him "Second Father."[20] The King of Ch'in was in his minority [*2510*] and the Queen Dowager frequently had illicit relations with Lü Pu-wei. Lü Pu-wei's household had ten-thousand house-boys.[21]

At the time, Wei had the Lord of Hsin-ling 信陵, Ch'u had the Lord of Ch'un-shen 春申, Chao had the Lord of P'ing-yüan 平原, and Ch'i had the Lord of Meng-ch'ang 孟嘗. They humbled themselves before knights and delighted in guests, attempting to sway them and move them. Lü Pu-wei, ashamed that Ch'in with its might was not their equal, summoned knights and treated them lavishly; in the end his household-retainers numbered 3000. At the time there were many orators among the feudal states, such as Excellency Hsün 荀 and his followers, who wrote books and spread them throughout the world. Lü Pu-wei thus had each of his retainers record their knowledge and compiled and edited it into 8 surveys, 6 discourses, and 12 records, in over 200,000 characters. He thought that these writings held all the affairs of Heaven, earth, and the myriad things, ancient and modern, and called it *Lü's Spring and Autumn* [*Annals*].[22] He posted it at the market gate of Hsien-yang and hung 1000 *chin* above it, then invited the wandering knights and retainers of the feudal lords; whoever could add or delete a single word would be given 1000 *chin*.

[2511] As the First Emperor (r. 246-210 B.C.) grew to maturity, the Queen Dowager's wanton behavior did not cease. Lü Pu-wei feared that the emperor would discover [matters] and disaster fall on him. He thus quietly sought out Lao Ai 嫪毐, a man with a large penis, as his houseman. He then held frequent performances of music and singing, had Lao Ai put his penis through the hole of a wheel of paulownia wood as he walked about, and let the Queen Dowager hear of this, tempting her. When the Queen Dowager heard of this, she did indeed wish to have him. Lü Pu-wei then presented Lao Ai and had a man falsely accuse him of a crime punishable by castration. Lü Pu-wei secretly told the Queen Dowager, "You could pretend to have him castrated and then he could wait on you in the palace." The Queen Dowager then granted lavish gifts to the officer in charge of castration. He pretended to carry out the sentence of castration, plucked his beard and eyebrows[23] as if he were a eunuch, and [Lao Ai] thus was able to wait on the Queen Dowager. The Queen Dowager had relations with him in

[20] Chung Fu 仲父. The famous statesman Kuan Chung was also called Chung Fu (see *Shih chi*, 79:2416), but in Kuan Chung's case, *chung* might refer to his *agnomen*. Similar confusion exists for the term Shu Fu 叔父 when King Chao-hsiang of Ch'in uses this to refer to Fan Sui 范睢, whose *agnomen* was Shu (see *Shih chi*, 79:2416). In the present case, Chung Fu may be an imitation of Kuan Chung's ancient title, may simply mean "Elder Paternal Uncle" or may imply "Second Father" as we translate (cf. the term Ya Fu 亞父 used by Hsiang Yü 項羽 to address Fan Tseng 范增 on *Shih chi*, 7:312).

[21] T'ung 僮. For a further discussion of this term, see C. M. Wilbur, *Slavery in China During the Former Han Dynasty*, Chicago: Field Museum of Natural History, 1943, and Cheng T'ien-t'ing, p. 461.

[22] Lü's book, *Lü-shih ch'un-ch'iu* 呂氏春秋 still survives. Surveys (*lan* 覽), Discourses (*lun* 論) and Records (*chi* 紀) are the titles of the three sections of *Lü-shih ch'un-ch'iu*. For a study of the textual history and organization of this work, see Michael Carson's preface to his *A Concordance to Lü-shih ch'un-ch'iu* (Chinese Materials Center, 1985, pp. ix-xliii). Ch'ien Mu, *Chu-tzu*, pp. 485-9, also provides discussion of Lü's motives in compiling this work.

[23] Takigawa (85:12) suggests that the phrase *hsü-mei* 鬚眉 just refers to the beard, and not the eyebrows. Wang Shu-min (85:2573) argues that eunuchs partially plucked their eyebrows for appearances. There are other references, however, which definitely refer to removing both the beard and eyebrows, in which aesthetics was not involved, such as the *Chan-kuo ts'e* story of Yü Jang (6:7a, *SPTK*); perhaps this was a part of the punishment. Shaving off hair was a form of "corporal punishment" (*hsing* 刑); examples include *nai* 耐 "shaving off the beard" and *k'un* 髡 "shaving the head and face."

secret and doted on him. When she became pregnant, the Queen Dowager feared others would learn of this, pretended that a divination had revealed she should avoid seasonal influences, moved out of the palace, and took up residence at Yung 雍.[24] Lao Ai always accompanied her. She bestowed lavish grants on him and all her affairs were decided by Lao Ai. Lao Ai's household had several thousand servants and over a thousand retainers seeking office became Lao Ai's housemen.

In the seventh year of the First Emperor (240 B.C.), King Chuang-hsiang's mother, the Queen Dowager Hsia, passed away. King Hsiao-wen's Queen, the Queen Dowager Hua-yang, had been buried together with King Hsiao-wen at Shou-ling 壽陵.[25] The Queen Dowager Hsia's son, King Chuang-hsiang, had been buried at Chih-yang 芷陽.[26] Thus the Queen Dowager Hsia was buried separately, east of Tu 杜.[27] [Before she died] she said, "To the east I will face my son, and to the west I will face my husband. A hundred years from now, there shall be a city of ten thousand households by my side."

[2512] In the ninth year of the First Emperor (238 B.C.), someone made the accusation that Lao Ai was not in fact a eunuch, that he regularly had illicit relations with the Queen Dowager, that he had sired two sons, both of whom he had concealed, and that he had plotted with the Queen Dowager, saying "If the king passes away, let us make our sons his heirs."[28] The King of Ch'in then sent the matter to his functionaries to handle; when all the facts were known, the Minister of State Lü Pu-wei was implicated in the matter.

In the ninth month, [the King] exterminated the three clans of Lao Ai, killed the two sons that the Queen Dowager had born, and transported the Queen Dowager to Yung. All of Lao Ai's housemen had their households confiscated and were transported to Shu 蜀.[29] The King intended to execute the Minister of State, but because of his great merit in serving the late king and the many retainers and orators who spoke out for him, the king could not bear to subject him to the law.

In the tenth month of the King of Ch'in's tenth year, he dismissed the Minister of State Lü Pu-wei. After Mao Chiao 茅焦, a native of Ch'i, advised the King of Ch'in,[30] the King of Ch'in greeted the Queen Dowager at Yung, recalled her to Hsien-yang, [*2513*] and sent the Marquis Wen-hsin out to his fief in Ho-nan.

After more than a year, the retainers and envoys of the feudal states seeking after Marquis Wen-hsin stretched down the roads. The King of Ch'in was afraid that he would rebel. He sent Marquis Wen-hsin a letter, saying:

> What was your merit in Ch'in that Ch'in enfeoffed you at Ho-nan with a hundred-thousand households for your provisions? How are you related to Ch'in that you are called 'Second Father'? You and your family are to move to Shu!"

[24] The former capital of Ch'in located south of modern Feng-hsiang 鳳翔, Shensi (see T'an Ch'i-hsiang, 1:43-4).

[25] North of modern Lin-t'ung 臨潼, Shensi (see Wang Li-ch'i, 85:1940; see also Ch'ien Mu, *Ti-ming k'ao*, pp. 243-4).

[26] About 10 miles northwest of modern Sian, Shensi (see T'an Ch'i-hsiang, 1:43-4).

[27] About 5 miles southeast of modern Sian (see T'an Ch'i-hsiang, 1:43-4).

[28] In *Shuo-yüan*, it was Lao Ai himself who revealed his relationship with the Queen Dowager. In a brawl during a drinking party, he shouted that he was the emperor's Chia Fu 假父, literally "substitute (or acting?) father" (see *Shuo-yüan*, 9:3b, *SPPY*).

[29] Shu was located in the central and western part of modern Szechwan province.

[30] This incident is recorded in *Shih chi*, 6:227. A more dramatic version is found in *Shuo-yüan* (9:6a-8a, *SPPY*).

Lü Pu-wei, judging that his position would be gradually eroded, and fearing that he would be executed, drank poison and died. After those who had incurred the anger of the King of Ch'in, Lü Pu-wei and Lao Ai, were both dead, the housemen of Lao Ai banished to Shu were recalled. In the nineteenth year of the First Emperor, the Queen Dowager passed away, was given the posthumous title[31] "Empress Dowager" and was buried together with King Chuang-hsiang at Chih-yang 芷陽.[32]

His Honor the Grand Scribe says: "Lü Pu-wei brought Lao Ai noble rank, and [Lao Ai] was enfeoffed as Marquis Ch'ang-hsin 長信.[33] When Lao Ai was accused, he heard of it. The King of Ch'in questioned his attendants, but nothing had yet come to light. When the king went to make sacrifice in the suburbs of Yung, Lao Ai, fearing that disaster would come, plotted with his confederates to forge the Queen Dowager's seal and send law officers to rebel at Ch'i-nien 蘄年 Palace.[34] [The King of Ch'in] sent law officers to attack Lao Ai. Lao Ai was defeated and fled. The law officers pursued [*2514*] and beheaded him at Hao-chih 好畤,[35] then his clan was destroyed. Lü Pu-wei's fall from power began with this. What Confucius called 'a man of renown,'[36] surely that was Lü Tzu?"

---

[31] Wang Shu-min, following "So-yin" and Liang Yü-sheng, believe that *shih* 謚 (posthumous title) should be read as *hao* 號 (title) because the First Emperor had abolished the practice of applying *shih* (see Wang Shu-min, 85:2575).

[32] This is the same as Chih-yang 芷陽 (see n. 39 above).

[33] Ch'ang-hsin was Lao Ai's title (see *Shih chi*, 6:227). The original reads Wen-hsin 文信, Lü Pu-wei's title, but our translation follows "So-yin's" suggestion that this be changed to Ch'ang-hsin. We also follow Wang Shu-min (85:2575) in treating *chi* 及 as a transitive verb.

[34] South of modern Feng-hsiang 鳳翔 County in Shensi (Wang Li-ch'i, 85:1941n.)

[35] Modern Ch'ien-hsien 乾縣, Shensi (see T'an Ch'i-hsiang, 1:43-4).

[36] This is a reference to *Lun yü,* 12/20, in which Confucius says: "As for a 'renowned' man, he appears humane, then diverges from it in his actions, yet has no hesitation in claiming it. Thus he is sure of 'renown' when serving both a state and a noble family."

TRANSLATORS' NOTE

This chapter expands on the story of Lü Pu-wei as told in "The Basic Annals of the First Emperor of Ch'in" (see our translation of Chapter 6 above). It is a story involving strategems, retainers, and literary accomplishment like many of the memoirs we have seen above. Yet here there are two additional factors: wealth and the mentality that produced it. Although the events resemble those in earlier chapters, the motivation does not. Even Lü Pu-wei's homilies reflect his merchant status: "A single comment that is equal to ten-thousand generations of profit." Lü's downfall, like that of the Lord of Ch'un-shen, comes as the result of his explotation of sex for his own interests, and it is on this affair that Ssu-ma Ch'ien focusses his final remarks, perhaps uncomfortable with the mercantile principles behind this life and realizing that his comment, too, would equal ten-thousand generations of censure.

BIBLIOGRAPHY

I. Translations

Bodde, Derk. *Statesman, Patriot and General in Ancient China.* New Haven: American Oriental Society, 1940, pp. 1-9.
Fukushima Yoshihio 福島吉彦, trans. *Shiki retsuden* 史記列傳. Rpt. Tokyo: Chikuma Shobō, 1986 (1969), 170-74.
Panasjuk, V. *Syma Czjan', Izbrannoe.* Moscow, 1956, pp. 189-96.
Watson, Burton. *Records of the Grand Historian: Qin Dynasty.* Hong Kong and New York: The Research Centre for Translation, The Chinese University of Hong Kong and Columbia University Press, 1993, pp. 159-165.

II. Studies

Bodde, *op. cit.*
T'ien Feng-t'ai 田鳳台. "Lü Pu-wei chuan k'ao" 呂不韋傳考, *Fu-hsing kang hsüeh-pao* 復興崗學報, 27(June 1982), 427-49.

The Assassin-Retainers, Memoir 26

Ts'ao Mo

[86:2515] Ts'ao Mo 曹沫[1] was a native of Lu. He obtained service with Duke Chuang 莊 of Lu (r. 693-662 B.C.) through his daring and strength. Duke Chuang delighted in [displays of] strength. Ts'ao Mo became a commander of Lu and fought with Ch'i, but he retreated in defeat three times. Duke Chuang was afraid and offered the territory of Sui-yi 遂邑[2] to make peace with Ch'i, but he still kept Ts'ao Mo as commander.

Duke Huan of Ch'i consented to meet with Lu at K'o 柯[3] and make a covenant. When Duke Huan and Duke Chuang had finished swearing the oath on the altar mound, Ts'ao Mo held up a dagger and seized Duke Huan of Ch'i. None of the duke's attendants dared to move; [the duke] then asked, "What do you want?"

"Ch'i is powerful and Lu is weak," said Ts'ao Mo, "but your great state has gone too far in its invasion! If the walls of Lu's capital were to collapse, they would crush the borders of Ch'i! Consider that, my lord!"

Duke Huan then promised to return all of Lu's captured territory. When he had finished speaking, Ts'ao Mo dropped his dagger, stepped down off the altar mound, faced north, and took his place among the assembled vassals. His expression did not change and his speech remained polite and formal.

Duke Huan was angry and decided to break the agreement. Kuan Chung said, "That will not do! If your greed leads you to satisfy yourself with petty profit [*2516] and you thus break your bond to the feudal lords, you will lose the world's support. It would be better to give them the land." After this, Duke Huan finally ceded Lu the land he had captured from it, and all the territory which Ts'ao Mo had lost in three battles was returned to Lu.

One-hundred-and-sixty-seven years later [515 B.C.] in the state of Wu there was the matter of Chuan Chu.

---

[1] We follow the pronunciation for Mo given in "So-yin." But Ts'ao first occurs as Ts'ao Kuei 劌 in the *Tso chuan* (Yang, *Tso chuan*, Chuang 10, 1:182-3), where his advice allows the Duke to rout the Ch'i army at Ch'ang-shao 長勺.

Three years later the *Tso chuan* (Yang, *Tso chuan*, Chuang 13, 1:194) gives its account of this covenant at K'o without mention of Ts'ao. Yang Po-chün in his commentary observes (following several traditional commentators) that there are no recorded battles between that at Ch'ang-shao and this covenant and thus Ts'ao Kuei/Mo could not have been defeated three times. The only other reference to these three defeats can be found in the *Chan-kuo ts'e* account (4:54a, *SPTK*). Although Ssu-ma Ch'ien does not refer to these three defeats elsewhere in the *Shih chi*, he does note Ts'ao's "extortion" of Duke Huan in *Shih chi*, 14:570 and gives similar accounts to that here on 32:1487 and 33:1531. But the convening of a covenant suggests that there had been recent strife which may simply have not been recorded in the *Tso chuan*. This tradition of Ts'ao threatening Duke Huan to regain territory is, moreover, fairly established in a number of other Warring States period texts (see Yang Po-chün, *Tso chuan*, 1:194 and Wang Shu-min, 86:2578). For a more detailed discussion of these problems, see Shih Chih-mien, pp. 1342-3 and our n. 35 to the translation of *Shih chi* Chapter 62 above.

[2] Wang Li-ch'i (86:1945) identifies Sui as the name of a city-state (Sui-yi) south of Fei-ch'eng 肥城 County in modern Shantung (see also T'an Ch'i-hsiang, 1:26). The *Tso chuan* mentions the destruction of Sui by Ch'i (not Lu!) in the summer of 681 B.C. after Sui failed to send representatives to the covenant held at Pei-hsing 北興 during the spring of that year (Yang, *Tso chuan*, 1:194).

[3] K'o was a town in Ch'i about 10 miles northeast of modern Yang-ku 陽古 County in Shantung (T'an Ch'i-hsiang, 1:26).

Chuan Chu

Chuan Chu 專諸[4] was a native of [the city of] T'ang-yi 堂邑[5] in Wu. When Wu Tzu Hsü[6] 伍子胥 fled from Ch'u to Wu, he recognized Chuan Chu's ability. When Wu Tzu Hsü had an audience with Liao 僚, King of Wu (r. 526-515 B.C.), he advised him that it would be to his advantage to attack Ch'u. Wu's Noble Scion Kuang 光 said, "This fellow Wu Yün's 員 father and elder brother both died in Ch'u. When Yün speaks of attacking Ch'u, he desires to repay his personal foes. He is incapable of acting on behalf of Wu!" The King of Wu then desisted. Wu Tzu Hsü realized that Noble Scion Kuang intended to kill Liao, King of Wu, and said, "This fellow Kuang has ambitions inside the state, he cannot yet be advised on matters abroad."[7] He then presented Chuan Chu to the Noble Scion Kuang.

[2517] Kuang's father was Chu Fan 諸樊, King of Wu (r. 560-548 B.C.). Chu Fan had three younger brothers; the first was Yü Chai 餘祭,[8] the second Yi Mo 夷昧,[9] and the third Chi Tzu Cha 季子札.[10] Chu Fan knew that Chi Tzu Cha was worthy and so he did not install an Heir, [but arranged for the throne] to pass to his younger brothers in succession, intending to eventually present the state to Chi Tzu Cha. When Chu Fan died, [the throne] was passed to Yü Chai and when Yü Chai died, it was passed to Yi Mo. When Yi Mo died, it should have passed to Chi Tzu Cha, but Chi Tzu Cha fled and refused to be enthroned. The men of Wu then enthroned Yi Mo's son, Liao, as king.

Noble Scion Kuang said, "If succession is from older brother to younger brother, then Chi Tzu should be enthroned. If the succession is to be among the sons, then I am the true and legitimate successor. I should be enthroned." He therefore sought the throne by secretly cultivating counselors.

After he had obtained [the services of] Chuan Chu, he treated him as a valued retainer. After nine years King P'ing 平 of Ch'u (r. 528-516 B.C.) died. In the spring [of 515 B.C.] Liao, King of Wu, decided to take advantage of Ch'u's period of mourning, and sent his two younger brothers, the Noble Scions Kai-yü 蓋餘 and Chu-yung 屬庸, to lead troops in the siege of the Ch'u [city] of Ch'ien 潛.[11] He sent Chi Tzu [Cha] of Yen-ling 延陵[12] to Chin to observe any changes [of alliance] among the feudal lords. Ch'u sent out troops to cut off the routes of the Wu generals Kai-yü and Chu-yung and Wu's troops could not return home.

---

[4] Chuan Chu also appears in *Tso chuan* (Yang, Chao 20 and 27, pp. 1409 and 1483-4) where his name is given as Chuan She-chu 鱄設諸. This event is also recorded in Wu Tzu Hsü's biography (*Shih chi,* 66:2174) and on *Shih chi,* 31:1462-3.

[5] Northwest of modern Liu-ho 六合 County in Kiangsu (Ch'ien Mu, *Ti-ming k'ao,* p. 589).

[6] See his biography in *Shih chi* Chapter 66.

[7] On *Shih chi* 31:1462 and 66:2174 Ssu-ma Ch'ien tells us Wu Tzu Hsü knew that Kuang had ulterior motives, but he does not have Wu mention them aloud. In the *Tso chuan* (Yang, Chao 20, p. 1409), however, Wu also utters his thoughts, but Legge (5:681) renders them as if they were an aside.

[8] This was his royal title; his *nomen* was Tai-wu 戴吳 and he ruled Wu from 547-544 B.C.

[9] In the Po-na Edition (86:2b) his title is Yi Mei 昧; he ruled Wu from 543-527 B.C.

[10] According to the *Shih chi,* 31:1449ff., Chi Cha was the youngest son of Shou Meng 壽夢, King of Wu (r. 585-565 B.C.) and the youngest brother of Chu Fan. Tu Yü's 杜預 (222-284) note in *Tso chuan* (Yang, Ai 10 [485 B.C.], p. 1656) claims he died in his nineties.

[11] Located 10 miles southwest of modern Liu-an City 六安市 in Anhwei (T'an Ch'i-hsiang 1:45).

[12] Chi Tzu Cha was enfeoffed with Yen-ling (*Shih chi,* 79:2424), located near the modern city of Ch'ang-chou 常州 in Chekiang (T'an Ch'i-hsiang, 1:30).

Noble Scion Kuang then said to Chuan Chu, "We can not lose this opportune time! If we do not seek, what will we gain? Moreover, I am the true and legitimate heir and should be enthroned. Even if Chi Tzu [Cha] comes, he will not depose me."

Chuan Chu said, "King Liao can now be killed. His mother is old, his son still young, his two younger brothers are commanding the troops attacking Ch'u, and Ch'u has cut off their rear. Now that Wu is hard pressed abroad at Ch'u, emptied of troops at home, and lacking in outspoken vassals, they can do nothing to us." Noble Scion Kuang struck his forehead against the ground and said, "My life is yours, sir."

[2518] On the *ping-tzu* day in the fourth month, Kuang concealed armored knights in his cellar, prepared wine, and invited King Liao [to a banquet]. King Liao had soldiers take up positions from his palace to Kuang's house. To the left and right, at the gates and doors, on the stairways and steps, all were King Liao's kinsmen. They pressed about him, standing in attendance, and all held long rapiers. When they were all in their cups, Noble Scion Kuang pretended to have a pain in his leg, entered the cellar,[13] and had Chuan Chu put a dagger[14] in the belly of a braised fish and present it [to Liao]. Arriving before the king, Chuan Chu pulled the fish apart, then stabbed King Liao with the dagger. King Liao died on the spot. His courtiers also killed Chuan Chu, and the king's men were thrown into confusion. Noble Scion Kuang sent out the armored men he had concealed to attack King Liao's followers, killing all of them. He then enthroned himself. He was known as Ho-lü 闔閭 (r. 514-496 B.C.). He enfeoffed Chuan Chu's son as a Senior Excellency.[15]

Some seventy years later there was the matter of Yü Jang in Chin.

Yü Jang

[2519] Yü Jang 預讓[16] was a native of the state of Chin. Formerly he served the Fan 范 and Chung-hang 中行 clans,[17] but found no means of gaining recognition. He left and served the Earl of Chih 智伯;[18] the Earl of Chih treated him with great respect and honor. When the Earl of Chih attacked Viscount Hsiang 襄 of Chao, Viscount Hsiang plotted together with Han and Wei to destroy the Earl of Chih. After the Earl of Chih had been destroyed, his land was divided three ways.[19] Viscount Hsiang bore the most resentment against the Earl of Chih; he had his skull lacquered and used it as a drinking vessel.[20]

Yü Jang fled into the mountains. He said, "Alas, a knight dies for the one who appreciates him, a woman dresses for the one who pleases her. The Earl of Chih appreciated me.

---

[13] Noble Scion Kuang went to the cellar partly for his own safety and to ready his armored men and partly because those who employ assassins traditionally avoided being present during the assassination.

[14] In the *Tso chuan* (Yang, p. 1484) he uses a sword 劍.

[15] *Shang-ch'ing* 上卿.

[16] Another version of this story occurs in *Chan-kuo ts'e* (6:7a-9a, *SPTK*) His name is given there as Pi 畢 Yü Jang and he is said to be the grandson of Pi Yang 陽.

[17] These clans were destroyed by Earl Chih (see n. 19 below and "So-yin").

[18] The major source for Earl Yao 瑤 of Chih is the *Chan-kuo ts'e* (see n. 19 which follows).

[19] The account of Earl Chih's conquest of Fan and Chung-hang and subsequent fall can be found in the *Chan-kuo ts'e* (6:1a-4b, *SPTK*).

[20] Other sources say a urinal. See Wang Shu-min, 86:2584. As "So-yin" notes, according to *Shih chi*, 123:3157, the Hsiung-nu khan did the same thing when he defeated the ruler of Ta-yüan.

Before I die, I will repay him by destroying his enemy. Then my spirits and anima will not suffer shame."

He changed his name, disguised himself as a convict-laborer, and entered the [viscount's] residence to plaster the outhouse. He stuffed a dagger inside his clothes, intending to stab Viscount Hsiang with it. When Viscount Hsiang entered the outhouse, he became uneasy; when [his attendants] seized and interrogated the convict-laborer who was plastering the outhouse, it was Yü Jang, holding a knife inside his garment: "I intended to repay the Earl of Chih's foe!"

The attendants prepared to execute him. Viscount Hsiang said, "This fellow is a man of principle. I will just be careful to keep him away from me. Moreover, when the Earl of Chih perished, he had no posterity, yet his vassal still seeks to repay his foe. This is one of the worthiest men in the world!" In the end he released Yü Jang and sent him away.

[2520] After a short time had passed, Yü Jang lacquered his body to produce skin ulcers, and swallowed charcoal to hoarsen his voice; having rendered his appearance unrecognizable, he went begging in the marketplace. His wife did not recognize him. On the road he saw his friend. His friend recognized him: "Aren't you Yü Jang?" "I am."

His friend wept for him: "With your talent, sir, you could have laid down your pledge and served Viscount Hsiang as a vassal; Viscount Hsiang would have been sure to trust and favor you. Once he trusted and favored you, you could have done as you wished. Wouldn't that have been easy? Then why have you crippled your body and afflicted your frame? To seek vengeance on Viscount Hsiang through means such as this, isn't this difficult?"

Yü Jang replied, "After laying down one's pledge and serving a man as his vassal, if you then try to kill him, that is serving one lord while owing fealty to another. What I have done is most difficult, but the reason I have done it is to shame those of later generations, wherever they might be, who serve men as vassals yet owe fealty to another."

[2521] A short while after he left [his friend], Viscount Hsiang was about to leave his residence. Yü Jang hid under a bridge he expected [Viscount Hsiang] would cross. When Viscount Hsiang reached the bridge, his [carriage] horses flinched. "This must be Yü Jang!" he said and sent a man to question him. It was indeed Yü Jang.

Viscount Hsiang then berated Yü Jang: "Didn't you once serve the clans of Fan and Chung-hang? The Earl of Chih destroyed them both, yet you didn't avenge them, but instead laid down your pledge and served the Earl of Chih as vassal. Now the Earl of Chih too is dead; why are you so determined to avenge only his death?"

Yü Jang said, "I served the clans of Fan and Chung-hang, and the clans of Fan and Chung-hang treated me as an ordinary man; therefore I repaid them as I would an ordinary man. As for the the Earl of Chih, he treated me as one of the greatest knights of his state, and so I will repay him as I would one of the greatest knights of the state."

Viscount Hsiang sighed deeply and wept: "Alas, Yü Tzu! Your actions on behalf of the Earl of Chih have already made your name, and when I pardoned you before, that was enough. Consider how you wish to die, I will not release you again!" He had his troops surround Yü Jang.

Yü Jang said, "I have heard that an enlightened ruler does not obstruct virtuous deeds and a loyal vassal has a duty to die for his good name. My Lord generously pardoned me in the past, and the world praised him as a worthy man. For today's affair, I naturally accept punishment, but I hope that I might ask for My Lord's garment and strike it, to show that it was my intention to seek revenge.. [If you grant this request,] then even though I die I will have no regrets. I do not dare to hope for this, I only dare to lay out my innermost desire."

Viscount Hsiang thought Yü Jang a truly principled man. He had a man take his garment and give it to Yü Jang. Yü Jang drew his sword, leaped in the air three times,[21] and struck the garment:[22] "Now I can go down and report to the Earl of Chih!" Then he fell on his sword and died. The day he died, when the resolute knights of the state of Chao heard of it, they all wept and sniveled for him.

[2522] Some forty years later there was the matter of Nieh Cheng in Chih 軹.[23]

Nieh Cheng

Nieh Cheng 聶政 was a native of Shen-ching Hamlet 深井里 in Chih.[24] He killed a man and fled from revenge with his mother and elder sister to the state of Ch'i, where he worked as a butcher.

Some time later, Yen Chung Tzu 嚴仲子[25] of P'u-yang 濮陽[26] served Marquis Ai 哀 of Han 韓 (r. *376-371 B.C.);[27] there was bad blood between Yen Chung Tzu and Han's Prime Minister Chia-lei 俠累.[28] Yen Chung Tzu feared execution; he fled and traveled about seeking a man who could repay Chia-lei for him.

When he arrived in Ch'i, someone told him that Nieh Cheng was a courageous and daring knight who had fled from revenge and retired among the butchers. Yen Chung Tzu went to his door and asked [for his help]. After going back several times, he prepared wine and offered it himself before Nieh Cheng's mother. When they were in their cups, Yen Chung-tzu took out a hundred *yi* of gold and stepped forward to present it as a gift to Nieh Cheng's mother. Nieh Cheng was amazed at his generosity and steadfastly declined Yen Chung Tzu's [gift]. Yen Chung Tzu steadfastly offered it, and Nieh Cheng declined: "I am fortunate enough to have my aged mother. My household is poor and as a wanderer abroad I must work as a dog butcher, but for now I am still able to obtain sweet and savory foods to care for her. Her needs are supplied and I would not dare to accept your grant."

Yen Chung Tzu had the others leave them alone and explained to Nieh Cheng:. "I have a bitter foe, and I have traveled to many of the feudal states. But when I reached Ch'i, I privately learned that you are indeed high principled, Honorable Sir. I would therefore offer

---

[21] We translate yüeh 躍 as "leaping in the air" but this may be another way of referring to the action of "stamping the feet" (*yung* 踊) which was a part of the ritual method of expressing grief after one's lord has died (see *Li chi Cheng chu*, 6:1a-b *SPPY*). Yü Jang evidently put off performing this action until he had made every attempt to avenge his lord.

[22] "So-yin" cites the *Chan-kuo ts'e* as follows: "Blood spurted out of every part of the garment. Viscount Hsiang turned his chariot around, but before its wheels had made a complete revolution he died." This passage is not part of the modern *Chan-kuo ts'e* account; if Ssu-ma Ch'ien saw this, he chose not to include it.

[23] Chih was north of modern Chi-yüan 濟源 in Honan (T'an Ch'i-hsiang, 1:36).

[24] This story also occurs in *Chan-kuo ts'e* (8:1b-5b, *SPTK*), and is mentioned in *Han Fei Tzu* and various other works.

[25] According to "So-yin," Chung Tzu was his *agnomen*; his *praenomen* was Sui 遂. In the *Chan-kuo ts'e* version, the Prime Minister's name was K'uei 傀. It also says that their rift came about after Yen Sui criticized K'uei in front of the marquis and K'uei then shouted at him. Yen tried to kill him and after failing fled the state of Han.

[26] A few miles southwest of the modern city of the same name in northeastern Hopei (T'an Ch'i-hsiang 1:36).

[27] According to the tables in the *Shih chi* (15:711) Nieh Chung killed Chia-lei in the third year of Marquis Lieh 列 (397 B.C.), the grandfather of Marquis Ai. The "So-yin" explains this discrepancy by postulating that Ssu-ma Ch'ien was drawing on differing versions of this story. In *Han Fei Tzu*, it is referred to the Marquis Ai.

[28] See Wang Li-ch'i, *Jen-piao*, p. 666.

this hundred *chin* for you to use in purchasing unhusked rice for your honored mother; if I may thus happily obtain your friendship, how would I dare hope to seek anything further?"

Nieh Cheng said, "The reason why I have lowered my ambitions and shamed myself as an itinerant marketplace and well hole butcher is only because I hope to care for mother. While mother is here, I dare not promise myself to anyone."

Yen Chung Tzu steadfastly pressed him, but to the end Nieh Cheng refused to accept his gift. Yet Yen Chung Tzu fulfilled the rituals of guest and host before departing.

[2523] After some time, Nieh Cheng's mother died. After she was buried and the period of mourning had ended, Nieh Cheng said, "Alas! I am a denizen of the marketplaces and well holes, banging a knife and butchering, and Yen Chung Tzu is minister to the feudal lords. Yet he did not consider a thousand *li* too far to trouble his carriage and outriders in order to make my friendship. The way I treated him was utterly inadequate! Even though I do not yet have any great merit worth mentioning, Yen Chung Tzu presented a hundred *chin* as a gift to my mother. Though I did not accept it, he could only have done this because he truly understood me. Here is a worthy man filled with repressed anger, eyes wide with fury, and he puts his trust in a miserable recluse. Can I silently end matters thus?. Moreover, in days past he enjoined me, and it was only mother that I thought of. Now mother has passed on after her full measure of years; I shall serve the one who understands me."

He went west to P'u-yang in Wey and saw Yen Chung Tzu: "The reason I did not promise myself to you in days past was only because my parent was still here. Now, unhappily, my mother has passed on after her full measure of years. Who is the foe you wish to repay? [*2524*] Allow me to be of service in this!"

Yen Chung Tzu told him everything: "My foe is the Prime Minister of Han, Chia-lei. Chia-lei is also the younger uncle of the Lord of Han. His clansmen are powerful and numerous, and his residence is elaborately guarded. I wanted to have someone assassinate him, but have been unable to do so. If I am fortunate enough that you will not abandon me, Honorable Sir, allow me to give you more chariots, outriders, and stalwart knights as your assistants."

Nieh Cheng said, "The distance between Han and Wey is not far at all. Now you intend to kill the prime minister of another state, and that prime minister is moreover the kinsman of the lord of the state; in such circumstances it will not do to take many men. If you take many men, disagreements are sure to arise; if there are disagreements, there will be loose talk; if there is loose talk, the entire state of Han will be your foe! How could you not be imperiled?" Declining his chariots, outriders, and followers, Nieh Cheng bade farewell and set out unaccompanied.

When he reached Han, using his sword as a walking stick, Han's Prime Minister Chia-lei was sitting in his offices. There were numerous men guarding him, armed with swords and halberds. Nieh Cheng went straight through the gates, climbed the steps, and stabbed and killed Chia-lei, throwing his attendants into complete confusion. Nieh Cheng gave a great shout and struck and killed dozens of them. He then flayed his face, dug out his eyes, chopped himself open, pulled out his intestines, and thus died.

[2525] Han took his corpse and exposed it in the marketplace. They asked who he was and offered a reward, but no one knew. Han then hung up notices offering a reward: "A thousand chin to the one who can name the killer of Prime Minister Chia-lei!" After some time, Han had still not learned who he was.

Nieh Cheng's older sister, Jung, heard that a man had stabbed and killed Han's Prime Minister. The assailant had not been captured [alive] and no one in the state knew his name; his corpse had been exposed in the market place, and notices offering a thousand *chin* [for his identity] had been posted. [His sister] was stricken with anguish: "Is this my younger brother? Alas, Yen Chung Tzu understood him well!"

She set out at once for Han. When she went to the marketplace the dead man was indeed Nieh Cheng. She bent over his corpse and wailed with the utmost grief, then said, "This is the one that [the people of] Shen-ching Hamlet in Chih called Nieh Cheng!"

The crowds passing by in the marketplace all said, "This man brutally murdered our state's Prime Minister and the king has hung up notices offering a thousand *chin* for his name. Haven't you heard this, My Lady? How do you dare come to identify him?"

Jung replied, "I have heard. But the reason why Cheng suffered shame and humiliation, casting himself among the peddlers of the marketplace, was that mother was happily still alive and well, and I had not yet married. When mother departed the world after her full measure of years and I made a home with my husband, Yen Chung Tzu discovered my brother and raised him out of his humiliation and straitened circumstances, making him his friend. His magnanimity was lavish indeed. What could [I] do [to stop him]? A knight will naturally die for the one who understands him! And now, because I am still alive, he has savagely mutilated himself in order to brush over his tracks. How could I let my worthy brother's name be buried forever just because I feared the penalty of death?"

Having dumbfounded the people in Han's marketplace, she gave a great shout of "Heaven!" three times and finally died beside Cheng, stricken with anguish and grief.

[2526] When Chin, Ch'u, Ch'i, and Wey heard this, they all said, "Not only was Cheng a capable man, his sister was also a valorous woman!"

If Cheng had earlier known that his sister had no intention of enduring in silence, thought nothing of having her bones lie unburied, was sure to cross thousands of miles of mountains in order to lay out his fame [before the world], and that older sister and younger brother would both lie exposed in the marketplace of Han, he might not have dared to promise himself to Yen Chung Tzu. As for Yen Chung Tzu, the expression "If you understand a man you can gain a knight" might well be applied to him!

Some 220 years later there was the matter of Ching K'o in Ch'in.

Ching K'o

Ching K'o 荊軻 was a native of Wey.[29] His ancestors were natives of Ch'i. [They] moved to Wey. The natives of Wey referred to him as Excellency Ch'ing 慶.[30] When he went to Yen, the natives of Yen referred to him as him as Excellency Ching 荊. [*2527*] He loved reading and swordplay. He spoke on the arts of politics[31] before Lord Yüan 元 of Wey, but Lord Yüan failed to employ of him. Later, Ch'in attacked Wei, established its Eastern Commandery, and moved the clansmen of Lord Yüan of Wey to Yeh-wang 野王.[32]

---

[29] Major parts of this story occur in a *Chan-kuo ts'e* narrative (9:41b-49a, *SPTK*).

[30] "So-yin" says says that Ch'ing 慶 was a Ch'i surname. Because Ching K'o's family was from Ch'i, the people of Wey called him by his Ch'i surname, Ch'ing. "So-yin" also notes that when Ching K'o's family moved to Wey, they changed their surname to Ching, because its pronunciation was close to their original surname.

[31] Some scholars take the word *shu* 術 here to refer to Ching K'o's swordsmanship.

[32] Near the modern city of Ch'in-yang 沁陽 30 miles northeast of Loyang (T'an Ch'i-hsiang, 1:36).

During his travels, Ching K'o once stopped in Yü-tz'u 榆次.³³ He discussed swords-manship with Kai Nieh 蓋聶.³⁴ Kai Nieh became angry and glared at him. Ching K'o left. Someone spoke of summoning His Excellency Ching again.

Kai Nieh said, "When I discussed swordsmanship with him just now while ago, we had a disagreement and I glared at him. Try and find him, but he should have left. He wouldn't dare to have stayed!" He sent a messenger to [Ching K'o's] host, but His Excellency Ching had already harnessed his horses and left Yü-tz'u. When the messenger returned to report, Kai Nieh said, "Of course he left. I stared him down."

Ching K'o visited the city of Han-tan. Lu Kou-chien 魯句踐 played *liu-po*³⁵ with Ching K'o and contended for lanes [on the board]. Lu Kou-chien became angry and shouted at him. Ching K'o was silent, then fled and never met with him again.³⁶

[2528] Having reached Yen, Ching K'o became fond of a dog butcher and a skilled dulcimer player, Kao Chien-li 高漸離. Ching K'o was fond of wine, and every day he drank with the dog butcher and Kao Chien-li in the marketplace of Yen. After they were well into their cups, Kao Chien-li would strike his dulcimer and Ching K'o would sing in harmony in the middle of the marketplace. They would enjoy themselves, then after a while they would weep, as if there was no one around. Although Ching K'o associated with drinkers, he was by nature recondite and fond of reading. In the [states of] the feudal lords to which he traveled, he established ties to all the worthy, powerful and respected men. When he went to Yen, Venerable T'ien Kuang 田光, a retired knight of Yen, treated him very well. [T'ien] knew that he was not an average fellow.

After some time had passed, it happened that Tan 丹, the Heir of Yen, who had been a hostage in Ch'in, fled back to Yen.³⁷ Tan, the Heir of Yen, had once been a hostage in Chao. Cheng 政, the King of Ch'in, was born in Chao, and in his youth had been very friendly with Tan.³⁸ When Cheng was enthroned as king, Tan was a hostage in Ch'in. But the King of Ch'in treated him badly, thus he bore resentment and fled [Ch'in], returning home. After his return, he sought a way to repay the King of Ch'in, but his state was small and his strength in-sufficient. After this, Ch'in daily sent troops east of the mountains, attacking Ch'i, Ch'u, and the Three Chin, gradually nibbling away at the feudal lords. When they were about to reach Yen, the Lord of Yen and his vassals all feared the arrival of disaster. The Heir Tan was dis-mayed and questioned his tutor Chü Wu 鞠武.

Wu replied, "Ch'in's lands cover the world and its majesty threatens the clans of Han, Wei, and Chao. To the north it has the strongholds of Kan-ch'üan 甘泉 and Ku-k'ou 谷口,³⁹

---

³³ Near the modern city of the same name in Shansi province (T'an Ch'i-hsiang, 1:38)

³⁴ "So-yin" merely reports that Kai and Nieh were his *cognomen* and *praenomen* respectively. This episode does not occur in *Chan-kuo ts'e*.

³⁵ On this game see n. 65 to our translation of Chapter 69 above.

³⁶ This episode, like that immediately above, is not in the *Chan-kuo ts'e*. Derk Bodde suggests that the incidents were added by Ssu-ma Ch'ien to show that Ching K'o, though brave in a righteous cause, was by nature of a gen-tle disposition (Bodde, *Statesman*, p. 24). Preferable is Han Chao-ch'i's explanation that these episodes portray Ching K'o's humility and depth of character (Han Chao-ch'i, p. 52).

³⁷ Yen returned to Yen in 232 B.C. (*Shih chi*, 15:754). Ching K'o's assassination attempt took place five years later in 227 B.C. (*Shih chi*, 15:755). A parallel account of the story which follows may be found in the *Chan-kuo ts'e* (9:41b, *SPTK*).

³⁸ This was the First Emperor of Ch'in. He was born in Han-tan (see *Shih chi*, 6:223). There is only a brief account in *Shih chi* Chapter 6 (6:233) about Ching K'o's attempt to assassinate the King of Ch'in and it contains few details.

³⁹ Kan-ch'üan is a mountain located northwest of modern Ch'un-hua 淳化 county in Shansi; Ku-k'ou is the point at which the Ching 涇 River flows out from the mountains northwest of modern Ching-yang 涇陽 county and

to the south the fertility of the Ching 涇 and Wei 渭 [river valleys]; it wields the wealth of Pa 巴 and Han 漢; tō the right[40] it has the mountains of Lung 隴 and Shu 蜀,[41] and to the left the redoubts of the Pass and Yao 崤 [Mountain].[42] Its people are numerous, its knights fierce, and it has a surplus of weapons and armor. Should an opportunity for its ambitions arise, there would be no place secure south of the Long Wall or north of the Yi 易 River.[43] How could you wish to rub its scales the wrong way[44] just because of your resentment at being humiliated?"

"Then what other way is there?" said Tan.

"Let me withdraw and consider it," he replied.

[2529] After some time had passed,[45] the Ch'in general Fan Wu-chi 樊於期 offended the King of Ch'in and fled to Yen. The Heir took him in and put him in a guesthouse. Chü Wu admonished the Heir:

"This won't do! The King of Ch'in's tyranny and accumulated anger against Yen are enough to chill the heart. How much more will this be so when he hears where General Fan is? This is called "throwing down meat to block a hungry tiger's path." Such a disaster would be beyond remedy. Even if you had Kuan Chung and Yen Ying,[46] they could devise no plans for you! I beg you, Heir, to quickly dispatch General Fan to the Hsiung-nu to eliminate any pretexts [for Ch'in to attack]. I ask you to form an alliance with the Three Chin to the west, join in coalition with Ch'i and Ch'u to the south, and come to terms with the Shan-yü 單于[47] in the north; only then can plans be laid."

The Heir said, "The Grand Tutor's plan is time-consuming. My heart is impatient and, I fear, cannot wait even a moment. But the problem does not only lie in this. General Fan, denied shelter by the entire world, has turned to me. I will never abandon an acquaintance whom I love and pity because I am pressed by mighty Ch'in. The day I settle him among the Hsiung-nu, this is surely the day I die. I hope that you might consider this once more, Grand Tutor."

Chü Wu said, "To risk hazard in pursuit of safety, to invite disaster in pursuit of good fortune, to make shallow plans yet harbor profound resentment, to maintain a newly formed friendship with a single man yet ignore a great threat to the royal family and state, this is what is known as 'feeding resentment and aiding disaster'! If you heat a swan feather over stove coals, it will surely soon disappear. Needless to say [what will happen] if you allow the raptor Ch'in to vent its cruel and resentful anger [on us]. Yen has a Venerable T'ien Kuang 田光, a man of deep wisdom and profound daring. You can consult with him."

northeast of modern Li-ch'üan 禮泉 county, both in Shansi (T'an Ch'i-hsiang, 1:44).

[40] At this time Chinese maps were oriented on South, so that "right" referred to the West.

[41] Although there is a range known as the Lung Mountains on the modern Shensi-Kansu border just north of the Wei River, this more likely refers to the mountains of the two commanderies of Lung-hsi (stretching across modern Kansu) and Shu (north of Chengtu; see T'an Ch'i-hsiang, 1:43-4).

[42] About 15 miles east-southeast of modern San-men-hsia 三門峽 City in Honan (T'an Ch'i-hsiang, 1:23).

[43] The Yi was a small tributary of the Yellow River joining it near modern Hsiung 雄 County about 50 miles south of Peking (T'an Ch'i-hsiang, 1:41). This river and the Long Wall demarcated the state of Yen.

[44] Watson (Qin, p. 169) adds a note that these are "the deadly scales that protrude from the throat of a dragon."

[45] Although there is no other record in the Shih chi of when Fan Wu-ch'i came to Yen, the conversations which follow must have taken place ca. 229 B.C., since Heir Tan tells Ching K'o that the King of Han has already been taken by Ch'in (230 B.C., see Shih chi, 15:754-5), but the state of Chao had not yet fallen (it fell in 228 B.C. according to Shih chi, 15:755). Ho Chien-chang (pp. 1314-5) dates his arrival in 228 B.C.

[46] See their biographies in Shih chi Chapter 62.

[47] The title of the leader of the Hsiung-nu.

The Heir said, "I hope that I might make the acquaintance of the Venerable T'ien through you, Grand Tutor. Is this possible?"

Chü Wu said, "I shall respectfully comply." He left and saw the Venerable T'ien, telling him, "The Heir hopes to consult with you on affairs of state, Venerable Sir."

"I respectfully receive his instructions," said T'ien Kuang, and set out.

[2530] The Heir welcomed him, and, walking backwards, led him [to his place], knelt down, bent over, and dusted off the mat.

When T'ien Kuang had taken his seat and there were no attendants present, the Heir moved off his mat[48] and made his request. "Yen and Ch'in cannot both exist! I hope you might devote your attention to this."

T'ien Kuang said, "Your servant has heard that a black stallion can gallop a thousand *li* in one day in its prime, but a plug can pass it when it is old and feeble. The Heir has heard of my prime and does not realize that my vigor has vanished. Although this is now the case, and I would not dare to allow you to consult me on affairs of state, my friend, Excellency Ching, could be employed in this matter."

The Heir said, "I hope that I might make the acquaintance of His Excellency Ching through you, Venerable Sir. Is this possible?"

T'ien Kuang said, "I shall respectfully comply."

He rose immediately and hastened out. The Heir escorted him to the gate and warned him, "What I have reported to you and what you have spoken of to me are crucial affairs of state, Venerable Sir. I beg you not to let them be known."

T'ien Kuang looked down and laughed. "I shall comply."

Bowed with age, he set off to see His Excellency Ching. "My friendship with you is known to all in the capital of Yen, sir. The Heir having heard of my prime, did not realize my frame is failing and instructed me, saying 'Yen and Ch'in cannot both survive, I would hope that you might devote your attention to this, Venerable Sir.' Presuming upon our friendship, I spoke of you to the Heir, Honorable Sir. I hope that you might call on him at the palace."

"I shall carefully receive your instructions," said Ching K'o.

T'ien Kuang said, "I have heard that the actions of a man of honor do not cause other men to doubt him. Today the Heir told me 'What we have spoken of are crucial affairs of state, I beg you not to let them be known, Venerable Sir.' Thus the Heir doubts me. When his actions cause other men to doubt him, this is no high-principled gallant."

Having decided to stir Ching K'o's resolve by killing himself, T'ien Kuang said, "I hope that you will hasten to call on the Heir, Honorable Sir, and inform him that Kuang has died to ensure his silence." He then slit his throat and died.

[2531] Ching K'o then met with the Heir, told him that T'ien Kuang had died, and conveyed Kuang's words. The Heir knelt and bowed twice, raised on his haunches and and crawled forward on his knees, weeping until snivel ran from his nose. He spoke only after some time. "The reason I warned Venerable T'ien not to speak was because I hoped that our vital plan might thus succeed. Now Venerable T'ien has ensured his silence with death; how could he have thought this was my intention!"

After Ching K'o was seated, the Heir moved off his mat, and knocked his forehead against the ground: "Venerable T'ien, ignoring my lack of worth, has made it possible for us to meet and to speak. It is in this way that Heaven takes pity on Yen and refuses to abandon its orphan."

---

[48] To indicate his respect.

"Ch'in is greedy for profit, its desires can never be satisfied. Not until it has exhausted the world's lands, enslaved the world's kings will it be satisfied. Ch'in has already captured the King of Han and appropriated every inch of his land. It has raised troops and attacked Ch'u in the south and confronted Chao in the north. Wang Chien 王翦[49] is leading a host of hundreds of thousands to the Chang 漳 [River] and Yeh 鄴,[50] and Li Hsin 李信[51] has invaded through T'ai-yüan 太原 and Yün-chung 雲中.[52] Chao is unable to resist Ch'in, and is sure to submit as a vassal. When it submits as a vassal, disaster is sure to strike Yen. And when Chao has gone under, Yen will stand next in line for disaster!

"Yen is small and weak and has frequently been hard pressed to defend itself. Now I calculate that mobilizing the entire state we would still be unable to withstand Ch'in; the feudal lords have submitted to Ch'in and none dare to join an alliance. By my own calculations I foolishly suggested that if we can obtain the world's bravest knight for a mission to Ch'in, and tempt Ch'in with great profit, the King of Ch'in, in his greed, is sure to desire this. If we are then able to seize the King of Ch'in and have him return all of the lands he seized from the feudal lords, as Ts'ao Mo did with Duke Huan of Ch'i, this would be best of all. If this is not possible, he might seize the opportunity to kill him. Ch'in's great generals are commanding troops abroad and when strife arises at home, ruler and vassals will doubt each other, allowing the feudal lords to join in alliance and ensuring the defeat of Ch'in. This is my greatest hope, but I do not know to whom I might entrust such a mission. May I ask that you consider this, Excellency Ching?"

After a long pause Ching K'o said, "This is a vital matter of state. Your servant is worn out and inferior and he fears he would be inadequate to take on such a task."

The Heir moved forward and knocked his forehead on the ground, imploring him not to decline, and in the end he agreed. He then made Excellency Ching a Senior Excellency[53] and lodged him in the upper lodge. The Heir appeared daily at his gate, supplied him with T'ai-lao,[54] offering other rare objects, and frequently presenting carriages, horses and and beautiful women, pandering to Ching K'o's every wish, all in order to meet his expectations.[55]

[2532] After some time, Ching K'o still showed no signs of setting out. Ch'in's general Wang Chien defeated Chao, captured its king, and seized every inch of his entire territory, leading his troops north, seizing land up to the southern border of Yen. Heir Tan was afraid and implored Ching K'o: "The troops of Ch'in will cross the Yi River any day. And when they do, even though I might wish to continue accompanying you, Honorable Sir, I will not be able to."

Ching K'o said, "Even if you had not spoken, Heir, your servant would have requested an audience with you." If I set off today, without a token of trust, I will be unable to

---

[49] See his biography in *Shih chi* Chapter 73. This campaign took place in 228 B.C. (*Shih chi*, 15:755).

[50] The Chang, which flowed along what is today the Hopei-Shansi border, probably marked the westernmost holdings of Chao at this time. Following the river course downstream would provide a route through the T'ai-hang Range into the North China Plain about 20 miles south of the Chao capital at Han-tan. Yeh was a county downriver in modern Hopei on the south side of the Chang (see T'an Ch'i-hsiang, 1:36 and 38). Wang Chien's forces were therefore striking along Chao's southern flank.

[51] Li Hsin is also mentioned in *Shih chi* Chapter 73, but there the focus is on his pursuit of Heir Tan *after* Ching K'o's assassination attempt failed (see *Shih chi*, 73:2339-41). See also Ma Fei-pai, pp. 248-9.

[52] This was a thrust against the northern reaches of Chao: T'ai-yüan was a commandery northeast of the modern city of the same name in Shansi and Yün-chung the commandery to the north and east of where the Yellow River bends west in northern Shansi (T'an Ch'i-hsiang, 1:37-8).

[53] *Shang-ch'ing* 上卿.

[54] See n. 14 to our translation of *Shih chi* Chapter 83 above.

[55] As "So-yin" notes, *Yen Tan-tzu* 燕丹子 (3:2b-3b, *SPPY*), a text of relatively late date, provides a lively description of the lengths to which the Heir went to please Ching K'o.

approach [the King of] Ch'in. The King of Ch'in has offered a thousand *chin* of gold and a manor of ten-thousand households for General Fan. If I could obtain General Fan's head and a map of Yen's Tu-k'ang 督亢[56] to offer to the King of Ch'in, the King of Ch'in is sure to be happy to see me and I will have my opportunity to repay you."

The Heir said, "General Fan has came to me in his time of trouble. I could not bear to offend my elder over my own private affairs. I urge you to reconsider, Honorable Sir!"

"Ching K'o knew that the Heir could not bear [to accept his plan], and saw Fan Wu-ch'i in private. "Ch'in's treatment of you may be called harsh indeed, General!" "Your parents and kinsmen have all been killed or enslaved. Now I hear he would buy your head for a thousand *chin* of gold and a manor of ten-thousand households. What will you do?"

Fan Wu-ch'i raised his face to the sky, gave a deep sigh, and with tears running down his face, said, "Each time I think of it, the pain cuts to my marrow! But I have no plan."

Ching K'o said, "If I could free the state of Yen from its peril and repay your foe with a single sentence, how would that be, General?"

Fan Wu-ch'i moved forward and said, "What is it?"

Ching K'o said, "I wish to have the General's head to offer to the King of Ch'in. The King of Ch'in is sure to be pleased and grant me an audience. With my left hand I will seize his sleeve, [*2533*] with my right hand I will stab him in the chest, thus the General's foe will be repaid and Yen's humiliation will be erased! Do you have such resolve, General?"

Fan Wu-ch'i bared one shoulder, gripped his wrist, and stepped forward. "Day and night I have gnashed my teeth and seared my heart for such a plan. At last I have been able to hear of it." Then he slit his throat.

When the Heir heard of it, he rushed in, leaned over the corpse, and wailed with the utmost sorrow. Since nothing more could be done, they put Fan Wu-ch'i's head in a box and sealed it. Earlier he had ordered a search for the sharpest dagger that could be found, and had purchased one from a man of Chao named Hsü Fu-jen 徐夫人 for a hundred *chin*. He ordered his artisans to coat the blade with poison and try it out on some men; though the thrust drew hardly enough blood to stain the robe of the victim, every one of the men dropped dead on the spot. The prince then began to make final preparations for sending Master Ching on his mission. There was a brave man of Yen named Ch'in Wu-yang 秦舞陽[57] who at the age of thirteen had killed someone, and was so fierce that no one dared even to look at him crossly. This man the prince ordered to act as a second to Ching K'o.

There was a man Ching K'o was waiting for, intending to have him go along. Though this person lived at a distance and had not yet arrived, [Ching K'o] made preparations for him in their journey.[58] Some time passed, but Ching K'o still did not set off. Thinking that Ching K'o had been delayed and suspecting that he had changed his mind, the Heir again went to ask [Ching K'o]: "There is no time left. Does His Excellency Ching still have his mind set on this? I would request to be allowed to send Ch'in Wu-yang on ahead."

Ching K'o was angered and roared back at the Heir: "What is this about the Heir sending [Ch'in Wu-yang ahead]? One who sets off without considering his return is a whelp!

[56] The traditional commentaries offer a number of speculations about the location of Tu-k'ang. T'an Ch'i-hsiang (1:41), however, believes it refers to the territory south and west of modern Peking, stretching from east of modern Yi 易 County to Ku-an 固安 County.

[57] Also known as 秦武陽. Ch'in was a rather unusual *cognomen* at this time and Wu-yang (as in this variant) the secondary capital of the state of Yen (T'an Ch'i-hsiang, 1:41).

[58] Here we follow the Chung-hua punctuation. This passage could also be read: "This person lived at a distance and had not yet arrived. [The Heir] made preparations for their journey." Who this person was is never determined.

Moreover, the reason I am delayed in carrying a single dagger into the unfathomably mighty Ch'in is I am waiting for my colleague who will go along. Now, since Your Majesty thinks I have been delayed, I beg permission to take my leave."

Then he set out.

[2534] The Heir and those of his retainers who knew of [Ching Ko's] affairs all wore white robes and caps to see them off. When they reached the Yi River, after sacrificing and choosing their route, Kao Chien-li plucked his zither and Ching K'o accompanied him in a song in the mournful key of F.[59] Tears streamed from the down the faces of all the knights. When they came forward [Ching K'o] sang for them:

> The wind cries soughs and sighs,
> The Yi River is cold.
> Once we hearties leave
> We'll never return to our fold!

Shifting to the key of A he became more energetic and the eyes of the knights glared and their hair bristled beneath their caps. At this time Ching K'o mounted his carriage and left, off, never once looking back.

When he arrived in Ch'in he presented gifts worth a thousand *chin* to the Counselor of the Palace,[60] Meng Chia 蒙嘉, one of the king's favorite vassals. Meng Chia [then] spoke first on his behalf to the King of Ch'in: "The King of Yen, trembling before the majesty of the Great King, has not dared to raise troops to oppose our armies, but wishes to to be allowed to sacrifice at and maintain the temple of his ancestors, the former kings [of Yen] by offering his state as a vassal to Ch'in, placing it among the ranks of the other feudal lords and presenting tribute and labor service like your commanderies and counties. In his trepidation he has not dared to speak in person, but has respectfully cut off Fang Wu-ch'i's head, and with it presents a map of the Tu-k'ang region in Yen. After [these things] were sealed in boxes, the King of Yen came forth and bowed respectfully in his courtyard, instructing his envoy to report [these things] to the Great King. He [now] awaits your orders, Great King."

When the King of Ch'in heard this, he was greatly pleased, put on his court robes and had nine-levels of officials[61] arrayed to receive the envoy of Yen in the Hsien-yang 咸陽 Palace. Ching K'o carried aloft the box with Fan Wu-ch'i's head, while Ch'in Wu-yang bore the case with the map case, advancing one after the other. When they reached the steps of the throne, Ch'in Wu-yang turned pale and began to tremble, and the assembled vassals felt it strange. Ching K'o looked at Wu-yang and smiled, then stepped forward to apologize: "This rustic fellow from the northern barbarian tribes has never seen the Son of Heaven, thus he is quaking. I ask that you, Great King, be a little tolerant of him and allow him to fulfill his mission here before you."

The king said to Ching K'o: "Get the map Wu-yang is carrying!" When Ching K'o took the map and presented it [to the king], the king unrolled map and at the end the dagger appeared. [*2535*] Accordingly Ching K'o seized the king's sleeve with his left hand, and with his right he picked up the dagger and stabbed at his chest.[62] Before [the dagger] reached [its goal], the King of Ch'in was startled and pulled himself to his feet, so that his sleeve tore

---

[59] Following Wang Li-ch'i's (86:1955n.) reading of *pien-chih* 變徵.

[60] *Chung shu-tzu* 中庶子.

[61] On the several interpretations of *chiu-pin* 九賓 see Wang Li-ch'i, 86:1955n.

[62] Han Chao-ch'i (p. 254) believes there is a passage missing here in which Ching K'o threatens the King of Ch'in and offers him conditions (in an action similar to Ts'ao Mo); see also n. 64 below.

away. He tried to draw his sword, but since it was too long, he [could only] grasp its scabbard. Since he was hurried at the time and the sword fit tightly in [its scabbard],[63] he was not able to draw it immediately. As Ching K'o pursued the King of Ch'in, the king went around a pillar and ran off. The assembled vassals were all startled, since this was sudden and unexpected, so that they completely lost their composure.

According to Ch'in law, none of the assembled vassals who waited upon the king in the upper hall were allowed to carry even the smallest weapon. All the palace attendants who carried arms were arrayed below the hall, and without a royal command they were not able to ascend. In the press of the moment the king had no chance to command the soldiers below and for this reason Ching K'o was then able to pursue him. And in their hurried alarm, [the assembled vassals] had nothing with which to attack Ching K'o, so they joined to strike him with their bare fists. At this time the attending physician, Hsia Wu-chü 夏無且, threw the bag of medicine he was carrying at Ching K'o. The king had just circled the pillar and in his hurried alarm did not know what to do. His attendants then said: "Put the sword on your back!" When had put it on his back, then he drew it and used it to attack Ching K'o, cutting open his left thigh. Ching K'o collapsed, then raised his dagger and threw it at the King of Ch'in, but it missed, hitting the bronze pillar. The King of Ch'in attacked Ching K'o again and Ching K'o was wounded eight times. Ching K'o, realizing that his attempt had failed, leaned against a pillar and laughed; his legs spread before him, he cursed [the king]. "The reason my attempt failed was because I tried without killing you to exact an agreement that I could take back to the Heir!"[64]   At this the king's attendants came forward to kill Ching K'o, [but] the king sulked for some time. After a little while he selected who had won merit [in this] and who among the assembled vassals those present to reward, but found them all wanting, then presented Hsia Wu-chü with two hundred *yi* of gold, saying "Wu-chü loves me, so he threw his bad of medicine at Ching K'o."

[2536] After this, the King of Ch'in, in a great rage, sent reinforcements to Chao and commanded Wang Chien's army to attack Yen with them. In the tenth month, they seized Chi-ch'eng 薊城.[65] Hsi 喜, the King of Yen (r. 254-222 B.C.), and his Heir, Tan, led their finest troops east and took refuge in Liao-tung 遼東.[66] Ch'in's general Li Hsin vigorously pursued and attacked the King of Yen. Chia 嘉, the King of Tai 代,[67] sent a letter to Hsi, King of Yen. It read:

> The reason that Ch'in pursues you so vigorously, Yen, is because of Heir Tan. If Your Majesty kills Tan and presents [his head] to the King of Ch'in, the King of Ch'in is sure to release you, and, if you are fortunate, your altars of soil and grain may continue to receive their blood sacrifices.[68]

Afterwards, when Li Hsin was in pursuit of Tan, Tan hid in the Yen River 衍水.[69] The King of Yen sent an envoy to cut off Heir Tan's head, intending to present it to Ch'in.[70]

---

[63] Following Wang Li-ch'i (86:1956n.).

[64] There is an inconsistency here. Above when Ching K'o is explaining his plan to Fan Wu-ch'i and when he attacks the King of Ch'in, he gives no indication that he has any plan except to execute the king.

[65] Yen's capital located near modern Peking (T'an Ch'i-hsiang, 1:41).

[66] A commandery stretching across what is now eastern Liao-ning and northwestern North Korea (T'an Ch'i-hsiang, 1:42).

[67] After Wang Chien took Han-tan in 228 B.C. and captured Ch'ien 遷, the King of Chao (r. 235-228 B.C.), the Noble Scion Chia set himself up at "the King of Tai" (see *Shih chi,* 15:755).

[68] *Chan-kuo ts'e* does not cite this letter, but simply refers to the King of Tai's plan (9:48b, *SPTK*).

[69] Now called the T'ai-tzu River 太子河, it flows northeast from Liao-tung Bay through modern Liao-yang 遼陽

Ch'in sent in more troops to attack him. Five years later [222 B.C.], Ch'in finally destroyed Yen and captured Hsi, the King of Yen.

The next year [221 B.C.], Ch'in conquered the world and established the title of "Emperor." Ch'in then began to pursue the retainers of Heir Tan and Ching K'o and they all fled. Kao Chien-li[71] changed his name and became [*2537*] a barkeep for someone, hiding in Sung-tzu 宋子.[72] After some time he was sick of his work and whenever he heard a retainer play the dulcimer in the hall of their house, he would linger, unable to leave, instead frequently muttering "He's got that part good, that part bad." The attendants told their master, "That barkeep knows music. He criticizes [the musicians]!" The lady of the house[73] had him come forward and play the dulcimer. Everyone seated there declared him excellent, and he was granted some wine. And Kao Li-chien, mindful of his long hiding and the endless poverty that lay ahead, retired, took out his dulcimer and his fine clothing from his bag, dressed himself and came forward. The seated guests were astounded and treated him as their equal, and he was made Senior Retainer.[74] They had him play the dulcimer and sing and every one of the guests wept before departing. Sung-tzu took turns hosting him and his renown reached the First Emperor of Ch'in. The First Emperor of Ch'in summoned him to an audience and someone recognized him and said, "It's Kao Chien-li!" The Emperor of Ch'in was taken with his skill at playing the dulcimer, granted him a great pardon, and had him blinded with acid. he had him play the dulcimer and all declared him excellent. [The Emperor] gradually drew closer and closer to him. Kao Chien-li put a piece of lead in his dulcimer. When he was presented again and able to draw closer, he lifted his dulcimer and struck at the Emperor of Ch'in, but missed him. [The Emperor] promptly executed Kao Chien-li and for the rest of his life never again allowed the men of the feudal states to draw closer to him.

[2538] Lu Kou-chien having heard of Ching K'o's [attempt] to assassinate the King of Ch'in, said privately, "Alas, what a shame he did not study carefully the method of assassination with a sword! How profound has been my failure to understand men! When I shouted at him before, he must have thought I was not [his kind of] man!"

His Honor the Grand Scribe says: "When our generation speaks of Ching K'o, they claim that the fate of Heir Tan was [a matter of] "heaven raining grain and horses growing horns."[75] This is going too far! They also say that Ching K'o wounded the King of Ch'in, which is equally false. At first Kung-sun Chi-kung 公孫季功[76] and Scholar Tung 董[77] studied with Hsia Wu-chü and all these events became known to them.

From Ts'ao Mo down to Ching K'o, some of these five men were successful and some of them not in their righteous endeavors. But it is perfectly clear that they had all determined upon the deed. They did not sell their goals short. How could it be perverse that their names should be handed down to later generations?"

(T'an Ch'i-hsiang, 1:42).

[70] *Shih chi,* 6:233 says Wang Chieh actually obtain the Heir's head.

[71] *Chan-kuo ts'e* here tells us simply in a single line that Kao Chien-li had audience with the Ch'in emperor and tried to kill him with his dulcimer (9:48b, *SPTK*).

[72] About 20 miles southeast of modern Shih-chia-chuang 石家庄 in Hopei (T'an Ch'i-hsiang, 1:38).

[73] Following "So-yin."

[74] *Shang-k'o* 上客.

[75] According to the story as recorded in *Yen Tan-tzu* (1:1a, *SPPY*), when Heir Tan was a hostage in Ch'in, the King of Ch'in told him he could only return home when "crows' heads turned white." When this strange phenomena actually occurred, the Heir was allowed to leave.

[76] This person is otherwise unidentified.

[77] I.e., Tung Chung-shu 董仲舒 (180-115 B.C.) with whom Ssu-ma Ch'ien probably studied.

TRANSLATOR'S NOTE

The "Assassin-Retainers" is the second of what are usually called *lei-chuan* 類傳 (classified biographies) in the *Shih chi,* which deal with several people sharing similar backgrounds, usually chronologically (the first is *Shih chi* Chapter 67, "Memoir of Confucius's Disciples"). Although this is one of the most famous chapters of the *Shih chi,* Ssu-ma Ch'ien received a great deal of criticism for his decision to include these men in his history, particularly from his famous successor Pan Ku, author of *Han shu,* who felt that these men were little more than hired thugs and murderers. Judging from the final sentence in his comments, he may have anticipated this. But this opinion was obviously not shared by the poets, dramatists, and authors of later generations, however, who found much inspiration in the fidelity and courage of Yü Jang, Ching K'o, and company.

Although the subject matter is obviously assassins, the theme--or at least one of the themes--of this collection of narratives is that a vassal will do his utmost for a lord who understands his worth. This is evident in all the accounts, but especially so in those of Yü Jang, Nieh Cheng, and Ching K'o. As Nieh Cheng's elder sister, Jung, put it, "A gentleman will always be willing to die for someone who recognizes his true worth!"

Derk Bodde (*Statesman,* pp. 41-2) and several Chinese scholars before him have noted that it is unlikely that the persons mentioned as witnesses to Ching K'o's attempt on The First Emperor's life could have lived long enough to discuss it with Ssu-ma Ch'ien. It may thus be possible that this piece comes from Ssu-ma Ch'ien's father, Ssu-ma T'an.

BIBLIOGRAPHY

I. Translations

Bodde, Derk. *Statesman, Patriot and General in Ancient China.* New Haven: American Oriental Society, 1940, pp. 23-38 (Ching K'o).

Dolby, William and John Scott, trans. *Sima Qian, War-Lords, Translated with Twelve Other Stories from His Historical Records.* Edinburgh: Southside, 1974, pp. 131-159.

Fukushima Yoshihio 福島吉彦, trans. *Shiki retsuden* 史記列傳. Rpt. Tokyo: Chikuma Shobō, 1986 (1969), pp. 175-186.

Liu, James J. Y. *The Chinese Knight-Errant.* Chicago: University of Chicago Press, 1967, pp. 23-38 (all but introduction and comments).

Watson, Burton. *Records of the Grand Historian: Qin Dynasty.* Hong Kong and New York: The Research Centre for Translation, The Chinese University of Hong Kong and Columbia University Press, 1993, pp. 167-178.

Yang Hsien-yi and Gladys Yang. *Records of the Historian.* Rpt. Hong Kong: The Commercial Press, 1985, pp. 385-402.

II. Studies

Bodde, *op. cit.*

McCraw, David. "Background for the Biography of Ching K'o," in *Chinese Social Relationships: The Ideal vs. the Real.* Honolulu: Center for Chinese Studies, 1988, pp. 21-35.

Li Ssu, Memoir 27

[87:2539] Li Ssu 李斯 was a native of Shang-ts'ai 上蔡[1] in Ch'u. In his youth, when he served as a legal officer in his commandery,[2] he saw that rats which lived in the privy of the officers' quarters ate filth and were close to men and dogs, who often frightened or startled them. When Ssu entered the granary, he observed that rats there ate the stored grain, lived under the great room and knew nothing of the worry of men and dogs. At this, Li Ssu sighed and said, "A man's worthiness or unworthiness, as with rats, rests merely with where he situates himself."

Li Ssu then studied the arts of emperors and kings with His Excellency Hsün 荀.[3] After completing his studies, judging that the King of Ch'u was not worth serving, that the Six States[4] were all weak, and that none of them could provide an opportunity to establish his merit, he decided to go west into Ch'in. He bade farewell to His Excellency Hsün: "I have heard that when one obtains opportunity he cannot be slothful. Now that the "Ten Thousand Chariots"[5] are vying with each other, the travelling [advisors] are masters of affairs. The King of Ch'in now desires to swallow up the world and rule with the title of Emperor. This is the time for commoners to gallop forth and the season of the travelling advisors. To be situated in a mean position and lay no plans, this is catching a deer just to look at the meat,[6] having a human face, but only being able to walk with difficulty. Thus there is no greater shame than a mean position, nor deeper grief than destitution. To remain for long in a mean position or state of destitution, criticizing the world [*2540*] and detesting profit, giving oneself over to Non-activity[7]--such are not the sentiments of a gentleman. Thus I will go west to advise the King of Ch'in."

Arriving in Ch'in just after King Chuang-hsiang 莊襄 (r. 249-247 B.C.) had died, Li Ssu then sought to become a Houseman of Lü Pu-wei 呂不韋, Marquis Wen-hsin 文信 and Prime Minister of Ch'in. [Lü] Pu-wei thought him worthy and appointed him a Gentleman.[8] Li Ssu was thus able to present his advice.

He advised the King of Ch'in [the future First Emperor]: "One who waits on others casts aside his opportunities. One who accomplishes great deeds does so through seizing flaws and chinks and concluding matters without mercy. Long ago, when Duke Mu 穆 of Ch'in (r. 659-621 B.C.) was Hegemon, he never went east to swallow up the Six States.[9] Why was

---

[1] Shang-ts'ai was a district capital located slightly southwest of modern Shang-ts'ai County in Honan (T'an Ch'i-hsiang, 2:7).

[2] The "So-yin" edition apparently read *hsiang* 鄉 "district" for "commandery" here. It also cites another annotator, Liu Po-chuang (seventh century A.D.) who says that Li Ssu had charge of the official documents of the district. Wang Shu-min (87:2617) reviews the variant readings and concludes that "district" is the better reading.

[3] On Hsün Ch'ing or Hsün Tzu, see his biography in *Shih chi* Chapter 73. For discussions on chronological questions related to Li Ssu, see Takigawa (87:2) and Wang Shu-min (87:2618).

[4] I.e., the states of Ch'i, Ch'u, Han, Chao, Wei and Yen.

[5] This metonymic expression originally referred to the *kings* of states large enough to maintain ten-thousand chariots and their teams. During the Warring States Period, because many feudal lords proclaimed themselves "kings" the expression was extended to include any feudal leader of a state.

[6] We read *ch'in* 禽 as *ch'in* 擒 following Wang Shu-min (87:2619).

[7] *Wu-wei* 無為 or "Non-activity" is a basic principle of Taoist philosophy.

[8] *Lang* 郎.

[9] This usage of "Six States" is anachronistic, since there were many more than six states east of Ch'in during Duke Mu's reign. The intent is to refer to the area subsequently held by the Six States during the Warring States Era.

this? The feudal lords were still numerous and the moral force of Chou had not yet decayed. Hence the Five Hegemons[10] arose one after another, but each in his turn respected the House of Chou. Since the time of Duke Hsiao 孝 of Ch'in (r. 361-338 B.C.), the House of Chou has declined, the feudal lords have annexed one another, east of the Pass has became the Six States, and for six generations Ch'in has followed through on its victories to control the feudal lords.[11] Today the feudal lords have submitted to Ch'in as if they were its commanderies and counties. Ch'in's might and your talent, Great King, like brushing off the top of a kitchen stove, are sufficient to destroy the feudal lords, to accomplish the imperial enterprise, and to bring unity to the world. This is the chance of ten-thousand generations! If you are negligent now and do not seize it at once, the feudal lords will regain their might and join together in alliance; then even though you were as worthy as The Huang Ti, you could not annex them."

The King of Ch'in then appointed Li Ssu Chief of Scribes,[12] listened to his stratagems, and secretly sent strategists, carrying gold and jade, to travel about advising the feudal lords. When the famous knights of the feudal lords could be bribed by material goods, [Ch'in's strategists] gained their friendship with rich gifts; when [the knights] were unwilling, [*2541*] they assassinated them with sharp swords. After [employing these] stratagems to alienate rulers and vassals, the King of Ch'in then sent his able generals following after them. The King of Ch'in appointed Li Ssu a Foreign Excellency.

At this time, a native of [the state of] Han named Cheng Kuo 鄭國 had come as an agent into Ch'in, [but] because he constructed a drainage and irrigation canal his status was discovered after a short while.[13] The clansmen of the House of Ch'in and the great vassals all said to the King of Ch'in: "Most of the men of the feudal lords who come to serve Ch'in seek to advise or spy on Ch'in for their own rulers. We ask that you expel all foreigners."[14] Li Ssu was also proposed as one of those to be expelled.

[Li] Ssu thus submitted a memorial which read:

I have heard that the officials propose to expel foreigners. In my humble opinion this would be a mistake. Long ago, when Duke Mu [of Ch'in] sought knights, he won Yu Yü 由余 from the Jung in the west,[15] obtained Pai-li Hsi 百里奚 from Yüan

---

[10] See n. 12 to our translation of *Shih chi* Chapter 68 above.

[11] These "six generations" of Ch'in's rulers were the six reigns of Duke Hsiao (361-338 B.C.), King Hui-wen 惠文 (337-311 B.C.), King Wu 武 (310-307 B.C.), King Chao-hsiang 昭襄 (306-251 B.C.), King Hsiao-wen 孝文 (250 B.C.), and King Chuang-hsiang (249-247 B.C.).

[12] *Chang-shih* 長史.

[13] This event is described in detail on *Shih chi*, 29:1408. According to the description there, Cheng Kuo was a hydraulic engineer sent by the state of Han to advise Ch'in on creating an irrigation system. Han's intention, however, was to weaken Ch'in by engaging its men and resources in this project. When the work was half completed, the ruse was discovered. The King of Ch'in wished to put Cheng Kuo to death, but Cheng noted that although the plan was at first something detrimental to Ch'in, its completion would also benefit her. When finished, it was called Cheng Kuo's Canal and was located approximately 25 miles north of modern Sian, between the Ching River and the Lo River (according to Tan Ch'i-hsiang, 2:5-6). See also Bodde, "Ch'in," pg. 44. and Yen Ch'ung-nien 閻崇年, "Ch'in Shih-huang yü Cheng Kuo chü" 秦始皇與鄭國渠, *K'o-hsüeh shih-yen* 科學實驗, 10(1975), 39-40.

[14] There seems to be an error here. According to *Shih chi*, 6:230, the matter of the irrigation canal took place in 246 B.C., but foreigners were not expelled until 237 B.C. Thus Cheng Kuo's actions could not have been the reason behind their expulsion. *Shih chi* 85:2512-13 states that foreigners were expelled because of the rebellious activities of Lao Ai and his cronies, primarily men from outside Ch'in.

[15] According to *Shih chi* 5:192, Yu Yü, whose ancestor was a native of the state of Chin who fled to the Jung, was sent by the King of the Jung tribes to assess Ch'in's strength in 626 B.C. Duke Mu thought him worthy. After he returned to the Jung, Yu Yü found that the King of the Jung had begun to indulge himself with beauties sent

宛 in the east,[16] [*2542*] welcomed Chien Shu 蹇叔 from the state of Sung,[17] and attracted P'ei Pao 丕豹[18] and Kung-sun Chih 公孫支[19] from Chin. None of these five gentlemen were born in Ch'in, but Duke Mu used them, swallowed up twenty states, and won hegemony over the Western Jung.

Duke Hsiao used the laws of Shang Yang 商鞅[20] to modify usages and change customs. The people thereby became prosperous and multiplied. The state thereby became wealthy and powerful. The families of the one-hundred cognomens served him with pleasure and the feudal lords submitted to him in person. [Duke Hsiao] captured the forces of Ch'u and Wei and occupied a territory of one-thousand *li* [on a side]. [Thus Ch'in] has remained powerful until the present day.

King Hui 惠 used the stratagems of Chang Yi 張儀[21] to take the territory of San-ch'uan 三川[22] and swallow Pa and Shu in the west.[23] He acquired Shang-chün 上郡 [Commandery][24] in the north and obtained Han-chung 漢中 [Commandery][25] in the south, embraced the Nine Yi,[26] and controlled Yen 鄢 and Ying 郢.[27] In the east he held the redoubts of Ch'eng-kao 成皋[28] and annexed fertile territory. He broke the alliance of the Six States, made them face westward and serve Ch'in, and his merit has extended down to the present time.

When King Chao obtained Fan Sui 范睢,[29] he dismissed the Marquis of Jang 穰 and expelled the Lord of Hua-yang 華陽.[30] He strengthened the ruling house and

him by Duke Mu of Ch'in and would no longer listen to his advice. Thus Yu Yü left the Jung for Duke Mu, helping Ch'in to deter the Jung in 623 B.C.

[16] A city in Ch'u near present Nan-yang 南陽 in Honan (T'an Ch'i-hsiang, 1:45).

On Pai-li Hsi, a native of Yüan, see our translation of *Shih chi*, 5:186ff.

[17] Chien Shu, a friend of Po-li Hsi, lived in Sung. He was welcomed from Sung in 655 B.C. on the advice of Po-li Hsi and subsequently became a Grand Master of Ch'in (see also *Shih chi*, 5:186).

[18] P'ei Pao was a son of P'ei Cheng 丕鄭, a Grand Master of Chin. Pao fled from Chin to Ch'in in 651 B.C. when his father was killed by the Duke of Chin; he became a general and led Ch'in troops in an attack on Chin in 645 B.C. (see *Shih chi* 5:187).

[19] Kung-sun Chih was a Grand Master and an advisor to Duke Mu (see *Shih chi* 5:188 and Wang Li-ch'i, *Jen-piao*, p. 261). He was apparently a native of Ch'in, but had been sojourning in Chin when he returned to his home state (see "Cheng-yi").

[20] See his biography in *Shih chi* Chapter 68.

[21] See the account of Chang Yi advising King Hui on *Shih chi*, 70:2282-83.

[22] San-ch'uan (Three Rivers) was a commandery seated near modern Loyang in Honan; it included lands north to the Yellow River, west to the upper reaches of the Lo 洛 River, south to the headwaters of the Yi 伊, and east to modern Chengchow (T'an Ch'i-hsiang, 2:6).

This seizure actually occurred in 308 B.C. (see *Shih chi*, 5:209).

[23] The taking of Pa and Shu, roughly covering modern Szechwan, was accomplished by the Ch'in general, Ssu-ma Ts'o 司馬錯 in 316 B.C. (*Shih chi*, 5:207). According to *Shih chi*, 15:736 Ssu-ma Tso put down a revolt in Shu in 301 B.C.

[24] See *Shih chi* 5:206. The commandery was located along the West bank of the Yellow River in modern Shensi (T'an Ch'i-hsiang, 2:6).

[25] According to *Shih chi*, 5:207, it was taken in 312 B.C. It ran from the modern city of Hsün-yang 旬陽 in Shensi to near modern Yi-ch'eng 宜城 in Hupei (T'an Ch'i-hsiang, 1:45).

[26] "So-yin" tells us the Nine Yi were nine non-Chinese tribes in Ch'u at that time, but we read it as reference to the area in which these tribes lived in following the general tenor of this passage as a description of the virtual conquest of Ch'u--from Han-chung through the area known as Nine Yi (T'an Ch'i-hsiang, 1:45) to the capitals of Ch'u (see also note immediately following).

[27] See n. 70 to our translation of *Shih chi* Chapter 66 above.

[28] Located near the modern city of Ssu-shui 汜水 in Honan (T'an Ch'i-hsiang, 2:16). This was a strategic place in ancient China near the south bank of the Yellow River about forty miles east of Loyang on the land route connecting lands to the east with Ch'in.

[29] See his biography in *Shih chi* Chapter 79.

sealed private doors.[31] He nibbled away at the feudal lords and enabled Ch'in to accomplish the imperial enterprise.

These four lords[32] all succeeded through using foreigners. Looking at it thus, how have foreigners betrayed Ch'in? If in the past these four lords had rejected the foreigners instead of accepting them, had ignored the knights instead of using them, it would have left the state without the realities of wealth and profit and Ch'in without a reputation for might and greatness.

[2543] Your Majesty has obtained jade from the K'un 昆 Mountains[33] and possesses the treasures of Sui 隨 and Ho 和,[34] wears the Bright-moon Pearl[35] and girds the T'ai-o 太阿 Sword.[36] You ride the horse Hsien-li 纖離,[37] fly flags decorated with feathers of the green phoenix, and set up drums made from the skin of the "divine alligator."[38] Ch'in does not produce one of these treasures, yet Your Majesty enjoys them. Why is this?

If only things produced by the state of Ch'in could be used, then jade rings which glow in the dark would not ornament the court and rhinoceros horn and ivory objects would not serve as your baubles. The women of the states of Cheng and Wey[39] would not fill the rear palaces, and excellent horses such as the *chüeh-t'i* 駃騠[40] would not occupy the outer stables. Copper and tin of the South would not be used, and pigments of cinnabar and bice from Western Shu would not be employed.

If that which can be used to ornament the rear palaces, to fill the lower ranks, to please the heart and mind, and to delight the ear and the eye must be produced in Ch'in to be acceptable, then these hairpins inlaid with Yüan 宛 pearls,[41] earrings with suspended elliptic pearls, clothing made with fine, plain O 阿 silk[42] and decorations made of embroidery and brocade would not be offered before you,[43] and the women of

---

[30] This story is told on *Shih chi,* 79:2404ff. and *Shih chi,* 72:2329.

[31] *Ssu-men* 私門, "private doors," refers *pars pro toto* to the homes of the noble families and relatives-by-marriage of the royal house.

[32] See their biographies in *Shih chi* Chapters 75-78.

[33] A famous site of jade production in ancient China, these mountains are today known as the K'un-lun 崑崙 and are located in Sinkiang (T'an Ch'i-hsiang, 1:31).

[34] Two of the greatest treasures of antiquity. The Sui treasure was a great pearl that had been presented to a Marquis of Sui (a small state in modern Sui County in Hupei) in an unknown time by a large snake in return for the marquis nursing its wounds (see Kao Yu's 高誘 [*fl.* 205-212 A.D.] commentary in the *Huai-nan Tzu,* 6:3b, *SPPY*).

The Ho treasure was a large piece of uncut jade which Pien Ho 卞和, a man from Ch'u, discovered and tried to present to two successive kings of his home state. Both believed he was trying to deceive them and each cut off one of his feet. Their successor, King Wen 文 (r. 689-675 B.C.) had faith in him and had the piece cut so that the quality of the stone appeared (see *Han Fei Tzu* 4:10b, *SPPY*).

[35] This is generally equated with the "treasure of Sui" mentioned just above; see n. 69 to our translation of *Shih chi* Chapter 83.

[36] One of three swords made for the King of Ch'u by two famous smiths during the Spring and Autumn era, Ou Yeh Tzu 歐冶子 and Kan Chiang 干將 of the state of Wu (see *Yüeh-chüeh shu,* "Pao-chien" 寶劍, 13:1b-2b, *SPPY*).

[37] One of the six famous horses of antiquity (see *Hsün Tzu,* 17:9a, *SPPY*).

[38] *Alligator sinensis,* the skin of which was used to cover drums.

[39] Generally noted for their musical talents and beauty.

[40] A fine breed of horse reared by the Northern Jung tribes (see Kao Yu's note in *Huai-nan Tzu,* 11:14b, *SPPY*).

[41] A city located near modern Nan-yang 南陽 in Honan (T'an Ch'i-hsiang, 1:29). The tradition of a famous pearl from Yüan seems to have been lost and some commentators (see "So-yin") believe this was the "treasure of Sui" mentioned above.

[42] This type of silk originated in O, located in Shantung province, northeast of modern Yang-ku 陽谷 (T'an Ch'i-hsiang, 1:39).

Chao, adapting to custom elegantly, beautiful and ravishing, shy and retiring, would not stand beside you.

Beating on jugs, tapping on jars, plucking the zither, [*2544*] and striking thigh bones while singing and crying "Woo! Woo!" to delight the ear, this is the true music of Ch'in. The [styles called] "Cheng," "Wey," "Sang-chien 桑間," "Shao 昭," "Yü 虞," "Wu 武" and "Hsiang 象" are the music of other states.[44] But today [the people of Ch'in] have abandoned beating on jugs and tapping on jars and have taken up the "Cheng" and "Wey." They refuse to pluck the zither and accept the "Shao" and "Yü." Why is this so? Simply to enjoy what is before them, to suit their taste. That is all.

But now it is not so in selecting men. Without asking whether they are suitable or not, without considering whether they are wrong or right, those who are not from Ch'in are to be sent away and those who are foreigners to be expelled. In this case, that given weight is feminine charms and music or pearls and jade, and that treated lightly is men. This is not the path by which you may overstride the lands within the seas or rule over the feudal lords.

[2545] I have heard it said that if the land is extensive, then grain will be abundant. If the state is large, then the people will be numerous. If the army is mighty, then the knights will be courageous. Thus Mount T'ai does not decline a clod of earth, and so is able to achieve its greatness. The rivers and seas do not choose among the tiny streams, and so are able to achieve their depth. A king does not send off the common people, and so is able to manifest his virtue. For this reason, when the land was not divided into four quarters and the people not divided into different states, the four seasons were filled with good things, and the spiritual beings bestowed blessings; this was the reason that the Five Emperors[45] and Three Kings[46] had no equals.

But now by abandoning the black-haired commoners, you aid enemy states; by sending away the foreigners you bring achievements to the feudal lords, cause the knights of the world to retreat and not dare to go west, cause their feet to be hobbled, and not to enter Ch'in. This is called "lending weapons to outlaws and offering provisions to bandits."[47]

There are many things which though not produced in Ch'in are still valuable. There are a host of knights who though not born in Ch'in still wish to be loyal [to it]. If foreigners are now expelled, thereby aiding enemy states, and your populace is reduced, thereby increasing your foes', then you would debilitate yourself at home and create more resentment with the feudal lords abroad. To seek in this way to free your state from danger will never do.

---

[43] According to the *Dai Kanwa jiten* (Gloss 41599.41, p. 12342), these four lines also occurred in the "Ch'in ts'e" 秦策 section of the *Chan-kuo ts'e* (entry repeated in *Chung-wen Ta-tzu-tien*, Gloss 42518.507, p. 15364). However, neither Takigawa nor Ōgawa mention this reference and the passage does not occur among those reconstructed sections of the *Chan-kuo ts'e* in Chu Tsu-keng (3:1744-1789). It is either a reference to a section of an edition held only in Japan, or an error (which the *Chung-wen Ta-tzu-tien* editors perpetuated). The following paragraph is also cited (*Dai Kanwa jiten*, Gloss 12466.39, p. 4979) as being from the "Ch'in ts'e."

[44] Cheng and Wey were states from which the noted female musicians mentioned just above came; Sang-chien refers to a place located in the southern part of modern P'u-yang 濮陽 County in Honan which had formerly been held jointly by Cheng and Wei. Shao and Yü were tunes supposedly transmitted from the time of Emperor Shun, Wu and Hsiang from the time of King Wu of the Chou dynasty (see Wang Li-ch'i, 87:1970n.).

[45] See the account of these rulers in our translation of *Shih chi* Chapter 1 above.

[46] The three kings were Yü, founder of the Hsia dynasty, T'ang 湯, founder of the Shang, and Kings Wen 文 and Wu 武 who jointly founded the Chou and are thus considered "the third king."

[47] Fan Sui, speaking to the King of Ch'in, uses this maxim in *Chan-kuo ts'e* (3:47a, *SPTK*).

[2546] The King of Ch'in then revoked the decree expelling foreigners, restored Li Ssu's position,[48] and eventually adopted his schemes. [His] position reached Commandant of Justice. After more than twenty years, [Ch'in] finally united the world,[49] honored its ruler as the August Emperor and made Li Ssu Chancellor. [The Emperor] leveled the city walls of the commanderies and counties and melted their weapons to show that they would not be used again.[50] He caused Ch'in to be without a single foot of land in fief, and did not invest his sons and younger brothers as kings, nor the meritorious vassals as feudal lords, to free posterity from the troubles of warfare.

In the thirty-fourth year of the First Emperor [213 B.C.] a feast was given in his palace at Hsien-yang 咸陽.[51] Chou Ch'ing-ch'en 周青臣,[52] the Supervisor of the Erudites,[53] and others extolled the First Emperor's majesty and virtue.

Ch'un-yü Yüeh 淳于越, a native of Ch'i, presented his admonition:[54] "I have learned that Yin and Chou, ruling as kings for more than one-thousand years, enfeoffed their sons, brothers and meritorious ministers to branch out as support to the court itself. Now Your Majesty possesses the lands within the seas, yet your sons and brothers are all ordinary men. If there were suddenly vassals like T'ien Ch'ang 田常[55] or the Six Ministers,[56] without support or aid [from your sons and brothers], who would there be to rescue you?[57] I have never heard that an affair can exist for long without following antiquity. Now Ch'ing-ch'en and these others increase the magnitude of your error still further by flattering you to your face. These are no loyal vassals."

The First Emperor sent his proposal to the Chancellor. The Chancellor thought his advice mistaken and rejected his explanations. He then submitted a memorial, saying:

> In ancient times when the world was unorganized and disordered, no one was able to unify it; thus the feudal lords all arose. In discussions, they censured the present by invoking the past and confused the truth by embellishing empty expressions. Men valued private teachings and based on these criticized what their superiors had established. Now Your Majesty has unified the world, discriminated between white and black,[58] and founded a single authority. Yet there are those with private teachings who join in criticizing the imperial decrees laying out laws and instructions. Upon hearing an ordinance has been issued, each immediately debates it according to his

[48] "Chi-chieh" cites a no longer extant passage from Liu Hsiang's *Hsin hsü* which notes that Li Ssu had been proposed as one of those to be expelled. After his memorial convinced the King of Ch'in, he was able to return to court.

[49] Bodde (*Unifier*, p. 21) and Wang Shu-min (87:2625, both point out that actually it was only seventeen years from the order for the expulsion of aliens (237 B.C.) to the final unification of the empire in 221 B.C.

[50] See *Shih chi*, 6:239.

[51] The Ch'in capital located northeast of the modern city of Sian in Shensi (T'an Ch'i-hsiang, 2:6).

[52] On this debate between Chou Ch'ing-ch'en and Ch'un-yü Yüeh see our translation of *Shih chi* 6:254 above.

[53] *Po-shih p'u-yeh* 博士僕射.

[54] This speech can also be found in *Shih Chi* 6.

[55] T'ien Ch'ang was a Grand Master of Ch'i. He killed Duke Chien 簡 of Ch'i (r. 484-481 B.C.) and usurped power (see *Shih chi*, 46:1883-4).

[56] The Six Ministers refers to the six noble clans of Chin during the Spring and Autumn period. They were Fan 范, Chung-hang 中行, Chih 智, Han 韓, Wei 魏 and Chao 趙. By sharing power they weakened the House of Chin. Eventually, only three clans, Han, Wei and Chao, emerged the power struggle to become feudal lords (403 B.C.).

[57] As Wang Shu-min (87:2626) points out, the text here seems corrupt; we follow his suggested emendation to read 六卿之臣, 無輔弼 for 六卿之患, 臣無輔弼. This emendation also approximates the version of this memorial on *Shih chi*, 6:254

[58] I.e., built a standard of right and wrong.

private teachings. Within they criticize it in their hearts and without they debate it in the streets. They make their reputations through criticizing their ruler, exalt themselves through their heterodox thought, and lead the assembled inferiors in devising slanders. If such a situation is not prohibited, then the ruler's authority will decline above and factions will form below. It would be appropriate to prohibit this. Your servant requests that all who own literary works, the *Book of Odes*, the *Book of Documents*, and the writings of the hundred schools, discard them as if they were waste. Those who have not discarded them within thirty days after the order is issued should be tattooed and sentenced to hard labor.[59] The writings which need not be discarded are those on medicine and pharmacology, divination by scapulimancy or plant stalks, and horticulture. Those who wish to study should take the functionaries as their teachers.[60]

The First Emperor approved his proposal. The *Book of Odes*, the *Book of Documents*, and the writings of the hundred schools were confiscated to keep the populace ignorant and to prevent the world from using the past to criticize the present. Clarification of the legal system and formulation of the laws and ordinances all came from the First Emperor. He unified the writing system and built separate palaces and villas throughout the world.

In the next year he again made a tour of inspection and drove out the barbarians of the four quarters. [Li] Ssu contributed much to this.

[2547] [Li] Ssu's eldest son, Yu 由, became the Governor of San-ch'uan. [Li Ssu's] sons all married Ch'in princesses while his daughters were all married to Ch'in princes. When the Governor of San-ch'uan, Li Yu, asked for leave to return to Hsien-yang, Li Ssu held a feast in his home. The heads of the hundred offices all appeared to offer gifts, and their chariots and horsemen in the courtyard behind his front gate numbered in the thousands. Li Ssu sighed deeply: "Alas! I have heard from His Excellency Hsün that 'Things should avoid flourishing too grandly!'[61] I was only a commoner in plain cloth from Shang-ts'ai, a black-haired one from the back alleys. His Highness did not realize my mediocrity and so advanced me to this post. Today, not one of the posts of his vassals is higher than mine; this can be called the acme of wealth and status. But when things reach their acme they decline. I do not know where I shall unhitch my horses."

In the tenth month of the thirty-seventh year of the First Emperor [211 B.C][62] his entourage left [the capital] to tour [Mount] K'uai-chi 會稽[63] and the seacoast, then went north, arriving at Lang-ya 琅邪 [Commandery].[64] Li Ssu, the Chancellor,[65] and Chao Kao 趙高,[66]

---

[59] *Ch'eng-tan* 城旦 may originally have referred to those convicts who worked until dawn on the Great Wall (see "Chi-chieh"), but seems to have become another general term for "hard labor" (a multi-year sentence) by this time (see also Hsü Chia-lu, p. 702 and n. 239 to our translation of *Shih chi* Chapter 6.

[60] There is a similar speech on *Shih chi*, 6:254-5.

[61] This saying is not in the extant text of the *Hsün Tzu*. There is, however, a similar saying in the *Mo Tzu* (1:1a, *SPPY*), suggesting that this idea was common during this period.

[62] Although the thirty-seventh year as a whole corresponds generally to 210 B.C., the tenth month was actually still in 211 B.C., because under the Ch'in Calendar the tenth month of the Hsia Calendar became the first month of the year. Ssu-ma Ch'ien calls it "tenth" because he depicts Ch'in time in terms of the Han Calendar (i.e., the T'ai-ch'u 太初 Reign Period [104-101 B.C.] Calendar), promulgated by Emperor Wu in 104 B.C., which also began the year in the same month as the Hsia Calendar. This explains why two paragraphs below the "seventh month of this year" can logically follow a depiction of the events of the "tenth month." See also n. 269 to our translation of *Shih chi* Chapter 6 above.

[63] See n. 56 to our translation of Chapter 66 above.

[64] See n. 170 to our translation of Chapter 6 above.

[65] According to *Shih chi*, 6:260, Li Ssu was the Chancellor of the Left.

[66] Chao was a eunuch who became extremely powerful during the reign of the Second Emperor of Ch'in. Although he has no biography in the *Shih chi*,, there are additional accounts of his life in chapters 6 and 88.

Prefect of the Palace Chariots,[67] concurrently Acting Prefect of the Department of the Imperial Seals and Tallies,[68] accompanied him.

The First Emperor had more than twenty sons. Fu-su 扶蘇,[69] the eldest son, because he had frankly admonished His Highness several times, was sent by His Highness to supervise military affairs in Shang-chün [Commandery] with Meng T'ien 蒙恬[70] as his commander. A younger son, Hu-hai 胡亥,[71] was the favorite. When he asked to accompany [the Emperor on tour], His Highness allowed it. None of the other sons accompanied [him].

[2548] In the seventh month of this year, when the First Emperor arrived at Sha-ch'iu 沙丘 (Sandy Hillock),[72] he became very ill. He commanded Chao Kao to write a letter to present to the Noble Scion Fu-su:

> Entrust the troops to Meng T'ien, come back to Hsien-yang to meet my funeral cortege and bury me!

When the letter was already sealed but not yet handed to the messenger, the First Emperor passed away. The letter and the imperial seals were both in Chao Kao's hands. Only [the Emperor's] son, Hu-hai, the Chancellor Li Ssu, Chao Kao, and five or six favored eunuchs knew that the First Emperor had passed away. None of the other officials knew. Li Ssu kept it secret because the Emperor had passed away outside [of the capital] and there was no true Heir. They put the body in the Heated and Cooled Carriage,[73] and the hundred officials presented petitions and offered food as before; the eunuchs approved all the petitions inside the Heated and Cooled Carriage [as if the Emperor were still alive].

Chao Kao thus kept the letter and the imperial seals, and said to the Noble Scion Hu-hai, "When His Highness passed away, he left only a letter for his eldest son, without issuing an edict to enfeoff his sons as kings. When the eldest son arrives, he will immediately be enthroned as emperor, while you, sir, will be left without an inch of territory. What's to be done?"

Hu-hai said, "This is only natural. I have heard that the perspicuous lord understands his vassals and the perspicuous father understands his sons. Since my father departed this life without enfeoffing his sons, what is there to be said?"

Chao Kao said, "Not so. Now whether the world's power can be preserved or lost depends only upon you, Sir, myself, and the Chancellor. I wish you to consider it. Furthermore, when it comes to enslaving men or being enslaved by men, controlling men or being controlled by men, how can the two be discussed in the same breath?"

Hu-hai said, "To remove [*2549*] an elder brother and establish a younger brother, this is unrighteous. To refuse a father's edict out of fear of death, this is unfilial. With an ability that is meager and a talent that is petty, to manage only by depending on others' merit, this is incompetent. These three run counter to virtue; the world will not submit [to me], I myself will probably be put in danger, and the blood sacrifices at our altars of soil and grain will cease."

---

[67] *Chung ch'e-fu ling* 中車府令.

[68] *Hsing fu-hsi ling* 行符璽令.

[69] See *Shih chi*, 6:258ff. and n. 260 to our translation of that chapter.

[70] See his biography in *Shih chi* Chapter 88.

[71] On Hu-hai see *Shih chi*, 6:260ff. and n. 272 to our translation of that chapter.

[72] Located on the west bank of the Yellow River about 5 miles northeast of modern P'ing-hsiang 平鄉 in Hopei (T'an Ch'i-hsiang, 2:38).

[73] A carriage which could control the temperature inside it by opening or closing windows (see "Chi-chieh").

Kao said, "Your servant has heard that when T'ang and Wu killed their rulers, the world proclaimed them righteous. This cannot be counted disloyal. The Lord of Wey killed his father, but the state of Wey honored his virtue and Confucius recorded it. This cannot be counted unfilial. In great matters one does not bother about petty formalities. With great virtue one does not observe basic courtesies. Towns and villages each have their own customs and the hundred offices their different tasks. Thus if one pays attention to what is small but forgets what is great, he is sure to be troubled later. If one is hesitant and uncertain, he is sure to have regrets later. If one is decisive and dares to act, then even the ghosts and spirits will shun him and he will gain success later. I hope that you might follow this."

Hu-hai sighed deeply: "Now the Grand Procession[74] has not set out and the obsequies have not come to an end. How can we bother the Chancellor with this matter?"

Chao Kao said, "The time! The time! There is not enough time to make plans! Even if we bundled up provisions and jumped on our horses, I am afraid we would still be too late!"

After Hu-hai had approved of Kao's words, Kao said, "I am afraid that the matter can not be successful unless we consult with the Chancellor. Allow your servant to consult with the Chancellor for you."

After this Kao told Ssu, the Chancellor, "When His Highness passed away, he left a letter for his eldest son [ordering him] to meet the funeral cortege in Hsien-yang and to be established as the successor. The letter has not been sent and, as His Highness has now passed away, nobody knows about it. The letter which was left for the eldest son and the imperial seals and tallies are all in Hu-hai's hands. The determination of the heir will come out of the mouths of Your Lordship and myself. What is to be done in this matter?"

[Li] Ssu replied, "How can you speak words which would ruin the state? This is not for vassals to discuss!"

Kao said, "If Your Lordship evaluated yourself, could you compare to Meng T'ien in ability? Could you compare to Meng T'ien in greatness of merit? Could you compare to Meng T'ien in planning for the future without error? Could you compare to Meng T'ien in incurring resentment nowhere in the world? Could you compare to Meng T'ien in the length of time you have held the trust of the eldest son?"

[Li] Ssu replied, "In all these five, I do not measure up to Meng T'ien. But why, sir, do you criticize me so sharply?"

Kao said, "I was originally but a servant of eunuchs. Fortunately, through my skill in writing with brush and scraper I entered the Ch'in palace where I have managed affairs for more than twenty years. I never saw a Chancellor or a meritorious subject whom Ch'in had dismissed retain his fief down to the second generation. Eventually they all were condemned to death.

"Your lordship knows all of the emperor's twenty-odd sons. The eldest son is resolute and [*2550*] steadfast, martial and courageous. He inspires trust in the people and instills spirit in the knights.[75] When he takes the throne, he is sure to employ Meng T'ien as Chancellor. It is all too obvious that Your Lordship will in the end lose the seal of a ranked marquis and return to your hometown. Since I received the edict to tutor Hu-hai and had him study legal matters for several years, I have never seen him commit an error. His kindness and sincerity are profound and immense. He disdains wealth, but honors knights. He is discriminating in mind, but slow in speech. He follows the rites to the fullest and respects

---

[74] Although *Ta-hsing* 大行, "The Grand Procession," can be used to indicate an emperor who has recently died but has no posthumous title yet, it refers here to the funeral cortege of the First Emperor.

[75] Wang Shu-min (87:2630) reads *shih* 事 "affairs" for *shih* 士 "knights." We take both *hsin* 信 and *fen* 奮 in a causative sense.

knights. Among the sons of [the House of] Ch'in, none measures up to this one. He would serve well as successor. Consider this, Your Lordship, and decide."

[Li] Ssu said, "Return to your post, Sir. I will obey the ruler's edict and accept the will of Heaven. What considerations are there to decide?"

Kao said, "Security may be endangered and the endangered secured. If he cannot determine security and danger, why honor the sage?"

[Li] Ssu said, "I was a commoner from the back alleys of Shang-ts'ai, yet was fortunate enough to be raised up by His Highness as Chancellor and enfeoffed as a ranking marquis while my sons and grandsons all obtained exalted posts and high emoluments. Thus [His Highness] wished to entrust me, his vassal, with the state's preservation and stability. How could I betray him? A loyal vassal would not trust to luck to avoid death, but a filial son should not put himself in danger through working too hard. A vassal attends to his duty, that is all. I hope you will not mention this again, Sir, lest it involve me in an offense."

Kao said, "Perhaps you have heard that the sage shifts about without norms. He takes advantage of change and follows the times. When he sees a branch, he knows the root; when he looks in a direction, he recognizes where it will lead. [All] things surely have this [rule of change]. How could they have an unchanging rule? For the moment, the world's balance and fate hangs from Hu-hai['s hand]; I can achieve my ambitions through him. Moreover, it is called misleading if one outside regulates one inside, rebellion if an inferior regulates a superior.[76] Thus plants and flowers wither with the descent of autumn dew, and all things become active with the stirring of [spring] water.[77] This is an inevitable outcome. Why is Your Lordship so slow in recognizing this?

[Li] Ssu said, "I have heard that when Chin changed its Heir they knew no stability for three generations;[78] when Duke Huan 桓 of Ch'i (685-643 B.C.) contested the throne with his brother, [his brother] was killed and his corpse exposed;[79] when Chow killed his kinsmen and refused to heed those who admonished him, his capital was reduced to ruins and his altars of soil and grain endangered.[80] These three defied Heaven, and their ancestral temples had no more blood sacrifices. I am no better than these other men; how am I be qualified to participate in this plot?"

[Chao] Kao said, "When superiors and inferiors are in harmony, they can endure for a long time; when inside and outside [the palace] are consistent, affairs will not be contradictory. If Your Lordship listens to my plan, then you will long hold the title of marquis, [your descendants] will designate themselves "The Lonely One"[81] generation after generation, and you are sure to have the longevity of [Wang Tzu] Ch'iao 王子喬 or [Ch'ih] Sung Tzu 赤松子,[82] and the wisdom of Confucius or Mo Tzu.[83] If you now renounce [this plan] and do

---

[76] Here Chao Kao suggests that since Fu-shu remained outside while Hu-hai was inside this was the best time to effect their plans.

[77] These two clauses explain the importance of taking chances.

[78] This refers to Duke Hsien 獻 of Chin (r. 676-651 B.C.) who forced his rightful Heir, Shen Sheng 申生, to kill himself and then established Hsi Ch'i 奚齊, the son of his favorite concubine, Li Chi 驪姬, as Heir (656 B.C.). This threw Chin into confusion for two decades (until 636 B.C.), when Chung Erh 重耳, another son of Duke Hsien, returned to rule the state (see *Shih chi,* 39:1645-6 for details).

[79] On the death of Duke Huan's brother, the Noble Scion Chiu 糾, see *Shih chi,* 32:1485-6.

[80] Chow, the last king of the Shang dynasty, killed his uncle Pi-kan 比干 and put the Viscount of Chi 箕 in jail because of their admonitions; see our translation of *Shih chi,* 3:107ff.

[81] A term used by kings and nobles to refer to themselves when speaking to their subjects. In other words, Li Ssu's descendants will maintain their noble status.

[82] Two immortals: see their biographies in *Lieh-hsien chuan* 列賢傳 (A:1a and A:12a-b, *Lin-lang Mi-shih ts'ung-shu* 琳琅秘室叢書 [in *Pai-pu ts'ung-shu chi-ch'eng* 百部叢書集成]).

not follow it, such disasters will overtake your descendants that it is enough to chill the heart. The skilled can make fortune out of disaster. How will Your Lordship handle matters?"

Li Ssu looked up to heaven and lamented, then wept and sighed deeply: "Alas! That I find myself in a disordered age! Since I have been unable to die [in the line of duty], to whom can I entrust my fate?"

After this [Li] Ssu heeded [Chao] Kao.

[Chao] Kao then reported to Hu-hai: "Your servant asks to notify the Chancellor of the Heir's perspicuous order. How could Chancellor [Li] Ssu dare disobey it!"

[2551] After this they planned things together, pretending to have received an edict from the First Emperor which ordered the Chancellor to establish the Emperor's son Hu-hai as the Heir.[84] They wrote another letter to present to Fu-su which said:

> "We are travelling on a tour of inspection around the world, praying and sacrificing to famous mountains and various spirits in order to prolong Our life. At present Fu-su and General Meng T'ien have garrisoned the border with a command of several hundred thousand troops for more than ten years. They are still unable to advance and more forward [our borders], but instead have lost many officers and soldiers without the merit of [gaining] a single inch of territory. Instead Fu-su has repeatedly sent Us letters frankly slandering what We have done. He harbors rancor day and night because he is unable to leave his post and return [to the capital] as Heir. As a son, Fu-su is unfilial. Grant him a sword and let him decide how to kill himself![85] General Meng T'ien has stayed outside [the capital] with Fu-su, yet has not rectified his behavior. He should have known of Fu-su's plot. As a vassal he is not loyal. Grant him death! Entrust the troops to the Lieutenant General, Wang Li!"

They sealed the letter with the imperial seal and sent Hu-hai's retainer to take the letter and present it to Fu-su in Shang-chün [Commandery].

When the envoy arrived, he unsealed the letter; Fu-su wept, went into his inner apartments and prepared to kill himself. Meng T'ien stopped Fu-su: "His Majesty is staying outside [the capital] and has not yet established an Heir; he sent me, his vassal, to command a host of 300,000 defending the border, and you, Noble Scion, as the Supervisor. This is the world's weightiest responsibility! Now with the arrival of a single envoy you are about to kill yourself. How do you know this is not a trick? I beg you to request confirmation. After you request confirmation, it will still not be too late to die."

The envoy pressed them several times. By nature, Fu-su was humane; he told Meng T'ien, "When a father grants his son death, how can [the son] request confirmation?" Then he killed himself.

Meng T'ien refused to die; the envoy delivered him to a legal officer who imprisoned him at Yang-chou 陽周.[86]

---

[83] This speech seems to be formulaic. In *Shih chi* Chapter 79 (2424), for example, Ts'ai Tse makes a very similar argument to Fan Sui.

There is a brief notice of Mo Tzu concluding *Shih chi* Chapter 74.

[84] There is a textual problem here. Wang Shu-min (87:2632) believe that the word "Chancellor" is an interpolation, the corrected text reading simply "They received an edict from the First Emperor to establish Hu-hai as the Heir."

[85] Allowing one to commit suicide had two advantages: the time and means of death could be chosen and no family members would be implicated.

[86] A county northwest of modern Tzu-ch'ang 子長 County in Shensi (Wang Li-ch'i, 87:1975n).

[2552] When the envoy returned and reported, Hu-hai, [Li] Ssu and [Chao] Kao were overjoyed. Having arrived at Hsien-yang and proclaimed the [Emperor's] death, the Heir was established as the Second Generation Emperor.[87] He made Chao Kao his Palace Prefect of Gentlemen and put him in charge of affairs.

When the Second Emperor was at leisure, he summoned [Chao] Kao to discuss affairs, and told him: "Man's life in this world is like galloping a six-horse carriage past a crack in a wall.[88] Now that I command the world, I desire to experience all that pleases the eyes and ears, to exhaust all that brings joy to the heart and mind, yet still secure my ancestral temples, please the ten-thousand families, and possess the world to the end of my natural span of years. Is there a way to do this?"

[Chao] Kao replied, "This is what only a worthy ruler can carry out, but it is forbidden to a muddled or confused ruler. Your servant asks permission to speak out; he does not dare to avoid execution at the chopping block, but hopes that Your Majesty might pay heed to [his words]. All the noble scions and great vassals have their suspicions about the plans we hatched at Sha-ch'iu. The noble scions are all Your Majesty's elder brothers[89] while the great vassals were appointed by the Late Emperor. Now Your Majesty is newly enthroned and these fellows are dissatisfied and refuse to submit. I am afraid there may be trouble.

"Moreover, Meng T'ien has already died, but Meng Yi 蒙毅[90] still commands troops stationed outside. Your servant trembles and fears only that there will be unnatural ends [for us]! How then could Your Majesty enjoy such pleasures?"

The Second Emperor asked, "What's to be done?"

Chao Kao said, "Make the laws more severe and the penalties harsher, have those who have committed crimes implicate each other in their punishment and include their entire clans. Exterminate the great vassals and distance yourself from your flesh and blood. Enrich the poor and honor the humble. Do away with all the old ministers of the Late Emperor and appoint in their place those whom you trust or feel close to. If you can do this, then Your Majesty will win all their hidden favor, your worries will be removed and treacherous plots cut short. All the officials will be blessed by your kindness, covered with your lavish favors, and Your Majesty can recline peacefully on a high pillow, giving free reign to your desires and favoring whatever you enjoy. No plan could be more outstanding."

The Second Emperor approved of [Chao] Kao's speech, and rewrote the laws. After this, whenever one of the assembled vassals or noble scions committed a crime, he was immediately turned over to [Chao] Kao to be interrogated and judged by him. He killed the great vassals such as Meng Yi and others. Twelve of the Noble Scions were killed and their bodies exposed in the marketplace at Hsien-yang. Ten of the princesses were dismembered at Tu. Their property was confiscated by the central government and the number of those who were implicated [in these crimes] was countless.

[2553] The Noble Scion Kao 高[91] wanted to flee, but he was afraid that he would implicate his clan and thus submitted a memorial saying, "When the Late Emperor was in good health, your servant was granted food upon entering [the palace] and allowed to ride in a chariot when leaving. The clothing of the Imperial Wardrobe your servant was able to obtain by

---

[87] This is based on the First Emperor's instructions regarding the titles of his descendants. From here on we will refer to him simply by the standard "Second Emperor."

[88] This is a variation of a maxim found in a number of pre-Ch'in and Han works (see Wang Shu-min, 87:2633).

[89] Some scholars believe that Hu-hai was not the youngest son (see Wang Shu-min 87:2633).

[90] Meng Yi was the younger brother of Meng T'ien (see also Ma Fei-pai, p. 251). According to *Shih chi,* 88:2569, Meng T'ien was still incarcerated at Yang-chou when Meng Yi was killed.

[91] A son of the First Emperor (see Ma Fei-pai, p. 126).

grant. The treasured horses of the Central Stable, your servant was able to obtain by grant. Your servant should have followed the First Emperor in death, but he was unable to. As a son, he has been unfilial. As a vassal, he has been disloyal. A disloyal person has no name on which to stand in the world. Your servant begs that he may follow [the Late Emperor] in death and be buried at the foot of Mount Li 酈.[92] He only asks that Your Highness should pity him!"

When the memorial was submitted, Hu-hai was delighted. He summoned Chao Kao and showed it to him, saying, "Is this what can be called 'a plight'?"

Chao Kao said, "When a vassal is constantly beset by thoughts of death, what trouble can he cause?"

Hu-hai approved his memorial and granted 100,000 coins for his burial.

The laws and ordinances, penalties and punishments were daily made more severe. Each of the assembled vassals felt himself in danger and there were many who wanted to revolt. [The Second Emperor] decided to build the O-p'ang 阿房 Palace[93] and lay out the Straight Road[94] and the Speedway.[95] Taxes became more burdensome and conscription and the corvee were without fixed terms. At this the garrison soldiers of Ch'u, Ch'en Sheng 陳勝[96] and Wu Kuang 吳廣[97] and their followers, rebelled, rising in revolt East of the Mount.[98] Men of ability stood up one after another, established themselves as marquises or kings, and revolted against Ch'in. When their troops arrived at Hung-men 鴻門, they were driven back.[99]

Li Ssu wanted to request a secret audience to admonish [the Second Emperor] several times, but could not get his permission.[100]

Then the Second Emperor reproved Li Ssu:[101] "I have some opinions of my own and also something which I heard from Han [Fei] Tzu; [Han Tzu] said[102] 'When Yao held the world, his hall was [only] three-ch'ih high.[103] His oak rafters were not stripped [of bark] and

---

[92] The location of the mausoleum of the First Emperor, about 25 miles northeast of modern Sian in Shensi (T'an Ch'i-hsiang, 2:6).

[93] See n. 244 to our translation of Chapter 6 above.

[94] On this road, which ran nearly 500 miles north from Yün-yang 雲陽 to Ch'in's northern marches, see Shih Nien-hai 史念海, "Ch'in Shih-huang chih-tao yi-chi te t'an-so" 秦始皇直道遺跡的探索, Wen-wu, 1975.10, 44-54. Shih presents several excellent maps and photos of the road (see also Shih chi Chapter 88).

[95] This was the system of roads which were 50 pu in width, the center 30 pu marked off by a line of trees for the exclusive use of the emperor, which eventually ran to the eastern and southern outer reaches of the empire (see Wang Li-ch'i, 6:125n., Takigawa, 6:32, and Chavannes, 2:138, n. 3). See also Bodde, "Ch'in," p. 101 and Ch'ü Shou-yüeh 曲守約, "Chung-kuo ku-tai te tao-lu" 中國古代的道路, BIHP, 2(1960), 143-52.

[96] The best account of Ch'en Sheng's rebellion can be found in Shih chi Chapter 48 (see also Ma Fei-pai, pp. 391-7).

[97] On Wu's role in the rebellion, see Shih chi, 48:1949-57 and Ma Fei-pai, pp. 391-7.

[98] Referring to Mount Hsiao 殽, located about 15 miles east southeast of modern San-men-hsia 三門峽 in western Honan (T'an Ch'i-hsiang, 1:35). Mount Hsiao and the Han-ku 函谷 Pass (often referred to as "the Pass"), about 20 miles southwest (ibid.) were the major natural barriers of the time, lands to the east being referred to as "beyond the Pass" or "east of the Mount."

[99] A slope located near modern Hsiang Wang Ying 項王營 (King Hsiang's Camp) just east of Li-yi 麗邑 (which became Hsin-feng 新豐 in Han times; see T'an Ch'i-hsiang, 2:6 and 15 as well as Wang Li-ch'i, 7:171n.). The rebels were defeated there by the Ch'in general Chang Han 章邯 (see Shih chi, 6 and 48 for details).

[100] According to Shih chi, 6:271, Li Ssu, the Chancellor of the Right, Feng Ch'ü-chi 馮去疾, and General Feng Chieh 馮劫 together admonished the emperor at this time.

[101] This speech, although it begins similarly with the reference to Han Fei Tzu's words, differs markedly from that cited on Shih chi, 6:271.

[102] This quotation approximates the text in the current version of the Han Fei Tzu (19:1b, SPPY).

[103] According to the Li chi Cheng chu 禮記鄭注 (7:15a, SPPY) such a platform for a king or emperor should be

his [roof's] thatch was not trimmed even. Even an inn for travellers could not be more frugal than this! In winter he wore a deerskin coat and in summer arrowroot cloth. His food was coarse grain and his broth made of weeds and leaves of pulse. He ate from a clay bowl and drank from a clay cup. Even that which maintained a gatekeeper could not be shabbier than this!'

"'When Yü dug through the Lung-men 龍門 [Mountains] and penetrated to Ta-hsia 大夏, he dredged the Nine Rivers and made dikes along the various bends of the Ho, releasing the accumulated waters and leading them into the sea.[104] His thighs were without fat and the hair had worn off his shanks. His hands and feet were callused and his face blackened. In the midst of this he died away from his home and was buried on K'uai-chi [Mountain].[105] Even the labors of a slave or captive could not be more arduous than this!'"

"If this is so, can it be that the reason men honor the one who possesses the world is that they want to mortify their frames and exhaust their spirits, rest their bodies in traveler's inns, feed themselves with a gatekeeper's provisions, or undertake with their own hands the labors of slaves? These are what the unworthy labor at, not what the worthy strive for. When a worthy man possesses the world, he directs his actions to one end: using the world as it strikes his fancy! This is why men honor the one who possesses the world. A man who is called a worthy man must be one who can secure the world and govern the ten-thousand people. Now if he cannot profit himself, how can he govern the world?

"Thus I wish to gratify my ambitions and expand my desires, and as long as I may, enjoy [*2554*] a world without trouble. How is this to be done?"

At that time Li Ssu's son, Yu, was the Governor of San-ch'uan. Wu Kuang and his followers, a group of bandits, swept over the lands to their west. When they passed by, he had been unable to stop them. After Chang Han had crushed and driven off the troops of Wu Kuang and his followers,[106] envoys went one after another to San-ch'uan to investigate whether he had any involvement [with the bandits]. They rebuked [Li Ssu] for occupying the post of the Three Masters[107] yet allowing the bandits to act like this. Li Ssu was fearful and he valued his noble rank and salary highly. Not knowing how to extricate himself, he pandered to the Second Emperor's whims, hoping to be treated lightly. He replied with a memorial:

> A worthy ruler must be one who is able to preserve [the ruler's] way while employing the art of calling men to account.[108] If the ruler can call men to account, then the vassal will not dare obey the ruler without doing his utmost. If the distinction between vassal and ruler is drawn, and the duty of superior and inferior is clarified, then no one in the world, worthy or unworthy, will dare to obey his ruler without doing his utmost to complete his tasks. In this way the ruler alone will control the world and

---

nine-*ch'ih* high.

[104] Located north of modern Ho-chin 河津 County in Shansi on the west (modern Shensi) side of the Yellow River (T'an Ch'i-hsiang, 1:35). Ta-hsia indicates the region in south-central Shansi. On the Nine Rivers see n. 112 to our translation of *Shih chi* Chapter 2, the chapter which generally traces Yü's efforts to regulate the flood waters.

[105] See n. 56 to our translation of *Shih chi* Chapter 66 above.

[106] This must have taken place in 208 B.C. (see *Shih chi,* 15:758).

[107] The Chancellor, the Grand Master of the Imperial Scribes, and the Grand Commander.

[108] According to "So-yin," *tu* 督 means "to supervise" and *tse* 責 "to punish." Wang Li-ch'i (87:1977) follows this interpretation. Bodde reads *tu* and *tse* as "supervising" and "holding responsible" (*Unifier,* p. 38, n. 3). But Wang Shu-min (87:2636) points out that *tu-tse* is a synonym compound verb with both *tu* and *tse* meaning approximately the same thing. We follow Wang Shu-min.

be controlled by none. He will be able to pursue his pleasures to their farthest reaches. The worthy and perspicuous ruler cannot fail to consider this carefully!

[2555] Thus as Shen Tzu[109] said, "Possessing the world without indulging desires is termed 'shackling oneself with the world.'" There is only one cause for this: [the ruler] is unable to call men to account, but instead wearies his frame on behalf of the world's people, as did Yao and Yü; thus he is called shackled. If one were unable to cultivate the perspicuous political arts of Shen [Pu-hai] and Han [Fei Tzu], practicing the way of calling men to account, with the sole end of using the world as it strikes his fancy, and instead vainly devoted himself to mortifying his frame and exhausting his spirit in obedience to the populace, this would be a servant of commoners, not one who makes the world his chattel. What is there worth honoring in this?

If he makes others obey him, he is honored and others are humbled. If he obeys others, he is humbled and others are honored. Thus one who obeys others is humbled, while one who is obeyed by others is honored. From ancient times until now, it has always been so. The reason for respecting worthy men is that their rank is honored, while the reason for disdaining unworthy men is that their rank is humble. Yao and Yü were ones who obeyed the world. If we respected them, we would thus be false to the motives which inspire men to respect the worthy. This can be called a great falsehood. Is it not reasonable that we call such men shackled? The fault lies in their inability to call men to account.

Thus Han Tzu said, "The loving mother has worthless sons, and the harsh household has no recalcitrant slaves."[110] Why is this? Because [the harsh household] is able to be consistent in applying punishment to its slaves. Thus according to the laws made by the Lord of Shang, one who discards ashes on the streets should suffer corporal punishment. Discarding ashes is a light offense, while corporal punishment is a heavy penalty. [The Lord of Shang] thought that only a perspicuous ruler could demand a thorough accounting for a light offense. Then if the offense was light yet the accounting was thorough, how much more would this be so for a heavy offense! Thus the common people did not dare to trespass [against his laws].

"Thus Han Tzu said, 'An ordinary man will not give up a *hsün* or a *ch'ang* of cloth, while Bandit Chih would not seize a hundred *yi* of molten gold.'[111] It is not that the thoughts of an ordinary man are weighty, or that the benefits of a *hsün* or a *ch'ang* of cloth are great, or that the desires of Bandit Chih are light. Nor should one take the actions of Bandit Chih to mean that he despised the value of a hundred *yi* of gold. If one's hands are sure to be mutilated in seizing it, even Bandit Chih would not snatch the hundred *yi*. Likewise, if the laws are not consistently put into practice, even an ordinary man would not let go of a *hsün* or a *ch'ang* of cloth. Thus, the city wall was only five-*chang* high, but Lou Chi 樓季[112] would not casually assault it. Mount T'ai is one-hundred *jen* high, but a lame ewe will graze [*2556*] on its summit. If even Lou Chi found a limit of five-*chang* difficult, how could a lame ewe find a height of one hundred-*jen* easy? Because the circumstances of the precipitous and the level are different. The reason a perspicuous ruler or a sage king is able to remain in an exalted

---

[109] Shen Pu-hai 申不害 (c. 400-337 B.C.), a native of the state of Cheng who also served as the Prime Minister of Han. A noted Legalist (see his biography in *Shih chi* Chapter 63 and Wang Li-ch'i, *Jen-piao*, p. 331) , his writings (*Shen Tzu* 申子) exist only in fragments (see also Ch'ien Mu, *Chu-tzu*, pp. 237-40).

[110] *Han Fei Tzu* (19:11b, *SPPY*).

[111] *Han Fei Tzu* (19:4a, *SPPY*).

[112] A younger brother of the Marquis Wen 文 of Wei (r. 445-396 B.C.) and a legendary man of strength and courage (see "So-yin" and Wang Li-ch'i, 87:1978n), he was also skilled with horses (see Li Shan's 李善 [d. 689] commentary to Mei Sheng's 枚乘 [d. 140 B.C.] "Ch'i-fa" 七發 [Seven Stimuli] in *Wen hsüan* 文選, 34:6b [Taipei: Hua-cheng Shu-chü,1982], p. 480). There is a statement similar to that in our text concerning Lou Chi in the same passage from *Han Fei Tzu* which was cited immediately just above (cf. *Han Fei Tzu*, 19:4a, *SPPY*).

position, wielding great power for a long time and monopolizing the benefits of the world for himself alone, is not that he has found a different way of ruling; he is able to rely solely on himself in reaching decisions, he is careful to call men to account, he is sure to punish severely, thus the world will not dare to trespass [against his laws]. If you now fail to devote yourself to the methods which others will not trespass against and instead labor at the means by which a loving mother ruins her child, this is just the sort who has failed to examine [the arts of] the sage. If one were unable to practice the political arts of the sages, then what could he do but be employed as a servant by the world? Is this not pitiful indeed?

[2557] Moreover, if there were men of thrift, integrity, virtue and principle standing in court, then wild and unrestrained revels would end. If there were vassals admonishing with arguments and evaluating rationales at one's side, then abandoned and reckless aims would be curbed. If the actions of ardent knights dying for their principles were renowned in the world, then the joys of extravagant pleasure would be abandoned. Thus a perspicuous ruler can go beyond these three and control his obedient vassals through wielding the ruler's arts, relying solely on himself, and polishing his perspicuous laws; thus his person is exalted and his power is weighty. All worthy rulers are sure to be able to brush off common wisdom and grind down customary behavior, abolishing what they dislike and establishing what they wish. Thus in life they have the power of the exalted and mighty, and in death they have the posthumous titles of the worthy and perspicuous.

Thus the perspicuous lord relies only on himself in reaching decisions, so his authority is not invested in his vassals.[113] Only when this is so can he obliterate the roads of humaneness and principle, silence the mouths of those who spout sophistries, repress the actions of ardent knights, stop up the ears of the keen of hearing, blinker the eyes of the keen of vision, and limit vision and hearing to himself alone.

Thus outside the court he cannot be moved by the humane and principled conduct of ardent knights and within the court he cannot be won over by the debates of those who passionately struggle to admonish him. Thus he is able to give the broadest rein to his unbridled desires at his own will and none will dare oppose him.

Only in this way can one be said to be able to understand the political arts of Shen and Han and to implement the laws of the Lord of Shang. I have never yet heard that laws were implemented and political arts understood, yet the world remained in disorder.

Thus while it is said that 'The King's Way is simple and easy to grasp' only an intelligent ruler can practice it. When this is the case, then it is said that if men are called to account conscientiously, one's vassals will have no evil intentions. When vassals have no evil intentions, then the world will be at peace. When the world is at peace, the ruler will be rigorously exalted. When the ruler is rigorously exalted, then the calling of men to account is certain. When the calling of men to account is certain, whatever is sought is obtained. When whatever is sought is obtained, state and house are made wealthy. When state and house are made wealthy, the Lord's pleasures are rich indeed.

Thus when the art of calling men to account is established, all that you desire will be satisfied. When the assembled vassals and the general populace haven't even the time to correct their faults, what disturbances would they dare to plan? When this is the case, the Emperor's Way is complete and one can be said to be able to understand the arts of lord and vassal. Even if Shen and Han were to return to life, they would not be able to do better [than this]."

---

[113] As Wang Shu-min (87:2639-40) notes, this line is similar to a citation from Shen Tzu in *Han Fei Tzu* (13:8a, *SPPY*).

When the memorial was presented, the Second Emperor was pleased. After this, the practices of calling men to account became harsher and harsher, and those who taxed the common people the heaviest became the most enlightened officers.

The Second Emperor said, "This is what should be meant by being able to call men to account." Men who had suffered corporal punishment made up half of those on the streets and the bodies of dead men piled up daily in the marketplace. Those who killed people in the largest numbers were regarded as the most loyal officials. The Second Emperor said, "This is what should be meant by being able to call men to account."

[2558] When Chao Kao was first made Prefect of the Palace Attendants,[114] the men he killed and the personal grudges he repaid were numerous. [Now] he feared that when the great vassals entered court they would submit petitions vilifying him. Thus he advised the Second Emperor: "The reason the Son of Heaven is honored is simply because only his voice can be heard, but none of his assembled vassals is able to see his countenance. Thus his title is "The Hidden One."[115]

"Furthermore, Your Majesty has a wealth of years left and may not entirely understand all affairs. If you were sitting today in court and one of your criticisms or recommendations, was inappropriate, you would be criticized by the great vassals. This is not how to demonstrate your supernatural perspicuity to the world. If Your Majesty remains at rest deep in the palace, attending to affairs with myself and others who serve in the palace and have a good knowledge of legal affairs, then when matters come up, there will be someone you can discuss them with. In this way the great vassals will not dare to petition on questionable affairs and the world will praise you as a sage ruler."

The Second Emperor adopted his plan, stopped attending court and giving audience to the great vassals, and stayed in the inner palace. Chao Kao was in regular attendance on the Emperor in the palace and wielded power; all matters were decided by Chao Kao.

When [Chao] Kao heard that Li Ssu was making noise about this, he saw the Chancellor and said, "There are many bands of robbers East of the Pass, while the Present Emperor urgently requisitions more and more corvee laborers to build the O-pang Palace and collects dogs, horses and other useless things. I wish I could admonish him, but my position is [too] humble. This is indeed a matter for My Lord, the Marquis. Why not admonish him, My Lord?"

Li Ssu said, "Certainly. I have wished to speak about it for a long time. But at the present, His Highness no longer sits in court and lives deep in the palace. Even if I had something to say, I would be unable to transmit it [to him]. Even if I wished to have an audience with him, he would not have free time for it."

Chao Kao told him, "If My Lord is indeed able to admonish him, allow me to watch for My Lord when His Highness has free time, and then inform My Lord."

After this, Chao Kao waited until the Second Emperor was in the midst of feasting and merriment, with women sitting before him, to send a messenger to inform the Chancellor: "His Highness has free time right now. You can present your petition."

The Chancellor went to the palace gates and sent in his visiting card. This happened three times. The Second Emperor became angry and said, "I often have days with much free

---

[114] *Chung-lang ling* 中郎令.

[115] Originally *chen* 朕 was an archaic form of the first-person pronoun. Beginning in 221 B.C., the First Emperor reserved it exclusively for the emperor's use (see *Shih chi*, 6:236). As "So-yin" points out (*Shih chi*, 6:272), Chao Kao appears to be using *chen* here in the sense of *chao* 兆 (this usage of *chen* is common in *Huai Nan Tzu*). *Chao* originally referred to the hairline cracks made by heating turtle plastrons for purposes of divination. This is where the sense of "hidden, portentous" is derived from.

time, but the Chancellor does not come. Just as I am having a private party, he suddenly arrives to make a request over some matter. Can the Chancellor think so little of me? Even think me a fool!?"

Chao Kao seized his opportunity: "If this is so, it is dangerous! The Chancellor participated in the plot at Sha-ch'iu. Now Your Majesty has already been enthroned as emperor, but the Chancellor's rank has not increased. His ambition perhaps is that he hopes to make himself a king by splitting [your] territory. If Your Majesty had not asked, your servant would not dare to mention this. The Chancellor's eldest son, [*2559*] Li Yu, is the Governor of San-ch'uan, while the Ch'u bandit Chen Sheng and his followers, are all sons of the neighboring counties of the Chancellor's hometown. Thus when the Ch'u bandits moved about openly, passing through San-ch'uan [Commandery], [Li Yu] guarded his cities and was unwilling to attack them. I have heard that there were letters exchanged between them. I have not gotten to the truth yet, so I did not dare to inform you. Furthermore, the Chancellor lives outside of the palace where his authority is more weighty than that of Your Majesty."

The Second Emperor believed this to be so. He wanted to have the Chancellor tried, but was afraid [Chao Kao's accusations] might not be accurate and thus sent someone to investigate whether there was contact between the Governor of San-ch'uan and the bandits. Li Ssu heard of this.

At the time, the Second Emperor was living at Kan-ch'üan 甘泉 [Palace],[116] watching performances of contests of strength and theatricals. Li Ssu was unable to gain an audience with him and he therefore submitted a memorial laying out Chao Kao's faults:

> Your servant has heard that a vassal equal to his lord will always endanger the state. A concubine equal to her husband will always endanger the household. At present there is a great vassal beneath Your Majesty who monopolizes rewards and punishments, so that there is no distinction between him and Your Majesty. This is utterly inappropriate.
>
> In ancient times when Tzu Han 子罕,[117] Minister of the City, became Prime Minister of the state of Sung, he personally handled punishments and penalties; in handling them he inspired awe, and after a year he snatched [power] from his lord.[118]
>
> When T'ien Ch'ang 田常[119] was the vassal of Duke Chien 簡 of Ch'i (r. 484-481 B.C.), his title and rank were without match in the state and the wealth of his private household was equal to that of the ducal house. By distributing his grace and bestowing his kindness, he won the favor of the common people below and the favor of the various officials above. Thus he secretly took the state of Ch'i, killed Tsai Yü 宰予 in the courtyard,[120] murdered Duke Chien at court,[121] and finally came to hold the state of Ch'i. These [events] are well known throughout the world.

---

[116] This was the Southern Palace 南宮 in Hsien-yang, not the Han palace located at Yün-yang 雲陽 (see Wang Li-ch'i, 6:121n., "Chi-chieh," *Shih chi*, 85:2513, Wang Shu-min, 6:195).

[117] Wang Li-ch'i, *Jen-piao*, pp. 285-6.

[118] See *Han Fei Tzu* (2:6b, SPPY).

[119] See *Shih chi*, 46:1883-4 and n. 39 to our translation of Chapter 67 above. An account of the story, paralleled to that of Tzu Han, can be found in *Han Fei Tzu* (2:6a-b, SPPY).

[120] Tsai Yü, *agnomen* Tzu Wo 子我, was a disciple of Confucius (see also Wang Li-ch'i, *Jen-piao*, p. 827).. According to *Shih chi*, 67:2195, Confucius was ashamed of him because he joined the revolt, but there is no mention that he was killed by T'ien Ch'ang. In the account on *Shih chi*, 46:1883-4, Ssu-ma Ch'ien claims T'ien Ch'ang killed both Tzu Wo and another Prime Minister, Chien Chih 監止. But some scholars (see "So-yin," *Shih chi*, 46:1884 and Yang, *Tso chuan*, Ai 14, p. 1683) believe Tzu Wo was Chien Chih's *agnomen* and that only he-- not Confucius's disciple of the same name--was involved in the revolt and then killed.

[121] According to *Shih chi*, 461884, Duke Chien was murdered when he fled from the capital.

Now [Chao] Kao's evil intentions and subversive acts are like those of Tzu Han when he served Sung as Prime Minister. The wealth of his private household is like that of the T'ien clan in Ch'i. His conduct combines the refractory ways of both T'ien Ch'ang and Tzu Han, and he snatches Your Majesty's power and [your subjects'] trust; his ambitions are those of Han Ch'i 韓玘 in serving An 安 of Han (r. 238-230 B.C.) as Prime Minister.[122] If Your Majesty does not lay plans for him, your servant fears that he will disturb the state.

The Second Emperor said, "How can this be? [Chao] Kao is indeed only a eunuch, but he is not self-indulgent in times of peace or faint-hearted in times of danger. By keeping his conduct pure and practicing virtue, he has brought himself to this [position]. He obtained promotion because of his loyalty and maintained his position with his fidelity. We truly regard him as worthy! Why do you, sir, doubt him?

Moreover, when We lost Our father, We were still young. We were ignorant and unpracticed in governing the common people, while you, My Lord, were already old. We truly feared that We would lose touch with the world. If We had not entrusted Ourself to Lord Chao, whom could We have relied on? Furthermore, Lord Chao [*2560*] by his nature is astute, incorruptible, strong-minded and forceful. He understands public feeling below and is able to put Us at ease above. Do not doubt him, My Lord!"

Li Ssu said, "Not so. [Chao] Kao was originally a base man. He has no understanding of reason, his greed is insatiable, and his pursuit of profit is unending. His rank and influence are second only to the ruler's and in his pursuit of his desires he will go to any extremity. Your servant thus called him dangerous."

The Second Emperor had trusted Chao Kao from the first, and feared that Li Ssu would kill Chao, thus he secretly told Chao Kao. [Chao] Kao said, "The Chancellor fears only me. Once I am dead, the Chancellor will soon wish to do what T'ien Ch'ang did."

At this the Second Emperor said, "Hand Li Ssu over to the Prefect of the Palace Attendants!"

Chao Kao handled the proceedings against Li Ssu. Li Ssu was seized, bound and thrown into prison. He looked up to the heavens and sighed: "Alas! Is it not sad? How can one make plans for an unprincipled lord! In ancient times Chieh 桀 killed Kuan Lung-feng 關龍逢,[123] Chow 紂 killed the Prince Pi-kan 比干,[124] and Fu-ch'ai 夫差, King of Wu (r. 495-476 B.C.), killed Wu Tzu Hsü 伍子胥.[125] Were not these three vassals loyal? Yet they could not escape death. They died, but those they were loyal to were in the wrong. Now my wisdom is not equal to these three gentlemen, while the Second Emperor is even more unprincipled that Chieh, Chow and Fu-ch'ai. It is only fitting that I die for my loyalty.

"Moreover, is not confusion the means of administration of the Second Emperor? In the past he wiped out his brothers and established himself on the throne, killed loyal vassals and honored humble men, built the O-p'ang Palace, and taxed the world. It is not that I didn't admonish him, but he didn't heed me. The ancient sage kings all used moderation in their drinking and eating, put a limit on the number of their chariots and utensils, and set a maximum size for their residences and halls. When they issued orders to initiate an undertaking,

[122] An (r. 238-230 B.C.) was the last ruler of the state of Han. There is no record of this event. Commentators have made a number of speculations, but they remain that. It is possible that the story was based on Li Ssu's personal experience.

[123] See n. 70 to our translation of *Shih chi* Chapter 83 above.

[124] See n. 98 to our translation of *Shih chi* Chapter 79 above.

[125] For details see our translation of *Shih chi* Chapter 66 above.

they forbid increases in expenditures if it did not increase the benefit to the people. Thus they were able to govern in peace for a long time.

"Now [the Emperor] engages in treachery against his brothers without regard for the consequences, illegally kills loyal vassals without considering the disastrous results, builds palaces and halls on a grand scale and taxes the world without a care for the cost. Having done these three things, the world will no longer heed him. At present the rebels already possess half the world, yet still [*2561*] his mind has not awakened and instead he makes Chao Kao his assistant. I am sure to see the invaders reach Hsien-yang and elaphures and deer wandering through the court!"

After this the Second Emperor had [Chao] Kao handle the case against the Chancellor. He inquired into his crimes, accused [Li] Ssu and his son Yu of plotting rebellion, and arrested all his clansmen and retainers. When Chao Kao interrogated [Li] Ssu, he had him beaten and whipped more than one-thousand strokes. [Li Ssu] was unable to bear the pain and falsely confessed. The reason [Li] Ssu did not kill himself was that he was confident in his own eloquence, had achieved merit, and actually had no intention to rebel. He hoped that with luck he could submit a memorial to explain himself and that the Second Emperor would then awake and pardon him.

Li Ssu thus submitted a memorial from prison which read:

> Your servant has been Chancellor and governed the people for more than 30 years, from a time when the territory of Ch'in was still narrow and constrained. In the reign of the late king, the territory of Ch'in was less than a 1000-*li* [on a side] and its troops numbered 100,000. Your servant did his best with his meager ability. He carefully pursued the laws and ordinances. He secretly sent out his plotters, provided them with gold and jade, and had them travel about advising the feudal lords. He secretly repaired weapons and armor, regulated policies and teachings, gave posts to fighting men, exalted meritorious vassals, and gave them rich rank and emolument. By all these various means, [Ch'in] finally coerced Han and weakened Wei, broke Yen and Chao, leveled Ch'i and Ch'u, and at last annexed the Six States, captured their kings, and established [the King of] Ch'in as the Son of Heaven. This was his first 'crime.'
>
> [Ch'in's] territory having been broadened to no small extent, he went on to manifest Ch'in's might by driving off the Hu and Mo tribes in the north and settling the Hundred Yüeh in the south. This was his second 'crime.'
>
> He consolidated a close relation [between the ruler and his officials] by honoring the great vassals and giving them rich ranks and emoluments. This was his third 'crime.'
>
> He manifested the worthiness of the ruler by establishing the altars of soil and grain and repairing the ancestral temple. This was his fourth 'crime.'
>
> He changed the form of the characters used in bronze inscriptions,[126] standardized the *tou* and *hu* measures of capacity and length and the written characters and established Ch'in's fame by propagating [these standards] throughout the world. This was his fifth 'crime.'
>
> He manifested the attainment of his ruler's ambitions by laying out the speedway and constructing pleasure palaces. This was his sixth 'crime.'
>
> He fulfilled his ruler's desire to win the hearts of the masses by easing punishments and penalties and lightening taxes and collections, and the ten-thousand people adored their ruler and did not forget him even in death. This was his seventh 'crime.'

---

[126] Our translation follows Ch'en Chih, p. 146.

This was the sort of vassal [Li] Ssu was; his crimes were long ago sufficient to warrant execution! Since His Highness allowed him to exhaust his abilities, he has been fortunate enough to live until now. May Your Majesty consider this!"

When the memorial was sent up, Chao Kao had the functionaries throw it away instead of presenting it, saying "How can a prisoner submit a memorial!"

Chao Kao sent more than ten of his retainers, pretending to be Imperial Scribes, Internuncios or Palace Attendants, to interrogate [Li] Ssu one after the other. Whenever [Li] Ssu changed his confession to state the truth, the men who had been sent beat him again. Later, when the Second Emperor sent a man to investigate [Li] Ssu's case, [Li] Ssu thought it would go as it had before, and in the end did not dare to retract his confession, but admitted his guilt. When the report came before His Highness, the Second Emperor was delighted: "If it were not for Lord Chao, we would have been deceived by the Chancellor!"

By the time the envoy whom the Second Emperor had sent to interrogate the Governor of San-ch'uan arrived there, Hsiang Liang 項梁[127] had already killed the Governor. When the envoy returned, the Chancellor had just been given over to the functionaries and Chao Kao [*2562*] had concocted [Li Ssu's] confession of his rebellion.

In the seventh month of the second year of the Second Emperor [208 B.C.] it was proclaimed that [Li] Ssu should be sentenced to the five punishments[128] and cut in half at the waist in the marketplace of Hsien-yang. When [Li] Ssu was brought out of prison, he was sent in custody [to the marketplace] with his second son. He looked at him and said, "Even if I wished once more to go out the eastern gate of Shang-ts'ai with you, leading our yellow dog[129] to chase a wily rabbit, how could I do it?" Father and son wailed together and his clan to the third degree [of relationship][130] was wiped out.

After Li Ssu died, the Second Emperor appointed Chao Kao as the Chancellor within the Palace.[131] All affairs major and minor were decided by [Chao] Kao alone. Realizing his immense authority, he presented a deer [to the Emperor], calling it a horse.

The Second Emperor asked his attendants, "This a deer!"

The attendants all said, "It is a horse."[132]

The Second Emperor was surprised. Thinking he suffering from a delusion, he summoned the Grand Diviner,[133] ordering him to divine by the diagrams.

The Grand Diviner said, "The reason matters have come to this pass is that when performing the suburban sacrifices [to Heaven and Earth] in the spring and autumn, and in offering sacrifices to the ancestral temple and its spirits, Your Majesty was not cleansed prior to fasting. Your Majesty should rely on his splendorous virtue and cleanse himself before fasting."

---

[127] One of the rebel leaders from Ch'u who was fighting Ch'in, see *Shih chi,* 6:269-70, 7:295-300 and Chapter 7 *passim* as well as Ma Fei-pai, pp. 407-11.

[128] See n. 346 to our translation of *Shih chi* Chapter 6 above.

[129] As Edward H. Schafer ("Falconry in T'ang Times," *TP,* 46[1959], p. 295) points out, there seems to have been a T'ang mss. of the *Shih chi* which read "leading our yellow dog and with gray hawk on arm" (*pi ts'ang-ying* 臂蒼鷹). We thank Charles Hartman for drawing our attention to this reference.

[130] Including his parents, brothers, wife and children.

[131] *Chung Ch'eng-hsiang* 中丞相; this position was especially established for Chao Kao, who, as a eunuch, could remain within the palace.

[132] Chao Kao was, of course, testing his influence with each of the Palace Attendants. The version of the story given on *Shih chi,* 6:273 is somewhat different.

[133] *T'ai-pu* 太卜.

At this [the Emperor] went into the Shang-lin 上林 (Sovereign's Forest)[134] to fast. He hunted and shot birds every day. A passerby entered Shang-lin and the Second Emperor himself shot and killed him. Chao Kao instructed his son-in-law Yen Le 閻樂,[135] the Prefect of Hsien-yang, to announce an investigation of the circumstances under which an undetermined person had murdered a man and moved the body to Shang-lin. [Chao] Kao then admonished the Second Emperor: "For the Son of Heaven to murder an innocent person without reason is what the Supreme Deity forbids. The ghosts and spirits will reject your sacrifices and Heaven will soon send down calamity. You should leave the palace and go to a distant place to ward off [the calamity]."

The Second Emperor then left the palace and resided in the Palace of Wang-yi 望夷 (Looking at the Barbarians).[136] After he had been there for three days, Chao Kao summoned the palace guards under false pretenses, then had them dress in unmarked clothes and hold their weapons facing toward the palace. He entered and informed the Second Emperor, "The troops of the bandits from East of the Mount have arrived in great force!"

When the Second Emperor mounted a lookout-tower and saw them, he was terrified. Chao Kao thus forced him to commit suicide.[137] [Chao Kao] took the imperial seal and hung it from his girdle, but none of the attendants or the hundred officials would obey him. When he ascended the audience hall, the hall seemed about to collapse three times. [Chao] Kao realized that Heaven did not support him and the various officials did not approve of him, and at last summoned a younger brother of the First Emperor and gave him the imperial seal.[138]

When Tzu-ying had ascended the throne, he was concerned about [Chao Kao]. He claimed that he was ill and could not administer affairs. Together with a eunuch, Han T'an, and his own sons, he plotted to kill Chao Kao. When [Chao] Kao sent in his card to ask about the illness, he was summoned to enter. [Tzu-ying] had Han T'an stab him to death, then exterminated his clan to the third degree.

Three months after Tzu-ying was enthroned,[139] the Magistrate of P'ei's 沛[140] troops entered the Wu 武 Pass.[141] When they reached Hsien-yang, the assembled vassals and the hundred officials all rebelled [against Ch'in] and did not resist. Tzu-ying, his wife, and his children tied silk cords around their necks and surrendered by the side of the Chih 軹 Road.[142] The Magistrate of P'ei handed them over to the functionaries. When King Hsiang 項[143] arrived, he beheaded them. Thus [Ch'in] lost the world.

His Honor the Grand Scribe says: "Beginning in a simple hamlet, Li Ssu traveled among the feudal lords, then came to serve Ch'in. 'Seizing flaws and chinks,' this was how he assisted the First Emperor. [The Emperor] finally succeeded in his imperial enterprise and

---

[134] Running along the south of the Wei from modern Hu 戶 County west for some 30 miles (T'an Ch'i-hsiang, 2:6).

[135] See also *Shih chi,* 6:274.

[136] Southeast of modern Ch'ing-yang 涇陽 in Shensi (Wang Li-ch'i, 87:1983n.).

[137] The version of these events given on *Shih chi,* 6:274 again differs from this.

[138] As "Chi-chieh" and "So-yin" both point out, Tzu-ying is elsewhere said to be the First Emperor's grandson and the Second Emperor's nephew (see n. 457 to our translation of *Shih chi* Chapter 6 above).

[139] *Shih chi,* 6:275 says "forty-six days" and Shih chi, 5:221 says "more than one month." See also Wang Shu-min (5:189).

[140] I.e., Liu Pang 劉邦, the founder of the Han dynasty.

[141] Located in modern Shang-nan 商南 County in Shansi (T'an Ch'i-hsiang, 1:44); it was one of the major routes from Ch'u into Ch'in.

[142] A relay station located about 10 miles northeast of modern Sian (Wang Li-ch'i, 87:1983n.).

[143] Hsiang Yü 項羽, see our translation of *Shih chi* Chapter 7 above.

Ssu became one of his 'Three Masters.'[144] He can be said to have been put to an exalted use indeed. Although Ssu knew the fundamentals of the *Six Arts*, he did not devote himself to an enlightened government with which to remedy his ruler's shortcomings. Holding the highest title and salary, he was slavish in his conformity and unscrupulous in his agreement, lent severity to [the emperor's] majesty and harshness to his punishments, then heeded [Chao] Kao's evil advice and removed the eldest son by the principal wife, installing another son in his place. When the 'feudal lords' revolted, Ssu finally wished to remonstrate. Was he not tardy indeed? Men all thought Ssu the epitome of loyalty, suffering the five punishments. If we search for the truth, it differs from the commonly held opinion. If he had not acted as he did, his merits could rank with those of [the dukes of] Chou 周 and Shao 召."[145]

---

[144] *San kung* 三公, indicating the three highest posts at the time (see Cheng T'ien-t'ing, p. 12).

[145] Who both helped to establish the Chou dynasty, see our translation of *Shih chi* Chapter 4 above.

TRANSLATORS' NOTE

This chapter indeed attributes Ch'in's successful unification of the world and its subsequent loss to Li Ssu. As an account of one of the major figures of Ch'in's government, it should also be read together with "Meng T'ien" (Chapter 88). "Li Ssu" has also been called an "unofficial annals" of the Ch'in dynasty and a "parallel biography" of Li Ssu and Chao Kao. It can also serve as an accompanying text for Chapters 5 and 6, "The Basic Annals of Ch'in" and "The Basic Annals of the First Emperor of Ch'in."

"Li Ssu" can also be seen in the tradition of the persuaders (a modern scholar has noted that 50% of the chapter is dialogue, 20% the text of memorials and only 30% narrative). He was certainly the persuader who achieved the most with his eloquence. But unlike Fan Sui and Ts'ai Tse who could foresee that their own time had reached its end, there were no limits to Li Ssu's ambition and greed (he learned well from the anecdote of the rats with which the Grand Historian begins this memoir). He is the arch-villain of the pre-Han *lieh-chuan.*

Nevertheless, it seems that it was Li Ssu's character (or lack of it) which enabled his success, since his rhetorical techniques differ little from those of kindred advisors we have seen in other chapters. The emphasis in this chapter is more on Li Ssu's written submissions, but the reader can detect little difference between letters, memorials, and the speeches these rhetoricians offered. This might lead to the conclusion that these texts were scripts for persuaders to study, were it not for the stock of allusions which seem to come from a now lost literature, a literature which may well have been transmitted orally by these persuaders and which died out when they and their tradition did.

BIBLIOGRAPHY

I. Translations

Bodde, Derk. *China's First Unifier, A Study of the Ch'in Dynasty as Seen in the Life of Li Ssu.* Leiden: E. J. Brill, 1938, pp. 12-55.

Creel, Herrlee G. "The Fa-chia: 'Legalists' or 'Administrators,'" *Studies Presented to Tung Tso Pin on His Sixty-Fifth Birthday, Academia Sinica, Bulletin of the Institute of History and Philology,* Extra Volume, No. 4, 1961, 636-707.

Fukushima Yoshihio 福島吉彥, trans. *Shiki retsuden* 史記列傳. Rpt. Tokyo: Chikuma Shobō, 1986 (1969), pp. 175-86.

Haenisch, Erich. *Der Herr von Sin-ling, Reden aus dem Chan-kuo ts'e und Biographien aus dem Shi-ki.* Stuttgart: Reclam, 1965, pp. 41-52 (partial).

Watson, Burton. *Records of the Grand Historian: Qin Dynasty.* Hong Kong and New York: The Research Centre for Translation, The Chinese University of Hong Kong and Columbia University Press, 1993, pp. 179-206.

II. Studies

Bodde, Derk. *China's First Unifier, A Study of the Ch'in Dynasty as Seen in the Life of Li Ssu.* Leiden: E. J. Brill, 1938.

Fields, Lanny B. "The Legalists and the Fall of Ch'in: Humanism and Tyranny," *JAH* 17 (1983), 1-39.

Itō Norio 伊藤徳男. Shiba Sen no Ri Shi, Mō Ten hiban ni tsuite 司馬遷の李斯蒙恬批判 について, *Suzuki Shun Kyōju kanreki kinen Tōyōshi ronsō* 鈴木俊教授還暦記念東洋 史論叢. Tokyo: Kan Gi Bunka Kenkyūkai, 1964, pp. 43-56.

Miyazaki Ichisada 宮崎市定. "*Shiki* 'Ri Shi retsuden' o yomu" 史記李斯列傳を讀む, *Toyoshi kenkyu* 東洋史研究, 35.4(1977), 29-60.

Meng T'ien, Memoir 28

[88:2565] Meng T'ien's 蒙恬[1] (?-210 B.C.) ancestors were natives of Ch'i. T'ien's grandfather Meng Ao 蒙驁 left Ch'i to serve King Chao 昭 ([of Ch'in] r. 306-251 B.C.) and his post reached Senior Excellency.[2]

In the first year of King Chuang-hsiang 莊襄 of Ch'in (r. 249-247 B.C.), Meng Ao led Ch'in's attack on Han and took Ch'eng-kao 成皋[3] and Ying-yang 滎陽,[4] which he made into San-ch'uan 三川 Commandery.[5]

In the second year (248 B.C.), Meng Ao attacked Chao and took thirty-seven cities.[6]

In the third year (244 B.C.) of the First Emperor ([of Ch'in] r. 246-208 B.C.), Meng Ao attacked Han and took thirteen cities.[7]

In the fifth year (242 B.C.), Meng Ao attacked Wei and took twenty cities, which he made into Tung-chün 東郡 [Commandery].

In the seventh year (240 B.C.), Meng Ao expired.

Meng Ao's son was called [Meng] Wu 武 and [Meng] Wu's son was called [Meng] T'ien. [Meng] T'ien had studied the penal codes and once prepared legal documents.

In the twenty-third year of the First Emperor (224 B.C.), Meng Wu was Ch'in's Adjutant General[8] and together with Wang Chien 王翦[9] attacked Ch'u. They crushed it and killed Hsiang Yen 項燕.[10]

In the twenty-fourth year (223 B.C.), Meng Wu attacked Ch'u and captured the King of Ch'u.[11]

Meng T'ien's younger brother was [Meng] Yi 毅.

In the twenty-sixth year of the First Emperor (221 B.C.), Meng T'ien, who, because of his lineage was able to become a general of Ch'in, attacked Ch'i and crushed it.[12] He was appointed Scribe of the Capital.[13] When Ch'in united the world [in 221 B.C.], [the First Emperor] sent Meng T'ien commanding an army of 300,000 troops to drive off the Jung and the Ti, and recover Ho-nan 河南.[14] He built the Long Wall[15] following the contours of the

---

[1] On Meng T'ien (?-210 B.C.) see also Ma Fei-pai, pp. 251ff. Ma is also useful on Meng Ao (pp. 250-4), Meng Wu (pp. 251f.) and Meng Yi (pp. 251-4).

[2] *Shang-ch'ing* 上卿.

[3] About 25 miles northwest of modern Chengchow in Honan (T'an Ch'i-hsiang, 2: 35-36).

[4] About 10 miles northeast of modern Chengchow in Honan (T'an Ch'i-hsiang, 2:35-36).

[5] See the parallel account on *Shih chi*, 5:219.

[6] This took place one year later according to *Shih chi*, 5:219.

[7] Cf. *Shih chi*, 6:224.

[8] *Pi chiang-chün* 裨將軍.

[9] See his biography in *Shih chi* Chapter 73.

[10] He was Hsiang Yü's 項羽 (see *Shih chi* Chapter 7) grandfather.

[11] This was Fu Ch'u 負芻, King of Ch'u (r. 227-223 B.C.). These events are also recorded in *Shih chi* 6:234, 15:756, 40:1736-7, *and*, in fragmentary form, on "Pien-nien chi," p. 7. The accounts in Chapters 15 and 40 are similar to that here, but in Chapter 6, the King of Ch'u was said to have been killed in 224 B.C. and Hsiang Yen to have committed suicide that same year. "Pien-nien chi" also records the King's death in 224 B.C. In chapters 15 and 40, Hsiang Yen was said to have been killed by Wang Chien in 224 B.C.

[12] Liang Yü-sheng (31:1322) notes that Wang Pen 王賁 was said to be the leader of this attack in other accounts in the *Shih chi*. He believes that Meng Yi was probably only a deputy for this campaign.

[13] *Nei-shih* 內史; this position was essentially that of the mayor of the capital (see also the long discussion of this title in Ochi Shigeaki 越智重明, *Sengoku Shin Kan shih kenkyū 1* 戰國秦漢史研究 [Fukuoka: Chūgoku Shoten, 1988], pp. 374-80).

[14] South of K'u-pu-ch'i 庫布齊 Desert and north of Mao-niao-su 毛烏素 Desert in modern Inner Mongolia

land, and controlling the land's redoubts and natural fortifications. It began at Lin-t'ao 臨洮[16] and reached Liao-tung 遼東[17] extending [*2566*] unbroken over ten-thousand *li*. [Meng T'ien] then crossed the Ho, occupied Mount Yang 陽,[18] and wound his way to the north.[19] He kept his troops in the field for more than a decade,[20] with their base in Shang-chün [Commandery]. At the time, Meng T'ien's majesty shook the Hsiung-nu 匈奴. The First Emperor profoundly respected and favored the Meng Clan. He trusted [Meng T'ien], relied on him, and considered him worthy. His relations with Meng Yi were very close. Meng Yi's post reached Senior Excellency. When the emperor went out, Meng Yi rode beside him in his carriage, and, when [the emperor] went in to court, Meng Yi would stand next to the imperial presence. [Meng] T'ien was in charge of external affairs while [Meng] Yi often made proposals concerning domestic affairs. They were famous for their loyalty and fidelity. Thus even the other generals and ministers did not dare contend with them.

Chao Kao 趙高[21] was a member of a distant branch of the Chao [ruling] family. Chao Kao and his brothers were all born into "the closed quarters."[22] His mother was implicated in a crime[23] and [his family] was permanently reduced to the basest rank. The King of Ch'in [i.e., the First Emperor], hearing that [Chao] Kao was strong and fit and had thorough knowledge of the penal codes, took him into service as Prefect of the Palace Chariots.[24] [Chao] Kao privately served Noble Scion Hu-hai 胡亥 and explained the judgment of legal cases to him. [Once Chao] Kao committed a serious crime and the King of Ch'in ordered Meng Yi to decide [the case] according to the law. [Meng] Yi did not dare bend the law and determined that [Chao] Kao's crime deserved the death penalty and removal from the register of officials. The emperor, considering [Chao] Kao to be diligent in his service, pardoned him and restored his position and rank.

When the First Emperor wanted to tour the world and to have a road built from Chiu-yüan 九原[25] straight to [Mount] Kan-ch'üan 甘泉,[26] he had Meng T'ien build the road from

(T'an Ch'i-hsiang, 2:35-36).

[15] I.e., the "Great Wall." As Liang Yü-sheng (31:1323) points out, most parts of the wall had been built during the Warring States period by various states; Meng T'ien linked the various sections .

[16] Modern Min 岷 County in Kansu (T'an Ch'i-hsiang, 2:5).

[17] A region on the Liao River in modern Liaoning (T'an Ch'i-hsiang, 2:42).

[18] Located just north of what was then Ho-pei 河北 at the northwest point of the "hump" in the Yellow River about 50-100 miles northwest of modern Wu-yüan 五原 in the Inner Mongolian Autonomous Region (T'an Ch'i-hsiang, 1:5-6).

[19] Bodde (*Statesman*, p. 54) reads "the Great Wall" as the subject of this sentence.

[20] Liang Yü-sheng (31:1323) notes that in *Shih chi*, 6:253 the First Emperor attacked the Hu 胡 (i.e. the Hsiung-nu) in 215 while Meng T'ien died in 210 B.C., and this was only six years in Chinese way of counting. However, as Shih Chih-mien suggests, the battle in 215 B.C. was probably just one of the many battles. Shih points out that in *Shih chi*, 110:2887 the chieftan of the Hsiung-nu was expelled to the north for more than a decade, and this agrees with this biography here (see Shih Chih-mien, p. 1368). Similar accounts are found in *Shih chi*, 87:2551 and 112:2954.

[21] On Chao Kao see also our translations of *Shih chi* Chapters 6 and 87 above.

[22] "The closed quarters" (*yin-kung* 隱宮) was where the eunuchs stayed to recover from castration (closed to protect them from breezes which were considered dangerous). Scholars have disputed whether Chao Kao and brothers were castrated in their infancy or later (for a summary of their arguments, see Takigawa, 88:4).

[23] Possibly implicated by Chao Kao's father (see "So-yin").

[24] *Chung ch'e-fu ling* 中車府令.

[25] About 5 miles west of modern Pao-t'ou 包頭, Inner Mongolia (T'an Ch'i-hsiang, 2:37-38).

[26] Kan-ch'üan was about 15 miles north-northwest of modern Ch'un-hua 淳化 in Shensi (T'an Ch'i-hsiang, 2:43-4). Bodde observes that Ssu-ma Ch'ien is referring to Kan-ch'üan as it was located during the Han dynasty (not during the Ch'in) here (*Statesman*, p. 55, n. 25 and 26).

Chiu-yüan to Kan-ch'üan[27] by cutting through mountains and filling up valleys for 1800 [*2567*] *li*. The road was not completed.

In the winter of the thirty-seventh year (210 B.C.), the First Emperor departed on an inspection tour to [Mount] K'uai-chi 會稽 and the seashore, then went north to Lang-ya 琅邪 [Commandery].[28] Along the way, he fell ill and sent Meng Yi back [to the capital] to pray to the mountains and rivers. Before [Yi] had returned [to the imperial party], the First Emperor passed away on his arrival at Sha-ch'iu 沙丘.[29] [His death] was kept secret, and none of the assembled vassals knew of it. At this time, Chancellor Li Ssu 李斯 (d. 208 B.C.),[30] Noble Scion Hu-hai, and Prefect of the Palace Chariots, Chao Kao, were in regular attendance on the Emperor. Kao had always been favored by Hu-hai and wanted to enthrone him. [Chao Kao] also harbored resentment against Meng Yi for handling him according to the law instead of on a personal basis, and thus bore him ill will. He plotted secretly with Chancellor Li Ssu and Noble Scion Hu-hai to install Hu-hai as Heir. After the Heir had been installed, he dispatched a messenger to grant Noble Scion Fu-su 扶蘇 (d. 210 B.C.) and Meng T'ien death for their offenses. After Fu-su died, Meng T'ien was suspicious and asked for confirmation.[31] The messenger handed Meng T'ien over to the responsible officials and took [Meng T'ien's] position. Hu-hai appointed Li Ssu's houseman as Commissioner of the Army.[32] The messenger returned to report, and Hu-hai, after hearing that Fu-su had died, wanted to release Meng T'ien. Chao Kao, afraid that the Meng family would regain its rank and exercise power again, harbored resentment against him.

When Meng Yi returned, Chao Kao, in accordance with "his loyal plan for Hu-hai," decided to exterminate the Meng family. He spoke [to Hu-hai]: "Your servant has heard that the late Emperor had long intended to choose a worthy man and install him as Heir, but [Meng] Yi admonished [the late Emperor], 'This will not do.' If [Yi] knew of a worthy man yet passed over him, instead of installing him, he was disloyal and deluded the ruler. In your servant's foolish opinion, it would be better to execute him." Hu-hai heeded him and put Meng Yi in bonds at Tai 代.[33] Earlier, Meng T'ien had already been imprisoned at Yang-chou 陽周.[34]

After the funeral procession reached Hsien-yang and [the late Emperor] had been interred, the Heir was enthroned as the "Second Generation Emperor," and Chao Kao became his intimate, attacking and denouncing the Meng Clan day and night and searching for offenses and errors in order to prosecute and impeach them.

Tzu-ying 子嬰 (r. 207 B.C.) presented an admonition:

[27] Meng T'ien was in the north and would therefore have his crews work south towards Yün-yang 雲陽 and Mount Kan-ch'üan. There may well have been some road suitable for military purposes already in existence and Meng's task would be to improve it and thereby create the famous "Straight Road" (Chih-tao 直道); see also *Shih chi*, 6:256, n. 94 to our translation of *Shih chi* Chapter 87, and the outline sketch of the road by T'an Ch'i-hsiang (2:5-6).

[28] On Mount K'uai-chi and Lang-ya Commandery see n. 56 to our translation of Chapter 66 and n. 170 to our rendition of Chapter 6, respectively.

[29] Located on the west bank of the Yellow River about 5 miles northwest of modern P'ing-hsiang 平鄉 in Hopei (T'an Ch'i-hsiang, 2:38).

[30] See his biography in *Shih chi* Chapter 87 .

[31] For a more detailed account of the story of the plot of putting Hu-hai on the throne, see *Shih chi*, 87:2548-52: it records how Hu-hai issued an edict in the name of the already dead First Emperor ordering Fu-su and Meng T'ien to take their own lives. Meng T'ien was skeptical and requested a second edict.

[32] *Hu-chün* 護軍.

[33] Tai was located about 5 miles northeast of modern Wei-hsien 蔚縣 in Hopei (T'an Ch'i-hsiang, 2:37-38).

[34] According to Wang Li-ch'i (88:1997), it was located northwest of modern Tzu-ch'ang 子長 County in Shensi.

I have heard that the former King of Chao, Ch'ien 遷 (r. 235-228 B.C.), killed his able vassal Li Mu 李牧 (d. 228 B.C.)[35] and employed Yen Chü 顏聚, that the King of Yen, Hsi 喜 (r. 254-222 B.C.), secretly used Ching K'o's 荊軻 (d. 227 B.C.) plot and broke the agreement with Ch'in,[36] and that the King of Ch'i, Chien 建 (r. 264-221 B.C.), killed the faithful vassals of former generations and used the proposals of Hou Sheng 后勝.[37] These three lords each lost his kingdom through changing precedents and brought calamities upon his own person. Now the Meng Clan were Ch'in's great vassals and counselors, yet the ruler intends to discard them in the space of one morning. Your servant privately feels that this will not do. I heard that 'Those who do not consider matters carefully cannot be used to govern a state and those who neglect others' wisdom cannot be used to preserve their lords.' To condemn and kill loyal vassals and establish a man without principle in his actions will cause the assembled vassals within the state to distrust each other and the warriors abroad to become alienated. Your servant privately feels that this will not do.

Hu-hai would not listen. Instead he dispatched the Imperial Scribe[38] Ch'ü Kung 曲宮 to go by post-carriage[39] to Tai and command Meng Yi, "The Late Ruler [i.e., the First Emperor] wanted to install an Heir but you objected, Excellency. Now the Chancellor considers you disloyal; this offense will involve your clan. We cannot bear [to carry out this penalty, but will grant you death, instead. You are fortunate indeed! Think this over, Excellency."

[Meng] Yi replied, "I am considered to have been unable to grasp the Late Ruler's intentions, but I became an official when I was still young, obeyed him, and received his favor until his departure from the world; it could be said that I grasped his intentions. I am held to have overlooked the worth of the Heir, but only the Heir traveled in attendance, touring around the world; in this he was far ahead of the other princes. There was no way for me to cast doubt on this. As for the Late Ruler's choice of the Heir, this built up over a number of years. What did I dare to say in admonition? What did I dare to consider in planning? [I am saying all this] not because I would dare evade death with specious excuses, but because I would bring disgrace upon the good name of the Late Ruler. I would hope that you might consider this for me, Grand Master, and allow me to find death as a result of my actual [crimes]. Moreover, to follow [reason] and to help fulfill a person's aims is what the Way exalts, to punish and kill is what brings the Way to an end.[40]

"Long ago, Duke Mu 穆 of Ch'in (r. 659-621 B.C.) killed the Three Worthies, then died himself;[41] he charged Pai-li Hsi 百里奚 with an offense he had not committed.[42] Thus [he] was given the posthumous title of 'The Wrongdoer.' King Chao-hsiang 昭襄 ([of Ch'in] r. 255-250 B.C.) killed Pai Ch'i 白起 (?-257 B.C.), the Lord of Wu-an 武安;[43] King P'ing 平

---

[35] For a brief account of Li Mu's life and the events leading to his death see *Shih chi*, 81:2526-36.

[36] See the account of Ching K'o's attempt to assassinate the First Emperor in 227 B.C. in *Shih chi*, Chapter 86. There the Heir, Tan 丹, not the King, employed Ching K'o.

[37] Hou Sheng was the Ch'i minister who first advised the king not to ally with other states in resisting Ch'in, and when the Ch'in attacked Ch'i, he persuaded the king to capitulate without resistance (see *Shih chi*, 46:1902-3).

[38] *Yü-shih* 御史.

[39] Emphasizing the urgency with which Hu-hai wanted Meng Yi put to death.

[40] Reading *tsu* 卒 as a verb meaning "to regard as a servant."

[41] See our translation of *Shih chi*, 5:194-5 above.

[42] Probably referring to Duke Mu's angry reaction to Pai-li Hsi's advice not to attack Cheng and the resulting events (see *Shih chi*, 5:190).

[43] See his biography in *Shih chi* Chapter 73.

of Ch'u (r. 528-516 B.C.) killed Wu She 伍奢;[44] Fu-ch'ai 夫差, King of Wu (r. 495-473 B.C.) of Wu killed Wu Tzu Hsü 伍子胥.[45] These four rulers all made great mistakes and the world condemned them, considering them unenlightened. Because of this they were notorious among the feudal lords.[46] Thus it is said, 'Those who employ the Way to rule will not kill the guiltless, nor will their punishments be inflicted on the guileless.' I would hope you might pay heed to this, Grand Master!"

The messenger, knowing the intention of Hu-hai, did not listen to Meng Yi's words and thus killed him.

The Second Emperor [i.e., Hu Hai] also sent a messenger to Yang-chou to command Meng T'ien:

Your faults are numerous and your younger brother [Meng] Yi has committed a great offense, Excellency; under the law you are involved, Scribe of the Capital.

Meng T'ien said, "From the time of my ancestors to [us] their descendants, we have accumulated merit and trust in Ch'in for three generations. Now I command over 300,000 troops and although I am confined and bound, my power is sufficient to raise a revolt. Yet knowing that I am sure to die, the reason that I still hold to my principles is that I do not dare to disgrace the teachings of my ancestors; thus I commemorate the Late Ruler. Long ago, when King Ch'eng 成 of Chou (r. c. 1067-1031 B.C.) was first enthroned, he was still in his swaddling clothes. Tan 旦, the Duke of Chou,[47] carried him on his back to attend court, and [King Ch'eng] eventually pacified the world. When King Ch'eng was gravely ill, the Duke, Tan, cut his own nails and dropped them in the Ho [River], saying, 'The King has no knowledge yet; it is I, Tan, who manage affairs. If calamity has been incurred through offense, I, Tan, will bear the ill-fortune.' He then wrote this down and stored it in the archives. He may be called faithful indeed. When the king was able to govern the state, a treacherous vassal said, 'Tan, Duke of Chou, has long intended to rebel; if Your Majesty does not prepare, there is sure to be a grave event.' The king was furious and Tan, Duke of Chou, fled and took refuge in Ch'u. When King Ch'eng looked in the archives, he found the text Tan, Duke of Chou had sunk [in the Ho River].[48] Weeping, he said, 'Who was it that said Tan, Duke of Chou intended to rebel!' He killed the one who had said this and recalled Tan, Duke of Chou. Thus the *Chou shu* 周書 (Documents of Chou) says, 'One must [consider things] three times and four times.'[49] Now my family has for generations had undivided loyalty, yet things have finally come to this. This is surely the way an evil vassal, disloyal and contumacious, usurps the Emperor's power. King Ch'eng erred, rectified it, and in the end prospered; Chieh 桀 [of Hsia] killed Kuan Lung-feng 關龍逢 and Chow 紂 [of Shang] killed Prince Pi-kan 比干[50] yet they had no regrets and when they died, their states perished. Thus I say, 'If at fault, one can

---

[44] See his biography in *Shih chi* Chapter 66.

[45] See *Shih chi*, 66:2171-3.

[46] Traditional scholars disagree on the meaning of the word *chi* 籍. Some read it as "recorded in books," while others interpret it as "to be notorious" (see Takigawa, 88:8).

[47] See the account of his role in the establishment of the Chou in *Shih chi* Chapter 33.

[48] This story appears also in *Shih chi*, 33:1518-20. There *ch'en-shu* 沉述 (literally, "sunk a written record") is written as *t'ao-shu* 禱述 (a prayer), referring to a *prayer* wrote out to accompany his nails.

[49] However, in the extant version of the *Yi Chou-shu* 逸周書, there is no such a saying.

[50] Chieh was the last emperor of the Hsia dynasty and Chow was the last emperor of the Shang. Both were tyrants. Kuan Lung-feng and Pi-kan were loyal officials of their time who were executed for their persistent remonstrations (see *Shih chi*, 2:88 and 3:108 and n. 96 to our translation of Chapter 79 above).

rectify it; if at fault, one can awake'⁵¹ [*2570*] To bear in mind [that things should be considered] three and four times, this is the way of the supreme sage. The words of your servant are not intended to seek to evade blame, but to admonish before he dies; he hopes that His Majesty, for the sake of the ten-thousand people, will think of following the Way."

The messenger said, "I received the imperial edict to apply the law to you, General; I do not dare convey the General's words to His Majesty."

Meng T'ien gave a great sigh. "What is my offense against Heaven that I should die without fault?"

After a long while, he said slowly, "My offense does indeed merit death. Beginning at Lin-t'ao and reaching to Liao-tung, I built walls and dug moats for more than ten-thousand *li*; was it not inevitable that I broke the earth's veins along the way? This then is my offense." He then swallowed poison and killed himself.

His Honor the Grand Scribe says: "I went to the north border and returned by way of the Straight Road. In my travels I saw the Long Wall and fortifications that Meng T'ien built for Ch'in, cutting through mountains and filling up valleys to open up the Straight Road. He was indeed careless with the populace's labor. When Ch'in first destroyed the feudal lords, the hearts and minds of the world were not yet settled and the injured not yet recovered, yet Meng T'ien, as a famous general, did not vigorously admonish, did not relieve the plight of the populace, did not nourish the aged, did not pity the orphaned, or labor at renewing harmony among the common people, but instead bent to the [Emperor's] whims and embarked on construction; was it not fitting that older and younger brothers should be condemned? Why blame the earth's veins?"

---

⁵¹ This is either a well known maxim or a citation from a work or part of a work no longer extant (see "So-yin").

TRANSLATORS' NOTE

This chapter deals with events also treated in Chapters 6 and 87, but this account focuses on the inverted morality that requires the usurper Hu-hai to be considered "loyal" and the Meng family, upon whom Ch'in had relied for generations, "disloyal," the guilty to succeed and the guiltless to die.

This structure and approach of this memoir also merit comment. The portrayal of a man's life by first discussing his ancestry, then his own deeds, and finally his death is one which became de rigueur in later dynastic histories. The Grand Scribe's typical method exaggerating praise and understating blame in the text devoted to that person can also be seen at work here. Meng Ao's defeat in the third year of King Chuang-hsiang of Ch'in (247 B.C.), is reported in the "Ch'in pen-chi" (Basic Annals of Ch'in, *Shih chi,* 5:219), but not in this chapter, whereas Meng T'ien is given credit for attacking Ch'in in 221 B.C., when it seems likely he was only a subordinate to General Wang Pen 王賁 (see n. 12 above).

But, in fact, this is no biography, but rather an account of that the Grand Scribe found memorable (i.e., a memoir) concerning the Meng Clan. Since most of the records he found concerned Meng T'ien, his name was chosen for the title.

BIBLIOGRAPHY

I. Translations

Bodde, Derk. *Statesman, Patriot, and General in Ancient China.* New Haven: American Oriental Society, 1940, pp. 53-62. [Complete, annotated translation of this chapter.]

Fukushima Yoshihio 福島吉彦, trans. *Shiki retsuden* 史記列傳. Rpt. Tokyo: Chikuma Shobō, 1986 (1969), pp. 203-6.

Watson, Burton. *Records of the Grand Historian: Qin Dynasty.* Hong Kong and New York: The Research Centre for Translation, The Chinese University of Hong Kong and Columbia University Press, 1993, pp. 207-213.

II. Studies

Bodde, *op. cit.*

Itō Norio 伊藤德男. Shiba Sen no Ri Shi, Mō Ten hiban ni tsuite 司馬遷の李斯蒙恬批判 について, *Suzuki Shun Kyōju kanreki kinen Tōyōshi ronsō* 鈴木俊教授還暦記念東洋史論叢. Tokyo: Kan Gi Bunka Kenkyūkai, 1964, pp. 43-56.

SELECTED BIBLIOGRAPHY

This bibliography is intended to be primarily of use to those studying the memoirs (*lieh-chuan*), specifically those of pre-Han China. A general bibliography is appended to Volume 1 of our translation.

This Selected Bibliography is divided as follows:

Chinese characters for publishers are given for the first occurrence only.

I. Translations of the Pre-Han *Lieh-chuan*

See also Timoteus Pokora, "Bibliographies des Traductions du *Che ki*, Chapitres 48-130," in *Les Memoires historiques de Se-ma Ts'ien*, Paris: Adrien Maisonneuve, 1969, pp. 113-146.

Ames, Roger, trans. *Sun-tzu, The Art of Warfare, the First English Translation Incorporating the Recently Discovered Yin-ch'üeh-shan Texts.* New York: Ballantine Books, 1993 (Sun Tzu).

Bodde, Derk. *China's First Unifier, A Study of the Ch'in Dynasty as Seen in the Life of Li Ssu.* Leiden: E. J. Brill, 1938.

_____. *Statesman, Patriot, and General in Ancient China.* New Haven: American Oriental Society, 1940.

Chan, Wing-tsit. *A Source Book on Chinese Philosophy.* Princeton: Princeton University Press, 1963, pp. 246-8 (Tsou Yen).

_____. *The Way of Lao Tzu.* Indianapolis: Bobbs-Merrill, 1963, pp. 36-37 (Lao Tzu).

Chang Yu-luan 張友鸞, *et al. Shih chi hsüan-chu* 史記選注. Peking: Jen-min Wen-hsüeh 人民文學, 1956.

Dolby, William and John Scott, trans. *Sima Qian, War-Lords, Translated with Twelve Other Stories from His Historical Records.* Edinburgh: Southside, 1974.

Dubs, H. H. "Sün-tzu," *The Moulder of Ancient Confucianism.* London, 1927, pp. 26-28.

Duyvendak, J. J. L. *The Book of Lord Shang.* London: Probsthain and Co., 1928, pp. 8-31 (Lord Shang).

Forke, Alfred. "Yen Ying, Staatsman und Philosoph, und das *Yen-tse Tch'un-ts'iu*," *AM, Hirth Anniversary Volume.* London: Probsthain and Co., 1924, pp. 101-44.

Franke, Herbert and Wolfgang Bauer. *Die Goldene Truhe.* Munich, 1962.

Fukushima Chūrō 福島中郎. *Shiki* 史記. Tokyo: Meitoku 明德 Shuppansha, 1972.

Fung Yu-lan. *A History of Chinese Philosophy.* Derk Bodde, trans. 2v.; Princeton: Princeton Univesity Press, 1952-53, v. 1, p. 132 (Ch'un-yü K'un, Ch'en Tao, Huan Yüan, T'ien P'ien, Chia-tzu).

Goodrich, Chauncey S. "The Biography of Wu Ch'i," *MS*, 35 (1981-83), 197-233 (Wu Ch'i).

Griffith, S. B., trans. *Sun Tzu: The Art of War.* Cambridge: Cambridge University Press, 1963, pp. 57-62 (Sun Tzu).

Haenisch, Erich. "Gestalten aus der Zeit der chinesischen Hegemoniekämpfe: Übersetzungen aus Sze-ma Ts'ien's Historischen Denkwürdigkeiten," *Abhandlungen für die Kunde des Morgenlandes,* XXXIV.2. Wiesbaden: Harrassowitz, 1962.

_____. *Der Herr von Sin-ling, Reden aus dem Chan-kuo ts'e und Biographien aus dem Shi-ki.* Stuttgart: Reclam, 1965.

Han Chao-ch'i 韓兆琪. *Shih chi hsüan-chu hui-p'ing* 史記選注匯評. Chungchow: Chung-chou Ku-chi 中州古籍 Ch'u-pan-she, 1990.

_____. *Shih chi p'ing-yi shang-hsi* 史記評議賞析. Huhetot: Nei Meng-ku Jen-min 內蒙古人民 Ch'u-pan-she, 1985.

_____. *Shih chi shang-hsi chi* 史記賞析集. Chengtu: Pa-Shu 巴蜀 Shu-she, 1988.

_____ and Lung Te-shou 龍德壽 (Asst.Ed.). *Shih chi wen pai-p'ing ching-hsüan* 史記文百評精選. Changchun: Chi-lin Jen-min 吉林人民, 1992.

Holzer, Rainer. *Yen-tzu und das Yen-tzu ch'un-ch'iu.* Frankfurt: Lang, 1983 (Yen Tzu, partial).

Ichikawa Hiroshi 市川宏. *Shiki* 史記. Tokyo: Meitoku Shoten, 1972.

Imataka Makoto 今鷹真. *Shiki retsuden* 史記列傳. Tokyo: Iwanami Shoten, 1975.

Jäger, Fritz. "Die Biographie des Wu Tzu-hsü, 66. Kapitel des *Shih-chi*)," *OE,* 7 (1960), 12-16.

_____. "Das 82. Kapitel des Schi-gi," *Sino-Japonica, Festschrift André Wedemeyer zum 80. Geburtstag.* Leipzig: Otto Harrassowitz, 1956, pp. 107-117.

Kaizuka Shigeki 貝塚茂樹. *Shiki retsuden* 史記列傳. Tokyo: Chūō Kōronsha 中央公論社, 1968.

Kou Pao-koh. *Deux sophistes chinois, Houei Che et Kong-souen Long.* Paris, 1953, p. 7 (Kong-souen Long).

Lai Hsin-hsia 來新夏 et al. *Shih chi hsüan* 史記選. Peking: Chung-hua 中華, 1990 (Preface 1983).

Lau, D. C. *Lao tzu, Tao te ching.* Baltimore: Penguin, 1963, pp. 8-10 (Lao Tzu).

Ma Ch'ih-ying 馬持盈. *Shih chi chin-chu* 史記今注. 6v. Taipei: T'ai-wan Shang-wu 臺灣商務 Yin-shu-kuan, 1979.

Margouliès, Georges. "Biographies de Kouan [Tchong] et de Yen [Ying]," *Le Kou-wen chinois.* Paris: Guethner, 1926, pp. 77-83.

Morgan, Evan, trans. "The Lives of Kuan Chung and Yen Tzu," in *A Guide to Wenli Styles and Chinese Ideals.* London: Probsthain and Co., 1931, pp. 117-127.

Nyitray, Vivian-Lee. "Mirrors of Virtue: Four 'Shih chi' Biographies." Unpublished Ph. D. dissertation, Stanford University, 1990.

Noguchi Sadao 野口定男. *Shiki* 史記. 2v. Tokyo: Heibonsha 平凡社, 1958.

Ōgawa Tamaki 小川環樹. *Shiki retsuden* 史記列傳. Rpt. Tokyo: Chikuma 筑摩 Shobō, 1986 (1969).

Panasjuk, V. *Syma Czjan', Izbrannoe.* Moscow: Nauka, 1956.

Plath, H. *Confucius und seiner Schüler, Leben und Lehre,* v. III, "Die Schüler des Confucius" (Munich, 1873), pp. 1-98. Not seen.

Pokora, Timoteus. "*Shih chi* 127, the Symbiosis of Two Historians," in *Chinese Ideas about Nature and Society, Studies in Honour of Derk Bodde.* Charles Le Blanc and Susan Blader, eds. Hong Kong: Hong Kong University Press, 1987, pp. 215-234.

Rudolph, Richard Casper. "The *Shih chi* Biography of Wu Tzu-hsü," *OE,* 9 (1962), 106-120.

_____. "Wu Tzu-hsü, His Life and Posthumous Cult: A Critical Study of *Shih chi* 66." Unpublished Ph. D. dissertation, University of California, 1942.

Sawyer, Ralph D. *The Seven Military Classics of Ancient China.* Boulder: Westview Press, 1993, pp. 193-6 (Wu Ch'i).

Sung Yün-pin 宋雲彬. *Hsiang Yü* 項羽. *Li-tai cheng-chih jen-wu chuang-chi yi-chu* 歷代政治人物傳記譯注. Peking: Chung-hua, 1962.
> A useful volume by one of the editors of the Chung-hua edition of *Shih chi.*

Tanaka Kenji 田中謙義 and Itsukai Tomoyosi 一海知義. *Shiki* 史記. 5v. [partial translation] Tokyo: Asahi 朝日 Shimbunsha, 1978.

_____. *Shiki: Shunjū sengoku hen* 史記: 春秋戰國篇. Tokyo: Asahi Shimbunsha, 1963.

Vandermeersch, Léon. *La formation du Légisme, recherche sur la constitution d'une philosophie politique caractéristique de la Chine ancienne.* Paris: Ecole Francaise d'Extreme-Orient, 1965 (Lord Shang Shen Pu-hai and Han Fei).

Wang Li-ch'i 王利器, ed. *Shih chi chu-i* 史記注譯. 4v. Sian: San Ch'in 三秦, 1988.
> There are a number of reviews of this volume (which was actually done by Wang Li-ch'i's students) in *Ku-chi cheng-li yen-chiu hsüeh-k'an* 古籍整理研究學刊, 1990.3, 1-13. Wang Li-ch'i himself reviewed the volume in the 1990.5 issue of the same journal (pp. 1-11).

Wang, Po-hsiang 王伯祥 (1890-1975). *Shih chi hsüan* 史記選. Peking: Jen-min Wen-hsüeh 人民文學 Ch'u-pan-she, 1957.

Ware, James R. *The Sayings of Mencius, A New Translation.* New York, 1960, pp. 10-11 (Mencius).

Watson, Burton. *Records of the Grand Historian of China, from the Shih chi of Ssu-ma Ch'ien.* 2v. New York: Columbia University Press, 1962.

_____. *Records of the Grand Historian, Chapters from the Shih chi of Ssu-ma Ch'ien.* New York: Columbia University Press, 1969.

_____. *Records of the Grand Historian: Han Dynasty I (Revised Edition).* 2v. Hong Kong and New York: *Renditions*-Columbia University Press, 1993.

_____. *Records of the Grand Historian: Qin Dynasty.* V. 3. Rev. ed. Hong Kong and New York: The Research Centre for Translation, The Chinese University of Hong Kong and Columbia University Press, 1993.

Yang Chung-hsien 楊鐘賢 and Hao Chih-ta 郝志達. *Wen-pai tui-chao ch'üan-yi Shih chi* 文白對照全譯史記. 5v. Peking: Kuo-chi wen-hua 國際文化 Ch'u-pan Kung-ssu, 1992.

Yang Hsien-yi and Gladys Yang. *Records of the Historian.* Rpt. Hong Kong: The Commercial Press, 1985.

Yoshida Kenkō 吉田賢抗. *Shiki* 史記. V. 1 and 2. Tokyo: Meiji 明治 Shoin, 1973.

II. Studies of *Lieh-chuan*

Bodde, Derk. "Further Remarks on the Identification of Lao Tzu," *JAOS,* 64 (1944), 24-27.

_____. "The New Identification of Lao Tzu," *JAOS,* 62 (1942), 8-13.

_____. *Statesman, Patriot, and General in Ancient China.* New Haven: American Oriental Society, 1940.

Chan Hsü-tso 詹緒佐. "*Shih chi* 'Lien Lin lieh-chuan' chu-shih, piao-tien chih-yi" 史記廉藺列傳注釋標點質疑, *Hsüeh yü-wen* 學語文, 1986.3.

Chan Li-po 詹立波. "Lüeh t'an Yin-ch'üeh-shan Han-mu chu-chien *Sun Tzu ping-fa*" 略談銀雀山漢墓竹簡孫子兵法, in *Yin-ch'üeh-shan Han-mu chu-chien Sun Tzu ping-fa.* Peking: Wen-wu 文物, 1976, pp. 10-18.

Chen Chu 陳柱. "*Shih chi* 'Po Yi lieh-chuan' chiang-chi" 史記伯夷列傳講記, *Hsüeh-shu shih-chieh* 學術世界, 2.2 (November 1936), 112-3.

Ch'en Han-nien 陳瀚年. "Lun *Shih chi* Meng-ch'ang Chün, P'ing-yüan Chün, Ch'un-shen Chün, Hsin-ling Chün" 論史記孟嘗君平原君春申君信陵君, *Kuo-hsüeh ts'ung-k'an* 國學叢刊, 10 (September 1942).

_____. "*Shih chi* 'Lu Chung Lien lieh-chuan' shu-hou (Erh-p'ien)" 史記魯仲連列傳書後〔二篇〕, *Kuo-hsüeh ts'ung-k'an*, 10 (September 1942).

Chiang Liang-fu 姜亮夫. "*Shih chi* 'Ch'ü Yüan lieh-chuan' shu-cheng" 史記屈原列傳疏證, in Chiang's *Ch'ü Yüan fu chiao-chu* 屈原賦校註. Peking: Chung-hua, 1972, pp. 1-26.

Ch'ien Mu 錢穆. *Hsien Ch'in chu-tzu hsi-nien* 先秦諸子繫年. 2v. Rpt. Peking: Chung-hua Shu-chü, 1985.

Chin Jung-hua 金榮華. "*Shih chi* 'Ch'ü Yüan lieh-chuan' shu-cheng" 史記屈原列傳疏證, *Shih-ta Kuo-wen yen-chiu-so chi-k'an* 師大國文研究所集刊, 9 (June 1965), 615-636.

Chu Hsüan 朱玄. "*Shih chi* 'Meng Hsün lieh-chuan' shu-cheng" 史記孟荀列傳疏證. *[Shih-Ta] Kuo-wen Yen-chiu-so chi-k'an* 師大國文研究所季刊, 10 (1966), 69-216.

Chu Yüan 朱瑗. "*Shih chi* 'Shang-chün lieh-chuan' shu-cheng" 史記商君列傳疏證, *Kuo-li Pien-i-kuan kuan-k'an* 國立編譯館館刊, 1 (1971.10), 39-58.

_____. "*Shih chi* "Shu-li Tzu, Kan Mao lieh-chuan' shu-cheng" 史記樗里子甘茂列傳疏證, *Kuo-li Pien-yi-kuan kuan-k'an,* 1.4 (December 1972), 101-58.

Dubs, Homer H. "The Date and Circumstances of the Philosopher Lao-dz," *JAOS,* 61 (1941), 215-221.

_____. "The Identification of the Lao-dz," *JAOS* 62 (1942), 300-304.

Fan Hsiang-yung 范祥雍. "Su Ch'in ho-tsung Liu-kuo nien-tai k'ao hsin" 蘇秦合縱六國年代考信 in *Chung-hua wen-shih lun-ts'ung* 中華文史論叢, 1985.4, 1-25.

Fields, Lanny B. "The Legalists and the Fall of Ch'in: Humanism and Tyranny," *JAH* 17 (1983), 1-39.

Fu Yi 傅義. "Tu 'Ch'ü Yüan lieh-chuan'" 讀屈原列傳, *Yü-wen hsüeh-hsi* 語文學習, 1956. 10.

_____. "Tu *Shih chi* 'P'ing-yüan Chun lieh-chuan'" 讀史記平原君列傳, *Yü-wen hsüeh-hsi,* 1956.8.

Fujita Katsuhisa 藤田勝久. "*Shiki* 'Jōkō retsuden' ni kansuru ichi kōsatsu 史記穰侯列傳に關する一考察," in *Tōhōgaku,* 71(1985), 18-34.

_____. "*Shiki* 'Shunshin Kun retsuden' no henshū katei" 史記春申君列傳の編集過程, *Tōhōgaku,* 77(Jan. 1989), 40-55.

Graham, A. C. "The Origins of the Legend of Lao Tan," in *Studies in Chinese Philosophy and Philosophical Literature.* Singapore: Institute of East Asian Philosophies, 1986, pp. 110-24.

_____. "The Tillers' Version of the Legend of Po Yi 伯夷 and Shu Ch'i 叔齊," in A. C. Graham, *Studies in Chinese Philosophy and Philosophical Literature.* Singapore: The Institute of East Asian Philosophies, 1986, pp. 86-90.

Hawkes, David. *The Songs of the South, An Anthology of Ancient Chinese Poems by Qu Yuan and Other Poets*. Rpt. Harmondsworth: Penguin Books, 1985.

_____. Review of *A Madman of Ch'u: The Chinese Myth of Loyalty and Dissent*, by Laurence A. Schneider, *CLEAR*, 4.2(July 1982), 245-7.

Hsü Shuo-fang 徐朔方. "Po shu 'Chao-kuo ts'e' ho *Shih chi* 'Su Ch'in lieh-chuan' 帛書戰國策和史記蘇秦列傳, in Hsü's *Shih Han lun-kao* 史漢論稿. Nanking: Chiang-su Ku-chi 江蘇古籍, 1984, pp. 334-354.

_____. "*Shih chi* 'Chang Yi lieh-chuan' ho *Chan-kuo ts'e*" 史記張儀列傳和戰國策, *Ibid.*, pp. 355-360.

Ichiguro Shunitsu 石黑俊逸. "*Shiki* 'Mōshi Junkei retsuden' no kōsei" 史記孟子荀子列傳の構成, *Shingaku kenkyū*, 12(1956), 1-4.

Ishida Hiroshi 石田博士. "*Shiki* no kijutsu to Kan Pi" 史記の記述と韓非, *Kambun Gakkaihō* 漢文學惠報, 28(1983).

Itō Norio 伊藤德男. Shiba Sen no Ri Shi, Mō Ten hiban ni tsuite 司馬遷の李斯蒙恬批判について, *Suzuki Shun Kyōju kanreki kinen Tōyōshi ronsō* 鈴木俊教授還曆記念東洋史論叢. Tokyo: Kan Gi Bunka Kenkyūkai, 1964, pp. 43-56.

Johnson, David. "Epic and History in Early China: The Matter of Wu Tzu-hsü," *JAS*, 40.2 (February 1981), 255-271.

_____. "The Wu Tzu-hsü *Pien-wen* and Its Sources: Parts I and II," *HJAS*, 40.1 (June 1980), and 40.2 (December 1980), 93-156 and 465-505, respectively.

Juan Chih-sheng 阮芝生. "'Po Yi lieh-chuan' hsi-lun" 伯夷列傳析論. *Ta-lu tsa-chih* 大陸雜誌, 62 (1981), 3, 37-42.

_____. "'Po Yi lieh-chuan' fa-wei" 伯夷列傳發微. *Wen-shih-che hsüeh-pao* 文史哲學報, 34 (1985), 1-20.

Kang Chou 岡周. "Tu 'Meng Hsun lieh-chuan' hou te chi-yi yi t'i-yao" 讀孟荀列傳後的稽疑及提要, *Chung-fa Ta-hsüeh yüeh-k'an* 中法大學月刊, v. 10, no. 4 (February 1937).

Kao Heng 高亨. "Lao Tzu cheng ku ch'ien-chi" 老子正詁前記, in *Ku-shih pien*. Ku Chieh-kang *et al.* 7v. Peiping: K'ai-ming 開明 Shu-tien, 1926-1938, v. 4, pp. 351-3.

_____. "*Shih chi* 'Lao Tzu chuan' chien-chien'" 史記老子傳箋證, in *Ibid.*, v. 6, pp. 441-73.

Kierman, Frank A., Jr. "Lu Chung Lien and the *Lu Lien Tzu*," in *Transition and Permanence: Chinese History and Culture*. David C. Buxbaum and Frederick W. Mote, eds. Hong Kong: Cathay Press, 1972, pp. 269-74.

Konrad, N. T. *Wu-tzu: Trattat o voennom iskusstve, perevod y kommentarij*. Moscow: Izdatel'stvo Vostochnoi Literatury, 1958 (gives brief biography of Wu Ch'i).

Kusuyama Haruki 楠山春樹. *Rōshi densetsu no kenkyū* 老子傳說の研究. Tokyo: Sōbunsha 創文社, 1979.

Lau, D. C. "The Dating of Events in the Life of Mencius" and "Early Traditions about Mencius," in Lau's *Mencius*. Middlesex: Penguin, 1970, pp. 205-213 and 214-219, respectively.

_____. "The Problem of Authorship," in Lau's *Lao Tzu, Tao Te Ching*. Middlesex: Penguin, 1963, pp. 147-162.

Liu, James J. Y. *The Chinese Knight-Errant*. Chicago: University of Chicago Press, 1967, pp. 23-38.

Li Shu-yi 李叔毅. "Tu *Shih chi* 'Meng Hsün lieh-chuan'" 讀史記孟荀列傳, *Ku-chi cheng-li yen-chiu hsüeh-k'an* 古籍整理研究學刊, 1985.4

Li Ling 李零. "Kuan-yü Yin-ch'üeh-shan chien-pen *Sun Tzu* te shang-ch'üeh" 關於銀雀山漢墓竹簡孫子的商榷, *Wen shih*, 7 (1979), 23-34.

Liu Pen-tung's 劉本棟. "*Shih chi* 'Chuang Tzu lieh-chuan' shu-cheng'" 史記莊子列傳疏證, *Yu-shih hsüeh-chih* 幼獅學誌, 5.2(1966), 42 pp. (no continuous pagination).

_____. "*Shih chi* 'Lao, Chuang, Shen, Han lieh-chuan' shu-cheng" 史記老莊申韓列傳疏證. Taipei: T'ai-wan Sheng-li Shih-fan Ta-hsüeh Kuo-wen Yen-chiu-so, 1966.

Lo Ken-tse 羅根澤. "Lao Tzu chi *Lao Tzu* shu te wen-t'i" 老子及老子書的問題, in *Ku-shih pien*, v. 4, pp. 449-461.

Lu Ting-hsiang 陸鼎祥. "Hsin-ling Chün 'ch'ieh-fu chiu-Chao' te chi-ke wen-t'i" 信陵君竊符救趙的幾個問題, *Yü-wen hsüeh-k'an* 語文學刊, 1985.

Maspero, Henri. "Le Roman de Sou Ts'in," *Études Asiatiques Publieé à l'occasion de vingt-cinquieme anniversaire de l'École française d'Extrême Orient*. Paris: G. Van Oest, 1925, v. 2, pp. 128-33 (127-41).

McCraw, David. "Background for the Biography of Ching K'o," in *Chinese Social Relationships: The Ideal vs. the Real*. Honolulu: Center for Chinese Studies, 1988, pp. 21-35.

Miao K'o-hsiu 苗可秀. "*Shih chi* 'Ch'ü Yüan Chia Sheng lieh chuan shu-cheng" 史記屈原賈生列傳疏證, *Tung-pei ts'ung-chien* 東北叢鐫, No. 16.

Naitō Shigenobu 內滕戊申. "Shinryōkun" 信陵君, *Ritsumeikan bungaku*, 1967, 735-56.

Nyitray, Vivian-Lee. "Mirrors of Virtue: Four 'Shih chi' Biographies." Unpublished Ph. D. dissertation, Stanford University, 1990.

Nieh Kan-kung 聶紺弩. "Tu 'Tu Meng-ch'ang Chün chuan'" 讀讀孟嘗君傳, *Chung-kuo She-hui K'o-hsüeh Yüan Yen-chiu Yüan hsüeh-pao* 中國社會科學院研究院學報, 71.6 (December 1985), 27 and 30.

Petersen, Jens O. "On the Expressions Commonly Held to Refer to Sun Wu, the Putative Author of the Sunzi Bingfa," *Acta Orientalia*, 53(1992), 106-21.

_____. "What's in a Name? On the Sources Concerning Sun Wu," *AM, Third Series*, 5.1(1992), 1-31.

Ryckmans, P. "A New Interpretation of the Term *Lieh-chuan* as Used in the *Shih-chi*," *PFEH*, 5(March 1972), 135-147.

Schneider, Laurence A. *A Madman of Ch'u: The Chinese Myth of Loyalty and Dissent*. Berkeley and Los Angeles: University of California Press, 1980.

Su Chen-shen 蘇振申. "*Shih chi* 'Chung-ni Ti-tzu lieh-chuan' shu-cheng" 史記仲尼弟子列傳疏證. M.A. Thesis, China Culture College (Taiwan), 1964.

Sun Tso-yün 孫作雲. "Tu *Shih chi* 'Ch'ü Yüan lieh-chuan'" 讀史記屈原列傳, *Shih-hsüeh yüeh-k'an* 史學月刊, 1959, No. 9.

Sun Tz'u-chou 孫次舟. "*Shih chi* 'Shang-chün lieh-chuan' shih-liao chüeh-yüan" 史記商君列傳史料抉原, *Shih-hsüeh chi-k'an* 史學季刊, 1.2 (March 1941).

Takahashi Hitoshi 高橋均. "'Chūji Teishi retsuden' ni tsuite" 仲尼弟子について, *Tōkyō Kyōiku Daigaku Bungakubu kiyō--Kokubungaku kambungaku ronsō* 東京教育大學文學部紀要--國文學漢文學論集, 77(1970), 79-116.

T'an Chieh-fu 譚戒甫. "*Shih chi* 'Meng Tzu Hsün Ch'ing lieh-chuan chiao-shih" 史記孟子荀卿列傳校釋, *Chung-kuo li-shih wen-hsien yen-chiu chi-k'an* 中國歷史文獻研究集刊, 1(1982), 84-96.

T'ang Lan 唐蘭. "Su Ch'in shih-chi chien-piao" 蘇秦事跡簡表 in *Chan-kuo tsung-heng-chia shu* 戰國從橫家書, Beijing, 1976, pp. 145-153

T'ien Feng-t'ai 田鳳台. "Lü Pu-wei chuan k'ao" 呂不韋傳考, *Fu-hsing kang hsüeh-pao* 復興崗學報, 27(June 1982), 427-49.

Wen, I-fan 溫一凡. "Tu 'Ch'ü Yüan lieh-chuan'" 讀屈原列傳, *Chiang-hsi Ta-hsüeh Hsüeh-pao* 江西大學學報, 1978.3.

Wu Yu 吳璵. "*Shih chi* Wei Kung-tzu chuan p'ing-hsi" 史記魏公子傳評析, *Ku-tien wen-hsüeh*, 1 (1979), 33-46.

Yang Tsung-yüan 楊宗元. "Kuei-ku Tzu shu-k'ao chi 'Su Ch'in, Chang Yi lieh-chuan' shu-cheng" 鬼谷子書考及蘇秦張儀列傳疏證. M.A. thesis, Chinese Cultural College, 1962.

III. Other Works

Allan, Sarah. *The Heir and the Sage*. San Francisco: Chinese Materials Center, 1981.

Ames, Roger, translator and editor. *Sun-tzu, The Art of Warfare; The First English Translation Incorporating the Recently Discovered Yin-ch'ueh-shan Texts*. New York: Ballantine Books, 1993.

Berkowitz, Alan. "Patterns of Reclusion in Early and Medieval China: A Study of the Formulations of the Practice of Reclusion in Early China and Its Portrayal." Unpublished Ph.D. dissertation, University of Washington, 1989.

Blanford, Yumiko Fukushima. "Studies of the 'Zhanguo zonghengjia shu' Silk Manuscript." Unpublished Ph. D. dissertation, University of Washington, 1989.

Goodrich, Chauncey S. "A New Translation of the *Hsün-tzu*," *JAOS*, 110(1990), 487-492.

Henry, Eric. "The Motif of Recognition in Early China," *HJAS*, 47(1987), 5-30.

Knoblock, John. *Xunzi, A Translation and Study of the Complete Works*. 2v. Stanford: Stanford University Press, 1988 and 1991.

Köhn, Livia. "Die Emigration des Laozi, mythologische Entwicklungen vom 2. bis 6. Jahrhundert," *MS*, 38(1988-89), 49-68.

Liang Ch'i-ch'ao 梁啟超 .. *Kuan-tzu chuan* 傳. Rpt. Taipei: Chung-hua, 1963.

Lung Yün-chün 龍運鈞. *Lu Chung Lien p'ing-chuan* 魯仲連評傳. Taipei: Cheng-chung 正中, 1969.

Rickett, W. Allyn, trans. *Guanzi: Political, Economic, and Philosophical Essays from Early China*. V. 1. Princeton: Princeton University Press, 1985.

_____. "*Guanzi xuekan*," in *Early China*, 14(1989), 201-11.

Rosen, Sydney H. "In Search of the Historical Kuan Chung." Unpublished Ph. D. dissertation, University of Chicago, 1973.

_____. "In Search of the Historical Kuan Chung,"*JAS*, 25(1976), 431-40.

Thompson, Paul M. *The Shen Tzu Fragments*. Oxford: Oxford University Press, 1979.

Vervoorn, Aat. "Boyi and Shuqi: Worthy Men of Old?" *Papers in Far Eastern History*, 28 (September 1983), 1-22.

_____. *Men of the Cliffs and Caves: The Development of the Chinese Tradition to the End of the Han Dynasty*. Hong Kong: The Chinese University Press, 1990.

Walker, R. L. "Some Notes on the *Yen-tzu Ch'un-ch'iu*," *JAOS*, 73(1953), 156-63).

Wu Chiu-lung 吳九龍. "Chien-pen yü ch'uan-pen *Sun-tzu ping-fa* pi-chiao yen-chiu" 簡本與
傳本孫子兵法比較交研究, *Sun Tzu hsin-t'an: Chung-wai hsüeh-che lun Sun Tzu*
孫子新 探: 中外學者論孫子. Peking: Chieh-fang Chün 解放軍, 1990, pp. 176-188.

INDEX

Place names such as Wei 魏 and dynastic titles such as Chou 周 occur too frequently in the text to be of use to the reader and are not included here.

This index is intended to afford access to our translation of official titles, which are all cross-listed by English translation and romanization.

A

Acting Minister of State, see *Chia-hsiang*
Acting Prefect of the Department of the Imperial Seals and Tallies, see *Hsing fu-hsi ling*
Adjutant General, see *Pi chiang-chün*
Ai-ling 艾陵, 56, 56 n.59, 225
"Ai ying" 哀郢 (A Lament for Ying), 7, 307
An 安 of Han, 353
An-men 岸門, 118
An-p'ing 安平, 275, 275 n.8
An-yang 安陽, 267, 267 n.16
An-yi 安邑, xviii, 90, 91 n.24, 92, 116, 117, 159 n.19, 162, 162 n.39, n.40, 163, 167 n.8
Analects (see also *Lun yü*), 63 n.1, n.3, n.4, n.6, n.9, 64 n.10, n.11, n.12, 65 n.18, n.21, 66 n.26, 67 n.30, 68 n.33, 70 n.42, 75 n.65, 77 n.74, 80 n.94, n.98, 81 n.107
Ao 昇, 78

B

Bandit Chih 盜跖, 4, 4 n.33, 290, 303, 349
Bissell, Jeff
Book of Changes (see also *Changes, Yi ching*), 5 n.44, 79, 298
Book of Documents (see also *Documents, Shang shu, Shu ching*), 1 n.4, n.5, 57 n.62, 252 n.124, 307 n.86, 341
Book of Odes (see also *Shih ching*), 81, 94 n.50, n.51, 302, 341

C

Chan Chiu-ming 陳照明, iii
Chan Ho 詹何, 261 n.38
Chan-kuo ts'e 戰國策, xvi, 33 n.2, 36 and *passim*
Chancellor within the Palace, see *Chung Ch'eng-hsiang*
Chang Ch'ou 張丑, 190
Chang Chü 長沮, 68, 68 n.33
Chang Erh 張耳, 176
Chang Hsiang-ju 張相如, 303 n.63
Chang Lu 張祿, 163, 233, 233 n.6, 234, 241
Chang Mao 張嫄, 295 n.5
Chang 漳 River, 100, 329
Chang-shih 長史 (Chief of Scribes), 336 n.12
Chang T'ang 張唐, 153, 154
Chang Wen-hu 張文虎 (1808-1855), viii
Chang Yi 張儀, 96, 103, 121, 123, 124,124 n.3, n.4, 125, 125 n.9, 126, 126 n.19, n.21, 127, 127 n.22, 129, 129 n.31, 130, 130 n.37, 131, 133, 134, 134 n.59, 135, 135 n.64, 136, 137, 138, 138 n.82, 141, 142, 143, 186, 297, 297 n.17, n.25, 298, 337, 337 n.21
Chang Yi 章義, 145, 147, 148, 148 n.35, n.36, 152, 153, 156
Ch'ang 昌, Earl of the West (see also King Wu of Chou), 3, 3 n.20
Ch'ang-kuo 昌國, 256
Ch'ang-lo 長樂 Palace, 147
Ch'ang Lu 長盧, 185
Ch'ang-p'ing 長平, 169, 169 n27, n.29, 170, 172, 173, 177, 178, 207, 207 n.19, 208, 208 n.26, 212, 212 n.34, 213, 216, 245, 245 n.82, 251, 269, 270, 284 n.17, 287, 287 n.33
Ch'ang-sha 長沙, 302, 302 n.56, 303, 304, 307
Ch'ang-shao 長勺, 319 n.1
Ch'ang-she 長社, 162, 162 n.42
Changes (see also *Book of Changes, Yi ching*), 225
Chao Chü 昭雎, 298 n.31
Chao Chuang 趙莊, 118
Ch'ao-hsien 朝鮮, 98, 98 n.10
"Chao hun" 招魂 (Summoning the Soul), 7, 307
Chao Kao 趙高, 341, 342, 343, 344, 344 n.76, 345, 346, 347, 351, 352, 352 n.115, 353, 354, 355, 356, 356 n.131, n.132, 357, 362, 362 n.21, n.22, n.23, 363
Chao-ko 朝歌 (Morning Song), 291
Chao K'uo 趙括, 170, 171, 171 n.39, 245 n.83, 269, 270, 273, 276 n.17
Chao Liang 趙良, 92, 93
Chao Pao 趙豹 (see also Lord of P'ing-yüan), 145 n.5, 169 n.24, 208 n.22
Chao Pass 昭關, 51, 237
Chao She 趙奢, 170 n.34, 245 n.83, 267, 268, 269, 273
Chao Sheng 趙勝, Lord of P'ing-yüan 平原, 169 n.24, 203, 204, 205, 206, 207, 208 n.22, 211, 211 n.31, 212, 212 n.34, 213
Chao Shih 趙郝, 208, 208 n.26, 209
Chao Ts'ung 趙蔥, 272
Chavannes, Édouard (1865-1918), v, ix
Che 輒 (see also Duke Ch'u of Wei), 68
Chen 軫, King Chao 昭 of Ch'u, 49, 52
Ch'en 陳, 45, 75, 82 n.111, 104, 104 n.53, 168, 168 n.15
Ch'en Chen 陳軫, 129, 130, 139, 139 n.88, 140, 141
Ch'en Chuang 陳莊, 126, 126 n.15
Ch'en-hsien 陳縣, 223
Ch'en Meng-chia 陳夢家, xv
Ch'en Sheng 陳勝, 175 n.74, 176, 347
Ch'en Ssu-pai 陳司敗, 82
Ch'en Tzu-ch'in 陳子禽, 70

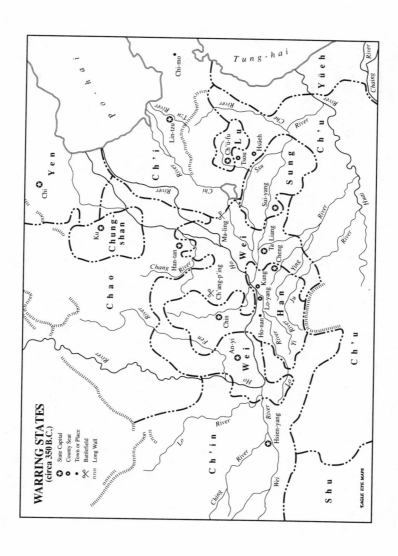

WARRING STATES
(circa 350 B.C.)

✪ State Capital
◉ ● County Seat
● Town or Place
✂ Battlefield
〰 Long Wall

Po-hai

Tung-hai

Chi ✪ **Yen**

Chao

Ku ✪ **Chung shan**

Chi-mo ●

Lin-tzu ✪

Ch'u-fu ✪ **Lu**
Tsou ◉ Hsieh ◉

Ch'i

Han-tan ✪

Ch'ang-p'ing

Chang River

Ma-ling ✂ Sui-yang ◉

Wei

Ta Liang ✪
Cheng ◉

Sung

Ch'u

Yüeh

Chin ✪

Kung ◉
Lo-yang ●

Han

An-yi ✪ Ho-nan ●

Wei

Fen River

Ch'in

Lo River

Hsien-yang ✪

Ching River

Wei

Shu

Ch'u

Huai River

Ying River

EAGLE EYE MAPS

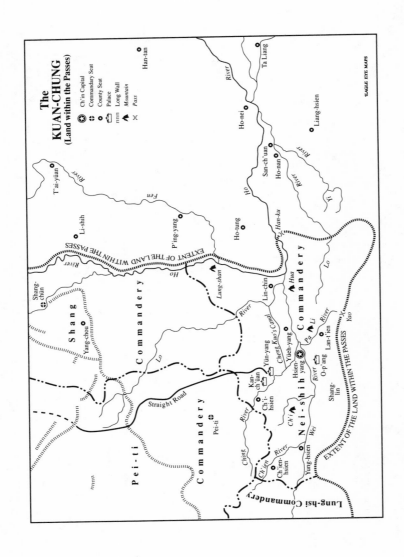

The
KUAN-CHUNG
(Land within the Passes)

Ch'in Capital
Commandery Seat
County Seat
Palace
Long Wall
Mountain
Pass

EAGLE EYE MAPS

Han-tan

Ta Liang

Ho-nei

Liang-hsien

San-ch'uan

Ho-nan

Ho

Yi

Han-ku

Lo

Hua

Commandery

Li

Pa

Lan-t'ien

Yao

EXTENT OF THE LAND WITHIN THE PASSES

Shang-lin

Wei

Yung-hsien

Lung-hsi Commandery

Ching River

Ch'i-yen

Ch'ien-hsien

O-p'ang

River

Nei-shih Commandery

Hsien-yang

Yüeh-yang

Cheng Kuo's Canal

Ch'i-hsien

Kan-ch'üan

Yün-yang

River

Pei-ti

Commandery

Straight Road

Lo

Pei-ti

Lo

Yang-chou

Shang

Commandery

Shang-chün

River

Lang-shan

Lin-chin

Lo

Ho

EXTENT OF THE LAND WITHIN THE PASSES

River

Ping-yang

Ho-tung

Fen

Li-shih

River

T'ai-yüan

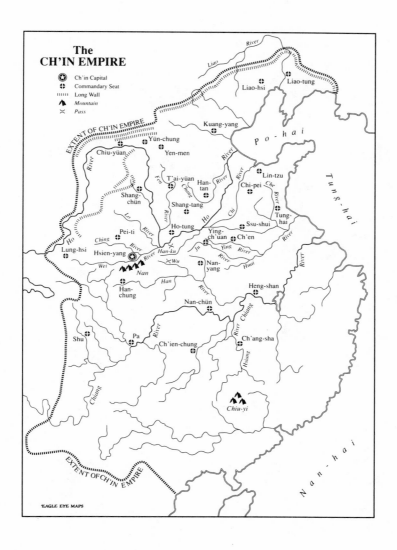

The CH'IN EMPIRE

- ⊕ Ch'in Capital
- ⊕ Commandary Seat
- ⫿⫿⫿ Long Wall
- ▲ *Mountain*
- ⤬ *Pass*

EXTENT OF CH'IN EMPIRE

Liao-hsi Liao-tung

Kuang-yang

P o - h a i

Yün-chung

Chiu-yüan Yen-men

T'ai-yüan Han-tan Lin-tzu

Shang-chün Chi-pei

Shang-tang *T u n g - h a i*

Ho-tung Ssu-shui Tung-hai

Pei-ti Ying-ch'uan Ch'en

Lung-hsi Hsien-yang Han-ku Nan-yang

Nan ⤬ *Wu*

Han-chung Heng-shan

Nan-chün

Shu Pa Ch'ien-chung Ch'ang-sha

Chiu-yi

EXTENT OF CH'IN EMPIRE

N a n - h a i

EAGLE EYE MAPS

DATE DUE

AUG 1 4 2005	
JUL - 7 2009	